END USER COMPUTING
Management, Applications, and Technology

ABOUT THE AUTHOR

Dr. Raymond R. Panko is on the undergraduate and graduate faculties of the College of Business Administration, University of Hawaii. Before coming to the University of Hawaii, he was an analyst at Stanford Research Institute (now SRI International). He received his Ph.D. from Stanford University.

He has been involved in end user computing since 1968, first as an early end user in an engineering department, and later as a researcher on text retrieval systems, Videotex, teleconferencing, office automation, data communications, and end user computing. His primary research concern is the fundamental shift that is now taking place in information systems from clerical support to professional support.

END USER COMPUTING
Management, Applications, and Technology

RAYMOND R. PANKO
College of Business Administration
University of Hawaii

JOHN WILEY & SONS
New York Chichester Brisbane Toronto
Singapore

Copyright © 1988, by John Wiley & Sons, Inc.

All rights reserved. Published simultaneously in Canada.

Reproduction or translation of any part of
this work beyond that permitted by Sections
107 and 108 of the 1976 United States Copyright
Act without the permission of the copyright
owner is unlawful. Requests for permission
or further information should be addressed to
the Permissions Department, John Wiley & Sons.

Library of Congress Cataloging in Publication Data:
Panko, Raymond R.
END USER COMPUTING

L.C. Subject Heading
Title and Series entries

ISBN 0-471-01102-9

Printed in the United States of America

10 9 8 7 6 5 4 3 2 1

To Romy, who helped in too many ways to count, and whose kindness and understanding really made this book possible. Also to Julia, who taught me how to use the Macintosh, and to David, who taught me how much fun a person can have with computers.

PREFACE

Computers are finally moving into the offices of managers and professionals. This revolution, which goes by the name **end user computing (EUC),** includes a broad range of applications:

- Personal computing
- Decision support systems (DSSs)
- Executive information systems (EISs)
- Nonclerical office automation
- Time-shared data and decision support applications on hosts
- Workstation-host data communications
- Local area networking (including PC networking)

EUC IN THE UNDERGRADUATE AND GRADUATE CURRICULA

Most business schools teach the basics of end user computing in their core information systems courses, along with traditional data processing. These introductory courses usually cover end user application packages (e.g., spreadsheet), the hardware and software knowledge needed by end users, and good practice in the development of EUC applications.

But the EUC picture beyond the business core is less happy. In the past, most schools only offered advanced courses in one or two specific EUC topics, notably decision support systems, office automation, personal computing, and data communications. It would take four or five single-topic courses to give a comprehensive picture of end user computing, and few students have the time for so many EUC courses. Worse yet, even students who take several courses often emerge with a scattered picture, instead of with an integrated understanding of end user computing and its management.

In response to the explosion in EUC applications and management theory, many courses that used to teach a single topic have been expanded, either officially or unofficially, to cover more material. Many DSS courses cover personal computing, while many office automation courses often cover PCs and perhaps data communications as well.

But this approach of expanding single-topic courses is far from ideal. It tends to leave some topics uncovered while other topics are covered in multiple courses. More importantly, the student tends to gain only a scattered understanding of EUC applications instead of a comprehensive understanding of EUC and its management.

At a more pragmatic level, expanded single-topic courses are hard to teach because most textbooks are limited to single applications, such as DSS or office automation. Hence, the teacher has to produce an endless stream of supplementary material. In many instances, these materials consist of magazine articles that assume a good deal of background that the student may or may not have.

THIS BOOK

This textbook, *End User Computing*, is designed to support a number of different strategies for teaching advanced EUC courses.

- Most obviously, it can be used in a two-semester course covering end user computing with an integrative perspective. A two-semester course can also cover application packages.

- It can also be taught in a one-semester overview course that discusses the management of end user computing broadly and also goes into depth in specific areas, for example, personal computing technology and applications. In this case, the teacher needs to be selective in assigning readings, because there is so much material to cover.

- It can be used as a textbook in expanded single-topic courses, either as the main text or as a supplementary text. A teacher who limits these courses to their classic 1970s boundaries would not find this book attractive, but a teacher who is striving to develop a broader perspective should find this book very attractive.

- In data communications, the textbook can be used as a stand-alone text by covering the early PC technology chapters as well as the data communications chapters and perhaps host-based applications. This focus gives a better understanding of how PCs approach data communications than many standard texts.

- Finally, this book can be used as a main text or as a supplement in multiple courses. Many MIS departments coordinate their advanced courses, and the use of *End User Computing* in several courses provides continuity as well as reduces the costs to the student.

Even courses that cover the entire book are likely to skip the topics covered in earlier core courses. In the PC hardware and software chapters, for instance, a professor might skip printers, except for laser page printers. This would avoid redundancy while freeing the time to focus on advanced topics, such as the graphics revolution. EUC is such a broad area and core curricula are so diverse that *End User Computing* could not be designed as a simple front-to-back textbook and still provide the material needed in different teaching strategies. Instead, it is *an organized resource to support diverse teaching strategies for end user computing courses.*

THE ACM AND DPMA MODEL CURRICULA

It is somewhat difficult to relate this textbook to the model curricula developed by the Association for Computing Machinery (ACM) and the Data Processing Management Association (DPMA). First, both of these curricula are still in the process of evolving beyond data processing. When the ACM's model curriculum, which is called the Computer Information Systems (ACM-CIS) curriculum, began in 1982, it was almost a pure DP curriculum, with only data communications and "modeling and decision systems" getting attention beyond the DP world. In 1986, the ACM-CIS curriculum expanded considerably, to include these courses of relevance to end user computing:

ACM-CIS/86-8	Microcomputer Applications for Business
ACM-CIS/86-9	Advanced Office Systems
ACM-CIS/86-10	Integrated Systems for Administration and Management
ACM-CIS/86-11	Introduction/Survey of Computer Graphics
ACM-CIS/86-12	Decision Support and Expert Systems
ACM-CIS/86-17	Techniques for Data Communication—A Survey
ACM-CIS/86-20	Information Center Management

Although this rush to EUC topics is encouraging, it is really too much of a good thing. Since no school can possibly offer all of these courses, there must be some rationale for grouping them together, and this rationale is missing from the CIS/86. The 1986 version still retains the schizophrenic piecemeal approach to end user computing that has long prevented corporations from adopting an intelligently integrative understanding of EUC.

DPMA also calls its model curriculum Computer Information Systems; hence, we will designate its courses as DPMA-CIS. In its 1986 revision, DPMA-CIS included the following courses with considerable EUC content:

PREFACE

DPMA-CIS/86-2	Microcomputer Applications in Business (core course)
DPMA-CIS/86-7	Information Center Functions (core course)
DPMA-CIS/86-9	Advanced Office Systems
DPMA-CIS/86-10	Computer Graphics in Business
DPMA-CIS/86-11	Decision Support and Expert Systems
DPMA-CIS/86-15	Distributed Intelligence and Communication Systems (In the description, data communications is only part of the course.)

DPMA is still in the process of defining its model graduate program, but initial drafts indicate that its graduate program is likely to be very similar to its undergraduate program.

Again, few business schools follow either the ACM or DPMA curricula exactly. Particularly in the areas covered by end user computing, they tend to create courses that cover two or more areas. In addition, both model curricula are still evolving rapidly, especially in the areas covered by end user computing. As a result, most schools lead the model curricula in EUC and other fast-changing areas.

COMPREHENSIVE TWO-SEMESTER COURSES

Two-semester courses can cover the entire book, or at least the parts of it not covered in the school's introductory course. They can also cover a number of application packages. My own experience is that students want to spend about one-half of the course learning new software packages or expanding their skills in packages already covered.

The book begins with several management chapters that can be covered in whole or in part, depending on the orientation of the course. During this period, homework can be given in packages taught in earlier courses, to help the student get back up to speed in these packages.

Next, the book goes through personal computing, beginning with hardware and software, and then moving into spreadsheet, data base, communication, and other PC applications. I generally stop at the end of PC applications that do not involve communications at the end of the first semester.

The rest of the book covers communications and the applications that use data communications. It begins with technology, covering PC-host communications, PC networking, and large issues, including LANS and comprehensive standards architectures. It ends with two chapters on host services.

I have sometimes given students one-semester projects, in which they build modest-sized applications in Lotus 1-2-3 macros. The project includes assessment, design, construction, and major aspects of implementation, including the development of training materials.

ADVANCED MICROCOMPUTING COURSES

An advanced microcomputing course would probably cover Chapters 1 and 2, then jump right into PC applications. It would probably include PC-host communications and PC networking, but probably would not include comprehensive data communications standards. This is a good deal to cover in one course if several software packages are to be mastered, but students who take these courses usually expect to be overworked in them.

The teacher will probably want to cover the introductory chapter on PC technology, but he or she will probably need to be selective in Chapters 7 and 8, which go into the details of PC hardware and software.

DECISION SUPPORT SYSTEM COURSES

Classes that deal with decision support systems and executive information systems tend to fall into two basic categories. Some deal with applications that are so complex that they must be created by information systems professionals. These are very hard to develop, and while the user takes a fairly active role, the IS professional is the real hero in the piece. *End User Computing* is not ideal for these courses.

Other DSS/EIS courses cover a much broader range of applications, including those developed by the ultimate user or by other end users in functional areas. This seems to be the dominant form of DSS and EIS in corporations today, and for these courses, *End User Computing* has a great deal to offer.

DSS and EIS normally include three components in varying degrees. First, there is data retrieval and perhaps the maintenance of the data base to be searched. Second, there is the analysis of the data, so that the use the data in whatever calculations are needed to solve a problem. Third, there are presentation tools, including analytical graphics.

Chapter 1 discusses the wider range of sizes in EUC applications, and Chapter 2 discusses how project development differs by size. It specifically addresses the problems encountered when the DSS must be developed by an IS professional. For PC-based systems, the PC technology, analysis, and data management chapters are important, while for larger systems, the data communications chapters and the chapter on host-based decision support applications is obviously germane. The communication chapters—Chapters 11 and 17—would not be covered. Nor would the chapter on other PC applications, Chapter 12, be covered, except perhaps for a few pieces.

DATA COMMUNICATIONS

Classic datacoms texts focus on technology. But a growing number of data communications courses focus on applications as well. Chapters 6, 13, 14, and 15, cover data communications technology in considerable depth. They focus on PC communications, and this seems reasonable, because it now appears that even host-oriented systems will use PCs as their workstations. Chapters 12, 16, and 17 then cover the kinds of applications users will encounter as they move into host communications and networking.

INFORMATION CENTER MANAGEMENT

The last major course that can be used with this book is a general course on information center management. The first five chapters cover this topic in depth, especially if the student is given an outside project. Because EUC applications will dominate corporate computer use in the future, it seems reasonable to devote a full course to this important topic.

These information center management chapters can also be covered as part of broader the "MIS courses" that focus both on EUC and on more traditional data processing and information resource management concerns. With this approach, traditional material would be covered with a second text or from class lectures.

Raymond R. Panko

ACKNOWLEDGEMENTS

I acknowledge the contributions of a number of individuals who helped extensively with this book, beginning with my reviewers: Fred Davis, University of Michigan; Malcolm Munro, University of Calgary; J. David Naumann, University of Minnesota; R. Ryan Nelson, University of Houston; Suzanne Rivard, Ecole Des H. E. C.; Paul W. Ross; Barbara J. Tante, B.J.T. Enterprises; Hugh Watson, University of Georgia; James Wetherbe, University of Minnesota.

    I also acknowledge the help given by numerous members of the Corporate End User's Support Group, especially Francis Natori, Joe Evans, Tom Wren, Don Fujimoto, Ron Letson, George Kvidera, Dick Burson, Gary Kuhn, Laurie Tenzer, Edna Tsukamoto, Laurie Lau, and Rene Katto. Their practical experiences were invaluable in preparing this book. I am also very grateful to the Honolulu staff of IBM, especially to Jann Boxold and Bill Sheeder, for the detailed help they gave me.

    I thank the many software companies that provided me with the software needed to produce the illustrations in this book, especially the Lotus Development Corporation, Ashton-Tate, Decision Resources, Inc., and Compu-Craft.

    Finally, I express my appreciation to the many professionals at Wiley who made this book possible, especially Nina Lewis, who got me started and excited, Joe Dougherty, who faced the rough job of getting the book finished, and Laura Gathagan, who somehow kept the pieces all together.

R.R.P.

CONTENTS

Chapter 1
THE END USER REVOLUTION 1

THE POST-DP ERA 1
  A Time of Change 1   Naming the Revolution 1   Outgrowing Early Concepts 2
THE END USER EXPLOSION 3
  Benjamin's Study 3   Can it Really Become That Large? 4   Can it Really Grow That Quickly? 4   Conclusion 6
BROAD USER NEEDS 6
  Taxonomy of Departments 6   Type I Departments 6   Type II Departments 8   The Type II Revolution 9   The Demographics of Office Work 10   National Data 10   The Need to Collect Corporate Data 12   Managers 13   Professionals 15   Secretaries in Type II Departments 15   Type II Support and the Information Center 15
TOOLS 17
  Computers 18   *Personal Computers, Hosts, and Microcomputers* 18   Applications 19   *Computers Versus Applications* 19   *Generic Applications Versus Specific Applications* 19   Verbal Communication 20   Analysis 20   Data Retrieval and Application Development 20   Activity Management 21   Graphics 22   Hybrid Applications 22   Patterns of Software Use 23   *Software Use Patterns on Time-Shared Hosts* 23   *Software Use Patterns on Personal Computers* 23
PROJECT DEVELOPMENT ENVIRONMENTS 24
  Project Development 25   The First Two Environments 26   The Third Environment: Mid-Range Projects 27   *Mid-Range Projects* 27   The Fourth Environment: Delegated Development 28   *Delegated Development* 28   *The Management Mix and Application Development* 31   The Fifth Environment: Department Management 32   *The Need for Departmental Planning and Management* 32   *The Management Mix and Project Development* 33

xvii

THE CHANGING INFORMATION CENTER 34
    The Early Years 34   *The 1960s* 34   *The 1970s* 34   *IBM Responds* 35   *The Information Center Concept Grows: 1980–1985* 36   *The PC Shock* 36   *The Information Center Explosion* 36   Broadening Vision of EUC Applications: 1985–1990 37   *DSS and EIS* 37   *Office Automation* 37   *Seeking a New Vision* 37   A Time of Challenge 38   Planning for Success 39   *Planning* 39   *Controlling User Activities* 39   *Becoming Proactive* 40   *The Role of IS Management* 41
CONCLUSION 41
    Themes 41   Organization of the Book 42
REVIEW QUESTIONS 44
REFERENCES 45

Chapter 2
APPLICATION DEVELOPMENT: END USER DEVELOPMENT, DSS, AND EIS 49

INTRODUCTION 49
    Stages in Application Development 49   *Assessment, Design, Construction, and Implementation* 50   *Assessment Versus Other Stages* 50   Sequential and Iterative Development 51   *Sequential Development* 51   *Iterative Development* 52   *Discipline in Iterative Development* 52   *Working Products in Iterative Development* 53   Application Development in Different Situations 53   *The Second Environment* 53   *The Third Environment* 53   *The Fourth Environment* 54   *DSS and EIS* 54
ASSESSMENT 54
    Identifying Candidates 54   *Depending on User Initiative* 55   *Systematic User Input* 55   *Critical Success Factors (CSFs) Analysis* 55   *Tactical Management Initiatives* 56   *External Contribution Analysis* 56   *Breakthrough Thinking* 56   *Identification in Perspective* 57   Selection 57   *Costs and Benefits* 57   *Objective-Critical Applications* 57   *Alternatives for Specific Applications* 57   *Technical Feasibility* 58   *Organizational Feasibility* 58   *Selection in Perspective* 58   Corporate Needs Assessment 58   *Structural Analysis* 58   *Application Identification Studies* 59   *End User Computing Data* 60
DESIGN 60
    Goals Clarification 61   Understanding the Current System 61   Identifying User Requirements 62   Designing the New System 63   Modular and Hierarchical Design 63   Design in the Second Environment 64   Design in the Third Environment 65   Design in the Fourth Environment 65
CONSTRUCTION 66
    Selecting Hardware and Software 66   Development, Testing, and Documentation 66   Construction in the Second Environment 67   Construction in the Third Environment 68   Construction in the Fourth Environment 68
IMPLEMENTATION 68
    Work Systems 68   *Components of a Work System* 68   *Changing Work Systems* 69   *The Organization* 70   Cutover 70   *User Preparation* 71   *Productivity Decline at the Cutover* 71

DEPARTMENT MANAGEMENT 72
   The Department Manager's Roles 73   The Secretary's Roles 73   Staff Members' Roles 74   Power Users' Roles 74   Department Management in Perspective 75
DSS AND EIS DEVELOPMENT 75
   DSSs and EISs 75   Three Versus Two Tools 75   Level of Clients 76   Tailoring to Decisions Versus Tailoring to Individuals 76   Distinctions in Perspective 76   Tailoring 76   Building DSSs and EISs 77   Tools 77   Roles 78   Development Approaches 79   Reactive Versus Proactive Development 79   DSS and EIS in Perspective 79
CONCLUSION 80
REVIEW QUESTIONS 81
REFERENCES 81

Chapter 3
MANAGING END USER COMPUTING: 83
BROAD CONCERNS 83
MANAGING IN A TIME OF CHANGE 83
   Cautious Growth 83   A Maturing Vision 84   Life Cycles 84   Life Cycles in Information Systems 85   Gibson and Nolan 85   Guimaraes 85   Henderson and Treacy 86   Life Cycles in Perspective 86
SERVICES, PROBLEMS, AND CRITICAL SUCCESS FACTORS 86
   Services 86   Leitheiser and Wetherbe 86   Brancheau 87   Sumner 88   Crwth 88   American Management Association 89   Services in Perspective 89   Problems 89   Guimaraes 89   Leitheiser and Wetherbe 89   Crwth 91   Computer Intelligence Corporation 91   Problems in Perspective 92   Critical Success Factors 92   Leitheiser and Wetherbe 92   Brancheau 92   Sumner 94   Critical Success Factor in Perspective 94   Services, Problems, and CSFs: A Recap 94
FUNDAMENTAL DECISIONS 95
   Personal Computers Versus Mainframes 95   Advantages of Mainframes 96   Processing speeds 96   Multiuser operation 96   Access to corporate data 96   Simpler technology 96   operator assistance 96   Advantages of Personal Computers 96   Consistent response time 96   Simpler day-to-day operation 96   more vivid and simpler 97   Seeking a Balance 97   Justification 98   Costs 99   Hard Benefits 99   Time savings 100   Softer Cost Savings: Tangible Benefits 101   Efficiency, Effectiveness, and Innovation 101   Trends in Factory Automation 102   Developing an Approval Process: General Direction 103   Developing an Approval Process: Individual Applications 103   Acceleration and Control 105   A Laissez-Faire Beginning 105   Acceleration Tactics 106   Control Tactics 106   Combining Acceleration and Control 106   Chargeback 106   Why Chargeback? 107   Developing a Costing Structure 107   Nuances of Chargeback 108   Should the Information Center Develop Applications? 109   Reasons for Not Offering Application Development 110   Reasons for Offering Application Development 110   Guidelines 111
PLANNING 112
   Planning Principles 112   The Mission 112   Specific Goals 112   User Needs 113   Technology Forecast 113   External Environment 114   Programs 115

Resources 115   *Balancing the Pieces* 115   *Measurement and Feedback* 115   *Feedback* 116   *Planning and Budgeting* 116   *The Planning Study* 117   *Proposal for a Planning Study* 117   *Information Gathering* 117   *The Charter* 118   *Specific Services and Internal Tasks* 119   *Staffing and Budgeting* 119   *Accountability and Oversight* 119   *Organization of the Proposal* 119   *The Presentation* 120   *Annual Planning* 121   *Data and Forecasting* 121   *The Annual Report* 121
CONCLUSION 122
REVIEW QUESTIONS 122
REFERENCES 123

Chapter 4
BUILDING THE INFORMATION CENTER 126
ORGANIZATION 126
   Placement in the Organization 126   *The Classic Infrastructure* 127   *Paradigm Lost* 128   *Differentiation* 128   *The Gap* 129   *The Bridging Function* 130   *The Marketing Image* 130   *The Contractor Image* 131   *The Information Center and Information Systems* 132   *The Role of the Information Center: A Summary* 132   *Work Space* 132
STAFFING 133
   Staff Size 133   *Selecting the Information Center Manager* 134   *Hiring Staff* 135   *Training the Staff* 135
MOBILIZING END USERS 136
   User Groups 136   *Formalizing the Functional Specialist Role* 138   *Rethinking the Functional Specialist's Role* 138
PROMOTION 139
   Special Events 139   *Walk-in Centers* 140   *Newsletters* 140
DEVELOPING THE TECHNOLOGICAL INFRASTRUCTURE 141
   Key Standards 141   *Philosophy of Control* 143   *Strict Enforcement* 143   *Open Enforcement* 143   *Product Research and Selection* 144   *Obtaining Samples* 144   *Initial Technical Testing* 145   *Establishing Evaluation Guidelines* 145   *Selecting an Evaluation Team* 146   *Pilot Studies and General Release* 146   *Purchasing* 146   *Advantages of Retailers* 147   *Advantages of Mail Order Firms* 147   *Purchasing Trends* 147   *Site Licensing* 148   *Stocking Goods* 148   *Installation* 149   *Software Upgrades* 150   *Purchasing* 150   *Maintenance* 151   *Comparisons* 151   *Detailed Arrangements* 151   *Maintenance Trends* 152   *Building the Technological Infrastructure: Conclusion* 152
ESTABLISHING KEY POLICIES 153
   Computer Abuse: Privacy, Security, Damage, and Theft 153   *Definitions* 153   *Host Security* 154   *Personal Computer Security* 155   *Unauthorized Software Copying* 155   *Ergonomics* 157   *The Display* 158   *Tables and Chairs* 159   *Other General Concerns* 159   *Radiation* 159   *Stress* 160   *Ergonomics in Perspective* 160
CONCLUSION 160
REVIEW QUESTIONS 161
REFERENCES 162

CONTENTS   **xxi**

Chapter 5
SUPPORT: CONSULTING, TRAINING, AND TROUBLESHOOTING   165
INTRODUCTION   165
     Major Themes   165   *The Support Mix*   165   *Life Cycle Support*   166   *The Skills Hierarchy*   166   Training Considerations   166   *Training Alternatives*   166   *Effectiveness in Training*   166   *Mobilizing End Users*   166
THE SKILLS HIERARCHY   167
     The Need to Understand User Skills   167   Basic Use Skills   168   Comfortable Use Skills   168   Good Practice   169   *Hardware and Software Knowledge*   169   *Data Management*   170   *Application Development*   170   *Domain Knowledge*   170   *Work Systems*   171   *Department Management*   171   *Roles in Corporate Systems*   171   *Conclusions about Good Practice*   172   Innovation   172   Conclusions About the Skills Hierarchy   172
TRAINING PRINCIPLES   172
     Harmon's Application of Piaget's Theories   173   *Concrete Operationalism*   173   *Formal Operationalism*   173   *Meta-Cognitive Understanding*   173   IBM's Minimalist Training Study   174   *Quick-Start Behavior*   174   *Naive Cognitive Models*   174   *Problems with Quick-Start Behavior*   175   *Using the Results*   175   Scharer's Less is More Study   175   *The Use of Cheat Sheets*   175   *User-to-User Training*   175   *Using the Results*   175   IBM's Training Wheels Word Processor Study   176   *The Training Wheels Word Processor*   176   *Results of the Research*   176   Tentative Conclusions   176   *Skills Hierarchy*   176   *Quick-Start Behavior*   176   *Users have Pre-existing Cognitive Models*   177   *Keep it Short and Simple*   177   *Compounding Errors*   177
TRAINING CONSIDERATIONS   177
     Trends   177   Organizational Responsibilities   178   *Should Training be Done within the Information Center?*   178   *Mobilizing End Users*   178   *Industry Patterns*   178   Diversity in Needs   178   *User Knowledge*   179   *Organizational Level*   179   *Typing Speed*   179   Modular Learning   179   *The Modularization of Courses*   179   *When to Teach the Machine and Operating System*   179   *Lengths of Modules and Sessions*   180   Skills Versus Concepts   180
TRAINING ALTERNATIVES   180
CLASSROOM TRAINING   180
     Advantages in Classroom Training   181   Disadvantages of Classroom Training   181   Internal Versus External Training   181   Techniques for Classroom Training   182
MEDIATED TRAINING   183
     General Characteristics of Mediated Training   183   *Advantages of Mediated Training*   183   *Disadvantages of Mediated Training*   183   Computer-Based Training (CBT)   183   *Authoring Programs, Presentation Programs, and Courses*   183   *Internal Development Versus Purchasing*   184   *CBT Use Patterns*   184   *Techniques of Computer-Based Training*   185   Audio and Video Training   185   *Audio Cassettes*   185   *Videotape and Videodisks*   185   *Considerations in Using VCR Training*   186   *The Future*   186
DEVELOPING A COMPREHENSIVE TRAINING PROGRAM   186
     The Introductory Course   187   Personal Computer Courses   188   *Using the Personal Computer and Its Operating System*   188   *PC Application Software Courses*   188   *Working with a Personal Computer*   188   Host Computing

Courses 189   Using a Host Computer and Its Operating System 189   Host Application Software Courses 189   Working with Host Computers 189   Management Courses 190   Personal Management 190   Departmental Management 190   Corporate Systems 190   Combining Levels 190
STANDARD POLICIES AND PLANS 190
DEVELOPING SUPPORT PROGRAMS FOR DIFFERENT ENVIRONMENTS 191
  Support in the Second Environment 191   Support for the Third Environment 191   Life Cycle Consulting 191   Life Cycle Workshops 192   The Fourth Environment 192   The Fifth Environment 193
CONCLUSION 193
REVIEW QUESTIONS 193
REFERENCES 194

Chapter 6
PERSONAL COMPUTER STANDARDS AND PRICES 196
INTRODUCTION 196
  Yesterday, Today and Tomorrow 196   Types of Personal Computers 199   Desktop Personal Computers 199   Portable Personal Computers 199   Engineering Workstation 200   Home Computers 200   The Necessity for Setting Standards 201
AN OVERVIEW OF PERSONAL COMPUTER TECHNOLOGY 201
  Major Circuits 201   The Microprocessor and Math Coprocessor 201   Memory Circuits 202   Adapter Circuits 202   Logical Organization: The Bus 203   Physical Organization: Mother and Expansion Boards 203   The Mother Board 203   Expansion Boards 204   Expansion Board Compatibility 205   Implications of Expansion Boards 205   Software 205   Loading and Terminating Programs 205   Division of Labor 206   Software Standards for Openness 207   Openness and Selection 208   Openness in Perspective 208
SETTING STANDARDS 209
  Standardization Tasks 209   Computer Families 209   Add-On Hardware 210   Software 210   Selecting a Family to Support 210   8-bit Personal Computers 211   The IBM PC Family 211   The IBM Personal Computer Desktop Line 211   The IBM Personal System/2 Line 213   Portable Computers 215   Specialized Machines 215   Networking 216   IBM PC Compatibles (Clones) 216   MS-DOS Compatibility 216   Full Program Compatibility 218   Expansion Board Compatibility 219   Apple Macintosh 219   The First Products 219   Problems 220   The Turning Point 220   The Explosion of 1987 221   Networking 221   Prospects 222   Other Computers 222
PRICE 223
  A Minimum Personal Computer 223   A Typical System 224   A High-End Personal Computer 225   Networked System 226   A Four-Year Budget 226   Price Trends 228   Historical Price Trends 228   Pressures on Prices 229   The Price Outlook 229
CONCLUSION 229
REVIEW QUESTIONS 230

Chapter 7
PERSONAL COMPUTER HARDWARE   231

ELECTRONICS   231
   The Bus   231   *Data Lines*   231   *Address Lines*   232   *Control Lines*   232   *Power Lines*   232   *IBM's Micro Channel*   232   *Apple Macintosh Busses*   232   The Microprocessor   233   *Microprocessor Technology*   233   *The Intel Family*   233   *The Motorola MC68000 Family*   237   Coprocessors   237   *Math Coprocessors*   238   *Graphics Coprocessors*   238   *Memory Management Coprocessors*   238   RAM   238   *Memory Limits*   239   *The Location of RAM*   239   *RAM Chips*   239   *Volatility*   239   ROM   240   *Bootstrap Programs*   240   *ROM Service Programs*   240   *Object Graphics Routines*   240   Expansion Boards   240   *Memory Boards*   241   *Adapter Circuits*   241   *Accelerator Boards*   243   *Peripheral Boards*   243   *Communications Boards*   244   *Multifunction Boards*   244   Board Compatibility   245   Power   245   *Capacity*   245   *Power Problems*   246   *Spikes*   246   *Prolonged High Voltage*   246   *Brownouts and Blackouts*   246   *The Quality of PC Power Supplies*   246   *The Cost of Power*   246

EXTERNAL MEMORY   247
   Why External Memory   247   Disk Technology   248   *Sides*   248   *Tracks*   249   *Sectors*   250   *Capacity*   250   *Clusters*   250   *The Macintosh Format*   250   Optical Disk Drive Formats   251   Floppy Disks   251   *5.25 Inch Floppy Disks*   251   *3.5 Inch Disks*   252   Hard Disks   252   *Capacity*   252   *Speed*   252   Hard Disk Backup   253   *Backup onto Floppy Disks*   253   *Tape Backup Units*   253   *Backup Software*   254   *Backup onto Hard Disks*   254   *Backup: Conclusion*   254   Other External Memory Technologies   255   *Bernoulli Drives*   255   *Optical Disks*   255

GRAPHICS TECHNOLOGY   256
   Introduction   256   Key Graphics Concepts   257   *Input/Output Systems*   257   *Pixel Output*   257   *Text Versus Graphics Adapters*   258   Memory Requirements and Processing Needs in Pixel Graphics   258   Resolution   259   *Pixels per Inch*   259   *Pixels per Screen or Page*   259   Bits per Pixel   260   *Monochrome Graphics*   260   *Gray Scale*   260   *Color Graphics*   261   Pixel Versus Object Graphics Software   262   *Objects*   262   *Representing Objects*   263   *Memory Requirements*   263   *Editability*   264   *Color*   264   *Output Quality in Printing*   265   *Printing Speed*   266   *Pixel Versus Object Graphics in Perspective*   266   Toward Graphics Standards   267   *The Complexity of Graphics Output*   267   *Emulation*   267   *PostScript*   268   *NAPLPS*   270   *VDI*   270   *SO Document Standards*   270   *Comprehensive Graphics Standards*   271   *Standards for Pixel Graphics Software*   271

DISPLAYS   272
   Cathode Ray Tube Technology   272   Computer Displays Versus Home Televisions   273   *General Differences Between Computer Displays and Home Televisions*   273   *The Resolution Problem*   273   Text Versus Graphics Displays   274   Monochrome Versus Color   274   *NTSC Color*   274   *RGB Display Systems*   274   Display Systems for IBMs and Compatibles   275   *IBM's Original Monochrome System*   276   *The Hercules Graphics Card*   276   *Color Graphics Adapter*   276   *IBM's Enhanced Graphics System*   276   *Multicolor Graphics Array*   277   *Video Graphics Array*   277   *Other Adapters and Displays*   277   Macintosh Display Systems   277   *The Original Apple Macintosh Display*

CONTENTS

System 278   Display Systems for the Macintosh II 278   Flat Panel Displays 278   Full-Page Display Systems 279   Projection Systems 280   Image Quality 280   Brightness 280   Monochrome and Color 280   Room Preparation 281
PRINTERS 281
Solid Font Printers 282   Golf Ball Printers 282   Daisywheel Printers 283   Letter Quality Printing 283   An Inability to Handle Graphics 284   Major Cost-Performance Categories 284   Other Cost Factors 284   Dot Matrix Printers 284   Dot Matrix Printing Technology 285   Graphics 285   Print Quality 285   Denser Print Heads 286   Multiple Pass Printing 287   Limits on Printing Quality 287   Other Dot Matrix Technologies 288   Cost Factors 288   Page Printers 289   Page Printer Technology 289   Performance 289   Low-Speed Units 290   Features 292   Plotters 293   Color 294   Market Dynamics 295
INPUT DEVICES 296
Keyboards 296   Pointing Devices 297   Light Pens 297   Touch Screens 297   Mice 298   Input Tablet 298   Scanners 299   Text Scanners 299   Graphics Scanners 300   Hybrid Scanners 300   Voice Technology 300   Voice Output 301   Voice Input 301
CONCLUSION 302
REVIEW QUESTIONS 302
REFERENCES 304

Chapter 8
PERSONAL COMPUTER SOFTWARE TRENDS   305

INTERNAL MEMORY CONCEPTS 305
The Address Space View 306   Address Spaces 306   Memory Map 307   Reserved System Memory 307   The Operating System 308   Other System Software 308   Application Programs 308   Unused Space 309   Actual Memory 309   The Layered View 309   Layered Calls 310   Efficiency 310   Consistency in User Interfaces 310   Combining the Two Views 310   Jump with Return 310   RAM-Resident Programs 311   Interrupt 311   Adding a Layer 312   Pop-up Programs 313   Conclusion 313
INTERNAL AND EXTERNAL MEMORY 315
Why External Memory? 315   Copying 315   Interactive Programs 316   Virtual Memory Operating Systems 317   Bank Switching 318   RAM Disks 319
SYSTEM SOFTWARE 320
General Considerations 320   Hardware and ROM Service Programs 320   Operating Systems 320   Selecting an Operating System 321   Simple Operating Systems 321   A Historical View 321   The Size Squeeze 322   Disk Operations 324   File Operations 324   MS-DOS Input/Output Operations 324   Hierarchical File Structure 325   MS-DOS Batch Files 326   Multitasking and Multiuser Operating Systems 326   Multitasking Operating Systems 326   Multiuser Operating Systems 327   Unix 327   Windowing Operating System 328   Single-Tasking Windowing 329   Task-Switching Windowing 329   Multitasking Windowing 330   Copying Across Windows 333   User-Friendly Operating Systems 330   The Initial Desktop 330   Windows 331   Operating on Windows 333   IBM's Operating System/2 335   Memory Management 335   Ease of Use 336   The Communications Manager 337   Data Base Functions 338

CONTENTS **xxv**

    IBM's Systems Application Architecture (SAA) 338   *The Systems Application Architecture Approach 339*   *SAA and OS/2 340*   *SAA in Perspective 341*   Environments Versus Operating Systems 341   Other System Software 342   *Keyboard Enhancers 342*   *Disk Managers 344*   *Disk Copying Programs 345*   *Programming Language Compilers and Interpreters 345*   *Integral Utilities 345*

INTEGRATION 346
    Incompatible Data File Formats 346   Integrated Software 346   Desk Accessory Programs 347   Screen Capture 349   *Text Screen Capture 349*   *Graphics Screen Capture 350*   *Macintosh Screen Capture 350*   *Dumb Terminal Screen Capture 350*   File Format Conversion 350   *ASCII Files 351*   *Spreadsheet File Formats 352*   *Lotus Worksheet Files 353*   *DIF Files 353*   *Word Processing File Formats 353*   *The General Situation 353*   *DCA 354*   *International Standards 354*   *Other Intermediate File Formats 354*   *Data Base 354*   *Graphics 354*   Windowing Environments 354

ARTIFICIAL INTELLIGENCE 355
    The Breakthrough of the 1980s 355   Limited But Important Problems 355   The Knowledge-Based System Approach 355   The Knowledge Base 356   *Overview 356*   *Knowledge Representation: Semantic Networks 357*   *Knowledge Representation: Frames 358*   *Knowledge Representation: Rules 358*   *Uncertainty and Inheritance 358*   The Inference Engine 359   *The Need for an Inference Engine 359*   *Forward Chaining 359*   *Backward Chaining 360*   *Advanced Inference 360*   The Dialog Management System 361   Languages for Building AI Applications 361   *LISP 361*   *PROLOG 362*   *Shells 362*   Major Applications 362   *Natural Language Input 362*   *Expert Systems 363*   *Anticipatory Software 363*

CONCLUSION 363
REVIEW QUESTIONS 364

Chapter 9
ANALYTICAL MODELING ON PERSONAL COMPUTERS   366

ANALYTICAL MODELING TOOLS 367
    Spreadsheet Analysis 367   Other Analysis Tools 368   Good Modeling Practice 369

ANALYTICAL MODELING PRINCIPLES 370
    Analytical Modeling 370   *The Benefits of Modeling 370*   *Dangers of Modeling 371*   Model Images 372   *Spreadsheet Image 372*   *Equations Image 372*   *Dependency Image 372*   *Images in Perspective 373*   Building Analytical Models 373   *Understanding the Problem 373*   *Identifying Variables 374*   *Quantifying Variables 374*   *Specifying Relationships Among Variables 375*   *Testing the Model 375*   Good Practice in Model Building 376   *Designing Equations Properly 376*   *Hierarchical Design 378*   *Modular Design 378*   *Documentation 379*   *Construction and Testing 380*   Interrogation 382   *Independent and Dependent Variables 382*   *What If Analysis 383*   *Sensitivity Analysis 384*   *How Can (Goal-Seeking) Analysis 385*   *How Best (Optimization) Analysis 386*   *Interrogation in Perspective 387*

SPREADSHEET CAPABILITIES: LOTUS 1-2-3 388
    Basic Capabilities 388   Model Building 388   *The Underlying Worksheet 390*   *Improving the Model's Appearance 390*   *Extending the Model's Logic 391*

What If Analysis 393   Analytical Graphics 394   Built-In Computational Functions 395   Financial @-Functions 395   Statistical @-Functions 396   Table Lookup @-Functions 396   Logical and String Handling @-Functions 398   Data File Tables 398   Keys, Menus, and Macros 399   *The Keyboard* 399   *Menus* 399   *Macros* 400
SELECTING SPREADSHEET SOFTWARE 402
    Lotus 1-2-3 Alternatives 403   *Direct Competitors* 403   *Value-Added Products* 404   Selecting Add-On Programs 405
SUPPORTING SPREADSHEET USERS 406
    Training 406   Teaching Simple Good Practice 406   Support for Larger Models 406
CONCLUSION 407
REVIEW QUESTIONS 407

Chapter 10
DATA MANAGEMENT ON PERSONAL COMPUTERS 409
INTRODUCTION 409
    Data 409   Data Management Tools 410   *Third-Generation Languages* 410   *Special Purpose Fourth-Generation Tools* 411   *Data Management Systems* 412   *Limitations on Fourth-Generation Tools on Hosts* 413   Personal Computer Products 413   Categories of Data Management Systems 414   *PC Versus Host Tools* 414   *Stand-Alone Versus Networked PC Products* 414   *File Management Systems* 415   *High-End Data Base Management Systems (DBMSs)* 415   *Mid-Range DBMSs* 415   *Data Management Products Embedded in Other Programs* 415   The Market 416   Steps in Developing Data Applications 416
DATA CONCEPTS 417
    Data Files 417   *The Table Image* 418   *Data Files: The Form Image* 418   *Repeating Fields* 419   Basic Relational Data Base Concepts 420   *The Need for Data Base Processing* 420   *Network Data Bases* 421   *Relational DBMS Terminology* 422   *Normalization* 423   *The Future is Likely to be Relational* 425   Relational Algebra 426   *File Extraction: Select and Project* 426   Relational Calculus 429
NEEDS IDENTIFICATION AND DATA MODELING 430
    Needs Identification 430   *The General Situation* 431   *Design Rules* 431   *Output Requirements* 431   *A Managerial Focus* 432   *New Versus Existing Applications* 432   Entity Identification 432   Designing Entity-Relationship Diagrams 433   *One-to-One Relationships* 433   *One-to-Many Relationships* 433   *Many-to-Many Relationships* 434   Refining the ER Diagram 434   *Removing One-to-One Relationships* 434   *Converting Many-to-Many Relationships* 434   Creating Primary Keys 435   *Natural Primary Keys* 435   *Artificial IDs as Primary Keys* 435   *Sequence Number Primary Keys* 435   *Avoiding Meaningful Keys* 436   *Multifield Primary Keys* 436   Setting Up Relational Tables 437   Adding Attributes 437   Assigning Attribute Types 438   *Text* 438   *Integer Numbers* 438   *Real Numbers* 438   *Binary Coded Decimal (BCD) Numbers* 439   *Date and Time Fields* 439   *Special Field Types* 439   Documenting the Schema 440
SETTING UP THE DATE BASE 441
    Entering the Schema 441   *dBase III Plus* 441   *Creating a Data Base by Giving Its Schema* 442   Entering Data 444   Editing Data and Changing File

Structures 444   *Basic Choices 444   Indexing a File 446   Retrieving
Information 447   Query Languages and Report Generators 447   Query
Languages 449   Report Generators 452   Creating Custom Applications 454
A Customized Application 454   Fourth-Generation Language (4GL) 455
Application Generators 456   Merging the Two Tools 458*
THE ROLE OF THE INFORMATION CENTER 459
   *Concepts and Terminology 459   Basic Concepts 460   Key Fields and Index
Files 460   Relational DRMSs 460   Teaching Specific Packages 461   Teaching
Programming 462   Support in Application Building 462*
CONCLUSION 463
REVIEW QUESTIONS 464
REFERENCES 465

Chapter 11
COMMUNICATION APPLICATIONS ON PERSONAL COMPUTERS   466
WORD PROCESSING 467
   *A Historical Perspective 467   Types of Word Processing Software 467   Text
Editors 467   Personal Programs 469   Standard Word Processing Programs 469
Advanced Word Processing Programs 469   Desktop Publishing Programs 470
Seeking Compatibility 470   Standard Programs 471   Basic Menu Operations 471
Text Entry 471   Formatting 472   Text Characteristics 472   Justification 474
Editing 476   Printing 477   Automated Operations 478   Import and Export 479
Advanced Formatting 479   Table Layout 479   Advanced WYSIWYG 480
Multiple Columns 480   Style Sheets 481   Page Description Languages 481
Graphics 481   Author Aids 482   Outlining 482   Revision Aids 482   Other
Useful Features 483   Word Processing in Perspective 483*
CONCEPTUAL GRAPHICS 483
   *Basic Distinctions 483   Analytical Versus Conceptual Graphics 483   Normal
Versus Presentation Graphics 484   Pixel Versus Object Graphics Software 484
Advantages of Pixel Graphics Software 485   Advantages of Object Graphics
Software 485   Hybrid Programs 485*
MACPAINT, A PIXEL GRAPHICS PROGRAM 486
   *The Initial Screen 486   The Text Tool 487   Shape-Drawing Tools 488
Layout Tools 489   Editing Tools 490   Add-On Products 491
Conclusion 491*
MACDRAW, AN OBJECT GRAPHICS PROGRAM 492
   *The Initial Screen 492   Object Drawing Tools 493   Free-Form Drawing
Tools 494   The Text Tool 494   Layout Tools 495   Arrangement
Functions 495*
DESKTOP PUBLISHING 496
   *Beyond Word Processing 496   The Limitations of Word Processing Programs 496
Page Layout 496   Desktop Publishing Versus Word Processing 497   Desktop
Publishing Software 497   The Computer 497   The Printer 498   The Future 498
Page Layout 498   Basic Elements 498   Text Creation and Importation 502
Graphics Creation and Importation 503   Editing 504   The Future 505*
CONCLUSION 505
REVIEW QUESTIONS 506

Chapter 12
OTHER PERSONAL COMPUTER APPLICATIONS 508

ONLINE SERVICES 509
   The Industry 509   Basic Information Retrieval 510   Advanced Information Retrieval 510   Electronic Mail 511   Reaching Online Services 511   *Public Data Networks 511   Modems 512   Terminal Emulation and Videotex 512   Communications Programs 513*   Managing the Use of Online Services 513   *Assessing Competing Services 513   Supporting Basic Services 513   Supporting Sophisticated Information Retrieval Services 513*

PC NETWORKING SERVICES 515
   Networking Basics 515   *The Main Components 515   Why PC Networks? 516   Printer Services 517   Communications Services 517   Disk and File Sharing Services 518   Basic Concepts 518   Volume Sharing 518   Sharing at Three Levels 519   Networked DBMS Programs 520   Managing Shared Disks 520   Electronic Mail 521   Managing a Networked Environment 521*

INTEGRATED PROGRAMS AND DESK ACCESSORY PROGRAMS 521
   Why Integrated Programs? 522   *Cost 522   Integrative Applications 522   Ease of Learning 523*   The Emergence of Integrated Programs 523   Problems 524   *Incompatibility with Existing Standards 524   Hardware Concerns 525   Learning Problems 525   Limited Attractiveness 525*   Managing Integrated Programs 526   Desk Accessory Programs 527

LESS COMMON APPLICATIONS 528
   Programming Languages 528   Project Management 530   Business Applications 530   Vertical Software 530   Expert Systems 531   *DEFT System 531   What Are Expert Systems 532   Expert System Shells 536   Development 537   Perspective 538*

REVIEW QUESTIONS 538
REFERENCES 539

Chapter 13
WORKING WITH HOST COMPUTERS 540

BASIC ISSUES 541
   Linking Workstations to Hosts 541   Transmission Speed 542   *Bits per Second 543   Bits per Second and Baud Rate 543   Duration and Noise 543   Throughput 544*

TERMINALS 544
   TTY Terminals 544   *Dumb Terminals 544   ASCII 545   Error Detection through Parity 546   Asynchronous Transmission 547   The RS232C Electrical Interface 547   Speed 548   Duplex and Echoing 549*   ANSI Terminals 550   Host-Specific Terminals 550   *Smart Terminals 550   EBCDIC 551   Synchronous Transmission 551   Host-Specific Interfaces 553   Line Sharing 554   Color and Graphics 555   The 3270 Terminal "Standard" 555   TTYs Versus 3270 Terminals: in Perspective 555*

PC TERMINAL EMULATION 555
   Approaches to Terminal Emulation 556   *TTY Emulation 556   Emulating Host-Specific Terminals 557   Protocol Converters 557   Communications Programs 558   Making the User's Life Easier 558*   The Need for Data Transfer 560   *Screen Capture 561   Uploading ASCII Disk Files 561   Nulls and*

XON/XOFF 561   File Transfer Protocols 562   Downloading with Format
Conversion 563   File Transfer in PC-Host Sister Programs 563   Micro-Mainframe
Links 563

THE TRANSMISSION FACILITY 564
Linking a TTY via Modems and the Telephone System 564   Modems 565
Modem Standards 566   Intelligent Modems 567   External and Internal
Modems 567   Callback Modems 568   Linking TTYs to Hosts Directly 568
RS232C Cables and Null Modems 568   Line Drivers 570   Short-Haul
Modems 570   Using Multiplexers 570   Fixed Allocation Multiplexers 571
Statistical Multiplexers 571   Linking 3270 Terminals to Hosts 572   IBM
Mainframes and the 3270 Family 572   Local Cabling for IBM 3270
Communications 572   Long Distance 3270 Communications 574   Personal
Computer 3270 Emulation 575   Linking Terminals via More Complex
Systems 575   Overview 575   Suppliers 576   Multiplexing and
Concentration 577   Microwave Bypass 577   Optical Fiber Bypass 578   Satellite
Bypass Systems 578

SUPPORT AND CONTROL 579
Security Software 579   Access Limitations 579   Multilevel Control 580
Security Administrator Features 580   Organizational and Planning Issues 580

CONCLUSION 581

REVIEW QUESTIONS 581

Chapter 14
NETWORKING AND COMPREHENSIVE COMMUNICATIONS STANDARDS 584

INTRODUCTION 584
Basic Concepts 584   Point-to-Point Communications Versus Networking 584
Networking Elements 585   Often-Overlooked Considerations 586   The
Importance of Moving Data Quickly 586   PC Networking Needs 586   PC
Networks, LANs, and Wide Area Networks 587   Personal Computer
Networks 587   Local Area Networks 588   Wide Area Networks 588   Switched
Versus Nonswitched Networks 589   Controllers 589   Standards 590
Protocols 591   Layered Approaches to Standardization 591   Bridges and
Gateways 593

BASIC TECHNOLOGICAL CONCEPTS 593
Transmission Media 594   Attenuation, Noise, Distortion and Interference 594
Twisted Pair Wire 594   Cable 594   Optical Fiber 595   Switched
Networks 595   Circuit Switching and Fast Circuit Switching 596   Virtual Circuit
and Datagram Service 596   Switching Topologies 598   Nonswitched Baseband
Networks 599   Baseband Versus Broadband 599   Bus Layouts 600   Ring
Topologies 601   Nonswitched Broadband Networks 602   CATV 602
Dual-Cable Broadband Networks 603   Single-Cable Broadband Networks 605
Engineering Broadband Networks 605   Access Methods for Line Sharing 606
Polling 606   Time and Frequency Division Multiplacing 606   CSMA/CD 606
Token Passing 607

STANDARDS 608
Standards Basics 608   The Protocol View 608   The Players 608   Layering 609
ISO/CCITT Reference Model for Open Systems Interconnection 610

Overview 610   The Physical Layer 611   The Data Link Layer 611   The Network Layer 611   The Transport Layer 611   The Session Layer 611   The Presentation Layer 612   The Application Layer 612   The X.25 and X.75 Standards 612   ISDN Standards 614   IEEE 802 Local Area Standards 615   The Overall Framework 615   802.3: CSMA/CD Bus Networks 617   802.4: Token Bus LANs 617   802.5: Token-Ring LANs 617   TCP/IP 618   IBM's Systems Network Architecture Overview 618   Overview 618   APPC 619   The Prospects for SNA 621
CONCLUSION 621
REVIEW QUESTIONS 621
REFERENCES 623

Chapter 15
NETWORKING PRODUCTS   624
PURCHASING PITFALLS 624
  The Any-to-Any Myth 625   Asynchronous and Synchronous Support 625   Controller Limitations 626   Channel Speed Limitations 627   PC Networking Needs 628   Network Management 628   Pitfalls in Perspective 629
PERSONAL COMPUTER NETWORKS 629
  IBM Personal Computer Networking 629   The IBM Personal Computer Network 630   The IBM Token-Ring Network for Personal Computers 630   The Token-Ring Network Adapter Board 631   Cabling for the Token-Ring Network 631   Software for the Token-Ring Network 632   Other Dedicated PC Networks 633   Token-Ring Network Compatibiles 633   Novell Network 634   3Com Etherseries 634   Microsoft's MS-NET and LAN Manager 635   RS232C PC Networks 635   Macintosh Networks 636   PC Networking Services on LANs 637   The Need for Adapter Boards 637   Server Support 637   Bridges Between PC Networks and LANs 638   Host-Based PC Networking 638
FULL LOCAL AREA NETWORKS 639
  General Considerations 639   Scope 639   PC Networking on LANs 639   Broadband LANs, Baseband LANs, and Data PBXs 639   Broadband LANs 640   CATV Cabling 640   Sytek's Broadband Products 640   Ungerman-Bass Net One 642   Wangnet 642   Baseband LANs 643   IBM's Token-Ring Network 643   Ethernet 643   Data PBXs 643   PBXs for Voice Communications 644   Data PBXs 644   High-Speed Data PBXs 645   Nonblocking PBXs 646
IBM'S DATA COMMUNICATIONS STRATEGIES 646
  IBM's Host-Based Strategies 646   Short-Distance Networking 647   Data PBXs 647   Openness 647   Slow Evolution 648
NETWORK PLANNING AND IMPLEMENTATION 648
  Initial Assessment 649   Benefits 649   Network Hardware and Software Costs 649   Server Costs 649   Planning Costs 650   Implementation Costs 650   Training Costs 650   The Costs of Discarded Software 650   Developing Network Administrators 651   The Bottom Line 652
CONCLUSION 652
REVIEW QUESTIONS 653
REFERENCES 654

Chapter 16
DATA AND DECISION SUPPORT APPLICATIONS ON HOST COMPUTERS 655

INTRODUCTION 656
   Difficulty of Learning 656   *Host Operating System Environments 656*   *Aging User Interfaces in Application Programs 657*   *Batch Operation 657*   *High Functionality 657*   *Improving Ease of Use 658*   Processing Speed and Multiuser Operation 658   *Processing Speed 658*   *Multiuser Operation 658*   Modular Pricing 659   Managing Host Data and Decision Support Applications 660

FINANCIAL ANALYSIS SOFTWARE 661
   Good Practice in Design 661   *Decision-Relevant Variables 661*   *NPV and IRR 662*   *Cash-Based Analysis 663*   *Other Pitfalls 663*   IFPS—A Financial Modeling System 663   *A Nonprocedural Language 664*   *Solving a Model 665*   *Interrogation 665*   *The Multiuser Dimension 667*   *IFPS in Perspective 668*   Training Support and Control 668   *Software Training 668*   *Content Training 669*   *Support 669*   *Control 670*

STATISTICAL ANALYSIS TOOLS 670
   Statistical Problems 671   *Nonparametric Statistics 671*   *Other Statistical Assumptions 672*   *Inferences 672*   *Multivariate Analysis Tools 673*   Problems in Perspective 673   A Comprehensive Package: SAS 674   Good Practice 676   *Faithfulness to Assumptions 676*   *Data Quality 676*

GRAPHICS 677
   Graphics Packages 677   Good Practice 678

DATA MANAGEMENT SYSTEMS 680
   The Evolution of Data Management Tools 680   *The Early Years 680*   *Types of Data Management Products 681*   End User Tools 682   *SQL 682*   *Simple Queries 682*   *WHERE 683*   *Advanced Retrieval 684*   *Multirelation Queries 686*   *Nonquery Operation 686*   *Overall 688*   FOCUS—Describing FOCUS Data Bases 688   *Defining Data Files 688*   *Describing a FOCUS Data Base—Overview 689*   *Defining a FOCUS Data Base—Describing Fields 690*   *Aids 691*   FOCUS—Queries and Reports 691   *Basic Retrieval 691*   *Advanced Retrieval 692*   Training, Support and Control 694   *Direct Support 694*   *Training Alternatives 694*   *Modularization in Training 695*   *System Maintenance 695*   *Control Policies 696*   *Assigning Personal Responsibility 696*   *The Application Control Document 696*   *Retention 696*

INTEGRATED DATA AND DECISION SUPPORT SYSTEMS 697
   The Drive for Integration 697   Tools 697   *Professional Data Tools 697*   *End User Data Tools 698*   *End User Analysis and Presentation Tools 699*   *PC/Workstation Tools 699*   *General Tools 699*   Roads to the Integrated System 700   *Multiple Integrated Systems 700*   *Full Standards 700*

CONCLUSION 701
REVIEW QUESTIONS 702
REFERENCES 702

Chapter 17
NONCLERICAL OFFICE AUTOMATION 703

INTRODUCTION 703
   The Two Worlds of Office Automation 703   Integrating the Management of OA and EUC 705

WORD PROCESSING CENTERS AND OTHER TYPE I DEPARTMENTS 706
    Services in Word Processing Centers 706   Central Dictation 706   Complex Jobs 707   Managing a Word Processing Center 707   Work Flow Management 707   Training 708   Automation 708   Integration with Corporate-Wide OA Systems 708   Managing a Service 708   Other Type I Operations 709   Records Management Centers 709   Reproduction 710   Mailrooms 710

ELECTRONIC MAIL 710
    Internal and External Mail 711   Public Record Services 711   Telegraph 711   TWX and Telex 711   Teletex 712   Other Record Services 713   Facsimile 713   Group 1 Facsimile 714   Group 2 Facsimile 714   Group 3 Facsimile 714   Group 4 Facsimile 714   Electronic Message Systems 715   Costs 715   User Reactions 716   EMS 716   EMS Products 717   Impacts of EMS 717   Organizational Problems 718   Computer Conferencing 718   Voice Messaging 719

STANDARDS FOR TEXT COMMUNICATION 720
    Basic Categories of Standards 720   Document and Mail Delivery Standards 720   Document Standards 720   Standards-Setting Organization 721   X.400 Standards 722   Mail Delivery Standards 722   The Interpersonal Message System Standard 723   The Office Document Architecture Standards Effort 724   The T173 Standard 724   Subsequent Office Document Architecture Standards Efforts 725   IBM Efforts 726   Conclusion 727

TELECONFERENCING 727
    The Audio Problem 728   Telephone Conferencing 728   Loudspeaker Telephones 728   Conference Calling 729   Room-to-Room Services 730   Portable Audio Conferencing Systems 730   Portable Video Conferencing Systems 730   Dedicated Audio Conferencing Rooms 731   Dedicated Video Conferencing Rooms 731   A Moderator's Role 731   When Does Teleconferencing Work? 732

INTEGRATED OFFICE SYSTEMS 733
    Services 733   Word Processing 733   Electronic Messaging 733   Group Meeting Scheduling 734   Document Storage and Retrieval 734   Other Personal Services 735   Administrative Services 735   Technology 735   Wang Office 736   Directory Services 736   Electronic Mail 736   Time Management 736   Other Features in OFFICE I 736   Wang Word Processing 737   Wang Office File Manager 737   IBM Products 737   PROFS, DISOSS, and Personal Services 737   PROFS 738   DISOSS 739   Personal Services 740   Perspective on Integrated Office Systems 740   Second-Generation Integrated Office Systems 741   Standards for Multivendor Environments 741   Multimedia Services 741   Extending Beyond Office Automation 742   PC Integration 742

STUDYING CORPORATE NEEDS FOR OFFICE AUTOMATION 742
    Mail Tagging 743   Personnel Questionnaires 743   Focus Groups 744   Research in Perspective 744

CONCLUSION 745
REVIEW QUESTIONS 745
REFERENCES 746
INDEX I-1

THE END USER REVOLUTION 1

THE POST-DP ERA

A Time of Change

In 1980, computers were the province of clerical workers, engineers, and a few "leading edge" managers and professionals. Today, in contrast, *most* office workers use computers. In another five years, it will be hard to find an office worker who does not.

Computers are not just being used *more* today; they are also being used *very differently* than they were in 1980. Before 1980, computing had been dominated by a single application, **data processing.** Today, non-DP applications are already about as large as data processing and will soon be much larger than DP in nearly every firm.

Unfortunately, many corporate **information systems (IS)** departments have failed to come to grips with this fundamental change. Instead of managing this **post-DP revolution** in an integrated way, they have tended to manage individual applications in isolation, fragmenting their thinking into separate strategies for personal computing, applications on time-shared hosts, decision support systems, executive information systems, and nonclerical office automation. This book attempts to build a more integrated picture of the post-DP revolution, treating all of these applications in a way that emphasizes the essential unity of the current revolution.

Naming the Revolution

The first problem in such a book is to give the revolution a name. The term "post-DP revolution" is one possibility, emphasizing that a fundamental change is occurring. On the other hand, this term merely says that what is happening is not DP. It tells us only what the revolution *is not;* we would rather have a term that emphasizes what this revolution *is.*

Another problem with the term "post-DP" is that some IS departments have a disturbing tendency to think that most new applications are really extensions of DP, believing that what users mostly want is access to corporate DP data bases. In fact, although corporate data bases play an important role in the post-DP world, they are used in only a fraction of new applications.

Another attractive term is "managerial and professional computing." Apart from office automation in clerical departments such as word processing centers, the revolution is aimed almost exclusively at managerial and professional departments and at individuals within these departments.

The term "managerial and professional computing" also has its problems. First, it is a jaw-breaker of the first order. More importantly, it is misleading because it focuses only on individual managers and professionals. In reality, the revolution is more concerned with computing in managerial and professional *departments*. Many problems and opportunities can be attacked only at the level of the department, not at the level of individual workers. In addition, there are many clerical workers in managerial and professional departments, especially secretaries. Secretaries are often pivotal users in this second wave of computing—a fact that the name "managerial and professional" fails to convey.

If we could somehow agree on a name for the kinds of *departments* that are the focus of the revolution, we would have a much better handle on the changes taking place. Later in this chapter, we will return to this problem in some detail, but for now, the important thing to emphasize is that the revolution is taking place in certain kinds of departments that are staffed primarily by managers, professionals, and their support staff.

Another possible name—the one we have selected for this book—is **end user computing (EUC).** When this term first appeared in the early 1970s, its meaning was restricted to data retrieval on time-shared hosts. Now, however, the term has expanded to embrace most or all of the applications that characterize the post-DP revolution, including applications on time-shared hosts, personal computer applications, nonclerical office automation, decision support systems, and executive information systems.

In addition, under the banner of end user computing, many firms have created specialized departments to manage end user computing. Called **information centers,** these departments now exist in most large corporations and many smaller ones. Although the term "end user computing" has given conceptual unity to the revolution, information centers have provided a rallying point for managing the revolution.

Outgrowing Early Concepts

Unfortunately, the terms "end user computing" and "information center" are not without problems. When IBM first promoted EUC in the early 1970s, its management advice was founded on a set of premises that we now realize are no longer universally true. Specifically, these premises were that:

- EUC applications are small and simple.
- EUC applications are developed by the ultimate user.
- EUC support and control should be directed to individuals.
- EUC applications are oriented toward corporate DP files.

Although these four premises hold true for many EUC applications, a good percentage of EUC applications violate at least one of these major premises, and quite a few violate all four. The problem is that EUC is not a monolithic phenomenon. Rather, it is an extremely heterogeneous group of applications with far more diversity than classical data processing. There is no way to even begin to manage EUC intelligently without accepting this diversity and developing a multifaceted management program that can provide appropriate support and control to different "clusters" of EUC applications with different characteristics. A major theme of this book is that end user computing cannot be managed adequately until a new set of premises is found for understanding the concept.

Managing the diversity of EUC applications may be better understood through an analogy from history. When the first Europeans reached Asia in the fourteenth century, they generally saw Asians as similar culturally and politically. Only when they began to appreciate the broad diversity that existed in this vast region did they begin to make headway in tapping its vast wealth. Today, IS is entering a continent that is much larger and more diverse than data processing—a continent with many small categories of applications instead of one overwhelming application such as data processing. It must develop different approaches to dealing with different types of EUC applications if it is to be successful at managing EUC.

Later in this chapter, we will look at the major "clusters" or environments of EUC project development that the information center must individually manage. Before we do that, however, we must understand the reasons for end user computing's enormous growth, the broad needs of end users, and the tools that support end users when they work.

THE END USER EXPLOSION

Despite the rapid growth of information centers, personal computers, and other indicators of EUC's growing size and importance, many organizations still view end user computing as a tactical problem to be addressed with fairly junior information systems professionals.

This book takes the view that end user computing is not a tactical problem but rather a strategic problem—perhaps the most strategic problem that faces IS today. As we will see, all the available evidence indicates that end user computing will soon surpass traditional data processing applications in both size and importance. Without a clear strategic vision of the implications of this end user computing revolution, strategic planning will be impossible for both EUC and for information systems in general.

Benjamin's Study

The long-term importance of end user computing was first underscored in 1981, when the IS heads of several major corporations gathered at MIT to hear Robert I. Benjamin of the Xerox Corporation. (6) Benjamin had just finished a major statistical study of computing in one of Xerox's operating units and presented his results at the seminar.

Part of his presentation dealt with end user computing. He began by saying that EUC had been negligible in 1970, a statement that surprised no one. But when he turned to data for 1980, his data set the audience at the edges of their chairs. In 1980, end user computing had risen to *nearly 40 percent of total central processing unit (CPU) cycles.*

His audience was understandably skeptical. But several listeners did some fast calculations, and most had to agree that his number was probably about right for their own firms. They had simply not asked the question before, and when they did ask it, the results forced them to reevaluate many of their most fundamental assumptions. In 1986, for example, Ronald Brzezinski of Quaker Oats described the surprise of his company at the results of a similar analysis in 1984. (15)

> A couple of years ago, we went through an assessment of all the money being spent at Quaker's information systems activity. We found that *MIS was paying a lot of the bills but managing only 40% of the total dollar figure. . . . It was an eye-opener. So end-user computing had been there for a long time but sort of under covers. Now, it's brought out.* (emphasis added)

Although the people in the room did not know it at the time, IBM Canada had done a similar study of its own internal computer use. In 1981, it estimated that 25 percent of its computer use was coming from end user computing. (25) This figure was lower than Benjamin's 40 percent, but it was still a surprising amount. Like Benjamin's study, it reflected an early stage of end user computing, before the "PC explosion."

Benjamin's study also looked to the future. From 1980 to 1990, he forecast that toal computer capacity would increase 20 times, while user computing would increase 40 times and would consume 75 percent of all CPU cycles. In other words, end user computing would be the *dominant* form of computing by the end of the decade.

Can It Really Become That Large?

At first, the notion that end user computing will eclipse data processing seems ludicrous. But DP has always been aimed at a small segment of corporate work, with most DP applications designed to support clerical workers. As discussed later in this chapter, in the section on managerial and professional work, clerical workers make up only about a third of all office workers, and many clerical jobs are not DP-related.

Although DP has always provided some management support, information from corporate clerical archives is only one of the many sources of information used by managers and professionals in the firm. In reality, DP dominated corporate computing in the past for only one reason: the highly structured and repetitive nature of clerical tasks was the only application domain that could be attacked successfully with early computer hardware and software. There was *never* any reason to expect clerical transaction processing or management access to corporate data to dominate corporate computing in the future.

Can It Really Grow That Quickly?

Even if end user computing is ultimately destined to dominate corporate computing, is it reasonable to assume that it can grow as *rapidly* as Benjamin

FIGURE 1-1 THE KEYBOARD EXPLOSION

Source: International Data Corporation.

has forecast? Or will the growth be far slower, so that data processing will continue to reign as the number one application for many years?

The answer is that Benjamin is at least in good company when he projects very rapid growth. A number of organizations have forecast the growth of computer use in U.S. organizations, and while they differ in details, they all project a very rapid growth for computers in the near future. Figure 1-1, for example, shows a growth forecast from the International Data Corporation (IDC). (33) This figure forecasts the number of keyboards that will be in use in the future. The total includes keyboards attached to personal computers, computer terminals, word processors, small business computers, and electronic typewriters. The last category, electronic typewriters, is debatable but represents only a small piece of the total. The total did not include keyboards at cash registers or other special-purpose keyboards.

Although computers began to appear during World War II, the computer did not come of age before 1980. At the start of this decade, IDC could only count 10 keyboards for every 100 office workers. (33) In addition, most of these keyboards were probably used by clerical workers in data processing applications and in word processing centers. By 1985, however, IDC saw the penetration of keyboards jump to 39 keyboards per 100 office workers, and for 1990, IDC forecasts that there will be 78 keyboards for every 100 office workers. (33) In other words, a majority of all office workers already have access to computers, and by the end of this decade, there will be only a few holdouts in large corporations.

IDC's projections understate computer use. Future Computing has found that for personal computers, at least, it is common to find several users sharing each keyboard. Based on telephone interviews and 45,000 responses to a mailed questionnaire, it found an average of 2.3 people sharing each personal computer in 1985. (14) Many terminals attached to minicomputers and time-shared mainframe computers are also shared by several people. In other words, the number of people using computers is probably much greater than even the large number of keyboards now in use.

Even if such forecasts are substantially off—and most firms are surprised when they look at their own use patterns and count at least half of all office workers already using computers—it is clear that computers are already in wide use and soon will be almost universally available.

Conclusion

All of these numbers boil down to a single conclusion: end user computing will soon be much larger than data processing, if it is not already. End user computing is the future of information systems. Those who fail to view it as a strategic fundamental change that will affect everything else within IS are failing at strategic IS planning itself.

BROAD USER NEEDS

Some years ago, the chairman of the Stanley Works told his board of directors, "Last year we sold four million drills that nobody wanted." After grabbing their attention with this remark, he went on to explain that drills are merely tolerated by buyers. They are purchased, despite their cost and difficulty of use, simply because of something else that buyers really want—holes. He was warning his board that Stanley would have to focus on user needs, not merely on tools.

In end user computing, there is also a tendency to think in terms of tools—personal computers, spreadsheet programs, personal computer networks, and the like. This tendency is so pervasive that few information center managers and staff members can even tell you how many managers and professionals there are in their firms, much less what their real needs are. Even when they do talk about needs, they tend to talk about such things as the "need for electronic mail," as if there was a need for tools as distinct from underlying work needs.

In this section, we will quickly survey some of the few facts that really are known about end user needs. We will look first at departments because, as discussed at the start of this chapter, EUC support and control is no longer a matter for individuals alone. Only afterward will we examine the needs of individual office workers.

Taxonomy of Departments

As discussed at the start of this chapter, the post-DP revolution was characterized by a shift in the *kind of department* being served by computers.

- During the first 30 years of IS, almost all applications were developed in a single kind of department, which is called Type I, because it was the first type computerized.
- Today, most development is taking place in a very different kind of department, called Type II to differentiate it from the departments originally served by IS.

Of course, no simple dichotomy can ever capture the richness of reality, but the simple Type I–Type II dichotomy explains the main thrusts of the EUC revolution surprisingly well. For a refinement of the Type I–Type II dichotomy into six more specific types of departments, see Reference 48.

Type I Departments

Type I departments handle the routine information processing chores of the firm. Examples are accounting, payroll, billing, the word processing center, the reprographics department, and the mailroom. Most workers in these departments are clerical, but there are also many nonclerical workers here, including managers and sometimes professionals. So calling these departments clerical would be at least somewhat misleading.

Data processing started here, in accounting, payroll, billing, and other Type I departments. Office automation started here, in word processing centers, records management centers, and reprographics departments. Even telecommunications had its earliest foothold here in the glory days of the telegraph, although the telephone brought telecommunications out of the clerical cloister before the start of this century.

Why did almost all types of IS begin here? Certainly not because Type I departments are the most important in the firm. Compared to the engineering department or the chief executive officer's staff, a word processing center or a billing department is a minor operation. Rather, IS began in Type I departments because the crude state of the art in computer technology in those early days allowed only the most routine work to be automated. This kind of simple routine work is common only in Type I departments.

Type I departments are also characterized by the high volumes needed to justify early IS equipment. The same transaction, once programmed, might be executed millions of times over the life of the program. In addition, workers in Type I departments worked at their machines over six hours a day. Utilization was even higher if there were two shifts. These factors were very important when computers were five to ten times more expensive than they are today and when even nondisplay processors cost over $20,000 in today's money.

The routineness of Type I work was even more important for a second reason—it has dominated thinking about application development. Systems analysis and similar application development disciplines in office automation were centered on the identification and automation of **procedures.** This made sense because procedures were not only pervasive; they were also *central.* If you automated these procedures, you were automating the heart of the work done in Type I departments, and you had a major impact on the performance of the office.

Another characteristic of Type I departments is that the work done in an individual Type I department rarely cuts across traditional IS tool categories. In word processing centers, there is one basic type of work, namely typing, so only office automation tools are needed. In billing departments, the work involves the handling of forms with fixed structures, so only data processing tools were needed. Even telecommunications got into the act, in Telex and facsimile rooms.

As noted earlier, Type I departments have a mixture of clerical and managerial workers, and sometimes professional workers as well. It would be a mistake to focus only on clerical workers, and in fact many ways of boosting productivity in Type I departments come from providing better information to the department's managers and professionals. As a result, it is at least misleading to describe Type I departments as clerical departments. On the other hand, it is true that most of the workers there are clerical workers and that the clerical workers do the main work; the managers and professionals are there mostly to support the clerical workers.

Type II Departments

Although Type I departmental support dominated IS in the early days, the growth tip in information systems today is a very different kind of information-handling department, the Type II department. Type II departments are very different from Type I departments, as summarized in Figure 1-2.

Although Type I departments handle the *routine* information processing chores of the firm—like paperwork assembly lines—Type II departments handle the organization's *knowledge work,* that is, its nonroutine policy-making and professional work. Type II departments include the offices of line managers; staff management offices such as finance, marketing, and corporate planning; and professional offices, such as legal and engineering departments.

Although Type I departments have *mostly clerical workers,* plus a few managers, Type II departments have a *mostly managers and professional workers,* plus some clerical workers (primarily secretaries). We could call Type II departments "managerial and professional" departments, but again the presence of other kinds of workers suggests that the more neutral term, "Type II" department, is preferable.

In Type I departments, procedures are pervasive, and the support of routine procedures is the key to enhancing performance. In Type II departments, this is not the case at all. Type II departments have broad repeating work patterns, for example, general approaches to developing advertising campaigns, but these can seldom be reduced to specific procedures. Although some procedures can be found in Type II departments, they are few in number, and their automation may have only a small impact on the performance of the department. Instead of having many simple routine transactions, Type II departments tend to have a relatively small number of complex nonroutine **projects** with only modest repetitive components, and even these

	Type I	Type II
Work	Routine paperwork	Nonroutine policy and professional
Workers	Mostly clerical	Mostly managerial and professional
Procedures	Pervasive, critical	Rare, secondary importance
Application development	Focuses on procedures	Nonprocedural focus
Tools	Fit traditional IS tool boundaries	Cut across traditional IS tool boundaries

FIGURE 1-2 TYPE I AND TYPE II DEPARTMENTS

repetitive components are typically ill-defined. In other words, the automation of procedures is not the right focus for effective support in Type II departments.

This noncentrality of procedures is crucial for selecting effective application development methodologies for projects in Type II departments. Most of our application development methodologies in both data processing and office automation are procedure oriented. Systems analysis innovations tend to focus on how to define and describe procedures rapidly and unambiguously. At the cutting edge in office automation, Petri nets and other methodologies for describing work flows are billed as being ideal for work processes that are not completely routine, but even they are useful only for quite routine processes and rarely work for anything like the majority of all activities in Type II departments. Even MIT's Office Analysis Methodology (55), which is designed for "semistructured" work, focuses quickly on procedures after an initial survey of needs.

From the historical perspective we have taken, it is fairly clear that procedure-oriented application development methodologies did not evolve in response to a total understanding of organizational information-handling work. Instead, these methodologies evolved because almost all early applications were created for Type I departments. Had we started in Type II departments, we would not have anything like today's fixation on procedure automation.

Worse still, individual projects in Type II departments, for instance, developing a marketing plan for a new product, require a mixture of work activities that *cut freely across even traditional boundaries between applications, for instance, the boundary between DP and office automation.* Word processing is not a *need* in a Type II department. It is merely a *tool* to help with certain projects, and although it matches certain project needs well, it plays only a small role in fulfilling other needs. Focusing on tools in Type II departments will always produce problems in the long run. Overall, the long dominance of Type I support has tended to cause IS to emphasize procedures, the automation of procedures, and the equation of tools with needs. Now that Type II support is growing, the situation is very different.

- We need to find ways to analyze needs that are primarily nonprocedural.
- We must learn to support work with tools that are not primarily procedural.
- We must create project development methodologies that assess needs in ways that are not biased by the equation of tools with needs.

The Type II Revolution

If Type II support was likely to remain small, compared to the support of Type I work, the problems raised in the preceding paragraph would be small concerns. But in fact, Type II support will soon be larger than Type I support, if it is not already larger. Given the data presented later in this chapter on job categories, it would appear that Type I departments cannot make up more than about a third of all office employment. Moreover, given clerical salaries (47), Type I departments cannot make up more than about a quarter of all office costs.

Most Type I departments are already well computerized. Although a good deal of work remains to be done, the easy gains have already been mined. In contrast, the support of Type II departments is only beginning. Given the work that lies ahead, Type II support will have an even larger share of the IS work to be done than demographic and cost figures would indicate.

The importance of Type II support is even more critical when the roles of Type II departments are taken into account. Type II departments, after all, make the key decisions that determine the fate of the company. Although the breakdown of a Type I paperwork assembly line can be disastrous, Type II departments are far more critical for the long-term success of the organization.

The Demographics of Office Work

The distinction between Type I and Type II offices captures the essence of the fundamental changes that are taking place in information systems today. But corporate IS plans must be built on a finer understanding of office work. In this section, we will look at the individual occupations that make up the complex and heterogeneous office workforce. Although IS plans must also extend beyond office work, those broader issues fall beyond the scope of this book.

National Data

Table 1-1 shows the general pattern of office work in the United States. This table gives highly aggregated results from an analysis (46) of 1985 data from the Bureau of Labor Statistics (BLS). (61) (For an earlier analysis by the author, see Reference 47. See Reference 54 for a similar analysis by Schement and Lievrouw.)

TABLE 1-1
U.S. OCCUPATIONAL STATISTICS: 1985 AVERAGES

CATEGORY	PERCENTAGE OF TOTAL EMPLOYMENT	PERCENTAGE OF OFFICE EMPLOYMENT
Type II Departments		
Managers	11.4	28.1
Professionals	6.4	15.8
Sales professionals	6.5	16.0
Secretaries	3.8	9.4
Subtotal	28.1	69.4
Type I Departments		
DP-oriented clerical	9.3	23.0
OA-oriented clerical	1.7	4.2
Other clerical	1.4	3.4
Nonsecretarial clerical	12.4	30.6
TOTAL	40.5	100.0

The table shows two columns of data. The first column is based on actual BLS data. The second column excludes job categories that are not likely to be considered office work by most people, for instance the jobs of grocery store clerks. Although there are a fair number of exclusions that not everyone would agree with, (46,47), it is likely that most allocations of BLS data to office work would present roughly the same final picture—that office work accounts for about 40 percent of all employment today in the United States. Widely quoted estimates that approximately half of all workers are office workers today are based on a careless use of BLS data that makes no exclusions.

The term "white collar work" is not used in Table 1-1 because the Bureau of Labor Statistics dropped this category when it adopted the new Standard Occupational Classification System in 1983. Although white collar work is fairly similar to the categories shown in Table 1-1, it is an outdated concept that can no longer be tied to national data and should not be used in demographic analysis.

Table 1-1 subtotals the four job categories found in most Type II departments—managers, professionals, professional sales workers, and secretaries. It also subtotals the kinds of clerical workers found in Type I departments. These figures hold a number of surprises.

- Managers form the largest category, but the number is not overwhelming. The traditional view is that offices consist primarily of managers and secretaries, but they account for only 37.5 percent of all office employment.

- There are about as many professionals and professional sales workers (as opposed to sales clerks and order-takers) as there are managers. In addition, many management jobs are really staff management jobs, such as finance and corporate planning, rather than line management jobs. These staff management jobs tend to be more similar to professional jobs than to line management jobs. When staff management jobs are added to the general "professional" category, the importance of line management shrinks even more.

- The BLS data show that nonsecretarial clerical jobs make up 30.6 percent of the U.S. office workforce. If we assume one manager for every ten of these workers (the categories already include many first-line supervisors), then it would seem that roughly one-third of all office workers spend their days in Type I departments and two-thirds in Type II departments. Given clerical salaries, (47) Type I departments probably account for only about a quarter of all office costs.

- Looking more closely at the nonsecretarial clerical category, we see that 23.0 percent of all office employment falls into DP-oriented clerical work. This may be an overstatement because, when in doubt, nonsecretarial clerical workers were placed in the DP-oriented category in order to get a reasonable upper bound on the market for clerical data processing. (46) In addition, although these jobs seemed to include the handling of record-structured data files, we do not know how many actually use computers. Overall, it seems that no more than a quarter of all office workers are directly involved in clerical data processing, and the real figure is likely to be much lower.

- The clerical category associated with office automation (OA) was dominated by typists, who, unlike secretaries, are likely to be found in word processing centers. The category also included other jobs that seem to be related to document filing and processing.

The purpose of this section is not to present a full discussion of the demographics of office work. Rather, it is to show the many surprises that even superficial looks at national data reveal. Even more surprises exist at lower levels of detail. No end user computing policy can hope to be rational unless it is based on a firm understanding of the firm's office demographics.

The Need to Collect Corporate Data

Although national data are good for understanding broad trends, they are not valid for individual industries, much less for individual firms. As shown in Table 1-2, many occupational categories are clustered in certain industries. (62) This is particularly the case for professional categories, although if staff managers were lumped with professionals instead of with line managers, this effect would probably be much smaller. Because of the limited data published in the Bureau of Labor Statistics' *Employment and Earnings*, occupational exclusions could not be done to the same extent they were for Table 1-1, so the two give slightly different pictures.

For individual firms, information centers need to develop profiles that are even more detailed than those shown in Table 1-1 if they want to speak rationally about the support of EUC and all other forms of office work. In

TABLE 1-2
INFORMATION WORK, BY INDUSTRY: ANNUAL AVERAGES, 1985

INDUSTRY	TOTAL EMPL*	PCT INFO WORK	PCT MGR	PCT PROF	PCT TECH	PCT SALES	PCT ADMIN
Finance**	7,005	93	24	2	2	24	42
Professional services	21,563	77	9	42	7	1	19
Wholesale trade	4,341	71	11	2	1	39	19
Public administration	4,995	68	21	13	5	1	28
Retail trade	17,955	59	8	2	0	42	8
Transport, pub. util.	7,548	50	10	6	3	4	27
Other services	10,504	47	15	10	3	5	14
Mining	939	43	15	10	5	1	12
Durables mfg.	12,586	39	11	9	4	2	12
Nondurables mfg.	8,293	37	10	6	2	5	13
Construction	6,987	22	12	2	1	1	6
Agriculture	3,179	8	2	2	1	0	3
TOTAL	105,895	56	12	13	3	12	16

SOURCE: Bureau of Labor Statistics
* In thousands
** Includes insurance and real estate

fact, occupational statistics need to be broken down by geographical site. To obtain such information, the information center will have to work with the corporate personnel department (increasingly called the "human resources" department).

Managers

Managers are often viewed as the main targets for end user computing, but the numbers in Table 1-1 do not support this notion. Managers constitute only about 28 percent of the office workforce. They are important, but they are only one support target.

In addition, managerial jobs vary so enormously that it is hazardous to make generalizations.

- Needs vary by *position in the hierarchy*. Higher-level managers with less structured needs than lower level managers.
- Needs also vary by *type of industry*. In tightly managed industries such as public utilities, even senior managers spend a great deal of time with numbers and models.
- Needs are also very different for *staff and line managers*. Although we have no good breakdown for staff versus line numbers, staff managers seem to be more numerous than line managers in a wide variety of firms. Staff managers are often specialists who do extensive computer work.

Unfortunately, BLS data do not provide many of the kinds of breakdowns we would really like to have. We cannot separate line from staff managers, for example, nor can we break things down by level in the hierarchy.

Although it is critical to divide the managerial "market" into several "market segments," each with different needs, we can say some things about managers in general. Since the early 1950s, a steady stream of **use of time** studies have looked at how managers spend their working days. As shown in Table 1-3, these studies are in strong agreement about general working patterns. The agreement is even higher when the systematic biases in some studies are taken into account.

First, managers spend about half their days in face-to-face communication, an activity that has so far resisted major inroads from technology. Although teleconferencing (Chapter 17), group decision support systems (Chapter 17), and presentation graphics to support meetings (Chapters 9, 11, and 16) have proven somewhat popular, this aspect of management work is not the most fruitful ground for information support.

Second, the rest of the manager's day is split about equally between mediated communication, that is, the telephone and written communication, and noncommunication activities. The Booz Allen-Hamilton study (8) looked more closely at noncommunication work. For managers and professionals combined, noncommunication work fell about equally into three categories: analysis, searching for information, and managing activities. As discussed later in this chapter, current use patterns among tools mirror the prevalence of these activities.

Use of time studies also show that activities vary in a predictable way among managerial job categories. Senior executives spend more time in face-

TABLE 1-3
USE OF TIME STUDIES OF MANAGERS AND PROFESSIONALS

| | Percent of Time in Communication Activities ||||
SOURCE	FACE TO FACE	PHONE	FTF & PHONE	READING & WRITING	TOTAL
Managers only					
Teger	47	9	56	29	85
Stogdill & Shartle	66	—	—	—	—
Engel, et al.	27	13	40	34	74
Stewart	54	6	60	28	88
Hinrichs	45	8	53	25	78
Burns	—	—	52	24	76
Horne & Lupton	54	9	63	24	87
Doktor	75	3	78	—	—
Dubin & Spray	55	6	61	5	66
Croston & Goulding	56	7	63	18	81
Ives & Olson	68	10	78	—	—
Mintzberg	64	6	70	—	—
Kurke & Aldrich	62	8	70	—	—
Kelley	61	—	—	—	—
Choran	36	17	53	—	—
Palmer & Beishon	54	6	60	15	75
Notting	—	—	59	17	76
Professionals only					
Case Institute	—	—	—	—	53
Teger	23	17	40	42	82
Engel, et al.	10	11	21	30	51
Hinrichs	25	5	23	47	70
Managers and professionals					
Xerox	18	5	23	47	70
Booz-Allen	—	—	46	21	67
Managers, professionals, secretaries, and clerical workers					
Klemmer & Snyder	35	7	42	26	68
Bair & Nelson	26	14	40	21	62

Note: Communication activity patterns add horizontally to total communication.

to-face communication than low-level managers, for example, and staff managers in areas such as accounting spend less time in oral communication than their peers in line management. These results are not unexpected, but they do provide confirmation for intuitive judgments.

Professionals

As noted earlier, the term "professional" is not well defined in the BLS data. Most of the people in the "Professional and Technical Speciality" category fit into the general image of professional workers. But so do sales workers who are "sales representatives." Sales representatives must have a high degree of product knowledge, as opposed to sales agents, who have small product expertise. In addition, many staff management jobs, such as corporate planning, marketing planning, and finance, have all of the characteristics of traditional professions such as engineering or law. If these staff management jobs are thrown into the professional category, it is clear that there are many more professional-type workers in the corporation than there are traditional line managers.

Table 1-3 shows that professional time-use patterns are similar to those of managers. The big difference is that professionals spend only about 30 percent of their day in face-to-face communication, and, as a result, they spend about 40 percent of their day in noncommunication activities—about twice the time that managers spend in noncommunication activities.

Secretaries in Type II Departments

In Type II departments, the role of secretaries has always been important, and with the advent of computers, it is becoming critical. The lead secretary in an office is rapidly becoming an office manager. He or she normally directs a miniature word processing center, has to worry about computerized file organization, and often has to know enough about computers to train others and to purchase the right kind of equipment for a particular need.

As shown in Table 1-4, secretaries have long had a great deal of variety in their jobs. Typing takes up less than half the day, but other forms of paperwork handling take up most of the rest of the day. In a Type II department, the secretary is not a clerical worker. The secretary is a paraprofessional and a critical member of the departmental team.

Type II Support and the Information Center

In the past, information centers have tended to define their charter in terms of tools and applications. From the discussion in this section, it would seem that a better definition of the information center's role would assign all Type II support to information centers. This will allow the information center to develop a comprehensive support program for all needs in these offices, in order to avoid the kind of situation in which the information center controls personal computing, the OA department controls office automation in these departments, the telecommunications department controls facsimile there, and so on.

THE END USER REVOLUTION

TABLE 1-4
USE OF TIME BY SECRETARIES

ACTIVITY	PERCENT OF TIME
Taking dictation	2
Telephone	20
Reading, writing	9
Typing	36
Other paperwork	25
Copying	8
Recordkeeping	6
Tabulating	5
Filing	4
Research	2
Other	8
TOTAL	100

SOURCE: Teger (1983)

More importantly, defining the information center's role as the support of Type II departments will help focus attention on the *market* instead of on *tools*. Most information center professionals come from IS and have strongly technical backgrounds. Defining the focus of information center work as the support of Type II departments will help information center personnel understand the need to focus on user needs before technical concerns.

The information center's role can also be defined as the support of managerial and professional work, but if this is done, two tendencies should be avoided. The first is the tendency to focus on individuals instead of on departments—a tendency that was imprinted on information center thinking in its early days but that is no longer sufficient for information center planning and implementation. The second is a tendency to exclude secretaries or at least fail to understand the critical and complex roles of support staffs in today's electronic offices.

Whether or not the information center is formally chartered to support Type II departments, it needs to work with the personnel (human resources) department to develop statistics on departments and individual work categories in the firm. The statistics presented in this section are national data that rarely fit individual firms. If the firm is geographically distributed, things are even more complex. Job and department analyses must be done for each major work site, so that the local information center department or outreach program can be tailored intelligently to the needs of that site.

It takes a great deal of work to develop a map of departments in the firm and to build profiles of occupations within each department, but the task is fundamental to good planning. The first job of the information center, whatever the second may be, is to understand its users.

TOOLS

When most people think about the Industrial Revolution, they envision huge factories powered by steam engines, or they think about locomotives drawing coal from mines drained by steam power. In other words, they think in terms of the tools that made the Industrial Revolution possible.

In end user computing, it is also natural to think of tools. Until today's hardware and software tools became available, little could be done for many of the problems that are now being solved by EUC. The PC, the time-shared host computer, and the application packages that run on these machines really are the steam engines of the end user revolution.

In data processing, most application development is done with third-generation languages like COBOL or fourth-generation languages (4GL) designed for information systems professionals. Both are oriented toward applications with data files and heavy transaction processing requirements.

End user computing embraces a much broader range of applications with a broad range of characteristic needs. As a result, it needs a much broader set of application development tools. These tools are so diverse, in fact, that it is sometimes difficult to find family resemblances among them. Because of this diversity, we will develop a taxonomy to describe the main dimensions along which these tools differ. This taxonomy is shown as Figure 1-3, which has two dimensions along which tools vary.

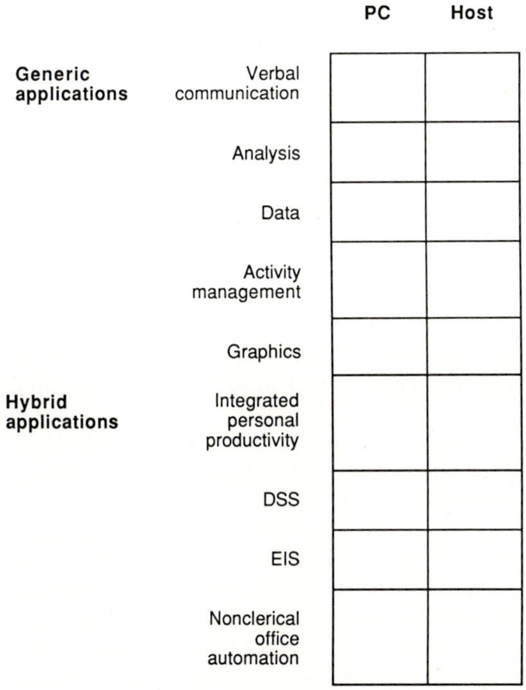

		PC	Host
Generic applications	Verbal communication		
	Analysis		
	Data		
	Activity management		
	Graphics		
Hybrid applications	Integrated personal productivity		
	DSS		
	EIS		
	Nonclerical office automation		

FIGURE 1-3 THE COMPUTER–APPLICATION MATRIX

- The first dimension is whether a personal computer or time-shared host computer is used. Although most applications can be accomplished either on PCs or hosts, these two machines have different strengths and weaknesses that must be considered when designing any specific application.
- The second dimension is the type of application. Five generic (common) application categories are listed. Also listed are four hybrid application categories, which tend to draw from two or more generic application areas.

The cells in this matrix represent tools, consisting of both a computer and application software. We will begin by looking at the horizontal dimension—the kind of computer being used. Although software is more important than hardware, hardware tends to restrict the kinds of application software that can be used.

Computers

Personal Computers, Hosts, and Microcomputers

End user computers fall into two broad categories. First, there are **personal computers** or **PCs.** Although many PCs can now work with larger computers, personal computers are not mere terminals. They have their own processing power and normally do almost all processing locally. Some PCs have more processing power than small minicomputers.

Second, there are **host computers** or **hosts.** Hosts are multiuser computers that can serve a number of users working at simultaneous terminals. The largest hosts are called **supercomputers.** These are usually limited to scientific and engineering work. The largest normally available for end user computing are **mainframes.** Mid-size hosts are **minicomputers,** and the smallest hosts are multiuser **microcomputers** or **micros.** (Note that not all micros are personal computers.) Hosts that fall between the major categories have such names as "supermini" and "mini-supercomputer."

Early hosts used batch processing, in which a user submitted a job to a waiting queue and then waited minutes or hours for it to be processed. Today, host-based end user computing is almost always done on **time-shared hosts,** which allow interactive processing of the type found in virtually all personal computer applications.

As discussed in Chapter 3, personal computers and hosts each have strengths not shared by the other. In the early days of personal computing, these differences led to tedious arguments about which type of machine was best. Today, in contrast, the tendency is to ask whether a specific application for a specific user should be done on a PC or a host, given not only the relative advantages of these two types of machines but also many other factors, such as the kinds of machine already familiar to the user. Tomorrow, many PC-versus-host discussions will be rendered moot by **cooperative PC–host software** that runs on both the PC and the host and combines the relative strengths of these two kinds of machines without worrying the user about the details of which machine is providing which underlying functions, but at least for now, whether to do an application on a host or a PC is still a major decision.

Applications

Computers are general-purpose machines, which can be employed in many different **applications,** that is, ways of using computers. To make a computer useful in a particular application, the user must have access to **application software.** To create and edit documents, for example, the user must have a word processing program.

Computers Versus Applications

The PC-versus-host distinction cuts across application categories. Word processing, for example, can be done either on PCs or on time-shared host computers. The same is true for filing applications, graphics, and nearly every other conceivable application.

As a result, any discussion of tools must be done in the context of a matrix like the one shown in Figure 1-3. Although many management concerns cut across cells horizontally or vertically, each cell has some particular management concerns that must be addressed separately by the information center.

Generic Applications Versus Specific Applications

The word "application" can be used either generically or specifically. **Generic applications** are broad categories of applications, such as "verbal communication" or "analysis." In contrast, **specific applications** are particular uses, such as an analytical model to study an acquisition. Because this book will focus on generic applications rather than specific applications, we will normally mean generic applications when we use the term "application" without qualification.

Figure 1-3 shows five generic categories of end user applications: verbal communication, analysis, data retrieval and application development, activity management, and graphics. Each of these generic application categories has a number of subcategories, which will be discussed later.

In addition to these widely-used **generic applications,** there are four **hybrid applications** that combine elements from two or more generic categories.

Integrated personal productivity applications.

Executive information system (EIS) applications.

Decision support system (DSS) applications.

Office automation applications.

We will look at the generic applications first and then turn to hybrid applications.

Verbal Communication

The first of the four major types of generic applications shown in Figure 1-3 is verbal communication. **Verbal communication** is human-to-human communication using *words*. It is subdivided into **written communication** and **oral communication.**

Use of time studies discussed earlier in this chapter indicate that managers spend half their days talking face to face, whereas professionals spend about 30 percent of their days talking face to face. Both groups spend a quarter of the day reading and writing and another 5 percent of the day on the telephone.

For supporting face-to-face communication, there have been few successful tools. As discussed in Chapter 17, such things as teleconferencing and electronic support for group meetings have some potential, but they are likely to remain small for some time to come.

For supporting *mediated communication,* the situation is entirely different. Word processing is the number one or number two application on virtually every list of PC software use, and several other mediated communication tools are becoming very popular, especially electronic mail. (See Chapter 11 for a discussion of PC communication tools, and Chapter 17 for tools that extend beyond personal computers.)

Analysis

Every manager or professional does at least some **numerical analysis.** As discussed earlier, about 6 percent of the manager's or professional's day is spent in analysis work, (8) and manual analysis can be extremely difficult and exhausting. Chapter 9 discusses analysis programs in general and then looks at spreadsheet analysis in detail. Chapter 16 discusses more advanced analysis tools.

Many desk accessories provide **pop-up calculators** for light work, but for most analysis tasks, users turn to **spreadsheet programs,** which are general-purpose modeling and analysis tools that can be used for a broad spectrum of problems ranging from the simplest calculations to fairly sophisticated analytical models.

For users with specialized needs, special-purpose analysis tools provide more functionality than spreadsheet programs. Although they are harder to learn, these special-purpose analysis tools are more productive under heavy use. Some examples of advanced special-purpose analysis tools are financial analysis programs, statistical analysis programs, and operations research programs.

Data Retrieval and Application Development

Every generic application has characteristic ways of organizing data. Word processing has the document, whereas analysis has the model. In traditional business applications, such as accounting, there is the **record-structured data file** and its more sophisticated cousin, the **data base.** These concepts are covered in most introductory IS courses, and they are reviewed in Chapter 10.

Data management programs on personal computers are discussed in Chapter 10, and host-based programs in Chapter 16.

Although the record-structured data file and the data base are only two ways to organize data, their universal use in traditional data processing applications has led DP professionals to call applications that use these structures **data applications.** Because EUC began with these applications, the practice of calling them data applications spilled over into the end user world. Today, the term "data application" is so embedded that there is no choice other than to use it.

Data management software is used to work with data files and data bases. The simplest data management programs can work only with individual files. The most complex data management programs can work with whole data bases. The latter are called **data base management systems** or **DBMSs.** Data management programs provide two basic sets of functions for end users.

- First, they provide tools for **data application development,** that is, the creation of full data processing systems that embrace data entry, data file, or data base structuring, reporting, administrative functions, and other work commonly involved in data applications built with COBOL or other traditional development languages.
- Second, they provide tools for **data retrieval.** Although data retrieval tools can be used to get information from end user data applications, they can also be used to extract data from corporate data processing files and data bases for accounting, payroll, and other needs.

Activity Management

Managers and professionals spend a great deal of time managing activities. Use of time studies indicate that they spend about 6 percent of their days doing this kind of work. (8) They manage their own activities with aids such as appointment calendars and "to-do" lists. They also manage group activities by coordinating meetings, scheduling their staffs, and managing projects. Computer applications for activity management tend to fall into four major categories.

1. Software for **personal activity management,** which includes online appointment calendars, "to-do lists," and telephone books.
2. Software for **group meeting scheduling,** which can greatly simplify the process of establishing a meeting among many people.
3. **Staff scheduling** software, which can allow supervisors to staff their shifts with people fitting various job requirements.
4. **Project management** software, which can allow a manager to keep track of the many things that must be done in a project or in a department's multiple projects.

Chapter 12 discusses some activity management programs on personal computers, whereas Chapter 17 looks at the kinds of activity management functions embedded in office automation programs.

Graphics

Until recently, graphics was extremely expensive, and it was used only in selected applications. Now, however, graphics technology is becoming very widespread on both personal computers and time-shared host computers.

Graphics applications may be divided into two distinct categories.

- **Analytical graphics,** which is used to summarize patterns in data. Pie charts and bar charts fall into this category. Figure 1-1, the keyboard forecast, is an example of analytical graphics. (Chapter 16 discusses analytical graphics.)
- **Conceptual graphics,** which represents relationships among concepts. Figure 1-3, our matrix of computers and generic applications, is an example of conceptual graphics. (Chapter 11 discusses conceptual graphics on personal computers.)

Although many dedicated graphics programs are now on the market, it is common to find graphics functions embedded in many word processing, analysis, data management, and even activity management programs. Often, the output from an embedded graphics function, such as a Lotus 1-2-3 graph, can be transferred to a dedicated graphics program for fine-tuning.

Hybrid Applications

As noted earlier, many application development tools cut across the generic application boundaries shown in Figure 1-3.

- **Integrated personal productivity** programs combine modules for word processing, simple analysis (especially spreadsheet analysis), graphics, simple data management, and communications with remote host computers (see Chapters 12 and 13). These modules can share data easily.
- **Executive information systems (EISs)** are designed to provide the specific information needed by managers, especially senior managers. Because of this top-level focus, executive information systems provide high visibility to the information center. In contrast to traditional management information systems (MISs), which focused on internal data processing information, EISs focus on whatever data the manager needs, including external data and information from marketing research studies, as well as data processing information.
- Although executive information systems only provide tools for two functions—data retrieval and presentation (graphics),—**decision support system (DSS)** tools add analysis to the mix. (56) Like executive information systems, decision support systems are normally developed by third parties, usually information center personnel or other IS personnel.
- DSSs and EISs also differ in another way. DSSs are developed for a *specific problem,* while EISs are developed for a *specific person.* A DSS may serve a problem faced by a number of people, for instance, budgeting. In contrast, an EIS may help the decision maker with several different decisions.

- Another major category of hybrid applications combining functions from several areas is **office automation.** Integrated office automation systems combine text communication, voice communication, and activity management tools into a single integrated multiuser system. Chapter 17 deals with office automation.

Patterns of Software Use

Now that we have looked at the major generic and hybrid applications of end user computing, we will turn to data on the kinds of application software which organizations use in practice. Although the specific numbers vary from survey to survey and from year to year, the pattern of applications has been relatively stable for the past few years and promises to remain reasonably stable in the future.

Software Use Patterns on Time-Shared Hosts

In 1985, Computer Intelligence Corporation (13) found the pattern of software use on time-shared hosts shown in Table 1-5. DSS and office automation products were not studied in the survey.

Other surveys cite different percentages and different orders, but most identify the products on the Computer Intelligence Corporation list as being the staples of host end user computing in the areas of data handling, analysis, and graphics.

Software Use Patterns on Personal Computers

Many sources list sales for various types of personal computer application software. Table 1-6 shows the results from one 1985 listing of popular application software. (20) This list of worldwide revenues is representative of what most sources now say.

As shown in the table, in first place in software sales in 1985 was word processing. Given the amount of time managers spend reading and writing, it is not surprising that word processing is first or second on most lists of application software use.

Next came spreadsheet software which can be used for the simplest kinds of analysis done on a calculator, as well as for the development of fairly

TABLE 1-5
SOFTWARE USED ON THE TIME-SHARED HOST COMPUTERS, 1985

TYPE OF SOFTWARE	PERCENT USING	PERCENT CONSIDERING
DBMS	73%	27%
Graphics	59%	20%
Information retrieval	59%	17%
Statistical analysis	50%	14%
Fourth-generation language	47%	30%
Spreadsheet	32%	16%
Financial analysis	27%	6%

SOURCE: Computer Intelligence Corporation

TABLE 1-6
SOFTWARE USED ON PERSONAL COMPUTERS, 1985

TYPE OF SOFTWARE	WORLDWIDE REVENUES (MILLIONS)
Word processing	$763
Spreadsheet	$741
Integrated software	$361
Data management	$311

SOURCE: DiNucci

sophisticated models. It is not unexpected that sales of spreadsheet software took second place.

The third category, integrated software, appears to be a very large category, with sales of $361 million in 1985. The reality, however, is that most of the revenues in this category come from Lotus 1-2-3 and other programs that are primarily single-function programs with a few simple extensions. Fully integrated programs such as Symphony made up only a fraction of total integrated sales. This distortion is present in most PC software figures.

Also strong was data management, with 1985 sales of $311 million worldwide. The data base market was, and still is, split into two distinct submarkets. First, there is the submarket for very simple **file management systems** that deal with only a single file at a time and emphasize ease of use over functionality. Software Publishing's pfs:file program dominated this submarket in 1985. Second, there is the submarket for high-end **data base management systems (DBMSs)**, which differ from file management systems by being able to handle several files at a time. DBMSs also differ by stressing high functionality, to the detriment of ease of use. Ashton-Tate's dBASE II and dBASE III dominated this submarket in 1985.

Published dollar figures somewhat understate the importance of data applications, since a number of spreadsheet, word processing, and integrated products have embedded file management features. On the other hand, there is a widespread belief that after the initial purchase spreadsheet and word processing programs are used far more intensively than data handling programs.

Other popular PC application software categories that rank high on most lists are graphics (often embedded in other programs), communications (to reach another computer via a communication line), project management, desk utilities, utilities for system-level functioning, and programs for such advanced analysis applications as financial analysis and statistics.

PROJECT DEVELOPMENT ENVIRONMENTS

In traditional data processing development projects, the user had a passive role in application development. A systems analyst studied the user's needs and designed an appropriate information system. A programmer then created a program to do the needed work. Finally, the systems analyst returned to manage the implementation of the entire information systems.

In end user computing, the situation is very different. The user has a much larger role to play in the development of projects as well as their ongoing implementation. In fact, end user control has often been taken as a defining characteristic of end user computing. Arnold Danberg of Transamerica Financial Services put it this way. (15)

> I would define end-user computing as an environment in which the user has free control and latitude over the process. He may use data that is interchanged through the mainframe or the MIS division, or he may create his own data. But he's in control, he's responsible for the product and the effectiveness of the use of the equipment.

When end user computing began, user control and initiative were fairly simple matters. Most projects were small and simple efforts that could be done adequately by the ultimate user, with very little support from the information center. The information center's support and control policies evolved to fit the needs of these small user-developed projects.

As discussed at the start of this chapter, many of today's EUC projects are no longer small, no longer simple, and no longer developed by the ultimate user. These "pathological" projects that refuse to fit into our traditional expectations about end user computing may now account for a majority of all EUC projects. In any case, they are widespread and cannot be neglected simply on the basis of preserving the theoretical purity of EUC definitions.

When a business person is faced by a very large market, he or she almost instinctively tries to subdivide the total market into a number of smaller "market segments," each having different needs and wants. He or she then develops an appropriate market offer for each individual segment. For example, car manufacturers base their plans on the premise that there is no such thing as a market for "cars." There are only market segments for low-cost transportation cars, high-performance luxury cars, roomy van-like cars, and so on. Failing to face the diversity that is present in almost any large market is likely to result in creating products that do not fit anybody very well.

In end user computing, we must now face the diversity that takes place in project development. The information center must face up to the task of subdividing development into a number of "environments" with different management requirements. The information center must then develop a separate management approach for each of the environments.

Project Development

Although each project development environment will require a specific management approach, all of these approaches will have to be built with four basic "building blocks."

Technological Infrastructure The information center must develop a mix of hardware, software, and communications to allow application development to proceed smoothly and efficiently.

Support The information must supply various kinds of support, including consulting, training, and hotline assistance when problems occur.

Control The information center must establish general policies and rules to ensure that harm does not come about because of a disregard for "good practice."

Promotion The information center must promote application development.

For any particular project, these four elements need to be specified individually and then blended together in exactly the right way—just as the ingredients in a cake mix must be selected and then blended together in exactly the right amounts. Instead of thinking of these four components as separate, it is important to think of them as constituting a **management mix** for each project—much like a cake mix for producing a particular type of cake. (This idea of a management mix is consciously borrowed from marketing theory, which uses a concept called a "marketing mix.") In this section, we will identify several "environments" of end user computing that require different approaches to infrastructure implementation, support, control, and promotion.

The First Two Environments

As discussed above, EUC projects were originally viewed as simple efforts created directly by the ultimate user. A manager creating a spreadsheet program to compare two investment decisions is a good example of this image.

For small projects, using the traditional "systems development life cycle" discipline would be like cracking open a nut with a nuclear bomb. Therefore, simpler development approaches had to be developed for simple end user computing projects. (These approaches are discussed in Chapter 2.) In addition, most of the work would have to be done by the users themselves, since no firm could afford to hire programmers to do all of the work that needs to be done in the firm's numerous EUC projects.

Because the management of EUC projects was so different from the management of projects to develop large **operational systems** in data processing, most information systems professionals believed that a simple dichotomy existed, in which large projects would have to be developed using traditional methodologies, while small projects would be developed using different methodologies. Rockart and Flannery (53) referred to this idea as the two-environment theory of project development, with the development of large systems constituting the **first environment** and the development of small simple EUC projects constituting a **second environment.**

In the second environment, all four elements of the management mix are relatively informal.

- The technological infrastructure usually consists of personal computers that do not push the state of the art, host computers, and widely-available application software, as well as communications approaches that do not require much expertise on the part of the user.
- Support usually consists of low-level initial consulting, training for the computer and application software package, some training in "good practice," hotline assistance when the user gets into trouble, and mundane support for such things as setting up computers, installing software packages, and preparing data extract files.

- Control is usually limited to establishing guidelines for good practice but may extend to occasional audits of compliance.
- Promotion consists primarily of newsletters, user groups, and product demonstrations in public areas.

Application development in end user computing is also simple. Instead of a long sequential process in which each step in the development process is completed before the next is begun, users often launch into simple projects with only modest initial understanding and initial design. They then build something and modify it until it fits their needs. Even if their initial design is badly off, they can easily start over without massive amounts of lost time. Although some discipline will improve productivity and safety considerably, intensive formal discipline is rarely enforced.

The Third Environment: Mid-Range Projects

Mid-Range Projects

In the early 1980s, Rockart and Flannery conducted a study of end users in seven large U.S. and Canadian organizations. (53) This study was a landmark effort in EUC because it exploded the "two environment" myth of end user computing.

- The study showed that only 31 percent of the applications, for example, were used by a single person for their own needs; 52 percent were used by several people in the department; and 17 percent were even used by people outside the department.
- In addition, 9 percent of the applications were large enough to be classified as operational systems, and another 50 percent were "complex analysis" projects. Only 35 percent fit the traditional image of time-shared applications as consisting of report generation, inquiry, and simple analysis.

These statistics were startling, and Rockart and Flannery argued that end user computing must be seen as having a **third environment** consisting of large end user projects. We will refer to these projects as **mid-range** projects because this size falls midway between operational systems and the traditional view of small end user applications.

Rockart and Flannery argued strongly that this third environment raises entirely new issues for end user support. Many of the information center practices that are appropriate for small efforts are not likely to work for larger projects. They argued that a separate information center strategy is needed to manage the third environment.

Although Rockart and Flannery's findings are critically important, several aspects of their methodology need to be understood. Most importantly, their study probably overestimated the prevalence of third-environment applications in the early 1980s. First, they did not take a simple random sample of employees or even users. Instead, they asked for "heavy and/or frequent users." It would be reasonable to assume that these heavy users are more likely to develop large projects than lighter users. Second, the study was done on users of time-shared computers. Time-shared systems were notoriously difficult to use in the early 1980s, and so relatively few small projects were likely to have been implemented on these systems. When another study team looked at personal computer applications after the Rockart and Flannery study was finished, they found relatively few mid-range applications. (52)

Nevertheless, the "power user" is now a well-recognized phenomenon, and it would be surprising if large projects were not fairly important today. Even if they constitute a small minority of projects, their size and the risks they represent would require corporations to build separate support approaches.

The third environment requires information centers to rethink their management mixes if these mixes have been set up primarily for the second environment. All four elements of the marketing mix must be adjusted at least somewhat.

- The technological infrastructure becomes more complex, first because power users tend to push the outer limits of their hardware and software, and second because power users may need different software packages that are more powerful than those normally provided to basic users, yet less powerful than those used by professional programmers.
- Support needs to be extended to include considerable initial consulting on needs analysis, design, and implementation because, as noted below, a more formal project development discipline is needed. Training also needs to be more extensive. For really sophisticated aspects of large projects, some coding may need to be done by the information center, either because the work is beyond the end user or because professional coding is needed for efficiency.
- Formal control is needed because large and complex models often present high risks that could be magnified by poor development and ongoing management practices.
- Promotion is needed to identify key projects that need to be managed more actively than second-environment projects as well as to encourage users to take on important projects that require more advanced skills.

Application development in the third environment needs to be more formal than development in the second environment. Unless good initial needs analysis and design are performed, the project can quickly get out of control. In addition, the development will need extensive testing at each step of the construction. Finally, implementation and ongoing management need to be planned and executed very carefully.

The Fourth Environment:
Delegated Development

Delegated Development

One of the great premises of information center management is that the staff should never do programming for users. Users, in other words, should be forced to do their own work. Originally, there were several reasons for this premise, but what they really boiled down to were that (1) end users were capable of doing the work themselves, and (2) the information center's staff would be swallowed alive by demand if it ever broke the No Programming rule and began to develop applications for users.

We now realize, however, that **delegated development**—in which the ultimate end user delegates the development of a project to someone else—is a very commonplace occurrence. Like the development of large projects, it raises issues that cannot be ignored for reasons of theoretical purity. Put bluntly, it is too large and raises too many issues to ignore.

The prevalence of delegated development was first quantified by Rockart and Flannery. (53) Developing earlier ideas by Codasyl, (12) Martin, (40) and McLean, (41) Rockart and Flannery proposed that there were six categories of end users.

1. **Data processing programmers.**
2. **End-user computing support personnel** (information center staff members).
3. **Functional support personnel** (power users who work in functional departments, outside of IS).
4. **End-user programmers,** who can write code.
5. **Command-level end users.**
6. **Nonprogramming end users.**

The first two categories do not represent end users at all. Rather, they represent IS professionals, including DP programmers and information center staff members. That leaves four categories of end users. Functional support personnel, end user programmers, and command-level end users all develop their own applications. The last category of users, nonprogramming end users on time-shared hosts, must turn to delegated development because, with the host-based tools studied by Rockart and Flannery, an inability to program means that someone else must develop the application.

In their data, Rockart and Flannery found very high levels of delegation in development. Of the 271 applications identified, 150 (55 percent) were used by nonprogramming end users and another 13 were developed for direct users by other people, raising to 163 (61 percent) the number of projects created by delegation. So in the Rockart and Flannery study, at least, *delegated development represented a majority of all project development tasks.*

In Rockart and Flannery's study, most delegated development was done by other members of the ultimate user's own functional department—Rockart and Flannery's "functional support personnel." (53) This fits the pattern seen in many departments today—a "lead user" or "power user" developing many of a department's applications.

Although empirical research on delegation is sparse, at least two studies have looked at delegated use. One is a study of electronic mail by Panko and Panko. (50) Another is a study of chauffered access to data bases on commercial online services by Culnan. (19) In both studies, delegation was extremely commonplace. Both studies found strong correlates between delegation and a number of user and situational variables. Unfortunately, the correlates they

THE END USER REVOLUTION

found were very different, and so we are still a long way from understanding the dynamics of delegated use. Neither study examined delegated development.

In addition, consumer research has long focused on heavy users, light users, and nonusers. Research has shown that all consumer products have nonusers, (60) and there is even a mathematical distribution, the negative binomial distribution, to describe this skewed use. (26) Marketers realize that there will always be a large number of nonusers, light users, and heavy users. Information center professionals, in turn, will have to understand that delegation is simply a core reality that will not go away with better training and other inducements.

Rockart and Flannery did not label delegated development and use as a separate environment, but because of the strong evidence for the importance of delegation, we will treat delegated development the **fourth environment** in this book. Figure 1-4 illustrates the relationships between the first four environments in terms of size and whether development/use is direct or indirect.

Forms of Delegated Development

Although we are calling delegated development a single environment, there are several reasons for doing delegated development, and each leads to somewhat different management approaches.

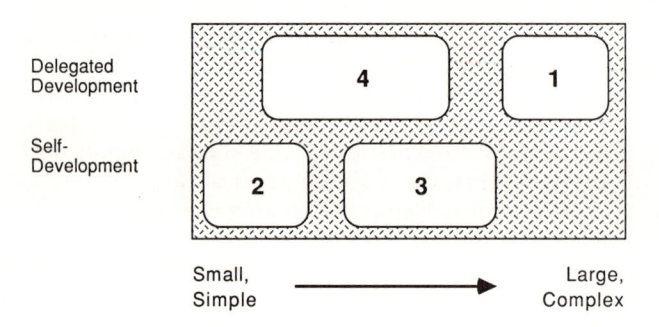

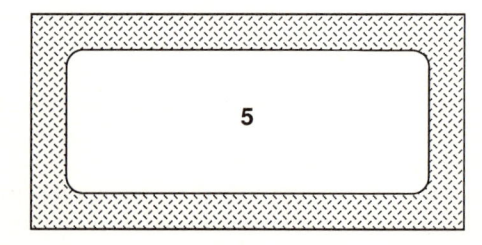

FIGURE 1-4 PROJECT DEVELOPMENT ENVIRONMENTS

The first reason for delegated development is that the work to be done is simply beyond the capabilities of end users. For decision support systems and executive information systems, development has long been done by IS professionals because of the technical complexity of the work.

Many firms, unfortunately, have no way to develop complex applications that lie outside the traditional domain of data processing. They can develop large DP applications, and they can support end user development, but they have no approval mechanism for creating complex analysis applications and other complex applications that may be crucial to the success of their organizations. In other words, for historical reasons, many firms have locked themselves out of potentially critical applications.

A second reason for doing delegated development is that the project is a large multiuser project. For multiuser projects, one individual has to do the development, and so most users become "delegators." Most multiuser projects are complex, although some are fairly simple.

The third reason for doing delegated development is the most controversial. This is that some users *simply choose* not to do their own development. This obviously flies in the face of the traditional No Programming orthodoxy and raises the spectre of the information center being deluged by development requests. Because this reason for delegation is so controversial, we will return to it later in the chapter and discuss it even more fully in Chapter 3.

The Management Mix and Application Development
Some delegated development projects are small, and others large. In general, the management mix and appropriate application development approaches for small projects is like that of second-environment projects, while the management mix and appropriate application development approaches for large projects in this environment is like the management mix for the third environment.

What separates the fourth environment from the second and third is the set of problems that appear when work is being done for another person or for several other people. For example, needs assessment must elicit the ultimate user's requirements, and this job has long been considered difficult even for professional systems analysts working with very structured data processing situations. For inexperienced end users working with fairly unstructured situations, things are likely to be even more difficult. There is a real danger that miscommunication will lead users to assume that the application works one way when it really works another way. This could easily lead to extremely faulty analysis.

The application also needs to be well documented because the developer may leave the organization, and without document, the user will have little hope of extending or perhaps even using the application. In a similar vein, the user or users need to be trained in how to use their application. Neither documentation nor training is easy to do well, and there is a danger that the prevalance of applications developed by people other than the ultimate user has already produced a large number of time bombs waiting to go off.

The Fifth Environment: Department Management

As shown in Figure 1-4, the first four environments deal with the development of specific applications. But organizations now find that a focus on individual applications is myopic. Broader issues of overall end user computing management must also be attacked at the department level. Department-level management for Type II offices is becoming so important that it represents a fifth environment for project development, as shown in Figure 1-4.

The Need for Departmental Planning and Management

In the early days of end user computing, very little thought was given to planning and development at the departmental level. Individual end users and the information center focused on single applications, and very little thought was given to the roles that should be assigned to different people in the department. As a result, a number of problems appeared when the use of computers exploded in each department.

Many of these problems appeared as a result of **application myopia,** that is, the focus on the development of individual applications without considering the broader problem of managing the department's broad portfolio of applications.

- First, a focus on individual problems often causes users to select "the best software and hardware for the job" for each application. This often results in a department's having several incompatible computers and incompatible application software packages running on even its compatible computers.

- Second, once a computer and application program are purchased, they tend to drive future application development decisions. Because this hardware and software represent sunk costs, users are often pushed to develop new applications on this hardware and software. In many cases, low-value early applications tend to constrain high-value application development projects that come later.

- Third, there is a danger that laissez-faire application development may be producing the wrong applications in a department. Without prior thinking, high-value applications may lay undeveloped while too much time is spent in the development of lower value applications.

Another source of problems has been a failure in many departments to develop clear roles for everyone in the department.

Management Although most managers today manage partially computerized offices (which in many ways are harder to manage than fully computerized offices), many lack the skills to see possible gains, foresee threats, develop security and privacy procedures, budget for equipment intelligently, or assign appropriate roles to individuals in the office. In many cases, this vacuum is filled by having "power users" make crucial decisions. But power users lack the manager's broad perspective and often tend to be junior employees who lack sensitivity to key issues.

Support Staff Unless secretaries are well trained, the department's computerized files are in danger of becoming chaotic. This could result in the "loss" of key data and a sharp loss in productivity in looking for information. In addition, poorly trained secretaries will not be able to purchase and maintain equipment intelligently or to handle work delegated by others. This will result in the inability to delegate work, so that the expensive time of professionals in the department will be wasted on work appropriate for secretaries.

Individual Users Individual users need to be trained to use their computers well. They must not just learn the rudimentary parts of their application software. They must also learn how to use their computer and operating system well, as well as understand good practice.

Power Users Power users are a major asset for departments today. But there is a growing danger that power users will "burn out," be diverted from their main functional work, or both. Secretarial delegation is critical, as is the insistence that individual users wean themselves from excessive dependence on power users.

Because of such problems, a number of information centers are beginning to develop support and control problems for the "fifth environment"—departmental development and management.

The Management Mix and Project Development

At the departmental level, the technological infrastructure must be built with foresight and a solid understanding of the department's current applications, needs, and selected development projects. Each individual may have his or her own equipment, but there will be shared equipment as well, and even if most equipment is individual, users with different machines must be able to work together smoothly.

Support is such a broad and unexplored issue that it is difficult to say anything about it briefly. Managers need to be trained to manage highly computerized offices, and others in the department must be trained in their roles as well. These problems are so big that the information center will probably have to work with the corporate human resources (personnel) and corporate planning departments to develop an appropriate portfolio of support programs.

Control at the departmental level is very difficult. First, because so many people are involved, privacy and security become difficult to enforce or even to understand. Second, if a critical application or a department-wide application fails, the entire mission of the department may be affected, and departments are more important than individual. Third, the department is the appropriate place to implement control mechanisms required in all four environments of end user computing, just as most other control processes in organizations depend on enforcement by the local department.

Promotion is needed simply to raise the consciousness of department managers and other employees, so that they can see the implications of departmental management. Since this issue has not received much attention in the popular press, the very idea of departmental management above the level of buying specific pieces of equipment and developing specific applications needs to be promoted heavily.

THE CHANGING INFORMATION CENTER

Although information centers are now widespread, they are still in their adolescence. In this last section, we will trace the development of information centers and discuss the changes they may need to make in the future to reach their highest potential and perhaps even to survive.

The Early Years

The 1960s
Although information centers are normally traced back to the 1970s, the first EUC applications appeared in the 1960s and perhaps even in the 1950s. With few exceptions, early end users were engineers and scientists, but their problems were remarkably like those of today's end users, and many engineering-oriented programs such as Boeing even established user's groups and support departments resembling information centers. (49)

The 1970s
During the 1970s, a number of line and staff managers began using computers.

- Falling computer costs made "inefficient" development and execution somewhat more acceptable to the data processing department, so users were allowed to write small programs.
- Service bureaus began to offer time-shared hosts, which provided much easier application development than the batch processing hosts that were then used in most firms. In addition, many corporations began to introduce time-shared host computers by the end of the 1970s.
- Fourth-generation tools such as report generators allowed users to develop small applications with only a moderate amount of training. By the late 1970s, many application packages such as financial analysis programs, statistical analysis programs, and graphics programs joined the earlier fourth-generation tools.
- The data processing department was unable to keep up with the stream of job requests coming from users, and a large **backlog** of applications awaiting development appeared in nearly every firm.

From the data processing department's viewpoint, the most important of these factors was the application backlog. Long delays harmed DP's relationships with other departments, and users were especially incensed that small requests took months to do—even if they could be jumped to near the top of the queue. The importance of the backlog was quantified in a study by Alloway and Quillard. (2) The study confirmed that backlogs existed and that they were very long. Worse yet, the study found that formal backlog was only the tip of the iceberg. There was also a large **invisible backlog** of jobs that users wanted to submit but did not bother submitting in the face of the enormous backlog of jobs to be done. This invisible backlog of jobs was actually much longer than the formal backlog.

Fortunately, the study confirmed that many jobs in both the formal and invisible backlogs were relatively small tasks. Many data processing heads had recognized the importance of small jobs long before the Alloway and Quillard study, and they came to believe that nontechnical end users could handle their own small jobs with fourth-generation tools designed for DP programmers. To test the possibility, they created small information centers staffed by only one or two people. These centers provided four basic services to users.

1. They provided tools—computer power, application software, and terminals to users.
2. When a user first came in with a project, they provided **consulting** to sharpen up the concept, explore costs and benefits, and select the right software tool for the job.
3. Next, the user was **trained** to use the tool.
4. If the user ran into trouble, **hotline assistance** would be available to solve specific problems.

Because the information center was seen as a way to let users get around the backlog without chewing into development resources too heavily, these information centers were careful to limit their services. Specifically, they refused to program. This **No Programming Dogma** made sense for backlog-oriented applications. It would not be fair or rational to tell one user to wait a year if the job was submitted formally but then turn around and write a similar application immediately for someone walking into the information center. Unfortunately, this No Programming Dogma was later applied to a wider array of applications, as we will see later. In at least some of these applications, the original rationale for the No Programming Dogma is at least questionable and is probably dead wrong.

Report generators were the most popular of the backlog-oriented tools. They could handle the majority of small user jobs, and they were relatively easy to use. But other tools were also used by more sophisticated end users, including fourth-generation application generators that created miniature DP applications for small needs, financial analysis programs, statistical analysis programs, graphics packages, and even third-generation programming languages. These tools are discussed in Chapter 16.

IBM Responds

In the early 1970s, IBM Canada built an "information centre" for its internal data processing needs. This center was so successful that IBM began to promote the concept among its clients, first in Canada and later in the United States. The vision promoted by IBM has tended to dominate general thinking about information centers. In addition to crystallizing the term "information center," IBM cast the No Programming Dogma in stone.

The Information Center Concept Grows: 1980–1985

The PC Shock

Although personal computers had been on the scene since the mid-1970s, their processing power was very low, and their role in corporate life was very limited. In 1981, however, IBM introduced the IBM Personal Computer, the first of a new generation of machines that broke the traditional 64 KB (kilobyte) barrier for internal memory and so allowed the creation of powerful and easy-to-use software. The combination of the IBM name and new processing power soon produced a flood of personal computers in corporations.

The central IS department was quickly numbed by the shock of assimilating hundreds of personal computers. These small machines from IBM and other companies required large amounts of technical competence for proper selection, setup and maintenance. This need was compounded by the hundreds of hardware and software options available on these machines. In addition, the IBM architecture had not yet achieved dominance, and most machines from different vendors were deeply incompatible.

In addition, training and consulting needs were enormous because most users were complete novices. Even when they achieved working competence, they constantly moved up to new levels of skills that required new training and consulting.

These problems had existed with time-shared host computing, but the large number of personal computers compounded support problems enormously, as did the tremendous diversity of PC options. Until 1985, few corporations had time to do more than basic support for PC users.

Where information centers existed, IS management usually handed over its PC headaches to these departments. In other companies, new units had to be created; they went by many names, but the term "information center" gradually became a generic name for the unit that supported both PCs and host time-shared applications. Of course, some firms still restrict the term "information center" to the subgroup dealing with host computers, but the clear trend has been to recognize "information center" as being synonymous with combined PC and host support.

The Information Center Explosion

At the start of the 1980s, even the broad concepts of end user computing and information centers were relatively unknown, and few IS managers put end user computing high on their list of management concerns. The Ball and Harris survey (5) of IS professionals could not find end user computing anywhere on the list of the top ten concerns.

The PC shock and the growth of host time-shared computing changed the situation dramatically. When University of Minnesota researchers conducted another survey in 1983, (21) they found that the management of end user computing had jumped to second place on this list, right behind overall IS planning. Only these two issues made the top ten on every respondent's list, and EUC was far ahead of the third place issue in the rankings.

This growth of interest was translated directly into action. By 1985, a number of sources indicated that at least half of all large companies already had information centers. (3,7,18,22,28,39,42) For 1990, most forecasts predicted almost universal implementation in large firms.

Broadening Vision of EUC Applications: 1985–1990

The personal computer was only the first new application to be added to the original concept of information centers. In many firms, the information center became the focal point for supporting all managerial and professional applications—applications in what we have called Type II departments.

DSS and EIS

As discussed earlier in this chapter, both decision support systems (DSSs) and executive information systems (EISs) require sophisticated programming beyond the capabilities of most end users. As a result, both DSSs and EISs are normally built by information systems professionals. The normal practice has been to create special corporate units that seek out fruitful applications and then develop them. In other words, the No Programming Dogma has never been part of the philosophies of either DSS or EIS specialists.

When DSS and EIS are absorbed into an information center, as is frequently the case today, their divergent views on development often produce intellectual stomach aches. In some cases, the result is a fruitful debate over when delegated development is appropriate. In other cases, the result is acrimony or simply coexistence without intellectual reconciliation.

In addition, DSS often focuses on *group* activities, for example, multiuser planning efforts. This fits into the fourth environment of development discussed earlier in this chapter—an environment that many information centers still fail to grapple with intellectually.

Office Automation

Office automation is also aimed at *group* applications; in fact, single-user activities in OA, such as using word processing to write a document, are normally just a prelude to group activities, such as distributing the document through electronic mail or placing it in a work group document base for later retrieval.

More importantly, OA has always spanned Type I and Type II departments, and office automation in such Type I departments as word processing centers is almost a separate field from Type II office automation, which is oriented toward managerial work station services and electronic mail. Although it might make sense to place Type II office automation under the information center and Type I office automation someplace else, this is rarely done. As a result, if the information center absorbs office automation, it usually finds itself managing clerical operations, and few information centers have any background in this area.

Seeking a New Vision

The addition of DSS, EIS, OA, and other services to the information center's early mix of time-shared host applications and PCs should force most information centers to rethink the range of services they will provide and to adjust their focus from individuals to groups. This has not always happened, however, and the merger of the new applications is often done in ways that merely place the old groups side by side, instead of reorganizing them on the basis of an underlying model of needs in managerial and professional departments.

A Time of Challenge

The euphoria of the early days was heady stuff for information centers. Demand for services was high, and, as noted above, end user computing was seen as among the most important issues facing IS management.

As end user computing began to mature, however, interest from senior IS management began to wane. Surveys of IS managers in 1985 and 1986 by Hartog and Herbert (29,30) found that EUC had slipped to fifth place in 1985 and to twelfth place in 1986. The information center placed even lower on the list of concerns—only twelfth in 1985 and fourteenth in 1986. Although these surveys had methodological differences from earlier surveys, many anecdotal comments from information center managers bear out the results of these two surveys. At least in the eyes of IS, end user computing is beginning to lose its luster.

General management above the level of IS also seemed to be growing impatient with end user computing. A 1985 survey by Crwth (18) found that mature information centers, which had been in business more than a year, were much more likely to cite budget justification pressure as a major problem than were pilot (startup) information centers.

Some of this loss in status was inevitable. A newborn baby always receives a great deal of attention, but soon it is no longer the newest child on the block and other newborns begin to steal its glamor. In addition, the list of IS concerns is basically a list of problems. Therefore, the fading of EUC and information centers on the list is, at least to some extent, a tribute to the success of information centers.

Even so, the fact remained that information centers were beginning to feel a great deal of pressure, and many began to feel that they were doing something fundamentally wrong. Joanne Kelleher summarized this feeling this way. (35)

> Most information centers started out with the goals of creating order amid the chaos of unsupervised minicomputer acquisitions and educated unskilled users in the elementary applications. Now that many of them have fulfilled their original calling, however, information centers are arriving at a juncture, a point that either signifies the beginning of their true vocation or the end of their original organizational usefulness.

In addition, not all information centers seemed to be doing equally well. Some seemed to have little control over end user computing and were experiencing endless problems. Others were generally seen as doing a better job. Daniel Couger described the situation. (16)

> Although computers have spread into every corner of the organization, although people have become more knowledgeable and enthusiastic

about them, many of their promises have not been fulfilled. End-user computing, which enables users to develop their own applications, has potentially the greatest impact of any development in the computer field. But for many organizations it has been far less effective and more costly than anticipated. Others have had good results.

Couger based this statement on a study of 17 large companies. Of these firms, 11 had serious problems with end user computing, in terms of proliferations of incompatible machines or uncontrolled cost growth. Six of the firms, however, seemed to be doing very well. Individuals firms need to be looking for ways to keep their own information centers in the winning column and out of the losing column.

Planning for Success

Although there is much disagreement about the best roads to take for information centers, there seems to be growing agreement on at least a few points, and we will close the chapter with a discussion of these points.

Planning

The first of these points is the importance of planning. The field of end user computing is changing at an enormous rate, both at the technical level and at the application level. Without good, solid plans, information centers will be whipped around like palm trees in a storm and will run into unforeseen problems and cost overruns almost daily.

Planning must begin with an understanding of the "market" that end user computing is attempting to serve—chiefly managers and professionals in Type II departments. This chapter has included a discussion of their general needs. Information centers must go beyond these generalities to develop a solid understanding of end users in their own firms. This understanding must include forecasts of demand for machines, various kinds of software packages, and various kinds of information center services.

The next step in planning is to forecast changing technology as well as possible. Although technology is changing at an awesome rate, some baseline forecasts have to be made for such things as average machine costs and communications capabilities. Many parts of the technological infrastructure, especially mainframe computers and networks, have to be planned several years in advance of actual implementation. To run out of power on a mainframe is more than a social mistake; it can affect the productivity of literally hundreds of users. Networking too late or too small can also pinch the firm's abilities. Of course, at the other end, buying far more capacity than needed and buying it too soon is also catastrophic.

Making baselines for demand and technology should allow the information center to staff up intelligently and, more importantly, to make hard choices about where it will spend its limited resources. Unless it wants to provide uniformly mediocre services, the information center must follow the most fundamental principle of planning: it is critical to say no.

Controlling User Activities

Couger's six successful firms had one thing in common—strong control over technology and applications development on the basis of "soft controls."

(16) Soft controls consist of items such as limiting support to a list of approved purchases and providing extra incentives, including electronic mail to complying personal computers. By offering a carrot as well as the stick, these firms were successful in guiding user behavior.

Of course, firms that exercised little or no control were doomed to proliferation and cost overruns, but Couger found that firms with very restrictive hard controls such as outright prohibitions on many kinds of purchases were also unsuccessful because they were unable to enforce their rules. Users simply got around them. By providing incentives, Couger's successful firms were able to enforce proper behavior.

Becoming Proactive

Another point that may be critical to success is avoiding the trap of being pinned down by vast user demand to mundane low-level activities that have comparatively small value to firms. Randy Castro, a consultant in Kansas, warned that many information centers "get caught up in a vicious cycle of installing PCs and delivering basic training and overlooking the need to identify strategic corporate resources." (35) In other words, these information centers failed to apply the first principle of planning: that of selecting where to spend resources to do the most good.

Although there is no way to avoid providing these services to a great extent, every information center needs to reserve a certain fraction of its resources in its annual plan for activities that will provide strategic benefits to the corporation and give it favorable visibility. Even if such a reserve is not approved by IS management, it must be created, or the information center will fade ever further into obscurity and will be type cast as a bit player.

One possibility, discussed in the next chapter, is to conduct needs analyses for individuals, departments, and larger work units. These studies will identify needs and help prioritize efforts that will have a major positive impact on the firms.

The information center should then make these high-priority applications happen, no matter what is involved. It may have to spend a great deal of time in the developers' offices, helping them see good ways of handling key design and implementing problems. It should also not hesitate to step in to do some or much of the actual work if the technical problems are formidable. In other words, it should not feel religiously bound to the No Programming Dogma.

At the same time, application development provided indiscriminately would be self-defeating. The information would soon end up with an enormous backlog and find itself even less able to break out of day-to-day work to make critical things happen. A strategic focus is needed to identify which projects should be taken on.

The basic concept is that the information center should shift from a reactive mode providing low-level service to a high proactive mode in which it helps users identify high-payoff areas and then helps them develop the applications as quickly and as well as possible.

Once the information center has produced benefits, it has to publicize them. It should ask end users to document hard dollar savings or softer benefits that are easily appreciated, such as a reduction in the time needed to do certain kinds of high-value work. It should then publish these successes in its newsletter and in an annual report.

Finally, the information center should help users manage benefits after a system is installed. At a negative level, it should enforce evaluations of systems after they have gone in. This is seldom done, but it can pinpoint trouble spots while providing even more success stories. More positively, the information center should work with developers to find ways of improving work systems after the application is implemented. This may consist of such mundane jobs as writing small programs to automate simple but repetitive tasks to helping the organization work out divisions of labor to offload as much work as possible from expensive managers and professionals.

The Role of IS Management

All of these things will mean nothing if EUC cannot get support from IS management. The information center needs to stress the strategic nature of end user computing to its IS bosses.

There is a basic dilemma that tends to cause the information center to have very low power within the IS department. This is the disparity between its importance and its size. Although end user computing is very large, it is accomplished largely outside the IS department, by end users. As a result, although EUC represents about half of all computing in a typical corporation, it rarely has even 10 percent of the IS staff. It is only human for IS heads to think of importance in terms of head count. This problem is compounded if the information center fails to take on strategic challenges, but it is present even if the information center does take on strategic work.

Even if the IS manager is convinced of the importance of EUC, additional persuasion may be needed for managers above IS. One vice president for information services was convinced of its importance and wanted to place his most senior lieutenant in charge of the information center. He reasoned that a person too junior for the job would not have the corporate maturity so steer EUC as a strategic innovation. Upper management argued that the information center director had to be more junior because he would only be managing two other people. It took a great deal of effort for the IS director to persuade top management to allow his staffing plan.

Both IS management and senior corporate management need to be convinced that end user computing is the most strategic problem facing information systems today, that it must take on strategic challenges instead of just doing low-level training and support, and that the information center director must have the organizational maturity needed to steer this critical family of innovations to achieve maximum benefits.

CONCLUSION

Themes

The first purpose of this chapter was to stress the strategic importance of end user computing within the broader world of information systems. EUC is already about as large as data processing and will soon be much larger. Yet in most firms today, the information centers that manage end user computing are staffed by very junior people and are limited to low-level support work.

In end user computing, there seem to be two basic **management objectives**. The first objective is to continue to provide the kinds of low-level support now given by information centers, including low-level consulting, training, hotline assistance, hardware and software selection, and policy setting, for smaller applications.

The second objective must be to support critical applications that fall outside the realm of data processing and yet are too complex for end users to develop themselves or will not be developed by end users for other reasons. For these kinds of systems, the information center will have to be a motivating force and may even have to do some development itself, just as DSS and EIS groups have long had to do development work for end users. This second objective is shared by only a fraction of information centers today.

Doing development and even motivating end users to work on strategic systems are frightening prospects for information centers that are already overburdened by work. But to fail to cause critical systems to come into existence is inexcusable when a large amount of money is already being spent supporting many lower-priority applications. If the information center restricts itself to critical applications, it will be able to avoid being swamped by excess demand.

A second theme of this chapter is that end user computing is not the simple phenomenon it is often depicted to be. When EUC began, most projects were small and simple enough to be developed by the ultimate users. Information centers responded with programs to support and control these simple user-developed projects. Today, however, EUC projects span a broad spectrum of sizes, and many are developed by people other than the end user. In addition, corporations are now beginning to realize that development needs to be managed at the department level, as well as at the level of individual workers and applications. Overall, end user computing is extremely heterogeneous, and it can only be managed with a multifaceted program in which different "management mixes" are developed for different kinds of projects. The information center that fails to develop programs for projects that are not small or user-developed is simply not fulfilling its role.

A third theme of this chapter is that information centers need to base their programs on a thorough understanding of user characteristics, needs, and desires. Relatively few information center staff members are likely to be able to say how many line managers, staff managers, professionals, secretaries, or other clerical workers there are in their corporations, much less how many of them use computers and how computer use varies among these groups. When EUC consisted of only a few simple applications and was limited to only a few people, a strategy based on tools may have been sufficient. But today computers have reached almost every office and are being used in almost every conceivable way, and a more formal understanding of user needs is required.

Organization of the Book

The information center today is in a period of uncertainty that will require many centers to rethink their basic patterns of doing business. The remainder

CONCLUSION

of this book looks at the many complex skills that information center staff members will have to manage if this strategic change in corporate life is to be fruitful.

Chapters 2 through 5 examine management issues.

- Chapter 2 focuses on needs analysis and application development methodologies. It presumes that the information center is taking the proactive stance discussed in the last part of this chapter.
- Chapter 3 surveys the fundamental issues that have to be faced when setting up an information center or reevaluating its role.
- Chapter 4 looks at the annual and day-to-day policies that need to be set for an information center to be successful.
- Chapter 5 examines the front line of information center services—support, including consulting, training, and hotline assistance.

The next seven chapters deal with personal computing.

- Chapter 6 introduces fundamental technical issues that pervade all other PC chapters, including the ensemble nature of personal computer systems.
- Chapter 7 focuses on the specifics of personal computer hardware.
- Chapter 8 carries on with the specifics of personal computer software technology.
- Chapter 9 introduces analysis applications and concentrates on spreadsheet programs.
- Chapter 10 looks at data management concepts and at personal computer DBMSs.
- Chapter 11 focuses on software for person-to-person communication, including word processing programs, conceptual graphics, and desktop publishing.
- Chapter 12 examines other personal computer applications.

The last five chapters deal with large systems.

- Chapter 13 discusses communications with host computers from terminals or personal computers.
- Chapter 14 presents basic technical issues for PC networking and larger networks.
- Chapter 15 focuses more closely on market alternatives and trends in networking.
- Chapter 16 surveys data and decision support applications on time-shared host computers—the original mother land of end user computing.
- Chapter 17 finishes the book with directions in office automation, especially electronic mail and document interchange.

REVIEW QUESTIONS

1. Why is "end user computing" a good name for the post-DP application explosion now underway? Why is it not a good name?
2. Why did it take so long to realize that data processing would eventually be surpassed as the main application in information systems?
3. Why are Type II departments more important than Type I departments? Why are they harder to automate? Why will traditional systems analysis approaches not work in Type II departments?
4. Looking at the office demographic data in Tables 1-1 and 1-2, what were the biggest surprises to you? Do you think that most information systems heads would be surprised by the data in these tables? If they are not familiar with these data, what mistakes do you think they are likely to make? What should companies do to get an understanding of their own office demographics?
5. When you looked at the use of time data in Tables 1-3 and 1-4, what were the biggest surprises to you? How do these tables help you explain the relative importance of different applications today? What do use of time studies fail to explain?
6. How would you differentiate the concepts of "manager" and "professional?"
7. Why is face-to-face communication difficult to automate? Why is activity management difficult to automate? Why are different types of analysis software needed?
8. In the computer–application matrix, what is the meaning of a cell? Why does each application have two cells? What is the difference between generic and hybrid applications?
9. What are the differences between an executive information system (EIS) and a decision support system (DSS)? How are they similar?
10. What are the differences between the second and third environments for application development? What complexities does the third environment add to the information center's management tasks?
11. What complexities does the fourth environment add to the information center's management tasks?
12. Why have the third and fourth environments often been overlooked by information systems? How are they the same? How are they different, in terms of support and control?
13. Why has the fifth environment been overlooked frequently in the past? In what sense is it the most crucial environment to manage?
14. Identify roles for the department manager, secretaries, all individual users, and power users.
15. In what ways did end user computing's initial set of applications blind it to some of the things that must be done today?
16. Why is end user computing declining somewhat in importance, in the eyes of IS management? What do you think is the most critical step for information centers to take in the future? Why? What do you think is the second most critical step?

17. What are the two management objectives discussed in the Conclusion? Which do you think is more important? Is this the objective that most information centers stress?

REFERENCES

1. ALAVI, MARYAN, PHILLIPS, JAMES S., AND FREEDMAN, SARA, "Strategies for Control of End-User Computing: Impacts on End Users," *Proceedings of the Seventh International Conference on Information Systems,* San Diego, December 15–17, 1986, pp. 57–66.
2. ALLOWAY, ROBERT M., AND QUILLARD, JUDITH A., "User Managers' Systems Needs," *MIS Quarterly,* June 1983, pp. 27–42.
3. American Management Association, *1985 AMA Report on Information Centers,* New York, 1985, cited in Crwth Computer Coursewares, "The Second Crwth Information Center Survey," *Crwth News for Better Training,* Vol. 3, No. 1, 1985.
4. BAIR, JAMES H., AND NELSON, KATHRYN, J., "User Needs as the Basis of Strategic Planning," Chapter 1 in Karen Tackle-Quinn (Ed.). *Advances in Office Automation,* Chichester: John Wiley & Sons, Ltd., 1984.
5. BALL, LESLIE, AND HARRIS, RICHARD, "SMIS Members: A Member Analysis," *MIS Quarterly,* March 1982, pp. 19–38.
6. BENJAMIN, ROBERT I., "Information Technology in the 1990s: A Long Range Planning Scenario," *MIS Quarterly,* June 1982, pp. 11–31.
7. BENSON, DAVID H., "A Field Study of End User Computing: Findings and Issues," *MIS Quarterly,* December 1983, pp. 35–45.
8. Booz-Allen and Hamilton, Inc., Booz-Allen Study of Managerial/Professional Productivity, June 1980.
9. BURNS, THOMAS, "Management in Action," *Operational Research Quarterly,* Vol. 8, No. 2, 1967, pp. 45–60.
10. Case Institute of Technology, *An Operations Research Study of the Scientific Activity of Chemists,* 1958.
11. CHORAN, I., "The Manager of a Small Company," Montreal: McGill University, unpublished MBA thesis, 1969.
12. Codasyl, *Codasyl End-User Facilities Committee Status Report,* North-Holland Publishing Company, Information and Management, Vol. 2, 1979, pp. 137–163, cited in Rockart, John F., and Flannery, Lauren S., "The Management of End User Computing," *Communications of the ACM,* Association for Computing Machinery, October 1983, pp. 776–784.
13. Computer Intelligence Corporation, *Information Center Market: CI Data File Analysis,* July 1985.
14. *Computerworld,* "Shared Micros Commonplace," March 25, 1985, pp. 1, 4.
15. *Computerworld,* "End-User Computing: MIS Answers the Call," August 18, 1986, pp. 41–55.
16. COUGER, J. DANIEL, "E Pluribus Computum," *Harvard Business Review,* September-October 1986, pp. 87–91.
17. CROSTON, J. D., AND GOULDING, H. B., "The Effectiveness of Communication at Meetings: A Case Study," *Operations Research Quarterly,* Vol. 17, No. 1, 1967, pp. 45–47.
18. Crwth Computer Coursewares, "The Second Crwth Information Center Survey," *Crwth News for Better Training,* Vol. 3, No. 1, 1985.

19. CULNAN, MARY J., "Chauffeured Versus End User Access to Commercial Databases: The Effects of Task and Individual Differences," *MIS Quarterly,* March 1983, pp. 55–67.
20. DiNUCCI, DARCY, "Environmental Impact," *PC World,* December 1985, pp. 224–231.
21. DICKSON, GARY W., LEITHEISER, ROBERT L., WETHERBE, JAMES C., AND NECHIS, M., "Key Information Systems Issues for the 1980's," *MIS Quarterly,* September 1984, pp. 135–147.
22. The Diebold Group, *Survey of MIS Budgets,* New York, 1985, cited in Crwth Computer Coursewares, "The Second Crwth Information Center Survey," *Crwth News for Better Training,* Vol. 3, No. 1, 1985.
23. DOKTOR, ROBERT, University of Hawaii, January 1984, private communication with the author. These data were taken from senior Japanese executives in Japan.
24. DUBIN, R., AND SPRAY, S. L. "Executive Behavior and Interaction," *Industrial Relations,* No. 3, 1964.
25. *EDP Analyzer,* "Supporting End User Programming," Canning Publications, Inc., 925 Anza Avenue, Vista, California, June 1981.
26. EHRENBERG, A. S. C., *Repeat Buying: Theory and Applications,* North-Holland Publishing Company, Amsterdam, and American Elsevier, New York, 1972.
27. ENGEL, G. H., GROPPUSA, J., LOWENSTEIN, R. A., AND TRAUB, W. G., "An Office Communication System, *IBM Systems Journal,* Vol. 18, No. 3, 1979, pp. 402–431.
28. GUIMARAES, TOR, "The Evolution of the Information Center," *DATAMATION,* July 15, 1984, pp. 127–130.
29. HARTOG, CURT, AND HERBERT, MARTIN, "1985 Opinion Survey of MIS Managers: Key Issues," *MIS Quarterly,* December 1986, pp. 351–361.
30. HERBERT, MARTIN, AND HARTOG, CURT, "MIS Rates the Issues," *DATAMATION,* November 1986, pp. 79–86.
31. HINRICHS, JOHN R., "Communications Activity of Industrial Research Personnel, *Personnel Psychology,* Vol. 17, 1963, pp. 194–204.
32. HORNE, JAMES, AND LUPTON, THOMAS, "The Work Activities of Middle Managers—An Exploratory Study," *Journal of Management Studies,* Vol. 1, No. 2, 1965, pp. 14–33.
33. International Data Corporation, cited in "The Paper Blizzard," *USA Today,* April 4, 1986, p. 1.
34. IVES, BLAKE, AND OLSON, MARGRETHE H., "Manager or Technician? The Nature of the Information Systems Manager's Job, *Management Information Systems Quarterly,* Vol. 5, No. 4, December 1981.
35. KELLEHER, JOANNE, "Information Centers—Their Choice: Justify Existence or Go Out of Business," *Computerworld,* August 11, 1986, pp. 51–59.
36. KELLEY, JOE, "The Study of Executive Behavior by Activity Sampling," *Human Relations,* Vol. 17, 1964, pp. 277–287.
37. KLEMMER, E. T., AND SNYDER, F. W. "Measurement of Time Spent Communicating," *The Journal of Communication,* Vol. 22, 1972, pp. 142–158.
38. KURKE, LANCE B., AND ALDRICH, HOWARD E., "Mintzberg Was Right," *Proceedings of the 39th Annual Meeting of the Academy of Management,* Atlanta, Georgia, August 1979.
39. LEITHEISER, ROBERT L., AND WETHERBE, JAMES C., "A Survey of Information Centers: Services, Decisions, Problems, Successes," Management Information Systems Research Center, School of Management, University of Minnesota, Minneapolis, Minnesota 1984.

REFERENCES

40. MARTIN, JAMES, *Application Development Without Programmers*, Prentice-Hall, Inc., 1982, cited in Rockart, John F., and Flannery, Lauren S., "The Management of End User Computing," *Communications of the ACM*, Association for Computing Machinery, October 1983, pp. 776–784.
41. MCLEAN, E. R., "End Users as Application Developers," *Proceedings of the Guide/Share Application Development Symposium*, October 1974, cited in Rockart and Flannery, "The Management of End User Computing," *Communications of the ACM*, Association for Computing Machinery, October 1983, pp. 776–784.
42. MELYMUKA, KATHLEEN, "The Information Center," *PC Week*, December 3, 1985, pp. 77–79.
43. MINTZBERG, HENRY, "Managerial Work: Analysis from Observation," *Management Science*, Vol. 18, No. 2, 1971, pp. B97–B110.
44. NOTTING, reported in Sune Carlson, Executive Behavior, Stockholm: Stromberg, 1951.
45. PALMER, A. W., AND BEISHON, R. J., "How the Day Goes," *Personnel Management*, 1970.
46. PANKO, RAYMOND R., "The Demographics of Office Work," Working Paper 87-1, Department of Decision Sciences, College of Business Administration, University of Hawaii, 2404 Maile Way, Honolulu, Hawaii, January 1987.
47. PANKO, RAYMOND R., "Office Work," *Office: Technology and People*, Elsevier Science Publishers, B.V., Amsterdam, September 1984, pp. 205–238.
48. PANKO, RAYMOND R., "38 Offices: Analyzing Needs in Individual Offices," *ACM Transactions on Office Information Systems*, Vol. 2, No. 3, July 1984, Association for Computing Machinery, pp. 226–234.
49. PANKO, RAYMOND R., "Why Asking Users to Define Requirements Rarely Works," Working Paper 71-5, Institute for Communication Research, Stanford University, Stanford, California, 1971.
50. PANKO, RAYMOND R., AND PANKO, ROSEMARIE U., "A Survey of EMS Users at DARCOM," *Computer Networks*, Vol. 5, No. 3, May 1981, Elsevier Scientific Publishers, Amsterdam, pp. 19–34.
51. PANKO, RAYMOND R., AND SPRAGUE, RALPH H., JR., "Toward a New Framework for Office Support," *Proceedings of the 1982 Conference on Office Information Systems*, Philadelphia, Association for Computing Machinery, June 1982.
52. QUILLARD, JUDITH A., ROCKART, JOHN F., WILDE, ERIC, VERNON, MARK, AND MOCK, GEORGE, *A Study of the Corporate Use of Personal Computers*, CISR Working Paper No. 109, Center for Information Systems Research, Massachusetts Institute of Technology, Sloan School of Management, 77 Massachusetts Avenue, Cambridge, Massachusetts, December 1983.
53. ROCKART, JOHN F., AND FLANNERY, LAUREN S., "The Management of End User Computing," *Communications of the ACM*, Association for Computing Machinery, October 1983, pp. 776–784.
54. SCHEMENT, JORGE REINA, AND LIEVROUW, LEAH, "A Behavioral Measure of Information Work," Telecommunications Policy, December 1984, pp. 321–334.
55. SIRBU, MARVIN, SCHOICHET, SANDOR, KUNIN, J., HAMMER, MICHAEL, AND SUTHERLAND, JULIET, "OAM: An Office Analysis Methodology," *Office Automation Conference 1982 Digest*, Association for Information Processing Societies, 1982, pp. 317–330.
56. SPRAGUE, RALPH H., JR., "A Framework for the Development of Decision Support Systems," *Management Information Systems Quarterly*, December 1980.
57. STEWART, ROSEMARY, "Managers and Their Jobs," London: Pan Books, 1967.

58. STOGDILL, R. M., AND SHARTLE, C. L., "Methods in the Study of Administrative Leadership," Columbus: Bureau of Business Research, Ohio State University, 1955, quoted in Kelley, Joe, "The Study of Executive Behavior by Activity Sampling," *Human Relations,* Vol. 17, 1964, pp. 277–287.
59. TEGER, SANDRA L., "Factors Impacting the Evaluation of Office Automation," *Proceedings of the IEEE,* Vol. 71, No. 4, 1983, pp. 503–511.
60. TWEDT, DIK WARREN, "How Important to Marketing Strategy Is the 'Heavy User'?" *Journal of Marketing,* Vol. 28, January 1964, pp. 71–72.
61. U.S. Department of Labor, Bureau of Labor Statistics, *Employment and Earnings,* February 1986, p. 80.
62. U.S. Department of Labor, Bureau of Labor Statistics, *Employment and Earnings,* February 1980, Table Q-21, Employed Persons by Occupation, Sex, and Age, p. 37.
63. Xerox Corporation, unnamed study cited in Ganz, John, and Peacock, James, "Office Automation and Business Communications," *Fortune,* October 5, 1981, pp. 7–80.

APPLICATION DEVELOPMENT
end user development, DSS, and EIS 2

Now that we have looked at end user computing broadly, we are ready to consider the central topic of application development. A major theme of Chapter 1 was the existence of several "environments" of end user computing (EUC) and the need for different application development approaches in different environments. We will expand on that theme in this chapter.

In addition to examining end user development, this chapter also looks at the development of decision support systems (DSSs) and executive information systems (EISs). DSSs and EISs, as discussed in Chapter 1, are too complex for end user development. At the same time, they are not classical data processing applications. Because they fall into a gap between end user development and data processing development, many firms have no standard way of developing them. We will treat their development in this chapter because DSS and EIS development are increasingly falling under the aegis of the information center.

INTRODUCTION

Stages in Application Development

Nearly every textbook on information systems (IS) argues that application development projects must be managed through a series of stages, beginning with an assessment of whether the project should be done and ending with its integration into ongoing personal and departmental work systems. Although different authors divide the overall process into different stages, nearly all agree on the specifics of what must be done over the life cycle of a project. Because this application development approach is oriented toward project life cycles, it is normally called the **systems development life cycle (SDLC).**

Assessment, Design, Construction, and Implementation

Figure 2-1 shows the SDLC model that will be used in this chapter. In this model, there are four stages.

Assessment In this stage, the individual or department decides whether the project should be undertaken. Since resources are limited, not every project can be done, even if its benefits exceed its costs.

Design In this stage, the developer lays out a plan for the final product. By planning carefully before moving on, time can be saved overall, and many disasters can be avoided.

Construction In this stage, the application is built. This includes not only programming, testing, and documentation, but also the purchase of hardware, software, and communication products.

Implementation In this last stage, the application is merged into the individual's or department's ongoing work systems. The cutover to the new system can be a traumatic experience unless this transition is managed carefully. After cutover, there is almost always a continuing need to extend the application, thus beginning a new development cycle.

Assessment Versus Other Stages

Although assessment can be viewed as merely the first stage in the SDLC, it is fundamentally different from other stages because assessment cannot be completed for projects in isolation. It has often been taught that development can proceed after it has been determined that benefits exceed costs, but the stark reality is that no individual or department has the resources to develop all of the applications that it would like to have. No work unit has enough resources to develop all applications whose benefits exceed their costs.

So priorities need to be set, both to ensure that only the most important projects are funded and to ensure that funds are not spread so thinly that nothing is developed very well. Setting priorities means that potential applications must be considered as a group, not just individually. This is why Figure 2-1 shows assessment cutting across individual projects, while design, construction, and implementation are tied to individual projects. Once assessment is completed, projects can be developed individually, although, as we

Project 1	Assessment	Design	Construction	Implementation
Project 2	Assessment	Design	Construction	Implementation
Project 3	Assessment	Design	Construction	Implementation
Project 4	Assessment	Design	Construction	Implementation
Project 5	Assessment	Design	Construction	Implementation

⎯Time⎯→

FIGURE 2-1 SYSTEMS DEVELOPMENT LIFE CYCLE

will see later, no project can be developed entirely independently of other existing applications and work in progress.

Of course, prioritization is important primarily for larger projects. For very small tasks, there is no need to set priorities in advance. At the same time, when creating the technological infrastructure in a department—specifically deciding what equipment and software to give to individuals—decision must be guided by the same reasoning presented in this section. Although an individual's small tasks need not be assessed at the level of departmental priorities, an individual's overall spectrum of tasks must be prioritized.

Sequential and Iterative Development

Although every project must go through all four stages of the SDLC, there are disagreements over whether these stages must always be done in sequential order or whether it should be possible to backtrack to earlier stages once later stages have been started.

Sequential Development

Classically, the SDLC has been taught as a strictly sequential process, in which every stage is completed before the next stage begins. Figure 2-2 illustrates sequential development. When a company builds a skyscraper, it develops its design very carefully before starting construction because, once the walls start going up, it is nearly impossible to make major changes in the design. The carpenter's old adage "measure twice, cut once" emphasizes the need for prior planning.

In data processing, sequential development has been touted for many reasons, but these reasons really boil down to two: most data processing projects are large, and the tools for developing them—chiefly COBOL—are extremely inflexible and make even small changes difficult. On large projects developed with rigid tools, sequential development is a critical safeguard.

Although it has always been recognized that some backtracking is inevitable, keeping it to an absolute minimum has always been a key goal in data processing. This goal is especially important in traditional situations in which the design is done by one person, namely, a systems analyst, and the construc-

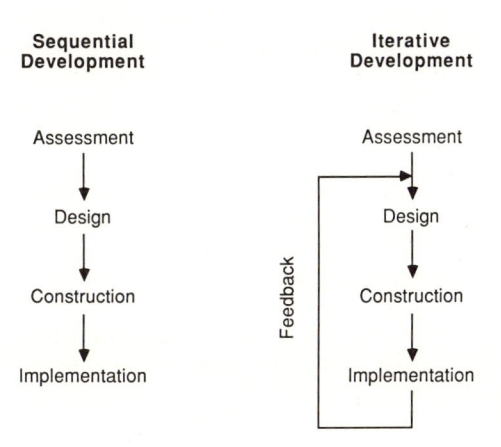

FIGURE 2-2 SEQUENTIAL AND ITERATIVE DEVELOPMENT

tion is done by someone else, a programmer. The failure to produce a clean handoff between systems analyst and programmer is almost always an invitation to serious problems. Furthermore, in many cases implementing the large data processing application is the job of yet a third person. Hence, there is a need for another clean handoff between the construction and implementation stages.

Iterative Development

In more recent years, there has been growing advocacy for nonsequential application development. Usually called **iterative development,** this approach to development not only allows backtracking to earlier steps; it actually makes backtracking mandatory. In iterative development, the application is developed through a series of cycles in which there are three basic steps.

1. A working product is developed for the user.
2. The user works with the product.
3. The developer extends the product in response to the feedback and gives the product to the user, thereby beginning a new cycle.

Iterative development was proposed when it became obvious that many data processing projects were relatively small and could be developed with flexible fourth-generation tools. Although it was recognized that backtracking could be disastrous, even in small products, advocates of iterative development argued that the benefits of feedback in development exceeded potential costs. Although iterative development was first proposed for small and midsize data processing projects, its use is very attractive for end user development projects, DSS projects, and EIS projects.

Discipline in Iterative Development

Iterative development is not the same thing as undisciplined development, in which backtracking is done at any time and in which the developer simply plows ahead with construction, without worrying much about earlier stages, on the grounds that earlier things can always be redone.

Instead, each iteration is a very distinct event. The user is not given a half-developed application. In good iterative development, the user is not shown anything until the application has been thoroughly tested and until at least minimum user documentation has been built. In other words, the user is not shown a rough sketch. Rather, he or she is shown a good draft final version of a project. Otherwise, it will be too hard to give meaningful feedback.

In addition, the developer does not simply go back, make many individual changes, and show the user the results after each small change. Instead, the changes are collected and incorporated into a distinct new version of the application. Therefore, feedback always revolves around a distinct version of the project.

There are several reasons for working only with tested applications that are produced in distinct versions, but in general, they center on control. Unless there are very distinct cycles, development is likely to get out of control, and there will be confusion over what changes have been made. But there are other important reasons besides control. If changes are not implemented immediately, undesirable changes are likely to be withdrawn before retrofitting begins. In addition, batching up changes allows the developer to fit changes into his or her schedule, instead of constantly being asked to make small changes.

Working Products in Iterative Development

Another mark of good iterative development is that even the first version should be a *full working product* that is directly useful. Its scope of activities may be limited, but what it does should be important, and it should do it well. Otherwise, it will not be used enough to allow the user to explore the problem domain in sufficient detail to understand what extensions are needed.

Successive iterations, in turn, will not be primarily bug fixing exercises. Although they will, of course, fix the errors that inevitably creep through testing, their main purpose is to add functionality. Successive versions primarily differ in doing more things than their predecessors. Iterative development does not simply produce successively better versions of a single set of functions. Instead, each cycle adds new functions to the application. This idea of getting quick gains and then moving on is becoming a major theme of the general management literature, not just the iterative design literature in IS. In their book *In Search of Excellence,* Peters and Waterman point out that successful firms do not waste time on long development projects that produce nothing until their ends. (9) Rather, they get quick results and real, harsh feedback. Afterwards, they either go forward or kill the project as not being worth the effort. Peters and Waterman call the specific process of taking small steps with concrete payoffs "chunking."

Application Development in Different Situations

The Second Environment

The second environment of project development in information systems consists of small and simple projects developed by the ultimate user. For trivially small projects, such as dashing off a memo, the stages of the SDLC collapse completely. But even for fairly simple projects, such as evaluating alternative personal computer purchases with a spreadsheet program, there should be at least some separation between assessment, design, construction, and implementation. Since every end user developer will eventually build nontrivial applications, they must all learn basic development disciplines.

The Third Environment

The third environment consists of mid-size projects that are less complex than the traditional operational systems of data processing but much more complex than the traditional image of EUC projects. Within the third environment, user-developers must be trained to use iterative development properly because there is a strong separation among the stages of assessment, design, construction, and implementation.

The Fourth Environment

In the fourth environment, the project is developed by someone other than the ultimate user. Typically, the developer is another end user in the ultimate user's functional department. In the fourth environment, the fact that the developer is no longer the ultimate user means that developers must be well schooled in the techniques for eliciting requirements from users and must be trained in the techniques of user documentation and user training.

DSS and EIS

In a sense, DSS and EIS are extensions to the fourth environment. Their development is different, however, because the developer is no longer a member of the ultimate user's department and the applications are too complex to be developed simply by applying a single tool, even a fourth-generation one. Although end users can develop simple decision-oriented applications and executive information-oriented applications, the terms "DSS" and "EIS" are normally reserved for complex projects beyond the scope of end user development. This chapter will respect that usage.

ASSESSMENT

Identifying Candidates

One old cookbook began a recipe for rabbit stew with the direction "First catch a rabbit." In assessment, the first step is to identify candidate projects for assessment. We will look at several methodologies for identifying candidates. These methodologies, which are listed in Figure 2-3, should be combined rather than viewed as exclusive alternatives. We will focus primarily on assessment at the departmental level, but the principles apply to the personal level as well. At the end of this section, we will extend the discussion to the larger corporate level.

Identifying Candidate Projects
- Depending on user initiative
- Systematic user input
- Critical success factors (CSFs) analysis
- Tactical management initiatives
- External contribution analysis
- Breakthrough thinking

Selection
- Costs and benefits
- Objective-critical applications
- Technical feasibility
- Organizational feasibility

FIGURE 2-3 ASSESSMENT

Depending on User Initiative

The simplest approach to identifying candidates is to depend on user initiative, considering only those applications that users propose. The advantage of this approach is that it only identifies applications that have user champions. Unless a project has a champion, it is likely to be quietly shelved for lack of interest, even if it is high on the final priority list.

The disadvantage of depending on user initiative is that it reflects only limited visions of departmental needs. It does not give the broad picture of potential applications that must be created for rational assessment. It specifically tends to ignore departmental priorities that are not individual priorities and applications that need to be done but that may be unpopular.

Systemic User Input

A more systematic approach is to bring a department's users together once a year and to develop a comprehensive list of candidates. In the first step, no attempt is made to weed out projects. Rather, a list of all possible candidates is developed through free-for-all brainstorming.

In the second step, the initial list is reduced not by elimination but by combining candidates that are essentially the same. In many cases, two candidates will either be identical or be aspects of a slightly large application. Again, the job of this step is not to say "no" to anything; it is to reduce the complexity of the assessment task.

In the third step, users develop a rough priority list by voting for the candidates they would like to see. This ranks user desires and gives a reasonably short list of things to be pursued in depth, but it neither attaches costs to alternatives nor reflects a detailed understanding of what is involved in each application. It is not the final say in setting priorities.

Critical Success Factors (CSFs) Analysis

One of the most popular techniques for identifying candidates is **critical success factors (CSFs)** analysis, which was suggested by Daniel (1) and developed by Rockart. (11)

The objectives of organizations are long-term goals that are hard to link to current actions. Daniel argued that in order to meet objectives over the long run, managers should identify the relatively few near-term actions that will make or break the effort to meet long-term objectives. If these critical factors are addressed well, long-term objectives are likely to be met, and if they are addressed poorly, long-term objectives are not likely to be met. Rockart formally named these actions "critical success factors."

In CSF analysis, managers are asked to name their long-term objectives. They are then asked to focus on the few things that are crucial in the short term for meeting these objectives. Hospital administrators, for example, might focus on staffing or cost reduction as their CSFs.

Once CSFs are identified, their information systems implications can be identified. For example, a staffing CSF might be critically dependent on an applicant data base. In this final step, the CSF approach produces candidates for application development.

Rockart (11) gives a good discussion of the CSF approach, but his discussion focuses on information needs, not processing needs. It is oriented toward the development of executive information systems more than toward decision support systems and other processing-intensive applications. Although this information focus was appropriate for the cases Rockart studied, CSF methodology is not limited simply to EISs.

Tactical Management Initiatives

A concept with some similarities to CSF analysis is the identification of **tactical management initiatives (TMIs).** Many companies have major strategic thrusts, for instance, to contain employment growth despite increases in business. In many cases, these **strategic initiatives** require a number of more specific initiatives, such as identifying managers who can cope with wider spans of control or developing a better understanding of how different work units relate to one another. These are called **tactical management initiatives** because they are tactical programs designed to implement broader strategic goals.

Many tactical initiatives require computer support. For instance, the identification of managers who can cope with broader spans of control may require the creation of a human resources data base that focuses on assessments of things pertinent to managing wider spans of control. In turn, understanding how different work units relate to one another might require the creation of a model that will allow "what if" analysis of how an increase of business might affect departments directly or indirectly.

In many cases, the computer applications identified through TMI analysis must be begun and put into place well in advance of the implementation of strategic initiatives. For instance, the human resources data base for managers may need to reflect several years of data before it can be used well. A major goal of TMI analysis is to identify applications with long lead times.

External Contribution Analysis

In his book, *The Effective Executive,* Peter Drucker argued that effective executives look externally rather than internally. (2) Instead of focusing on the internal efficiency of their own departments, they ask what their department can do to make *other parts of the firms* work more effectively. This focus on **external contribution** recognizes the fact that no work units exist for their own sake. They exist only to provide services to customers and other units of the firm. Therefore, only by focusing on external contributions can a department identify what is important. In external contribution analysis, a department looks at the needs of its clients instead of its internal processes, and this must include *asking* its clients for suggestions.

Breakthrough Thinking

In many cases, making small changes through information systems is not worth the cost. Three percent gains often have equal or greater costs. With information systems, it may be better to identify **breakthrough strategies** that produce large gains that would probably not be possible through a series of small incremental improvements. (8)

The classic example is airlines reservation taking. In the past, requests for reservations were handled by passing the paperwork through a series of people, each with a specific job to do. Computerizing this sequential process would have resulted in small gains. Instead, computerization was based on a total redesign of the work, so that one person could do all tasks and give immediate replies. The productivity benefits were enormous.

Identification in Perspective

The purpose of this discussion has been not to propose a specific program for identifying needs, but rather to show the diversity of possible approaches and to emphasize that most of these approaches take a hard look at the way things are now being done instead of simply adding a few patches to the current work system. They are not limited to identifying applications whose dollar benefits exceed their dollar costs. Rather, they focus on objectives, and they identify innovations that are needed to meet critical long-term and short-term objectives.

Selection

Once candidate applications are identified, the next step is to set priorities and decide which ones will be undertaken.

Costs and Benefits

An obvious step is to measure the costs and benefits of different alternatives. Obviously, all costs should be measured as well as possible, so that there are few surprises later. But quantifying benefits is often difficult or even impossible, and to focus simply on costs and benefits that can be quantified would be myopic. In fact, the quantification of benefit is somewhat dangerous unless there is an equal emphasis on "softer benefits." Otherwise, there is the danger of falling into the old analysis trap: "numbers drive out thinking."

Assessing soft benefits is not an exact art. Different organizations have different ways of dealing with soft benefits at the philosophical level. Deciding how to do cost-benefits analysis is not a matter of technique. It is a fundamental decision for information center management, and we will discuss it in Chapter 3, together with other fundamental decisions.

Objective-Critical Applications

Even if costs and benefits can be weighed exactly, the specific net benefit of a project may be far less important than whether it is critical to a specific objective of the department. Objective-critical applications may wind up high on the priority list even if their net dollar benefits are very low and their other soft benefits are low.

Although it may be possible to treat the relationship between an application and important objectives as being just another soft benefit, the relationship to objectives is different in kind from other kinds of benefits, and it links projects directly to the mission of the department.

Alternatives for Specific Applications

Another complexity of selection is that individual applications may present several subchoices, in the form of alternatives. For example, it may be possible to do an application on a PC or a host, or it may be possible to build either an advanced system or a simple version of the application. When setting priorities, it is important to study different alternatives for each project.

Technical Feasibility

For complex projects, a key issue is whether the department has the technical expertise to develop the project. The question is not whether the project is technically feasible in the abstract, but whether it is technically feasible for *this particular department at this particular time.*

Organizational Feasibility

For some projects, development may generate discomfort and controversy. Although it is often necessary to implement projects that not everyone wants, resistance should be taken into account in project selection. For some projects, resistance may be so strong that the project is completely infeasible within a department.

Selection in Perspective

Overall, there is no magic methodology for setting priorities. Managers must weigh costs, benefits, and relationships to missions, as well as the technical and organizational feasibility of various alternatives. This need to weigh many things is "messy," but it is nothing new to managers. Few managerial decisions in which priorities have to be set boil down to dollars and cents "bottom lines." Managers are quite accustomed to looking at good cost analyses, lists of benefits, relationships to objectives, and practicality in order to arrive at a decision that involves the selection of alternatives. End user computing is no different than other managerial decisions.

Corporate Needs Assessment

Although we have focused on needs assessment at the departmental level, needs assessment is also critical at the corporate level. The information center can only develop a balanced program of support if it understands the corporation's needs very broadly. Corporate needs assessment is very complex, but we will describe in broad generalities two major approaches to corporate needs assessment: structural analysis and application identification studies.

Structural Analysis

In **structural analysis,** the information center develops data on the general structure of the corporation and its employees. This approach resembles market research in that it tries to understand the general quantitative dimensions of its client. It provides a general framework for the research needed to understand individual needs. The chief priority of the information center, whatever its second priority may be, is to have a good understanding of information work in the corporation, and structural analysis is a good initial step in that direction.

The first task in structural analysis is to develop an **occupational profile** of the corporation's employees, especially its office employees. Chapter 1 showed broad occupational patterns for the U.S. economy as well as for individual industries. For planning purposes, an information center must develop a much finer breakdown of job categories than was shown in Chapter 1, and this finer breakdown must be completed for different job sites within the firm if the corporation is geographically decentralized. The information center must work with the personnel department (often called the human resources department) to develop a good occupational profile for the firm.

The second task in structural analysis is to develop a **work unit profile** for the firm. In a work unit profile, all departments or comparable work units are identified and classified. Classification should include factors such as office versus nonoffice, Type I versus Type II, and line versus staff. If possible, a detailed job breakdown should be created for each department.

The third task in structural analysis is not likely to be performed in most firms because of its cost. This is **unit–relationship analysis,** in which relationships among units are described at both traffic levels (number of messages or business forms) and more substantive levels, such as dependencies for particular guidance or information. Unit–relationship analysis will essentially create a planning model for the firm.

Wherever the information center stops, structural analysis brings reality into needs assessment. Very few corporate managers or information systems professionals have a very good understanding of work in their firms, and this leads to major misperceptions, such as those discussed in Chapter 1. Even stopping at occupational profiles can be very enlightening.

The need for structural analysis goes far beyond the information center. The entire information systems department needs it, and it is required in a wide variety of corporate planning tasks outside of information systems. Given this broader importance, it would seem best if the information center were only a coordinator of an effort by many departments, chiefly personnel.

Application Identification Studies

A more straightforward way to study corporate needs is to take a good sampling of individuals in many departments and to discuss their desires for new applications. This approach is widely used for information systems planning in corporations because it does not involve complex methodology. It is generally good at identifying major unserved needs in the corporation.

Live interviews are necessarily limited in number, however, and even if three to five dozen people are studied, it is possible to get highly misleading results. Bias is even more likely if the sample is skewed toward power users, fails to include remote sites, or has other problems with representativeness. It is not necessary to have a statistically random sample, but it is very important to balance the sample so that many different types of people in different types of departments are queried.

It is always a good idea to supplement face-to-face interviews. One way to do so is to select **focus groups,** in which a group of people is brought together to exchange ideas about their needs. Focus groups work well, provided the following safeguards are used.

- Make sure that everyone in a group is of comparable status
- Keep a few dynamic people from dominating the discussion.
- Make sure that quiet people are brought into the conversation.

The normal way to implement the last two safeguards is to pose a question and then go around the room asking each person in turn for an answer. During this period, no other comments are allowed. That is left until everyone has answered the question. If these safeguards are enforced, focus groups will allow people to build on one another's comments and discuss differences openly. This interchange is the primary purpose of focus groups.

Even focus groups have the problem of small size. The way to overcome this problem is to conduct a formal questionnaire of many users, based on results achieved during the personal interviews and focus groups. Provided the response rate is sufficiently high, questionnaire surveys can provide a much safer picture of application desires.

In all cases, results must be treated carefully because users are acting on the basis of perceptions that fail to reflect costs and probably fail to include an understanding of application details. As in departmental needs assessment, identifying application candidates is only the first step.

End User Computing Data

Another valuable source of information about user needs is to collect data on actual use for machines and various kinds of application software. The information center should take a census of technology and application software, and it would not be too difficult to add a very simple survey that asks what applications people use and how often they use them. This can be done with a telephone survey, which is cheaper than mail surveys when all costs are added. In addition, telephone surveys are faster and give a better response rate. Although EUC data stress what is rather than what is needed, this information is valuable in and of itself. In addition, year-to-year trends can tip off the information center to emergent use patterns if the survey is sufficiently precise.

DESIGN

After assessment has set priorities, users can begin to develop their applications. The first step in this process is design. Before large projects are undertaken in any field, it is important to design the final system in great detail before construction is begun. Otherwise, there will be constant backtracking that will be expensive and can even be fatal.

Spending time on design saves overall time on the project. In data processing, it has been established that the *more time* spent on initial design, the less time spent on the entire application. (6) In data processing, the average amount of time spent on design is about 20 percent, (6) but the data indicate that this is less than the optimum percentage. Comparable studies have not been done in end user computing, but similar results would probably be obtained in EUC.

Even for smaller projects, design is needed. For reports of any length, a writer must first create an outline, or his or her report will simply ramble on without clear flow or logic. In turn, someone building a spreadsheet of even modest size must outline the basic logic of the spreadsheet before entering it into the computer. With regard to the data base, it is even more important to worry about initial design before committing the data base schema to the DBMS.

DESIGN   **61**

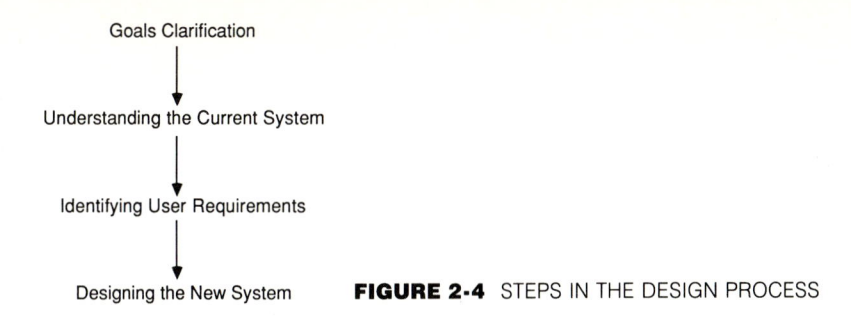

```
Goals Clarification
        │
        ▼
Understanding the Current System
        │
        ▼
Identifying User Requirements
        │
        ▼
Designing the New System
```
FIGURE 2-4 STEPS IN THE DESIGN PROCESS

As shown in Figure 2-4, design is a multistep process. A number of things have to be done, roughly in sequence, to produce a good design.

Goals Clarification

Before doing anything else, the designer must clarify the goals of the system. There are usually two problems with initial goals statements. The first is that many are too hastily conceived and so are too brief to guide design. Good design requires a comprehensive understanding of what is to be accomplished by the project, and few projects at the end of their assessment stage have goals sufficiently detailed to guide design work. It is important for design work to begin with a detailed statement of goals, although users often resist going into the extra detail on the belief that it is not necessary compared to other kinds of tasks they have to do in their busy days. This resistance is even true, perhaps especially true, when an end user develops an application for his or her own use.

The second problem with goal statements is that they are often simply incorrect. In a surprising number of cases, a complete system is designed, only to be terminated because late in the process of development it is realized that the application is not doing what is needed. For example, one bank started to do research on charging for ATM (automated teller machine) services. The research was well underway when the marketing department correctly pointed out that the bank's objectives were to increase use of the ATMs. (This was in the early days of ATMs.) Increased use was important for a larger reason—the need to get as many people out of teller lines during the day time. When these issues were discussed, the project was scrapped because charging was likely to interfere with the bank's higher objective.

Even in a small second-environment project, it is important to spend a reasonable amount of time writing out the explicit goal of the project and then studying it carefully to see if the goals are sufficiently detailed and make sense in terms of broader goals.

Understanding the Current System

The second step in design is the most prosaic. It is to understand the current work system—the way people are doing the task now. The current work system may be computerized, or it may be manual, but in either case, there is no sense in going forward until the current work system is understood.

Work system analysis is usually undertaken by asking people about what they currently do and by studying paper records. It is common to get different pictures from different people because different workers often have very different understandings about what is now going on. In addition, managers often have very different understandings than the people doing the work. Because of these differences, it is important to talk to everyone who is involved in doing the work or in using the results of the current work system.

One problem in understanding the current system is that users may unwittingly leave out important information. In their studies, Holzman and Rosenberg (5) found that users were systematic about what they accidentally left out. First, they left out things that were so routine that they fell below users' thresholds of attention. People badly underestimated such data as the amount of time spent refiling documents and updating data. Second, they left out exceptions that should not occur but did. They failed to realize how often missing data, missed telephone calls, interruptions, and other exception conditions occurred. Simple interviews are not likely to ferret out these routine and exception conditions that must be addressed in system design. Instead, time logs, observations, and other tools must be used. This task is too complex for most end user projects, but for important projects, routine and exception conditions must be studied extensively.

Perhaps the biggest problem with understanding the current system in end user computing is the poorly structured nature of work in Type II departments. In these departments, many problems are solved individually, so no procedure is established. Although certain habits and tendencies do carry over from problem to problem, these are far more tentative than the procedures so often found in Type I clerical departments.

This lack of procedures has been a major stumbling block for formal methods office analysis, such as MIT's Office Analysis Methodology (OAM). (12) When OAM was tried on a number of offices, it was found that it worked well only in Type I departments. (7) In Type II departments, it was difficult to apply and did not produce solid results. The problem was that OAM, like most other office analysis methodologies, can be used only where there is enough structure for procedures to emerge. Although these methodologies are designed for less structured environments than classical systems analysis methodology in data processing, they still require a great deal of structure. In Type II departments, either this structure does not exist at all or it exists only in fairly peripheral subtasks.

At the same time, where there is at least a reasonable amount of structure, the insights and sometimes the specific methods proposed by office analysis methodologies can be of great value. Important sources in this area are Sirbu et al.'s article on the MIT Office Analysis Methodology, (12) Harris and Brightman's study of bottlenecks in a fairly unstructured environment, (4) and a number of excellent papers by William Sasso at New York University.

Identifying User Requirements

After the current system is completely understood, the next step is to understand exactly what users want from the new system. In contrast to the earlier task of goals clarification, identifying user requirements moves down to the lower levels of report format design and other details. This work must lead to a very explicit and written set of **user requirements.** It is even important to do this when developing a system for personal use because it forces the user–developer to think carefully about the specific requirements of the system.

For data applications, requirements would include such considerations as reports to be produced by the system, sample queries, the schema of the data base, the length of time data are to be kept in the system, and data entry screens. For other applications, different types of requirements would be specified, but in most cases, output requirements are the focus of the requirements definition, since output is the reason for the application's existence. All other requirements are there to ensure the quality of output.

Designing the New System

Once the old system is understood and requirements have been set, the developer can design the new system. Before doing so, however, it is often a good idea to change the existing system immediately if problems have been found during the analysis of the existing system. This is particularly true if the new system will take some time to build, so that the existing system will be in place for some time. It may even be that a new system is not needed if the old system is changed appropriately. One company decided to move its mailing list from a commercial service bureau to its own computer because of high error rates in data entry at the service bureau. Initial analysis, however, showed that the high error rate existed simply because the company had once decided not to pay for "verification," in which each record is typed twice to catch errors. By switching to verification at a modest increase in cost, the company avoided having to convert to a PC system.

Design documentation should appear in two forms. First, there should be an overview document that illustrates the main components of the application's design. This should be simple and clear enough for someone to understand quickly if they want to understand the system generally. If the application is developed for other users, this document will become the tool for users to understand the application.

Second, there should be a detailed design document that has enough detail to guide someone who maintains the system later. Even in self-development, a detailed design document is critical. First, it will refresh the developer's memory when changes are needed later. Second, and more importantly, it will guide the construction of the application. A good and detailed design will smooth the construction process.

Modular and Hierarchical Design

A basic principle of all forms of design is to break up large problems into smaller problem and then solve the smaller problem. Figure 2-5 shows a design that embraces this principle in the form of modularization and hierarchical design.

First, the problem is broken down into small pieces called **modules.** Each module represents a distinct unit of work and must be logically complete and separate from other activities. Breaking a problem down into logically distinct modules can be extremely difficult.

64 APPLICATION DEVELOPMENT

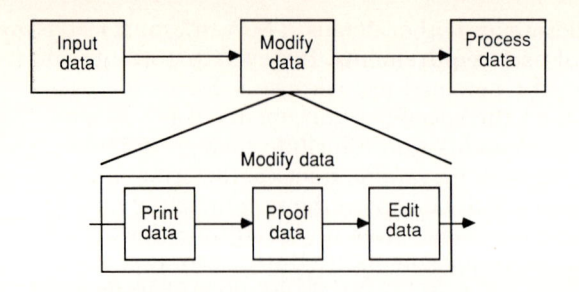

Notes:

Each module has one entry point, one exit point.

Each module may contain submodules. Here, only the "Modify data" module's submodules are shown.

FIGURE 2-5 MODULAR AND HIERARCHICAL DESIGN

Another characteristic of modular design is that modules should have only one entry point and one exit point. This means that both their inputs and outputs are well known. If this design principle is followed, then relationships among modules can be expressed fairly simply by pointing the output of each module at appropriate inputs of other modules.

This limitation of inputs and outputs into two points also makes life easier during the construction phase of the project. First, each module can be developed and tested separately. Building small subcomponents is easier and much safer than building a large application and then trying to debug it. With modularization, each module can be tested in isolation, simply by giving it dummy inputs and observing whether outputs conform to paper and pencil calculations. Although it would be nice simply to study the logic of a module and declare that it is correct, only actual testing will produce confidence in the correctness of the design.

It is also normal to organize modules hierarchically, as shown in Figure 2-3. Each module essentially has submodules within it. Hierarchical design allows the fairly rapid understanding of designs even if there are dozens or even hundreds of modules. Hierarchical design allows someone who is trying to understand the design to focus first on the broad picture and then to move down to the level of individual modules.

Design in the Second Environment

Some second-environment applications are so simple that there is no formal design phase beyond a few minutes' thought. But even in the second environment, at least a brief design phase is necessary. Otherwise, users tend to develop applications too hastily, often ignoring important objectives or building models and other information structures that must be redesigned entirely later or that become so patched together that understandability becomes very low and the danger of unseen errors increases.

At the very least, there should be a clear statement of objectives of the new application, and this statement should be based on at least an hour's reflection about what is to be accomplished. In many cases, the user finds that the application will not really answer his or her needs or that his or her original idea about was needed was seriously in error. The statement of objectives should be sufficiently detailed that it is not a platitude but rather a platform for development.

In addition, there should be a fairly detailed sketch of the information structure to be built (model, data base schema, document outline, etc.), so that flaws can be discovered before the actual construction begins. Information structures must never be allowed to grow like Topsy, without a clear plan.

Design in the Third Environment

In the third environment, the underlying situation is sufficiently complex to require careful analysis of the current system, a detailed explication of requirements, and a clear design document that lays out the design at both broad and detailed levels. There is no way to cut corners and still come out of the design stage well poised for construction.

In the third environment, it is also important to design the application so that it can be extended easily at a later time. Large operational systems are constantly extended. Accordingly, DP developers have long been schooled in the need to do everything possible to make their design general, so that it can be extended easily. In EUC, extension and the need to design for generality are equally or more important. For any large project, the designer must think through possible extensions for the application and build the model so that they can be added easily later. In the second environment, it is common to rebuild the application from scratch if its internal design gets too muddled because of modifications. In the third environment, the costs of redoing the system are likely to be extremely high. It pays to spend a good deal of time thinking about how an application is likely to be extended.

Design in the Fourth Environment

In the fourth environment, the situation is complicated by the fact that the developer is not the ultimate user or is only one of several ultimate users. In the clarification of goals, the analysis of the current situation, the specification of requirements, and the detailed design, it is critical to poll everyone involved. Because most people are poor at describing what is currently happening and what they really need, the developer must aggressively push for detail and clarity. The root problem is that most users fail to understand the level of detail needed to create complex applications.

The written statement of user requirements and the design document become critical communication tools in the fourth environment because they provide tangible documents that the user must accept or reject before any more time is spent on the project. The more specific these descriptions are, the better users are able to react to them. Even for small projects, it is important to put requirements and the general design into writing and to go over this material with the user.

In the fourth environment designing with future extension in mind is as important for large projects as it is in the second. In the fourth environment, however, it is not enough for the developer to think about potential extensions. He or she must also get the client to do so, and this can be extremely difficult—first because the ultimate user will not understand the importance of thinking through extensions, and second because the user will not have looked at the application as closely as the developer by the end of the design stage and so will not realize the level of detail needed in the design.

CONSTRUCTION

The design phase sets the stage for construction when hardware and software are purchased and custom programming may be done.

Selecting Hardware and Software

Most textbooks teach the need to pick the best software for each job and then choose hardware on the basis of the software that has been selected. In practice, this is rarely done, nor should it be done. "Pick the best tool for the job" is a dangerous myth, not a valid prescription.

The major problem is that picking the best software and then picking the best hardware to run it only make sense if you will develop one and only one application. In practice, this is almost never the case. Most individuals and departments have several applications, perhaps dozens. If the first application were the basis for selecting hardware, the department or individual might end up with a machine totally unsuited to later applications. If the best software and hardware were picked for each application, then departments would become Towers of Babel with many incompatible machines. Carried to its logical conclusion, picking the best tool for each job would lead to several computers or terminals on each individual's desk.

In selecting hardware and software, it is critical to begin with some insight into the user's or department's likely application mix in the future. Only with a broad view can a department set standards for what hardware and software will be purchased.

Development, Testing, and Documentation

Every application requires some development. In analysis, models must be created and entered. In data base, the schema must be entered, after which reports and data entry screens must be created. In creating a large word processing document, the outline must be turned into prose. This development can be the longest stage of the systems development life cycle.

In addition, development may extend to the use of the embedded programming languages in the selected application software. Some of these embedded programming languages are simple, but others are quite complex. If the goal is to make ongoing use easy, considerable time may have to be spent in custom programming.

Testing must go hand in hand with development. In fact, development should always be done in modules, and testing should be done after each module is constructed. Testing should never be left until the end. As discussed earlier, modularization simplifies testing. Each module can be given test inputs with known outputs, to test whether the module is working. If testing is left until the end, even modularization will not make it easy to track down errors.

In testing, it is important to observe three basic principles.

1. It is important to work with round numbers instead of actual data because it is much easier to tell whether the results make sense when round numbers are used than when real data are used.
2. The range of numbers used in testing should be at least as great as the range used in practice.
3. Special cases should be identified and tested, for instance, zeros or negative numbers if these occur.

The last step is to document the application. A design document was created in the design stage in order to guide the development work. The documentation at the end of the development stage has a different purpose. Its first purpose is to describe the actual construction of the application in sufficient detail that a future maintainer will be able to see how changes can be implemented without having to study the actual code in detail. This is even important if the developer is also the user because memory grows cold, and even after a few weeks, it is difficult to understand the logic of one's own application. A maintenance document should at least describe the overall organization of the application and the general organization of important submodules. It should also have a section with notes on tricky parts of the model that are likely to be hard to understand or that are likely to be misinterpreted later. Except for very large applications, it is probably not worth the effort of documenting logic in the middle ground between broad organization and critical details.

The second purpose of the final documentation is to produce a user's guide that will tell the user how to use the system. This is even important if the developer is the only user but may put the system aside and not use it again for some time. Because user documentation is more of an implementation than a construction issue, we will defer its discussion until the section on implementation.

Construction in the Second Environment

In the second environment, construction, testing, and documentation are likely to be simple. However, there must be at least minimum documentation, and the need for full testing is imperative. Computers allow analysts to build much larger applications than they could have built manually. This is true not only in analysis, but also in data management applications, word processing, and many other kinds of applications. Even in the second environment, projects are much larger than most traditional manual projects. In nearly all kinds of large applications, it is extremely easy for small but serious errors to appear unless full testing is done and documentation performed at least to some extent.

The kind of documentation needed varies from application to application. (Documentation needs are discussed in later application chapters.) Most of these needs, however, are common sense. For instance, in spreadsheet applications, the basic logical structure of the model should be described. In data applications, the schema should be stated explicitly, and in all printouts, there should be date and time labeling, as well as a labeling of what files and fields were used in the output. In financial modeling, to give one last example, it is important to state whether the first year was considered as Year 0 or Year 1 in discounting calculations.

Construction in the Third Environment

In the third environment, the construction process must be extremely disciplined, with hierarchical and modular construction and testing performed within each module. In addition, because the internal logic is likely to be so complex, documentation for future maintainers must be extremely detailed.

Construction in the Fourth Environment

In the fourth environment, users are likely to pressure the developer to "get things done" and to hand over the system before it is tested and documented. In addition, they may not know how to express what kinds of data to suggest for testing—for example, what data ranges are reasonable. Yet documentation and testing are critical. Particularly in multiuser applications, correctness is extremely important, for there may be a tendency to trust the output. In addition, maintenance of core department systems is critical, and without documentation, maintenance abilities may die if the original developer leaves the department.

IMPLEMENTATION

After an application has been built, tested, and documented, it is placed in operation, either in an individual's life or in the day-to-day work of a department. In iterative development, the initial implementation is normally followed by a new cycle of design and construction, but even when iterative development is used, the initial implementation can be a critical time for the ultimate success of the application.

Work Systems

A great deal has been written about implementation. Much of this writing has focused on a concept that goes by several names and that we will call a **work system.** Figure 2-6 illustrates this concept.

The Components of a Work System

Figure 2-6 shows that a work system is the combination of technological tools (hardware, software, and communications) with the department's or individual's human system (people and organization) and information resources. Just as a football team requires a group of people to work together to achieve an objective, a work system combines technology, people, information, and organizational tools to meet specific objectives.

A department is a work system. Work systems can be larger, involving several departments. (In fact, the entire organization is a work system.) They can also be smaller, revolving around specific tasks, such as presenting an

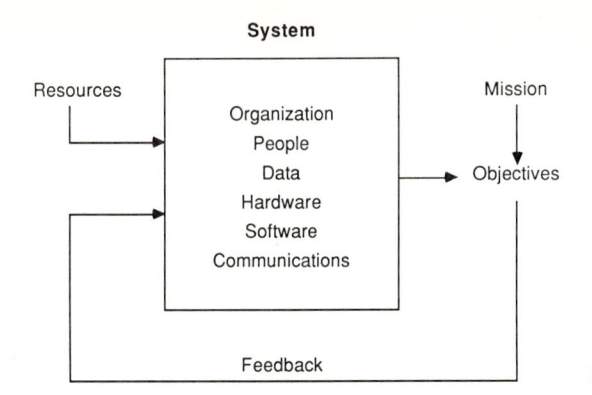

FIGURE 2-6 WORK SYSTEM

annual plan. They can even be personal work systems, including a person's overall job and specific tasks, such as creating documents. The work system idea is a framework for talking about all kinds of work in an organization.

Changing Work Systems

There are very few totally new applications. In almost every case, an application is created to improve an existing work system. This existing system may be manual, but it is increasingly common to find computer-intensive work systems replacing other computer-intensive work systems.

When a work system already exists, it is impossible to change just one of its components. If a football team's star running back is hurt, everyone else on the team needs to make adjustments. If they do not make these adjustments, or if they make them poorly, the results can be very bad. Similarly, it is never enough to drop a new computer or application into an existing organization without carefully thinking through how the work system should change and how it should not change.

In some cases, not only will the components change, but the very objectives of the work system will change. Computer support may allow radically new changes, allowing new objectives to be added or even shifting objectives from one work system to another. The work systems that use the results from the work system being changed can also be affected sufficiently to change their objectives. Overall, it is not enough to take objectives as givens. It is not even enough to design work systems in isolation.

For large applications, it may be necessary to redesign the entire work system instead of merely modifying it. This is particularly true when many people are involved. Otherwise, the structure of the information might be inappropriate (the old data model may be inappropriate), people might not have clear roles and may forget to do such critical things as backing up data, and there might not be adequate attention given to training.

Many writers place the design of work systems before the design of the computer application. There is a great deal of merit to this approach, and even at the assessment stage, part of the assessment should involve the cost of changing the work system and the desirability of various alternative work systems, not just the hardware, software, and communication components of these work systems. In design and construction, too, it is important to have a clear idea of what the work system should be like. But it is during the implementation stage that the fine details of work system design fall into place.

Organization

There are four aspects of organization: roles, management, policies, and procedures. **Roles** are general responsibilities assigned to individuals in the work system. For example, one person might be assigned the role of managing data entry and another the role of doing backup. When good employees are given clear roles, they can work out most of the details of what needs to be done to achieve their roles, minimizing the need for other forms of organization.

Management means the work system's chain of command. If there is a conflict or even mere uncertainty over what should be done, the overall manager of the work system must be brought into the picture. Ideally, the manager will act primarily to bring people together so that they can resolve the issue. In some cases, however, the manager will have to make a formal decision.

If a certain type of situation comes up repeatedly, a **policy** may have to be set. Basically, a policy casts an employee's or manager's decisions in concrete, providing a framework that can guide everyone's actions without recourse to more detailed enforcement. For example, a policy may be set discouraging the use of a Macintosh attached to a laser printer for graphics development if it is overused and is the department's primary tool for printing.

When certain situations arise again and again, it is often best to establish specific **procedures** for dealing with them. For example, a procedure might be established for backing up the hard disk. Procedures have several advantages. First, they allow efficiency because they minimize what must be done by providing forms, check lists, and other rapid ways of handling information. Second, they provide consistency, so that the proper thing will be done even if people change or if someone forgets something (the procedure should catch such lapses). Unfortunately, there is a tendency to create procedures even when these benefits do not outweigh the costs of going through the procedures. Procedures should not be used when policies are sufficient, and policies should not be used if the assignment of roles and management referral is enough.

For second-environment projects, organization can be more informal, but even individuals soon find themselves establishing at least rough policies for what they should do and specific procedures for often-repeated tasks that are highly structured. In addition, even second-environment applications are often sufficiently important to get a department manager involved in the process. In the third and fourth environments, the full panoply of roles, management, policies, and procedures must be considered carefully.

Cutover

The most critical time in implementation is the actual time of **cutover** from the old system to the new system. Several issues need to be addressed at this point.

User Preparation

The first issue is how to prepare users for the change. Obviously, there is a need for training, particularly if the change is a major one involving several people. For example, one division that implemented word processing gave little training at the time of cutover. Although many people eventually picked up the system, a vast amount of worker time was lost unnecessarily because of a refusal to train people in order to conserve computer expenditures. Chapter 5 discusses training in some detail.

Equally important is user documentation. As discussed in Chapter 5, detailed procedure manuals with long sections are not very likely to be useful, but quick-start guides, manuals that are broken up into many small sections, and "cheat sheets" that describe the step-by-step operations to do specific things are a great help and must be provided.

Like the application code itself, training and documentation must be tested before being delivered. The existence of small errors can waste a great deal of the users' time and destroy the credibility of an otherwise exemplary use guide or training program.

For large multiuser projects, an important part of user preparation is **motivation.** The best way to get motivation is to get early user involvement and to keep users involved throughout the project. Although this problem is primarily one of the fourth environment, fourth-environment projects are sufficiently common for motivation to be a major concern.

The Productivity Decline at Cutover

It is extremely important to realize that cutover will create a great deal of additional work. It is sometimes supposed that productivity will rush forward after cutover. In fact, productivity usually declines sharply after cutover, and it may take several months to achieve real gains.

The first reason for this productivity decline is the need in many cases to convert data from the old application to the new. Data files may have to be imported into the format of the new program, and even if there is software to do this job easily, the process can be extremely time consuming. In turn, when moving from manual to computerized applications, months of data may have to be punched into the computer before actual work can begin.

The second reason is the need for at least some parallel operation, in which the old system is left in place while the new system is first used. Nearly every text agrees that it is suicidal to pull the plug on the old system before users certify the new systems as acceptable. In some cases, it is necessary to cope with major problems in the new system by keeping the old system or at least part of the old system in place. Of course, parallel operation is a serious drain on staff time, especially for large applications.

The third reason is the effort needed to learn a new computer application. Training is time consuming, and even after training is completed, users are slow on their systems until they develop real proficiency. In addition, it is common to lose data initially or to do other things that require substantial rework.

A fourth reason for the initial decline in productivity is the time it takes for the work system to get straightened out, including roles, policies, and procedures. There will be job overlap, inefficient work procedures, and confusion.

APPLICATION DEVELOPMENT

To cope with productivity decline, several steps can be taken. First, major applications should never be implemented in busy periods. Santa Claus, for example, would never be wise to implement a new inventory system in December (or even in October, because new applications are often late). If there are lulls in the annual or monthly cycles, those are good times to implement new applications because their productivity declines will come when lost productivity can be best afforded.

Training and the careful design of the work system can also help by directly reducing the productivity decline. More intensive training can slash the period in which people are learning how to use the application efficiently, while designing roles, policies, and procedures in advance can reduce the confusion of the initial period.

Even careful budgeting can be a help. In the annual plan, the individual or department can consider tradeoffs between suffering through the productivity decline and getting help, including temporary help, overtime, and the use of services such as data conversion services.

DEPARTMENT MANAGEMENT

Just as assessment needs to be addressed at a broader level than individual applications, implementation of applications into the work system must be considered at the broader levels of personal and departmental management. We will focus on departmental management, which is more complex than personal management.

We will base our discussion of department management issues on Figure 2-7, the department management matrix. This matrix shows that roles must be assigned to the department manager, secretaries, ordinary professionals,

	Department manager	Secretary	Staff professional	Power user
Application planning				
Technology planning				
Application development				
Control				
Support				
Data management				
Daily work				

FIGURE 2-7
DEPARTMENT MANAGEMENT MATRIX

and power users. These roles must include application planning, technology resource planning, application development, control, support, data management, and daily work.

The Department Manager's Roles

The most critical roles are those of the department manager. As discussed earlier, a good department manager does not hesitate to make decisions when needed but prefers to allow the department's staff members to work through decisions and reach a concensus that also fits broader department objectives.

In application planning and technological resource planning, the department manager must play the lead role in deciding what applications will be developed and what technological resources will have to be purchased. The goal is to select the best possible applications and develop a technological infrastructure that will support the department's needs within its limited budget.

In application development, the manager is likely to play a passive role, stepping in only to monitor the progress of projects and to ensure that good development discipline is being maintained. A critical job for the manager in application development is to ensure that important applications are not lost when a developer leaves the department. Every exit must be preceded by a formal delegation of responsibility for important projects. In the future, the large amount of application development in most departments will also require increased attention to the issue of how efficiently each application is being developed.

In the policy areas of control and support, the department manager must see first that the company's broader policies are implemented in these areas and second that department control and support policies and procedures are set and enforced. As privacy, security, damage, and other matters grow in importance, the department manager must learn a great deal about departmental computing policies.

In the final areas of data management and daily work, the department manager must ensure that backup, data entry, the creation and maintenance of a hierarchical filing system for electronic information, and other mundane areas are well managed. This means that procedures must be set up, roles clearly defined, and agreements enforced.

Unfortunately, few managers are trained in any of these areas. Most have little or no background in technology, policy, or good practice principles that relate to computer-intensive work systems. Although nearly every manager now manages a partly automated office, which is harder to manage than a fully automated office, few corporations train their managers in the skills needed in computer-laden departments.

The Secretary's Roles

The secretary's basic job is to take as much delegation as possible, so that professional staff members will not be overburdened. This job of taking delegation is most obvious in daily work, such as backup, and data entry and data management, including developing a filing system for electronic information.

The secretary will also be important in other areas. One of the most time-consuming tasks of managers and professionals is selecting and purchasing computers, software, or add-on equipment for their computers. Many secretaries have little training in the purchase or installation of computers and software packages and in the future will have to be better trained to avoid this major time drain. Similarly, secretaries should also be able to build batch files and other time-saving automation tools.

In support, secretaries may become major trainers and problem solvers, although this may create problems in some departments, since many senior managers and staff members are reluctant to be dependent on secretaries for help that demonstrates their technical weaknesses.

Secretaries can even be very important in application development if they can type spreadsheet code or enter data base schemas for applications developed by others in the department. This requires training, since it is almost impossible to enter information without understanding at least the basics of analysis tools, data base tools, and other tools.

Just like managers, secretaries need far different kinds of training than they have had in the past. In addition, more help will be necessary to free the secretary to do advanced tasks. The lone secretary is being replaced by the secretary who is really an office manager, plus one or two helpers to do detailed and routine work.

Staff Members' Roles

Staff members must accept responsibility for developing and following the general rules laid down for the kinds of tasks they need to do. They must also handle, as a practical matter, a good deal of data management and daily work tasks. Although it is very important to encourage and prod professional staff members to delegate as much as possible, it is senseless to believe that most professionals will have enough secretarial support to delegate everything.

Nonetheless, the department manager must see that there is enough secretarial staff to handle a great deal more delegation than is now possible in most departments. Too much time is lost in such mundane tasks as formatting disks and changing ribbons in printers, either because secretaries lack the training and charter to do such tasks, or simply do not have the time. Now that so much work is computerized, this lack of delegation capability is no longer acceptable.

At a broader level, professional staff members must take an active role in application planning and technological resource planning. These are difficult jobs that have wide implications for the future of the department, and it is important not to let individuals, not even the department manager, control the process.

Power Users' Roles

In many departments, there is a **power user,** sometimes called a lead user or functional specialist. This kind of person is both a blessing and a curse to management. The positive virtues of having such a person are obvious and enormous, but the department manager must also address some problems surrounding these people.

The first problem is how to prevent burnout. Power users often have to do so much computer work that they burn out from excessive work. This can be prevented by requiring other staff members to do most of their work, turning to power users only for major matters, and having secretaries handle as much low-level work as possible, so that power users will not have to do such things as change cartridges in laser printers.

The second problem is how to prevent diversion. Power users are still first and foremost members of functional departments. They have functional jobs to do, and these must be done. It is important both to assign computer support as one of their functions and to prevent computer support from cutting into their other work. This is a delicate problem that few managers and power users solve to their mutual satisfaction.

The third problem is how to prevent dominance. In selecting applications for development, in planning for the technological infrastructure, and in other areas, power users tend to dominate decision making. The department manager must somehow bring the power user's superior knowledge to bear without allowing this person to overshadow quieter and less technologically adept department members who still have cogent information and insights.

Department Management in Perspective

A recurrent theme of this discussion has been the lack of training given to today's managers, professionals, and secretaries. The end user (Type II) revolution has appeared so suddenly that few corporations have yet developed programs to provide the necessary training. Unfortunately, problems will not wait for those programs to be created and implemented.

DSS AND EIS DEVELOPMENT

DSSs and EISs

One of the fastest growing areas of information systems, and one of the most perplexing, is the creation of custom-tailored tools for managers, specifically decision support systems (DSSs) and executive information systems (EISs). Although these tools are similar, there are also important differences between them.

Three Versus Two Tools

One way to distinguish DSSs and EISs is by the number of generic application areas from which tools are taken. In this view, decision support systems combine tools from three generic applications: data management, analysis, and presentation. (13) For example, an important recurrent decision at International Harvester (now Navistar) is bidding on fleet contracts. (3) This takes a good data base on costs, the ability to do various types of basic and what if analyses, and a good system for presenting complex results. The company's DSS group developed a decision support system to help executives making fleet bidding decisions in the early 1980s.

In contrast, executive information systems combine only two tools: data management and presentation. Typically, EISs pull information from various sources and package this information through a program with a simple user interface and rich graphics. For example, Firestone's EIS group has developed a sophisticated EIS for senior managers. (10) Originally, this system had limited goals, namely, to access the Dow Jones News/Retrieval Service. Over time, however, the system became a front end to many forms of information, including a large relational data base with color graphics retrieval access and a large-scale budgeting and forecasting system. About two dozen executives use this mainframe-based system via personal computers.

Although three tools versus two tools is a good way to distinguish between DSS and EIS, both terms are often used loosely. Often, one term is used to describe both types of tools. In addition, individual projects may be hard to describe with a two-tool versus three-tool distinction. For example, the Firestone system has some forecasting capabilities. Does this limited analysis capability make it a DSS?

Level of Clients

Other analysts distinguish between DSSs and EISs on the basis of client level within the company. These analysts restrict the term "EIS" to applications for very senior managers, and they use DSS to describe tools for middle managers and staff analysts. For these writers, EISs focus primarily on two tools because senior executives want information and leave the analysis to middle managers and staff managers, who naturally need three-tool systems.

Tailoring to Decisions Versus Tailoring to Individuals

A third way in which DSS and EIS differ is that DSSs are tailored to *specific decisions,* EISs are tailored to the needs of *specific decision makers* and cut across several of the decisions they may make. Many systems classified as DSSs or EISs also fit this mold.

Distinctions in Perspective

In this section, we will use the three-tool versus two-tool theory. Although the executive versus manager distinction is also useful, the discussion is somewhat easier to present in terms of the kinds of tools employed. In any case, it is common for a single group to build both DSSs and EISs, so the distinction between the two applications is not critical in many firms.

Tailoring

More important than the distinctions between DSS and EIS are the characteristics they have in common, and the first of these is **tailoring**. Both DSSs and EISs are tailored to individual decisions or individual decision makers. After interviews with several senior executives, Edward Wakin gave this comment. (16)

> The more executives discussed decision making, the clearer it became that each put his or her individual imprint on the process. In addition to personal style, the company setting and situation make a difference. A take-charge executive in a highly competitive market must move faster and with less consultation than does an executive in a mature company in a relatively stable market.

So a DSS or EIS is not simply a collection of tools from two or three generic application domains. Rather, it is a specific application linked to a specific decision or person.

Complexity

Another characteristic shared by DSSs and EISs is **complexity.** Producing a tailored system from two or three application domains and combining the needed capabilities into a smoothly-running package is too complex a task for individual end users. It almost certainly requires the coordination of tools from several different software vendors and perhaps hardware vendors as well. Even data processing application programmers may lack the skills needed to do this kind of integration. Precisely this complexity separates end user development from DSS and EIS development.

Building DSSs and EISs

The key question, of course, is how to develop individual DSS and EIS applications. Although it can be said simply that DSSs and EISs are created through iterative development and so represent a "super fourth environment," the complexity of the DSS and EIS environments raises several issues not discussed earlier.

Tools

In his article, "A Framework for the Development of Decision Support Systems," Sprague argued that it is important to distinguish three levels of tools (as shown in Figure 2-8, which is adapted from that paper). (9) The major difference between the figure and Sprague's art work is the replacement of the term "DSS" with "DSS/EIS," to emphasize that Sprague's model extends to EISs as well as DSSs.

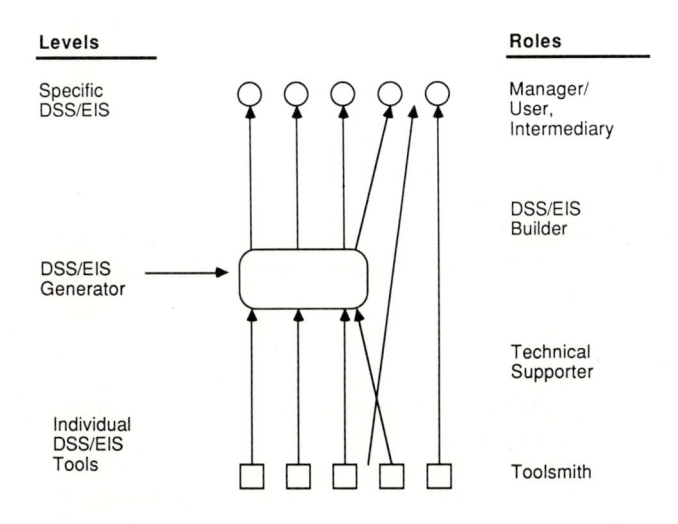

Levels

Specific DSS/EIS

DSS/EIS Generator

Individual DSS/EIS Tools

Roles

Manager/ User, Intermediary

DSS/EIS Builder

Technical Supporter

Toolsmith

Source: Sprague (1980)

FIGURE 2-8 DSS/EIS TOOLS AND ROLES

At the lowest level, there are **DSS/EIS tools.** These are individual tools, including data base management systems, statistical analysis programs, analytical graphics programs, and other tools that must be combined to produce working products for users.

At the highest level, actual working products are labeled **specific DSSs/EISs.** These are specific applications custom tailored to specific decisions or specific individuals. The fleet bidding system at International Harvester is a specific DSS, and the Firestone system is a specific EIS.

It is possible to build specific DSSs/EISs directly from DSS/EIS tools, and this is often done. But it is more economical to develop an intermediate product called a **DSS/EIS generator.** The generator combines the individual tools with a tailoring capability, so that specific DSSs and EISs can be built rapidly once the generator is created.

Sometimes generators are built by the DSS/EIS group. In other cases, commercial products are purchased. As discussed in Chapter 16, host-based tools are often sold as "suites" of products that contain analysis, data management, and graphics in one package. In addition, these software suites often import data from other software products on host computers. Some even have personal computer front-end programs. Although these products lack some of the capabilities envisioned by Sprague for the ideal generator, (15) they serve the needs of many DSS/EIS groups.

Roles

Sprague identified five roles for the development of DSSs. (12) These same roles exist in EIS development. Although they are not present in every specific application, all are rather common.

Manager or User This is the client for the system—the person who ultimately needs the information or needs to make a decision.

Intermediary This is a person who helps the user by doing the actual terminal work. This can be a clerical worker or professional staff member.

DSS/EIS Builder This is the person who creates the specific application using the generator or individual tools. This person is primarily in charge of design, construction, and implementation. The builder must work intimately with the ultimate user and with the intermediary if one is present.

Technical Supporter This is the person who adds new capabilities to the generator, for instance, a new data base management system or links to a DBMS.

Toolsmith This is the person who develops new tools.

The roles of builder, supporter, and toolsmith tend to be combined in many organizations, owing to small staff sizes. But different skills and temperaments are needed for the three roles. The builder must be able to work very well with users and must have strong application knowledge. For this person, technical knowledge is important, but strong technical knowledge is no replacement for user interaction skills and knowledge of the application domain.

The intermediary level exists in only a small fraction of all cases, but when it does exist, it is extremely important. For a complex system and a time-pressed executive, intermediaries make a great deal of sense. In addition, it is very common to use secretaries or other clerical staff members to do at least some work in many systems. Although these people are not full intermediaries, systems must be designed to fit their knowledge and skills as well as the needs of the client.

Development Approaches

Sprague and Carlson note that different DSS/EIS groups have somewhat different philosophies about how to go about development. (14) Although nearly all groups use iterative development for interactions with clients, their technical approaches can be very different. Sprague and Carlson specifically list three major approaches.

Quick-Hit In this philosophy, specific applications are built where there is high need and tools are available. This approach produces quick payoffs but does not lead to the creation of a generator.

Staged In this philosophy, a specific application is built but with advanced planning, so that part of the effort can be reused in other applications. This approach slows the rate of application creation initially, but by producing a protogenerator, it leads to faster development later.

Complete In this philosophy, a full-service generator is built, as well as the organizational structure for managing it, before any individual application is built. This delays all initial application development but lays a strong foundation for later development.

Reactive Versus Proactive Development

Another difference between DSS/EIS groups is that some are reactive, waiting for users to come to them with needs, while others are proactive, going out to important managers and looking for problems that have two characteristics: they are high payoff areas, and they are amenable to computer assistance. One reason for a proactive search is that it purposely looks for the most important applications. Another reason is that users are often incapable of understanding technology enough to realize that some problems that were not actionable before are now amenable to computer support.

DSS and EIS in Perspective

We have not gone into the specific development of DSSs and EISs because it closely resembles iterative development in the fourth environment of end user development. Instead, we have emphasized how these applications are different at the levels of technology and organizational management than systems developed by end users in functional departments.

Because of these technical and management characteristics, specific applications are not likely to come into being without a conscious decision to create a DSS/EIS group. If such a group does exist in the firm, the information center is likely to have it as a subfunction. If such a group does not exist, however, the information center should seriously consider creating DSS and

EIS construction services, including the creation of generators. Many critical corporate needs can only be developed through the classic DSS/EIS development approach.

If the information center does create a DSS/EIS development service, it is crucial to staff it with DSS builders that are capable of working with very senior management. This argues for both age and general business experience more than for technical experience. In addition, strong analytical modeling skills are very important because many DSSs require the building of large analytical models that require strong knowledge of the software, model development, statistical reasoning, and financial reasoning.

CONCLUSION

Application development is one of the most fundamental topics in end user computing. This chapter examined both end user development and application development for DSS and EIS.

One central concept is the systems development life cycle model, in which applications are developed in a series of stages. In this book, the stages are described as assessment, design, construction, and implementation. Even the developers of small second-environment projects must go through all four stages instead of simply being created by sitting down at a computer system and composing an analytical model, data base schema, or large document. For large applications, extremely strong discipline is needed.

Almost all user-developed, DSS, and EIS applications are created using **iterative development,** in which the developer builds a small working system and refines it through a series of iterations. This does not mean constant backtracking instead of solid initial design. Iterative development must begin with good initial design, it should present the user with tested working products instead of buggy rough drafts, and iterations should come in the form of occasional new versions instead of constant changes. Each iteration should not just fix bugs—it should add new capabilities to the product.

Assessment is different from other stages in that it cannot be done for individual projects in isolation. No organization has the resources to do all of the application development it wants or even needs. Before any large applications are undertaken, the department must prepare a strategic plan to prioritize applications and select only those that can be done well within budget constraints. Costs and benefits should be one factor in selection, but there should also be other factors, including links to key objectives.

At the implementation end, a departmental perspective is also needed. Although each application has a distinct implementation phase, all implementation must be done in the broader context of managing the departmental work system. A key concept in departmental management is the assignment of roles to the department manager, secretaries, professional staff workers, and power users. Although these roles are complex, and the growing use of computers makes role clarification critical, few organizations have training programs for department managers, secretaries, or professional end users.

Decision support systems and executive information systems are too complex for end users to develop because they tend to stress the limits of technology and to integrate tools from different vendors. Many organizations have no mechanism in place for developing these kinds of applications, which fall into a gap between DP development and end user development. Those that do develop these groups must struggle with a number of issues, including staffing, tool selection and development, and the assignment of roles within the DSS/EIS group.

REVIEW QUESTIONS

1. What are the four stages of the systems development life cycle presented in this book? How is the assessment stage different from the other three?
2. What is iterative development? What are its advantages and disadvantages? What common misconceptions do people often have about it? What is the truth for each of these misconceptions?
3. What are the chief methodologies for identifying candidate applications for development? Which do you think is the best? The easiest to implement? The hardest to implement?
4. What are the main considerations in selection?
5. Compare the strengths and weaknesses of structural analysis and application identification studies as methodologies for corporate needs assessment.
6. Describe the main steps in the design process. What are the advantages of modular and hierarchical design, and how are the two related?
7. Why is it *not* desirable to pick the best software for a particular application and then the best hardware?
8. Describe testing considerations in the development stage.
9. What is a work system, and what are the implications of this concept for implementation?
10. What are the four elements of organization, and how do they work together in a complete organization strategy for a work system?
11. Summarize the things that must be done and the problems that tend to occur at cutover.
12. Write a sentence or two for each cell in the department management matrix.
13. Compare and contrast application development in the four environments. (This information is scattered throughout the chapter. Your job is to bring it together coherently.)
14. What are the ways of distinguishing DSSs from EISs? What do they have in common? What separates them from end user development?
15. Characterize the considerations in building DSSs and EISs. Specifically discuss tools, roles, and development philosophies. How are these different from the considerations in fourth-environment development?

REFERENCES

1. DANIEL, D. R., "Management Information Crisis," *Harvard Business Review,* October 1961, pp. 111–121.

2. DRUCKER, PETER F., *The Effective Executive,* Harper & Row, 1967.
3. *EDP Analyzer,* "Interesting Decision Support Systems," March 1982.
4. HARRIS, SIDNEY, E., AND BRIGHTMAN, HARVEY J., "Design Implications of a Task-Driven Approach to Unstructured Cognitive Tasks in Office Work," *Transactions on Office Information Systems,* July 1985, pp. 229–306.
5. HOLZMAN, DAVID L., AND ROSENBERG, VICTOR, "Understanding Shadow Functions: The Key to System Design and Evaluation," *Proceedings of the Palo Alto Research Center Workshop on Office Automation,* Xerox Palo Alto Research Center, May 13–15, 1976.
6. MCKEEN, JAMES D., "Successful Development for Business Application Systems," *MIS Quarterly,* September 1983, pp. 47–65.
7. PANKO, RAYMOND R., "38 Offices: Analyzing Needs in Individual Offices," *ACM Transactions on Office Information Systems,* Vol. 2, No. 3, July 1984, Association for Computing Machinery, pp. 226–234.
8. PANKO, RAYMOND R., "Rethinking Office Automation," *Administrative Management,* July 1982, pp. 22–24, 71–72.
9. PETERS, THOMAS J., AND WATERMAN, ROBERT H., JR., *In Search of Excellence,* Harper & Row, 1982.
10. RINALDI, DAMIAN, AND JASTRZEMBSKI, TED, "Executive Information Systems: Put Strategic Data at Your CEO's Fingertips," *Computerworld,* October 27, 1986, pp. 37–51, passim.
11. ROCKART, JOHN F., "Chief Executives Design Their Own Data Needs," *Harvard Business Review,* March–April 1979, pp. 81–93.
12. SIRBU, MARVIN, SCHOICHET, SANDOR, KUNIN, J., HAMMER, MICHAEL, AND SUTHERLAND, JULIET, "OAM: An Office Analysis Methodology," *Office Automation Conference 1982 Digest,* Association for Information Processing Societies, 1982, pp. 317–330.
13. SPRAGUE, RALPH H., JR., "A Framework for the Development of Decision Support Systems," *Management Information Systems Quarterly,* December 1980.
14. SPRAGUE, RALPH H., JR., AND CARLSON, ERIC D., *Building Effective Decision Support Systems,* Prentice-Hall, Inc., 1982.
15. SPRAGUE, RALPH H., JR., AND PANKO, RAYMOND R., "Criteria for a DSS Generator," *Proceedings, 13th Annual Meeting of the American Institute for Decision Sciences,* Atlanta, Georgia, 1981.
16. WAKIN, EDWARD, "Decisions, Decisions: How Top Execs Make Them," *Today's Office,* September 1982, pp. 66–74.

MANAGING END USER COMPUTING: BROAD CONCERNS 3

The first two chapters introduced end user computing and discussed the general process of analysis and development. The next three chapters deal with the general management of end user computing.

In this chapter, we will discuss the broad concerns that must be faced by information center managers, including the basic organizational context of information center management, the fundamental decisions that must be made before other decisions can be settled, and the general process of planning. The next two chapters look at the nuts and bolts of implementing successful information centers.

MANAGING IN A TIME OF CHANGE

As early as 1985, surveys were in unanimous agreement that more than half of all large firms already had information centers. (1,2,8,10,14,25,30) In 1985, the American Management Association (1) concluded that information centers tend to appear when a critical mass of about ten personal computers is installed. Even small firms have gone far beyond that critical mass today, and the information center is now a ubiquitous part of corporate life.

Cautious Growth

At the same time, today's information centers are far from mature. In nearly every case, information centers start small, with limited budgets and services. The main reason for this cautious start has been senior management fears that costs will run out of control. As one Army general said, "I will give you $50,000 on faith, but then I want to see some results, and I want to see them soon." As a result of such caution, most information centers have a lot of growth ahead of them.

83

End user support represents a massive investment for corporations—an investment that is extremely difficult to measure and justify. In order to obtain the funding it needs to give good service, a major part of the information center's internal mission is to demonstrate the successes that have occurred as a result of current investment levels.

A Maturing Vision

Information centers are also changing because few started with clear long-term visions for end user computing and their role in EUC. Even those that did have a clear initial vision have been forced to backtrack constantly, just as first-time parents, whose children "would never act that way" must learn the fallibility of their perceptions. Although most information centers do have definite mission statements, these statements and people's interpretations of them change constantly over time.

It is not only the information center's internal vision of itself that is being transformed. Users' visions of its role are also changing, and the role that top management assigns to the center is unstable as well. It is important to keep lines of communication open, especially during the information center's early years, so that shifts in perceptions can be understood and treated as appropriate.

Life Cycles

Another source of change is the fact that end user computing is still in an early stage of its life cycle. Just as people go through the life cycle of birth, childhood, adolescence, adulthood, and death, most institutions also experience a series of stages over time.

The life cycle concept derives from research on the diffusion of innovations (35) and from marketing. (26) Diffusion research tends to focus on the people in charge of adopting the innovation, whereas the marketing literature tends to describe life cycles from the point of view of markets and institutions. In this book we will employ the marketing view, since we are interested primarily in the management of an institution, the information center, and a "market," end users.

The Life Cycle Concept

According to the life cycle concept, an industry or a specific product undergoes five distinct life stages. These are:

Introduction In the introduction stage, growth is slow and uncertain. People who adopt during this period tend to be different from later adopters. (35) End user computing underwent this stage in the 1970s and early 1980s.

Growth In the growth stage, many people begin to adopt the innovation. The rate of growth actually increases from year to year.

Early Maturity In the early maturity stage, growth continues, but the rate of growth falls each year. Many people think that end user computing has passed from growth to early maturity, but it is always difficult to identify this transition, since growth often accelerates again when maturity is believed to have settled in.

Late Maturity In late maturity, growth is small to negligible.

Decline During the decline stage, use actually decreases with time. The product may die away entirely at this point, its role replaced by other products. Careful studies by Cox (7) of a wide variety of products indicates that true decline is uncommon. Normally, rebounds occur when decline is believed to have set in, and these rebounds may be larger than the original peak. Some industries begin rebounds even earlier, during late maturity, and their growth continues almost without interruption.

Life cycles are very important in planning. During the early stages of the life cycle, neither customers nor vendors really understand what they are doing. Customer astuteness is low, and vendors rarely turn to true market segmentation research. During the maturity stages, however, and sometimes even during the growth stage, customers' preferences become more complex, and unless segmented product strategies are pursued, a firm will lose market share rapidly. At later stages, marketing practices have to become ever more sophisticated to keep up with users.

Life Cycles in Information Systems

Gibson and Nolan

Gibson and Nolan (13) first popularized the idea that information systems products go through a life cycle. Focusing on data processing, they identified the stages in the life cycle as introduction, contagion (growth), control, and integration. This taxonomy centered on the management of data processing and the gradual imposition of controls on exploding data processing demand. The authors' postulated fourth stage, integration, in which DP would become an integral part of corporate life, was simply their guess about the future.

Although the Gibson and Nolan model is similar to the product life cycle, it is not identical to it. It appeared at a time when control was just beginning to come to data processing, and it focused almost exclusively on that issue. Because the Gibson and Nolan model is well known among IS professionals, IS planning often revolves around control, to the detriment of other aspects of life cycle thinking.

The model has not stood up well under close scrutiny. King and Kraemer (23) published a review of a number of studies that tried to confirm or invalidate it; collectively, these studies produced little support for the full Gibson and Nolan model.

Guimaraes

Guimaraes proposed another model in 1984, this time for information centers. (14) In the first phase, there was no support for users and no way to get to data. In the second phase, there was access to data but very little support for end users. In a future third stage, Guimaraes argued, there would be full support, including application development services. Again, Guimaraes was concentrating on a single issue, the broadening of services.

Henderson and Treacy

A more recent model for end user computing is much closer to the classical life cycle model. (18) In this model, Henderson and Treacy focus on four clusters of issues:

- The support infrastructure (services to users)
- The technological infrastructure (hardware and software)
- The data infrastructure
- Evaluation, justification, and planning

They argue that support concerns were dominant in the early stages of end user computing, followed distantly by the technological infrastructure. Over time, however, they expect support concerns to wane dramatically in *relative* importance, and they expect technological concerns to peak and then fall off. Overtaking them will be justification/evaluation and data.

Life Cycle in Perspective

Overall, information centers are still in a high state of flux, and very few policies and support strategies are permanent. Every year, the information center must review at least some of its policies and practices and devise better arrangements.

SERVICES, PROBLEMS, AND CRITICAL SUCCESS FACTORS

Services

To users, the information center is seen primarily in terms of the services it offers.

Leitheiser and Wetherbe

Figure 3-1 lists a number of services commonly offered by information centers. In 1984, Leitheiser and Wetherbe (25) asked 25 information center managers whether they offered each service and, if so, how much time each service consumed, with "1" meaning heavy time consumption and "5" meaning little time consumption.

The survey shows that the seven services fell into two distinct tiers. The first tier consisted of services that were offered by nearly all respondents. These were consulting, training, troubleshooting, and research for product selection. Of these first-tier services, however, only consulting and training were rated as highly time consuming.

The second tier of services was offered by about two-thirds of the organizations surveyed. These were application development, data extraction, and newsletters. Of these, only application development was rated as highly time consuming. Application development is a highly controversial service, and we will examine it in more depth later.

SERVICES, PROBLEMS, AND CRITICAL SUCCESS FACTORS

Service	Percent Offering	Staff Time Median (1=high)
Consulting	100	2
Training	96	2
Troubleshooting	95	3.5
Product research	95	5
Programming/development	65	2
Data extraction	63	5
Newsletter	61	6

Other services mentioned:

    Office automation support
    Electronic mail
    User's group
    Departmental needs assessment
    Coordinate end user data access
    User advocate for data processing department
    Document and distribute end user software

Sample: Size varied with question, from 19 to 25.

Source: Leitheiser and Wetherbe (1984).

FIGURE 3-1 LEITHEISER AND WETHERBE'S SERVICE LIST

Brancheau

Later, these categories together with word processing support were used in a survey of 50 end users (as opposed to information center professioanls). Figure 3-2 presents the major results from that survey. (3) The first column of data lists the average rank given to each service, a measure of its perceived importance to the respondent. The second column shows the percentage of users using the service.

Troubleshooting and consulting were at the top of the list, with training close behind. Data extracts and programming/development come next, with lower average ranks. Neither data extracts nor programming/development was mentioned frequently, but this may be misleading, since data extracts are

Service	Percent Offering	Average Importance Rating
Troubleshooting	77	6.8
Consulting	73	6.6
Training	64	6.4
Data extraction	33	6.4
Programming/development	28	5.8
Product research	33	5.3
Newsletter	28	4.7
Word processing support	16	4.9

Sample: 53 end users in five companies.

Note: Development was not offered in one firm and was discouraged in two others.

Source: Brancheau, Vogel, and Wetherbe (1985).

FIGURE 3-2 BRANCHEAU'S SERVICE LIST

MANAGING END USER COMPUTING: BROAD CONCERNS

Service	Number Offering
Training	13
Consulting	13
Technical and operations support	11
Hotline assistance	11
Management of data	10
Microcomputer software development	10
Debugging assistance	9
Newsletter	8
Information clearinghouse	6
Prototyping	5
Data dictionary for user applications	3
Documentation support for user applications	3

Sample: 13 St. Louis Information Centers.

Note: All information centers had been in operation at least two years.

Source: Sumner (1985).

FIGURE 3-3 SUMNER'S SERVICE LIST

pertinent to only some applications, and since one of the five information centers used in the study did not offer development at all and two others strongly discouraged it. Product research, newsletters, and WP support were not mentioned frequently, and their importance ratings were low.

Sumner

In her survey of 13 information centers in the St. Louis area, Sumner obtained the results shown in Figure 3-3. (39) Again, the familiar litany of services appears, including training, consulting, technical and operations support, and hotline assistance. Close behind are data management, microcomputer software evaluation, debugging assistance, and the newsletter. Application development was not included in the list of services studied.

Crwth

Crwth, (8) in its survey of information center staff members, recorded the services listed in Figure 3-4. It is difficult to compare this list with the

Service	Percent Offering
Training	86
Analyze end user requirements	79
Demonstrate hardware and software	79
Provide hotline for end users	78
Provide microcomputer support center	74
Select end user hardware and software	67
Provide user graphics facilities	59
Provide access to data bases	58
Centralized buying of equipment	49
Provide network & connection to mainframe	43
Provide application programming	16
Provide capacity planning	14

Sample: 1080 individual respondents.

Source: Crwth (1985).

FIGURE 3-4 CRWTH'S SERVICE LIST

others because it breaks service categories down into finer subunits, but training, consulting, and hotline assistance stand out as usual. Application development is probed in this survey; only 16 percent of the information center staffers reported that application development was supported.

American Management Association
Finally, in the American Management Association's survey, the top five tasks mentioned were: (30) general PC training, evaluation of micro hardware and software, selection of hardware and software, micro software training, and mainframe training.

Services in Perspective
In general, there seems to be strong agreement about the kinds of services offered by information centers, although there may be wide differences in what kinds of specific services are offered under each category. Training is done almost universally, as are consulting of various types, troubleshooting, and product selection. The picture for promotion, application development, and data extraction is somewhat less clear, but a fair number of information centers do provide these services.

Problems
When information center directors get together, their conversation usually focuses on the problems they share. The information center is not the place for people who want a simple and smooth existence.

Guimaraes
Figure 3-5 lists some of the problems seen in an early survey of information center managers. (14)

Leitheiser and Wetherbe
A slightly more recent survey, conducted by Leitheiser and Wetherbe in 1984, (25) after the early confusion over end user computing had abated somewhat, gave a somewhat different picture. Figure 3-6 presents the results of this study. The one issue that received by far the most frequent mention was the disproportionate demand for services relative to the resources available in most organizations. Nevertheless, other factors such as staffing and control problems, support, and the difficulty of getting users to develop their own systems were also mentioned frequently.

Leitheiser and Wetherbe reclassified this large number of problems into three major categories.

- **Political problems,** such as lack of top management support, resistance by MIS, and poor definition of responsibilities
- **Service problems,** such as high user expectations, inappropriate use of the center, and inability to reach top management
- **Internal problems,** such as high staff turnover and hardware incompatibility

MANAGING END USER COMPUTING: BROAD CONCERNS

Index of Concern	Problem
4.8	Lack of company plan for personal computing
4.7	Lack of user education regarding a companywide and long-term perspective about personal computing
4.6	Poor maintainability of user-developed systems
4.6	Unnecessarily high cost to the company due to users learning by trial and error about lack of compatibility with mainframe
4.5	Lack of communication between MIS and user departments
4.4	Overwhelming growth of user requests for assistance
4.3	Unnecessarily high cost to the company due to users learning by trial and error how to use available software packages
4.2	Contamination of corporate data on the mainframe
4.2	Mismatch of user applications to other possible computing alternatives, such as mainframe packages or the traditional approach for system development
4.2	MIS has image problem with users
4.2	Lack of equivalent or better mainframe software packages to compete successfully with microcomputer software
4.2	Lack of adequate training on products, computer concepts, etc.

Sample: 52 MIS managers at a seminar on information center management.

Source: Guimaraes (1984).

FIGURE 3-5 GUIMARAES' PROBLEM LIST

Percent	Problem
48	Demand for services exceeds supply.
28	Center staff can't get users to develop their own systems.
20	Developing staff with appropriate skills is difficult.
20	Existing controls for user development are inadequate.
16	User expectations about center services are unrealistic.
Others:	Difficult to get top management support.
	Procedures for software development not formed.
	Resistance in the DP department.
	Inappropriate applications developed in the center.
	Not enough publicity.
	Responsibilities not clearly defined.

Sample: 23 information centers.

Source: Leitheiser and Wetherbe (1984).

FIGURE 3-6 LEITHEISER AND WETHERBE'S PROBLEM LIST

Crwth

Crwth Computer Coursewares (8) obtained similar results from its large survey of information center staff members. Their list of major problems is especially interesting because it is different for pilot (new) information centers and mature information centers. Pilot information centers ranked their problems as follows:

- Lack of end user awareness
- Shortage of DP trainers
- CPU shortage
- DP resistance
- Management resistance
- Lack of chargeback system
- Insufficient disk storage

Mature information centers produced the following ranking, illustrating a transition from growing pains to chronic operational difficulties:

- Shortage of DP trainers
- Lack of end user awareness
- Management resistance
- CPU shortage
- DP resistance
- Lack of chargeback system
- Insufficient disk storage

Computer Intelligence Corporation

Another view of problems comes from a 1985 survey by Computer Intelligence Corporation (CIC), (6) which queried information center managers. The CIC survey showed that the following areas were of most concern.

- 64% User training
- 59% User awareness
- 59% Management support
- 53% Staffing
- 48% Budget
- 41% Security
- 34% Software limits
- 9% Hardware limits
- 26% Technical support
- 25% User resistance

CIC also examined these issues from the point of view of the number of end users surveyed. User training made the list of the top three concerns in every size category, and user awareness made the list in all but the next to largest category, 500 to 999 end users.

For very small information centers, those serving fewer than 50 end users, budget was on the list of the top three concerns. Budget did not make the top three in larger information centers. In contrast, management support appeared on the list in all size categories beyond 50 end users, perhaps suggesting that, as information centers grow, overall management support replaces the specific issue of budget or that Gibson's and Nolan's (13) prediction that control will follow early growth is accurate.

Problems in Perspective

Again, there is fair agreement about the major problems facing information centers, namely, training, user awareness, organizational support, concerns over the quality and safety of user development, and technology.

Critical Success Factors

Obviously, information center management needs to pay close attention to these pressing concerns, but it must also be concerned about long-term goals that may not show up in its list of serious problems. Unfortunately, however, the list of concerns and goals is very long, and unless management focuses on those that have the highest priority, its time will be spread too thin.

Rockart, (33) following some early suggestions by Daniel, (9) argued that most managers could identify relatively few elements that were critical to their success. By identifying these "critical success factors" and making sure that they were handled well, a manager would have a good chance of overall success.

Leitheiser and Wetherbe

Leitheiser and Wetherbe (25) asked their 25 respondents to list the critical success factors for their information centers. The results, shown in Figure 3-7, failed to produce any clear consensus, but they did reveal several prevalent themes, namely, providing whatever services users need in a timely way, developing a competent staff, selecting and supporting software, conducting training, monitoring and coordinating end user development, and obtaining the support of top management.

Brancheau

Later, Brancheau *et al.* asked information center *users* to rate their organizations' critical success factors. (3) Although some results were the same, users emphasized staff and completely ignored control. Of the 147 CSFs listed by the 50 respondents (see Figure 3-8), 62 were related to staff. The only other category of any consequence was availability, which was cited by 28 respondents. Training, selecting appropriate equipment, research, and management support were rarely mentioned, and only the large number of responses in the "other" category diminished the overwhelming importance of staff and availability. Users seem to have different agendas than information center managers.

When we look at staff more closely, we see that technical skills received by far the greatest number of mentions—26 which is about the same as the next three categories combined. Only business understanding and an orientation toward service received many mentions as important staff issues.

SERVICES, PROBLEMS, AND CRITICAL SUCCESS FACTORS   **93**

Percent	Problem
36	Provide whatever services are needed in a timely way.
36	Develop a competent staff.
28	Select and support the "right" application packages.
24	Do effective end user training.
20	Monitor and coordinate end user development.
20	Obtain the support of top management.

Others: Quickly respond to development requests.
Effectively promote information center services.
Establish good communications with EU departments.
Deliver solutions in a cost effective way.
Create a comfortable environment for users.
Maintain good system performance.
Know users' businesses and problems.
Get organizational acceptance of information center.
Manage user expectations.
Provide service to distributed sites.
Successfully implement electronic mail.
Clearly define center's purpose.

Sample: 23 information centers.

Source: Leitheiser and Wetherbe (1984).

FIGURE 3-7 LEITHEISER AND WETHERBE'S CSF LIST

Number	Critical Success Factors
62	Staffing
28	Availability
12	Training
9	Appropriate equipment
5	Research
4	Management Support

Staff-Related CSFs

47%	Technical skills
17%	Business understanding
16%	Service-oriented
11%	Communication skills
8%	Current knowledge
5%	Quality people

Sample: 53 end users in five organizations.

Source: Brancheau, Vogel, and Wetherbe (1985).

FIGURE 3-8 BRANCHEAU's CSF LIST

The Brancheau *et al.* findings indicate that users want *results*. They want the staff to know what it is doing, and they want the staff to be available when called. They also want staff people that, while technically superb, can understand their business needs and have a genuine service orientation.

Sumner

Sumner (39) also looked at critical success factors, but she presented raw data instead of analyzing patterns. The advantage of this approach is that it reveals little consistency among the CSFs of the 13 information center managers she surveyed. Each manager seems to be focusing on very different things, and although some weak patterns can be teased out of the data, it is the absence of strong patterns and consistency that is most important in her study. If other studies show similar divergence, the CSF approach should be used with caution.

Critical Success Factors in Perspective

Based on the Leitheiser and Wetherbe, Brancheau *et al.*, and Sumner results, we can draw a tentative general picture of what is important in information centers.

The important factor, from the user's point of view, is fast, effective service. Users want help when they need it, they want knowledgeable help, and they want help from people who speak their language and who are service oriented. The focus of this service is troubleshooting, a service that information center managers mention less frequently than users. Perhaps this reflects the concerns of users who have already selected their hardware and software and have already received their training. Since many end users are in this position, however, this post-novice user segment needs to be heeded.

At the same time, information center managers have many other concerns that must be handled. Training, staffing, product selection, top management support, and promotion of end user computing are all necessary if the information center is to survive. So is controlling end user computing, a factor that the Brancheau *et al.* users *completely* ignore. Management must neither be dominated by intense demands for help on specific applications nor fail to give these demands high attention.

Services, Problems, and CSFs: A Recap

Overall, there seems to be very wide agreement on the kinds of services that information centers should offer. The only major point of contention seems to be whether the information center staff should attempt application development.

On problems, there is less agreement, but a few major problems seem to show up consistently, including staffing, training, managing end user expectations, and getting end users to do their own work. Because there was little agreement on other specifics, the Leitheiser and Wetherbe taxonomy of service, internal, and political problems seems to provide a good framework for helping individual information center managers organize their own assessments of problems.

The CSF approach has been touted as a way to help managers focus their attention more specifically on the few things that most need to be accomplished amid their broader range of concerns. Studies have found only slight agreement on these CSFs. This indicates either that the method is not likely to be broadly useful during this chaotic early period of information center development, or simply that, although it works for individuals, situations in different information centers are too different for broad trends to emerge. Somewhat disturbingly, the Brancheau *et al.* study indicates that users and information center managers may have quite sharply different ideas of what is critical.

Since the information center is still in an early stage of its life cycle, we can expect services, problems, and critical success factors to change constantly. Most of the surveys that studied information centers in detail were conducted early in the life of end user computing. Their results should be viewed as starting points for the analysis of situations in information centers today, not as ways to build hard guidelines for this year's services and policies.

FUNDAMENTAL DECISIONS

Before other decisions can be made, a corporation needs to make five fundamental decisions that cut across many long-term and day-to-day decisions. The choices made in these fundamental decisions establish the basic "personality" of end user computing in the corporation and of the information center itself. These decisions are the following.

- When should host computers be used, when should personal computers be used, and how should the two be viewed over the long run?
- How is justification to be done, that is, how can a corporation decide how much to spend for end user computing in general and for specific applications?
- Should the information center's role be to accelerate end user computing, control it, or both?
- How should information center support be financed? Directly by the organization as an overhead expense? Through chargeback? And, if through a combination of the two, when should chargeback be used?
- Should the information center develop applications for users? If so, under what circumstances and using what procedures?

Personal Computers Versus Mainframes

Only mainframes existed during the early years of end user computing. Host computing, which we have defined as consisting of data applications (retrieval and application development), analysis, and graphics, was the meat and potatoes of end user development in the 1970s and early 1980s.

When personal computing began to explode, fueled in large part by analysis tools, battle lines were often drawn between "mainframe bigots" and "PC bigots." Only a few firms completely escaped philosophical battles over the relative advantages of hosts and PCs, and in some firms, these battles were so severe that separate information centers sprang up to serve host and PC applications.

Advantages of Mainframes

The advantages of hosts stem from their processing speeds, multiuser operation, access to production data, simpler technology, and operator assistance.

Processing speeds of several millions of instructions per second on mainframes and even large minicomputers means that these machines can do processing jobs that would take hours on personal computers. For large and complex models, the mainframe is likely to be the only alternative, although advanced PCs are beginning to eat into this advantage.

Multiuser operation, in turn, means that users scattered across a corporation can work together to develop a budget or keep track of product changes in a data base. Since multiuser applications are very common, as discussed in Chapter 1, this multiuser capability is widely needed.

Access to corporate data is also critical. In her survey of mainframe-intensive information centers, Sumner found that 43 percent of all applications needed access to corporate data, (39) and if the application works on the host, it should be easier to collect the data needed for an application.

Simpler technology does not mean that hosts are inherently simpler; it only means that the complexity of hosts can be hidden from end users. End users do not have to configure the computer, add boards, learn most of the complexity of the operating system, or know the many other things that PC users have to learn.

The last point, **operator assistance,** is very important in cutting down maintenance-type work such as doing backup restoring archived files, loading printers with paper, installing new software, adding updates to software, and diagnosing problems. Few PC users are or want to be aware of how much time these activities take.

Advantages of Personal Computers

Personal computers, in contrast, offer the benefits of consistent response time, simpler day-to-day operation, more vivid application software, and simpler application software.

Consistent response time means that actions always take the same amount of time when they are initiated. Although large hosts have immense processing power, this power is spread over many users. Response time changes remarkably, even from second to second. This is especially disconcerting for simple activities such as word processing and spreadsheet operation. Imagine using a typewriter that sometimes runs fast, sometimes slow.

In addition, end users are normally given low priority, in order to avoid degrading the performance of production operations on the host and to contain the danger of runaway queries, in which a single query traverses many data files, absorbing many CPU cycles from other applications. Although some host administrators promise very high priority, few give it in practice. Worse yet, "acceptable" response times are often considered to be a half second to a second, which is totally unacceptable for highly interactive work such as word processing and spreadsheeting.

Simpler day-to-day operation means that users do not have to become enmeshed in the complex administrative paperwork and procedures that seem to attend the use of nearly all host computers.

Although host operators do a great deal of work, such as making backups nightly, host administrators normally create a fair number of operational procedures to be followed for account billing, security, and other matters. These procedures are especially burdensome for intermittent users, who may only need to use an application every three to six months. Between uses, several procedures are likely to be changed, and although these procedures are documented in monthly newsletters, intermittent users are not likely to read these newsletters.

The final points are probably the best reason for using personal computers: their application software tends to be **more vivid and simpler** than host software. Many host packages were designed for dumb TTY (teletypewriter) terminals (see Chapter 13) and so make little or no use of the advanced screen handling that makes PC packages so attractive, such as pop-up windows, real-time line justification in word processing, and graphics-oriented user interfaces such as the Macintosh interface. Further hampering the attractiveness of host application software is the fact that many host programs were designed in the early 1970s, when user interface design was crude, and have evolved since then in ways that have not radically altered their ease of use.

These same factors also tend to make PC application software easier to learn and use than host software, but an even bigger reason why PC software is easier to use is that PC application developers have long had to cater primarily to users demanding simplicity and limited functionality. Most PC programs have simple "core metaphors," such as accounting spreadsheets or blank pages for typing, which are easy to comprehend. Many host packages such as SAS and IFPS, however, have long appealed to people who want power computing and are willing to spend more time learning to get higher functionality. These vendors increase sales by adding functionality, and many of these packages are really collections of a dozen or more large modules.

In addition, the PC world represents such a large market that larger numbers of application developers are attracted to it, giving a wider range of offerings and a faster pace of evolution.

Seeking a Balance

Few firms support only PCs or host computing. A survey of information center managers by Computer Intelligence Corporation in 1985 found that only 23 percent of the managers they surveyed supported only micros or mainframes. (6) In 1984, 24 percent of the information center managers surveyed by Leitheiser and Wetherbe supported only micros or mainframes. (25) Today, dual support is even more the rule. The question, then, is not which delivery technology to support but rather *when* to use PCs and mainframes in particular applications.

For **individual applications,** the balance usually tips toward personal computers for personal productivity applications that are highly interactive and where superior application software exists. This is especially true when ease of learning and interface attractiveness are important.

Applications requiring **vast processing** must turn to hosts, whereas for multiuser applications, the issue is whether the application spans a department's boundaries. If it is exclusively departmental, a single PC or PC network may be attractive, whereas applications that involve many people or people who are widely scattered geographically must turn to host computers.

Yet another consideration is **data.** If the data are purely personal or departmental, a PC can be used. But if data are needed by several different departments, putting the application on a PC could greatly retard necessary data access.

Many corporations have established guidelines to help information center staffers and end users decide when to use a PC and when to use a host. These guidelines tend to stress the considerations given in the preceding paragraphs.

It is also wise to make individual decisions on the basis of how **other applications** of the user or department are currently being handled. If a person uses IFPS (a host-based financial analysis package) for most work and needs simple word processing, host power should probably be used, whereas a person who does mostly spreadsheeting or word processing on a PC might be well advised to stay with PCs for an occasionally larger financial analysis.

Furthermore, all guidelines need to be changed constantly because the relative tradeoffs between host computers and personal computers are changing rapidly. Personal computers in the PS/2 Model 80 and Macintosh II range and beyond now have so much processing power that some of the processing advantages of the host are being eroded rapidly. In addition, some host packages are developing better user interfaces, and many now have versions running on PCs that offer both improved user interfaces and simple cooperative operation with their host cousins.

The existence of products that run on both PCs and hosts raise their own set of problems. Few are as comfortable to use as the existing and new PC products with which they compete. In addition, several "ported" host products are an order of magnitude more difficult to learn and use, because they have the extensive functionality demanded of power users, and so are daunting to users with simpler needs. Forcing users to use these products often makes little sense other than making micro-mainframe exchanges easier.

More importantly, hosts and PCs are beginning to converge toward a multitier technical support structure, in which the PC is becoming the standard workstation, with hosts acting as file servers for some applications, and the main processing source for others. Software will eventually appear in modules that can shift work between the workstation and remote host automatically and transparently.

The real problem for the present is how to set guidelines during a time of rapid change. Guidelines are critical, and they must stress current tradeoffs. But case-by-case decision making must also take into account what other software users already have. In addition, the guidelines must also change rapidly to fit the evolving state of hardware and software technology.

Justification

Justification involves both costs and benefits. In end user computing, costs are usually quantifiable, but in many cases, benefits are not. As a result, strict cost/benefits analysis can only be done for some applications.

This limitation leads to two basic choices for justification. The first is to restrict end user computing to applications in which quantifiable cost/benefits justifications can be done. Firestone has taken this approach, with rigid guidelines that no project can proceed without a 16 percent return on investment, with no more than 10 to 20 percent of the benefits coming from time savings, and with no allowance for cost avoidance. (21)

The other approach is to try to face up to the problem of soft benefits. This involves developing methodologies for assessing soft benefits where reasonable or developing justification procedures that permit line managers to make decisions based on semiquantified benefits, as they now do in many other areas of business.

End user computing is far from unique in its inability to quantify most benefits. Perhaps a majority of all business decisions are made on the basis of unquantified or semiquantified benefits. But DP has long used cost/benefits analysis, so it is simply assumed that end user computing will do the same.

Another consideration is that the scale of EUC investments is becoming so large in many firms that senior management now demands at least as much rationality as possible.

Costs

Although some costs are elusive, every proposal should be able to estimate costs with some accuracy.

For **hardware costs**, it is important to cost out a fully loaded system, with all of the options needed. For both mainframes and personal computers, "base prices" are almost meaningless. For PCs, base prices are only half or less of the ultimate price of the machine, including peripherals and expansion boards. (PC pricing is discussed in Chapter 6.) Hosts are also sold as ensembles, and base prices that merely reflect the CPU or a system with insufficient memory or peripherals are deeply misleading.

For **software costs**, it is important to identify all packaged software and the costs needed to develop programmed applications or to customize applications using the internal customization procedures of packages. If packages are used and no development is done, software may be as little as 25 percent the cost of the hardware. Development can make software's cost twice that of hardware.

Ongoing costs are also important. If the equipment is leased, the lease will reflect hardware amortization, finance charges, and maintenance charges. Even if the equipment is purchased, there will be maintenance charges, and some firms have internal finance charges on capital purchases. The cost of paper, ribbons, and supplies will also be considerable.

The most difficult costs to assess are **human costs.** It is very expensive to develop a major application, both for department members and for the information center. After initial development, there is training, the development of procedures, and various forms of hotline assistance or deeper problem diagnosis. The information center should develop guidelines for these personnel costs, based on data collected in actual projects.

Hard Benefits

The hardest benefits are those in which a clearly identifiable current cost can be avoided by replacing an existing operation with computerization. For instance, external time-sharing costs can often be replaced by internal computing with clear savings. (15,29,30) A strong case can also be made for **current cost avoidance** in many other areas, as the following examples indicate.

> Security Pacific National Bank's commercial loan staff was able to support 20 percent more loan volume with no increase in staff. (4)
>
> A textile manufacturer was able to reduce clerical costs by $134,000 with a $90,000 investment in personal computers. (37)
>
> Holiday Inn managers normally keep four or five rooms in their "back pockets" to adjust for reservation problems. With better information, these can be released much earlier, improving the occupancy rate. (27)
>
> Wendy's International was able to save 0.25 percent of total food cost by purchase planning. (41)

Although these firm cost savings that can be quantified in detail are useful, in many cases actual quantification is difficult, but there are some variables whose value is open to debate. For instance, Wendy's International was able to allocate its staff better, putting people on duty at the most critical times and in the best numbers. (41) Although precise quantification would have been difficult, reasonable "what if" analysis showing probable savings under several scenarios could have been used to give a rough quantification of potential savings.

Cost avoidance is also difficult to handle. In **cost avoidance**, extra hiring, or some other cost that would be created, is avoided. The quality of cost growth avoidance arguments depends almost entirely on how firmly programmed the avoided cost is. If the cost is already programmed into a budget, avoidance is likely to be persuasive. But if the cost is due to a proposed program that may or may not be implemented or that is suspected of being "padding" in a budget proposal, real cost displacement is questionable. In addition, there is the concern that the cost may not be avoided at all, even if the system is implemented. Therefore, cost avoidance proposals should be carefully audited afterward.

Time savings arguments are important but must be evaluated carefully. Today, a PC or time on a host system can be justified if it saves as little as 10 percent of an end user's time in many cases. But it is not clear how that 10 percent of released time will be spent. For clerical workers, it is common for new work to appear. For instance, when word processing is introduced, the cost per line may plummet, but the volume of work often grows, resulting in no net cost displacement. Although the new work may be worth the cost, this is a separate issue. The bottom line is that, unless cost displacement can be accompanied by a budgeted decrease in head count, it is not likely to be a real cost decrease, although the soft benefits may be worthwhile.

One way to implement hard cost savings without detailed cost/benefits analysis is to give department managers broad discretion over their budgets. This will allow, for instance, a department manager to purchase a computer that allows the reallocation of work, keeping costs from rising or even decreasing overall costs. If the total budget is fixed, control over internal allocation gives the manager freedom to innovate within a no-added-cost framework.

Softer Cost Savings: Tangible Benefits

Having discussed hard cost savings, we can now turn to softer savings: those that cannot be quantified.

The term "soft" is somewhat misleading because it really consists of two different kinds of costs—intangible and tangible. **Intangible savings** are those like customer good-will which are very difficult to assess even intuitively. **Tangible savings** are those that can be "felt," though not quantified. For instance, if customer backlogs are growing because of an inability to process information rapidly, it might be difficult to quantify the benefits, but the problem of the backlog may be felt so tangibly that the cost of the system seems justified.

In tangible benefits decision making, the manager must compare a known and quantified cost with a benefit that is known and felt keenly but not quantifiable. This is a common decision situation in business and one that most line managers are at least reasonably comfortable making. As a result, when bottlenecks or other tangible (felt) benefits exist, it may be reasonable to expect line managers to do justification as well as they justify most other things, without going to quantified benefits.

Efficiency, Effectiveness, and Innovation

In its information center literature, IBM lists three levels of justification: efficiency, effectiveness, and innovation. (20) Each shift to a higher level means less quantification in benefits but higher potential payoffs.

The lowest level is **efficiency,** in which both costs and the value of benefits are known. An amount of money that can be estimated can be saved. Benefits, however, tend to be relatively small.

At the next level, **effectiveness,** the goal is not to do a job with less cost but to do it better. Effectiveness often produces bigger benefits than efficiency because it leads to better and faster decision making, and other benefits that can improve a company's overall position. Compared to efficiency, effectiveness is a higher risk benefit with higher potential payoffs.

In effectiveness, someone or some organization does its work better, but in basically the same way. In the highest form of benefits, **innovation,** the very way the individual or organization works is restructured. For example, at SmithKline Beckman, the goal of using PCs is to monitor research much earlier, to weed out unpromising projects, and to expedite promising ones. (42) The company's ultimate objective is to change the broad drug development process. The benefits of innovation are difficult to assess, but the potential payoffs can be enormous.

IBM lists several examples of innovation, drawn from a *Business Week* special report. (5) These include restructuring a company to use fewer layers of management, amalgamating sales districts through improved communication, and developing a new customer service for corporate clients that will allow the customer service group to reduce its staff almost 20 percent.

Innovation is difficult to evaluate, first because not even its costs are measurable, since many of them are human costs. Risks are also difficult to assess, as they are in any organizational innovation. Sassone (38) argues that change often has three phases. In the first, technology substitutes for tasks already done; in the second, new tasks are performed, using the capabilities added by the technology; and in the third, the way the organization does its business changes fundamentally. If Sassone is correct, by the time an organization reaches the innovation stage, it will have considerable experience with technology.

Trends in Factory Automation

The search for "hard benefits" is often viewed as a way to manage offices as efficiently as firms already manage their factories. Ironically, factory automation has thrown capital purchasing in production environments upside down, and new justification procedures for end user computing are likely to flow from conceptual advances in factory automation.

In his seminal article, "Do's and Don'ts of Computerized Manufacturing," Gerwin points out that traditional cost-benefits analysis cannot be used effectively in factory automation. (12) Gerwin notes that computer-aided manufacturing (CAM) changes "accounting procedures, production scheduling, quality control, maintenance, foundary and assembly operations, plant management, and job structure." (12) This represents a total restructuring of the way an organization works and involves high risk. It is therefore senseless to treat it as merely a routine capital budgeting situation. It is a global change that must be assessed globally.

Another problem, pointed out by Richardson and Gordon, (32) is that return-on-investment (ROI) arguments are valid only in certain firms. An ROI argument "is true only if the firm is competing on the basis of cost and productivity." If product innovation were instead the basis for competition, then reliance on an ROI measure could be misleading.

Richardson and Gordon (32) propose that firms measure their "total manufacturing performance" with multiple measures of performance relevant to particular situations. To the extent that productivity is crucial, it should be factored in, but the productivity index should be only one of many indices. In their survey of Canadian manufacturing firms, they found that the more effective measures of manufacturing performance were those that compare achievements to objectives.

Gerwin provides simpler guidance for dealing with pressure from above for short-term results. (12)

- Reduce the visibility of proposals by including them in other larger capital improvement proposals.
- Project a confident image with unswerving commitment. This makes management feel more confident despite a lack of solid cost and benefit numbers.
- Maintain credibility by being realistic because once faith is lost, top management will review details closely and subject all innovations to intense scrutiny.
- Appear to be rational by preparing rudimentary financial analyses and a written evaluation of merits, even if exact, because this helps satisfy corporate guidelines for rationality.

The "bottom line" is that CAM is a strategic matter. It must be driven by overall strategy, and it may change overall strategy. Although end user computing, by its high diversity, will have a much harder time demonstrating strategic implications, many of the adoption arguments being developed in factory automation may show us better ways to justify end user computing.

Developing an Approval Process: General Direction

So far, we have talked about general theoretical issues. Justification is not a theoretical problem, however; it is a practical, pressing problem. Moreover, the cost of justification should not be overly burdensome.

IBM argues, and most analysts would agree, that justification should be a two-stage process. (20) In the first stage, upper management sets its objectives for justification and end user computing in general. In the second stage, the justification of specific innovations is completed.

Top management sets objectives in several ways. First, senior executives are likely to make their general philosophies known on an individual basis. If the CEO opposes rapid growth, rapid growth is not likely to take place, and justification is likely to be very detailed and selective. If the CEO wants to push modernization in the firm, growth is likely to be rapid, and justification may focus on effectiveness and innovation.

Second, general management is likely to exercise control through its normal budgeting process, particularly with regard to capital expenditures. The budgeting office is likely to have overall growth or retrenchment targets for various organizational units. Justification will obviously be easier in areas slated for growth. In addition, because capital budgeting is so critical to corporate cash flow, some firms allocate capital budgets on a unit-by-unit basis, including capital expenditures for information technology.

Top management also gives direction by its general philosophy on centralized versus decentralized management. If the firm has a strategy of decentralized management, this will mean giving individual managers far more control over all their resources. The central justification process may be weak or nonexistent in this case, with individual managers making individual decisions within their allocated budgets.

These general guidelines will help the information center establish a justification process for individual innovations that will fit the desires and decisions of senior management. Even if the direction offered by senior management does not affect the paperwork to be done, it will affect the rate at which proposals are accepted and what kind of initiatives will be supported.

Developing an Approval Process: Individual Applications

For individual applications, the information center should have a simple form that lets the user describe the application, its costs, and its benefits. Although justification is important, it must not be too expensive, or real benefits will be chewed up in the process. Jim Hall-Sheehy has proposed the following simple application format for a personal computer. (16)

- Identify the primary applications.
- Name the user for each application.
- Tell how frequently each application will be used.
- List software (to see if it is consistent with the application).
- State how much time the PC will be used each month.
- Describe the benefits.

Although costs are not explicitly on this list, they are probably computed by the information center staff. It would probably be much better to force the user to estimate costs at the time of the proposal, perhaps using a template supplied by the information center.

There will probably be different types of justification for different levels of expenditures. For example, a $200 expenditure should get only a cursory check on compatibility with corporate standards, whereas a $75,000 departmental minicomputer or $100,000 department plan to overhaul its operations completely should be given close scrutiny. The sources of funds may also make a difference. At Grumman, for instance, a PC required on a contract will obtain faster approval than one paid from general funds. (36)

In many cases, the actual justification process is designed not so much to evaluate individual cases, but rather to force users to think through their applications and to prevent end-of-period budget money from being burned off at the end of the year with little thought. Even one company proud of its "tough" justification process requiring seven signatures turned down only two requests, (37) and at Wendy's International, not one request had been turned down through 1985. (41) In these and other companies, some applications were undoubtedly withdrawn because, after scrutiny, their proposers found they were not worth their cost. Some firms even provide free help to users who are developing the business case for an innovation, in order to help users see their ways clearly.

Since the information center looks bad if many poor applications reach senior management, most information centers review each questionable application in depth with the proposer, and quite a few will readily turn down applications. After all, the information center's credibility is at stake. In other words, although most users will withdraw weak applications, direct quality control is also likely to be necessary, using the detailed guidelines distributed to users.

A minor but important decision is how to compute cost/benefits figures when they are used. The simple measure is the **payback period**—how many months or years will it take before cumulative benefits surpass cumulative costs. Net present value (NPV) and internal rate of return (IRR) are also attractive, but if these measures are not used widely in the corporation, their theoretical advantages will be outweighed by training costs and the risk of error from incorrect use. Even if the simple mechanical discounting functions in programs such as Lotus 1-2-3 and IFPS are used, the way the initial year is treated by the program—as year zero or year one—can distort results by 5 percent to 20 percent, depending on the firm's cost of capital (see Chapter 16).

Many information centers are taking creative approaches to justification. For instance, Bloomingdale's will often give loans to applicants when it doubts the payoff from an application. (28) It will require a use log to be kept for six months, at which time it will review the application. These creative approaches should become more common in the future, as information centers become more comfortable with their basic justification processes.

Acceleration and Control

One fundamental decision is whether to promote the growth of user computing actively, whether to control its growth carefully, or whether to take a position in between. To a considerable extent, this decision stems from the corporation's stance on the justification issue.

In explaining the results from interviews with 40 managers in 10 organizations, (31) Munro and Huff drew the matrix shown as Figure 3-9. According to this matrix, acceleration and control are independent dimensions, so that firms can be high on both dimensions, low on both, or high on one and low on the other.

A Laissez-Faire Beginning

Munro and Huff found that all firms started with both low acceleration and low control. They call this the laissez-faire corner because the corporation is essentially letting end user computing alone, giving it neither significant support nor control. Munro and Huff point out that firms start here by definition, since this simply represents the absence of a corporate policy, and before end user computing becomes significant, there is no reason to create a corporate policy.

From the laissez-faire corner, firms tend to move either clockwise or counterclockwise, either becoming expansionist with little control or following a containment policy with strong control and little acceleration. Acceleration is normally pursued to spur overall corporate productivity, whereas a policy of restraint is adopted because of lack of resources, nervousness about high demand, the desire to limit risks, and the feeling that there is no need for acceleration, since end user computing is already spreading like a grass fire.

	Control High	Control Low
Acceleration High	Expansionist	Controlled growth
Acceleration Low	Laissez-faire	Containment

Source: Munro and Huff (1985).

FIGURE 3-9 MUNRO AND HUFF'S ACCELERATION VERSUS CONTROL MATRIX

Again, fundamental decisions made on the justification issue will greatly affect the choice.

Acceleration Tactics
Munro and Huff list several acceleration tactics.

- Promote information flow with newsletters, trainers, user groups, and good manuals.
- Subsidize costs to users or even give hardware and software free. (A number of firms subsidize personal purchases.)
- Speed the acquisition process and open a wide spectrum of good products to users doing acquisition.
- Provide good user support and assistance, with consulting, training, hotline assistance, and in general take responsibility for finding solutions to users' problems.

Control Tactics
The control tactics identified by Munro and Huff focus on controlling acquisition by restricting choices, using veto power in specific instances, and flatly forbidding certain forms of acquisitions. Sometimes, the goal is to restrict PCs in favor of mainframes, which is done by offering a broader range of software on the host and promoting the mainframe in other ways.

Combining Acceleration and Control
Again, it is important to note Munro and Huff's basic observation that support and control are not mutually exclusive but are independent dimensions. Some firms have rigid restrictions on what can be purchased and yet also turn to such acceleration tactics as providing extensive information center support and a broad range of excellent products within the domain of what can be purchased. From their observations, Munro and Huff believe that most firms will end up somewhere near the middle of the box, with moderate degrees of control and acceleration. The overall goal is not to speed up or slow down end user computing but to make a distinction between the things that make sense and those that do not and to do the things that make sense as rapidly as resources allow.

Chargeback

Support services can be financed in two basic ways: (1) offer services through overhead, not charging the individual user departments; and (2) use chargeback, in which the individual user department pays for the services it receives.

There is a growing trend toward the use of chargeback. In 1984, Leitheiser and Wetherbe (25) found that 48 percent of the information centers they sampled employed at least some form of chargeback. Sumner (39) found a similar degree of chargeback use in her sample, which was taken about the same time. There is a general, though undocumented, feeling that chargeback will become the normal way of financing information center services in the future.

Why Chargeback?

Hammond (17) argues that chargeback has several benefits. In general, it helps organizations understand their costs and plan for future costs. More specifically, it establishes that the information center is not a free resource, and it helps monitor and control usage, establish and demonstrate the value of the information center, perform capacity planning and projections, and determine productivity trends.

In 1985, Corning Glass's information center billed its users at the following rates. (40)

- Training and consulting at headquarters: $40 per hour per staff member used
- Road shows: $400 per person per day, plus expenses
- General consulting on site: $350

These costs are probably representative of what is being charged elsewhere. For instance, Security Pacific National Bank charges $200 per user per day for training. (4)

Developing a Costing Structure

To perform chargeback well requires cost analysis in the information center. Figure 3-10 shows a sample calculation. In this calculation, the staff member's salary is $30,000 per year. General statistics indicate that this person will work about 240 days per year, giving a per day cost of $125. To this cost must be added the cost of fringe benefits, including sick leave and insurance, which typically runs about 30 percent of salary, raising the cost of the staff member to $162 per day.

Chargeback must also pay for desk space, computers, training materials, and the other costs of running the office where the person works. In addition, it must pay for the management needed to support the person, as well as the secretaries and other clerical workers needed to make the person productive. These numbers must be computed accurately. Figure 3-10 uses a value of 50

Annual salary	$30,000
Divided by: workdays per year	240
Gives cost per working day	$125
Times: fringe benefit rate	30%
Gives fringe benefits per day	$37
Cost/day with fringe benefits	$162
Times: rate for other costs (work space, clerical help, management overhead, etc.)	50%
Gives other costs	$81
Total cost per working day	$243
Divided by: billable percentage	60%
Gives cost per billable day	$405

FIGURE 3-10 A SAMPLE COST CALCULATION

percent of personnel costs for illustrative purposes, bringing the cost of the person to $243 per working day.

Not all working time will be billable. If the person is a trainer, he or she can only train about two days a week. The rest of the time is spent learning the technology, creating teaching material, and simply waiting, which represents lost time when the training schedule is not completely filled. Consultants, in turn, cannot be working 100 percent of the time, or there will be excessive waiting during peak load periods. A careful evaluation of billable time must be done. In Figure 3-10, we assume that 60 percent of the staffer's time will be billable, giving a cost per billable day of $405 to cover the real cost of the person.

During the first year of billing, the goal will be to assess the basic assumptions made in the initial chargeback system. For each person, billable time must be carefully tracked, and this time must be broken down into time spent on specific types of projects and even specific projects. For support workers, time spent on billable projects in general and on specific projects and support people in particular must be tracked. All other costs must also be carefully monitored, especially equipment and training facility costs. This tracking system is difficult to follow and even more difficult to enforce, but without it, chargeback will always be suspect. In consulting firms, data collection is simply a normal fact of life.

In addition to developing parameters for the chargeback system, tracking highlights the profitability of various "lines of business" such as training, helping the information center understand when it is not cost effective to provide certain types of services internally.

After the first year or two under chargeback, clear measures of the information center's productivity can be quantified. This evaluation is important in justifying that the information center is doing a good job, is controlling its costs, and should be awarded more funding.

Nuances of Chargeback

Although chargeback is generally desirable, a number of subtle factors need to be taken into account.

For instance, it is probably best to offer certain services free, first because billing would be too burdensome, and second because it is in the corporation's best interests to encourage their use. For instance, Corning Glass does not charge for telephone calls to its hot desk. (40) This simplifies billing and encourages users to call when they have a problem instead of wasting hours on the answer to a simple question. In addition, "seed" projects are often handled free to promote end user computing in a specific targeted area.

Chargeback is very burdensome for new applications. When a department is starting end user computing in general, putting in new equipment, and developing some initial applications, the consulting time will be considerable, escalating the startup costs to the department. The information center management must decide whether all charges should be paid for startups, because these costs are certainly real, or whether startup departments should be subsidized initially. Chargeback can also be burdensome for other applications, but this reflects the real nature of startup costs for applications.

One issue is how to finance intrastructure activities such as evaluating new software or developing training modules. In some cases, where the activity can be traced to a specific line of business, for instance, training, the cost should be built directly into chargeback. But few firms charge for the evaluation of new software packages. This leads to the question of whether these general costs should be lumped together with the overhead costs used in chargeback billing or whether the firm as a whole should subsidize them.

More broadly, the firm needs to decide whether the information center should be completely self-sustaining or whether it should have "capital investment" from general funds during its growth stage. During growth phases, full absorption costing could strongly overcharge the early users, retarding growth. Even more mature information centers may have certain areas of high growth that would be retarded by full absorption costing.

Another issue is whether the information center should be able to run at a profit. In most cases, profits are returned to a general fund, but in other cases, profits allow the information center to invest in new resources. Of course, excessive profit would mean overcharging for services.

Chargeback can also distort decision making. For instance, if all chargeback for support is done during the year an application is created, users may find it advantageous to skimp on early development or even to use a mainframe instead of purchasing a PC in the initial year, even if long-term total costs are higher for a mainframe. Chargeback and purchasing are part of the broad issue of how end user computing should be financed in the organization.

Some firms "lease" personal computers and software to individual departments instead of requiring purchases, as a way of preventing first-year costs from distorting project decisions. A lease spreads costs evenly over the life of the project. Other firms put depreciation costs instead of cash payments in departmental budgets. This has the advantage of integrating departmental planning with the firm's overall method of accounting for the fact that capital purchases produce benefits over a long time period.

Other firms are not concerned with startup costs, since most departments are implementing a steady stream of new applications and intrastructure innovations. As a result, there is a uniform pattern of startup costs. Nevertheless, during budget crunches, charging PC and software purchases to single years gives a strong incentive to cut out new applications.

Finally, and most importantly, chargeback only makes sense if end user departments have flexibility in how they use their budgets. If they do not have the overall freedom to allocate spending within their overall budget, they will not be able to respond to training and unexpected consulting needs. Chargeback policy cannot be separated from the firm's overall budget-setting policy.

Not all costs are controllable. Many applications cannot be avoided, and the user department simply says so and gets whatever it needs added to its budget. In such cases, the advantages of chargeback disappear.

Should the Information Center Develop Applications?

One of the most hotly debated issues among information center managers is whether the information center should develop applications for users. Although this issue has already been discussed elsewhere in this book, this section pulls together the arguments for and against information center application development.

As discussed in the introduction to this chapter, application development is neither rare nor common. It is offered by a minority of information centers, but enough centers offer it that it cannot be dismissed as an oddity. In addition, as we will see below, there are some very strong reasons for doing application development. Thus, even if the practice is far from universal, it needs to be considered carefully.

Reasons for Not Offering Application Development?

Three reasons are commonly cited for not offering application development for users. The first is that it breeds dependency, while the information center's job is to breed self-reliance among end users. Although application development might make sense in a particular case, its long-term consequences are counterproductive. "Just one more time," many users plead after initial help. (22)

The second reason for not doing application development is resource constraints. Nearly all information centers operate on very tight budgets. If application development is done, the information center will have to cut off other services to users or support fewer users, unless there is a major increase in budget. (22) This is a major problem, and even information center directors that have done application development extensively and approve of it heartily cite this as a serious problem.

The third reason is philosophical. Early information centers were not aimed at a broad spectrum of applications but were focused on data processing applications. There was a long backlog of these applications, and the information center was seen as a way to reduce the backlog for simple jobs, thereby freeing programmers to develop other applications. To use information center time to develop applications would counteract this original purpose. Because the DP application backlog is not the major justification for information centers today, this argument should have far less force than it once did, but having been promulgated so long it is still potent. Interestingly, IBM, which long espoused the No Programming Orthodoxy, discusses application development as a part of its proposed management approach to end user computing. (19)

Reasons for Offering Application Development

There are several reasons for offering application development. One of the strongest is that it is far more efficient for the information center to do application development under many circumstances. Learning a package well takes at least six to twelve hours of instruction, plus hands-on exercises. In addition, even after a package is learned, users will not be very productive in their initial work. Thus, delegated development is likely to make sense if the end user will not engage in certain work extensively. If the user has a one-time need, the up-front investment is very difficult to justify. Moreover, many users are **intermittent users**, who only need to use a product every year or so. By the time they return after the first application, they will need extensive retraining, and they may even have to unlearn certain procedures if an updated version of the program is in use, if hardware has changed, or if the application exists on a host and the host authority has changed use procedures. Certainly, it is important to compare learning costs with other alternative approaches to developing one-time or infrequent applications. The argument also holds for the use of advanced and rarely used features, especially on host products that have many modules. Delegated development may be done on parts of a project that are particularly difficult.

Another reason for doing some development work is that many EUC languages can produce very inefficient and expensive programs on host computers. If the information center staff is active in application development, it may be able to save a great deal of money by producing midrange programs or at least by fine-tuning existing programs. (11)

Naomi Karten (22) offers a number of other reasons for doing application development. The first is that many users are not able to do things themselves. She characterizes many host products billed as fourth-generation languages as merely 3.35th generation languages that are very hard to use. Among her rules for when to do application development are to consider development if the software is not very user friendly, if the information center has not developed adequate training, or if processing is required on two computers.

Another consideration is that application development makes the information center more knowledgeable, both of their products and of user needs. As Karten says, "Would you feel comfortable with a vendor hotline where the vendor's solution to your problem is accompanied by "Trust me, I've heard it works this way?'" In addition, by knowing users better, the information center is able to anticipate their future needs.

Strategically, one of the most important reasons for doing development, especially for senior executives, is the effect of development work on the image of the information center. Dawn Lepore, who manages the information center for Charles Schwab, put it this way. (24)

> Quite honestly, you have to do these things if you are going to make your information center a success. . . . Otherwise, you are just perceived as a small testing and training organization, or as someone who coordinates the purchase of PCs.

Guidelines

For information centers that have decided not to rule out application development, the question to be faced is *when* to do it. Every situation will be different, but the key issue is to determine when it is cheaper for the information center or someone else to handle application development. If the cost of application development by the information center is much less than the cost of direct user development and if the learning that the user would go through does not seem justified in terms of future uses, application development probably needs to be done.

When to do application development will also be dependent on the way the information center is financed. If chargeback is used for application development, and if the corporation has a rational approach for doing departmental budgeting, it should probably be left up to individual departments whether to do purchase application development services. This is especially true in corporations that have a strong philosophy of management decentralization. Managerial decentralization is impossible without the freedom to spend budgets in ways the manager deems proper.

In any case, application development should not be considered the normal form of application support. It should be backed by a firm philosophy of requiring users to become more and more self-sufficient. Even if a user is given a menu-driven application based on a microcomputer DBMS, the person should probably be required to take some training. For instance, he or she should learn how to use the computer and operating system, and perhaps also learn the DBMS's simpler commands, if there is any indication that the DBMS will be used in other ways in the future.

Although we have focused on whether the *information center* should do the development, Rockart and Flannery (34) have demonstrated that delegated development by end users for other end users is a normal process and may even be the most prevalent development practice. After developing a philosophy of when delegated development should be done, the policies discussed later for using end user functional specialists or outside consultants need to be set.

PLANNING

Planning is the most universal job of managers. It is also the hardest. There are never enough funds to support everything, so managers have to make tough decisions about what will not be done.

Priorities need to be set on the basis of realities—especially user needs, but also technical realities and broader organizational realities. A "plan" that merely adds a few programs to what is already being done is no plan at all in today's rapidly changing environment.

Some general planning principles must be mastered in both annual planning and in the initial planning to start an information center. We will look at these general principles, and then turn to the specific work needed to establish an information center and to do its annual planning.

Planning Principles

Figure 3-11 illustrates the general planning process. We will examine the main parts of this figure and then discuss the process that links them together.

The Mission

At the broadest level is the overall mission of the planning unit. Like any good definition, it declares that certain work falls outside the unit, and other work within its province.

Specific Goals

The mission statement only gives broad direction. The unit also needs to set specific measurable goals to give it concrete direction for the next planning period.

FIGURE 3-11 THE GENERAL PLANNING PROCESS

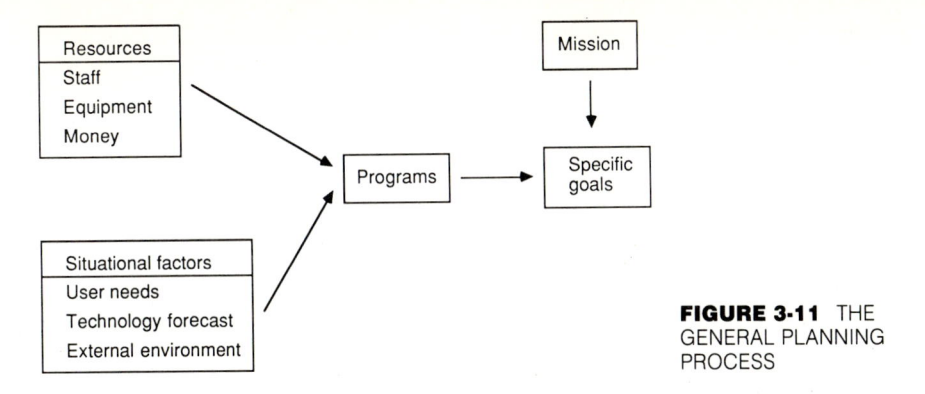

Measurability is critical. Among the goals are "train 50 users each month," "hire three more people," "reduce average response time on the host by an eighth of a second," or "reduce the ratio of users to information center staff members by 10 percent." Although it is useful to begin with such soft objectives as "improve relationships with top management," specific measurable goals need to be generated.

In a well-run organization, attaining goals is the basis for evaluating the unit and its managers. For example, for a manager to get an excellent performance review, he or she may need to meet a certain percentage of goals. Ideally, bonuses should be awarded if most or all goals are met.

User Needs

Another part of the diagram shows three **situational factors** that need to be understood and taken into account in creating the plan. The first of these is **user needs.** (Chapter 2 discussed the techniques needed to assess user needs.)

User needs change constantly in end user computing, people shift among market segments, and new market segments keep appearing. Although holding a few meetings with key people may identify gross changes and major unserved needs, a finer degree of user needs assessment is required in such a rapidly changing arena. Even holding a few meetings is better than nothing.

An end user computing plan that is not based on recent direct contacts with users is unacceptable. "We meet with users every day" does not do the job either, since few of these casual encounters produce directed information exchange and since not all end users contact the staff equally.

Technology Forecast

The technology forecast should begin with some price forecasts for hardware and software already being offered. Prices for PCs, per hour charges for the host, transmission costs, and networking charges should all be placed on a per unit basis and then aggregated up to total spending estimates.

The forecast also needs to reflect changing configuration mixes to be credible. If a larger percentage of PCs delivered next year will be ATs, for instance, the forecast must be made on the basis of the expected mix.

New products also have to be factored into the picture. Because there will not be an existing user base for these products, forecasting will be more tentative.

Ideally, the information center will build a demand model, based on user desires and a complete history of technology and costs, which will offer two or three years of data to help in forecasting. Not many information centers, however, are likely to go all the way to price elasticity and econometric modeling.

The demand forecast is critical to corporate capital planning, because end user computing represents a significant fraction of total capital spending. The finance department may be able to help in the forecasting work and may even do the bulk of it, relying on the information center primarily for price estimates and configuration mix estimates.

During the initial establishment of the information center, the kinds of data needed for detailed annual forecasting will not be available, but a major initial objective should be the establishment of the needed data base.

External Environment

The preferences and constraining influences of three groups external to the information center need to be taken into account in planning.

The closest of these groups is the **information systems (IS)** department as a whole. Although the information center will play a role in such decisions as whether to adopt SNA or OSI as a data communications framework (see Chapter 15), it will only be one voice among many. Once basic technical decisions are made, they determine the range of actions that the center's staff can take.

Since budgeting and planning are inherently top-down activities in practice, the information center will be competing for resources with other, often much larger, IS units. Senior IS management will mediate internal allocations and will also have to fight for additional resources with senior management. Obviously, it is important to get IS management behind the information center's efforts.

It is also critical to *listen* to the guidance that IS management gives on its vision of the information center. IS management is concerned with overall IS planning, and its broad vision needs to mesh with information center planning. Although some decisions may be best for end user computing, IS management may choose other alternatives to fit broader needs.

A second external group is **corporate management.** Although information center management understands technology and the needs of individual users, corporate management needs to balance end user computing needs against other corporate needs and against the general condition of the corporation. Corporate management will also dictate whether end user computing will be judged on the basis of efficiency, effectiveness, or innovation, using the taxonomy of benefits discussed earlier in this chapter.

A third set of external groups includes unions and governmental agencies. These will set ergonomic standards, privacy regulations, and other constraints on the information center.

During planning, the information center staff needs to understand the requirements of each of these external groups and to anticipate any major changes in their requirements.

Programs

Based on its objectives on the one hand and user needs, technology, and the external environment on the other hand, the information center must decide what to do.

We will use the general term "programs" to describe the actions the center will take, including service offerings, research projects, and numerous other actions.

Each program should be linked to one or more of the information center's goals, and it should be molded by user needs, the technology forecast, and environmental factors.

Resources

The last piece in the picture is **resources.** There are three basic resources in any organization: **staff, equipment,** and **money.** Generally, money is the basic measure of resource, but organizations usually have separate controls over headcount and equipment purchases, as well as a few other elements such as office space.

Balancing the Pieces

Needs, technology, the environment, objectives, resources, and programs are not separate concerns. Rather, they are six simultaneous equations that must be solved jointly to come up with a solution. Unlike simultaneous equations, however, these factors cannot be solved by some well-defined mathematical procedure. Instead, they are balanced by political negotiations.

The information center tries to create objectives that mirror the demands of user needs, technology, and the environment. It then proposes a number of programs as well as the resources it feels these programs demand.

Higher management is not likely to approve everything. It may counterpropose a lower level of resources that will force certain objectives to be dropped, and it is likely to suggest that most programs could be handled with fewer resources.

During the planning and budgeting period, the information center and senior management try to reach a common accord on resources, programs, and objectives, and the end result is normally a compromise of different views.

Measurement and Feedback

Once a plan is accepted, the real work begins—implementing the plan. Unless the staff is strongly behind the plan, implementation will be very difficult. As a result, information center management should involve the staff early, so that it will feel that it "owns" the resultant plan or at least was party to the compromises it dislikes. Since information center staffers tend to have strong personalities, "participative management" is both difficult and essential.

Management should also communicate strategically. U.S. organizations tend to communicate only what the next lowest level needs to know, but Japanese firms believe that the lower one goes in the corporation, the *more* one needs to communicate strategically. People at the top learn overall strategy by osmosis, whereas people at lower levels need to be cultivated if the core strategy is to be kept on course.

Feedback

Figure 3-11 shows one element we have not looked at until now. Engineers call it **feedback.** Management theorists call it **accountability.**

During the year, either goals will be met or they will not. Since goals are supposed to be measurable, it should be possible to tell whether they are met. In well-managed organizations, bonuses and other rewards are linked closely to objectives. This is called **management by objectives,** or **MBO.**

To work well, MBO must be accompanied by considerable freedom for managers. You cannot tell managers what color paper clips to use or sharply limit how they can spend their budgets and then hold them accountable. This makes true MBO very dangerous because, unless accountability is strictly enforced, the combination of budgetary freedom and lack of imposed overall discipline can lead to disastrous results.

If objectives are not established, then one or more changes need to be made during the next planning and budgeting period:

- Objectives can be scaled back.
- Resources can be increased.
- The unit can be made more efficient in using its resources.

Again, human judgment is needed to decide which of these three alternatives should be pursued. Dropping objectives will hurt other parts of the organization that need the information center's services. Increasing resources is expensive and may not even be fruitful if the unit is inherently inefficient. Finally, deeming a unit inefficient is demoralizing. When objectives are not met, action has to be taken, but there is no easy solution. Making such tough calls is a basic function of management, and it is certainly the least pleasant.

Without feedback, planning makes little sense. Yet in many organizations, perhaps a majority, there is little or no feedback on the attainment of specific goals. Without the accountability this provides, planning becomes little more than an elaborate ritual.

On the positive side, an information center that creates specific objectives and publishes its successes and failures will soon get a reputation for being well managed. A good feedback system will help the information center when top management reviews its budget. Although cost/benefit analysis is admirable, a good deal of budgeting is still done on the basis of perceived trustworthiness.

Planning and Budgeting

Up to now, we have not distinguished between "planning" and "budgeting," but the two are very different.

- **Planning** is used to refer to broad decision making about what should be done. Price tags are set but not in detail. The goal is to get the "big picture" right.
- **Budgeting,** in contrast, refers to the detailed work of establishing specific, detailed budgets and tracking actual spending. Planning is done first, with most arguments being considered at a high level of abstraction. Then, detailed budgeting is done on the basis of planning decisions.

If organizations skip one of these steps, it is usually planning, with the result that budgeting is made primarily on the basis of the previous year's budget instead of on more global considerations.

Because planning and budgeting systems deal with such radically different levels of data aggregation, many organizations now have separate computerized planning and budgeting systems, with the planning system used initially and its rough output put into a more detailed budgeting system. Trying to do planning with a computerized budgeting system's detail is extremely impractical.

The Planning Study

Today, most large corporations have information centers, but a few do not, and quite a few smaller organizations have not yet established information centers. In addition, the steps that are required to establish an information center essentially need to be repeated each year, although in much less detail.

Proposal for a Planning Study

The first step in creating an information center is to do a planning study that will help build the information center on a solid foundation of knowledge. The study period will be short, only four to eight weeks. Yet during that time, it will be possible to collect much of the information that is available for easy collection in the firm.

Before the study is undertaken, a proposal to do it must be formulated. This proposal will first, provide the money to do the work; second, legitimize the project, and thereby lessen the chance that the study team's working time will be shunted off to other projects; and third and most importantly, establish lines of communication with IS management and upper corporate management.

This communication will work both ways. First, it will educate IS and corporate management briefly in the importance of end user computing and in the importance of information centers. The arguments made in Chapter 1 and to a lesser extent in this chapter will help the proposer build a strong initial case for information centers to manage end user computing.

Second, the communication will give management a chance to indicate what it expects to see from the study and to indicate its initial reaction to end user computing. If top management stresses the importance of tough empirical cost/benefits analysis in end user computing and in information center support, then minimal form of support is likely to result, and planning for full-support information centers is not likely to be fruitful. If top management instead stresses the need to support radical ongoing or planned corporate changes, then the information center will have a very different role.

Information Gathering

After funding and staffing for the planning study are approved, the data gathering begins. (The analysis of end user needs is discussed in Chapter 2.) The purpose of assessing needs is to help set priorities and uncover unusual applications. For instance, a study done for a hospital found that staff scheduling and PC-host links were unusually strong needs, which indicated that the information center would have to be a leader in these two areas.

A technological forecast, in turn, will try to predict cost trends, integration trends, and significant turning points such as shifts from XT-generation PCs to 80286 and 80386 generation machines. The technological forecast should provide a basis for predicting what applications are likely to flower and what services will be needed to support these applications.

In addition to studying user needs and technology, the study team needs to understand corporate directions. The corporate strategic plan, the IS strategic plan, and knowledge about large changes such as major reorganizations are all critical inputs. For instance, if a subsidiary is likely to be sold in the near future, investing heavily to serve its particular needs is not likely to be productive. In addition, the study team has to understand the company's basic management philosophies. If the company places a high premium on decentralized decision making and decision making by lower managers, the information center is not likely to be able to impose strict controls over individual choices.

By the end of the information-gathering phase, the information center should have a good understanding of the priorities with which the information center will need to attack problems and opportunities. To a lesser degree, it should also be able to specify the likely demand for end user computing, including how many users will need to be served and how much capital spending will need to be budgeted to support end user computing.

The Charter

The next stage in the planning study should be to develop an information center charter to present with the study results. A charter has three purposes. First, it establishes the information center's sphere of responsibility. Second, it specifies how the fundamental decisions listed toward the start of this chapter will be settled. Third, it lays out the relative responsibilities of the information center and of users.

The charter should distinguish between the work of the information center and the work of other organizations within IS. As discussed earlier in this chapter, the information center should serve most or all needs in Type II (managerial and professional) office departments. Demarcation should not be based on small versus large applications, because this would muddy the information center's responsibilities for mid-range applications of the third environment and the fifth environment of department computing.

The charter itself will not describe the specific services to be offered, but it will specify the relative roles of PCs and host computers, chargeback philosophies, whether application development will be done, and other far-reaching decisions that need to be made through broad policies to prevent endless debates later.

Hammond (17) emphasizes that the relative roles of end users and the information center should be laid out as general commitments which each agrees to make. For instance, Hammond states that users must commit themselves to doing most or all of their own development work, whereas the information center must commit itself to ensuring that the data needed in an application will be ready as needed. The metaphor of commitments is a very powerful way to phrase the relative roles of end users and the information center.

Specific Services and Internal Tasks

Along with the charter, the proposal should list initial services to be provided. It is important not to bite off more than the information center can chew during its first chaotic year. A relatively short list of services should be proposed, along with a step-by-step plan for implementing each. Implementation will consist of detailed needs analysis for the particular service, selecting hardware and software, developing training, doing the technical and organizational pilots discussed earlier in the chapter, promoting the service broadly, and, finally, rolling it out widely. The proposal should also include the internal tasks needed to staff and administer the information center. During the initial year, a great deal of time will be spent on internal matters.

Staffing and Budgeting

Based on the work to be performed and external studies of how many end users an information staffer can support on the average, the proposal next projects the staff and budget needed to implement the planned work.

It is important to develop full budget estimates. Obviously, there are direct salaries, but there are also fringe benefits, overhead of various types, office space, equipment, renovation, telephone charges, travel costs, supplies, clerical workers, and everything else that goes into the budget of a department. The salaries of the main professionals rarely constitute much more than 60 percent of total costs.

In staffing, job descriptions should be laid out, so that appropriate pay levels can be established. The personnel department will probably have to complete this part of the proposal.

Accountability and Oversight

The information center will need to establish ground rules for accountability. These may include key ratios such as the number of users trained during the years, performance measures such as the average time to respond to user requests for help, and user satisfaction surveys. Although it will be impossible to set very detailed targets initially, it will be critical for the information center to identify key measurements to assess its importance and to collect data on these indicators.

Part of accountability is the establishment of oversight mechanisms to make sure that the information center stays on course. IS management will provide direct oversight, but it also seems highly advisable to establish an **oversight committee** to make sure that clients are also represented in assessing the information center's importance. Many organizations already have oversight committees for IS as a whole. The information center oversight role can be assigned to such a committee, but if this is done, the balance of committee members should be adjusted to reflect the reality that end user computing will represent the bulk of corporate computing in the future.

Organization of the Proposal

There are no hard and fast rules for organizing the proposal and the plan it creates, but Hammond suggests a format that covers most of the items an organization is likely to consider important. (17)

General Statements (Examples)

Creating an environment to assist people to use personal computer products.

Defining the cooperative interface between the information center (I/C) and project teams.

Planning expansion based on usage and user input.

Providing ongoing advice and consulting to personnel using the I/C so they can make financially justified use of the facility.

Developing and maintaining a strategic statement for the usage of the I/C environment.

"Marketing" the I/C within the organization.

Source: Hammond (1982).

FIGURE 3-12 HAMMOND'S ELEMENTS OF A MISSION STATEMENT

First, he recommends a **mission statement** of no more than three "typed, moderately spaced" pages. This statement includes a general mission, steps to be taken, and criteria for work appropriate to the information center. Figure 3-12 illustrates some of the elements he suggests including under these headings.

Second, he recommends the creation of a more detailed **overall operating plan** with these sections:

- Background and mission
- Terms and definitions
- Roles and responsibilities
- Strategic direction
- Education
- Data security and availability
- Package selection
- Packages supported
- Potential package support
- Accountability for usage
- Chargeback considerations.

This overall operating plan will serve as a reference for anyone in the organization who wants to understand the information center. It lays out what the center does, the specific elements supported, and the conditions for getting support. Although Hammond's general organization seems oriented to the particular needs of host-oriented information centers, it illustrates the kind of information needed and clarity of organization.

The Presentation

After the proposal is completed, it should be delivered in written form, and there should also be a full face-to-face presentation of the results. The presentation should cover needs, the proposed charter, proposed fundamental decisions on key policies, specific services to be offered and other work to be done, the staffing, budget, and other resources needed to implement the plan, and, finally, the accountability indicators to be used to judge the performance of the information center.

After the presentation, IS management and senior management are likely to deliver certain caveats on the results, ranging from wholesale scaledowns in what will be provided to modest guidance on priorities and how quickly solid results are expected to appear. If the information center wishes to retain management backing over the years, this management direction needs to be followed or additional dialogue needs to take place if certain management directions seem likely to produce real harm.

Annual Planning

Annual planning has much in common with strategic planning. It differs strongly, however, in detail and in a stress on shorter term considerations. Annual planning contains much greater detail because a basis of experience and data are now available. Shorter term thinking is likely to be more the case because only a few fundamental decisions have to be rethought each year and because technological forecasts probably need only minor modifications from those of previous years.

Data and Forecasting

The information center's data base on how it is using its own resources and what other resources end users need should be a boon to corporate resource planning. As individual departments become more adept at capacity and application planning, the information center's consolidation of these plans should become even more valuable in overall corporate planning.

With good data, the information center should be able to forecast its own budgetary needs and user capacity needs in the coming year. Since resources will constrain demand, these forecasts represent not a classic demand forecast but tradeoffs between user needs, corporate priorities, and planned additions to services.

It may even be necessary and desirable to set overall goals for capacity increases for major corporate units, say the number of PCs to be purchased in specific divisions. It is questionable, however, whether so much power will be delegated to the information center. It seems more likely that the corporate planning and budgeting officer will use information center inputs but retain these decisions in its own shop.

The Annual Report

In addition to planning for services and budgets, the annual planning process should produce an overall report for the preceding year. This report should emphasize successes, particularly if outstanding case studies can be found and documented. Although cost savings speak for themselves, many of the higher level benefits of end user computing can only be communicated well through minicases that show the benefits possible in practical situations.

The report should also present data on the main accountability indicators agreed on to measure information center performance. Goals met or not met, favorable or unfavorable changes in key ratios, and other quantitative information need to be presented.

CONCLUSION

Before an information center can turn its attention to day-to-day business, it needs to confront a number of broad concerns that will influence its basic philosophy. Many of the specific policy decisions discussed in the next chapter require that more fundamental decisions be made on these broad concerns.

At the broadest level, the information center needs to decide what services to offer, anticipate its problems, and determine what actions will be most critical to its success. These three issues of service, problems, and critical success factors will vary as the information center moves through its life cycle from its embryonic beginnings, through its rapid growth, and finally to its steady state or decline.

Next, the information center must decide a number of fundamental issues, including the following.

- When should PCs or hosts be used?
- How should project justification be done?
- Should the center try to accelerate EUC, control it, or both?
- How should the information center be financed?
- Should the center develop applications for users?

These issues cannot be decided individually. The information center must have a well-conceived strategic plan to place everything else in perspective. The last section of this chapter discussed the creation of a planning study to develop a long-term strategic plan. Such a study would be done when starting a new information center. Since the environment is changing so rapidly, a planning study should also be conducted every two or three years. Of course, the information center must also develop its annual plans to guide its operations and decisions during the following years.

REVIEW QUESTIONS

1. In what life cycle stage do you think most information centers are today? What problems will be raised by the transition to the next stage?
2. What are the main services provided by information centers? The main problems of information centers? The critical success factors of information centers? Draw data from the chapter to give your answer, but also give your own judgment.
3. What are the relative advantages of hosts and PCs? Why are the tradeoffs between using PCs and hosts likely to be reduced in the future?
4. How should justification be done for individual applications?

5. Should the information center's role be to accelerate end user computing, control it, or both?
6. How should the information center be financed? Include a discussion of when chargeback should be done.
7. Should the information center develop applications for users? If so, under what circumstances and using what procedures?
8. Describe the general planning process.
9. Describe the planning study and the annual planning effort.

REFERENCES

1. American Management Association, *1985 AMA Report on Information Centers,* American Management Association, New York, 1985, cited in Crwth Computer Coursewares, "The Second Crwth lnformation Center Survey," *Crwth News for Better Training,* Vol. 3, No. 1, 1985.
2. BENSON, DAVID H., "A Field Study of End User Computing: Findings and Issues," *MIS Quarterly,* December 1983, pp. 35-45.
3. BRANCHEAU, JAMES C., VOGEL, DOUGLAS R., AND WETHERBE, JAMES C., "An Investigation of the Information Center from the User's Perspective," *Data Base,* Fall 1985, pp. 4-17.
4. BRYANT, SUSAN, "Security Pacific National Bank," *PC Week,* November 26, 1985, pp. 59-62.
5. *Business Week,* "Business Week Special Report, Office Automation Restructures Business, October 8, 1984, cited in IBM, *The Management of End-User Computing: Justification,* First Edition, January 1985.
6. Computer Intelligence Corporation, *Information Center Market: CI Special IC Manager Survey,* July 1985.
7. COX, WILLIAM E., JR., "Product Life Cycles as Marketing Models," *Journal of Business,* October, 1967, pp. 375-384.
8. Crwth Computer Coursewares, "The Second Crwth Information Center Survey," *Crwth News for Better Training,* Vol. 3, No. 1, 1985.
9. DANIEL, D. R., "Management Information Crisis," *Harvard Business Review,* October 1961, pp. 111-121.
10. The Diebold Group, *Survey of MIS Budgets,* New York, 1985, cited in Crwth Computer Coursewares,"The Second Crwth Information Center Survey," *Crwth News for Better Training,* Vol. 3, No. 1, 1985.
11. *EDP Analyzer,* "Supporting End User Programming," June 1981.
12. GERWIN, D., "Do's and Don'ts of Computerized Manufacturing," *Harvard Business Review,* March-April 1982, pp. 107-116.
13. GIBSON, CYRUS F. AND NOLAN, RICHARD L., "Managing the Four Stages of EDP Growth," *Harvard Business Review,* January-February 1974, pp. 76-88.
14. GUIMARAES, TOR, "The Evolution of the Information Center," *DATAMATION,* July 15, 1984, pp. 127-130.
15. GUTTMAN, MICHAEL K., "American Medical International," *PC Week,* November 5, 1985, pp. 63-66.
16. HALL-SHEEHY, JIM, "Some Justification Is Better Than None," *Information Center,* May 1986, pp. 22-25.

17. HAMMOND, L. W., "Management Considerations for an Information Center," *IBM Systems Journal*, Vol. 21, No. 2, 1982, pp. 131-161.
18. HENDERSON, JOHN C., AND TREACY, MICHAEL E., "Managing End-User Computing for Competitive Advantage," *Sloan Management Review*, Winter 1986, pp. 3-14.
19. IBM, *The Management of End-User Computing: Support Organization*, First Edition, IBM Corporation, White Plains, New York, October 1984.
20. IBM *The Management of End-User Computing: Justification*, First Edition, January 1985.
21. JENKINS, AVERY, "'Rust Bowl' Behemoth Uses PCs to Keep Budgets Low, Creativity High," *PC Week*, July 16, 1985, pp. 45-47.
22. KARTEN, NAOMI, "Confessions of a Code Writer," *Information Center*, May 1986, pp. 62-64.
23. KING, JOHN LESLIE, AND KRAEMER, KENNETH L., "Evolution and Organizational Information Systems: An Assessment of Nolan's Stage Model," *Communications of the ACM*, May 1984, pp. 466-485.
24. LAPLANTE, ALICE, "Dealing with Top Management," *InfoWorld*, June 9, 1986, pp. 31-32.
25. LEITHEISER, ROBERT L., AND WETHERBE, JAMES C., "A Survey of Information Centers: Services, Decisions, Problems, Successes," Management Information Systems Research Center, School of Management, University of Minnesota, Minneapolis, Minnesota, 1984.
26. LEVITT, THEODORE, "Exploit the Product Life Cycle," *Harvard Business Review*, November-December 1965, pp. 81-94.
27. LITTMAN, JONATHAN, "PCs Fill a Vacancy at Holiday Inn," *PC Week*, July 30, 1985, pp. 41-53.
28. MANDELL, PATRICIA, "Surviving the Retail Downturn in PC Style," *PC Week*, July 23, 1985, pp. 33-36.
29. MCCARTNEY, LATON, "The New Info Centers," *DATAMATION*, July 1983, pp. 30-46.
30. MELYMUKA, KATHLEEN, "The Information Center," *PC Week*, December 3, 1985, pp. 77-79.
31. MUNRO, MALCOM C. AND HUFF, SID L., "Information Technology Assessment and Adoption: Understanding the Information Center Role," *Proceedings of the Twenty-First Annual Computer Personnel Research Conference*, co-sponsored with Business Data Processing, Association for Computing Machinery, May 2-3, 1985, pp. 29-37.
32. RICHARDSON, PETER R., AND GORDON, JOHN R. M, "Measuring Total Manufacturing Performance," *Sloan Management Review*, Winter 1980, pp. 47-58.
33. ROCKART, JOHN F., "Chief Executives Define their Own Data Needs," *Harvard Business Review*, March-April 1979, pp. 81-93.
34. ROCKART, JOHN F. AND FLANNERY, LAUREN S., "The Management of End User Computing," *Communications of the ACM*, October 1983, pp. 776-784.
35. ROGERS, EVERETT M., *Diffusion of Innovations*, New York: Free Press, 1962.
36. RUBY, DANIEL, "Grumman's Productive PCs," *PC Week*, August 20, 1985, pp. 33-36.
37. RUBY, DANIEL, AND CALL, BARBARA, "Micros at the Mill," *PC Week*, December 24, 1985, pp. 25-31.
38. SASSONE, PETER G., *Cost Benefit Analysis for Office Information Systems*, College of Management, Georgia Institute of Technology, May 1984, cited in IBM, *The Management of End-User Computing: Justification*, First Edition, January 1985.

39. SUMNER, MARY, "Organization and Management of the Information Center: Case Studies," *Proceedings of the Twenty-First Annual Computer Personnel Research Conference,* co-sponsored with Business Data Processing, Association for Computing Machinery, May 2-3, 1985, pp. 29-37.
40. WHITE, LEE, "End User Computing Is Transparent at Corning Glass," *Computerworld Focus,* October 16, 1985, pp. 51-54.
41. ZARLEY, CRAIG, "Wendy's International, Inc., *PC Week,* February 4, 1986, pp. 29-33.
42. ZARLEY, CRAIG, "SmithKline Beckman," *PC Week,* December 10, 1985, pp. 49-52.

4 BUILDING THE INFORMATION CENTER

Now that we have presented a broad discussion of the management of end user computing, we can turn to the nuts and bolts of creating the information center. We will look at these specific topics.

- Organizing the information center
- Staffing the center
- Mobilizing end users
- Promotion
- Developing a technological infrastructure
- Creating key policies

ORGANIZATION

Firms must take a number of steps to organize an information center, including deciding where to place the center organizationally, formalizing its role relative to other organizational units, and obtaining office space. Although some of these are one-time activities, others need to be redone or at least reexamined every time a new round of strategic planning is completed.

Placement in the Organization

Nearly everyone agrees that the information center needs to be a distinct organizational unit. If it is not, two consequences are possible. (20) First, its staff will be constantly pulled from end user support to fight DP fires. Second, it will not have the identity in users' minds that must be created if users are to come to it for support. The question, then, is how to organize this unit once the need for a separate organizational unit has been identified.

In most organizations, the information center is placed under the information systems (IS) department. A 1985 survey by Computer Intelligence Corporation found that 86 percent of all information centers fell under IS, with another 4 percent under finance, 4 percent under administration, and a final 5 percent under the "other" category. (6) As technological issues multiply in the future, it seems likely that the IS department will become even more dominant.

Saying that the information center is likely to fall under IS however, tells only part of the picture. In many organizations, the relationship of the information center to the rest of the IS organization is muddled or was at least established without much clear thought. We will look at major alternatives for information center roles. Before we look at specific roles, however, we need to discuss the historical evolution of IS, and to understand where the information center is likely to find its best niche.

The Classic Infrastructure

When information technology began to appear in business in the late 1960s and early 1970s, its management was scattered across the firm, as indicated in Figure 4-1. (This figure and the general flow of this section of the book derive from two papers by Panko and Sprague.) (38,39)

Data processing was normally handled by the corporate controller. Telecommunications was under a telecommunications administrator who was often subordinate to the facilities manager because the biggest issue in telephony was where to run the wires and place the wiring closet. Office products fell into two categories: (1) specialized office products such as word processing center machines and centralized duplicators, and (2) general office products such as typewriters. Both types of office products were usually handled by the administrative vice president, although they were often managed independently.

This schizophernic infrastructure made sense in those early days. The technology of computers had little in common with the technology of telephones, typewriters, or duplicators. System development details were also radically different, and prices had little in common. Perhaps most impor-

Product/Service	Authority	Vendors	Users
Data Processing			
Transaction processing	VP of data	IBM	Accounting
Fixed format reports	processing	Digital	Inventory
Specialized Office Products			
Mailroom equipment	Administra-	Kodak	Mailroom
Duplicators	tive VP	3M	WP center
Microfilm			
WP center equipment			
General Office Products			
Copiers	Administra-	Xerox	Most
Typewriters	tive VP	IBM	offices
Telecommunications			
Telex	Facilities	AT&T	Telex,
Telephones	Manager	GT&E	Most
PBXs			offices

FIGURE 4-1 THE CLASSIC INFRASTRUCTURE

tantly, most offices served by these technologies were Type I clerical departments (see Chapter 1) that needed only one major technology, so integration was a nonissue.

Paradigm Lost

During the 1970s and early 1980s, the factors that had selected for a fragmented infrastructure gave way to forces selecting for integration. The technology of MIS, office automation, and even telecommunications began to be similar in technical content, price, and development disciplines. Products also began to cut freely across previously defined lines of demarcation, making it difficult to decide where to place them. Perhaps most importantly, information technology began to penetrate into Type II managerial and professional offices (see Chapter 1), where needs cut freely across traditional product boundaries, making traditional product-based distinctions not just obsolete but positively misleading. This mismatch between products and Type II office needs was brought into sharp focus when personal computers began to appear, offering analysis, data management, word processing, graphics, and other services long viewed as being under different management realms.

By the late 1970s, researchers and practitioners discussed the need to develop integrated management approaches, under the banner of information resource management (IRM). Although the IRM name largely failed to catch on, most large firms had integrated their IS management under a single IS department by the mid-1950s.

Differentiation

Once the IS department was created, a new basis for differentiation needed to be created. There were too many people to treat as a unit, especially since many had specialized technical backgrounds.

Figure 4-2 illustrates a typical outcome of the reorganization. Most of these boxes come straight from MIS and telecommunications, with systems development and computer operations mirroring the classical organization of these two units.

The last box, information center, has caused the most problems because it has integrated a number of disparate areas, specifically:

- Personal computing
- Time-shared data management, analysis, and graphics
- Office automation
- Executive information systems
- Decision support systems

Most of these activities grew out of traditional activities. Decision support systems (DSS) and host computing were spinoffs of MIS and operations research/management science, and office automation came from traditional clerical office products activities. Personal computing was a new area that tended to muddy the entire picture after its explosive emergence in the early 1980s.

We will call this box the information center because that is its most common title. But it is given many other titles in corporations, including the information resources center, the office services center, decision support, and

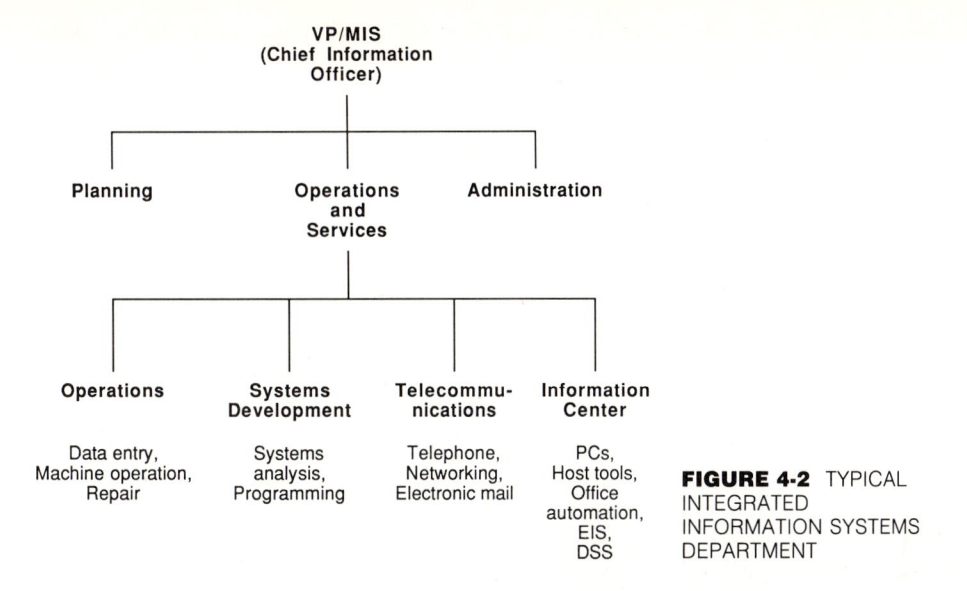

FIGURE 4-2 TYPICAL INTEGRATED INFORMATION SYSTEMS DEPARTMENT

office automation. The name is likely to reflect the traditional group having the most power at its formation.

The Gap

As shown in Figure 4-3, even this reorganization failed to address at least one of the major problems facing IS, namely, how to deliver its services to users. The classic integrated structure of 1980 did not speak to users with a unified voice. It was almost as if all producers in an industry had decided to build a

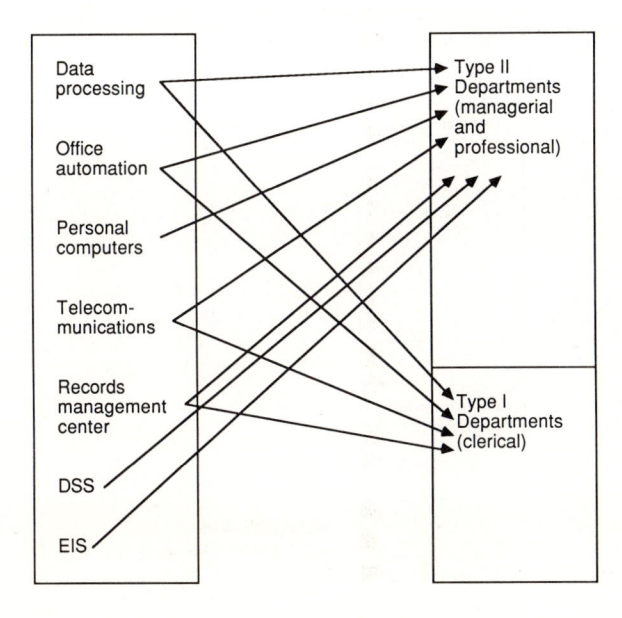

FIGURE 4-3 THE IS–USER GAP

monopoly but had forgotten to worry about marketing channels to deliver these products to consumers.

As a result, users in both Type I and Type II departments were still spoken to by a confusion of voices, each voice promoting and delivering a different service.

The Bridging Function

The information center's best role is to act as a bridging function, as shown in Figure 4-4. Its basic purpose is to bridge the gap between suppliers on the one hand and consumers on the other.

More specifically, we the information center is primarily a bridging function for Type II office needs. There are two bases for this argument. The first is that Type I office needs are still handled well by the traditional systems analysis role of MIS, so that only a few functions need to be added, such as user training. The information center can absorb these few functions without becoming deeply enmeshed with Type I office support.

Second, the integrated nature of needs in Type II offices requires an entirely new focal point for services. The functions that make up the information center—DSS, host computing, personal computing, electronic mail, and so on—are used mostly in Type II offices. The information center offers a way to serve all Type II office needs while speaking with a single voice. Our conclusion, then, is: **The information center is fundamentally the support arm for tools used in Type II nonclerical office departments.**

The Marketing Image

From the field of marketing, we can begin to draw possible roles for the information center. If Figure 4-4 were a marketing system, the information

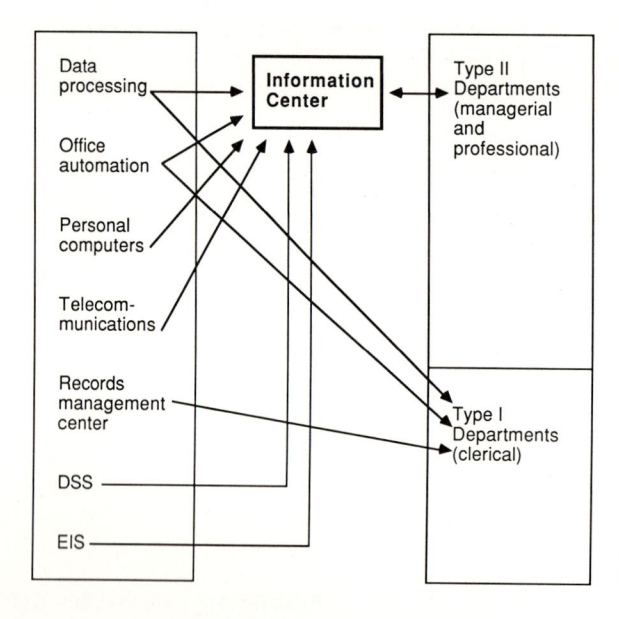

FIGURE 4-4
BRIDGING THE GAP

center would basically act as a wholesaler and retailer, delivering information technology to users in a way that fits their specific needs.

A retailer, for instance, has to target specific market segments with tailored "market mixes" employing product tailoring, service, pricing that reflects services offered, promotion, and delivery. In the same way, the information center may be able to deliver a number of different offers to different communities in the organization.

The retailer also has many other functions, including buying in bulk and then breaking bulk, installing, training, offering use advice, and many of the other tasks we now see being performed in information centers. Overall, the retailer idea offers many analogies that could be used to guide thinking about information centers. We have mentioned only a few here.

Before leaving the marketing image of the bridging function, we should note that most products reach consumers through multiple lines of distribution. Computer software, for instance, is sold directly by vendors, through dealers, and through mail order houses. Each channel offers some advantages, such as price or support, that will appeal to different people. Although few organizations have organized multiple information centers, it may be better to allow users to bypass the basic information centers to seek support from outside organizations instead of buying it internally.

The Contractor Image

Another image that might help guide our thinking about the information center is that of the contractor. Contractors take on a job, such as building a house. They delegate specific work such as plumbing to subcontractors, but they provide the integrative role, creating tailored systems for individual needs.

DSS has always performed such a role, producing systems tailored to specific decisions and specific decision makers. DSS has drawn together tools from three areas traditionally thought to be separate, including modeling, data management, and graphics—offering the user not a tool box but an integrated tool designed for a specific need.

The information center may also take the lead in developing complete integrated systems. When one IS manager saw the bridging function idea in Figure 4-4, he said, "Great, the information center can assess needs, then pass the user onto the appropriate tools organization." But a little reflection made him add, "Of course, that won't work at all if needs require more than one tool. You can't expect the tool people to be the integrator."

The contractor image actually has roots in the IS literature. As discussed in Chapter 1, delegated development has long been the norm in decision support systems.

The contractor image suggests that the information center may not be subordinate to the other IS components, and this may in fact be the case. Just as a contractor can turn to any supplier, the information center may be able to draw on outside resources, perhaps even if the same resource is available internally but at a higher price or with other undesirable service conditions.

If such independence is not built into the corporate information center, functional units are likely to build their own "wild information centers" that bypass the formal information center. Many of today's corporate information centers began life that way, and as long as users obeyed general policies on technology and good use practice, it would be difficult to stop functional units from developing their own contracting agencies.

Independence can also allow the information center to put pressure on other parts of IS to provide services in a certain way. IS has long been criticized for unresponsiveness to user desires, and although this criticism has generally been overstated, it remains true that few organizations have built specific mechanisms to allow users to put pressure on IS to act in certain ways. Building reasonable independence into the information center could provide this line of control.

The Information Center and Information Systems

The preceding paragraph raises the possibility that the information center has a role to play relative both to IS and to users. It has long been recognized that the information center should play a role in planning even such things as local area networks (LANs), which it will not control directly. For such broad infrastructure decisions, the information center must represent its constituents in deliberations.

In addition, the information center may be the first part of IS to develop strong competence in such tools as fourth-generation languages that will have applicability in operational systems. If it does not help the rest of IS adopt these tools, it may be missing a good part of its role in the firm. (23)

The Role of the Information Center: A Summary

To summarize this section, the information center's role is not as well defined or as obvious as it is often painted. We have sketched just a few possible images of how the information center can serve as the bridging function between IS and Type II office departments. Now that most organizations have established information centers based on thin conceptualizations of their roles, it seems time to explore a number of analogies to see what new possibilities they raise.

Work Space

One of the first steps in creating an information center once its role has been defined is the most prosaic: finding office space.

The IS department is often housed far from corporate headquarters and operating divisions. But the information center is a high visibility organization that needs to be located very near users if it is to be successful. Relatively few users will willingly travel several blocks to a warehouse location, and even several floors can be a hindrance. In addition, unless the center is located in a place where many people can see it, the promotional value of the physical center will be reduced.

An information center needs a good deal of working space. First, there must be offices for all professional staff members, secretaries, and other support workers. Because these people will have computers on their desks and will have to entertain visitors, each office must be large. The receptionist's placement is also important, since there will be many drop-in visitors.

The center will probably have both a demonstration area and an education area where machines will be placed. If the two are combined, users may find themselves unable to look at equipment when they drop in. The training area, discussed in the next chapter, needs to be large, especially if computer-based training enhanced by video presentations is to be implemented. In addition, if executives are to be trained there, nice furnishings and even private work spaces may be required. The demonstration area, in turn, should have ample room for people to walk around and sit comfortably in small groups around each system. There should also be sufficient acoustical treatment, so that people can work comfortably.

The center will need a conference room that will serve as both an enclosed demonstration area and a meeting place for small teams such as product evaluation teams. This room will need computer equipment to serve its purposes.

Many information centers have libraries with technical reference documents, popular magazines, rating service reviews of software and hardware, and even loanable software and computer-based and video-based training materials. This library will need space to hold these materials as well as for reading chairs and perhaps a computer and video machine for training or software evaluation.

Finally, a set-up and maintenance area is needed to handle new machines and machines being repaired. Although this area can be located away from the main site, room is needed at the center itself for a repair person on site as well as some light inventory of test equipment and commonly needed components.

STAFFING

Staffing involves two basic considerations: how many people to have, and what kind of people to get.

Staff Size

IBM recommends one staff member for every 50 or so end users. More precisely, IBM recommends the following staffing. (22)

- 500 : 1 Consulting
- 100 : 1 Product support (PCs)
- 100 : 1 Workstation support (PCs)
- 200 : 1 Administration
- 500 : 1 Technical support

So an organization with 400 end users, half of whom work on PCs, would need one consultant, two product support specialists, two workstation support specialists, two administrative workers, one technical support specialists, and one overall manager. Nine people for 400 end users gives a ratio of just under 50 : 1.

Another way to look at staffing requirements is to see the ratios of users to staff members in actual firms Here are some actual ratios:

- 118 : 1 John Hancock Financial Services, 1986. (25)
- 67 : 1 IBM Canada, 1981. (13)
- 125 : 1 Lincoln National Life (office automation), 1981. (13)
- 100 : 1 Unknown, 1985. (40)
- 56 : 1 "Canadian Company," 1981. (2)
- 167 : 1 Grumman, 1985. (41)

Obviously, there is no agreement, although articles that describe small ratios (2) tend to discuss demonstrated successes, whereas articles with high ratios (41) tend to have comments like "difficult at best." Since not even IBM Canada sports a 50:1 ratio, a good support ratio is probably something like 75 : 1 or 100 : 1.

Of course, much will depend on the spectrum of services provided. If few services are provided, the ratio can be much higher. Much will also depend on how much work is borne by support workers in user departments, as discussed below. Given these and other factors such as the maturity level of end users, all published ratios are merely checkpoints for consideration.

Selecting the Information Center Manager

Once the rough size of the staff is known, the next question is what kind of person to hire to run the information center and what kind of people to hire to staff its support and policy-making functions.

Computer Intelligence Corporation has found that most information center managers have a data processing background. Seventy-four percent came from data processing, and about half of these were staff members rather than managers before taking over the information center. (6) Only 8 percent came from end user management, with the other 18 percent coming from outside the company or from other sources. (6)

Whatever the manager's background, the key issue is how senior a person to select to run the information center. There is often a problem hiring a person with sufficient seniority to run the information center, because, although the center will support hundreds of projects and will need high-level management, its headcount is small. In many organizations, someone who will only lead three to ten people is automatically viewed as a very junior manager. As a result, sharp salary limitations are placed on the position, and the person selected to head the information center must be relatively junior.

Even the IS department may overlook the importance of the information center due to its low headcount. When the IS manager walks into the IS area and sees dozens of busy programmers and technicians and only a handful of information center workers, it is very hard to remember that end user computing has most of the organization's applications and uses most of the firm's information resources. Since the information center is often located away from the main IS department, the problem of perception may be even worse than headcount alone would tend to dictate. If the manager is considerably more junior than other IS area heads, the problem of perception will be compounded immeasurably.

Some organizations have faced up to the **importance/headcount paradox** by assigning senior people to run the information center. One vice president of information services in a large corporation, after much agonizing, assigned his top subordinate to the position. It took intense convincing to get senior management to assign an appropriate salary to the position. Fortunately, many firms have senior staff members who supervise only a few subordinates, and, although it may be difficult to extend this practice to a part of the IS, this may be the most valid way to proceed.

It may not be entirely inappropriate to staff the information center with a junior person because younger people may be more energetic and flexible. But while assigning a junior person may be tactically smart, such a person is not likely to be mature enough to provide the strategic guidance needed for end user computing, or capable of participating effectively when working with senior management on strategic planning. Unless the importance/headcount paradox is faced directly, the strategic impact of the information center may be severely compromised.

Hiring Staff

Information centers have been more eclectic in their hiring of working staff members. Although 79 percent hire staff members from data processing, 44 percent hire from end user departments. The information center manager may be from information systems, but a fair number of staff members may come from end user departments. (6)

The strong position of IS professionals in the information center means that technical issues are likely to be handled well. It is unclear, however, whether IS staff members have a sufficiently broad understanding of other functional areas to be able to help end users define their opportunities. There is at least a danger that the information center staff will focus on technical issues and low-level policy issues such as backup and application development steps, to the exclusion of helping users improve the performance of their functional areas by developing insights into how computers can be used to innovate effectively.

No single individual can have all of the skills needed to support users, ranging from high technical competence to interpersonal skills and teaching skills. As a result, most information centers hire a mix of staff members, some being more technically oriented and others more interpersonally oriented. This situation has touched off debates over whether it is easier to give technical people interpersonal skills or nontechnical people technical skills, but this point is not likely to be settled to anyone's satisfaction. The debate only serves to underscore the necessity that everyone in the information center have a broad mix of skills with no one being a "pure people person" or a "pure techie."

Training the Staff

Although staff members will be selected for their knowledge, they will still need a good deal of training, both initially and on a continuing basis.

It will be easiest to provide training on detailed technical matters, since many external suppliers provide courses in such subjects as PC repair and Lotus 1-2-3. It will be much harder to provide training in the general principles of information center management. Fortunately, a number of for-profit corporations provide multiday seminars on broader issues. It is good practice to send all new employees to such seminars.

For ongoing training, the basic sources for initial training are also good sources of advanced training and training in areas that have emerged since initial training. In addition, many trade journals and national conferences provide continuing ongoing education.

The important point about training is to establish a clear training policy from the start and to include training as a line item in the annual budget. Training needs to be institutionalized within the information center, just as it needs to be institutionalized in user departments.

MOBILIZING END USERS

Even the earliest information centers realized that most end users turn first to other end users when they have a problem. Typically, the most computer-adept person in a functional department would serve as a primary contact point for questions and problem resolution. It did not take information centers long to realize that by mobilizing end users they could extend the reach of their services, serving more people with their limited staffs and resources. So far, this mobilization has focused on the creation and support of user groups and the formalization of "associates" roles in functional departments. But these are likely to be only the first two steps in a longer term effort to get users to resort to more self-support.

User Groups

When host computing and, later, personal computers burst onto the scene, many end users formed **user groups** that met monthly or more often to hear about new developments, share insights, ask questions, and in general huddle with other people sharing the same problems and enthusiasms.

User groups usually started in cities or sections of cities, but soon in-house user groups started to evolve in individual companies. In-house user groups can focus on common concerns related to their specific business problems. They can also discuss company-related matters that cannot be discussed in an open forum. (42)

Some companies welcomed these in-house user groups, providing space to meet and encouraging participation in company newsletters. In many cases, however, support was given only on the provision that the user groups meet outside of normal business hours, either during lunch time or during the evenings.

In many cases, support began grudgingly but later flowered. The Bendix Users Group, for instance, attracted top management's attention when it saved the company $40,000 by specifying options from third parties that were cheaper but performed as well as the primary vendor's options. (42)

The role of the information center in user groups varies widely. In some cases, the user group maintains fierce independence, even acting as a power balance between users and the information center. In other cases, the information center staff is invited on a guest basis to answer questions and give presentations. The information center newsletter, discussed later in the chapter, may even be the vehicle for club news. In some cases, links are even closer. Santarelli points out that the information center has the time to create a good agenda and minutes and so in some cases actually runs the meetings, (42) but this seems to be the exception, not the rule.

A typical meeting will include a period for handling club business and a formal presentation by the information center, a vendor, or one or more end users. Since many presentations will involve product demonstration, it is very helpful to have large screen video projectors or at least screen capture software and a reproduction budget.

Many get-togethers also provide the opportunity for less formal information sharing. Typically, this will include:

- Tips from users and information center staffers on new products and tricks with existing products.
- Questions thrown open for comment and help.
- New information center policies and product releases.
- Information on who has bought new equipment or software or who has developed an interesting new application.

Although user groups are valuable and deeply ingrained in the life of many corporations, they are associated with several problems that are difficult to solve. The first is how to handle user groups in companies that are geographically distributed. Obviously, travel makes it impossible to have a single user group, so there must be some level of coordination of user groups in various locations, and special attention must be given to small centers. One approach to this problem is to issue an information center newsletter that combines news from all groups. (9) Another approach is to have members from the central information center attend meetings at outlying locations.

An even bigger problem is how to handle meetings in which users have vastly different levels of expertise. Too technical a program will terrify novices, whereas too elementary a program will bore the company's power users. Inland Steel copes with this problem by scheduling a roundtable discussion at each meeting, asking each attendee what they would like to ask or bring up. (42) Another approach is to establish a newcomer's group that people can come to while they are still novices. Membership in the newcomer's group can be limited in time, or people can gradually shift their attendance to the regular user group. Because the best talent in the newcomer's group constantly "graduates," these groups are likely to be run directly by the information center.

In some cases, a subgroup of users may have a sufficient commonality of interest to create its own user group. Secretaries, in particular, may feel reluctant to talk at general meetings attended by managers and professionals, and secretaries have special needs that they do not share with other users.

Formalizing the Functional Specialist Role

Another approach to mobilizing end users in order to extend the reach of the information center is to formalize the role of functional specialists—the "super users" or "power users" who have a great deal of technical knowledge and experience but who work in functional departments such as marketing and finance.

Departments have long turned to their functional specialists for advice and guidance on an informal basis, but now many firms have formalized the functional specialist role.

Intel, for instance, has a "Super User Program" that had 175 members in 1985, compared to only 40 information center staff members. (40) One Intel official said that these super users are essentially running information center franchises in their local areas. The information center provides a number of special services, including formal registration in the program, priority support, and special attention from consultants. There are also monthly meetings. In other companies, it is becoming common to support registration at local trade shows and even limited travel to distant trade shows.

In formal programs, the functional specialists' manager needs to give formal approval to membership, agreeing to have the functional specialist give part of his or her time to fulfill the responsibilities created in these programs.

Functional specialist programs greatly reduce the workload of the information center. In addition, Intel reports that its users, being much closer to the software, teach the information center as much as they learn from the center. (40)

Rethinking the Functional Specialist's Role

When the functional specialist role first evolved, only two skills were needed: (1) the ability to train users in basic hardware and software operation and to solve use problems; and (2) the ability to develop applications. Today, however, the situation is more complex, and it is not clear that a single functional specialist can or should do what needs to be done.

As discussed in Chapter 1, nearly every manager already manages an automated office. Policies must be set, procedures hammered out, impacts on budget and performance assessed, and so on. Because power users are not always department managers, they can help only indirectly. There seems to be no way around developing an information management role for all managers. In the "fifth environment" discussed in Chapter 1, the department manager has to be involved.

Secretarial roles are also changing. Secretaries are acting more as office managers, handling the details of storage strategies and day-to-day preventative maintenance, placing trouble calls, and, most importantly, specifying the configurations of PCs and other equipment. Although some of these functions could be delegated upward to higher priced power users who are managers and professionals, that hardly seems appropriate. In too many cases, computer-adept professionals spend such large amounts of time doing low-level technical and information management roles that their productivity suffers considerably. In addition, power users are often highly specialized in their knowledge and could not handle such matters without additional study.

Another role that is evolving is that of **technological gatekeeper**. Communication research has long shown that the communication of information tends to be a two-step process, with "opinion leaders" reading and listening more and passing on advice to other people. Opinion leadership is highly specific to topics. A person who is an opinion leader in one area may not be one in another. Allen has shown that opinion leadership exists at the level of technology transfer in firms, (1) and this probably extends to end user computing information. The "technological gatekeeper"—the term Allen uses—may be a manager, professional, or even secretary in the case of end user computing. Or this role may not exist. If a technological gatekeeper role emerges in a department for end user computing or for specific emerging areas such as graphics, the person or persons in this role will greatly influence the department's thinking.

Because information is a two-step process, the information center's informational campaigns should be addressed to these opinion leaders if they can be found, and information should be geared to the high level of sophistication these people want.

Overall, the next stage in mobilizing user support in most firms is likely to be the formalization of several roles within the department, beginning with the overall manager and continuing to the department secretary. This formalization is likely to be done in conjunction with today's functional specialist programs that aim at traditional power users.

Another development may be the cataloging of computer talent so that new positions can be filled in-house instead of by outside hiring. When General Electric found that almost a fifth of its employees spent *most* of their time working with computers, it began its Computing People Project to keep track of computer-adept people. (7) It has a skills data base and a way of matching job openings with people who need or want to change jobs. Since the cost of hiring a technology worker from the outside is $40,000, including fees and training, and since the turnover rate among computer people was 20 percent higher than it was for corporate employees as a whole, this program has provided solid benefits to the company.

PROMOTION

Although most information centers are already overworked, it is important to promote the center effectively so that if users are not served, they can be excluded in a rational way, instead of just because they did not know that services exist. Information centers promote themselves in many ways, but we will focus on just three: special events, walk-in centers, and newsletters. The user groups and functional specialist programs just discussed are also promotional tools.

Special Events

When an information center first starts, begins a major phase of growth, or introduces new products, it is common to hold a special event to publicize the change.

When the Queen's Medical Center in Honolulu started its information center, for example, it held a major Computer Fair in which people were invited to drop by to see new products in actual operation. There were fliers, balloons, and even a door prize—a Commodore 64 home computer. This event generated great interest and strong attendance.

Many information centers hold annual computer fairs, in which they give people a chance to look over old as well as new products. Staff turnover is 20 percent annually in many firms, and even if people have seen a product demonstrated before, they may not remember it. In many cases, end users demonstrate the applications they have developed in order to help share information and to help potential users appreciate the potential of particular tools for solving business problems.

Another popular event is the cafeteria demonstration. During lunch hour, equipment is set up in a corner of the corporate cafeteria. At lunch time, people can stop by and see quick demonstrations, as well as try things out themselves.

Special courses or seminars are also offered on an occasional basis, but these are normally part of broader training programs. They will be treated in the next chapter, which deals with training and support.

Special events provide a way to generate awareness and interest, so that users can move to the next step—examining a potential application in detail with the information center's staff.

Walk-in Centers

Many information centers have walk-in facilities, often called "toy stores," with working PCs, terminals, and software, so that users can literally sit down and explore products on their own or with the close guidance of the information center staff. These walk-in centers make new applications concrete for users and give them a chance to try things before making actual purchase decisions.

The walk-in center needs to be located where users normally pass, to make it convenient and attractive for them to stop in. Walk-in centers often double as the corporate training facility for classes, but at least a few machines should be available even when classes are in session. Of course, if some people are using the machines for computer-based training, the others are still free to serve as exploration stations.

Some information centers even have "loaners" that can be checked out for reasonable periods of time. Users can take these loaners with them and use them in their offices for a set time before deciding whether to make a purchase.

Newsletters

In a 1984 survey of 25 information centers, Leitheiser and Wetherbe found that over 60 percent already provided newsletters to end users. (27) Today, the percentage of information centers that provide newsletters is probably much higher.

A newsletter helps the information center publicize new products and promulgate new policies. It also lets users ask questions and see the answers to questions that others have asked. It publicizes applications in order to help users see how computers can be used to solve practical business problems and in order to help people avoid "reinventing the wheel" when someone else has already solved a problem.

Boeing has gone beyond the simple newsletter, offering a full catalog listing supported products, computer-based training tools, and other valuable information. (35) This catalog is updated annually.

One issue is whether the newsletter is to be limited to the information center or whether it should be a broader MIS publication vehicle. Restricting it to the information center gives it more focus, lessening the danger that users will throw it away because it contains too much irrelevant material to wade through. Broadening it to include IS will give users a wider view of IS in the corporation.

DEVELOPING THE TECHNOLOGICAL INFRASTRUCTURE

The IS department, including the information center, must develop an underlying **technical infrastructure,** consisting of hardware, software and communications. End users should be able to employ this **technostructure** with a minimum of bother and with confidence that all the pieces will work together. Metz has described Boeing's goal of developing standards for technical and office protocols (TOPs), for instance:

> What's desired, in essence, is a situation in which PC users can sit down at their workstations and immediately begin to transact business: no sign-on to the host, no knowledge of multiple operating systems, no job control language or construction of intricate command statements. (35)

Although it will take many years for fully integrated environments to appear, many corporations are trying to build at least limited "islands of integration." The Electrical Power Research Institute (EPRI), for instance, has developed a standardized workstation consisting of either an IBM PC/XT or PC/AT with 640 K, MS-DOS, Lotus 1-2-3, and Crosstalk (26). Other packages, including dBASE III, Framework, and Symphony, are standard options. EPRI will deliver and install fully configured workstations, with all software installed and even a menu front end that allows the user to select software without dealing with DOS.

In most firms, the goal is much simpler. An effort is made to develop key standards for individual hardware and software categories, testing the individual standards for compatibility and building at least rudimentary bridges among key pieces of this piecemeal technical infrastructure.

Key Standards

Since the setting of individual standards is the norm today, we should at least list the key standards that need to be established. PC hardware and software standards discussed in Chapters 6 through 12 include the following.

- Basic PC hardware families
- Optional PC equipment
- Spreadsheet software
- Word processing software
- File and data base software
- Analytical and conceptual graphics software
- Integrated packages
- Operating system
- Key utilities
- Programming languages
- Standards for specialized PC software
- PC–host communications hardware
- PC networking hardware and software

For host computers the decisions discussed in Chapters 13, 16, and 17 include the selection of software in the following areas.

- The operating system
- Security software
- Query software
- Report generation software
- Host data file and data base software
- Analysis software: spreadsheet, financial analysis, statistics, etc.
- Graphics software
- Electronic mail software
- Group calendar management software
- Integrated office support software
- PC–host links for uploading and downloading information

Finally, there needs to be an appropriate data highway, as discussed in Chapters 13, 14, and 15, including the following.

- Terminal–host cabling
- Personal computer networking
- Local area networking
- Wide area networking
- Higher level data communications standards

Although the information center will only take an advisory role in the selection of large-scale hardware and software systems such as host hardware, host operating systems, local area networking, and wide area networking, its advisory role will be crucial to the success of end user computing. For example, if the host is an IBM mainframe, the VM operating system will offer a much wider range of software choices than the MVS or DOS operating systems. To give another example, if a company has many IBM PCs and can only select a local area network (LAN) that forces these PCs to work through RS232C interfaces, the effectiveness of PC–PC communications will be strangled. It is important for the information center to be strong enough to play an intelligent role in decisions beyond its complete control.

On the other hand, most of the decisions listed above are under the direct control of the information center. Every year, an information center makes three to six key infrastructure choices, and even when there is a standard for every item on the list, the job is still not finished. Even before that time, technical progress will have overtaken earlier decisions, forcing the information center to migrate to updated versions of the selected products or to choose entirely new products.

Philosophy of Control

In addition to selecting standards, the information center must develop a general philosophy for how strongly to enforce standards. Very few centers have a completely laissez-faire policy, letting users buy anything they want. With few exceptions, there are published standards for hardware and software. The degree to which these standards are enforced, however, and the methods used to enforce standards vary widely.

Strict Enforcement

Some companies take a very hard line, forbidding the purchase of nonstandard hardware and software. Their reasoning is that selecting "the best system for the job" may lock the user into a deadend system in the longer term, precluding further applications from being added. By taking a hard line, they will ensure the integrity of the basic technical infrastructure.

Strict standards control also simplifies user support and the enforcement of other management decisions.

- For instance, in order to avoid backup problems, Nabisco forbade the use of hard disks. Only Bernouli Boxes, which always come with a main and backup drive, were permitted. (45)
- Training and support have also been improved. It is impossible to provide training and support if dozens of products are in use in each category.
- Careful option control will make it easier for the information center staff to discover harmful interactions between hardware options and to maintain parts in its inventory for rapid maintenance support.
- According to Schnorr of General Foods, standards help the information center protect the company from advocates of "vaporware"—products that are advertised but not actually delivered. (12)

Open Enforcement

Other firms set standards but try to implement them with carrots instead of sticks. Their approach is to make volume purchases that reduce the cost of selected hardware and standards. They pretest products for their performance and compatibility with other products by providing services such as setup. Most importantly, they refuse to support nonstandard software. If the user has a problem with a system containing nonstandard hardware and software, the user must return to the dealer to solve the problem.

Some information centers refuse to provide support if a system contains even a single nonstandard component. But this is likely to alienate users and often for good reason. Most will provide basic services, but if the problem is traced to a nonstandard component, an additional service charge may be made.

Some companies are even more liberal. The Queen's Medical Center in Honolulu, for instance, will at least help a user purchase nonsupported hardware and software, in order to avoid basic bad purchase practices. It will not, however, pass judgment on the quality or applicability of a particular product.

Many firms have whole areas in which user choices are left completely open. Many firms, for instance, refuse to become involved in the selection of special-purpose software for particular applications, although they may have certain general guidelines—for instance, the requirement that no software can be purchased unless the user has first tried it. This openness allows the end users to respond quickly to changes in the market, without being burdened by standards that are not likely to be appropriate anyway.

Product Research and Selection

Because three to ten standards may have to be established each year, information centers need to develop structured processes for selecting standards.

The first step is to set priorities for standards. This flows from the user needs study discussed later in this chapter. Because user demands for standards are likely to outstrip the ability of the information center to establish standards, it is important to set priorities carefully.

The rest of the process involves obtaining samples of standards candidates and seeing if they meet the organization's needs. Because it is generally harder to evaluate software than hardware, owing to the presence of soft user preferences and the complexity of software, we will focus on software selection, although the basic steps are the same for hardware selection.

Obtaining Samples

Unless the organization has actual working hardware and software to evaluate, it cannot make an informed decision. A few mail order houses allow companies to rent software for a month or so, but most vendors refuse to give samples for evaluation. Many of the ones that do provide samples merely provide stripped-down demo packages that only show the product's strong features. As a result, it is nearly always necessary to purchase a piece of hardware or several software packages for evaluation. This is a relatively expensive proposition, but it represents only part of the cost of doing an evaluation.

It is important to limit the number of candidates to be considered. Obviously, it is more expensive to evaluate many candidates, in terms of both purchase costs and organizational costs. More importantly, it is very difficult to evaluate more than three to six alternatives in the depth needed to guide decision making.

Most companies develop an initial list of potential candidates from lists of top-selling software, evaluations in magazines, and product evaluation services such as Software Digest. These help screen out poor products, and detailed reviews help the organization prescreen products for special needs which the company has in the standards area.

Initial Technical Testing

Before the product is sent to a larger evaluation team, the information center often conducts initial technical testing. According to Jim Smith of Security Pacific Computer Solutions, initial technical testing answers three basic questions. (26)

- Does it work?
- Does it do what is claimed?
- How easy is it to use?

Establishing Evaluation Guidelines

Each candidate will be evaluated by several people, so it is important to develop evaluation guidelines to provide some consistency in their evaluations. The user needs study should have pinpointed some key criteria, and there are also some general factors such as ease of use and the presence of training materials. In addition, each software area has a number of features commonly offered, such as the ability of word processing systems to generate personalized form letters.

Some firms have a ratio scale by each criterion and even give a weight to each, so that an overall score can be obtained. Others force the user to go through a detailed check list, and then ask for a half dozen or so general evaluations on ease of use, power, and other broad factors. This allows one or two finalists to be selected for detailed and open-ended evaluations.

When creating criteria, it is important to focus on items that are pertinent to the firm's most pressing needs. No software package has all possible features, and if the evaluation criteria resemble a long shopping list of nice features, fully featured systems are likely to be selected, regardless of how good they are.

To provide focus, all evaluators should work on a real problem that is representative of the organizational work that must be supported by the product. Every candidate is evaluated on this benchmark problem, for both suitability and speed of operation.

Another trap in the check list-oriented evaluation is that it focuses on current versions of the product. All viable software products evolve over time, through a series of updates. Although it is wrong to evaluate products on the basis of promised features that may or may not be delivered, it is equally wrong to ignore the long-term viability of a product. A product that has good sales and comes from a well-established firm can be expected to improve over time. A good product that few people are buying is not likely to improve, and customer support could eventually die with the product.

Selecting an Evaluation Team

The next step is to create an evaluation team consisting of both end users and information center staff members. The information center people will ensure that the standard selected makes sense from a broader standpoint, whereas the end users will validate the usefulness of the product in day-to-day use.

At Grumman, the role of end user testing is highly formalized. The company has a number of selected "test pilots," a term appropriate to the company's military aircraft orientation. (41) In other firms, end user testers are drawn from the general body of users. In either case, there are certain dangers to look for in end user testing. Naturally, testers tend to be more technically adept than is the norm, which causes them to focus on advanced features. They may not even be aware of some potential problems for less knowledgeable users. At some point during the evaluation process, less knowledgeable users *must* be brought into the picture.

Pilot Studies and General Release

Even after a product is selected, it should not be released to the corporation as a whole. Instead, release should be gradual. First, there should be a **technical pilot,** in which a technically advanced department implements the product. During this technical pilot stage, the focus is on the product. If fatal deficiencies are found, the product can still be killed. If nonfatal deficiencies are found, technical fixes may be created, or at least warning notices and procedural fixes can be developed.

The next step is the **organizational pilot.** Although the technical pilot focuses on the product, the organizational pilot focuses on the applicability of the product to real problems and the procedures that must be developed to use it effectively. Several departments should be chosen as organizational pilots. These departments should have appropriate needs that are pressing and matched to what the product offers, and they must not be coerced into participation, but the goal is to use representative organizations without unusual technical competence. Before this is done, however, the information center itself should be well trained, create dialogues, develop user guides, and produce all training material. (19) The organizational pilot is also a pilot of the information center's support program for the product.

The pilot stage should end with a full report documenting whether or not the product should be rolled out to the general users in the organization. (19) This will require, during the pilot stage, the collection of appropriate data on satisfaction, problems, and demonstrable payoffs from using the product. (19)

Finally, the rollout can be planned. Before the product is released, training materials need to be refined, and promotional materials geared to key market segments must be created. Purchase arrangements, maintenance facilities and parts, and other basic support mechanisms must also be in place. Then the product can be released with appropriate fanfare.

Purchasing

After a product has been selected, purchase conditions must be negotiated. Purchase conditions are part of the evaluation process because cost can tip the balance between two close alternatives.

Advantages of Retailers

In general, goods can be purchased through two basic marketing channels—retail stores and mail order firms. Retail stores offer purchasers a number of advantages. (16)

- A retailer can help you clarify your needs by talking with you first about the kind of work you need to do.
- A retailer can test the whole system in the store.
- Many retailers charge lower repair rates for the goods they sell.
- Retailers know the products they sell
- Retailers offer more convenient service than mail order houses, which often require you to mail back the part to be repaired.

This is an impressive list, but it is marred by the fact that many dealers, pinched by falling profit margins, have steadily reduced the quality of their staffs. In many cases, salespeople are not very knowledgeable about the products they sell, and the retailer may not even have tested various expansion boards being sold for compatibility with one another. A good retailer can indeed offer superior knowledge and service, but selecting such a dealer can be very difficult.

Advantages of Mail Order Firms

The most obvious advantage of mail order firms is lower price. Not faced with store space, elegant displays, or the costs of salespeople, mail order firms offer prices that are 20 to 40 percent lower than those in retail stores, although large purchasers can often obtain retail discounts near the levels of mail order discounts.

Another major advantage is selection. Although most retail stores stock only a narrow range of products, mail order firms stock hundreds of items. In general, they are also better able to keep these items in stock, although some mail order firms sell the product before locating a source.

In addition, many vendors prohibit mail order sales of their products, and although their products can often be purchased through mail order sales anyway, these "grey market" sales void the manufacturer's warranty. Some mail order firms offer their own warranties.

Mail order products are delivered directly to the buyer's desk, avoiding a trip to the retail store every time a purchase is made. This can be a significant advantage for volume purchasers.

Purchase Trends

Basic computers are most often purchased through local dealers because maintenance is a major consideration in the selection of products. This can be an important factor in the selection of products. Many companies are highly decentralized, and they need to standardize products that can be supported in most or all locations. Other companies are in pocket markets where some candidate products are not available.

Broadly used software and expansion hardware, however, are often purchased from mail order houses in order to get the lowest possible cost on products that are basically commodities. In the case of software vendors, it may even be more desirable to get better support through direct dealer purchases than to purchase the product from dealers who are not as familiar with it as they should be.

Although the retailer/mail order dichotomy is a fundamental one, the line between the two is becoming blurred by low-end retailers who offer discounts of 10 percent to 20 percent compared to that of full service retailers but who offer at least some of the traditional advantages of retailers. At the high end, some retailers offer full list prices but provide exceptional help in product selection and exceptional service. Over time, the options for purchase should expand considerably.

Site Licensing

There are two broad alternatives for dealing with software vendors: (1) enter into a **volume purchase arrangement** and (2) acquire a **site license.** The difference between the two revolves around who does the copying. (31) In volume purchase arrangements, the manufacturer delivers an agreed-upon number of copies. In site licenses, the user does the copying or installs the product on a hard disk for general use.

Good site license terms can be obtained because the user organization absorbs many costs traditionally incurred by vendors, including marketing, distribution, billing, carrying credit, and accounting. (30) In addition, many vendors see licensing as a way to become an instant corporate standard. (31) Although the cost per copy sold is low, the overall price obtained is good, and many services are frequently unbundled, for instance, support and documentation.

On the negative side for vendors, many vendors fear piracy if they give a copiable disk to customers. Some provide disks that make only a certain number of copies, while others require users to keep audit reports of where each copy goes as evidence of good control. (31)

On the negative side for users, the cost of copying and distribution can become very significant and difficult to predict, and vendors may be slow to service site licenses, since further sales may not be likely. In addition, large firms may have so much bargaining power that site licensing may not provide major cost savings, (30) although it may be needed for networking.

Many legal stipulations must be incorporated in a site licensing contract, including whether updates are included or will have a guaranteed price, whether vendor support is included, and whether documentation is included.

Stocking Goods

Some organizations even purchase goods so that they will have stock on hand when the user needs hardware and software, instead of waiting until a need appears to begin ordering goods. Stocking can provide a great deal of responsiveness and good-will.

Of course, if goods are overstocked, inventory costs will be high and will have to be factored into prices charged to users. In addition, if the inventory becomes obsolete, it will have to be written off or sold at "fire sale" rates. This, too, will raise the general price of stocked goods. If either of these factors becomes too large, stocked goods will be prohibitively expensive.

Some firms stock used computers. When a person upgrades to a new model, the information center will buy back equipment on a depreciated basis. This will make upgrades easier in departments where the old machine cannot be used. It also provides a ready stock of starter machines to get people up and running quickly and at low cost.

Installation

A major issue is how to deliver products to user. One option is to give users computers and terminals in their shipping cartons and to deliver software that is still shrinkwrapped. This reduces information center costs, but it also imposes very high costs on users, for whom "simple" installation tasks are very time consuming and daunting.

As a result, many information centers now install hardware at user sites. A PC, for instance, is taken out of the carton and wired together. The installer then runs diagnostics—something most users are likely to skip over. This whole process may take an installer 15 or 30 minutes, but it might take a user several hours. Later, while the hardware is still under warranty, the installer may return to ask about malfunctions. Users frequently do not realize that their machine has a serious problem during the warranty period. They simply note something mildly annoying.

In personal computers, expansion boards are also installed frequently. Again, an installer can do the work in a fraction of the time taken by the user, and the installer will also be sufficiently experienced to know about potential interrupt conflicts among boards and how switches should be set given different hardware configurations.

Software, in turn, usually comes in a very raw state. It normally has no operating system, so the first step is to install DOS on the program disks or copy both DOS and the program disk onto a "boot disk," depending on whether or not the disks are copy protected. The next step is likely to be "installation," in which the software is configured to a machine's basic hardware. The last step is to make backup copies as appropriate and to store original disks in a safe place. This too can be done far more rapidly by information center staffers than by users.

Overall, it may take a user one or two days to set up a personal computer and its software. Not all of this work will be done at once, but as expansion boards and new packages are added, the work will mount considerably. This can probably be cut to an hour or two if the information center staff does the work.

Among the costs to the information center, obviously, there is the installer's time. Less obviously, it is often best to check out hardware and software at a central location instead of at the user's site. This is especially true for software. Central preparation requires considerable work space and probably several PCs as well.

To give a practical example, Pacific Bell's information center provides the following services for users. (29)

- Purchases machines
- Determines proper configurations
- Installs boards

- Installs software
- Tests machines
- Repairs machines

This broad spectrum of services requires Pacific Bell to keep an 11,000 square foot warehouse to handle the several hundred PCs it installs each month. (29)

Host applications require much less setup at each user's site, but they may also be expensive to install. Most importantly, many packages need a half-time responsible systems programmer, or at least an applications programmer, to maintain, reconfigure when additions are made, and customize user profiles. In addition, as the PC becomes the standard workstation in the firm, hardware and software may have to be installed at each PC, especially for data downloading applications or if a package comes with both host and PC versions that can share models or data.

Software Upgrades

Most software packages, both on PCs and hosts, go through a series of refinements which come out as **upgrades**—new releases of the product. These upgrades must be purchased and distributed, and users must be trained to use them.

Since most organizations have at least a dozen major software packages, each with one or more upgrades each year, the number of upgrades that need to be handled is enormous. Melymuka has summarized the situation. (34)

> Software upgrades are a little like grasshoppers: You tolerate them because they get rid of bugs, but cringe when they appear in groups because the little critters become a nuisance; in great numbers, a blight.

Purchasing

The first step in purchasing is to know that a new upgrade is available. One advantage of centralized setup of software is that upgrade notices come to the information center, but many vendors do not even have a systematic way of releasing notices of upgrades.

The next step is to test the new upgrade in order to be sure that it works and does not introduce new bugs. (34) Although the upgrade may work on some hardware, it may not work on all configurations, or it may conflict with other standardized software. Many are not even compatible with older versions, so that the company must upgrade all packages or none.

Next management approvals must be obtained. With 500 PCs, upgrades can cost $75,000 to buy and 250 person-hours to install. (34) Senior management may balk at such huge outlays, requiring more time to be spent on justification.

Then come the mechanics of distribution. Without a good data base of software users, distribution can be impossible, but even with one, it will be difficult. It may not specify whether the software should move with people when they switch departments or stay with the department that made the original purchase. In addition, the software must be delivered and probably installed. It may even be necessary to collect old disks or manuals and return them to vendors. Networked environments will take care of some of these complications, but networking or downloading from a host solves only some of these problems.

After the product is delivered, users must be trained. Obviously, it does little good to spend a great deal of money for capabilities no one understands. Moreover, upgrades sometimes require users to change the way they do the things they already do.

Host software retains many of these problems. Although physical distribution of software is not a problem, setup can be tricky, since upgrades often come as patches to existing systems. Training and the distribution of manuals also need to be handled. Another consideration is that host programs tend to be very large, and so nearly all have at least a few bugs that must be fixed or at least documented.

Maintenance

Personal computers and terminals occasionally break down. Three types of maintenance service are available to deal with these breakdowns:

- **Service contracts** with external vendors, which provide unlimited repairs for a given period of time, in return for a flat annual fee.
- **Per call maintenance** from external vendors which provides repairs on a **time-and-materials** basis
- **In-house maintenance** staffs which provide maintenance work for end users within the organization

Comparisons

Service contracts give peace of mind and guarantee that a department's budget will not be thrown out of kilter because of a major repair. On the downside, service contracts are much more expensive than the expected annual cost of repairs. For instance, Kemper Insurance paid only $25,000 one year in per call charges, whereas a comparable service contract would have cost $250,000. (44) Although this case may be unusual, it probably indicates the general pattern. Complicating the cost picture is the fact that service contracts that do on-site repair are more expensive than service contracts that require the user to bring the equipment into the vendor's shop.

Time-and-materials costs may be lower, but there is some chance that users who use this method will receive less prompt service from vendors.

In-house maintenance is probably the cheapest over the long run, and it gives prompt service if done correctly. However, the initial cost of setting up such a service can be high, and ongoing space and other requirements can also be expensive. Another advantage of in-house maintenance is that the company has a repair history of each machine. (44)

Detailed Arrangements

Although general differences between the three basic service schemes are important, the way each is implemented can make a considerable difference.

For instance, service contracts cost less if the user carries the equipment into the vendor's shop. Since service contracts are insurance policies, many firms may prefer to gamble on service not being needed very often and so stay with bring-it-in service contracts. On-site contracts cost more, especially if there is a guaranteed time to appearance, say two or four hours.

Service contracts are especially high if the service agency agrees to give the user a temporary replacement. Downtime is frequently more important than repair costs, so replacement clauses are often added to contracts, at least in applications where downtime is very expensive. Contracts that merely require repair people to appear in four hours do not guarantee when the equipment will be running again.

Other clauses that may be important in service contracts are requirements to establish a stocked maintenance area on site (15) or to spend a certain amount of time on site each day (44) for fast access and to handle minor irritations during nonbusy periods.

Some companies combine an on-site staff with per call maintenance. An on-site employee checks each call, often finding that the problem is a loose cable or misunderstood software. (44) Only real problems are sent out for repairs.

Many companies also keep in stock those parts that fail the most frequently. (44) Studies have shown, for instance, that printers account for 32 percent of all support requests and storage devices for another 17 percent. (43) It is common to keep replacements for printers and floppy disk drives for rapid response to common problems.

Some distributed companies keep a stock of parts on hand at a central location. Thanks to a data base on all machines and their configurations, for instance, Travelers' Insurance can assemble a replacement on the spot and deliver it the next day. (44)

Local area networks (LANs) are especially difficult to maintain because equipment and software from many vendors are likely to be involved, and it may be very difficult to identify the problem component. It may not even be possible to get service contracts on LANs. Most organizations find that they need a full-time administrative staff for LANs and that they even need half-time administrators for PC networks. These administrators can do initial diagnostics, turning to a central staff for more complex work.

Maintenance Trends

There is no clear pattern to the choices organizations are making, and different research organizations give different figures for the percentage of companies pursuing each option. (44) Although in-house maintenance is small at the time of this writing, maintenance contracts and per call repair seem to be about equal. In time, as LANs become more commonplace and integrated multivendor equipment becomes the norm, in-house maintenance may become considerably more important because only in-house maintenance may be able to cope with the diversity that exists.

Building the Technostructure: Conclusion

In the minds of many people, building an effective infrastructure means selecting hardware and software standards. But we have seen that the process is much broader and more difficult than that. Selecting standards is not only just the first step, but it is also a very difficult first step if done well.

The real costs may come once the standard is selected. Although it is possible to drop most of the work on end users, few end users are very technically adept. It is far easier for the information center staff to do most setup and administrative work for the user, beginning with the purchase mechanics, continuing to hardware and software setup, and ending with ongoing maintenance. A full life cycle approach to support is more expensive for the center, but it can slash overall corporate costs and, perhaps even more importantly, it can avoid a great deal of user anguish that can easily lead to people stopping computer use or at least not moving up to later innovations.

ESTABLISHING KEY POLICIES

After organizing itself and developing a program for implementing the basic technical infrastructure needed in end user computing, the information center needs to develop policies in a number of key areas, including security and privacy, unauthorized software copying, departmental management rules, and the development of small, mid-range, and contract applications.

Computer Abuse: Privacy, Security, Damage, and Theft

Definitions

Computer abuse is a broad concept that embraces several practices: privacy, security, damage, and theft. Privacy and security, the first two types of abuse, involve unauthorized access.

- **Privacy** is the unauthorized access to personal information that an individual does not wish to be released.
- **Security** is the unauthorized access to corporate or client information that the corporation or a client does not wish to be released.

Privacy concerns are becoming more important because of the growing number of lawsuits by employees, suppliers, and customers. Medical records are often private, but so too are salaries and in some cases telephone numbers and addresses. The general rule is that if the person about whom the data are kept does not want the information released or even recorded, their desires should be respected except with good reason. Several countries, including Sweden, have strict privacy laws, and, at least in the federal government, privacy regulations have become so strict that it is becoming difficult to establish any data bases involving people in federal and military organizations.

In contrast to privacy and security, **damage** goes beyond access. It involves the unauthorized damage or destruction of data or other resources. This damage can be done by insiders or outsiders, and it may be either malicious or accidental. Although the classic image of damage is a teenage "breaker" who erases critical corporate files, the concept includes accidental data erasures and the loss of data because of a failure to do timely backup. Corporate executives have long been responsible for the security of their "vital records," without which the company would fail to operate. In the future, we can expect to see an increasing number of stockholder lawsuits if security breaches result in damage.

Theft, in turn, is the unauthorized use of resources or the taking of resources. Theft may involve data, programs, or equipment. Note that using a computer for personal work without authorization is included in the definition of theft. Theft of equipment seems to be on the rise because of the high value of computer equipment, but theft of programs and data can be extremely devastating, and unauthorized resource use for personal purposes can be very large in the aggregate.

Host Security

Although mainframe authorities outside the information center in most corporations are responsible for maintaining host security, the information center still has a number of reasons to take a role in establishing security procedures such as the following.

1. End user computing is dramatically broadening access to mainframes, creating new and perhaps unforeseen levels of privacy and security dangers.
2. Some information centers have their own host computers with data extracts. If so, the information center may have a primary role in establishing host security.
3. The information center may have to lay down specific rules on how often end user passwords change and in general help set security and privacy profiles for their users.
4. The information center will have to lay down privacy and security policies for use in end user projects.

The matter of controlling individual applications can begin to be addressed in the user's initial proposal to develop an application. If corporate data or data under the control of a particular department are needed, the information center will require that this need be declared in the initial application. This will allow the information center to decide whether data should be accessed or help coordinate the decision if several parties are involved.

If the user is developing a data base, in turn, the information center can decide on whether privacy or security concerns are present. It can also pass judgment on how the user intends to lock up sensitive data, recover from machine crashes, keep data secure from disasters, and limit access. If the user's plan is inadequate, it can help the user prepare an adequate plan.

After the project is started, procedures and policies can still be brought to bear on end users. The information center itself may do all extracts from sensitive data in order to avoid unauthorized access, accidental damage of data, and so on. The cost of this service is high, however, and information center extraction is likely to be limited to high-risk cases. In addition, the information center may periodically audit all applications over a certain risk level in an attempt to ensure compliance with corporate standards.

A number of technologies are available to improve security on host computers, including callback modems and special security packages. These technologies are discussed briefly in Chapter 13. But use procedures and protections such as requiring passwords to be changed often and preventing the use of a person's name as a password are probably more important than technology in ensuring privacy and security on mainframes.

Personal Computer Security

Personal computer systems represent high privacy and security dangers. First, there is no way for the information center to determine whether unauthorized fields have been added to a data base, except through a direct audit. Second, if hard disks are used, backup to prevent loss is not likely to take place easily. Third, if either floppy disks or hard disks are used, it is often easy for someone to gain unauthorized access during off-duty periods.

Again, several technological procedures are available to improve privacy and security. Mandatory backup devices on all hard disk computers, encryption, passwords in software, and the locking up of removable hard disks can all be used. More important, however, are procedures such as backup schedules that are enforced and audited occasionally.

Now that many departments have minicomputers or supermicro file servers on networks, some of the "large machine" problems formerly seen on hosts are beginning to appear at the departmental level. Someone in the office, probably the department manager working with a secretary, will have to enforce rules laid down by the information center.

PCs also have one problem that is virtually unknown in the larger system world: the physical theft of equipment. The organization may wish to impose rules mandating insurance and the physical attachment of machines to tables or other difficult-to-move objects.

Unauthorized Software Copying

A hot issue in information management is the unauthorized copying of software, a practice that is often known by the more colorful name of software **piracy.**

A major study conducted by Future Computing for the Association of Data Processing Services (ADAPSO) estimated that half of all programs in use are unauthorized copies. (14) This conclusion was drawn from a study in which 75,000 questionnaires were sent to households. By comparing the software that people reportedly had against known sales patterns, the ratio of unauthorized to sold copies was estimated. Although this is not a clean methodology, most people agree that unauthorized copying is a pervasive problem.

In 1985, DiNucci at *PC World* wrote a major paper on unauthorized copying based on a survey of *PC World* readers. (11) This is admittedly an atypical group.

Among the respondents, 57 percent admitted that they had made unauthorized copies; this percentage was the same in large and small companies. Advanced users were more likely to report having made unauthorized copies. At work, an average of 10.5 programs were being used, 2.2 of which were unauthorized. At home, an average of 11 programs were being used, almost half of them unauthorized.

More interesting, however, were the *reasons* why people made unauthorized copies. Here are the percentages of respondents who made unauthorized copies by the reasons posed by DiNucci as important:

70% Wanted to make backups
68% Wanted to try before buying
60% Wanted to experiment
51% Wanted to put on hard disks
49% Program was overpriced
43% Wanted for home use
31% Could not afford the program
10% Office provided copy
9% Copy was free

The importance of making backups and installing the system on a hard disk was cited most frequently by the respondents. Although license agreements on many software packages forbid this practice, it is hardly appropriate to describe it as "piracy". It may be forbidden and may even be illegal (court tests are pending in various stages), but making a backup copy for personal use or installing the program on a personal hard disk is not an inherently malicious act. The importance of putting the program on a hard disk is probably understated by the numbers, since well under half of all PCs had hard disks at the time the survey was done.

The second and third reasons—trying before buying and wanting to experiment—are also difficult to classify as piracy, although some revenue is lost by the manufacturer. Of the respondents to the survey, 72 percent said they did not want to risk money on a program they had never used. In addition, many purchased the program after a trial.

Having a copy for home use is also difficult to categorize. If the program is not being used simultaneously at home and at work, this may violate the letter of the license agreement, which often states that a license is specific to a single machine. It is not the same as piracy as traditionally viewed, however. All the same, since it does lose revenues for the vendors, it is a major problem.

Other reasons fall into the category of pure and simple piracy. People who complain about program price, citing the freeness of the copy and giving other avaricious motives for copying, account for a large share of the unauthorized copying. Software vendors might argue that these are the true motives behind today's widespread piracy.

DiNucci also asked why people purchased when they could have copied. Among the responses were:

79% Wanted the user manual
66% Wanted updates
65% Found the price reasonable
41% Wanted support
27% Knew that company policy forbade couping
20% Felt copying to be immoral

9% Did not trust copy

1% Feared getting caught

A firm can adopt several policies to retard unauthorized copying. The first is to avoid firms whose practices and license agreements make unauthorized copying likely, including those that are copy protected or cannot be installed any number of times on a hard disk; those that do not provide adequate demonstration copies of their programs for evaluation; and those that do not have a program for purchasing copies for home use at a lower price. Unfortunately, since few vendors would still qualify, this type of action is unlikely. Without it, however, enforcement will continue to be very difficult.

It is important to have a very firm and well-publicized policy against unauthorized copying. In accordance with DiNucci's findings, this policy should point out that unauthorized copying is illegal, immoral, and counter to company policy. There should also be specific sanctions, with the toughest reserved for pure piracy and the weakest imposed for actions such as making backup copies and installing the program on a hard disk for personal use.

One of the simplest ways of reducing piracy is to make users specify software when they specify a computer and to require an adequate amount of software to be purchased with the machine. This is good practice simply from the viewpoint of cost justification, and it tends to eliminate the most flagrant forms of piracy, in which a department buys several machines and only one copy of each software package it needs. In addition, if the information center keeps an inventory list of equipment and legal software in each department, as well as a list of applications, it should be possible to catch obvious cheating.

On the positive side, the firm should have a "loaner library" of programs, so that potential users can test drive the product before making an actual purchase. The firm should also guarantee that it will provide backup copies if the original is accidentally destroyed, and it should maintain a library of backup programs to make this guarantee rapid and credible. Finally, it should stress the importance of manuals, vendor help lines, and other positive reasons which DiNucci cited for purchasing software.

On host systems, unauthorized copying is a major problem only when piracy is done at the institutional level. A number of companies have adopted the practice of wholesale piracy in both PC and host software. Fortunately, these firms seem rare.

Although preventing piracy is expensive and resource draining, the spectre of being caught in a lawsuit because of individual piracy should be viewed very seriously. It is not even necessary for a software vendor to prove actual damages, since significant statutory damages can be assessed even if damage amounts are not proven. Firms without aggressive anti-piracy stances that include stiff penalties for piracy are extremely vulnerable to being turned in by disgruntled employees or ex-employees with an axe to grind against their own departments.

Ergonomics

At some point, a firm must face up to **ergonomics**—the fitting of equipment and work situations to human characteristics, not the other way around. In the past, the office automation department has been the primary focus of ergonomics concerns. In the future, the information center may be assigned the role of establishing ergonomics standards.

Unions are already beginning to press for ergonomics in work rules, and a number of states have been considering regulations. Unless firms take the lead in developing internal economic standards, they may have these standards set for them by outside forces. More positively, the National Institute of Occupational Safety and Health (NIOSH) has demonstrated that good ergonomics can spur productivity. In one controlled laboratory experiment, people working under good conditions received 25 percent more incentive pay based on performance than people working under ergonomically poor conditions. (8)

A company will have to establish clear ergonomic rules for people who spend many hours a day at computers, but for light users, who spend less than an hour a day or so at the machine, a different set of rules might be enforced. Unfortunately, ergonomics is still an inexact world with some rules but few solid research conclusions.

Ergonomics is not a single concern but rather a group of related issues. In thee United States, health concerns among VDT (video display tube) users have received the most attention but have not been proven despite considerable testing, while other problems have been amply demonstrated. After reviewing available studies in 1983, the National Research Council of the National Academy of Sciences concluded that evidence for radiation effects was completely lacking. There was ample evidence, however, of problems caused by the quality of equipment, the design of workstations, and job design. (24) We will begin with those problems first.

The Display

Most surveys find that eyestrain is the most common complaint among VDT workers in America. (18,33) Over half of all workers in these surveys mention this problem. One of the biggest sources of eyestrain seems to be glare. A good way to see how much glare is present is to look *into* the display screen as if it were a window, instead of concentrating on its surface. You will often see the reflections of overhead lights, windows, and other "bright spots." Glare causes a great deal of eyestrain and fatigue.

Glare screens that fit over the surface of the display slash glare dramatically and yet cost only $30 to $80. Even these devices , however, cannot work against heavy glare from open windows. Unless the screen can be tilted away from strong light sources that cause problems after a glare screen has been fitted, the display must be moved or the source of offending light covered.

There are debates over the best combinations of colors (green on brown, amber on black, etc.), but these are probably less important than display height and distance. For instance, the screen should be no less than 14 inches away and no more than 22 inches away, (10) and its height should be set for the kind of work the person does. If the person will be looking at the screen most of the time or at papers at screen level, the *top* of the screen should be at eye level, so that the person will be looking slightly down. If the person is working with papers on the desktop (this is not advisible, but it is common), the screen should be much lower to reduce the number of times the person must move his or her head.

Ambient light is important, although different experts disagree about the amount of light that should be provided in offices where people work some of the time with paper and some of the time with video screens.

Tables and Chairs

Glare screens are cheap to provide, whereas most other changes to lighting are vastly expensive. The costs of tables and chairs fall in between, with good chairs priced at $250 to $500, unadjustable desks $200 to $400, and adjustable desks $600 to $1200.

Ideally, persons will sit with their feet on the floor and their knees making a 90 degree angle with the upper legs. The upper legs, in turn, will make a 90 degree angle with the torso. This position will provide good circulation. The forearm will be horizontal and should make a 90 degree angle at the elbow.

To achieve this position, the chair should be adjustable, within the range of 15 inches to 19 inches, or it should be 17 inches in the uncompressed state if it is fixed in height. (10) Adjustment should be easy, and it should be possible while the person is sitting.

The desk should also be adjustable, between 25 and 30 inches high; if it is fixed, it should be 25 or 26 inches high for typing and 28 inches high for writing and other general deskwork. (10)

The chair should also have good lower and middle back support, and this support should be easily adjustable while the person is sitting. The chair should have arms for support. It should also have a nice cloth seat and should roll, but not too easily.

It is important that the desk be large—with ample storage space for manuals, enough room for papers (many computer desks have little or no other work room), space for a printer if one is present, and closable drawers for supplies.

The display itself should be adjustable, able to swivel up and down, left and right, so that it can always be viewed at a comfortable angle. To increase comfort and decrease fatigue during keyboarding, wrist support may be desirable.

Other General Concerns

One of the most common "minor" problems with computers is noise. Printers, fans, hard disk drives, and other sources of noise can disrupt ordinary office environments. Sound hoods for impact printers should probably be mandated in policies, and if sound levels are still too high, acoustical materials can be added to ceilings and walls. When planning new buildings, masking noise generators should be included in specifications.

Heating, ventilation, and air conditioning are also important. Temperature is critical, but so is the circulation that comes with good ventilation. In addition, the air must not be too dry for work. These considerations should be part of general business design.

Radiation

When color television sets first became available, parents warned their children not to sit too close to the screen because of X-rays. Although early

TVs did emit X-rays, these emissions were eliminated almost completely in later sets. VDTs emit no measurable ionizing radiation, (37) although it is probably good practice to check for radiation on request, just to maintain good relationships and piece of mind.

Although ionizing radiation cannot be considered a health menace, many people are now concerned about the fluctuating magnetic fields created by the electromagnets in the VDT. Dr. Jose Delgado in Madrid reported damage to chicken embryos in an experiment with a fluctuating magnetic field different from that found on VDTs. (32) When Sweden's National Board of Occupational Safety and Health did a more controlled experiment on mouse fetuses, it first announced damage. (5) This study received much publicity, but when the board completed its analysis, it found no measurable effect. (4)

Despite these negative findings, people, especially pregnant women, continue to be afraid of harm. On the one hand, there are the negative results already cited, together with negative results from studies such as the one by Finland's Institute of Occupational Health that examined the cases of 1475 mothers who had malformed children. (5) On the other hand, the secretarial organization called "9 to 5" has reported isolated cases of clusters of maternity and delivery problems and has conducted a survey with only a 15 percent response rate that claims a significant miscarriage rate. (18) Unfortunately, a long-planned NIOSH study to study the matter in more detail has been postponed several times, in large part for lack of an adequate control group. (4)

Stress

One issue that NIOSH has raised has not been given much attention. This is stress. Even in its earliest studies since the mid-1970s, it found very high levels of stress in clerical departments using VDTs. In fact, although it sees no links between radiation and miscarriages, it has noted that high levels of stress can indeed cause miscarriages. (21) Although the information center is not likely to supervise clerical offices directly, there is a possibility that it may do so in some firms. In the quest for productivity, clerical workers are often subject to heavy tension. One early NIOSH analyst who asked not to be named said, after studying insurance companies, that he had never seen such high levels of stress on assembly lines.

Ergonomics in Perspective

Overall, the field of ergonomics is confusing and, at the time of this writing, filled with questions. There are some cheap fixes that should probably be universal, including glare screens, intelligent display placement, and sound hoods over printers. But if workers spend any significant amount of time at their desks, a more comprehensive, and expensive, program of support must be provided, including investments in tables and chairs that may range from $1000 to $2000 per worker.

CONCLUSION

The information center's manager needs to deal with a great mass of detailed organization and policy matters. The first of these, of course, is how the information center should be organized. This chapter argues that the organization of traditional information systems (IS) departments leaves a gap between the IS department and Type II user departments. It also argues that the information center should be specifically designated as the unit that bridges this gap, handling all support for Type II departments through a single organizational interface with these departments. Finally, the chapter argues that the information center should broaden its self-image, seeing itself not only as a consulting and training group, but also as part of a marketing (including distribution) system and as a general contractor when multi-tool applications are constructed.

In staffing, the key problem is the size/headcount paradox. Although end user computing is or will soon be the dominant form of corporate computing, only one person is needed in the information center for every hundred or so end users. As a result, the information center is normally a small unit within the IS department and so has little political power. Further complicating this problem is the fact that the unit is normally headed by a junior person within IS and is often viewed as a low-level service group instead of a critical unit responsible for the largest part of corporate computing. It is also viewed as being technically uninteresting compared to the data base and large application development groups within IS. Because of all of these factors, many information centers lack the corporate "clout," even within IS, to manage end user computing as a strategic part of IS and corporate development in general.

Although it is critical to hire and train the information center staff, it is equally crucial to mobilize end users to help one another. User groups, newsletters, and other linking devices can help end users with similar problems work together. It is especially important to develop a special program to organize and support functional specialists (also called power users and lead users), so that they can execute their unique roles within their departments.

The information center must cope with a number of important policy issues, including privacy, security, damage, theft, and piracy. Each of these matters has the potential to provoke serious lawsuits, and the corporation will be in a bad legal position if it has no strong program to deter these problems. Without such programs, low-level misconduct by end users can get the corporation into serious trouble. The information center must combat these problems not only with penalties that are strictly enforced but also with positive measures, such as providing loaner copies of software to prevent unauthorized software copying done simply to try out new programs.

In ergonomics, the corporation should have strong plans for glare, lighting, chairs, work surfaces, noise, heat, air flow, and other problems that may reduce on-the-job productivity. The corporation should also state its position on the question of radiation, particularly for pregnant workers. These issues are far more serious in Type I than Type II departments. Hence, ergonomics policies should be set at the IS level or above the IS level by a corporate human resources committee, not at the level of the information center.

REVIEW QUESTIONS

1. Explain why it would be desirable to define the information center's role as being the support arm for tools used in Type II nonclerical office departments.

Describe the various images that are possible for this role, adding your own images if possible.

2. What is the importance/headcount paradox? Why is it a serious threat to the management of end user computing as a strategic IS thrust? What steps can IS management take to prevent this paradox from being harmful?
3. Describe staff hiring and training.
4. Why is it critical to mobilize end users? What specific programs should an information center implement to mobilize end users? In particular, why is it especially critical to organize functional specialists (power users), and what programs should be implemented to mobilize them?
5. What can an information center do to promote end user computing?
6. What are the key technological infrastructure standards to set? What process should be used to set them? What general philosophical alternatives are there for enforcement?
7. Discuss alternatives for purchasing and maintenance. Discuss the specific problems of installation and software upgrades.
8. Distinguish between privacy, security, damage, and theft. What steps can be taken to deter each?
9. What are some reasons for unauthorized copying? Why is it critical to deter piracy? What can be done to deter piracy?
10. Do you think that radiation is harmful? Back your answer with data, but give your own opinion on the subject. What are other ergonomic problems, and what can be done to reduce them?

REFERENCES

1. ALLEN, T. J., *Managing the Flow of Technology*, MIT Press, 1977.
2. BEELER, JEFFREY, "Information Centers Seen Commonplace," *Computerworld*, October 26, 1981.
3. BENSEN, DAVID H., "A Field Study of End User Computing: Findings and Issues," *MIS Quarterly*, December 1983, pp. 34-45.
4. BETTS, MICH, "Federal Office Delays Study on Pregnancy Risks of VDT Use," *Computerworld*, February 24, 1986, p. 15.
5. BETTS, MICH, "Report Links VDTs, Birth Defects," *Computerworld*, February 17, 1986, p. 13.
6. Computer Intelligence Corporation, *Information Center Market: CI Special IC Manager Survey*, July 1985.
7. CRAIG, JEFFREY L., "GE's Electronic Corporate Ladder," *DATAMATION*, April 15, 1986.
8. DAINOFF, MARVIN J., *Visual, Musculoskeletal, and Performance Differences Between Good and Poor VDT Work Stations*, National Institute for Occupational Safety and Health, 1982.
9. DECH, LEANNE, "Companies Find PC Newsletters Foster DP-User Communications," *PC Week*, March 25, 1986, p. 47.
10. DIFFRIENT, NIELS, *Human Scale 7/8/9*, MIT Press, 1981.

REFERENCES

11. DiNucci, Darcy, "Copying Software: Who's Right?" *PC World,* September 1985, pp. 84-90.
12. Ditlea, Steve, "Befriending the Befuddled," *DATAMATION,* June 15, 1985, pp. 84-90.
13. *EDP Analyzer,* "Supporting End User Programming," June 1981.
14. Frazier, Donald, "Piracy Study: 50% of All Software Copied Illegally," *PC Week,* January 22, 1985, pp. 1, 6.
15. Gable, David, "Maintenance Contracts," *PC Week,* September 24, 1985, pp. 75-76.
16. Gabel, David, "Better Deals: Do Retail Dealers or Mail-Order Firms Give You More for Your Money?" *PC Week,* May 14, 1985, p. 43.
17. Gerwin, Donald, "The Do's and Don'ts of Computerized Manufacturing," *Harvard Business Review,* March-April 1982, pp. 107-116.
18. Haber, Lynn, "Survey by 9 to 5 Links VDTs, Health Problems," *Computerworld,* February 27, 1984, p. 12.
19. Hammond, L. W., "Management Considerations for an Information Center," *IBM Systems Journal,* Vol. 21, No. 2, 1982, pp. 131-161.
20. Head, Robert V., *Planning and Implementing Information Resource Centers for End User Computing,* QUE Information Sciences, Inc., 1985.
21. Hoard, Bruce, "Niosh: No Links Between CRT, Health Hazards," *Computerworld,* July 26, 1982, p. 7.
22. IBM, *The Management of End-User Computing: Support Organization,* First Edition, IBM Corporation, White Plains, New York, October 1984.
23. Karten, Naomi, "Information Centers: Problems or Solutions?" *Computerworld,* December 5, 1984, pp. 37-40.
24. Kendall, Richard M., "The Office Revolution: Health Hazards Coming into Focus," *Occupational Hazards,* October 1983, pp. 79-83.
25. LaMotta, Toni, and Bernknopf, Jeff, "Performance, not Flash," *Information Center,* May 1986, pp. 17-20.
26. LaPlante, Alice, "Corporate Micro Labs Offer Solutions," *InfoWorld,* April 28, 1986, pp. 47-50.
27. Leitheiser, Robert L., and Wetherbe, James C., "A Survey of Information Centers: Services, Decisions, Problems, Successes," Management Information Systems Research Center, School of Management, University of Minnesota, Minneapolis, Minnesota, 1984.
28. Lewensetin, Bruce V., "The Ethics of Software Piracy," *PC Magazine,* April 30, 1985, pp. 179-187.
29. Littman, Jonathan, "Pacific Bell: Networking PCs," *PC Week,* January 22, 1986, pp. 33-38.
30. Littman, Jonathan, "PG&E Utility Gains Power with PCs," *PC Week,* January 8, 1985, pp. 39-42.
31. Mandell, Patricia, "Site Licenses," *PC Week,* April 9, 1985, pp. 43-46.
32. McEnaney, Mura, "Study Suggests VDT Emissions Have Adverse Biological Effect," *Computerworld,* October 29, 1984.
33. Meilach, Dona Z., "Ergonomics . . . The Science of Safe Computer Use, *Interface Age,* July 1983, pp. 49-53.
34. Melymuka, Kathleen, "The Upgrade Upheaval," *PC Week,* February 4, 1986, pp. 47-49.
35. Metz, Richard, "Boeing's PC Practices," *DATAMATION,* January 15, 1986, pp. 85-88.

36. Munro, Malcom C., and Huff, Sid L., "Information Technology Assessment and Adoption: Understanding the Information Center Role," *Proceedings of the Twenty-First Annual Computer Personnel Research Conference,* Association for Computing Machinery, May 2-3, 1985, pp. 29-37
37. NIOSH, *Potential Health Hazards of Video Display Terminals,* June 1981.
38. Panko, Raymond R., and Sprague, Ralph H., Jr., "A Marketing Perspective on Information Systems Management," Working Paper 85-1, Decision Sciences Department, University of Hawaii, 2404 Maile Way, Honolulu, Hawaii, 1985.
39. Panko, Raymond R., and Sprague, Ralph H., Jr., "Toward a New Framework for Office Support," *Proceedings of the ACM SIGOA Conference on Office Information Systems,* Association for Computing Machinery, June 21-23, 1982, pp. 82-92.
40. Petrosky, Mary, "Demand for Micro Managers Increasing," *InfoWorld,* June 1, 1985, pp. 30-34.
41. Ruby, Daniel, "Grumman's Productive PCs," *PC Week,* August 20, 1985, pp. 33-36.
42. Santarelli, Mary-Beth, "In-House User Groups," *Information Center,* May 1986, pp. 33-36.
43. Shipley, Chris, "PC Replacement Seen as Way to Cut Maintenance Costs," *PC Week,* April 15, 1986, pp. 33-36.
44. Stemps, David, "Who's Maintaining the Micros?" *DATAMATION,* April 15, 1986, pp. 83-86.
45. Winkler, Connie, "Cooking with Custom PCs," *PC Week,* January 14, 1986, pp. 29-36.

SUPPORT
consulting, training, and troubleshooting 5

Chapter 1 identified four major roles for the information center.

- Building a technological infrastructure
- Supporting end users
- Controlling end user computing
- Promoting end user computing

Chapter 4 concentrated on three information center roles: building a technological infrastructure, control, and promotion. This chapter focuses on support—the role that most directly concerns users.

INTRODUCTION

Major Themes

The Support Mix
This chapter has three major themes. The first is the need to create a "support mix" to assist users. As the studies cited in the previous chapter indicate, nearly all information centers provide three support services.

- **Consulting** in application development
- **Training** in tools and higher level concepts
- **Troubleshooting** after the development effort gets underway

These should not be viewed as three separate services. Rather, they should be regarded as three components of the **support mix** needed by end users. Just as a cake mix requires precisely the right ingredients in precisely the right proportions and order, the support mix needs to combine these three basic services into a cohesive program of support.

Life Cycle Support

The second major theme of this chapter is the need to develop **life cycle project support.** As discussed in Chapter 2, projects proceed through a series of predictable stages, beginning with a hazy initial idea about what should be done and culminating in implementation and ongoing use. At each stage, there are different degrees and different types of consulting, training, and troubleshooting needs. Information centers need to develop life cycle support programs for various kinds of projects. In general, they need to tailor life cycle support programs to the four different environments of end user computing introduced in Chapter 1. (The other environment discussed in Chapter 1 was the data processing development environment.) They will also have to tailor their support mixes to the needs of individual users.

The Skills Hierarchy

The third major theme of this chapter is the existence of a hierarchy of skills that end users need to master. Some skills, such as the ability to format a disk, are very basic and easily mastered. Other skills, such as the ability to create a model whose flow is clear and that correctly describes the real situation, are far more difficult to master.

If the user lacks some of the skills needed to do a project, then either training must bridge the gap, or additional consulting or troubleshooting will have to be provided.

Training Considerations

Although training is only one form of support, it is the most time-consuming support service for most information centers.

Training Alternatives

The first problem is that there are many ways to provide training: internal classroom training, classroom training from vendors, classroom training from third parties, computer-based training (CBT), and video-based training. Each has strengths and weaknesses that need to be matched to the needs of the task and the individual.

Effectiveness in Training

The second problem is that we do not have a good theory of end user learning. As a result, although research suggests some guidelines, it is very difficult to say what will be effective in training. Most ideas about training effectiveness derive from practical experience, and like all ideas born from practical experience, they have both the advantages of springing from actual working knowledge of training situations and the disadvantages of personal viewpoints and limited exposure to different kinds of situations.

Mobilizing End Users

The third problem is how to help end users teach one another more effectively. User-to-user training has many advantages, and if the information

THE SKILLS HIERARCHY

The Need to Understand User Skills

When most people begin to work with computers, their skills are just good enough to get by. Within a few weeks or months, however, most users graduate beyond basic skills, to the advanced skills needed to use computers well. A few even become "power users" whose knowledge in specific areas is likely to exceed the knowledge of the information center's staff.

Research is badly needed to understand what skills users need in their daily work. Unfortunately, the research we need has not been done. As a consequence, every information center must consider needed skills and develop the training users need. It must also develop support programs that users need but cannot be expected to handle themselves.

Figure 5-1 shows one possible taxonomy of user skills. It is expressed in the form of a hierarchy, with low-level skills at the bottom and mastery skills at the top. Other ways of viewing user skills are possible, and skill models do not even have to be viewed as hierarchical, but our discussion will be limited to the skills hierarchy model shown in Figure 5-1.

In general, users rise through the skills hierarchy over time. But it would be a mistake to think that users jump completely from level to level. Even after a long period of time, most users have only basic skills in certain areas, while they have advanced skills in other areas. Thus, the levels shown in Figure 5-1 exist primarily to help classify *individual skills* and to pinpoint lower level skills that users should have but do not. It is not meant to describe the progress of *individual users*.

Innovation

Good Practice
Hardware and software knowledge
Data management
Application development
Domain knowledge
Work systems
Department management
Roles in corporate systems

Comfortable Use Skills

Basic Use Skills

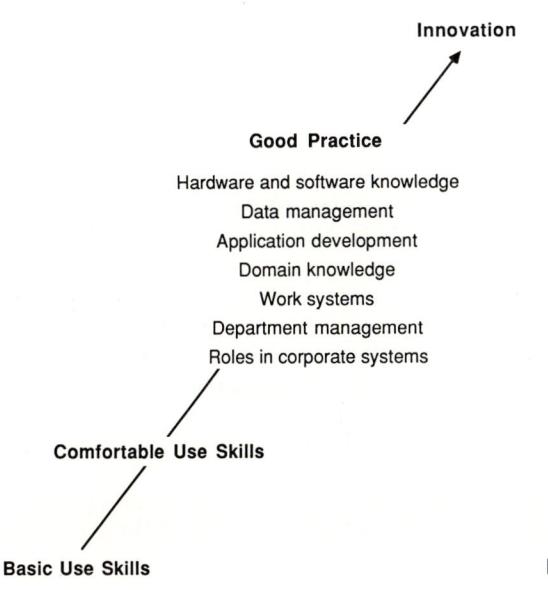

FIGURE 5-1 SKILLS HIERARCHY

Basic Use Skills

The lowest level in the hierarchy is **basic use skills.** These are the skills that users should have after taking two courses: (1) an introductory course on using the computer and its operating system and (2) an introductory course on an application software package.

It would be nice to say that these two courses make the user reasonably competent to do useful work, but that is often not the case. In many cases, the user emerges from these two courses with a crippled understanding of the computer, its operating system, and the application software. Because these courses teach only a few possible functions, most graduates can only work inefficiently, wasting time in blocks that are small but eventually add up to a large amount of wasted effort. In addition, they often lack the training to work safely. They may not understand when to save their work or even know that they need to save their work.

Many users skip the basic course on using the computer and its operating system and jump immediately into an application software course. During the advanced course, the user will have to do so much backtracking that he or she will learn neither how to handle the application program nor how to use the computer and its operating system.

It may be best to teach the computer and operating system course in two modules. A short startup module would be taught before application software courses, and the prerequisite would be rigorously enforced. Later, the second part of the introductory computer and operating system course would be taught. It is easier to enforce the taking of a short course than a longer course, and users will be better prepared to understand more advanced introductory operating system concepts once they have had some experience working with an application program.

Comfortable Use Skills

The second level in the hierarchy is **comfortable use skills.** At this level, the user graduates from the very limited understanding that he or she had initially. To a great extent, this growing comfort comes from use. As the user becomes more and more familiar with the computer, its operating system, and application software, patterns of working "fall into place" in the user's mind. This brings growing comfort with the system and usually the confidence to explore new features. In addition to experience, comfort grows as users learn tricks and principles from other users in their departments and as they take advanced modules in the use of the computer, its operating system, and application software.

A potential problem at this level is **plateauing**—stopping at an incomplete understanding of the hardware and software. Some word processing users, for instance, may never learn the program's embedded programming language. As a result, they have a crippled understanding of the product, which limits their efficiency. Plateauing is particularly important when a company is thinking about upgrading to a new software package with more features than the current software. There is no point trying to make such a change if users have already plateaued far below the limits of their current tool.

To prevent plateauing, advanced modules in use skills should be encouraged. Many advanced skills are difficult to master, and without formal training, users are not likely to "get over the hump" to learn them. In some cases, advanced learning should be mandatory. Secretaries, for instance, should know most of the advanced features of their word processing system. In most cases, however, advanced modules should be kept optional. A large amount of discretion must be given to managers, professionals, and clerical workers in the modern firm.

In any case, it is far better to encourage than to mandate. The information center needs to make advanced modules very accessible through live instruction and mediated training, and it must publicize these modules. In promotional material, it should sell the benefits of learning particular advanced modules.

A worse limitation of comfortable computer use is that it still represents only a small part of what computer users need to know to work effectively in an organizational environment. Users at this stage still do not know how to select computers, organize their data files, do data modeling, develop applications, set policies for backup and the delegation of routine work, or any of the other skills that are critical to keeping computers from becoming major problems instead of major opportunities. These skills come at the next higher level, good practice.

Good Practice

Good practice goes beyond the skills needed to work with the computer, its operating system, and its application software. It involves all of the knowledge that users must have to work with computers efficiently and safely.

Hardware and Software Knowledge

It is not enough to know how to push the right buttons to get a document to print. Users must have a wide variety of other hardware and software skills.

- They must be able to decide whether to use a PC or mainframe and what kind of application software package will best serve their needs. This requires a thorough understanding of the relative advantages of alternatives.
- They should be able to specify their personal computer and terminals, down to the level of individual options and their costs. Although it would be ideal to leave this to the information center, users need to take some control of their destinies.
- They should be able to install new computers, hardware options, and software packages. Physical setup is usually easier than the complex and sometimes mystifying task of trying to get an application package working on a particular personal computer.
- They should realize the need to automate frequent operations, and, they should have the skills to automate these operations by using embedded programming languages such as DOS batch files and Lotus 1-2-3 macros.

- They should be able to do day-to-day maintenance, including fixing problems, changing ribbons, and following a schedule of preventative maintenance.

Data Management

The managing of a person's or department's data is not a matter of technology at all. Rather, it depends on intellectual organization and is too central to a department's needs to be left to an information center staff member. Yet, few users are trained in personal and departmental data management.

- They should be able to plan file organization for floppy disks and hard disks, in order to avoid the chaos and lost time that result when old files are difficult to find. This is particularly important when networking is present, on host computers, and on personal computers that are placed in common areas to be shared by several people in a department.
- They should have the technical knowledge to create hierarchical file structures, including knowing when it is desirable to have a file organization software utility (see Chapter 8).
- They should be able to develop a retention schedule for files, both to avoid disks being overloaded and to reduce the time needed to find a particular file.
- They should be able to maintain a paper description of the files on disks, as well as descriptions of record-structured data files (see Chapter 10).
- On PCs, they should be able to understand the need for backup and know how to develop a backup system, including schedules, personal responsibilities, and procedures for dealing with disaster recovery, including switching to other computers for essential tasks and recreating the hard disk.

Application Development

Chapter 2 discussed the process of prioritizing applications for development and developing individual applications. Users should know these processes, both in general and in detail. They should especially understand the importance of design before construction, documentation for future maintainers, and documentation for users if other people will be using their application.

Domain Knowledge

When users work in a particular application domain, such as analysis, they need knowledge that is specific to that particular domain, for example, knowledge about financial concepts or statistical inference. Domain-specific knowledge, which is discussed to varying degrees in subsequent chapters dealing with particular applications, must be mastered to avoid serious mistakes that no amount of knowledge about computers can avoid.

Every course that deals with a particular application software product must go beyond button pushing and face up to the complexities involved in that particular application domain. Exercises should reinforce this domain knowledge.

Yet, few application software courses teach domain knowledge. In part, it may be felt that users should already possess such knowledge—a poor assumption in light of the many users who now use financial, statistical, and other advanced packages without a solid foundation in domain knowledge. In part, this failure to teach domain knowledge may also be traced to trainers' ignorance. Most trainers are IS professionals with limited domain knowledge in the many software packages they must teach. It is highly desirable for functional departments to work with the information center and to ensure that domain knowledge in their field is taught well, even if a functional specialist must be brought in to give the lecture.

Work Systems

As discussed in Chapter 2, few computer uses are completely new. In most cases, a manual system is already in place for doing the work, and often a computerized system is already ongoing. In either case, roles, policies, and procedures will already be established, and it is impossible to change one piece of the work system—the computer and its software—and expect other aspects of the work system to remain unchanged. Many aspects of the work system will have to be redesigned.

- **Roles** for various people must be defined; once responsibility is established, users can reason out most of what they should do on an ongoing basis. For instance, once a secretary is given responsibility for backing up a network server, he or she can usually develop efficient processes and schedules for doing so.
- General **policies** need to be laid down to help guide individuals, say policies for labeling private information and for safeguarding files with private information.
- At a finer level of details, specific **procedures** must be given for common tasks, to ensure both that they are done properly and that they are done efficiently.
- As much as possible, these roles, policies, and procedures should be aimed at **delegating work** at as low a level in the department as possible.

Department Managers

As discussed in Chapter 2, each individual must be trained in the specific responsibilities of his or her general department role. Managers must learn exactly what decisions and policies need to be made to ensure good operation. Staff members must understand their responsibilities in application selection, development, and use. Secretaries must also understand their many roles. It is especially important to clarify power users' roles since they are a valuable resource and yet can also be abused, with a resultant loss of personal and departmental productivity.

Roles in Corporate Systems

Workers in Type I clerical departments are likely to work heavily with large corporate data processing systems, such as accounting applications. Even Type II departments, commonly have one or two large applications. Workers need to be trained to understand their roles in the creation and use of these systems. Specifically, they need to learn how to work with systems analysts in the all-important design and implementation stages of data processing application development.

Conclusions About Good Practice

Overall, good practice is a very large area with many different kinds of concerns. Unless an information center spends a great deal of effort to identify these good practice knowledge requirements, it cannot begin to plan intelligently for user training.

Worse yet, if the information center fails to understand the existence or importance of teaching good practice, it will be doing only a fraction of its job. It is not even enough to teach traditional good practice for application development. Although most textbooks still stop there, that is only the beginning of good practice in end user computing.

Innovation

As discussed in Chapter 2, good practice stops at efficiency and safety. It fails to take the last and most critical step of **innovation**—changing the very way the person or department works in response to the capabilities of new technologies. Sharing innovation insights, critical success factors, external contribution analysis, and breakthrough thinking are all important to teach. They are, of course, also very difficult to teach.

Conclusions About the Skills Hierarchy

In the final analysis, as many users as possible must be brought as close as possible to the level of innovation, given the resources of the information center and the willingness of users to move up the hierarchy. In particular, the information center should do the following.

- Mandate and enforce adequate hardware and software training, so that every user goes through full basic skills training without skipping the introductory computer and operating system course, and so that an adequate number of advanced modules are taken.
- Have nonskills training that goes beyond use skills to good practice and innovation skills.
- Move as much domain knowledge and good practice as possible into application software courses, even if this means hiring trainers with domain knowledge for the whole course or for a module on domain knowledge.

TRAINING PRINCIPLES

We will now look at a few studies that present learning principles to help guide information center planners. Although these few studies fall far short of providing a complete theory of training, their general agreement with one another and with the practical experiences of many teachers gives good support for a number of widely held beliefs while challenging other beliefs.

Harmon's Application of Piaget's Theories

The skills hierarchy discussed above is not based on formal theory, but the idea of stages of learning is found in many aspects of education. Paul Harmon, in a *Computerworld* article, discussed the implications of Piaget's work on stages in learning, adding insights from later scholars. (9) Although Piaget is known for his studies of childhood and adolescent training, his basic categories have been found to carry over into adult life. (9)

Concrete Operationalism

Piaget found that when children learn a subject such as mathematics, they first go through a stage called **concrete operationalism,** in which they learn to do steps by rote, with little recourse to any underlying theory of what they are doing. Harmon notes that adults experience this stage when learning to drive in a new city (9). They often learn just a few specific routes. They are trying, in other words, to do their work with mechanical algorithms; there is no understanding the basic principles behind what they are doing.

Formal Operationalism

At the next stage, children reach **formal operationalism,** in which they begin to understand the principles behind what they are doing and begin to apply these principles to true solving of problems, instead of using fixed algorithms. Like the driver in a new city who finally studies a map, the learner who reaches formal operationalism develops a broad ability to work with the sphere of knowledge. The learner who reaches formal operationalism can do true problem solving instead of following concrete behavior patterns. (9)

Until a person reaches formal operationalism, he or she may draw the wrong conclusions from experience. A teenage driver who makes a dangerous pass on a curve and does not have the underlying knowledge of the danger of passing on curves may conclude that passing on a curve is safe. (9) End users who use their equipment while at a fairly operational level of skills frequently misinterpret what they see taking place on the machine's screen. (2)

Meta-Cognitive Understanding

Harmon follows other cognitive psychologists in adding a third stage to Piaget's model. This third stage, meta-cognitive understanding, denotes adult learning in which the learner monitors, evaluates, and ultimately directs his or her learning. (9) Harmon combines this skill with the ability to manipulate two formal systems, such as having formal knowledge of both programming and accounting. Harmon calls this combination of self-direction and the formal mastery of two domains **meta-formal thought.**

A major advantage of Harmon's model seems to be the implication that users engage in concrete, formal, and meta-cognitive thinking in sequence, so that trainers must first get people up to the level of concrete operations when they work with computers and only later try to move them up to formal thinking and problem solving.

In EUC training, it may be best to get users going quickly, using simple step-by-step "cheat sheets" on how to perform key actions. Later, as users become more comfortable, they can be led from concrete to formal operationalism by adding conceptual frameworks. For example, it may be best to drill users in formal DOS commands before adding the idea that some commands are internal while others are external. If theoretical constructs are taught while users are still at the level of concrete operationalism, they may understand little and retain even less.

IBM's Minimalist Training Study

Trainers can also take guidance from a series of studies conducted by researchers at IBM's Thomas J. Watson Research Center. Although these studies focused on word processing, their results probably have much wider applicability.

Quick-Start Behavior

When IBM researchers studied people learning a new word processing system, (2) they found much to their surprise that people did not work through the formal manual. Typifying users' responses to the manual was a comment by a person who skipped over several pages of the manual saying that it was "just information." Instead, learners jumped the gun and began working with scarcely a glance at the manual. When they did read the manual, they typically jumped around, skipping to parts that interested them.

Adding to their impatience was a desire to do real work instead of learning about the system. One learner complained, "I want to do something, not learn how to do everything." (2) Another said, "I could have typed 3,000 words by now." (2)

Although this kind of behavior causes the designers of carefully paced tutorials to roll their eyes in dismay, quick-start behavior has some obvious advantages. Most importantly, by plunging in until they have a problem, users do not waste time on working exercises teaching them what they see immediately. Why learn what you already know? Unfortunately, as we will now see, quick-start behavior can lead to a number of problems that quickly eat up gains in learning time.

Naive Cognitive Models

Even when the learners studied by IBM were in doubt, they reasoned what would probably happen instead of reading the manual. Needless to say, they got into considerable trouble, and even then, they continued to ignore the screen, as they had done all along.

In effect, most users seem to be working with a cognitive model of how the system *should* act. They use this cognitive model to guide their actions, backtracking to the manual or seeking human help only when their model clearly breaks down. These "naive cognitive models" are useful to the extent that they are right, but they can lead to disaster because they tend to blind users to the feedback given by the system if this feedback does not fit their expectations. Things that do not fit the theory are ignored, or, if they are not ignored, the user tends to go past them and hope that everything will be all right anyway.

The use of naive models by learners has been recognized in science education. (12) In physics, for example, students try to apply naive models to problems instead of what they are thought. In addition, over time prior naive models tend to take over from formal models. (12) It is very important to teach proper models and have students apply them until they become second nature. Shallow learning dies too rapidly.

Where users tend to use naive theories, it is important not only to teach correct theory, but also to reinforce it through exercises and repetition at intervals of time. Between each repetition, many users will have reverted to the use of naive theory.

Problems with Quick-Start Behavior

Although one can argue that users were learning the system efficiently, the IBM study found that people who followed this approach got into constant trouble. They had a great deal of time getting out of trouble once they got into it because they had probably completed a series of steps incorrectly before they realized they were in trouble. (2)

Using the Results

The study team responded to the results of the research by radically changing their approach to documentation. Instead of a massive reference manual, they produced a minimal manual with as little verbiage as possible (2). They broke it into small chapters of two or three pages so that people could jump around as they were bound to do. The manual also tried to get users to look at the screen by asking questions about it. (2)

Scharer's Less Is More Study

The Use of "Cheat Sheets"

In another study, Scharer (16) studied several dozen users that had to be trained on more than 20 online systems. Like the IBM researchers, she found that only 10 percent to 15 percent of the users looked at the formal manuals during their training periods. Instead, they listened carefully during demonstrations and took notes. When the demonstration ended, the only sheet of paper they used extensively was one holding the telephone number of the systems analyst who did the demonstration.

User-to-User Training

In general, users helped one another when they got into trouble, and they even trained new users when they came on board The people who originally read the manual stopped doing so and wrote up some "cheat sheets" for common problems. These sheets, rarely even typed, were copied and widely distributed.

Using the Results

Scharer noted that, although the formal manual was a failure, the users were highly attentive during the demonstrations and were natural teachers. She also noted that this approach was probably successful because so many users were already experienced with computers. They were able to walk into the demonstrations with a good idea of how the system was likely to work, and their notes were confined to exceptions and very specific information. Scharer responded by creating manuals that were basically cheat sheets with as few words as possible, plus some later memos stapled to its end.

IBM's Training Wheels Word Processor Study

The Training Wheels Word Processor

In another study by IBM, building on the minimalist training study described earlier, the IBM researchers developed a training wheels word processor in which they attempted to block the most common quick-start errors found in the study by disabling certain functions in the system. (3)

Results of the Research

This action of blocking errors dramatically speeded learning time. When office temporaries with no word processing backgrounds were given the same instruction manual and letter to type, learning time was much faster in the group using the "training wheels" version of the word processor. The group with the commercial system took 116 minutes, on the average, to do the work, whereas the group with the training wheels system took only 92 minutes. The difference, as expected, seems to be attributed almost exclusively to the time commercial system users spent recovering from nonblocked errors. The group with training wheels also had higher comprehension scores and work-attitude scores, and they had a higher completion rate on advanced work. (3)

Tentative Conclusions

Although little research has been done to date on user learning, the work just described has reinforced several ideas commonly proposed by experienced trainers.

Skills Hierarchy

The first conclusion is the existence of a skills hierarchy. Harmon describes a growth in understanding over time that follows Piaget's work and research on adult learning. His approach is different from the skills hierarchy presented earlier in the chapter. Blending the two together, we would expect the growth from concrete understanding to meta-cognitive understanding to take place in most or all individual areas discussed in the skills hierarchy. Users would go through these steps when learning how to use their computers, again when learning how to use a specific application package, and yet again when working on data modeling or selecting a personal computer.

Quick-Start Behavior

The second conclusion is that users rarely follow long tutorials. They like to jump ahead and try things out, jumping backward and forward through material covered in the tutorial. This practice is so pervasive that training materials should be devised to fit this user behavior. How-to manuals with clear organization and many small sections that can be mastered quickly and with a minimum of reading need to be devised, so that people can move around quickly. Instead of viewing quick-starting as a problem, it should be viewed as the normal way of learning and should form the basis for training.

Users Have Preexisting Cognitive Models

The third conclusion is that users always approach each situation with an underlying model of how the system works, even if they have little background on the type of software being used or on computers in general. In some cases, reasoning by this intuitive model produces the right results, but in other cases it leads to major errors, and when errors do occur, they often go unrecognized. In general, these intuitive models seem to be based on analogies drawn from knowledge the user already has. For example, users who are familiar with typewriters habitually try to move the cursor on a word processor by hitting the space bar and carriage return keys, just as they do on a typewriter.

Since user learning is likely to be heavily influenced by preexisting models, teachers have to be sensitive to how their students are approaching various situations, in order to try to understand what models they are using. If this can be done, these models can be confronted directly and used as desirable. It is also likely to be beneficial to try to create some simple vivid analogies when teaching how something operates, so that the person will have a strong substitute model to use when approaching the system.

Keep It Short and Simple

The fourth general result is that users like things kept short and simple, with directions that can be used without extensive reading and that contain a minimum of words. When to add more advanced concepts or attack underlying naive user theories has not been explored, but the best time definitely seems to be after the user has become comfortable with the mechanical workings of the system. This suggestion fits both our skills hierarchy and Harmon's analysis.

Compounding Errors

The fifth and last general result is that users will make complex errors. The combination of racing ahead and not understanding when things have begun to go wrong tends to lead users into making a sequence of errors, often producing an error state from which recovery can be possible only with heroic efforts. This last result implies that training should be done only when there are experienced users around who can extract the person from problems. Otherwise, the user is likely to grow extremely frustrated.

TRAINING CONSIDERATIONS

Now that we have considered some of the theoretical issues and basic principles behind user learning, we can attack the problem of *how* to train end users—more specifically, we can look at the training alternatives that are available to information center managers.

Trends

Training is not new to U.S. information workers. A 1984 study by the Bureau of Labor Statistics (1) showed that 35 percent of all information workers had undergone skill training of all types, with 12 percent receiving training in school, 11 percent in formal on-the-job programs, and 14 percent in informal on-the-job training. Not surprisingly, managerial, professional, and higher skilled sales workers were the most likely to receive the additional training. Spending figures on end user training are more difficult to obtain, but in 1984, it was estimated that $3 billion was being spent on personal computer training alone. (12) Today, the training bill is far higher.

Organizational Responsibilities

Should Training Be Done Within the Information Center?

In many organizations, the information center is responsible for end user training. Quite a few firms, however, already have well-established training departments with excellent facilities, and it is becoming common to see end user training based there. Pacific Bell is one company that follows this practice. (14) Its end user training falls in the human relations department.

When the management of training is centralized in the information center, organizational choices still remain. Should the information center trainers be a distinct subunit, or should all information center staffers share the training work? More importantly, should some or all of the training be done externally? Managing does not necessarily mean doing.

Mobilizing End Users

Because so many firms have taken great pains to mobilize their end users to help one another, it is very common to find training formalized through this process. For example, Pacific Gas and Electric (PG&E) has a three-tier program to support its thousands of PCs spread over 94,000 square miles. (11) At PG&E, users are trained directly by local supervisors, who in turn are trained by divisional micro coordinators, who meet as a group monthly. The divisional micro coordinators are trained by central trainers.

Industry Patterns

When Efroymson and Phillips asked information center managers who did training in their firms, "all of the above" best describes the results they got. (8)

- More than half listed training in three or more corporate departments.
- All but one did training in the information center.
- Half trained in MIS or DP
- Half trained in human resources, personnel, or corporate training.
- Half trained locally through resident experts
- Half used outside training firms.

Diversity in Needs

In selecting training alternatives, it is important to consider the highly diverse needs of end users. This chapter focuses on differences in training needs in the four environments of end user computing, but several other dimensions of end user needs also need to be taken into account.

User Knowledge
The first dimension is user knowledge. At one end of the scale are the novice users who have little or no computer literacy. At the other end are the power users, whose party jokes revolve around arcane technical matters. Some trainers feel that users at the two extremes cause the most problems—novice users because of their lack of knowledge and power users because of their constant demands. (6) Other trainers believe that the biggest problems come from intermediate users, who are frustrated by what they do not know. (6)

Organizational Level
A second dimension of user differences is whether the person is a clerical worker or a professional. Most firms train secretaries separately from managers and professionals, both to avoid uneasiness in mixing these people together in a peer-like environment and in order to deal with the different needs and educational levels among these groups. Top management, in turn, is often given one-to-one tutoring to avoid putting them into a class with subordinates as well as to cater to their hectic time schedules.

Typing Speed
In classroom training situations that involve hands-on computer use, typing speed can be an important consideration. Unless classes are segregated by typing speed, the slowest typists are likely to fall behind, feel embarrassed, and become demoralized.

Modular Learning

The Modularization of Courses
If the user is faced with a complex product, such as using Lotus 1-2-3, it is inefficient to teach every feature of the program initially. An overload of detail early in the training period will often result in the user losing even basic information. Users need to be given a series of modules that are timed to match their use patterns. In addition, not every user is likely to need every module. Many Lotus 1-2-3 users, for instance, feel little need to learn macros. A typical 1-2-3 program would therefore begin with an introductory module that everyone must take, followed by a universal module for such items as absolute references in copying, printing well, and doing simple graphics. These two modules would be followed by a series of optional modules, such as macros.

When to Teach the Machine and Operating System
In both PC and host applications, an important issue is when to teach the machine and its operating system. The user should have these skills before taking an application software course, but many users enroll without prerequisite training, and those who do take basic machine and operating system training complain that they have no motivation for learning the material. Perhaps a good approach is to teach some machine and operating system skills

initially, allow the user to take a basic module on an application package, and then require an in-depth course on the machine and its operating system before allowing enrollment in advanced application software modules.

Lengths of Modules and Sessions

Modules should be limited to about six hours, and even these short modules should be divided into two or three hour segments, since skills learning is so exhausting. Given their time constraints, however, many users choose to take an exhaustive (and exhausting) three-day course instead of breaking up their days for several weeks of intermittent training.

Skills Versus Concepts

Training focuses on two basically different entities: **skills** in using computers and **concepts,** such as system development disciplines and data structures. Most corporate training focuses on skills, providing little to support the conceptual development of users. This emphasis is likely to create major problems in the long run, unless users can get needed conceptual information informally or unless information centers switch to conceptual teaching as the user base becomes comfortable at the skills level.

Skills and concepts need to be taught differently. For example, linear presentations on video tape without hands-on computer use are deadly for teaching computer use skills. On the other hand, linear presentations are often very good ways to teach concepts.

More important than the way knowledge is taught is making sure that it *is* taught at all. Most commercial courses focus almost exclusively on skills, and the information center may have to supplement commercial courses with in-house knowledge training.

TRAINING ALTERNATIVES

Users may be trained in many ways, ranging from classroom courses to computer-based training. Each has its advantages and disadvantages. One possible option is not to train at all, at least formally. Instead, users can be asked to teach one another or to learn by reading manuals and the tutorials that application software vendors supply with their software. The problem with this approach is that users lose a great deal of time, since this form of learning is inefficient. By not doing formal training, costs are transferred from the information center to the functional departments of the corporation. Many users will not use the system unless formal training is provided, and many others will develop such narrow skills that they will be limited to only a few features—as if they were driving a Ferrari without knowing how to take it out of first gear. Faced with these problems, few firms fail to do any training at all.

CLASSROOM TRAINING

Classroom training with a live instructor is a popular alternative for user training.

Advantages of Classroom Training

Classroom training has several strong advantages over other forms of training, which do not use live instructors.

- Feedback is immediate when problems occur. Learners can ask questions, and the teacher can ask questions to gauge the group's understanding.
- The teaching can be tailored to the learners by adding company-specific examples or job-specific examples.
- The classroom is a familiar and acceptable environment for most people.

Disadvantages of Classroom Training

On the negative side, classroom instruction also has a number of strong disadvantages.

- It is usually more expensive than mediated training without instructors. A typical instructor can only teach one or two days a week; the rest of the time is spent in preparation. In addition, training facilities are expensive, particularly if hands-on computer training is to be done.
- Users have to wait until a class starts to get them the training they need. This is impractical in many circumstances, say when a new secretary is hired and needs to learn word processing immediately.
- Teaching quality can vary considerably from course to course.

Internal Versus External Training

If the company decides to sponsor training, the next step is to decide whether to do it internally or whether to contract the training out to external vendors. Many firms use internal training because it has several important advantages.

- There is greater control over quality. If there are quality problems, these can be overcome. With external training, there is less control over quality.
- Courses can be tailored to the corporation by including company-specific information.
- Although the cost of maintaining staff, offices, classrooms, and training computers is large, internal training can be cheaper than external training when extensive training is done.
- Although external training vendors may not offer courses in unusual software packages purchased by the corporation, an internal staff will develop such courses.
- Internal courses can be designed to include the good practice and innovation concepts left out of many external training classes.

On the other hand, external vendors offer a number of advantages over internal training.

- If internal training is done in geographically decentralized organizations, a great deal of travel may have to be necessary to reach remote locations. In contrast, the use of external vendors can provide cheaper local training when popular application software packages or the basic use of the computer are to be taught.
- Unless a firm has a very large training program, external training will be less expensive.
- For popular software packages or basic machine use, external vendors will offer courses almost continuously, whereas internal programs may offer these courses less frequently.

Techniques for Classroom Training

Classroom training is the traditional forum for learning, and it works quite well for conceptual training. The students need not have computers, and the instructor can use traditional audiovisual aids. Some advanced aids would be highly desirable, for instance, a big-screen projector that shows the screen image on the kind of screen normally used for an overhead projector. A big-screen projector lets the teacher demonstrate a program while the entire audience views the results of each key stroke.

For learning skills, however, the participants almost must have computers right at their desks, so that users can repeat the demonstration immediately on their own. Again, a big-screen projector can be extremely valuable because it allows (1) the students to see exactly what they must do and (2) the instructor to interrupt an exercise and show how to get out of a particular problem.

In addition to the benefits of applying what is said immediately, the fact that the instructor is present while the students are doing exercises means that they can get immediate help. Immediate help is especially important when participants make a series of errors that require complex recovery procedures.

A variation on the computer-on-the-desk theme is the approach of doing a bit of classroom training, followed by a retreat to a computer room. This is done in many university courses. However, most trainers agree that there should be no more than ten minutes of talking between hands-on exercises. This is impossible in a traditional classroom setting.

When participants are doing hands-on exercises, they require a lot of help. Most trainers advocate one trainer for every five participants during exercises. Often, this means having ten students supported by a master teacher and an aide.

There is disagreement over whether each individual should have his or her own machine or whether two participants should work at each machine. If there are two participants, they can help one another, reducing both the amount of time to do exercises and the amount of help the instructor must give. If there are two people at each machine, however, the instructor needs to be especially diligent about making sure that they take turns, instead of one person doing most of the work or constantly "teaching" the other person, who should be learning primarily by doing.

MEDIATED TRAINING

In mediated training, the teacher is replaced by a computer disk, video recorder, or other devices.

General Characteristics of Mediated Training

Advantages of Mediated Training
Several features make mediated training attractive.

- It is always available, so users who need to master a software package immediately do not have to wait for a course to start.
- In geographically decentralized organizations, there is no need to send trainers to remote sites or to worry about the quality of local training by external vendors in out-of-the-way sites.
- For the information center, it is usually much cheaper than live training, although users may spend more time learning the material through media.
- Pacing is individualized. People can go through the material at their own speed.

Disadvantages of Mediated Training
On the negative side, mediated training has two serious disadvantages. First, all the advantages of classroom teachers are lost, including perhaps the most important reason for having a life teacher—learner motivation. A good teacher's first job is to stimulate his or her students. Second, the learner will invariably get into trouble as he or she works. Because mediated instruction often takes place in ordinary offices, there may be no one around to help.

Computer-Based Training (CBT)

Computer-based training (CBT) uses the computer as the training vehicle. In CBT, the user is taken through a series of exercises in which the computer is not only a tool the user can employ to do sample work, but also the coordinator of the training process.

Authoring Programs, Presentation Programs, and Courses
In CBT, the course creator uses an **authoring program** to develop a series of presentations and learning exercises for students. The data file created by this program is called a **course.** To use this course, each user must have a **presentation program,** which plays back the course on the user's screen.

In some cases, the presentation program is bundled with each copy of the CBT course. In the best case, the user simply boots the computer and is taken directly to the lesson. In other cases, the user must first learn the presentation program and then the CBT course. This extra learning can be a burden, especially if different CBT courses are written for different presentation programs.

Internal Development Versus Purchasing

CBT courses can be authored within the information center. If authoring is done internally, the training can be geared to the corporation through the selection of examples. The problem with internal authoring is cost. First, the authoring software is expensive. Second, and more importantly, each hour of instruction requires 25 to 250 hours of authoring and testing time. (7) Although newer authoring programs are reducing the amount of time needed to develop high-quality courseware, the time needed to produce and test good CBT courses is still great. Unless the information center serves many users, the cost of internally authored software is likely to be prohibitive.

Because of the cost and complexity of internal authoring, CBT courses are usually purchased from external vendors who sell hundreds or thousands of copies of each CBT course. Their price per course is therefore far more attractive than the price of internally developed courses.

Unfortunately, the quality of CBT courses now on the market remains uneven. In many cases, their products are very poor, forcing the user into lock-step learning, thereby frustrating users who want to work actively and in general throwing away many of CBT's advantages. Many do not even simulate the product being taught.

In other cases, CBT vendors offer a broad curriculum of excellent CBT modules. Some vendors even develop their courseware with popular authoring languages, so that buyers can alter the courses to fit their companies' specific needs.

A major problem with vendor CBT is that there is no standard presentation program. In the IBM mainframe world, the popularity of IBM's Interactive Instructional System (IIS) has created something of a de facto standard, and many vendors build products that run under IIS. For other hosts and for PCs, however, nothing like this exists. A user firm may have to purchase a number of presentation programs to show vendor software.

Overall, the biggest problem facing CBT is the fact that it is not the "normal" way people have been taught. Most people have learned exclusively from classroom instruction and from reading books. The few that did experience CBT, moreover, did so mostly in the 1960s and 1970s, when the state of the art was limited to crude drill-and-practice programs. CBT can be a hard sell and can be uncomfortable for many employees.

CBT Use Patterns

The use of computer-based training seems to be on the rise. A 1985 Crwth survey found that 57 percent of all respondents were already using CBT, 5 percent were planning to introduce it, and 25 percent were exploring it. (5) About two-thirds of the CBT courses were standard CBT vendor packages, and another quarter was authored. (5) Fewer than 10 percent were created under contract.

Not surprisingly, Crwth found that the number of trainees served each year by an information center was a good predictor of whether CBT was used. Among information centers without CBT, only 30 percent trained more than

200 users. In contrast, among the centers that did use CBT, 45 percent trained more than 200 users each year.

In its 1985 survey of information center managers, Computer Intelligence Corporation (CIC) obtained similar results. (4) In the CIC survey, 61 percent of all information center managers reported that they were using micro-CBT, and 40 percent reported using mainframe CBT.

Techniques for Computer-Based Training

EDP Analyzer, after discussions with a number of experts in the CBT field, drew three conclusions about good CBT designs. (7)

1. They are **interactive**, meaning that the user is free to jump around and take the initiative in controlling what will be learned and in what order. In contrast, **reactive** programs control the instruction, and the user does what he or she is told. The learning research on quick-start behavior cited earlier in this chapter bears out the conclusion that interactivity is critical.
2. They do not use testing because testing wastes time and creates anxiety. Instead, learners should decide when they have mastered the material.
3. They **simulate** the software product being taught, instead of just talking about it. The learner does not just answer questions about the system; he or she carries out the actions needed to accomplish goals.

Many CBT courses now on the market, including several of the most popular, are reactive instead of interactive, provide no simulation, and have mandatory testing.

Audio and Video Training

In contrast to CBT, which uses the computer's processing power, audio and video instruction uses separate players to present information. For conceptual training, such as teaching users how computers work, no computer needs to be involved at all. For teaching computer use skills, audio and video instruction presents information while leaving the computer free for exercises.

Audio Cassettes

Some training courses are offered on standard audio cassettes. Cassette users can listen to the tape while looking at the computer screen and perhaps following a written guide that accompanies the tape. Although audio courses lack the appeal of video courses, they can be run on a standard tape player in the user's office.

Videotape and Videodisks

Other training courses are offered on videotape or videodisks. A late bloomer, video training is beginning to move rapidly into the corporate world. **Videotape**—the technology used in home VCRs—is cheap and widely available, but it is essentially a sequential access medium. In contrast, **videodisk** is a random access medium, but it is valuable only when it is under computer control, and computer-controlled videodisk systems are expensive and rare.

Considerations in Using VCR Training

Video adds visual appeal, but VCRs are expensive and computer-controlled videodisk players are even more expensive. As a result, users normally go to a training area to use the instructional materials. This can be inconvenient, but at central sites trained people are usually available to help when the user needs help.

It must also be recognized that there are two popular VCR standards, namely, VHS and Beta. VHS, being more popular, is likely to be a better choice, but many vendors of VCR training materials will supply tapes in both formats.

The Future

In the long term, computer-controlled videodisks will eventually provide an extremely rich working environment, marrying the advantages of visual images and the flexibility and individualization of computer control. If the CD-ROM format for computer-controlled videodisks (discussed in Chapter 7) becomes a popular storage medium, then computer-controlled videodisk training may become available in nearly every office.

Rogers (15) notes that a standard videodisk can hold 54,000 images, retrieving any one in 1.5 seconds and displaying an image as good as one would get from a one-inch broadcast videotape. He notes that regular motion video, stills, animation, and slow motion can be combined in a single lesson. In addition, Rogers notes, computer-generated text can overlay the screen, information on the screen can be highlighted, a procedure on the computer screen can be synchronized with video action, and there are two audio tracks, so instruction can be done in two languages.

Unfortunately, there are as yet no standards for computer-controlled videodisks. IBM's Vision system, Sony's VIEW, and other products are vying for attention, but the situation is still too embryonic to make computer-controlled videodisks an attractive training vehicle.

DEVELOPING A COMPREHENSIVE TRAINING PROGRAM

As discussed earlier in the chapter, end users need a great deal of training to work well. This training cannot be limited to hardware and software use skills. It must also embrace good practice and innovation—the management of end user computing at the personal and departmental levels.

Given these requirements, it seems critical to develop a comprehensive training program that offers courses in all required areas. Figure 5-2 gives one possibility for a comprehensive training program. We will discuss this specific program in this section, but the basic comments should be applicable to most broad designs.

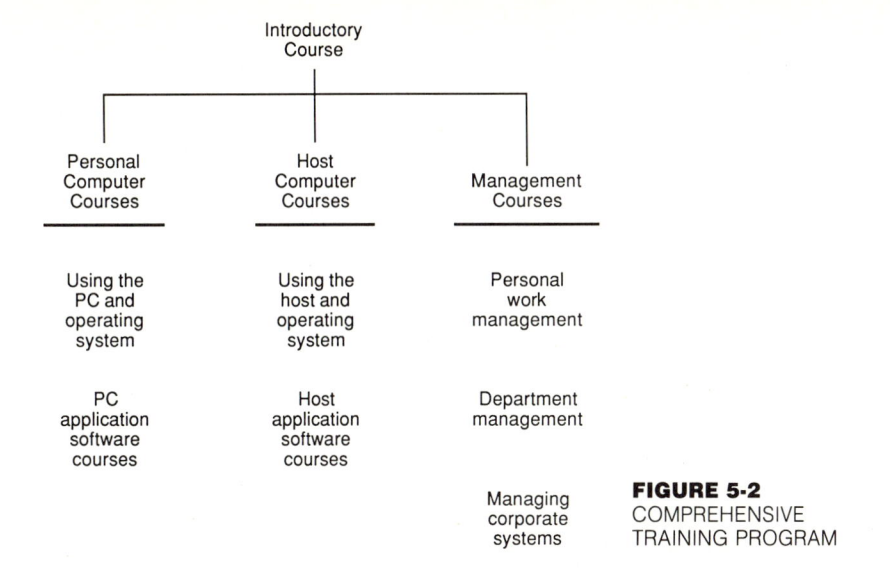

DEVELOPING A COMPREHENSIVE TRAINING PROGRAM **187**

```
                    Introductory
                      Course
        ┌───────────────┼───────────────┐
    Personal          Host          Management
    Computer        Computer         Courses
     Courses         Courses
    ─────────       ─────────       ─────────
    Using the       Using the        Personal
    PC and          host and          work
    operating       operating       management
    system          system

    PC              Host             Department
    application     application      management
    software        software
    courses         courses

                                     Managing
                                     corporate
                                     systems
```

FIGURE 5-2
COMPREHENSIVE TRAINING PROGRAM

The Introductory Course

Everyone in the corporation should take an introductory course that covers the major issues in end user computing, lays out what they must know to work with computers effectively, explains why each skill or knowledge domain is important, and spells out the policy ground rules for end user computing in the firm. Ideally, this course will be part of the training given to all new employees, although when it is first created, it must also be given to existing employees.

The introductory course will have a large amount of ground to cover, but realistically, it must be held to approximately one day. This means that it is critical to stick to main points and not dwell on minor concerns. The following topics are likely to be covered in the course.

- The computer explosion and the shift to end user computing in Type II (managerial and professional) departments.
- A broad survey of computer and communications terminology.
- A survey of EUC and corporate applications, including a bit of hands-on use or at least demonstration to emphasize the importance of major applications.
- The end user's role in general and in different EUC applications.
- Application development for EUC and for larger data processing systems, with an emphasis on the end user's role.
- Specific issues in the management of personal and departmental computing.

- The specific services offered by the information center and how to use these services.
- Corporate policies on privacy, security, damage, theft, piracy, and other key matters.

Personal Computing Courses

There should be a stream of courses for personal computer users. Each should have both basic and advanced modules.

Using the Personal Computer and Its Operating System

As discussed earlier it is critical to teach users how to use their machines and operating systems before allowing them to take application software courses. Although advanced PC and operating system courses can be taken after a basic course in application software, it is critical to take at least the basic course in the use of the PC and its operating system before going on to application software. It is also critical for users to come back to advanced PC and operating system courses instead of simply mastering basic skills.

PC Application Software Courses

Application software courses, as discussed earlier in the chapter, should be divided into a basic module and several advanced modules. Only some users may need to take specific advanced modules. In Lotus 1-2-3, for example, the awkward "data base" function would only be used by some employees.

When teaching application software, it is critical to teach not just button-pushing skills, but also good practice and especially application development. Although the general process of application development will have been taught in the introductory course, it needs to be reinforced. The domain-specific aspects of application development must also be taught.

In data base applications, for example, it is important to teach file and data base concepts, the difficult skill of data modeling (see Chapter 10), and the importance of managing data entry and verification, among just a few skills. The application development process is a natural way to introduce both the functionality of the program and domain-specific knowledge. Unfortunately, as discussed above, many commercial and even internal courses ignore these higher level skills and deal only with simple hardware and software use skills.

Working with a Personal Computer

Working with a personal computer is somewhat different from working with a mainframe. Among the specific skills that must be mastered by PC users are the selection of personal computers, the installation of hardware and software, day-to-day PC maintenance, and sharing information among PCs through networking or disk exchange. There should be a module that deals with precisely this information. Although it is possible to pick up this knowledge "by osmosis," important information may not be acquired without specific training. We are beginning to see the emergence of "old wives' tales" about buying and using PCs that differ sharply from reality.

Host Computing Courses

A stream of courses for host computer users is also needed. Some of these courses will be similar to the courses for PC users, but there will be some differences as well.

Using a Host Computer and its Operating System

As discussed in Chapter 13, host computers are both easier and more difficult to use than personal computers. If the information center installs a terminal on the user's desk, complete with a transmission facility to link the terminal with the host, the user will encounter few difficulties. If the user must use a TTY (teletypewriter) terminal and must arrange his or her own transmission facility, however, he or she will have to deal with many settings on the terminal as well as with modems, telephone lines, cabling, and perhaps the use of a public data network. These problems are compounded when a PC is to be used to emulate a terminal. As far as possible, the information center should hide users from the details of working with a terminal and transmission facility, but users must learn at least a little about terminal and transmission terminology.

Some operating systems on host computers are easy to master, but even when the mechanics are simple, users must still be familiar with the computer's file and data organization terminology, as well with such matters as why the host is sometimes so slow. Some operating systems, in turn, are extremely difficult to use, and these must be taught in detail—unless the information center buys user-friendly shells to shield the user from operating system details. The best shells work on the PC itself, but even shells on the host can greatly reduce what a user needs to know.

Host Application Software Courses

As discussed in Chapters 16 and 17, host application software tends to be harder to learn than PC software. First, most host products have very high functionality, so there is a lot to learn. Second, many were developed many years ago. They often use batch operation, in which creation and execution are separate phases. Even when they have added an overlay of ease of use, the underlying archaic designs of many products continue to poke through.

Because power users are often utilize host tools, it is even more important to teach domain-specific knowledge for these programs than it is to teach this knowledge when training users in PC application software.

Working with Host Computers

In many ways, host computers reduce the amount of day-to-day working knowledge required by users. There is nightly data backup by the host computer staff, and the central staff also fixes technical problems. On the other hand, users must be intimately familiar with the administrivia required by most host authorities. This is particularly a problem for intermittent users who turn to the host only occasionally. Each time they use the host, policies and procedures are likely to have changed. In addition, because hosts encourage the use of multiuser software and data file sharing, it is important to impose working discipline on all users to prevent chaos.

Management Courses

The details of managing computers and applications should be taught in the PC and host computer streams. It is important, however, to have courses that draw these details together and to present other information that is taught only at a broad level.

Personal Management

Users must be taught how to manage *their own* end user computing. Different courses should be devised for department managers, professional staff members, power users, and secretaries because each has different roles to play.

Department Management

Everyone in the department needs to understand that departments are complex work systems that rely on teamwork. They also need to understand one another's roles. This department-level training is not widely given, either to individuals or to department managers. This failure to train department managers is particularly dangerous.

Corporate Systems

Employees also need to understand corporate-wide systems, including data processing applications, office automation applications, and other applications, such as planning and budgeting systems. They need to understand the importance of these systems and their roles in designing and using these systems. Again, different training should be given to people with different roles. Department managers, middle managers, and executives need special training.

At this level, the traditional process of application development must be taught, in order to teach the roles of users in systems design, the roles of information systems personnel—including systems analysts, programmers, operators, and data entry operators—and the all-important process of implementation. These topics were discussed in Chapter 2.

Combining Levels

It may be best to put all three management modules in one course, so that users can see the interrelationships that exist between management needs at different levels, and understand the need to avoid focusing myopically on the personal level.

Standard Policies and Plans

In all courses that deal with policies and plans, it is desirable to furnish "boilerplate" documents. For example, for data applications, there should be a standard procedure manual specifying roles, backup, and other considerations. Within these boilerplate documents, there can be spaces to be filled in with variable information. In addition, the department manager should be free to modify the document to fit his or her own situation. The purpose of the boilerplate is not to restrict the department manager so much as to guide the user and save time.

There should also be model documentation for applications—both for training guides for users and for detailed descriptions of the system to aid future maintainers. Again, the goal is to provide guidance to simplify developers' lives.

DEVELOPING SUPPORT PROGRAMS FOR DIFFERENT ENVIRONMENTS

The preceding section discussed the creation of a comprehensive training program for end users. In this section, we will look not only at training but also at the other elements in the support mix—consulting and troubleshooting. We will also discuss the support mix separately for the different project development environments of end user computing.

Support in the Second Environment

As discussed in Chapter 1, the second environment consists of small and simple applications. As long as the project developer takes the courses in the comprehensive training program, the second environment presents relatively simple support requirements. Initial consulting should take place, both to help the user select the most appropriate tools and to help the user clarify his or her thinking about the project, do a reasonable initial design under the review of a consultant, and produce a realistic assessment of the costs and value of the proposed project. There should also be troubleshooting later when the user gets into inevitable difficulties. While extracting the user from problems, the troubleshooter should train the user in how to solve the problem if the problem is one the user is likely to encounter again.

Support for the Third Environment

The third environment consists of major applications that are large in size, critical to important objectives, or both. Because of the importance and complexity of third-environment applications, a great deal of support is needed beyond training.

Life Cycle Consulting
Although initial consulting should take place, the consulting given by the information center should not stop there. The consultant and developer should agree on a staging schedule for the project, and after each major stage, the consultant should review the work done to that point in order to identify any serious errors. The consultant is there mainly to provide support, but he or she must also enforce proper discipline. This task is a difficult and sensitive one.

For complex tasks, the consultant is likely to play a very active role. For example, in data modeling, the consultant may even take over the lead in entity identification, entity-relationship modeling, and defining the detailed data base schema (see Chapter 10). Unless the user is quite experienced in these matters, serious problems are likely to arise later.

The consultant is likely to be very influential in the implementation stage, helping the user understand what documentation to produce, how to manage the transition to the new system, and what specific policies to lay down.

Troubleshooting will be needed when developers jump into advanced areas. In many cases, developers will simply be in over their heads technically. In others, they will be pushing the limits of their application software. In both cases, active intervention is needed. If the problem is a rare one that the user is not likely to see again, the troubleshooter may handle the entire problem.

Life Cycle Workshops

Since consultancy time is limited, one way to leverage this time is to offer **workshop** programs tailored to a specific type of application, say a large data application. These workshops would draw together six to twelve people working on this type of application, who would meet regularly for training, to share their progress, and to get feedback.

For users, a major advantage of workshops is interaction with other users. By the end of the workshop, each user will have seen several other applications being developed, learning from other users and simply having seen unique problems arising in other situations. For the longer term, the workshop is likely to provide a much more solid base than individual consulting or training courses.

This greater depth has a price. Workshops, like courses, can only be scheduled several times a year, and everybody in the workshop must work at about the same pace, finishing each stage together. For large applications, this is not likely to be an overwhelming problem. Because most large applications take a year or more to develop, timing is not always a critical factor. In addition, the lock-step discipline of the workshop approach may be desirable in and of itself.

The Fourth Environment

In the fourth environment, developers develop systems for others. For these projects, it is good to have a course that teaches important features of delegated development, principally the eliciting of design information and the process of turning over the project to the ultimate user.

How to elicit information can be taught in case studies and in role-playing exercises. Since this is a difficult skill to teach to IS professionals, it is not clear how much training end users will need. Until people have done delegated development, they tend to underestimate the difficulty of eliciting information from users. Therefore, no amount of training is likely to overcome all problems. The consultant should sit down with the developer and ultimate user(s) and go over the design after the developer has created a written statement of requirements.

At turnover, the developer must provide training and documentation, including quick-start guides and a miniature manual. This is particularly important in large and multiuser applications. Even for small applications, however, delegated development makes documentation crucial—including the documentation to assist future maintainers, who may not be the original developer.

The Fifth Environment

The fifth environment is the management of computing at the department level. Although the principles of department management will be taught in courses, problems tend to come to a head during the creation of the annual department plan (see Chapter 3). Active involvement from information center consultants may be needed in the creation of a plan, particularly the first time the department or department manager must create it. It is also desirable for the information center to review the plan and give feedback.

If all annual planning is to be done at once in the corporation, the workshop approach may be desirable to help department managers create their department plan. This workshop would probably not be divided into stages. There should be an initial meeting to lay out planning considerations and current policies, as well as to teach department managers how to use the current version of the planning document outline. Subsequent meetings might be held to answer general questions, share insights, and voice frustrations and problems.

CONCLUSION

Consulting, training, and troubleshooting must be blended together like ingredients in a cake mix, to form a "support mix" for end users. As the user proceeds through the stages of a project—assessment, design, construction, and implementation—the support mix must change to match the changing needs of each stage.

Training is likely to be the largest component of the support mix. An information center must weigh the costs and advantages of several training alternatives—internal classroom training, commercial classroom training, CBT, audio instruction, and video instruction. It must use each as appropriate.

Research has shown that users come to courses with preliminary models for how the system will work, jump around through exercises, get themselves into complex problems, and move gradually to full understanding on simple topics. Training must reflect these and other realities.

Most importantly, the information center must recognize that users must move upward through a complex hierarchy of skills. A program to serve all computer use skills and conceptual skills must be developed.

In the learning hierarchy, the use of computers and software is only the beginning. Users must also be taught to work efficiently, safely, and innovatively. These skills go far beyond the systems development life cycle disciplines taught in most textbooks. Because few external training programs teach these good practice and innovation skills, every information center must have a specific plan for teaching them.

REVIEW QUESTIONS

1. What are the three main components of the support mix, and why is the support mix described as being like a cake mix?

2. What are the four levels in the skills hierarchy presented in this chapter? What distinguishes each from the immediately lower level? Do users move completely from stage to stage?
3. What are the major components of good practice, and what are the subcomponents of each area? Can you add subcomponents to any major areas? Can you add any major areas?
4. Distinguish between concrete operationalism, formal operationalism, and metacognitive understanding. What are the implications of these stages for training?
5. What is quick-start behavior? How would you use it to guide documentation? Training? What are its dangers, and how can they be controlled?
6. Discuss the problems with naive cognitive models. How can these problems be controlled?
7. What are the main organizational choices for end user training? What are the advantages and disadvantages of each? How can these advantages and disadvantages be blended together to reduce problems?
8. What are the dimensions of diversity in user needs? How do these affect training?
9. Discuss the importance of modularization and considerations in implementing modularization for individual courses and for programs of courses.
10. Compare the advantages and disadvantages of internal and external classroom training.
11. What advice would you give to an information center setting up an internal classroom training program for computer use skills and conceptual training?
12. Compare the relative advantages and disadvantages of live classroom training and mediated training? CBT, audio, videotape, videodisk, and computer-controlled videodisk training?
13. What are authoring programs, courses, and presentation programs? When does internal development make sense in CBT?
14. Discuss the main elements of a comprehensive training program. Can you make any additions to the basic categories of courses shown in Figure 5-2? Any additions to the detail discussed in the text? Develop your own list of topics for an introductory course that would be required of everyone. How long would the course be? The individual modules?
15. Discuss support programs for the different environments of end user computing. For the third environment, be especially detailed in your discussion, describing the advantages and disadvantages of each alternative and adding your own alternatives if possible.

REFERENCES

1. CAREY, MAX, AND ECK, ALAN, "How Workers Get their Training," *Occupational Outlook Quarterly,* Winter 1984, pp. 3-21.
2. CARROLL, JOHN M., "Minimalist Training," *DATAMATION,* November 1, 1984, pp. 125-136.

3. CARROLL, JOHN M., AND CARRITHERS, CAROLINE, "Training Wheels in a User Interface," *Communications of the ACM,* August 1984, pp. 800-805.
4. Computer Intelligence Corporation, *Information Center Market: CI Special IC Management Survey,* July 1985.
5. Crwth, "The Second Crwth Information Center Survey," *Crwth News for Better Training,* Vol. 3, No. 1, 1985.
6. DITLEA, STEVE, "Befriending the Befuddled," *DATAMATION,* June 15, 1985, pp. 84-90.
7. *EDP Analyzer,* "Computer Based Training for End Users," October 1983.
8. EFROYMSON, SHARON, AND PHILLIPS, DAVID B., "Here a Course, There a Course," *Information Center,* September 1985, pp. 48-52.
9. HARMON, PAUL, "Training: Psychology Meets Technology," *Computerworld,* May 19, 1985, pp. In Depth 7/16.
10. LITTMAN, JONATHAN, "Pacific Bell: Networking PCs," *PC Week,* January 22, 1986, pp. 33-38.
11. LITTMAN, JONATHAN, "PG&E: Utility Gains Power with PCs," *PC Week,* January 8, 1985, pp. 39-42.
12. *PC Week,* "Training," April 3, 1984, p. 33.
13. RESNICK, LAUREN B., "Mathematics and Science Learning: A New Conception," *Science,* April 1983, pp. 477-478.
14. ROCKART, JOHN F., "The Management of End User Computing," *Communications of the ACM,* October 1983, pp. 776-784.
15. ROGERS, JAMES L., "Computer-Based Training Moves Within Reach," *Information Center,* September 1985, pp. 29-36.
16. SCHARER, LAURA L., "User Training: Less Is More," *DATAMATION,* July 1983, pp. 175-182.

6 PERSONAL COMPUTER STANDARDS AND PRICES

As discussed in Chapter 3, almost all information centers set PC standards. Chapter 4 discussed the organizational issues involved in setting standards, freeing us to concentrate on technical issues in this chapter and the two that follow.

This chapter looks at technical issues broadly, while Chapter 7 looks in greater depth at hardware issues and Chapter 8 does the same for software. After discussing the need for standards, this chapter surveys the features of PC design that lead to the openness that both delights and plagues organizations that work with personal computers. It then looks at the major families of personal computers on the market, including IBM micros, IBM compatibles (clones), and Apple Macintoshes.

The chapter ends with a discussion of costs. Power and functionality are wonderful, but there are costs attached to them. Many organizations badly underestimate the costs of personal computers. The discussion of costs will examine the purchase costs of several popular configurations and will also look at life-cycle costs for a typical personal computer.

INTRODUCTION

Yesterday, Today, and Tomorrow

In 1975, MITS produced the first popular personal computer, the Altair 8800. Shown in Figure 6-1, this machine was unbelievably crude. It was slow. It had a bank of flashing lights instead of a display. It used these lights to give its output in binary code. It also had a bank of switches for binary input, instead of a keyboard. To top everything off, it came as a kit that the user had to solder together.

INTRODUCTION 197

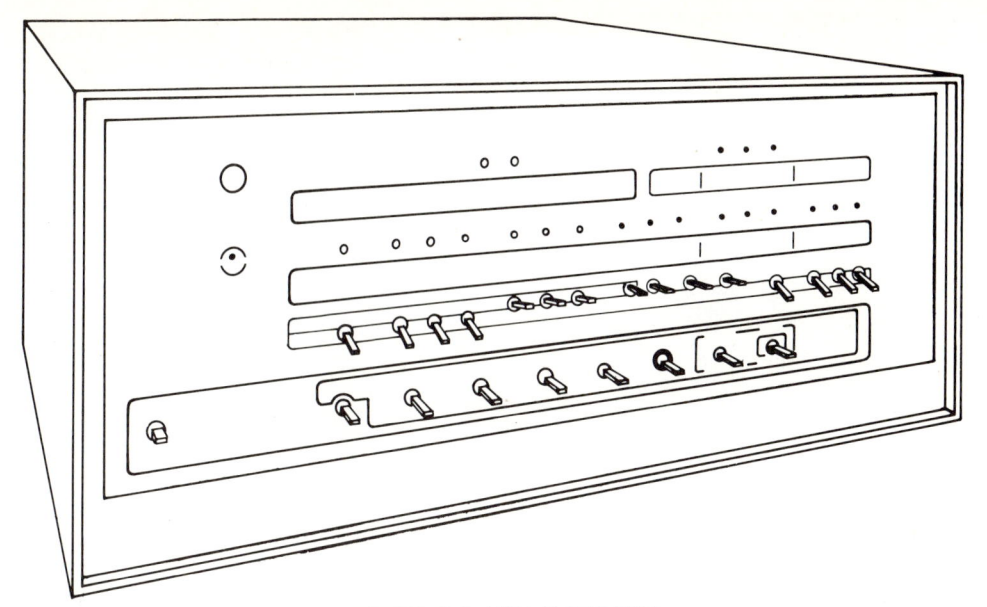

FIGURE 6-1 MITS ALTAIR 8800

Compare this with the situation in 1987, just 11 years later. As shown in Figure 6-2, IBM's main line of microcomputers, the **Personal System/2 (PS/2)** family, came slickly packaged and had 10 to 20 times the power of the MITS Altair. Apple's Macintosh SE, shown in Figure 6-3, and Macintosh II, shown in Figure 6-4, gave comparable improvements in finish and speed.

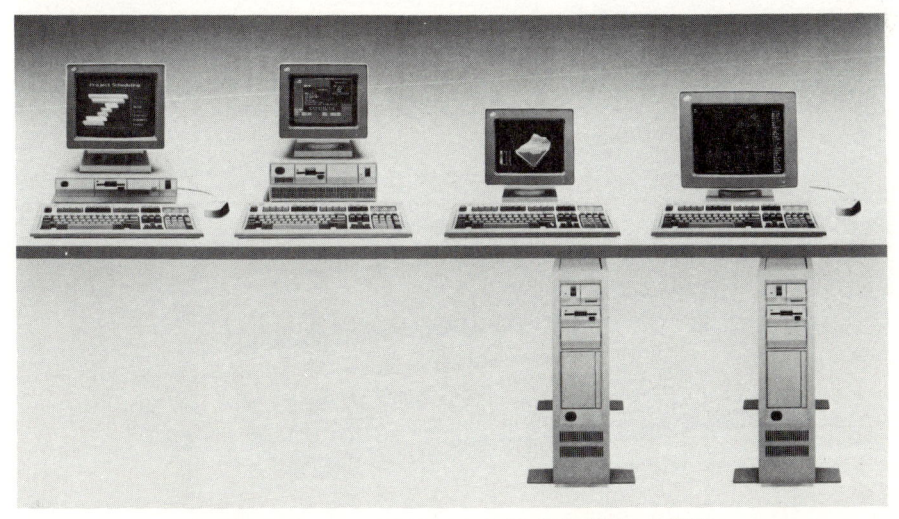

FIGURE 6-2 IBM PERSONAL SYSTEM/2 (PS/2) SERIES

198   PERSONAL COMPUTER STANDARDS AND PRICES

FIGURE 6-3   APPLE MACINTOSH SE

FIGURE 6-4   APPLE MACINTOSH II

INTRODUCTION

While the Altair 8800 was a machine for only the most determined hobbyists, the Macintoshes were literally easy enough to be used by three-year-old children. Although the IBM PS/2 line lacked this interface in 1987, IBM announced that it would add this kind of interface in 1988 or 1989.

At the same time that power and ease of use improved enormously, costs fell dramatically. In 1981, when the original IBM PC was introduced, a full system cost about $6000. By 1987, the cost had fallen to about $1100 for machines of somewhat superior power. If the user did have $6000 to spend in 1987, he or she could buy a high-end PS/2 or Macintosh II computer offering more than six times the speed and memory of the original IBM PC.

In addition, the PC is no longer a stand-alone machine living in splendid isolation. Many are linked to host computers (minicomputers, mainframes, and the like), and many others are linked with other PCs in personal computer networks. As discussed in Chapters 13–15, PC communications is still very crude and limited, but it is no longer rare.

Only a fool or charlatan would forecast the state of the art in the future, but we can make at least three predictions with confidence.

1. Price–performance ratios will continue to improve by 20 percent to 30 percent each year. Entry-level machines will be far cheaper, and high-end machines will have immense power. The average system in three to five years will be two or three times as powerful as today's average purchase.

2. Future machines will be far easier to use. Interfaces like the Macintosh's will be widely available and will be supplemented by full animation and a good deal of artificial intelligence. This growing ease of use will be critical in improving the productivity of current users and in attracting people who have so far resisted computers. It will also help current users expand to more complex applications and technological environments, such as networking.

3. Communications will be an integral part of the PC's hardware and software, instead of being an add on as it is today. Communications will be far easier to use, and there will be good standards for linking computers from different vendors.

Types of Personal Computers

There are three basic types of personal computers—**desktops, portables,** and **engineering workstations.**

Desktop Personal Computers

Desktop PCs sit on desks and are rarely moved, being large and bulky. (It has been said that they are called "desktops" because they take up the entire desktop.) Desktops vary considerably in power. The fastest are five to seven times as fast as the slowest. There are similar disparities in memory capacity and graphics capabilities.

Portable Personal Computers

As the name suggests, portable computers can be moved easily from place to place. Desktops can also be moved, but the process is cumbersome because of their multiple components, and constant movement can be hard on them. Like desktops, portables vary considerably in processing power and memory, but the most obvious feature of portable computers is size. Older portables tend to be **suitcase-size portables** that can only be moved with difficulty. Newer portables tend to be **laptop** units no larger than an attache case.

Laptop machines can be moved easily from place to place. For easy portability, laptops use small flat panel displays. These displays tend to be both expensive and hard to read, as discussed in Chapter 7. Although laptops should eventually be very popular, their adoption has been restricted by their expensive and low-quality liquid crystal displays (LCDs), by the high cost of their peripherals, and by their poor keyboards, which have fewer keys than desktops and suitcase-size portables, and which lack the good tactile "feel" needed for fast typing.

Engineering Workstations

For most business users, today's PCs have ample power, but for scientific and engineering users, high-power **engineering workstations** are needed. These machines have two to ten times the power of a high-end desktop, and they also have superior graphics. They achieve this power with 32-bit microprocessors that run at 10 MHz to 40 MHz, plus special circuitry for graphics and floating point operations. With this high capability comes a price tag—$10,000 to $40,000. As noted above, high-end desktops are beginning to attack the engineering workstation market. They use the same microprocessors as engineering workstations, and they have optional high-quality display systems. Still, they only fall at the low end of the engineering workstation performance spectrum, because their design is not optimized for the kinds of things done with engineering workstations.

We will not cover engineering workstations in this book because few information centers deal with them. Nonetheless, engineering workstations give us a glimpse of tomorrow's personal computer. Future generations of personal computers will have all of the power of today's engineering workstations.

Home Computers

When we use the term "personal computer" in this book, we refer to office PCs rather than home computers. In the past, the distinction between office and home machines was primarily one of power. Office machines used 16-bit microprocessors, whereas home machines used 8-bit microprocessors. Today, however, many home machines have more power than office PCs. For example, the Commodore Amiga and the Atari 520ST use the Motorola MC68000, which has 32-bit internal processing, a 16-bit data bus, and a cycle speed of 7 MHz or more. This same microprocessor is used in the Macintosh, and it is much more powerful than the microprocessors used in IBM PCs and PC XTs.

The distinction between office and home machines today revolves around their relative emphases on technology and software. Home machines put their power into color, graphics, and sound, whereas office machines emphasize data crunching. Home machines are attracting games and educational software rather than business application software. It is this lack of business software that makes home computers ill suited to general office use.

The Necessity for Setting Standards

Although the pace of technological change is extremely heartening to promoters of personal computing, it is a source of endless frustration for those who must set corporate standards for hardware and software. The purpose of standards is to allow personal computers to work smoothly with the other PCs, hosts, and other machines. Without clear standards, the office will become a Tower of Babel, in which no machine will be able to talk to any other.

If two people doing the same application, for example, word processing, want to be able to work together smoothly, four different sets of standards must be enforced.

1. Both users have to use the same or compatible **application programs.** If their word processing programs are incompatible, it makes little difference if they are using the same computers.
2. In many cases, application programs are usually tied to the operating system, so both users may need to have the same or compatible **operating systems.**
3. In many cases, application programs are linked to the computer's hardware, both users may need to have the same computers or compatible **computers.**
4. Both users need to have the same or compatible **data transfer devices,** which may be as simple as disk drives, if the data are to be hand-carried, or as complex as local area networks for electronic transfers.

In any specific case, only some of these four sets of standards need to be enforced, but when all of the many interactions among PC users in a corporation are considered, it becomes imperative to set standards in all four areas.

AN OVERVIEW OF PERSONAL COMPUTER TECHNOLOGY

Major Circuits

Before discussing the specific standards that need to be set, we will look at the internal workings of personal computers. Although these internal workings are normally hidden from users, they are very important in setting standards. We will examine these topics only briefly in this chapter, using Figure 6-5 as our guide. The details of hardware technology are discussed in the next chapter.

The Microprocessor and Math Coprocessor

The heart of the PC is its **microprocessor.** A microprocessor is sometimes called a "computer on a chip," but this is an overstatement. It is really the computer's **central processing unit (CPU)** on a chip. It has all of the circuitry needed to decode program instructions and direct the rest of the

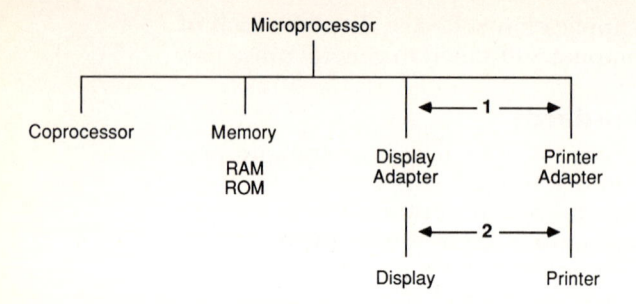

FIGURE 6-5 LOGICAL ORGANIZATION OF A PERSONAL COMPUTER

Notes:
1. Simple and general commands and replies
2. Complex and specific commands and replies

computer to carry out the demands of each task. It not only controls electronic circuits within the computer's electronics unit, but it also controls the **peripherals** that lie outside the electronics unit, including displays, printers, and modems.

The microprocessor has more than the computer's CPU on a single chip. It also has an **arithmetic logic unit (ALU)** on the same chip. This ALU is sufficient for most tasks, but for heavy floating point arithmetic, most microprocessor vendors sell a **math coprocessor** that works with the microprocessor. The math coprocessor for the Intel 8088 and 8086, for instance, is the Intel 8087. In some computers, the math coprocessor is standard, but on most machines, it is an extra-cost option, and some PCs do not even support math coprocessors as an option.

Memory Circuits

A PC needs large amounts of **internal memory,** both **random access memory (RAM)** and **read-only memory (ROM).** User demand for RAM is growing explosively because of (1) the emergence of larger and more sophisticated programs, (2) the benefits of keeping more than one program at a time in memory, and (3) the popularity of various RAM-based programs that can accelerate the performance of peripherals. The amount of RAM in a PC is usually optional. Today, most users have 256 kilobytes (KB) to 8 megabytes (MB) of RAM.

Adapter Circuits

The microprocessor, RAM, and ROM are taught in virtually all introductory textbooks, but for standards setting, another group of circuits, namely, **adapter** circuits, are equally critical. Adapters are needed because the microprocessor knows nothing about the specifics of peripherals, such as printers or displays. To the microprocessor, a peripheral is merely a **port**—an address to which a few simple commands can be given. An adapter circuit must be provided for each peripheral to be attached. As shown in Figure 6-5, the adapter stands between the microprocessor and the peripheral, translating the microprocessor's terse instructions into the detailed information the peripheral needs to do its work.

Other Circuits
The PC has numerous other circuits, including timing circuits and memory management circuits. Because these circuits rarely figure into standards for configuring PCs, we will ignore them in this book.

Logical Organization: The Bus
How do all of these circuits communicate with one another? The answer is that they all communicate via a set of transmission lines called **the bus.** As shown in Figure 6-6, every circuit is connected to the bus. The bus acts as a party line, and when any circuit talks, every other circuit can hear it. To prevent chaos, the microprocessor directs who can talk and who may not.

Before busses were used, computers had to be rewired every time a circuit was added or dropped. Today, they are simply connected to the bus or disconnected from it.

Physical Organization: Mother and Expansion Boards
Most PCs today have **open designs** that allow—and even encourage—other hardware vendors to add electronics to the basic system. They do this primarily by allowing other vendors to build **expansion boards**—printed circuit boards with additional electronics—to be plugged easily and quickly into the basic computer.

The Mother Board
These expansion boards are plugged into something called a **mother board,** which is a single printed circuit board with most or all of a computer's

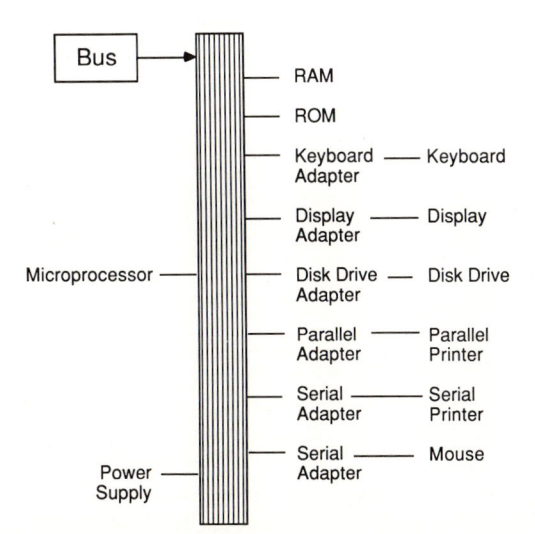

FIGURE 6-6 THE BUS

basic circuitry. This board contains the microprocessor, the system's ROM, and at least some RAM. It may also contain adapters for displays, disk drives, and other peripherals. In the future, it will even feature networking adapters and other communications adapters. In general, newer PCs pack more circuitry into their mother boards than older machines.

Expansion Boards

As shown in Figure 6-7, the mother board has **expansion slots,** into which **expansion boards** can be inserted. So the mother board not only has a broad spectrum of functions to perform, but it is also the link point for expansion boards.

Installing an expansion board is very easy. The first step is to remove the cover from the PC which usually requires only a screw driver. The next step, installing the board, is also very simple. This can normally be done with fingers alone, although it may be necessary to tighten one or two screws. The last step is to tell the microprocessor that a board has been added and to specify what kind of board it is. As noted earlier, this step requires the setting of a switch in older machines. In newer machines, it only requires running a special "setup program." Mechanically, boards can be inserted in ten minutes or less, although the whole process is likely to take an hour or more for someone who has never installed an expansion board or when the expansion board has to be set up carefully to avoid conflict with other circuits in the computer.

Because expansion slots are directly linked to the bus, all circuits,

Mother Board

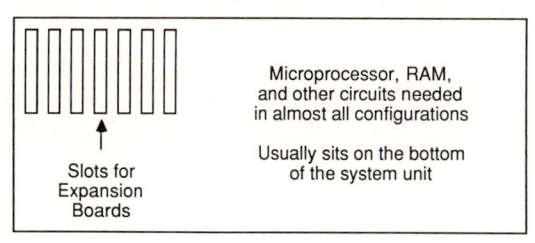

Slots for Expansion Boards

Microprocessor, RAM, and other circuits needed in almost all configurations

Usually sits on the bottom of the system unit

Expansion Board

Circuits needed in only some configurations

Connector to fit into expansion slot

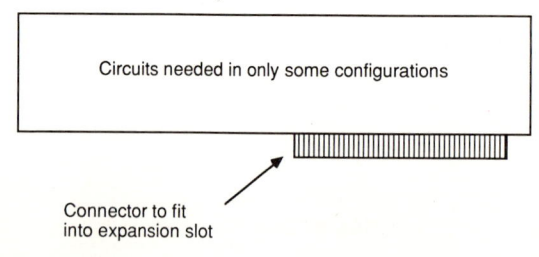

FIGURE 6-7 MOTHER BOARD AND EXPANSION BOARDS

whether on the mother board or on expansion boards, can talk on an equal footing. It literally makes no difference where any circuit is physically located. Tying expansion boards to the mother board via the bus marries the logical and physical designs of the personal computer. It is this combination of expansion boards and the easy addition of these boards via the bus that creates an open design and encourages constant evolution.

Expansion Board Compatibility

As discussed in Chapter 8, when expansion boards want to speak to the microprocessor, they electronically "raise their hands" by placing signals on certain control lines on the bus. These are called **interrupt lines** because they interrupt whatever program is currently in use and require the computer to service the interrupt before returning to the program currently in operation. Often, this servicing consists merely of putting the interrupting board on hold.

A PC bus has a limited number of interrupts, and if several expansion boards are added, two boards may try to use the same interrupt. This is especially common when complex boards such as communications boards are added. Interrupt conflicts and some other hardware and ROM conflicts must be diagnosed and corrected when they occur. As a result, each new board should be tested with existing boards, and conflict "fixes" should be developed before giving new expansion boards to end users.

Implications of Expansion Boards

The internal workings of a PC are discussed here, ahead of standards, because these internal workings keep popping up when standardizing hardware. For every peripheral to be added, there must be an adapter circuit, often on an expansion board. In addition, expansion boards are key options in and of themselves, giving additional memory and other internal capabilities. They sometimes even contain peripherals, including modems and hard disks.

Software

Although a computer's logical and physical designs are important in openness, software is also critical to openness in design. Just as PC vendors have been careful to provide an open environment in hardware, these vendors and third parties have worked to provide openness in software.

Loading and Terminating Programs

When a computer is running, it is *always* under the control of a program. During a user's session on a computer, a series of programs will operate the computer, passing control from one to another.

- When the computer is first turned on, control is given immediately to a ROM program that performs internal diagnostics.
- When this ROM program finishes, it loads the operating system from disk and passes control to the operating system.
- When the user types the name of an application program, the operating system loads the application program and passes control to it.

- When the application program is finished, it passes control back to the operating system. Because the operating system normally remains in memory while the application program is running, there is usually no need to load the operating system when an application program terminates.

During a typical user session on a PC, a half dozen or more programs may find themselves in control of the computer. At any moment, however, only one can be in control.

Division of Labor

The operating system is not the only program that may remain in RAM after it passes control to another program. When any program terminates, it does so by issuing either of two calls to the operating system. One call tells the operating system to reuse the section of memory used by the application program. This effectively erases the application program.

The other, called **Terminate but Stay Resident (TSR)** tells the operating system to let the program code stay in RAM. Other programs that are loaded must be loaded into other areas of RAM. So RAM can hold several programs at any moment.

The full implications of TSR programs are discussed in Chapter 8. For now, they are important because they mean that several programs in RAM can act like a team. Although only one program can be in charge, it can call other programs to have them do specialized work, just as a contractor can call in a plumber or carpenter to do a specific task. Division of labor, so important in human work, is also important in computer work.

Figure 6-8 illustrates a simple example of this teamwork process, printing a document on a printer. Different printers use different ASCII codes to denote boldface, subscripting, carriage returns, and other formatting information. So output must always be in the format required by the printer.

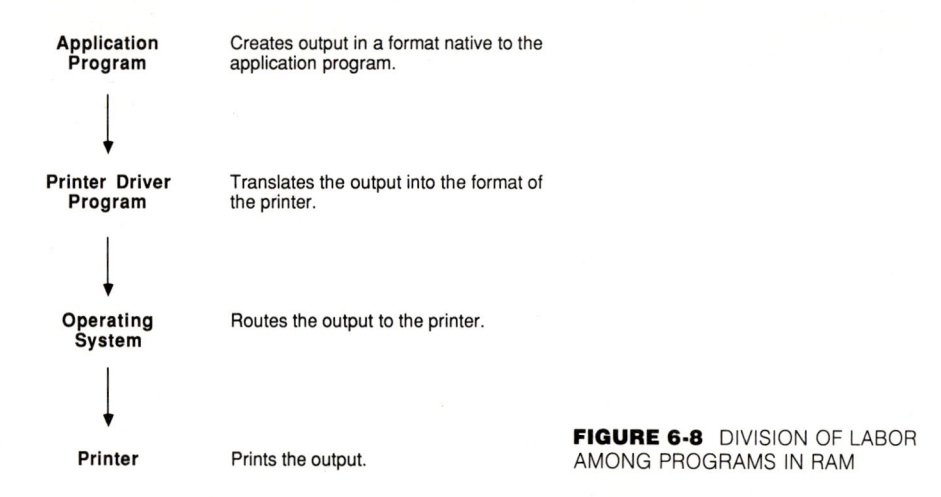

Application Program — Creates output in a format native to the application program.

↓

Printer Driver Program — Translates the output into the format of the printer.

↓

Operating System — Routes the output to the printer.

↓

Printer — Prints the output.

FIGURE 6-8 DIVISION OF LABOR AMONG PROGRAMS IN RAM

As shown in the figure, the printing process requires several programs to call upon others to do specialized work.

- First, the application program produces its output in its "native" format, no matter what format the printer demands. It sends this native format output to another program, called a **printer driver.**
- Second, the printer driver changes the format of the output, translating between the native format of the application program and the format of the printer. There must be a different printer driver for every application program–printer pair. Typically, an application program is sold with many printer drivers.
- Third, the printer driver passes the output to the operating system.
- Fourth, the operating system passes the output to the correct adapter, which handles the details of delivering the output to the printer. This adapter, as discussed earlier, handles the fine details of the delivery, including pausing if the printer cannot keep up with the output.
- Fifth, and finally, the printer accepts the output and prints it.

Many program interactions in RAM are far more complex than this. To store information on a disk drive, for example, the operating system would probably have to call on several ROM service programs in addition to passing the information stream to the disk drive adapter. But despite its simplicity, our printer example illustrates the basic elements of the process.

To appreciate why this division of labor is desirable, imagine what things were like before division of labor was introduced in software. In those early days, every application programmer had to "reinvent the wheel" by writing routines to move bits to the printer. In addition, every time a printer was added, the programmer had to modify the application program.

With division of labor, however, the operating system programmer determines the best ways to handle common chores. These excellent routines are then available simply through calls from the application programmer.

Second, if there is a change in the system, such as the addition of a printer, the programmer simply writes another printer driver. The main program is not modified. This is important, because the main program is likely to be so big and complex that any change could have unforeseen consequences, even if the programmer is very careful.

Software Standards for Openness

For division of labor to work well, low-level programs must be completely standardized, and the allowable calls to them must be published. This allows programmers working at higher level to program with the confidence that what they call for will be provided.

For example, DOS has become a de facto standard for operating system calls. Each version of DOS has its own calls, but newer versions still execute old calls, so that application programs do not have to be rewritten every time the operating system is updated.

In addition, ROM service programs are standardized so that calls to them will behave predictably. While it might be good if only the operating system were allowed to call ROM programs, this is not the way things are done in practice.

At a higher level, PC networking (see Chapters 12 and 14) requires the addition of special software to handle networking functions. This "network operating system" must be standardized so that application programs can work with it.

In addition, intelligent laser page printers (see Chapter 7) require much more complex output formatting than the dot matrix and daisywheel printers that printer drivers have traditionally had to deal with. To reduce problems, most intelligent laser page printers accept output in a single format. This is a proprietary format called PostScript, which is discussed in Chapter 7. As a result of this de facto standardization, a programmer who wants to send a program's output to an intelligent laser page printer only has to write one complex device driver, which will translate from the application program's native format into the PostScript format.

Openness and Selection

If the information center selects PC software standards intelligently, it will provide a solid foundation upon which to add new application programs. But if it sets the wrong standards for low-level programs such as the operating system and the network operating system, it could find itself locked out of application programs that cannot work with these programs. When selecting low-level software, the information center should be less concerned with technical merit than with the base of application software that can work with the low-level software. If few application programs work with the system software, its technical merit will be cold comfort to users who find little or no application software that will work with it.

Openness in Perspective

Most modern PCs are very open environments that are designed to be added to easily by the PC's vendor and by other companies as well.

- Bus designs allow circuits to be added and dropped easily, making the creation of new circuits a fairly easy task.
- Expansion slots allow circuits to be packaged conveniently and also allow users to install new circuits easily.
- The use of adapters means that an improved or totally new peripheral can be added simply by creating a new adapter and adding it to the system.
- Division of labor among application programs, the operating system, ROM service programs, and other programs in RAM allows application developers to develop new programs quickly and with the confidence that their programs will receive the services they want when they are called.

Although openness leads to development by third parties and these third party products take some sales away from the original vendor, the flood of products that are produced by third parties usually make the computer far more valuable to customers and ultimately increase the original PC vendor's sales.

When Apple tries to reverse this trend by closing the design of the original Macintosh by installing no expansion slots and by not publishing the machine's technical specifications, the backlash almost killed the machine. Not until Apple published its specifications and encouraged third party development did Macintosh use explode.

SETTING STANDARDS

Standardization Tasks

Computer Families

The first item that must be standardized is the kind of computers that users may buy. In practice, this means standardizing on one or more **families** of personal computers. *A Family is a series of machines that maintains* **upward compatibility.** *That is, when new machines are added to the family, they can use all of the software and peripherals purchased for earlier machines.* Upward compatibility protects the users' investment in software, hardware, training, support, and maintenance.

Of course, newer machines in a family will be able to do things that older machines cannot. Over time, newer features may become so important that older machines will be phased out.

Within a family, growth over time is smooth and rather painless. But changing a family standard, say from the Apple II family to the IBM PC family, is wrenching. Entirely new software and peripherals must be purchased, complete retraining must be done, and data files must be laboriously converted. Furthermore, if the conversion is not done all at once, there will be incompatibility among users during the transition.

To preserve corporate sanity and to avoid creating a situation in which employees cannot work together, most firms standardize on one or two families. Family selection is usually drawn from three major alternatives.

1. IBM has one major family, which began with the first IBM Personal Computer in 1981 and has embraced most subsequent PCs from that company.
2. A number of other companies produce IBM "compatibles" or "clones" that are compatible, to varying degrees, with the IBM PC family. Many firms view IBM PCs and compatibles as being members of a single family.
3. Apple Computer has one major business family, the Macintosh family. Until recently, most large firms standardized on IBM PCs and compatibles. In many large firms, however, the Apple Macintosh has risen to the status of a second standard. Apple's Apple II family, which is incompatible with the Macintosh family, is aimed primarily at the home and school markets.

A number of other vendors have attempted, like Apple, to maintain families that are not IBM compatible, but few have been successful with this strategy. Most are either moving to full IBM PC compatibility or at least toward coexistence through compatible file transfer.

Add-On Hardware

The second item that must be standardized is add-on hardware, including expansion boards and peripherals, such as printers and displays. Standards need to be set (1) to assure compatibility among the many add-ons that can be purchased and (2) to allow the information center staff to learn the products well enough to give good support.

Software

The third thing that must be standardized is software, beginning with the system software and the most important piece of system software, the operating system. In the IBM PC and compatibles world, the MS-DOS operating system is the normal standard. Other operating systems are available, but they are rarely selected. The main reason for selecting MS-DOS is that most application programs require it. IBM sells MS-DOS under the name PC-DOS. The dominance of MS-DOS once made operating system decisions simple, but IBM's introduction of Operating System/2, which has multitasking and other features, and Microsoft's announcement of a similar operating system for other computers have reopened the operating system issue.

Application software is the next thing to standardize. There must be clear standards for all widely used forms of application software, for example, word processing software. For software used in limited parts of the firm, standards may or may not be set.

Standardized software is complicated by the fact that most software vendors release **updates** every few months. These updates are new versions of the program with enhanced features. When setting standards, a specific update version must be specified. Every time a new update is released, the information center must decide whether to shift some or all of the user base to the new update. Handling software updates is a major headache for most information centers.

Selecting a Family to Support

In selecting a family to support, the most important consideration is *software*. Since users rarely write their own programs, a family must have both a wide variety of excellent packaged software and good prospects for a continuing flood of programs. Unless a computer is selling well, it will not attract good software; therefore, it does not make sense to select a machine with low sales, no matter how good its technology is.

The second consideration is *support*. Is there ample training available locally for the machine and its most popular software? Is maintenance readily available and available from several sources? Like software, good support is available only for popular families of PCs.

A third consideration is an *open design and the availability of add-on hardware from third parties*. Again, a good market share is critical, but so is the machine vendor's commitment to an open design.

A fourth consideration is *total price*—not just the price of the machine itself, but the price of a fully configured computer, including both software and add-on hardware. For popular computers, stiff competition among third-party suppliers of hardware and software creates both low retail prices and heavy discounting through mail order houses. Some unpopular machines and machines with closed designs have attractive base prices, but the cost of software and add-on hardware becomes excessive because there is only one seller and because there are no economies of scale for hardware and software development.

A fifth consideration is the presence of *special features*, such as exceptional ease of use or graphics. Special features, however, must not blind the standards developer to the other considerations listed in this section.

8-bit Personal Computers

The first rule of selecting a family to support is never to standardize on an old 8-bit family. Early personal computers used either the Intel 8080 microprocessor or microprocessors that tended to imitate its design. These PC's were called **8-bit** computers because these microprocessors processed information in 8-bit chunks.

The use of the term "8-bit" is something of a red herring, however. These machines were not limited by 8-bit technology per se, but rather by one particular design decision made by Intel when it created the 8080—a design decision copied by other microprocessor producers. This design decision was totally unrelated to 8-bit technology.

The decision was to limit the size of the microprocessor's "address register" to 16 bits. This allowed the microprocessor to address only two to the sixteenth power memory locations directly. Two to the sixteenth power is 65,536 (64 K). Because each memory location holds one byte, these early machines were limited to 64 KB of directly addressed memory.

Today, most personal computer programs need at least 256 KB to 512 KB of storage to run at all. Even if a firm can "get by" with an 8-bit PC for a short time, the costs of converting data to the formats required by more powerful and incompatible systems will be excessive.

The IBM PC Family

Since August 1981, IBM has produced a steady stream of personal computers. Several, including the original IBM Personal Computer, the XT, and the AT, have become de facto standards in the industry and have sold in the millions. Other products have failed miserably in the market, some being pulled out of production less than a year after introduction. We will look at the IBM family in three major sections. First, we will consider the IBM Personal Computer desktop line that includes the PC, XT, and AT. Second, we will examine the IBM Personal System/2 line that was introduced in 1987. After discussing these two main desktop lines, we will look at other PCs that IBM has produced.

The IBM Personal Computer Desktop Line

IBM has produced a number of desktop computers that have "IBM Personal Computer" in their names. Table 6-1 summarizes the characteristics

TABLE 6-1
IBM PERSONAL COMPUTER DESKTOP SERIES

SYSTEM UNIT CHARACTERISTIC	PC	PC XT	PC AT
Microprocessor	8088	8088	80286
Cycle Speed (MHz)	4.77	4.77	6/8
Processing (bits)	16	16	32
Data Transfers (bits)	8	8	16
Coprocessor	8087	8087	80287
Free Expansion Slots	2/3	5/6	5
Standard Memory (KB)	256	256	512
Maximum Memory (KB)	640	640	640
Standard Floppy (KB)	360	360	1,200
Hard Disk Drive (MB)	None	10/20	20/30
Access Time (msec)	N/A	80	30
Can Run OS/2	No	No	Yes

of the most important of these desktops. These characteristics are discussed briefly in this chapter and are examined in more detail in Chapters 7 and 8.

IBM began its PC line in 1981, with the introduction of the **IBM Personal Computer.** This machine was still being sold at the time this book was written, but it is now out of production and is being phased out of the IBM inventory. The machine uses a slow microprocessor, has few expansion slots, and has a weak power supply.

Although the basic PC launched an era, its limitations quickly became obvious, and in 1983 IBM introduced a modified version of this machine, the **IBM Personal Computer XT.** The XT added three more expansion slots, a larger watt power supply, and ROM to handle an optional 10 MB (later 20 MB) hard disk drive. Otherwise, the machine was identical to the PC.

Although the PC and XT have been superseded in the performance by newer machines, millions of these machines may be found in offices, and there are millions of clones of these machines as well. Most large and small firms continue to view these mundane but inexpensive machines as their basic personal computers, setting software standards with these machines in mind. The original PC and XT have become the workhorses of the modern office.

In 1984, IBM introduced an entirely new machine, the **IBM Personal Computer AT.** Using Intel's more powerful 80286 microprocessor, this machine offered very high performance. For most jobs, the AT was two to three times as fast as the original PC and XT. The AT, despite its high initial price, quickly became the favorite of power users with big jobs.

The AT came standard with a large 1.2 MB floppy disk drive. This large floppy drive was designed to make floppy-to-hard disk data transfers more convenient. Two more drives could be added; most users adding two more drives chose one hard disk and one 360 KB floppy disk drive for data transfers with basic PCs and PC XT's, but some purchased two hard disk drives for even higher storage capacity. To keep up with the fast microprocessor of the AT, its 20 MB hard disk drive (later expanded to 30 MB) had an access time of 30 milliseconds—about half that of XT drives. To round things off, the microprocessor speed, which was initially pegged at 6 MHz, was later increased to 8 MHz.

The Achilles' heel of the Personal Computer family has been its displays. IBM originally offered only a monochrome display, and although its resolution was very high, it could do no graphics at all. IBM apparently believed that the PC would double as a games machine using low-resolution home TVs (an adapter for home TVs was included in the mother board) and as an office machine using a monochrome text monitor. Although other firms, particularly Hercules, built display adapters capable of showing graphics on the display, IBM never did.

Matters improved only slightly when IBM introduced its color graphics adapter (CGA) and IBM Personal Color Display. Although the display could show four colors, its resolution was miserable. Even in two-color mode (monochrome), the resolution of the system was very poor. In 1984, IBM tried again with its enhanced graphics adapter (EGA) and enhanced color display. This system offered 16 colors and resolution that were nearly equal to those of the original monochrome system. EGA use grew slowly at first because its initial cost was very high. After 1986, however, its popularity grew enormously, thanks both to plunging costs and growing demand for high-resolution graphics.

The IBM Personal System/2 Line

In 1987, IBM introduced an entirely new line of personal computers. It called these computers the IBM Personal System/2 line to emphasize the intended links between these machines and the System/36, System/38, and System/370 lines of computers. These machines were clearly intended to be IBM's main line for the future.

This line introduced several new technological advances, including surface-mounted technology in which chips are mounted directly on the board, instead of on carriers, and multichannel data busses. However, we are more concerned with the technical characteristics of these machines summarized in Table 6-2. These characteristics are discussed in more detail in Chapters 7 and 8.

The smallest machine in the family, the Model 30, differs sharply from other models because it is so limited. Its 8086 microprocessor limits it to 640 KB and precludes the use of Operating System/2, which will even be able to run on older ATs. It also uses 720 KB floppy disks that are smaller than the 1.44 MB floppy disks used in other PS/2 models. The Model 30 uses a graphics adapter, the MultiColor Graphics Array (MCGA), which is not the main adapter of any other IBM computer, so little software may appear for it. Since this adapter fails to emulate EGA, the user must drop all the way back to the poor-resolution CGA technology for programs that do not support MCGA. In addition, the machine has only three expansion slots. The only advantage that the Model 30 offered was thrift. Its performance was almost twice that of

TABLE 6-2
IBM PERSONAL SYSTEM/2 SERIES

SYSTEM UNIT CHARACTERISTIC	MODEL 30	MODEL 50	MODEL 60	MODEL 80
Microprocessor	8086	80286	80286	80386
Cycle Speed (MHz)	8	10	10	16/20
Processing (bits)	16	32	32	32
Data Transfers (bits)	16	16	16	32
Coprocessor	8087	80287	80287	80387
Free Expansion Slots	3	3	7	7
Standard Memory (KB)	640	1,024	1,024	1,024
Maximum Memory (KB)	640	7,168	15,360	16,384
Standard Floppy Drive (KB)	720	1,440	1,440	1,440
Hard Disk Drive (MB)	20	20	44/70	44/314
Access Time (msec)	80	80	30	30
Can Run OS/2	No	Yes	Yes	Yes

an XT and came within 30 percent of AT speeds, despite a price far below that of IBM ATs (and, more to the point, competitive with the prices of AT clones).

The Model 50 really begins the PS/2 line. It uses the standard 1.44 MB floppy disks and the standard Video Graphics Array used in large models. It also uses the 80286 microprocessor that allows up to 16 MB of internal memory and the use of Operating System/2. At the same time, the machine has only three expansion slots. One of these will be taken up by a memory expansion board, since the Model 50 mother board only holds 1 MB of RAM, and at least 2 MB of RAM are needed to work well with Operating System/2. It would be very easy to run out of slots in the Model 30. Another problem is the Model 50's use of a slow 20 MB hard disk as its standard second drive. This should degrade the machine's performance.

The Model 60 fixes these limitations, boosting the number of expansion slots to seven and making a faster 44 MB or 70 MB hard disk standard, depending on the specific submodel purchased. The Model 60 is likely to be the standard machine in most organizations.

Although the Models 50 and 60 use the same microprocessor as the AT, they perform about 60 percent faster than an AT in benchmark tests. Their performance is therefore more than four times greater than the performance of an XT. Models 50 and 60 are definitely power machines.

The Model 80 is an entirely different machine. Although Model 50 and Model 60 use the Intel 80286 microprocessor used in the AT, the Model 80 uses the more powerful Intel 80386, giving a performance boost of about three compared to Models 50 and 60 and a seven-to-one performance ratio over an XT. This performance places the Model 80 in the same category as the Macintosh II discussed later in this chapter. Its standard hard disks range from 44 MB to 314 MB, depending on the model. The top model can support two hard disk drives giving up to 628 MB on a single Model 80.

When it introduced the Personal System/2 line, IBM was careful not to repeat its earlier display woes. For all products but the Model 30, it put a new **Video Graphics Array (VGA)** adapter on the mother board. Because this adapter uses analog signalling, it is not limited to 16 or so colors. It can produce up to 256 colors at a time. Its best resolution is 640 pixels horizontally by 480 pixels vertically. This is almost equal to the horizontal monochrome monitor's resolution, and its vertical resolution is 37 percent greater. It also provided several displays capable of working with VGA. As noted earlier, the Model 30 uses a different adapter on its mother board, the MultiColor Graphics Array (MCGA).

The most difficult machine in the PS/2 family to discuss is the Model 25. The Model 25 is not a business machine. Rather, it was created for the educational market. Basically a limited and lower-cost version of the Model 30, the Model 25 was released with an extensive corpus of educational software reported to be able to use the machine and its MCGA adapter. While the Model 25 may be useful for training within the information center, most information centers prefer to train users on the equipment they will actually be using in their offices.

Portable Computers

IBM was slow to produce a portable computer. This gap in its line spurred the initial growth of the compatibles discussed later in this chapter. When IBM did introduce its **IBM Portable Computer** in 1984, the machine's sales were poor and the product was eventually discontinued. It was not competitive with other suitcase-size portables.

In 1986, the same year that IBM announced the demise of its first portable, the company introduced the **IBM PC Convertible,** a 12-pound laptop using an 80C88 microprocessor clocked at 4.77 MHz. This machine introduced new 720 KB disk drives with a 3.5 inch diameter floppy disks. It can be purchased with a flat panel display or a CRT display. Add-in electronics usually plug into the back of the unit, instead of being added as internal expansion boards. These are equivalent to expansion boards, however, because they are linked directly to the bus.

Specialized Machines

In addition to its main desktop and portable lines, IBM has introduced a number of specialized machines.

- The **IBM PCjr** was a semicompatible home machine that failed to find a market.
- The IBM 3270 PC, introduced in 1983, combines a standard desktop PC with a 3270 terminal. This product is used primarily by IS programmers.
- The IBM XT 370 and AT 370, introduced in 1983 and 1985, respectively, are desktop machines that can act as desktop PCs or as miniature System 370-series mainframe computers running the VM operating system. They are used mostly by IS professionals for development work.

- The **IBM PC RT,** introduced in 1986, is a reduced instruction set technology machine that is geared toward scientific and engineering applications. Its name is somewhat confusing; the IBM PC RT is not part of the regular IBM PC family because it is not compatible with the other machines in the family at the time of this writing.
- Another specialized machine is the **System 36 PC,** a hybrid machine that can function as a PC, a small System 36 minicomputer, and departmental file server. It was introduced in 1986.

Networking

IBM currently has two personal computer networking products. The first to be introduced was the **IBM Personal Computer Network,** and the second was the **IBM Token-Ring Network.** Only the Token Ring-Network experienced good sales. (Both products are discussed in Chapter 15.)

IBM PC Compatibles (Clones)

As noted earlier, the IBM PC's popularity and its open design have enticed a number of firms to build **compatible** personal computers or **clones** that act like the IBM PC. For the user, these "clones" offer two advantages.

- First, they tend to run at least 20 percent cheaper than comparable IBM products, and some are even cheaper.
- Second, most compatibles perform better than comparable IBM products, in terms of speed or special features such as integral graphics.

Compatible vendors tend to adopt one of two basic competitive strategies. Some opt for higher performance than the IBM PC for a slightly lower price. Others opt for big cost reductions, with little if any performance improvement and in some cases clearly inferior components.

Despite their advantages, compatibles have two major disadvantages. The first is a high vendor mortality rate. When buying a clone, many firms rate stability of the vendor higher than all technical criteria. Mortality may become worse in the future if IBM lessens its commitment to an open architecture. For example, it applied for a patent on its AT keyboard, and it used many proprietary chips in its Personal System/2 line. However, the PS/2 machines should not be prohibitively difficult to clone, and these are IBM's flagship machines for the near future. Cloning should therefore remain healthy, although the number of compatible vendors should decline in the future.

A second problem is that many "compatibles" are not fully compatible with IBM products. There are several degrees of compatibility, and, as in marriage, a low degree of compatibility can be disastrous. Most compatibles fall into one of three major levels of compatibility: (1) MS-DOS compatibility, (2) full program compatibility, and (3) expansion board compatibility. We will concentrate on clones of the original Personal Computer line, but the same principles hold for the cloning of all machines.

MS-DOS Compatibility

As noted earlier, the most popular operating system on IBM personal computers and compatibles is MS-DOS, which is sold as PC-DOS by IBM.

This operating system is produced by Microsoft, which has also written versions of MS-DOS to run on PCs from other vendors, including Wang Laboratories and Digital Equipment Corporation. These versions of MS-DOS are compatible with the versions that run on the IBM PC.

Application programs are written to work with a particular operating system. Thus, a program written to run on the Unix operating system will not run on MS-DOS, or vice versa. Although the IBM PC can run other operating systems than MS-DOS, little end user software is available for these other operating systems.

MS-DOS compatibility simply means that a computer uses the MS-DOS operating system. A certain class of application programs, called **well-behaved programs,** can run on any machine that uses MS-DOS. As shown in Figure 6-9, well-behaved programs talk only to the operating system, letting the operating system handle all communication with the machine's hardware and ROM. For such programs, it does not matter in the least that the underlying hardware and software look nothing like the IBM PCs. The operating system shields the users from these differences. As a result, some companies that sell MS-DOS machines with incompatible underlying hardware bill their systems as "IBM compatible." This is obviously a misnomer, since they are merely MS-DOS compatible, and MS-DOS is not even an IBM product.

More seriously, not all programs are well behaved. As shown in Figure 6-10, many programs—including almost all of the very best programs—occasionally reach "under" the operating system to work with the PC's basic circuits and ROM programs. If the machine is only MS-DOS compatible, these **badly behaved programs** will grind to a halt. Although vendors of MS-DOS compatibles can claim that their machines can run *most* programs written for the IBM PC, they can usually run only a small fraction of the **most popular** programs created for the IBM PC.

It is possible to rewrite "badly behaved" programs to run on machines whose underlying hardware and ROM programs are incompatible with IBM's

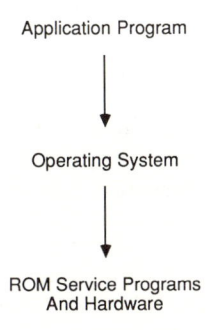

Application Program
↓
Operating System
↓
ROM Service Programs And Hardware

Note:
A well-behaved application program never deals directly with ROM service programs or the computer's hardware (such as RAM working memory for the display adapter). It always works through the operating system.

FIGURE 6-9 WELL BEHAVED APPLICATION PROGRAM

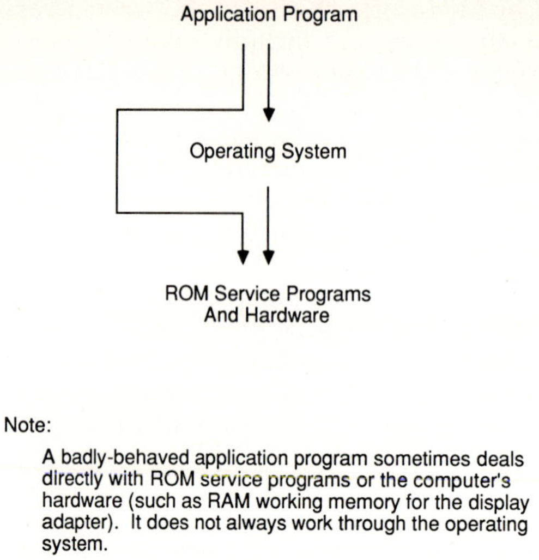

```
          Application Program
                 |
                 v
          Operating System
                 |
                 v
          ROM Service Programs
             And Hardware
```

Note:
A badly-behaved application program sometimes deals directly with ROM service programs or the computer's hardware (such as RAM working memory for the display adapter). It does not always work through the operating system.

FIGURE 6-10 BADLY BEHAVED APPLICATION PROGRAM

hardware and ROM programs. But only a few of the most popular badly behaved programs have been rewritten, and even these have only been rewritten to work with the most popular MS-DOS compatibles.

Full Program Compatibility

The next level of compatibility is **full program compatibility.** Even badly behaved programs can run at this level, providing two requirements are met.

1. That underlying hardware be identical to the hardware of the IBM PC or at least be functionally equivalent.
2. That ROM service programs be functionally equivalent to IBM's ROM service programs.

Functionally equivalent means that hardware or software is not an exact copy but still functions the same way as the original. For example, in ROM service programs, a call to a compatible's particular ROM interrupt (see Chapter 8) must produce the same results as a call to this interrupt on a comparable IBM computer. Functional equivalency is rarely perfect, and for advanced applications such as networking, a few problems may appear. As a result, clone makers use functional equivalency only when exact copying is impossible.

In general, exact copying is normally done for hardware. IBM did not copyright its hardware designs for its PC and PC XT, and it has moved very slowly toward copyrighting features of its advanced models. It has taken a few steps in this direction, but at least through the PC AT, exact copying of hardware is possible for nearly all components.

IBM PCs, at least through the PC AT, have been built almost entirely from standard, off-the-shelf components. As a result, clone makers have not even faced barriers owing to component production in the past. This situation is changing, now that the Personal System/2 line of machines uses proprietary chips, but this will only shake out "mom and pop" clone companies.

Exact copying means that the same circuits are used and are wired together in the same way, but in some aspects of design, this limit still allows innovation. For instance, more circuitry can be packed onto the mother board. To give another example, faster microprocessors can be used, as long as it is possible to slow them for speed-sensitive applications.

In contrast to hardware, IBM has copyrighted its ROM service programs and has vigorously protected its rights. Therefore, for ROM, building functionally equivalent programs is the only viable approach for clone makers. Fortunately, IBM has programmed its ROM through the PC AT fairly loosely, so building functionally equivalent ROM has been straightforward. As noted earlier, however, functionally equivalent ROM is never completely equivalent to the original, and compatibles may balk at some advanced programs.

Expansion Board Compatibility

Until the mid-1980s, full program compatibility was sufficient, but now that so many add-on expansion boards are being used, a higher level of compatibility is needed. This higher level of compatibility is **expansion board compatibility**—the ability to take expansion boards designed for the IBM PC. Networking boards, 3270 terminal emulation boards, and other advanced boards are becoming essential, and vendors are producing hundreds of good and inexpensive expansion boards for IBM PCs and expansion board compatibles. Unless a compatible can take these boards, the user is likely to be locked out of tomorrow's world. As a result, most corporations limit compatible purchases to personal computers with this third level of compatibility.

For everyday use, most expansion board compatibles work very well. But some expansion boards, particularly the advanced communications boards discussed in Chapters 13 through 15, sometimes push compatibility beyond its limits. Before a specific compatible is purchased, rigorous compatibility testing is needed for computers that are to be placed in communications-intensive environments.

Apple Macintosh

Apple has billed the Macintosh as "the computer for the rest of us." This slogan implies that its ease of use is so great that anyone can use it without being "one of them"—computer junkies. Even when we discount marketing claims, the Macintosh is easy to use. Its basic user interface approach was created by Alan Kay and others at the Xerox Palo Alto Research Center specifically as a way for children to use computers.

The First Products

Apple introduced a similar machine in 1983, the Lisa. Although the Lisa was superior to the Macintosh in many ways, its price tag was prohibitive, and even its AT-class microprocessor failed to give its advanced features adequate performance. The Macintosh was a more realistic effort that balanced capabilities, price, and performance.

The Macintosh offered impressive features even in its earliest versions. It had an AT-class 7.8 MHz Motorola MC68000 microprocessor and 3.5 inch microfloppy drives with 400 KB of capacity apiece. Instead of a slow RS232C serial port, it offered a higher speed RS449/422A port for communication with the outside world.

More importantly, it introduced the mouse and the iconic interface (see Chapter 8) to the general public, in the form of a user interface so simple and intuitive that many analysts at first underestimated the processing power of the machine. This user interface approach is beginning to enter the IBM PC world.

Problems

When the Macintosh was introduced in 1984, its sales were disappointing. A number of factors contributed to this early disappointment. First, the machine was designed for 256 Kbit chips, which were not widely available when the machine was first sold. As a result, the Macintosh was originally limited to 128 KB of RAM. This was totally inadequate, so the application software needed to make the machine viable was slow in emerging. Later, when Apple introduced 512 KB Macintoshes ("Fat Macs") and introduced upgrade kits for older machines, software developers began building in earnest, but the Macintosh proved to be a difficult machine to design for.

Second, the Macintosh abandoned the open design philosophy. It had no expansion boards at all, and third-party hardware designers found it difficult to come up with products for the new machines. Hard disk drives were few and expensive, and until Apple introduced its LaserWriter page printer, output was limited to dot matrix printers.

Third, the Macintosh was completely incompatible with IBM machines. Apple did not even provide an external 5.25 inch drive for disk-to-disk file transfers. For many potential Macintosh users, this was the most serious problem of all, and things did not get better until 1987.

The Turning Point

The turning point came in 1986. Software suddenly became good and plentiful, and third-party hardware also began to proliferate. In addition, Apple introduced its Macintosh Plus, a machine that had a megabyte of memory, 800 KB disk drives, and new ROM programs for faster operation. Particularly when used with a hard disk drive, the Macintosh Plus was an entirely new ball game. Even with floppy disk drives, the ample memory of the Plus allowed the use of RAM disks (see Chapter 8) to speed performance dramatically.

To match these better graphics engines, Apple introduced the LaserWriter page printer and later the LaserWriter Plus, giving output rivaling that of print shops in quality. As discussed in Chapters 7 and 11, the LaserWriter has embedded hardware and software for handling PostScript, a page description language. This dramatically increases its ability to produce graphics compared to earlier laser printers.

Another reason for the rebirth of the Macintosh had nothing to do with Apple. This was the emergence of desktop publishing (see Chapter 11) as a major application. Because the Macintosh and LaserWriter were eminently suited to this application, software developers built their first programs for the Macintosh. Not until 1987 did reasonably competitive programs appear on the IBM PC, and even then, the pace of development in the Macintosh world was exploding.

The Explosion of 1987

In 1987, Apple introduced the Macintosh SE, which outwardly resembled the Macintosh Plus but added a number of important new improvements. The most dramatic was a single expansion slot, which allowed expansion boards into the Macintosh world for the first time. Into this slot could go a card with a math coprocessor, an accelerator card, and even cards to emulate IBM PCs. The cards would generally be sold with an external 5.25 inch floppy disk drive, for data transfer between Macintoshes and IBM PCs. This finally provided the compatibility or at least exchange path that the Macintosh family had lacked for so long. In addition, the SE allowed *two* internal drives to be installed, removing the need for the clumsy external drive of earlier models. The machine also incorporated many other advances.

The SE was overshadowed by the announcement of the Macintosh II. This name was created to remind buyers of Apple's earlier flagship line, the Apple II, and most analysts agree that this is Apple's Macintosh of the future. Although its price was originally high, it represented an entirely new architecture.

Its processing power was about three times greater than that of earlier Macintoshes, which are themselves in the AT class. This made the Macintosh II as powerful as an IBM PS/2 Model 80, the top of IBM's line. In addition, it had six expansion slots for virtually unlimited expansion, including expansion to AT compatibility and external disk drive. It had no standard video output because its design allows a vast array of graphics adapters to be built for it. Apple did introduce two displays with the machine, including a high-resolution monochrome display and a high-resolution color display, but these were only viewed as the first steps toward tomorrow's graphics output.

Another computer development in 1987 was the first delivery of portable Macintoshes. These machines were not sold by Apple itself, but rather by third parties who bought Macintoshes or components from Apple and packed them into portable computers. These portables are costly and fall halfway between suitcase-size portables and laptops in size, but for applications where at least luggability is needed, they are likely to prove popular.

Table 6-3 shows the technical characteristics of the original Macintosh 128K and those of the active products in the Apple Macintosh series at the time of this writing. The technical improvement in the Macintosh are obviously dramatic. These technical characteristics are discussed further in Chapters 7 and 8.

Networking

About the time the SE and Macintosh II appeared, the last pieces of Apple's networking fell into place. Even the first Macs had been sold with **422A** ports (see Chapter 14), which allow very high speed transfer. Although the transfer was limited by software, it was still possible to do networking at a quarter million bits per second at the cost of only $50 to $100 per machine.

TABLE 6-3
APPLE MACINTOSH SERIES

SYSTEM UNIT CHARACTERISTIC	MODEL 128 K*	Plus	SE	II
Microprocessor	68000	68000	68000	68020
Cycle Speed (MHz)	8	8	8	16
Processing (bits)	32	32	32	32
Data Transfers (bits)	16	16	16	32
Coprocessor	None	None	None	Yes
Free Expansion Slots	0	0	1	5
Standard Memory (KB)	128	1,024	1,024	1,024
Maximum Memory (KB)	512	1,024	4,096	8,192
Standard Floppy Drive (KB)	400	800	800	800
Second Internal Drive	No	No	Yes	Yes

* Original 128 KB model is out of production; data are included for comparison.

The AppleTalk network from Apple was offered soon after the first Macintoshes, but the server software for the network was not solidified until 1987. Today, it is possible to use the network to link not just Apple machines but IBM machines as well, although IBM machines require a more expensive adapter card because they lack a high-speed two-way communications interface like 422A. This allows several IBM and Macintosh PCs to be linked together for file exchange and to use the LaserWriter printer. It provides a quick way to get a department into networking with immediate payoffs to IBM users, who now get access to the LaserWriter. Macintosh networking is discussed further in Chapter 15.

Prospects

At the very least, the Macintosh will push IBM toward ease of use and consistent user interfaces. IBM is already moving in this direction, but its new operating system's graphics features will not be delivered until 1988. In this time, the Macintosh would continue to solidify its software lead, particularly in the top-end area, where the Macintosh II offers supurb graphics performance.

Other Computers

Although the IBM PC and its compatibles dominate the corporate world today, a number of vendors besides Apple offer their own incompatible machines. Most of these are producers of mainframes, minicomputers, and word processing systems. These vendors hope to leverage their installed base of host users into buying PCs. Others hope to exploit retail strength (for example, Tandy) or low prices (for example, Kaypro). Few of these other vendors, however, have been successful, and most are moving rapidly toward full PC compatibility.

PRICES

PC pricing is very confusing because there are so many hardware, software, and service options to consider. In addition, many quoted prices reflect stripped-down "base systems" that would be of little use in practice. For example, many base systems fail to include displays or omit hard disks in machines that are normally purchased with hard disk drives.

In this section, we will look at the prices of several representative configurations. Prices for 1987 will be shown in the examples. For low-end systems, prices should fall about 10 percent to 20 percent per year. For high-end options, prices should decrease 20 percent to 30 percent annually.

A Minimum Personal Computer

When users hear about systems with "base prices" of $900 or less, they often rush out to purchase one. But they normally return with a machine that costs twice as much, and they often have to spend several hundred dollars more during the first year to bring the machine up to usable form. Information centers naturally discourage this practice. One way to discourage low-balling is to have a standard price for a minimum personal computer. Table 6-4 reflects the going price of a minimally-useful PC and refers to a PC with the following attributes.

- A basic IBM PC XT (or compatible) with 640 KB of internal memory. Although many programs still run with 256 KB of internal memory, the number that can do so is shrinking rapidly. An XT is specified instead of a basic PC because IBM no longer produces the basic model, and nearly all compatibles are really XT compatibles.

TABLE 6-4
PRICE OF A MINIMUM PERSONAL COMPUTER (1987)

System Unit (PC XT Compatible)	
640 KB RAM	
Two 360 KB floppy drives	
Serial and parallel adapters	
Total	$900
Display	
Monochrome display	$125
Monochrome display adapter	$75
Total	$200
Printer	
Low-end printer	$300
Software	$350
Glare screen for display	$30
TOTAL	$1780

- Two floppy disk drives. This is mandatory because programs take up almost a full disk, thereby requiring a second drive for data disks. It is also mandatory because backup is almost never done on machines with a single drive.
- A monochrome display and display adapter
- A low-end dot matrix printer or a slow daisywheel printer. Neither is good for more than light printing.
- A software budget for the operating system and one or two application programs.
- A simple glare screen to reduce glare from the display. This is a tiny investment that should be mandatory.

For minimum configurations, a "base price" of $900 or less is often quoted. This normally includes the system unit and nothing else, and sometimes it includes only a single floppy disk drive. As shown in Table 6-4, a full minimum system is twice as expensive. To make matters worse, minimal systems are often purchased by exactly those novice users who do not understand the ensemble nature of PC purchasing.

A Typical System

Even when fully loaded, a base system is still inexpensive, and many organizations conclude incorrectly that computers cost only about $2,000. But minimum systems are not good enough for many users, and the "average" system is much more expensive. Table 6-5 shows the type of computer that represents a typical purchase in corporations today. We will call it a **typical system.**

- The basic computer is an IBM PC XT compatible—not a PC AT. It is purchased with 640 KB of internal memory, one 360 KB floppy disk drive, and a 20 MB hard disk. It also has a serial and a parallel adapter.
- Also added is a monochrome graphics board, so that graphics can be displayed on the standard monochrome display. This allows the user to see graphics in shades of green. Care must be taken when buying a monochrome graphics board, since only some graphics products may work with many graphics boards for monochrome displays.
- A good, near letter quality dot matrix printer with adequate speed is added, plus a sound hood to mute the loud noise made by this printer.
- Communications is becoming commonplace, so communications must be included in the typical system. The "communications board" price is roughly the price of either a sophisticated terminal emulation board (and software), in order to let the terminal work with an IBM host computer, or an adapter board for a local area network or PC network.
- There is a software budget sufficient to purchase two major programs and one or two small programs to boost performance, plus adequate furniture that is slightly more expensive than the minimum configuration's.
- In addition to a glare screen, there is a low-cost ergonomic table that is not adjustable.

TABLE 6-5
PRICE OF A TYPICAL PERSONAL COMPUTER (1987)

System Unit (PC XT Compatible)	
640 KB RAM	
One 360 KB floppy drive	
One 20 MB hard disk	
Serial and parallel adapters	
Total	$1200
Display	
Monochrome display	$125
Monochrome graphics display adapter	$100
Total	$225
Printer	
Medium-range printer	$500
Sound hood	300
Total	$800
Communications board and software	$900
Software	$600
Furniture	
Glare screen	$30
Ergonomic table	$300
Total	$330
TOTAL	**$4055**

This configuration is a good deal more expensive than that of a minimum personal computer and far more expensive than the $900 base price often cited. Yet it is almost typical of what corporations buy today.

A High-End Personal Computer

Many users have heavy demands that require the purchase of high-end systems. These machines are expensive, as Table 6-6 indicates.

- The machine is an IBM Personal System/2, Model 60.
- Its RAM has been expanded to 2 MB.
- It has a 360 KB (5.25 inch) floppy disk drive, a 1.44 MB (3.5 inch) floppy disk drive, and a 44 MB hard disk.
- A tape backup unit is included because failure to back up such a large system could be disastrous.
- An 8512 color graphics display compatible with the Video Graphics Array adapter is included.
- A communications board is included.
- A typical page printer based on laser technology is included.
- A software budget reflecting more expensive programs is included.
- An adjustable ergonomic work station is included.

TABLE 6-6
PRICE OF A HIGH-END PERSONAL COMPUTER (1987)

System Unit (PS/2 Model 60)	
2 MB RAM	
One 1.44 MB floppy drive	
One 360 KB floppy drive	
One 41 MB hard disk	
Serial and parallel adapters	
Display and other adapters	
Total	$6,190
Display	
VGA color display	$685
Printer	
Page printer	$2500
Communications Board and Software	$900
Tape Backup Unit	$1500
Software	$2000
Furniture	
Glare screen	$30
Fully ergonomic table	$1200
Fully ergonomic chair	$600
Total	$1830
TOTAL	**$15,605**

Networked System

Networking is often touted as a way to reduce costs, but it is expensive, as shown in Table 6-7. An IBM Token Ring Network is used in this example.

- A network communications adapter card is needed for each user PC.
- Networking communications software is also needed for each user PC.
- Server software and network management software are needed for the server PC.
- Cabling is needed to link the computers together.

Although the costs of networking hardware and software are high, the real cost of networking usually stems from the server. For the number of PCs shown in Table 6-7, a dedicated Personal System/2 Model 60 is needed. It will be used so heavily that it cannot be used simultaneously as a user PC. This cost is often overlooked in PC network planning.

These costs have not included the costs of network planning and installation, which can be considerable. At least 10 percent of the purchase cost should be added for planning, installation, and training.

A Four-Year Budget

Tables 6-4 to 6-7 are only the beginnings of a PC purchase budget. First, they only show the first year, and costs continue well beyond the first year. Second,

TABLE 6-7
PRICE OF A NETWORKED SYSTEM (1987)

Server (PS/2 Model 60)	
System unit	
VGA color display	
Page printer	
Tape backup unit	
Communications board and software	
Total	$11,775
User PCs (6)	
One floppy drive	
Monochrome display system	
No printer	
Total ($1000 per PC)	$6000
Application Software	$4000
Networking	
Adapter boards (7)	$4200
Network software (7)	$400
Server software	$2000
Network management software	$1000
Cabling	$700
Total	$8300
TOTAL	$30,075
COST PER USER PC	$5,012

they fail to show such "soft" costs as supplies, training, and information center support. Table 6-8 shows a realistic four-year budget for a typical personal computer.

- The budget shows that hardware and software spending almost invariably continue beyond the first year, as users add to their original systems.
- Ongoing costs include not only supplies but also maintenance. Our figure is the cost of a typical maintenance contract, which is more than the expected cost of repairs, but repairs and maintenance cannot be avoided and must be budgeted.
- The "support costs" include training expenses, lost time due to training, and the prorated cost of the information center staff (using a ratio of one staff member for every 100 end users).
- The time spent specifying the purchase, justifying purchase, and installing the computer can easily run to 20 percent of hardware and software costs.

Overall, the four-year budget shows that the average *annual* cost of a standard PC is a major investment that needs to be budgeted and justified carefully.

Our figures assume that the PC is used by a single person. What if the PC is shared? Obviously, the hardware and software costs per person will decline

TABLE 6-8
FOUR-YEAR BUDGET FOR A TYPICAL PC (1987)

CATEGORY	1987	1988	1989	1990
Computer System				
Hardware	$3125	$300	$300	$300
Software	$600	$300	$300	$300
Furniture	$330	$0	$0	$0
	$4055	$600	$600	$600
Ongoing Nonlabor Costs				
Supplies	$300	$300	$300	$300
Maintenance	$400	$400	$400	$400
	$700	$700	$700	$700
Labor				
Purchase/justify/install	$800	$120	$120	$120
Information center	$400	$400	$400	$400
Course tuition	$240	$120	$120	$120
Training time	$500	$250	$250	$250
	$1940	$890	$890	$890
Total for Year:	$6695	$2190	$2190	$2190

TOTAL COST $13,2655
ANNUAL COST $3316

proportionately. But support costs will increase directly with the number of people supported, and even ongoing supplies and maintenance costs should rise. As the cost of hardware and software falls compared to the cost of support, even PC sharing will not produce extensive cost savings.

Price Trends

As noted at the start of this section on prices, we have only included 1987 data to make the price analysis concrete. Prices are falling rapidly, and by the time you read this book, its specific numbers will be obsolete, although the logical structure of the price analysis should remain valid.

Historical Price Trends

A good way to anticipate future price declines is to look at the past. For example, when the IBM PC first came out, in late 1981, a 256 KB machine with two floppy disk drives, a monochrome display, and a cheap dot matrix printer cost $5,817. In late 1986, five years later, a clone with 640 KB and a better low-end printer cost only $1500. So in five years, the price fell to only 24 percent of its original level. This represents a compound annual price decline of 25 percent.

This price decline understates the true dynamics of prices. A 1986 clone still basically used 1981 technology, so 1986 clones did not reflect the true state of the art in 1986. A better picture can be drawn by comparing the 1981 PC with the PC AT introduced three years later. An AT with a single floppy disk drive and no hard disk in 1984 cost almost exactly the same as a single-floppy PC did in 1981. Yet the AT has roughly three times the performance of a PC. This threefold improvement in price–performance represents a compound annual rate of about 45 percent. The jump from AT to PS/2 has shown a similar leap in price–performance.

Pressures on Prices

Why are prices falling so rapidly? First and foremost, the large size of today's market allows new technology to be introduced very rapidly, and each generation produces major improvements in price and performance.

Second, below the level of new technology, growing market size produces major economies of scale in manufacturing and delivery. Even without new technology, PC prices would be decreasing rapidly.

Third, the large size of the PC market has encouraged low-cost producers, wholesalers, retailers, mail order houses, and bulk sellers to work cheaply and to accept low markups. Although this change produced its biggest benefits in the mid-1980s, there are still some marketing economies to be found. In the future, it will be very hard for IBM and other vendors to maintain profit-skimming prices on new models, as they did in the early years of the PC revolution.

The Price Outlook

The rate of price decline depends on the specific components in a machine. High-price components such as hard disk drives and fast microprocessors are falling much more rapidly in price than low-cost components such as floppy disk drives and slower microprocessors.

As a result, the definition of "low-end" system is changing constantly, as noted at the start of this chapter. In 1981, many early PC users bought systems with 64 KB of RAM and a single floppy disk drive. In 1987, few firms even bought the minimum systems shown in Table 6-4. Almost all PCs purchased by large corporations had hard disk drives.

Another result is a constant shift in the "typical system" purchased by a firm. Today, a typical system is a PC XT or clone with a monochrome display. By 1990, it may be a Macintosh II or Personal Series/2 with a high-resolution color display. In addition, this machine will offer advanced software using a user interface similar to that of a Macintosh. Despite these advances, the typical machine should be cheaper than it is today.

The high end will also change constantly. Machines running advanced microprocessors will soon bring the equivalent of today's engineering workstations to departments with intense analysis needs, large data bases, or processing-hungry graphics applications.

CONCLUSION

This chapter sets the stage for all subsequent PC chapters and the data communications chapter as well. We have now looked in general at technology, standards, and prices. In future chapters, we will flesh out the details.

Two key themes of this chapter are the open designs of most PC families and the difficulty of speaking intelligently about PC prices. Open design has led to a flood of hardware and software options, resulting in purchase confusion, configuration headaches, and incompatibility nightmares. In addition, it has created the "ensemble approach" to PC purchasing, which gives buyers great flexibility but also requires very careful attention to configuration specification when estimating costs.

We close by mentioning one technique that many corporations are using to simplify these compatibility and pricing difficulties. This is restricting user purchase to one of a half dozen or so **standard configurations.** These standard configurations have well-defined price tags. In addition, their components will have been tested extensively for mutual compatibility. Even if some compatibility problems exist, these will at least be well documented. If these standard configurations come complete with software, then the information center can even develop simplified menu systems that allow users to turn on their computers and select application programs or operating system functions by pointing to menu choices.

REVIEW QUESTIONS

1. Make the case that laptop computers will eventually replace desktop computers. Now make the case that they will not.
2. Contrast desktop computers, engineering workstations, and home computers.
3. The adapter, the bus, and the mother board/expansion board design, and division of labor in software have combined to bring great openness to computer design. Explain why each brings openness and discuss how the three all work together to bring openness.
4. Why is an open design important to buyers? What problems does it bring to buyers?
5. What is a computer family? Why is the IBM PC and compatibles family the most popular family today? Why is the Apple Macintosh family gaining?
6. Distinguish between MS-DOS compatibility and full program compatibility. What does "functionally equivalent" mean? Why is full program compatibility not enough for the future?
7. What are the characteristics of a minimum personal computer? Which of these characteristics do you think most first-time buyers are likely to overlook when shopping around? Which of these characteristics do you think will be the first to go as companies move up to new minimum PC configurations? Why?
8. How do you think the typical personal computer of 1992 will differ from the typical system of 1987?
9. What are the components of a networked system? Why is networking not a sure way to reduce total hardware costs? What networking component do you think is the most frequently overlooked by purchasers?
10. Looking at life cycle costs, which costs do you think will fall most swiftly over time? Most slowly?
11. Given the way that many costs are falling, what do you think the PC you are personally likely to buy in 1990 will be like, and what do you think it will cost? Give a four-year budget for the purchase.
12. What are the advantages of creating standard configurations? The disadvantages?

PERSONAL COMPUTER HARDWARE 7

Now that we have discussed PC standards and prices in general, we will look in detail at the hardware of personal computers. We will begin with the PC's system unit, which houses its electronics and its disk drives. Afterward, we will examine the peripherals attached to the system unit, including printers, displays, and advanced input/output (I/O) devices.

Graphics technology is undergoing enormous change today. Before discussing I/O peripherals, we will present a broad view of graphics because many graphics concepts and principles appear constantly in the discussion of these peripherals.

ELECTRONICS

The heart of any computer is its electronics—its central processing unit, its RAM and ROM memory, its adapter circuits, and the other circuits attached to its bus. These circuits were mentioned in Chapter 6. In this chapter, we will examine them somewhat more closely.

The Bus

As discussed in Chapter 6, the **bus** is the key to flexibility in modern computers. Because the bus forms a central data path used by all circuits, adding a circuit or dropping one is simply a matter of plugging it in or taking it out. In modern PCs, it is not even necessary to set switches to signal the change.

Data Lines

Most personal computers have between 60 and 100 lines in their busses. Of these lines, the most important are the **data lines** that carry data in parallel. The IBM PC has eight data lines for parallel data and instruction transfers. This feature allows it to transfer a whole byte in each clock cycle. The IBM PC AT, the Macintosh SE, and other machines that use the Intel 80286 or Motorola MC68000 microprocessors have 16 data lines for parallel transfers. Both the IBM PS/2 Model 80 and Apple Macintosh II have 32 data lines, to accommodate their Intel 80386 and Motorola MC68020 microprocessors, respectively. This allows them to transfer 4 bytes of data or instruction code in a single clock cycle.

Address Lines

Other lines are used to specify memory addresses or port addresses. Whether memory addresses or ports are being specified depends on the nature of the command being executed. The number of lines is dictated by the address register of the microprocessor. Computers using Intel 8086 and 8088 microprocessors have 20 address lines on their busses. Computers with Intel 80286 microprocessors have 24 address lines. Machines using Intel 80386 or Motorola MC68020 microprocessors can have 32 address lines, although many use fewer, thus limiting themselves to smaller address spaces than their microprocessors support.

Control Lines

The bus's **control lines** act as traffic managers, dictating when devices may transmit their signals. Some control signals pass from the microprocessor to subsidiary circuits. Others, called **interrupts,** are sent by subsidiary circuits to the microprocessor, to indicate that they have something to say—much like a student raising his or her hand in class.

Power Lines

The bus not only sends data and control signals, but it also serves as an electrical power utility for the computer's electronics. Several lines act as grounds, whereas others supply power at different voltages. These power lines allow individual circuits to draw power without the creation of a separate wiring system for electrical power.

IBM's Micro Channel

With its PS/2 line, IBM introduced a patented bus architecture called Micro Channel. In contrast to earlier bus designs, which could send only one piece of data at a time, Micro Channel is like a multilane freeway, allowing more than one data transfer to share the bus in a single clock cycle.

Apple Macintosh Busses

Early Macintoshes, through the Macintosh Plus, provided no expansion slots. In 1987, this changed dramatically with the introduction of the SE and Macintosh II. The Macintosh SE had a single expansion slot, whereas the Macintosh II offered six slots, one of which has to be used for a video adapter board.

Although both machines use 96-pin busses, these busses are extremely different. The SE uses the Eurocard Type C bus, whereas the Macintosh II uses a subset of the IEEE NuBus standard designed for minicomputers. One of the chief characteristics of NuBus is that any slot on the bus may be selected as holding the master board. Thus, it is possible to add a board that emulates an IBM PC and to designate this board as the temporary master. That board will then control the computer.

The Microprocessor

The microprocessor is the most important group of circuits in the computer. It, more than anything else, determines the throughput of a particular computer model. Although simple measures of performance, such as processing speed and number of bits processed in parallel, fail to predict throughput in a way that can be computed precisely, the only way to get a quantum leap in performance is to move up to a computer with a more powerful microprocessor.

Microprocessor Technology

In 1971, a Japanese company approached Intel with an idea for an all-electronic "hand calculator." This calculator would need several new integrated circuit chips to handle its major functions. The Intel engineer assigned to the project, Ted Hoff, quickly realized that the required chips would have so many functions that they could not be produced economically. After thinking about the problem for some time, however, Hoff realized that there was an alternative to building dedicated circuits for each function. A computer, he reasoned, does not have dedicated circuits for each calculation. Instead, it has a **control unit** to execute a limited group of operations called an **instruction set.** To execute a specific calculation, a programmer must write a set of commands in the instruction set. This program would be slower than dedicated circuits doing the same thing, but with programming, there is no limit on functionality.

Although the Japanese company lost interest in the product, Intel turned Hoff's idea into a product. It labeled the product a **microprocessor,** billing it as a "computer on a chip." The computer-on-a-chip label was stretching truth considerably, since the microprocessor had only a control unit and arithmetic/logic unit. In other words, it was only a central processing unit on a chip. It had virtually no memory and needed a host of auxiliary circuits such as timing circuits and memory management circuits to resemble anything like a computer.

The Intel Family

As shown in Table 7-1, Intel has introduced a series of microprocessors over time, each becoming successfully faster and more capable. The major factors in performance are (1) clock speed in megahertz (MHz), (2) number of bits that can be processed in parallel internally within the microprocessor, (3) number of bits in the computer's data bus for parallel data transfers with primary memory and peripherals, (4) the address space it can address directly, and (5) its virtual memory address space.

Another way to see the incredible pace of progress in microprocessor technology is to look at the number of transistor circuits packed on each microprocessor chip.

- The Intel 8088 has 5,500 transistors.
- The Intel 80286 has 134,000.

TABLE 7-1
INTEL MICROPROCESSORS

MODEL	TYPICAL SPEED (MHz)	INTERNAL PROCESSING (BITS)	DATA BUS (BITS)	ADDRESS SPACE	VIRTUAL MEMORY	MULTI-TASKING
4004	1	4	4	NA	None	No
8008	2	8	8	64 KB	None	No
8086	5–10	16	16	1 MB	None	No
8088	5–10	16	8	1 MB	None	No
80186	6	16	16	1 MB	None	No
80286	6–12	32	16	16 MB	1 GB	Yes
80386	16–25	32	32	4 GB	64 TB	Yes

- The Intel 80386 has 275,000.
- The Intel 80486, still under development at the time of this writing, will have at least 1,000,000 and may have as many as 1,250,000.

Early Intel products Intel's first microprocessor was the Intel 4004, a very limited 4-bit microprocessor that was popular as a terminal controller. After an interim product called the 8008, Intel introduced the Intel 8080 microprocessor, an 8-bit machine that was used in the MITS Altair 8800 and was widely used in other personal computers. Most other microprocessors in the 1970s were designed along the general lines laid down by the 8080. Many were only improved versions of the 8080.

The Intel 8086 and 8088 microprocessors When Intel moved beyond the 8-bit world of its 8080 microprocessor to the 16-bit world, it hedged its bets by producing two microprocessors, the Intel 8086 and the Intel 8088. The 8086 was a full 16-bit microprocessor, with 16-bit internal processing and a 16-bit data bus. Its 16-bit data bus raised a production problem. Almost all of the proven, available, and inexpensive auxiliary circuit chips on the market were designed to work with 8-bit data buses. For a 16-bit data bus, a whole new set of expensive auxiliary chips would have to be built.

Because the computer market was extremely price sensitive in the early 1980s, when the 8086 was created, Intel also built a similar chip, the 8088, which processed information internally in 16-bit chunks but only transferred data in 8-bit chunks. This slowed processing somewhat, but it allowed existing auxiliary circuits of low cost to be used, thus lowering the cost of a full computer dramatically. When IBM built its first personal computer, it used the 8088. (Six years later, it returned to the original 8086, albeit a modernized version running at 8 MHz, for the least powerful member of the PS/2 line, the Model 30.)

The original IBM PC used a version of the 8088 clocked to operate at 4.77 MHz. Today, as just noted, much faster versions of both the 8088 and 8086 are on the market. Many IBM PC compatibles use an 8086 running at 8

MHz or even higher, giving better performance. For timing-sensitive programs, however, these compatibles usually have a switch to return the computer to 4.77 MHz.

The 8086 and 8088 were built to run with a **coprocessor,** the 8087. This chip is essentially an extended arithmetic logic unit, permitting faster computation for floating point operations. Application software has to be specially written to work with the 8087.

Breaking the 64 KB barrier IBM's adoption of the 8088 sparked a debate over whether the chip should be called a 16-bit microprocessor, since it has only an 8-bit data bus. But this debate missed the real importance of the chip, namely, its ability to address more than 64 KB of internal memory. Almost all previous microprocessors had been limited to 64 KB of internal memory, and this meant small programs of limited functionality and ease of use.

The problem had not been 8-bit technology per se but a specific design choice made by Intel when it created the 8080. Specifically, Intel decided to make the **address register,** which specifies memory locations, only 16 bits long. This meant it could address only two to the sixteenth power memory locations—65,536 or 64 K. Because each memory location held one byte, this gave an internal memory limitation of 64 KB—a small address space that had to be shared by all ROM programs, reserved system RAM, the operating system, the application program, and the application program's data.

Again, there was nothing in 8-bit technology that dictated the 16-bit address register in the 8080. This was simply a design choice based on the "enormous" size of 64 KB when the 8080 was designed. When other 8-bit microprocessors were built, they could have chosen different sizes for their address registers, but nearly all chose to follow Intel's lead.

By the time the 8086 and 8088 microprocessors were built, it had become clear that 64 KB was not really such an enormous address space after all, so a 20-bit address register was selected for these machines, giving a directly addressable address space of 1 MB. On the IBM PC, only 640 KB is available for user programs, the rest being reserved for system use, as discussed in the next chapter. *The importance of the 8086/8088 revolution, then, was not speed or 16-bit processing. It was the breaking of the 64 KB barrier.*

The Intel 80186 Intel quickly moved beyond 8086/8088 technology and soon produced a better version of the 8086. It called this new microprocessor the Intel 80186.

This microprocessor had a somewhat faster cycle time than its predecessors. More importantly, advances in integrated circuitry allowed the functions of several auxiliary chips to be built into the 80186. This integration of functions reduced the total computer cost and improved throughput.

The improvements produced by the 80186 were too modest to attract most computer vendors. Although a few vendors built computers around these chips, IBM and most others did not. As a result, the 80186 is found mostly on expansion cards, including advanced network adapter boards (see Chapters 14 and 15) and a few of the accelerator boards discussed later in this chapter.

The Intel 80286 In 1984, IBM produced the PC AT, based on a radically new microprocessor, the Intel 80286. The Intel 80286 was like two microprocessors built into one because it operated in two very different modes, one of which offered a quantum leap in functionality.

In the simpler "real" mode, the 80286 acts primarily as a faster 8086. It has a faster clock cycle, generally 8 MHz to 12 MHz, depending on the model. In addition, it has on-chip circuitry to handle many functions previously handled on auxiliary chips, for example, memory management. In addition, memory management was improved to increase performance even more. An AT has two to three times the performance of an IBM PC or PC XT equipped with an Intel 8088.

The second mode is called the "protected" mode.

- The protected mode allows programs to make use of the 80286's 32-bit internal processing bus, 16-bit data bus, and 24-bit address register. The 24 bits in the address register give an address space of 16 MB.
- The protected mode makes use of on-chip circuits to provide true multitasking and virtual memory operation (see Chapter 8), giving computers running the 80286 in protected mode many of the characteristics of minicomputers.

When 80286 computers were first released, in 1984, MS-DOS was incapable of handling the protected mode's special features. Therefore, MS-DOS users who switched to the PC AT and other 80286 machines merely had much faster standard personal computers. This faster raw speed was important to people with large data bases, large models, and other processing-intensive jobs. As a result, PC ATs and compatibles sold very well.

In 1987, IBM announced its new Operating System (OS)/2, which is designed to break the "640 KB barrier," along with providing many other advances discussed in the following chapter. Microsoft, in turn, announced that it would release an operating system offering a subset of OS/2 features. Both advanced operating systems, which have not actually been released at the time of this writing, will only run on computers using the Intel 80286 and subsequent Intel microprocessors, since earlier microprocessors lack the protected mode that forms the heart of OS/2 and Microsoft's advanced operating system. Even the PS/2 Model 30, which runs a high-speed 8086, will not be able to run OS/2.

The Intel 80386 and beyond The Intel 80186 and 80286 were only the first salvos in Intel's attack on advanced microprocessing. Machines today are beginning to use Intel's next release, the Intel 80386. In real mode, the 80386 offers speeds of 16 MHz to 25 MHz, giving blazing performance well within the minicomputer range. The first 80386 machines have been used for massive processing applications, file servers in networks, and even scientific and engineering workstations.

The 80386 supports the full protected mode, providing a few extensions as well—especially extensions in memory size. After several painful experiences with "ample" address spaces that later proved too small, Intel went for broke on the address register. The 80386 can support an enormous 4 gigabytes of directly addressed internal memory and 65 *terabytes* of virtual memory. These numbers are orders of magnitude beyond today's memory technologies. For example, to fill up virtual memory, you would need about 100,000 ATs with 20 MB disks. To fully populate 4 GB of RAM would require 2000 memory boards, each with 2 MB of RAM.

The 80386 added what is essentially a third mode to the 80286's real and protected modes. This is the **virtual 8086** mode, in which the memory space can be divided into many 1 MB sections, each running a different program in what appears, to the programs in these sections, to be real mode. Special on-chip circuitry allows almost instantaneous switching between virtual 8086 partitions. Strictly speaking, virtual 8086 operation is a subset of protected mode, but it is so radically new that it is usually accorded the status of a third mode.

When the virtual 8086 mode was announced, Intel stated that different partitions could run different operating systems. It has since taken back this claim on the 80386 but has promised multiple operating system support in its next-generation product, the Intel 80486.

In 1986, Compaq and several other corporations announced 80386 computers that were compatible with older IBM machines, such as the AT. When IBM introduced its first 80386 computer, the Personal System/2 Model 80, it used a radically different design. Customers buying 80386 computers therefore need to understand what computers are compatible with their purchases. It is not enough to use the same microprocessor; the entire design of the computer must be the same if programs that bypass the operating system (see Chapter 6) are to run properly.

The Motorola MC68000 Family

Although the Intel family dominates the personal computer market, as a result of their adoption by IBM, the Motorola MC68000 family of microprocessors has been used in many high-end PCs. The Motorola family is attractive to builders of advanced PCs because it tends to be one jump ahead of the Intel family at any given moment.

The Macintosh, for example, is built around the original MC68000, which has 32-bit internal processing, a 16-bit data bus, and, in the model used in the Macintosh, a 7.8 MHz clock speed. *In other words, in terms of raw processing power, the MC68000 resembles an Intel 80286 operating in real mode.* This is one reason why most IBM PC software that mimics the Macintosh can only run acceptably on IBM PC ATs and compatibles. On older 8088 and 8086 machines, these programs work too slowly to be useful.

Motorola has advanced members of the MC68000 family, including the MC68020 and MC68030. Just as the MC68000 is comparable to the Intel 80286, the MC68020 is comparable to the Intel 80386. The Apple Macintosh II, released in 1987, uses a 16 MHz MC68020 microprocessor. Later machines are likely to run faster versions of this microprocessor.

Coprocessors

A coprocessor is like a second CPU. Although it is subordinate to the main microprocessor, it has a definite mind of its own. The microprocessor merely sends it data and a generalized signal requesting what action should be taken.

The coprocessor then takes over and runs its own program to get the desired results. In some situations, the microprocessor and coprocessor can operate in full parallel mode, essentially turning the computer into a multiprocessor system.

Math Coprocessors

The most popular coprocessors to date have been **math coprocessors,** which do floating point arithmetic between 10 and 100 times faster than the arithmetic/logic portion of the microprocessor. For computationally intensive chores, math coprocessors bring radical performance boosts.

Math coprocessors must be matched to the computer's microprocessor. As microprocessor speed increases, so does the need for a faster math coprocessor. The Intel 8086 and 8088, for example, use the Intel 8087 math coprocessor, but the faster Intel 80286 and 80386 use the faster Intel 80287 and 80387 math coprocessors, respectively. IBM computers have traditionally been sold with math coprocessors as expensive options.

The Macintosh did not offer even an optional math coprocessor before the SE model introduced in 1987. The SE itself was not designed around a math coprocessor, but its open slot has enticed vendors to offer expansion boards that include coprocessors. In contrast to this timid approach, the Macintosh II faces the math coprocessor situation directly, incorporating the MC68881 math coprocessor as a standard feature.

Graphics Coprocessors

For high-speed screen refreshes and special effects, a number of home computers, including the Commodore Amiga, have turned to graphics coprocessors that free the host from the task of handling the display screen. At the time of this writing, graphics coprocessors have yet to be included in major office PCs, but it is probably only a matter of time until this happens. As noted later in this chapter, high-resolution color displays place such a heavy processing burden on the computer that screen refreshing becomes very sluggish unless either a very high-speed microprocessor or a graphics coprocessor is used. Two promising graphics coprocessors are the Intel 82786 and the Texas Instruments 34010.

Memory Management Coprocessors

Another heavy processing chore is the management of memory in a way that simplifies the work needed to do virtual memory and multitasking. The Intel 80286 and 80386 put this memory management circuitry right in the microprocessor, but the Motorola MC68020 does not incorporate these features. Instead, Motorola offers the MC68851 **memory management coprocessor,** which handles these features. Future multitasking operating systems for the Macintosh will almost certainly require this chip.

RAM

One of the most basic issues for a PC buyer is how much internal **random access memory (RAM)** to purchase. Most users today have 256 KB to 4 MB of RAM on their machines, and the average RAM capacity of PCs is doubling about every two years.

Memory Limits

In real mode on newer Intel microprocessors and on older machines such as the PC and PC XT, there is a limit of 640 KB of user RAM. This limit was noted earlier. Although the Intel 8088 can address 1 MB of internal memory, IBM reserves 384 KB for ROM, display management, and other system needs, resulting in the 640 KB limit. As discussed in Chapter 8, there are several roundabout ways to use more than 640 KB of RAM, including RAM disks and bank switching. Furthermore, once advanced versions of MS-DOS become widely used, today's 640 KB limit will become a historical anachronism.

The Location of RAM

The mother board on the original PC and PC XT could hold a maximum of 256 KB of RAM, whereas a PC AT can hold 512 KB on the mother board, and most PS/2 models from IBM can hold one or two megabytes on the mother board. For more RAM than the mother board can hold, the user must buy an expansion board.

RAM Chips

When users buy expansion boards, they often buy them only partially filled with memory chips. They run buy their own chips to add the memory themselves. Although computer memory is measured in bytes, RAM chip capacity is measured in bits. If you want to use 64 Kbit chips to get 64 KBytes of internal memory, you will need nine 64 Kbit chips—the ninth chip being used by the computer for error checking.

The earliest PCs used 16 Kbit RAM Chips. The IBM PC and most machines of its generation use 64 Kbit chips. Newer machines usually have 256 Kbit chips. Although 256 Kbit chips are more expensive than 64 Kbit chips, they are not four times as expensive; it is therefore cheaper to use 256 Kbit chips to increase memory than 64 Kbit chips. IBM's PS/2 Model 80 computers use 1 Mbit memory chips. In time, 1 Mbit chips will eclipse 256 Kbit chips.

RAM chips are also classified by speed. Fast microprocessors use very fast RAM chips operating at 80 nanoseconds or less. These chips are more expensive than the slower chips used by older machines, whose speeds may be as slow as 190 nanoseconds.

Volatility

RAM is **volatile** memory, meaning that when power is turned off, the information in RAM is lost. This is unfortunate because the growing use of internal memory is playing more and more information into RAM, including user data.

Because of volatility problems, manufacturers are beginning to produce **persistent RAM** which maintains itself by a small battery when the main power is off. Persistent RAM uses **C-MOS** integrated circuit technology instead of the **N-MOS** RAM technology used in most PCs. C-MOS technology uses much less power than N-MOS to keep the information in RAM alive. Many portable PCs use the Intel 80C88 microprocessor, in which the "C" stands for C-MOS technology.

Persistent RAM is sometimes confused with ROM, but the two are very different. Read-only memory (ROM) is written at the factory and is never erased, even when all power is off. Users may neither write on nor erase ROM. In contrast, persistent RAM is full user memory, which users can both write on and erase. In addition, persistent RAM needs at least a small trickle charge from internal barriers to keep it alive.

ROM

Read only memory (ROM) is not erased when the computer is turned off. So programs that must always be available are stored in ROM.

Bootstrap Programs

When the computer is turned on, control passes immediately to a **bootstrap program** that does some internal diagnostics and then looks for an operating system on disk, loads it into RAM, and passes control to it. In effect, the bootstrap program starts itself, "picking itself up by its bootstraps."

ROM Service Programs

As discussed in Chapter 8, most computers have ROM service programs that provide commonly used low-level services, such as checking a disk drive to see if it is ready to receive data. These ROM service programs are created to serve the operating system, but they can also be called by other systems software and even application programs.

When application programs call ROM service programs directly, this can increase their performance, but application program calls to ROM can also result in system crashes, because what the application program does may conflict with the actions of other programs. And, as discussed in Chapter 6, "badly behaved" programs that bypass the operating system and work directly with ROM require a higher level of IBM compatibility in clones than do well behaved programs.

Object Graphics Routines

As noted earlier in this chapter, object graphics require a good deal of processing, because each line, circle, and text character must be painted individually from its stored description.

The Macintosh attacked this problem vigorously by creating a large body of object graphics processing routines and placing them in ROM. These are called the QuickDraw routines. They provide fast screen changes, plus a standard way for application programs to handle object graphics. As a result of this standardization, almost all Macintosh object graphics programs work in exactly the same way. Some laser page printers (discussed later in this chapter) can work directly with QuickDraw routines.

Expansion Boards

There are literally dozens of kinds of expansion boards for personal computers. In this section, we will describe only the most popular kinds of expansion boards.

Expansion boards are designed for specific computers. An expansion board designed for an IBM PC XT, for example, will not work in a Wang Professional Computer or even an IBM PS/2 Model 50. As discussed in the last chapter, some "IBM compatible" PCs are not sufficiently compatible to accept expansion boards designed for the IBM machines with which they are touted as compatible.

Memory Boards

Memory boards provide more RAM than the mother board can hold. On a basic IBM PC, the mother board is limited to 256 KB. Other machines have different limits on their mother boards.

Memory boards have traditionally brought total RAM up to a maximum of 640 KB. But 640 KB is now a very cramped space for many users. As a result, board makers have introduced memory boards with 2 MB to 8 MB. OS/2 allows this added space to be used directly on 80286 and 80386 PCs, but for the time being, other approaches to breaking the "640 KB barrier" are still very popular because most PCs still use 8088 and 8086 microprocessors, which will not be able to run OS/2.

One approach is to use the memory above 1 MB as a RAM disk. As discussed in Chapter 8, a RAM disk is an area of RAM set aside to act like a very fast floppy disk. In effect, the RAM disk software fools both the application program and the computer into acting as if the section of RAM managed by the RAM disk utility was a read disk drive. Neither the application program nor the computer needs to be changed in any way. RAM disks are popular because they are up to a hundred times faster than a floppy disk drive and up to five times faster than a hard disk.

Another approach to using memory above 1 MB without resorting to OS/2 is to utilize the Lotus/Intel/Microsoft bank switching approach called the expanded memory specification (EMS). Also discussed in Chapter 8, the EMS divides memory above 1 MB into 16 KB "frames." It then swaps them into and out of a reserved 64 KB area in normal memory. Both RAM disks and EMS require a good deal of memory swapping, and this degrades performance somewhat. Nevertheless, RAM disks and EMS are widely used to support high-capacity memory boards.

Adapter Circuits

As noted in Chapter 6, adapter circuits provide flexibility in computer designs by allowing the microprocessor to give a few generalized commands to any peripheral. The adapter translates these few commands into the detail needed by specific peripherals. The adapter also translates peripherals requests and instructions into a form the microprocessor can understand.

Adapters fall into two categories. First, there are **specialized adapters** that work with specific peripherals, for example, a display adapter designed to work with a particular kind of display. Specialized adapters tend to be complex circuits. If they are not on the mother board, they tend to require entire expansion boards.

Second, most computers are designed to support a few **standard adapters,** which can be used by many different kinds of devices. These standard adapters tend to be rather simple, and it is common to find them built into the mother board and sold as add-on features on expansion boards built for other purposes.

Computers support at least two types of standard adapters: (1) a standard **serial adapter,** which sends one bit at a time, taking eight clock cycles to send a single byte of data; and (2) a standard **parallel adapter,** which uses several lines to send a whole byte or more in each clock cycle.

Parallel adapters The IBM PC was designed with two generic adapters that are used by a wide variety of peripherals. These are IBM PC parallel and serial adapters. The IBM PC's **parallel adapter** uses the **Centronics interface,** which was created by Centronics for its own printers but is now used by many printers from different companies. Parallel adapters have eight data lines in their cable, allowing them to send an entire byte in a single clock cycle.

Because the parallel interface was designed for communications with printers, it is basically a one-direction interface. The printer can only send a few control signals in the other direction, for example, to ask the parallel adapter to stop sending temporarily.

An IBM PC running MS-DOS can have up to three IBM parallel adapters, called LPT1, LPT2, and LPT3 in MS-DOS commands. This means that a single IBM PC can operate three parallel printers.

Serial adapters The IBM PC also has a generic **serial adapter,** which uses the popular RS232C standard discussed in Chapter 13. This adapter sends information serially, one bit at a time.

In contrast to IBM's parallel adapter, which is designed for one-way communications with a single kind of peripheral, IBM serial adapters are designed for full two-way communications with a wide variety of peripherals, including mice, modems, and some printers. Because printers can use either parallel or serial adapters, it is important to be sure a user's PC has the correct adapter before purchasing a printer.

An IBM PC is limited to only two IBM serial adapters, named COM1 and COM2. (COM1 can also be called AUX in MS-DOS commands.) This limit is inherent in both the IBM PC design and in MS-DOS. This limit of two serial ports made sense initially, when there were few peripherals and when the most common peripherals, namely, printers, normally used parallel adapters. Today, however, the limit of two serial adapters is problematic because many peripherals now use this interface. A number of vendors now offer **multiport serial cards,** which allow several peripherals to share a single serial adapter.

Macintosh serial adapters The Apple Macintosh also has two generic adapters. Originally, the Macintosh was released with only one, a two-way serial adapter using the RS449/422A interface (see Chapter 14) instead of the RS232C interface used by the IBM PC's serial adapter. Although RS232C is limited to only 19,200 bits per second, RS449/422A is a high-speed interface that can send data at several million bits per second. The Macintosh's software limits transmission speeds to 230,000 bits per second, but this order of magnitude is still faster than IBM's serial adapter speeds. Although these speeds are somewhat slow for PC networking, the Macintosh serial adapter allows networking without the addition of the expensive network adapter boards that must be purchased for networking in the IBM PC world. To add networking to several Macintoshes and an Apple LaserWriter printer costs only $50 per device.

The Macintosh SCSI parallel adapter The Macintosh Plus introduced another generic adapter, the **small computer system interface, SCSI.** A SCSI (pronounced "skuzzy") adapter is a two-directional parallel adapter that can multiplex up to seven peripherals onto a single socket and can move data at 320,000 bytes (not bits) per second. SCSI is now used mostly for hard disk drives, but it can be used by a wide variety of peripherals. In fact, the SCSI limit is not seven peripherals; it is really eight devices. Although this can be one Macintosh and seven peripherals, it can also be three Macintoshs and five peripherals. In other words, SCSI can be used to build a miniature network.

Accelerator Boards

One of the newest and most exciting types of expansion board is the **accelerator board,** which literally accelerates the speed of the personal computer. Most of these boards are designed for PCs and PC XTs, extending their useful lives in an age of ever faster microprocessors. Accelerator boards can boost speeds anywhere from 100 percent to 300 percent.

Accelerator boards have faster microprocessors than the standard PC and PC XT. In general, the faster the microprocessor and the faster it is clocked, the faster the accelerator will run and the more expensive it will be. The cheapest accelerator boards use 8086 microprocessors, whereas the most expensive use 80286 and even 80386 microprocessors. Those in between typically use the 80186 microprocessor.

The faster the microprocessor, the faster its RAM must be, and the more it will benefit from a 16-bit or even 32-bit data bus. Accelerator boards with fast microprocessors often have their own memory with up to a megabyte of very fast RAM, linked via a data bus of 16 or 32 bits. Obviously, the more RAM there is and the faster it will run, the more expensive the board will be.

Because some programs are speed sensitive, most accelerator boards can slow to the traditional 4.77 MHz. Some do so very easily, but others only with considerable difficulty.

Lower price boards typically take up a half slot and double a PC's speed for a price of $300 to $900. Higher price boards range up to $2000. They produce bigger gains, but their price approaches the price of an AT clone, and many have operational problems. If even $300 is too much, users can buy faster 8088s and faster timing crystals for their PCs and get speed gains of about 30 percent for under $50.

Peripheral Boards

Shrinking electronics have even allowed devices that are normally considered peripherals to be put on expansion boards. Board modems and board hard disks (such as the Hardcard in Figure 7-1) are two examples of this trend. By packaging a peripheral on a board, the cost of enclosures is eliminated, reducing prices dramatically.

244   PERSONAL COMPUTER HARDWARE

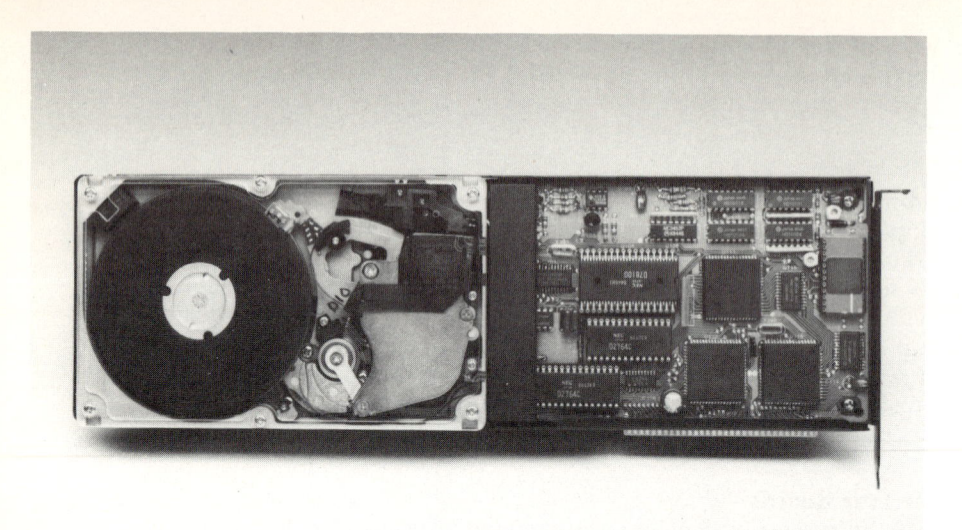

Hardcard,™ 10 megabyte hard disk drive on a plug-in card. (Shown with exposed head disk assembly.)
© 1985 Plus Development Corporation. All rights reserved.

FIGURE 7-1 HARD DISK ON AN EXPANSION BOARD

Communications Boards

Terminal emulation for sophisticated terminals requires a terminal emulation board. Similarly, networking usually requires a network adapter board. These communications boards are discussed in Chapters 13 through 15.

Multifunction Boards

In the early days of personal computing, each function (memory, parallel adapter, etc.) required its own expansion board. Today, the ability to pack more and more circuits onto individual chips has allowed us to pack several functions onto a single expansion board. These boards are called **multifunction boards**.

Early expansion boards had up to 384 KB of RAM, a serial port, a parallel port, a clock and calendar (so that the user does not have to give the date and time every time the system is booted), plus software to use parts of the RAM as a RAM disk or print spooler (see Chapter 8).

Now, however, it is common to find multifunction boards with up to 4 MB of RAM, several serial and parallel adapters, software for windowing, desk accessory software (see Chapter 8), and the traditional clock and calendar. Although more expensive than older multifunction boards, they are very popular.

In fact, we are beginning to see circuits that once had a hard time fitting on a single board packed into multifunction boards with several other circuits. An example of a high-end multifunction board is IDEAssociates' All Aboard product, which can combine serial and parallel adapters, a clock and calendar, 2 MB of EMS memory, an EGA display adapter (discussed later in the chapter), and a hard disk controller.

Multifunction boards are usually sold in a base configuration, with certain features optional. In the earliest multifunction boards, the base configuration usually had sockets for RAM but no RAM. The user could then purchase RAM with the board or install RAM after the purchase. Game paddle adapter circuits were another common option. Today, the list of options on a typical multifunction card reads like an options list on an automobile. Options must be understood clearly before a purchase is made.

Boards sold with "0 KB" of RAM require the user to understand how RAM chips are sold. As noted earlier, RAM chips come in different storage capacities and speeds, so the user must know if the expansion board requires 64 Kbit chips, 256 Kbit chips, or 1 Mbit chips and how fast these chips have to run. The user must also keep in mind that, because chip capacities are measured in bits and that parity is used in storage, that a given byte capacity, say 256 KB, requires nine times that number of bits.

Board Compatibility

Users who have several boards from different vendors must be sure that their machine's power and heat exchange software are up to the load. Some new boards, particularly accelerator boards and hard disk controllers, use a good deal of power and generate considerable heat.

Two or more boards may want to use the same interrupt line on the bus, and the result can be chaos or at least some real headaches for the technical staff of the user firm.

Finally, some boards are "fat," taking up more than a full slot and preventing a full board from being placed in the slot next to them. This is particularly true of boards that are really sandwiches made of a main board and one or more piggy back boards.

Power

The heaviest part of the system unit is the **power supply,** which takes AC wall current and translates it into the various DC voltages needed by system unit components.

Capacity

The basic IBM PC has a power supply rated at 85 watts. This is sufficient for a machine with floppy disk drives and most of its expansion slots full. The PC XT, however, has 130 watts, and this power is needed if the user has an internal hard disk and many expansion boards. The IBM PC AT has a 150-watt power supply. The PS/2 Model 30 has a 70-watt power supply, which is somewhat limited despite the use of newer technologies that require less power; the Model 50 has a somewhat more ample 94-watt power supply; and the Models 60 and 80, over 200 watts.

Power Problems
In many areas, the power coming from the electrical company is not uniform. In addition, power disturbances can be produced by local equipment, including heavy machinery and even room air conditioners.

Spikes
To protect themselves from power problems, many users buy **spike suppressors,** which are also called **surge suppressors.** These devices are designed to filter out very short duration (millisecond) power spikes, such as those caused by lightning or the starting of equipment with electrical motors. Spike suppressors spread out the power surge over a longer period of time, so that the power at any millisecond is smaller than it would have been with the spike.

Prolonged High Voltage
Spike suppressors do nothing for prolonged high voltage, which can also damage the machine and its data. Even a power increase lasting a quarter of a second will flow right through a spike suppressor. To protect against prolonged high current, special devices that shut off the computer are needed.

Brownouts and Blackouts
Spike suppressors are also ineffective with regard to low current, including **brownouts,** in which voltage falls to 80 percent or less of its normal value, or **blackouts,** in which power is completely interrupted.

For full power protection, **uninterruptable power supplies, UPSs,** are needed. These provide extensive protection against spikes, prolonged high current, brownouts, and even blackouts. Unfortunately, the price tends to run at about $1000 per PC, making them too expensive for all but the most sensitive applications.

The Quality of PC Power Supplies
Personal computers vary in their abilities to shield users from power problems. Some, including the IBM PC, have very good power supplies that shield users from modest voltage fluctuations. They also shield the user from **noise,** that is, tiny random fluctuations caused by nearby equipment. If this noise got through the power supply, it could be interpreted by the microprocessor as data. A few PCs, however, have cheap power supplies that do not protect the user. Furthermore, when any power supply is stressed to its limit by adding many options, its protection is likely to suffer at least somewhat.

The Cost of Power
One last warning about power is in order. PCs, their printers, and other peripherals consume quite a bit of power. Users may want to factor this cost into their purchase decision, although few do. More practically, if several PCs and their peripherals are placed in a room, an extra electrical circuit may have to be added to avoid constant circuit breaker shutoffs that wipe out internal memory.

EXTERNAL MEMORY

Upgrading Power Supplies

Many users are now upgrading their original power supplies, for example, adding 130-watt power supplies to standard IBM PCs. If an upgrade is being considered, the user may wish to look at products that allow the computer to be switched on via telecommunications. When these power supplies are linked to a telephone, they allow a remote user to turn on and then work with the PC.

EXTERNAL MEMORY

Now that we have looked at the personal computer's central electronics, we will consider the computer's electromechanical peripherals.

Why External Memory

Microprocessors are extremely fast, so the memory that is directly accessed by the microprocessor also has to be extremely fast.

But fast memory is expensive memory, so most computers have comparatively little **internal** or **primary memory** able to work directly with the microprocessor. To cope with this limitation, computers use three types of memory: primary, secondary, and tertiary (Figure 7-2).

First, as just noted, there is a small amount of very fast primary memory—just enough to hold what the microprocessor is currently working on. There may not even be enough primary memory to hold the entire program being run, and many data files are also too large to fit in their entirety. Primary memory on a personal computer is normally limited to between 256 KB and 8 MB.

The second tier of memory in Figure 7-3 is **secondary memory.** This is like a waiting room for primary memory. Programs and data that may be needed in primary memory at any moment are stored in secondary memory. Although the microprocessor can access any location in RAM in less than a microsecond (millionth of a second), it takes a millisecond or more to reach a memory cell in secondary memory. To compensate for slowness, secondary memory's cost per bit is a small fraction of primary memory's unit storage cost. As a result, secondary memory is often far larger than primary memory.

	Retrieval Speed	Cost
Primary Memory	nanoseconds	high
Secondary Memory	milliseconds	medium
Tertiary Memory	minutes	low

FIGURE 7-2 MEMORY TIERS

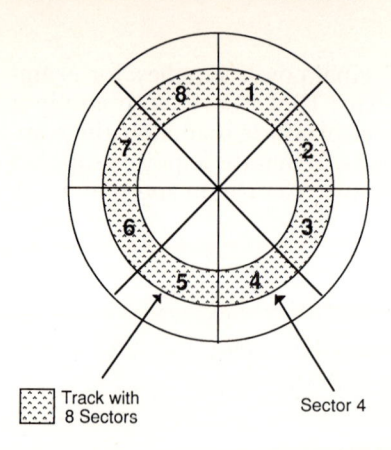

FIGURE 7-3 MAGNETIC DISK

In contrast to primary memory, which is entirely inside the CPU, secondary memory is **external memory** outside the CPU. Although many types of secondary memory are physically located in the PC's system unit, they are still outside the electronics of the CPU and must be connected to the computer's processing electronics via an adapter, just like any other peripheral.

The most popular form of external memory is disk memory, which is discussed below. Magnetic tape, often used as secondary memory on the cheapest home computers, is far too slow to be used for an office machine's secondary memory. Today, two types of disk memory are popular. The first is low-capacity, low-speed floppy disk memory. The second is high-capacity, high-speed hard disk memory. In the longer term, ultrahigh-capacity optical disk memory is expected to be important as well.

For the long-term storage of programs and data files that may not be needed for some time, there is **tertiary memory** or **archival memory,** which is the slowest form of memory but which is also the cheapest and highest capacity member of the team. Floppy disk stored on a shelf constitutes the tertiary memory for many personal computers. Magnetic tape is also very useful for archival storage.

Disk Technology

Apart from RAM and tape, all forms of external memory use disk drives. As shown in Figure 7-3, a disk resembles a phonograph record. It has a doughnut-shaped recording band, like the recording area on a phonograph record. Although disk diameters vary from 3.5 inches to 8 inches, the width of the recording band is rarely more than an inch.

Sides

The earliest 5.25 inch disks used in personal computers were single-sided floppy disks, meaning that only one side had a recording band. Although it is not expensive to produce two-sided disks, which have recording bands on both sides, it was originally very expensive to produce disk drives that could work with double-sided disks. As a result, double-sided disks were rare until 1982. Since then, however, nearly all 5.25 inch floppy drives on

EXTERNAL MEMORY

office PCs have used double-sided floppies. When 3.5 inch drives came out in the mid-1980s, they, too, were briefly limited to single-sided operations, but they quickly graduated to a double-sided operation.

Double-sided disk drives require double-sided disks. Many single-sided disks are still sold in stores because quite a few home computers still use single-sided disks and so purchases must be made carefully. Because many disks sold as single-sided are physically double-sided, some users buy single-sided disks and use them as double-sided disks. But many of these disks have a manufacturing flaw on one side, and this is why they are sold as single-sided. Disks sold as single-sided should never be used as double-sided disks.

For hard disks, the situation is more complex. Most hard disks use several disk platters, arranged like a lazy susan. Figure 7-4 illustrates this arrangement. As a result, hard disks tend to have four to ten sides, with five sides being very common on PC hard disk drives.

Tracks

As shown in Figure 7-3, the operating system divides recording bands into a number of concentric circles called **tracks.**

- A typical 5.25 inch diameter floppy disk with 360 KB of capacity will have 40 tracks in the recording band.

FIGURE 7-4 HARD DISK WITH MULTIPLE PLATTERS

- IBM's 1.2 MB floppy disk introduced with the PC AT has 80 tracks.
- Most hard disks have 300 to 600 tracks within their recording bands.

Sectors

The operating system further divides each track into several sectors, as shown in Figure 7-3. Versions of MS-DOS beginning with 2.0 divide ordinary floppy disks into nine sectors per track. IBM's 1.2 MB floppy has 15 sectors per track, whereas hard disks usually have 15 to 20 sectors per track.

The sector is the ultimate unit of storage in MS-DOS. MS-DOS never reads or writes less than one sector at a time. Every sector on a disk managed by MS-DOS has 512 bytes, regardless of whether it is a floppy disk or a hard disk.

Capacity

The combination of number of sides, number of tracks per side, number of sectors per track, and number of bytes per sector defines the capacity of the disk. Here is a typical calculation, for a double-sided, double-density floppy disk with 360 KB of capacity.

```
2 sides
40 tracks per side (80 tracks total)
9 sectors per track (720 sectors total)
512 bytes per track (368,640 bytes or 360 KB)
```

Clusters

Although the sector is the smallest unit that MS-DOS *can* use, MS-DOS restricts itself to larger units of storage called **clusters.** Clusters typically range from one or two sectors on floppy disks to eight sectors for some hard disks. Both read and write operations work on entire clusters. In effect, although the sector is the basic unit of storage, the cluster is the basic unit for read and write operations.

The Macintosh Format

It may seem odd, at first, that outer tracks, which are larger than inner tracks, have the same capacity. It would seem that outer tracks should be given more capacity.

The important consideration, however, is how long it takes for a sector to pass under the read/write head for recording or reading. Although outer tracks are larger, they are also spinning faster. If we think of a byte as a fraction of a second under the read/write head, instead of as physical space along the track, we have a better understanding of the realities of recording information. On a floppy disk rotating at 360 RPM, both inner and outer tracks are 1/6 of a second long. In a 360 KB disk, with 4 KB per track, each byte is 1/24000 of a second long—whether it is on the innermost track or the outermost track.

In order to squeeze more room into the Macintosh's 3.5 inch diameter floppy disks, Apple took a different approach. It constantly varies the speed of the drive as the read/write head moves from track to track, slowing down near the circumference to take advantage of the larger physical space there and speeding up as it moves nearer the center of the disk. The outermost tracks have 12 sectors per track, and the innermost tracks only 8.

Optical Disk Drive Formats

Optical disk drives use yet another format. Optical disk drives were designed for television and audio recordings, and their basic formats merely add error checking to their basic TV and audio formats.

The most popular optical disk technology is CD-ROM, which is discussed later in this chapter. CD-ROM's information is stored along a spiral, instead of in concentric circles. This mirrors the familiar spiral groove of phonograph records.

In a spiral, diameter changes constantly. At the outer edge, CD-ROM has 20 sectors along the circumference; at the inner edge of the recording band, it has only 9. To complicate life further, CD-ROM achieves constant linear velocity along the spiral by changing rotation speed constantly as the read head moves along the spiral. Speed varies from 200 RPM to 500 RPM along the radius.

For sequential reads covering many sectors, these complexities cause no problems. Once the first sector is located, data can be transferred at 150 KB per second—about as rapidly as typical hard disk can transfer data.

For random access, however, the computation of a sector's physical location from its relative sector location along the groove is a nightmare. An average seek takes almost a second, compared to between 20 and 90 milliseconds for a hard disk.

As a result, CD-ROM is excellent for reading in large sequential files, but for applications such as random access to data base records, word processing pages, or video images, CD-ROM's slow random access—a trait it shares with other forms of optical disk—is a major problem.

Floppy Disks

As the name suggests, a floppy disk is flexible, allowing it to adjust to imperfections on the disk drive's service. This buys low cost at the penalty of low performance. A floppy disk spins at 360 RPM—only one-tenth the speed of a hard disk drive.

The original floppy disks were 8 inches in diameter. Today it is rare to find a machine with a floppy greater than 5.25 inches in diameter. In fact, most newer computers use 3.5 diameter floppy drives.

5.25 Inch Floppy Disks

Until 1984, almost all floppy disk drives used 5.25 inch diameter disks. These disks fell into several capacity categories, the type of disk to be used depending on the drive. Drives can work with higher capacity disks but not lower capacity disks.

- Single-sided, double-density (1S/2D) disks usually hold 100 KB to 200 KB of data.
- Double-sided, double-density (2S/2D) disks—the most popular—usually hold 300 KB to 400 KB of data. IBM's traditional 360 KB disk drive uses 2S/2D disks.
- Double-sided, high-density (2S/HD) disks usually hold 1000 KB to 1500 KB of data. IBM's 1.2 MB floppy disk drive uses 2S/HD disks.

3.25 Inch Disks

The smallest floppy disks used commonly on PCs today are 3.5 inch diameter disks. Because 3.5 inch drives are physically smaller than 5.25 inch drives, the whole computer can be smaller, taking up less space on the desk. Most new personal computers are being built with 3.5 inch diameter floppy disk drives.

Another plus for the 3.5 inch "microfloppies" is that they are encased in rigid plastic cases that protect them from damage. Traditional 5-¼ inch disks are notoriously susceptible to damage, thanks to their thin casing and many exposed surfaces.

Just as in the case of 5.25 inch diameter floppy drives, the capacity of 3.5 inch microfloppy drives has increased constantly.

- Early 3.5 inch drives were single-sided, double-density drives. For example, the original Macintosh drive used an 1S/DD drive giving 400 KB of storage.
- These were quickly followed by double-sided drives; MS-DOS provides 720 KB on such drives, whereas Macintoshes put 800 KB on them.
- More recently, IBM has introduced a 1.44 MB double-sided, high-density drive (2S/HD) for all but the low end of its PS/2 line. This is likely to be IBM's workhorse drive of the future. Although Apple has not followed suit at the time of this writing, its drives in both the SE and Macintosh II are clocked for 1.6 MB disks.

Hard Disks

Capacity

As the name suggests, hard disks are rigid. This allows the read/write head to be positioned very precisely, so that much more information can be written per square inch. A single hard disk platter can hold 2 to 10 megabytes, and a hard disk drive usually holds several disk platters on a single shaft, as discussed earlier in the chapter. Typical hard disk capacities are 20 MB to 115 MB.

Speed

Not only do hard disks hold far more than floppies, but they also spin ten times faster than floppy disks. As a result, it takes less time for the proper information to pass under the read/write head once the head is positioned at the right track. Typically, hard disk drives store and retrieve data five to ten times faster than floppy disk drives because they spin ten times faster. For many large programs and data bases, information is constantly shuffled between disk and internal memory. Practically speaking, these programs and data bases cannot be run adequately on floppy disks, even if the disks have sufficient capacity.

In fact, hard disk drives spin *too* fast for most personal computers. To slow down the transfer rate, most hard disks are **interleaved.** This means that sectors that are logically adjacent are stored every second, third, or even fourth sector apart. This effectively slows down the transfer rate without slowing down the rotation speed of the disk. An interleaving factor of one means no interleaving, an interleaving factor of two means that information is written in every other sector, and so on.

Older hard disks, such as those used in the IBM PC XT and IBM PS/2 Models 30 and 50, tend to have average access times of 60 to 90 milliseconds (ms). In contrast, newer hard disks such as those used in the IBM PC ATs, most PS/2 models, and Macintoshes, tend to have access times of 20 ms to 40 ms. These higher speeds are needed to keep up with today's faster microprocessors.

Hard Disk Backup

Hard disks do have one major problem—they are hard to backup. If a floppy gets ruined without being backed up onto another floppy, a user may lose several days of work. But if a hard disk goes down without being backed up, a user may be out months of work. A small firm can literally go bankrupt because of the loss of records.

Backup onto Floppy Disks

Computers with hard disks always come with at least one floppy disk drive, so that files can be backed up onto floppy disks. If users have the discipline to backup as they go, the time burden of backup is not too great, but few people have that kind of discipline. The other alternative is to backup the entire hard disk onto floppies every day or so, but this can take a half hour or more.

Tape Backup Units

A better solution to the backup problem is a **tape backup system,** which dumps some or all of the hard disk's contents onto magnetic tape, with little or no human intervention once the backup starts. Tape backup systems fall into two categories.

- **Image** tape drives backup the hard disk sector by sector, track by track, without regard to file organization.
- **File-by-File** tape drives back up and retrieve information one file at a time.

Image drives are faster and cheaper, but they cannot recover individual files. This is a serious failing, because users cannot recover from accidental file erasures by turning to their last backup tape—unless they restore the entire disk, and this erases the disk's current contents. In contrast, file-by-file systems usually allow individual files to be recovered. Virtually all minicomputers and mainframes use file-by-file tape backup, simply because lost files are far more common than actual disk crashes and other disastrous erasures. Today many drives can do both file-by-file and image backup. If file-by-file backup is considered desirable, a policy prohibiting the use of the faster image backup method must be instituted.

A major consideration in selecting a tape backup unit is its ability to detect and correct errors. After a major hard disk crash, discovering that the last backup tape did not record properly is, to say the least, an unpleasant surprise. The most popular error-checking formats for ¼ inch tape drives are the approach used by the popular Irwin Magnetics units and the QIC-24 standard of the Quarter Inch Compatibility Standards Committee. Some vendors use proprietary error-checking formats that are equal or better, but some do very little error detection and correction.

Backup Software

Whether floppy or tape backup is used, users may benefit from special backup software. These backup packages can dramatically slash backup time when floppies are used. They can sometimes bring dramatic gains to tape backup units as well.

Backup onto Hard Disks

A third alternative for hard disk backup, in addition to floppy disk and tape backup, is to buy a second hard disk and use the second disk for backup. This produces ultrafast backup at costs at or below those of tape units. Care must be taken, however, to make sure that the backup drive is securely parked when not in use, so that vibration and power outages will not damage it. (If the backup disk is not parked most of the time, it is very likely that both the original and backup disks will be damaged by a hard jolt or by a blackout.) It must also have its own controller (adapter), and for good measure, it should be backed up onto floppies every month or so.

Most hard disk drives are **Winchester** drives in which the hard disk is sealed and is not removable. Because the distance between the read/write head and the disk surface is smaller than a smoke particle or piece of dust, it is critical to seal the actual disk from contamination. Sealing the entire drive is the cheapest way to do so.

In contrast, **cartridge** drives have removable disks. This is not a cure for backup problems, however, unless users have *two* hard disk drives—the original and a backup cartridge drive—because backup only takes place with any speed if users are backing up from one disk to another. If users back up on one disk drive, they must insert the original cartridge, load one RAM-full of disk memory into internal memory, and then remove the original and insert the backup. This flip-flop process continues for many shuffles.

Backup: Conclusion

As a result of the trend toward networking hard disk drives, the sharing of 30 MB to 100 MB drives by several users takes much of the sting out of buying a good backup system. In any case, given the horrendous consequences of hard disk failure and the reality that few people have the discipline to back up when backup is difficult, buying a good backup system should be viewed as inseparable from the decision to buy a hard disk.

Other External Memory Technologies

Although floppy disks, hard disks, and backup units are the main tools of external memory today, they are not the only external memory technology in use.

Bernoulli Drives

One alternative to cartridge hard disk drives requires some discussion. This is the Bernoulli Box by the IOMEGA Corporation. This strange drive uses a floppy disk but has the performance of a hard disk drive.

The Bernoulli Box employs aerodynamic principles to let an 8 inch diameter floppy disk drive rotate at 1500 RPM without becoming unstable. Although 1500 RPM is only half the speed of a typical hard disk drive, an interleaving factor of four is used, compared with six for an XT disk and three for an AT disk. As a result, performance is comparable to that of an XT hard disk. Bernoulli Box cartridges are removable. This is ideal if several large data bases must be used, and it also makes the Bernoulli Box attractive as a backup device. Although IOMEGA pioneered this type of drive, several other vendors are introducing products using the same basic technology.

Optical Disks

Both floppy disks and hard disks are magnetic media. The read/write head is a tiny electromagnet that magnetizes a section of the disk or reads a magnetic pattern already recorded there.

Optical disks record in a different way. A laser burns tiny spots into the disk. Because laser beams can be focused very precisely compared to the "large" magnetic footprints of electromagnetic read/write heads, it can record far more information per square inch, just as you can write more on a piece of paper with a pencil than with a paint roller.

CD-ROM The cheapest optical disk drives are **read-only** units. There are few applications for read-only memory devices on computers today, although they could be ideal for reference manuals and for storing dozens of programs. The most popular units are called **CD-ROM** drives. They feature the same basic technology as audio compact disk drives, but they use sophisticated error control software to improve recording quality. CD-ROM units have been standardized at 4.72 inch diameter disks (120 mm) with 550 MB of data—about the same as 1500 typical floppy disks or a quarter of a million pages of text. Grolier Electronic Publishing has already published its 21-volume Academic American Encyclopedia on CD-ROM.

WORM drives More expensive are **write once, read-many (WORM)** optical disks drives, which allow the PC to write on the disk but not to erase the information after it is written. This is wasteful, but because such units can usually store a gigabyte (1024 MB) or more, users could go a very long time between disk changes. Early WORM drives were very expensive, costing $12,000 or more. Newer units can fit into a standard floppy disk slot, but they are still very expensive.

Erasable optical disk drives **Erasable** optical disks will eventually be a reality, but forecasts of when they will become an important market force vary widely. Many techniques are being tested, including several that combine optical and magnetic technology.

Other Technologies

Although optical disks are exciting, several newer magnetic recording strategies promise to bring a tenfold increase in capacity at a doubling in price. Thus, whether or not optical disks thrive, we should soon see dramatic increases in capacity and dramatic decreases in the cost per bit stored.

GRAPHICS TECHNOLOGY

The remainder of this chapter considers **input/output (I/O)** peripherals, including printers, displays, and nonkeyboard input devices. Because many of these peripherals use graphics technology, we will examine the general technology of graphics before looking at individual peripherals.

Introduction

Most early personal computers were limited to **alphanumeric** information—text and numbers. Although many users wanted interactive graphics to create more complex visual portrayals of information, two technical barriers stood in the way.

1. For reasons discussed below, graphics technology was very expensive, so few ordinary users could afford graphics.
2. Common output devices either could not do graphics at all or could only do it poorly, giving grainy output.

Time has destroyed both of these barriers. Graphics technology today is only moderately more expensive than text-only processing. In addition, laser-based page printers have brought high-resolution output into the budgets of most offices.

The use of graphics is not simply a cosmetic improvement designed to add pretty pictures; graphics, as we now realize, is integral to good computing.

- First, the Macintosh and subsequent products from other vendors have demonstrated that tremendous ease-of-use gains are possible when graphics are used to improve the user interface (see Chapter 8). A better user interface slashes learning times and encourages users to learn their programs well.
- Second, following the ancient Chinese saying, "One picture is worth a thousand words," it is probably true that many concepts and relationships among concepts are far easier to portray visually than to describe

GRAPHICS TECHNOLOGY 257

in writing. Imagine a textbook without illustrations. Chapter 11 discusses the importance of graphics in ordinary communication, and Chapter 16 explores a more limited topic—using graphics to portray numerical information.

Although the late 1980s has brought a flowering of graphics, the full fruition of graphics technology is not expected until the 1990s. Images of photographic quality and subtle color shading will be able to move in full animation across the screen, bringing even greater advances in ease and use and communication potency.

Key Graphics Concepts

Before we discuss graphics in detail, we need to discuss three basic concepts that underlie all PC graphics—I/O systems, pixels, and text versus graphics adapters.

Input/Output (I/O) Systems

To input or output graphics information, a PC must have an **input/output system,** also called an **I/O system.** These systems are made up of two components.

1. An **I/O device,** such as a printer, a display, or a mouse. This is the obvious component in an I/O system.
2. An **adapter** consisting of hardware (often on an expansion board but sometimes on the mother board) and related software. Adapters, discussed in Chapter 6, are often a bigger impediment to graphics than I/O devices; it is common to find an I/O device capable of handling graphics hobbled by an adapter that cannot handle graphics or cannot handle it well.

Pixel Output

With few exceptions, graphics devices employ the same basic method to produce graphics images. As shown in Figure 7-5, a graphics image is drawn

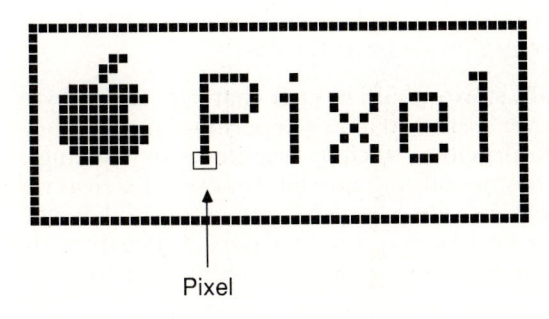

Pixel

Note:
This figure illustrates letters, a rectangle, and a shape (the Apple icon from the main menu of the Macintosh)

FIGURE 7-5 PIXEL GRAPHICS

as a group of dots, called **picture elements,** or **pixels.** This method is similar to the way Impressionist painters created scenes with dots of color. The pixel approach can also be used to input graphics information, for instance, through the scanners discussed later in this chapter.

Figure 7-5 illustrates how pixels can be used to portray almost any kind of information—including **images,** such as the apple from the Macintosh menu, **letters,** such as "Pixel," and **geometric shapes,** such as the box surrounding the apple and the word "Pixel." Of course, the pixels on a real output or input device are much smaller, so that images look like they are continuous instead of consisting of many dots.

Text Versus Graphics Adapters

As noted above, many adapters are incapable of producing graphics images, even on graphics devices. Instead, these adapters are limited to **alphanumeric** images—letters, digits, and punctuation signs, just as a typewriter is limited to the letters and other symbols assigned to its keys. Alphanumeric adapters are usually called **text adapters,** although they handle numbers as well as text.

Text adapters have a fixed character set of 90 or so characters. This limits their usefulness but also lowers their cost. In the early days of personal computing, I/O systems with text adapters were far less expensive than graphics I/O systems, and graphics processing was much slower than alphanumeric processing. This is why IBM's first PC display system used a text adapter. Today, cost and speed are less problematic, although most graphics I/O systems also have a text mode to speed up information portrayal if purely text information is being shown on a screen.

On a pixel-oriented output device, such as a CRT display or dot matrix printer, even text adapters paint each character as a matrix of dots. On a CRT screen, for example, it is common to divide the screen into **character boxes** that are typically about 9 pixels across and 14 to 16 pixels down. The text adapter then paints the appropriate character in each box by turning on the proper pixels in the box.

Memory Requirements and Processing Needs in Pixel Graphics

As discussed earlier, graphics processing places heavier burdens on hardware than does text processing. There are two reasons for this.

1. Although text systems usually store only 16 bits per character (a one-byte code to identify the character in the adapter's repertoire and another byte to represent special information, such as brightness or blinking), graphics I/O systems need to store one or more bits for every pixel, as we will see later. Although text I/O devices need only about 2 KB per printed page, graphics I/O devices may need to store a megabyte or more of data. Although memory costs are falling rapidly, megabytes of memory are still costly.

2. More importantly, although a text adapter only needs to process about 2 KB of data for every page printed, a graphics adapter has to process thousands or millions of bytes of data. As the number of bits in storage

rises, processing slows down dramatically—unless a more powerful processor is used. This is why most graphics programs require at least a PC AT or a Macintosh (which has PC AT power.)

Resolution

To keep processing requirements low, it is desirable to keep the number of pixels as small as possible. But this goal clashes with a more important goal—making the number of pixels as *large* as possible to improve image quality. The larger the number of pixels, the smaller each one will be, and the finer the image will look. If there are too few pixels, individual pixels will show, and the picture will look grainy, but if there are enough pixels, the individual dots will be too small to see, and the image will be very smooth.

Pixels per Inch

The density of pixels is called the **resolution** of an input or output device. Resolution is measured in two ways: either as the total number of pixels horizontally and vertically, or as the number of pixels per inch (**ppi**) horizontally and vertically.

- Professional photocomposition devices have resolutions of at least 1000 ppi horizontally and vertically. This gives photographic quality, and even fine curved lines show no signs of jaggedness. No common personal computer peripherals attain this resolution, although some professional photocomposition devices can take output from a personal computer.

- Page printers (often called laser printers) are the densest printing devices commonly used with PCs. They usually have resolutions of 300 ppi horizontally and vertically. This produces true letter-quality output for text, making it virtually indistinguishable from typewriter output. For graphics, 300 ppi gives excellent quality for all but fine curved lines.

- Most dot matrix printers can produce only 100 ppi to 250 ppi horizontally and vertically. Printers at the high end of this range are called near letter-quality printers, but their text output is not quite as good as that of a typewriter. Their image output is somewhat grainy, with "jaggies" appearing when circles and straight lines are drawn at arbitrary angles. Printers at the low end of this range are useful only for producing initial drafts, and their graphics quality is very poor.

- Display screens have even lower resolution. Modern display systems typically have 50 to 150 ppi vertically and horizontally.

Pixels per Screen or Page

It is also useful to think of resolution in terms of the number of pixels on an entire display screen or a printed page, because these are the numbers that determine the memory and processing requirements of graphics-based computers.

- Typical modern display systems paint 640 pixels across each display screen and 480 pixels vertically, for a total of 307,200 pixels—0.3 Mpixels (megapixels).

- An 8.5 by 11 page of text with 300 ppi resolution horizontally and vertically has 2550 pixels horizontally and 3300 pixels vertically, for a whopping 8.4 Mpixels.

Bits per Pixel

Now that we have looked at the number of pixels required to produce a desired level of resolution, we will turn to the number of bits per pixel. As we will see, the number of bits per pixel depends on only one thing, color. Simple monochrome graphics requires the least number of bits per pixels, whereas the use of many colors or gray scale levels multiplies the number of bits per pixel rapidly.

Monochrome Graphics

The simplest graphics devices are limited to **monochrome** graphics in which there is only a single color against a contrasting background. Popular monochrome combinations are green on black, amber on black, and black on white. In monochrome graphics, pixels are either on or off. If they are on, they take the foreground color—black, green, or amber. If they are off, they take the background color—white or black. *Monochrome graphics requires only one bit to be stored in memory for each pixel.*

For a monochrome display screen with 0.3 Mpixels, 300,000 bits or about 40 KB of storage and processing will be required. An entire monochrome printed page with a resolution of 300 ppi requires a staggering 8 Mpixels or about 1 MB of data to be stored and manipulated in I/O operations.

When entire pages are stored in memory, data compression techniques may be used to reduce storage requirements. Unfortunately, although this reduces storage requirements, it can dramatically increase processing requirements because of the processing needed to do compression and decompression.

Gray Scale

Traditional "black and white" photographs are not really monochrome. They also have **gray scale,** meaning that each point on the screen varies in darkness from pure white to pure black. In pixel graphics, gray scale requires several bits to be stored per pixel.

- Three bits per pixel gives eight levels of gray, which is marginal but superior to pure monochrome graphics.
- One byte per pixel gives 256 gray scale levels, which is the limit of common PC output devices.
- Two bytes per pixel defines 65,536 gray scale levels—better than photographic quality.

A display screen holding 0.3 Mpixels will therefore require 0.6 MB of storage if 65,536 gray scale levels are used (0.3 MPixels times 2 bytes per pixel)—a sixteenfold increase in the number of pixels to store a display screen in simple monochrome. This same sixteenfold increase holds for entire pages

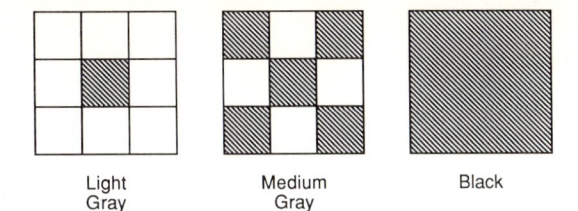

FIGURE 7-6 DITHERING TO MIMIC TRUE GRAY SCALE

stored in gray scale, raising the number of bytes per page to a staggering 16 MB.

To reduce the memory penalty of gray scale, a process called **dithering** is often used. As shown in Figure 7-6, dithering addresses a group of pixels instead of a single pixel. In this case, a 3 by 3 pixel box is addressed. If all pixels are on, the block is pure white. Turning on only the middle pixel gives very light gray. Turning on a cross pattern gives medium gray. When all pixels are on, the box is pure black. A 3 by 3 dithering box gives 10 shades from pure white to solid black.

The problem with dithering is that it wastes resolution. If a 3 by 3 dithering box is used, horizontal and vertical resolution are slashed to a third of their original values, and the number of overall pixels is slashed to a ninth of its original value.

Color Graphics

Color graphics are produced by combining the three primary colors. For devices that use light, for example, displays, the three primary colors are red, green, and blue. This is why color displays are called RGB displays. For devices such as printers that use pigment, the primary colors are cyan, magenta, and yellow.

If there are three bits per pixel, each of the three primary colors can be turned on and off independently, giving eight colors. Adding more bits allows each color to be given a different intensity (like a gray scale). This intensity variation multiplies the number of colors. One byte per pixel gives 256 colors, whereas two bytes per pixel gives 65,536 colors.

Both IBM's Video Graphics Array and the color graphics adapter released with the Macintosh II have resolutions of 640 by 480, with 16 colors. These 0.3 Mpixels require 1.2 Mbits (about 150 KB) of storage and processing for every screen image.

Some early color graphics systems balanced the memory penalty of color graphics by reducing resolution. The classic example was the IBM Color Graphics Adapter and Color Display, IBM's first color/graphics display system. When it shows color, this display system has only 320 pixels across and 200 pixels down—about half the horizontal and vertical resolution of IBM's monochrome display systems or newer new color/graphics display systems. Even IBM's Video Graphics display balances the memory penalty of color by dropping to 320 by 200 resolution in its most prolific color mode, in which it can produce a quarter of a million different colors.

Pixel Versus Object Software

Pixels must be manipulated at the levels of both system software and application software. At the system software level, it is necessary to handle pixel-oriented I/O systems with pixel-oriented graphics. At the application software level, however, another approach to manipulating pixel graphics image is possible. This is the **object** manipulation. As we will see below, object manipulation does two things. First, it slashes the memory required to hold application data files. Second, it makes it easier for the application software to work with high-resolution output devices, such as laser-based page printers.

Objects

Instead of storing pixel-by-pixel information, **object graphics** programs store images as a series of objects. The most common objects handled by these programs are text strings, lines, and geometric forms.

Text To store a text string, the object graphics program must store a code symbol for each character. This symbol is normally taken from the popular ASCII code for alphanumeric information, a successor of old Morse code used in telegraphy. This takes a single byte per character. In addition, the object graphics program needs to store certain information about each character, including its type face, size, emphasis (such as boldface, underlining), and color (if applicable).

If text information is cut and pasted among files produced by the same application program or a compatible application program, characteristics will be retained, not just the ASCII codes. Consequently, boldfaced Helvetica type in 12 pitch (see Chapter 11 for text characteristics) will retain this distinctive form when it is copied.

Lines Lines can be viewed as a connection between two points, but they have a number of characteristics that must be stored with them.

- The most obvious of these characteristics is width. Some lines can be hair-thin, and others thick.
- Lines can be solid, dashed, dotted, or filled with other patterns.
- Lines may come in various shades of gray or colors.
- Finally, it is common to put arrows at the ends of lines, either in one or both directions.

Polylines A **polyline** is a string of lines joined head to tail. If the individual lines in a polyline are small enough, a polyline will look like a smooth curve, although some jaggedness almost always remains. Polylines normally have the same characteristics as lines, and one set of characteristics normally applies to all line segments in the polyline.

Boxes and ellipses Boxes and ellipses, of which squares and circles are special cases, are enclosed by lines that may have many of the characteristics just described for lines. Boxes and ellipses may also be filled with color, shades of gray, or complex patterns. Both are defined by a start point (corner or center), an end point, and a few characteristics.

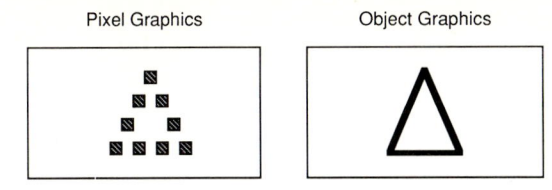

FIGURE 7-7 PIXEL VERSUS OBJECT GRAPHICS

Representing Objects
Figure 7-7 shows two triangles, one represented by pixel graphics and the other by object graphics. The pixel graphics program represents it as a series of dots, and the object graphics program as a series of lines.

Memory Requirements
As shown in Figure 7-8, all graphics application programs create data files. Pixel graphics programs produce pixel graphics data files, whereas object graphics programs produce object graphics data files.

Storage for individual objects Individual text strings, lines, boxes, and ellipses stored as objects take up far less memory than the same information stored by pixel programs. For example, consider a text string of 100 characters. In object programs, there must be one ASCII byte for each character, as well as several characteristic bytes for every **run** of text characters with the same characteristics. Typically, about 150 bytes will be needed to hold a 100-character text string.

If these same 100 characters were stored in pixel mode, each would be represented by at least a 9 by 14 character box. This would require over 1500 bytes even if color were not used. If there were 16 colors, the object storage would still be around 150 bytes, but the pixel storage requirements would jump to over 6000 bytes.

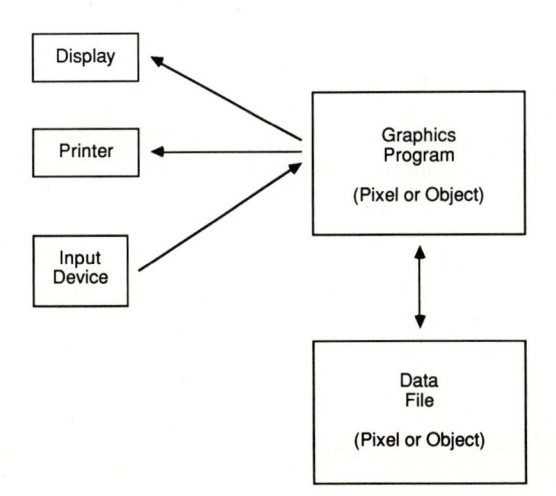

FIGURE 7-8 GRAPHICS PROGRAMS AND DATA FILES

There are similar economies for storing lines, boxes, and ellipses. All three are characterized by a start point and end point, and a half dozen or so characteristics, but each might require hundreds or even thousands of pixels to represent in pixel modes.

Storage for whole screens and pages The situation is only somewhat different at the level of whole screens and pages. For display screens, a pixel graphics program may need 150 KB to store a single screen image in color, and it may need 1 MB to 8 MB to store an entire page of information. It will need to store this much regardless of how much or how little actual graphics information is stored on the page, unless sophisticated file compression is used.

In contrast, the amount of storage required for an object graphics program is normally far less. A general rule of thumb is that object graphics programs need only about 10 percent as much storage capacity to store a page or screen as a pixel graphics program. In the figures created for this book, for example, pixel graphics figures averaged about 20 KB, whereas object graphics figures averaged around 2 KB.

For extremely dense object graphics images, the gap between object and pixel graphics storage decreases, and it is even possible for object graphics pictures to require more storage than pixel graphics images. These situations are extremely rare, however. In all but a few odd cases, object graphics programs require far less storage.

Editability

Pixel and object graphics programs vary in their editability. Pixel graphics programs generally allow the user to edit individual pixels, turning them on or off or changing their colors. As a result, pixel graphics programs are ideal for producing complex art with shading and complex detail that cannot be defined easily in terms of text or simple geometric forms. DaVinci would have used pixel graphics in his work.

Object graphics programs have a different editing advantage. In pixel graphics programs, an object's identity is lost once it is drawn. Its pixels merge with those already on the canvas. After a square is drawn in an area that already has pixels, it cannot be moved. In contrast, object graphics elements never lose their identity. An object graphics square can be moved around on the canvas, duplicated, or placed in front of or in back of another object. In addition, most object graphics programs allow several objects to be **grouped,** so that they can be treated as a single object in editing operations.

Color

Just as pixel graphics program provide vivid images by the use of free-form drawing, they also excel in color. The best pixel graphics programs use thousands of colors to produce fine shadowing with graded color darkness, various types of washes, and numerous other artistic effects. As color becomes more important, this advantage will grow more pronounced. Although some object graphics programs use color, they can rarely handle complex shading and fine details such as those found in shadowing.

Output Quality in Printing

For on-screen images, both pixel and object software are limited to display resolution, which is 50 to 75 pixels per inch. But even dot matrix printers can produce twice this resolution, and laser-based page printers can produce 300 pixels per inch. We would like our printed output to be adjusted to the maximum resolution of the output device, instead of being limited to the resolution of the screen.

Pixel graphics printing The ability of a pixel graphics program to print well on high-resolution output devices is usually determined by the format of its data files (see Figure 7-8). If the data file format is limited to screen resolution, with one data element per display screen pixel, printing is also likely to be limited to display resolution, no matter how good the printer's intrinsic resolution is.

In MacPaint, for example, the popular pixel graphics program on the Macintosh, the data file is limited to the resolution of the Macintosh screen, which is 72 ppi. On dot matrix printers, output resolution is also limited to 72 ppi, although the printer can give twice this resolution. On the LaserWriter, MacPaint output is still limited to 72 ppi (actually 75 ppi, since the printer must work with fractions of 300 ppi). Therefore, although the small dots on laser printers make output look reasonably crisp, resolution is nothing like 300 dots per inch.

For the IBM, the situation is often worse. At least MacPaint treats the screen as only a small window on the entire page. In contrast, many IBM pixel graphics programs treat the screen as a full page of output, instead of just as a section of a full page. As a result, the 60,000 to 300,000 pixels on the screen are translated into the same number of pixels on the printer—only a fraction of the 8 million pixels possible on a laser printer.

The situation does not have to be this way. A pixel graphics program could support data files with very high pixel densities, say 300 ppi. They would then translate these dense images to the screen, dot matrix printer, page printer, or other output device, using the full resolution of each device.

This approach would require storing and processing a megabyte of information per page in monochrome, and far more if color or gray scale were used. This is completely impractical. In addition, the time needed to translate the dense data file into less dense screen images and the time needed to translate screen editing operations into data file changes would result in extremely sluggish performance. As a result, screen resolution normally acts as the default for pixel graphics designers.

An interesting compromise is represented by SuperPaint, which offers a normal screen density pixel graphics mode as well as a high-density pixel graphics mode called LaserBits. The LaserBits mode gives 300 ppi densities, but only for areas about 2 inches on a side. This allows small regions of superdensity pixel images to be added to a data file.

In the end, although there are ways to get around the tyranny of screen resolution in pixel graphics, they are seldom used. With rare exceptions, *pixel graphics programs cannot use the full resolution of output devices.*

Object graphics printing Most object graphics programs unlike pixel graphics printing, can adjust their output to work with the full resolution of the output device. Since object graphics files *always require* translation to be shown on a display screen, there is nothing about the display screen that creates a de facto standard. Any good object graphics program will have a rich set of translation options to match the output of screens, dot matrix printers, and high-resolution page printers. *On high-resolution output devices, good object graphics printers product output at the full resolution of the output device—thus producing printed images that look far better than screen images.*

Object graphics programs can often scale their output. For example, most of the object graphics figures in this book were done for full-size paper and were then scaled down to the size of book figures. The most common form of scaling is reduction, in which printing is done at a fraction of the original size. However, it may also be possible to scale output so that it is twice or three times its normal size, in order to produce posters or large signs.

Printing Speed

Printing resolution is one thing, but printing speed is quite another. Because pixel graphics programs normally do not do translation from data file to screen, dot matrix, or page printer output, they print very rapidly.

In contrast, object graphics programs must always translate from their data files to output devices, as just noted. Although this allows very precise output, it also takes a good deal of time. Object graphics programs give excellent quality, but they often take several minutes to print.

One way to avoid this penalty is to use a printer with built-in translation hardware. Many laser printers can be purchased with these boards as options. Although these boards add $1000 to $1500 to the cost of a page printer, they improve processing time by an order of magnitude, and are mandatory for intense object graphics printing, desktop publishing, and other high-resolution graphics needs.

Even painting an image on the screen can be excruciatingly slow if the computer lacks special tools to speed the translation from object data file to screen image. Fortunately, many computers have these tools. The Macintosh, for instance, has a rich set of ROM-based QuickDraw routines to translate objects into screen images. Computers with the graphics coprocessors discussed earlier in this chapter are even faster. On most IBM microcomputers, however, there are neither ROM nor hardware aids from translating object graphics files into screen images, and many object graphics programs on IBM micros are extremely sluggish and move only in spurts.

Pixel Versus Object Graphics in Perspective

On balance, the most potent argument for object graphics appears to be its high quality. For excellent quality output, there is no choice, and the laser printer is making high-quality output increasingly the norm.

Pixel graphics programs do win out for one type of image—free-form graphics that require color, shading, and detail that cannot be captured adequately with lines and other geometric objects. For drawing artwork involving people, animals, trees, and other realistic details, pixel graphics is the best option.

As discussed in Chapter 11, however, a third choice may be available in some situations. This is to use a **hybrid graphics** program that combines both pixel and object graphics. A good example of such a program is **SuperPaint,** which has two overlapping layers—one based on pixels and having associated pixel editing tools, and the other based on objects and having associated object editing tools. These two frames can overlap transparently, giving the best of both worlds. In addition, as noted earlier, SuperPaint adds editing at 300 pixels per inch over very small areas.

Toward Graphics Standards

The Complexity of Graphics Output

Chapter 6 described how text application programs deal with the multiplicity of text printers on the market. These application programs output text in a single format called the **native format** for that program. This native format output is then passed to another program sold by the vendor of the application program, a **printer driver.** The printer driver translates the native format into the format used by a particular text printer. Most programs are sold with a rich set of printer drivers, and as new printers appear on the market, the application program vendor creates and distributes additional printer drivers.

For text programs, printer drivers are fairly easy to build. Text output is basically a stream of ASCII characters, and formatting consists largely of embedding a few control codes within the ASCII stream. One control code, for example, would turn on boldface printing, while another would turn boldface off. In this simple environment, translation consists largely of substituting control codes. Proportional spacing adds only somewhat to the complexity of the translation process.

Building printer drivers for graphics printers is much more complex. There is nothing analogous to a simple stream of ASCII text in graphics printing. Graphics printers print a pattern of dots, and resolution is different for every printer on the market. Each device driver must be carefully and painfully built. Not just a theoretical problem, this difficulty has slowed the growth of graphics device drivers. Printer standards are badly needed, so that application designers can concentrate more of their energy into basic application program functionality and less into the construction of printer drivers. Standards are also needed so that builders on new printers can construct their machines with confidence that they will be able to work with a wide range of application software. And finally, standards are needed so that buyers will be able to make purchases with the assurance that their application programs and printers will be able to work together.

Emulation

It is said that imitation is the sincerest form of flattery. Imitation is also the easiest way for printer builders to work with application software. Most printers, in addition to working in their own basic formats, can also emulate popular printers on the market. The emulating printer can take a print stream designed for the printer being emulated and translate this stream into its own basic format. It can then print the output.

In emulation, then, there are two translations. First, the application program's printer driver translates the output into the format of the printer being emulated. Then, the emulating printer translates the translated output into its own printer format. There is obviously the danger that something will be lost in translation, but even with double translation, emulation is a good way to provide basic program–printer compatibility.

Text printers have long used emulation. Most, for example, can emulate the IBM Graphics Printer and several daisywheel printers. In graphics printing, the IBM Graphics Printer has again become a standard, but this is a low-resolution, low-functionality machine and gives only a lowest common denominator. As printers move toward very high resolution, the IBM Graphics Printer standard will become even more inadequate.

For page printers, the enormous popularity of the Hewlett-Packard Laserjet and Laserjet Plus has made these machines de facto standards, and most laser printers can emulate these machines. But emulation of graphics printers is very difficult, and some Laserjet and Laserjet Plus emulations are less than adequate.

More importantly, even very clean emulation cannot avoid the biggest pitfall of all emulation. This is the fact that emulation limits a printer's features to those of the printer it is emulating. Because only popular printers are emulated and because it usually takes some time to achieve popularity, the printers emulated are usually fairly old and behind the functionality curve. Emulation essentially strips a printer of the new functionality it brings to the market.

PostScript

The Adobe Corporation attacked the problem of graphics compatibility in a different way, by creating a single graphics format called **PostScript.** Adobe built extremely high functionality into PostScript, so that machines would take several years to press its limits. It has since updated PostScript constantly, to keep ahead of printer technology.

As shown in Figure 7-9, application programs who use PostScript as their natural output format simply send their output to PostScript printers. Others build a single PostScript printer driver to reach any PostScript printer.

PostScript is a **page description language (PDL).** This means that it is designed to describe complexly formatted pages. This makes it ideal for desktop publishing (see Chapter 11). But PDLs are also very useful for analytical and conceptual graphics programs (see Chapter 11). Their richness makes them ideal for a wide variety of graphics output operations.

PostScript output does not consist of a pixel map to be printed. PostScript is designed for object graphics software. When it sends an alphabetic character, for instance, it sends a description of what the letter should look like in terms of the arcs and other patterns needed to draw it. As a result, PostScript is not useful for pixel graphics software, although PostScript printers nearly always have a native pixel output format that programs can use.

Typically, printers are not built from the ground up to use PostScript. Instead, the printer manufacturer builds a special-purpose microcomputer into the printer. This microcomputer, using ROM-based software, translates

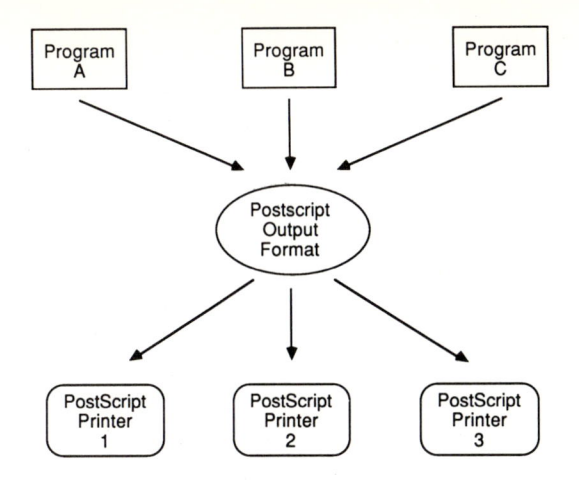

FIGURE 7-9 POSTSCRIPT OUTPUT FORMAT

PostScript output into the native format of the printer. This takes the user back to the double translation problem of emulation, but this time the processing is very rapid, because it is handled outside the PC in the printer. In addition, because PostScript is so rich, little or nothing should be lost in emulation.

In a few cases, the processing circuitry and ROM software are not built into the printer. Instead, they are placed on an expansion card within the PC. The expansion card works in parallel with the PC's microprocessor, so that the PC is not tied up during translation. Placing the processing inside the PC allows a special high-speed interface to be used to link the PC with the printer. But it means that only this single PC can work with the printer. If the processing is done within the printer, however, several PCs can be connected with simple A-B-C switches, and each will enjoy PostScript processing without the addition of special hardware.

PostScript is not the only PDL format. Several others are struggling to gain a foothold, but in general they are achieving only small market shares. When Hewlett-Packard adopted PostScript after a spirited fight to promote its own PDL, and when IBM adopted PostScript for its first desktop publishing product, PostScript's future seemed assured. In addition, many photocomposition output devices with ultrahigh resolution have adopted PostScript, giving this PDL an even stronger competitive edge over its competitors, who are largely limited to page printers. Any program that uses PostScript output is not limited to office page printers.

Now, however, this popularity is producing clones—processors that can accept PostScript format and convert it into the format of a particular printer. They can do this because they do not duplicate Adobe's program code, which is copyrighted, but only work with PostScript format, which is probably not protected by law. Adobe originally charged very high royalties for PostScript, somewhat retarding the growth of graphics printing. Competition should produce lower royalty payments and lower printer prices.

For the foreseeable future, however, costs for PostScript seem destined to remain fairly high. Even if royalties fall, the processor itself is still quite expensive, having microcomputer power and complexity. Although today's premium of $1500 to $2500 for PDL capability will soon be a thing of the past, prices for PDL will continue to remain high.

NAPLPS

Although PostScript now dominates the page printer market, several international standards for object graphics are emerging and promise to be important in the 1990s.

The most promising of these output standards is **NAPLPS** (the North American Presentation-Level Protocol Standard). NAPLPS is an object graphics standard designed for Videotex, an information retrieval service discussed in Chapter 12. This makes it a specialized standard, but there is the possibility that NAPLPS will be used in a much wider variety of user applications, including electronic mail.

NAPLPS, unfortunately, faces two major problems. First, most NAPLPS terminals use slow telephone lines, so screen representations must be kept simple. Although NAPLPS is capable of high resolution and complex output, telephone-based services will not be able to use these capabilities. Second, few online services are popular today, despite a vast installed base of TTYs that can use these services in text mode today. While NAPLPS proponents argue that NAPLPS will bring the vividness needed to make these services attractive to a much wider audiences, online service vendors are reluctant to act in light of the high cost of technical delivery equipment and the even higher costs of producing visually rich information services. While NAPLPS may become popular in the 1990s, even its long-term future is far from assured.

VDI

Another promising output standard is **VDI (Virtual Device Interface).** While PostScript is oriented toward printers and NAPLPS is oriented toward display screens, VDI uses a common output format for all devices. This means that programmers will not have to toil twice to produce output, once for printers, once for displays. It should also mean that display representation will be more faithful to printed output. Not only an output standard, VDI is also used for input devices, so that the information input into the computer can be processed easily by software that is compliant with the standard.

VDI is achieving some popularity in computer aided design (CAD), but it has yet to make a major dent in the general graphics market. When IBM supported VDI within its EGA adapter, many felt that VDI would spurt forward, but that did not happen. VDI, like NAPLPS, will be a future player if it will be a major player at all.

Document Standards

Because of the growing popularity of desktop publishing and other text services that require complex page layout, ISO (the International Organization for Standards) is now working on an **Office Document Architecture (ODA)** that will embrace the functionality of desktop publishing programs. This standard is discussed in a little more detail in Chapter 17. The standard embraces a page description language standard that could give PostScript competition in the 1990s, but it remains to be seen whether ISO's effort will bear fruit.

Comprehensive Graphics Standards

VDI, NAPLPS, and ODA are only pieces in a much broader standardization effort by the International Organization for Standards (ISO). Figure 7-10 shows the major standards now under development at ISO.

In ISO's picture, the application program would not even have to do its own detailed graphics creation. Instead, it would send rather simple graphics definitions to a **graphics utility program,** which would flesh out the details of the graphics. This will be a major boon to word processing programs and other programs for which graphics is only a minor task. The interface between the application program and the graphics utility program is called the **graphics kernel standard (GKS).**

The graphics utility program also produces its output in standard form. For printers, output can be in VDI, NAPLPS, or the PDL standards now being developed for ODA.

There is even a standard for filing object graphics data on external storage media. This is the **virtual device metafile (VDM)** standard. Once data are stored in VDM format, any program can work with them, not just the original. VDM may prove to be an important intermediate file format for transfers among programs, but that will only be true if it becomes popular.

Standards for Pixel Graphics Software

PostScript, VDI, NAPLPS, and GKS are restricted to object graphics. For pixel graphics, they provide no help at all. PostScript, VDI, NAPLPS, and GKS do nothing for these programs. In other words, current standards are still no panacea for the translation problem.

As a result, de facto standards tend to govern the market to the extent that the market is governed at all. In the Macintosh world, MacPaint has set a

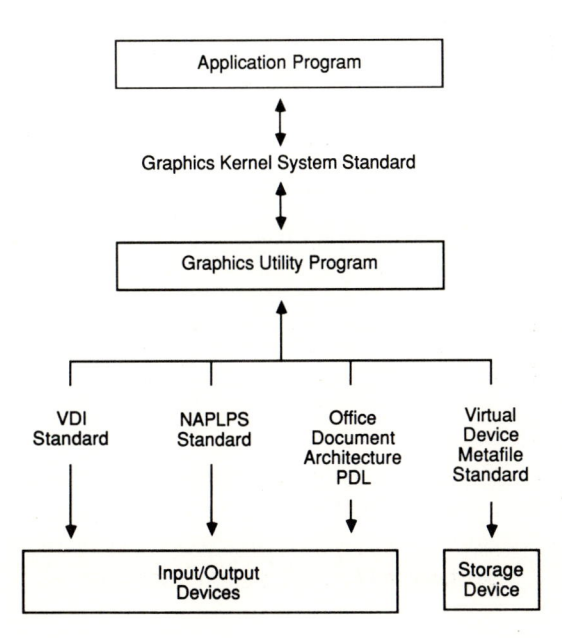

FIGURE 7-10 COMPREHENSIVE GRAPHICS STANDARDS

de facto standard for pixel graphics, and almost all pixel graphics programs that run on a Macintosh are based on the MacPaint file structure. Two-way compatibility is rarely guaranteed, however, since these programs offer other features. In the IBM world, the only common denominators are the screen resolutions of various IBM adapters.

DISPLAYS

Every personal computer is equipped with a display, and the purchaser normally has several options when making the purchase. Display choice can limit the kind of software that can be used on the machine. It can also either promote or prevent eyestrain.

Cathode Ray Tube Technology

Most computer displays use **cathode ray tube (CRT)** technology. As shown in Figure 7-11, there is a screen covered with phosphors that will glow when an electron beam hits them. There is also an electron beam that sweeps over the screen constantly, scanning from left to right, top to bottom. As the intensity of the electron beam is varied, phosphors glow brighter or darker, forming an image on the screen.

In a monochrome display, there is a single electron gun, and all phosphors glow the same color. In a color display, there are phosphors that glow red, green, or blue, and there are three electron guns each of which illuminates phosphors of different colors. Because there are three electron beams,

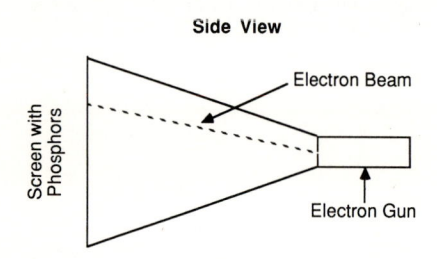

FIGURE 7-11 CATHODE RAY TUBE DISPLAY

and because the phosphors must be arranged carefully on the face of the screen, color displays are much more expensive than monochrome displays.

Computer Displays Versus Home Televisions

Each personal computers used ordinary television sets as displays, and many home computers continue to use ordinary TVs. Many users ask why they cannot use ordinary TVs with their office computers today.

General Differences Between Computer Displays and Home Televisions

In the United States and some other countries, both black and white and color home television sets use the **National Television Service Committee (NTSC)** standard. This standard provides 525 horizontal scan lines that are refreshed 30 times each second. Refreshing is needed because phosphors lose their brightness quickly after they are illuminated.

These 525 scan lines are painted in two passes. The odd-numbered lines are painted on the first pass, and the even-numbered lines on the second. This process, called **interleaving,** means that half of all scan lines are one-sixtieth of a second old or less.

Displays created for computers use different numbers of scanning lines than home television sets. The actual number of lines depends on the particular display adapter. In addition, many adapters do no interlacing because the long-persisting phosphors used in computer displays do not lose their brightness as quickly as the phosphors on home television sets. Another reason is that, unless interlacing is done very exactly, the odd and even lines will tend to overlap, reducing the vertical resolution of the display.

The Resolution Problem

So far, we have merely looked at how home televisions differ from computer displays, but we have not asked why home TVs cannot be used as displays. Now we turn to that core issue. Put briefly, the problem with ordinary TVs is that the picture signal has a "bandwidth" of only four megahertz (4 MHz). This means that the signal changes only four million times per second. At the *maximum,* then, only four million changes can be sent per second. We will do a calculation to see the implications of a 4 MHz transmission speed.

- Because only four million changes can be sent per second, a maximum of four million pixels can be sent per second.
- A screen is refreshed 30 times per second, so each screen can have a maximum of 133,333 pixels (four million divided by 30).
- Each TV screen has 525 lines, so each line can have a maximum of 254 pixels (133,333 divided by 525).
- If each character is five pixels wide, and if there is one pixel between each pair of characters, each line can show a maximum of about 40 characters (254 divided by 6 is 42.3). This is only about half of a printed page—too small a window on the world for business applications.

Although computer displays use basic television technology, their circuits are able to handle higher "bandwidths" (signal speeds in MHz), so they can display 80 or more characters per line. Most displays operate at about 15 MHz. Although high-definition television standards which will double the resolution of broadcast television are now before standards committees, office computer demands will probably have moved beyond the capabilities of these approaches before a high-definition broadcast standard is ratified.

Text Versus Graphics Displays

As discussed earlier in this chapter, **display systems** consist of two components: the display itself and the adapter inside the computer. All displays produce output in pixel form, as shown in Figure 7-12. (This way of producing pixels through scan lines or "raster lines" is sometimes called **raster graphics,** but it is nothing more than a way to produce pixel graphics.)

As noted earlier, whether or not a display system can show graphics depends not on the display itself but on its adapter. Some adapters only have **text modes,** in which they can merely paint letters, numbers, punctuation signs, and other special symbols from a limited character set on the display screen. These are called **text display systems.**

Others, called **graphics display systems,** usually have both a text and a graphics mode. In most cases, the entire screen must be in either text or graphics mode at any moment. Some graphics display systems, such as the one in the Apple Macintosh, have no text mode at all. They produce everything in graphics mode.

The distinction between text and graphics display systems will grow less important over time, since all new display systems are graphics systems. Many text display systems are still in offices today, however, and for adapters that have text modes, it is important to understand how text modes handle the screen.

Monochrome Versus Color

As noted earlier, **monochrome** (from the Greek for "one color") I/O systems, including displays, show information in one color against a contrasting background. In contrast, **color displays** have three electron guns, one each for red, green, and blue.

NTSC Color

It is possible to show color output in an NTSC home television set. Unfortunately, in addition to the resolution problem discussed earlier, the NTSC standard mixes colors together and requires the television set to unmix them on delivery. This process usually results in constant color variations. This problem is so severe that NTSC has been described as an acronym for "never twice the same color"

RGB Display Systems

Until 1987, nearly all popular color displays systems for computers were **RGB** monitors, in which the red, green, and blue signals came in via separate wires. In pure RGB signalling, only the three colors are possible. By combining them two or three at a time, a display can produce eight colors.

It is more common to see **IRGB** displays, in which the "I" stands for "intensity." These display systems add a fourth line to give intensity information. Typically, the line has two signal levels, one for normal, another for bright with the eight basic colors and two intensity levels, 16 distinct colors can be produced.

Analog Displays

The RGB approach is a digital approach because it uses only a few discrete signal levels. It is simple to implement, but it only produces a few colors. Since 1987, most new display systems have been **analog systems,** in which the signals on the RGB and intensity wires can take on any value over a wide range. Analog systems can produce hundreds of thousands or even millions of colors. Most, however, produce only a few hundred.

Display Systems for IBMs and Compatibles

Figure 7-12 summarizes the characteristics of adapters for popular display systems created for IBM computers and compatibles. All except one were created by IBM but have become the basis for numerous clones from other vendors. The one exception is the Hercules Graphics Card, which serves a niche ignored by IBM, namely, monochrome graphics.

Adapter	Mode	Horizontal Pixels	Vertical Pixels	Colors
Monochrome Display Adapter	Text	720	350	2
Hercules Graphics Card	Text	720	350	2
	Graphics	720	348	2
Color Graphics Adapter	Text	640	200	4
	Graphics	640	200	2
	Graphics	320	200	4
Enhanced Graphics Adapter	Text	640	350	16
	Graphics	640	350	16
	Graphics			
Multicolor Graphics Array	Text	640	400	16
	Graphics	640	480	2
	Graphics	320	200	256
Video Graphics Array	Text	640	400	16
	Graphics	640	480	16
	Graphics	320	200	256
8514A	Text	1024	768	256
	Graphics	1024	1024	256

Notes:
  Two colors is monochrome output.
  The Hercules Graphics Card is not produced by IBM.
  Most adapters can support less dense graphics modes.

FIGURE 7-12 POPULAR DISPLAY ADAPTERS FOR IBM PERSONAL COMPUTERS

IBM's Original Monochrome System

The original IBM PC was sold with the **monochrome display adapter,** which could only handle monochrome text on an **IBM Personal Computer Display.** Although the display had a resolution that was not surpassed for many years by IBM's color products, its lack of graphics was a major problem for many users, including many Lotus 1-2-3 users, who wanted to see their graphs on-screen before printing them.

The Hercules Graphics Card

Sensing that many users wanted a low-cost way to do graphics, several companies built adapters that could handle graphics as well as text on a standard IBM Personal Computer Display. The dominant entrant was the Hercules Graphics Card, which supported a graphics mode with 720 by 348 pixels. Many vendors began offering "Hercules compatible" display adapters, and prices for monochrome graphics adapters plunged. Hercules tried to shake off competitors by introducing the Graphics Card Plus in 1986. This new card offered built-in routines for generating text very rapidly.

Other vendors have built monochrome graphics adapters that mirror the lower resolution of IBM's original color graphics system, which is discussed next. Although software does not have to be rewritten for these cards, as it has to be for the Hercules Graphics Card and Graphics Card Plus, these products suffer from the low resolution of IBM's original color graphics system.

Color Graphics Adapter

In 1983, IBM produced its first color graphics system, consisting of the **color graphics adapter (CGA)** and **IBM Personal Computer Color Display.** In one move, IBM introduced both color and graphics.

Because color and graphics prices were so high at that time, IBM's design cut many corners. It could only show four colors, and when it did show color, its resolution was only 320 pixels across and 200 pixels down—about half the horizontal and vertical resolution of the monochrome system. The color graphics system also allowed graphics at 640 by 200 resolution, but only by reverting to monochrome. Because of these weaknesses, the growth of color and graphics in the IBM world was very slow.

IBM's Enhanced Graphics System

In 1984, IBM came back to the market with an improved graphics system, consisting of an **enhanced graphics adapter (EGA)** and an **enhanced color display.** This system is normally called EGA, after its adapter.

- EGA can show 640 pixels across and 350 down—almost equal to the resolution of the original monochrome system.
- EGA can show 16 colors at a time.
- EGA is also fully compatible with older software for the original monochrome and for CGA. Of course, in compatible mode, it is reduced to the limitations of those adapters.

The cost of the system was very high when it was released. The adapter, which had to do extensive processing, cost more than $900 in usable form.

The display needed small (0.31 mm) diameter phosphors for high resolution, and this raised its cost to over $800 initially. Soon, however, clones began to hit the market at much lower costs. Most of these used a new chip set from Chips and Technologies to slash production costs, and these savings were matched by low markups from the clone vendors. By the start of 1987, adapter prices had already fallen to $300, and display prices had decreased to about $500. Although these prices were still high, users began to turn to the enhanced graphics system with enthusiasm. Further price declines have continued to fuel the growth of enhanced graphics products.

Multicolor Graphics Array

In 1987, IBM introduced the **multicolor graphics array (MCGA)** adapter for its Personal System (PS)/2 Model 30. This adapter was built right into the computer's mother board. Because MCGA was not sold with any other PS/2 model, the incentive for developers to produce MCGA-compatible software was weak. Another drawback is that MCGA cannot run EGA applications—only applications that use CGA modes, with their limited color and resolution.

Video Graphics Array

For all PS/2 models above the Model 30, IBM introduced a different adapter on the mother board. This was the **video graphics adapter (VGA)**. VGA offers high resolution at 16 colors, as well as a mode with a quarter million colors that unfortunately drops the machine to CGA resolutions. It is also compatible with EGA, so that it can run programs that handle EGA but not VGA.

As PS/2 machines proliferate, VGA's popularity should spread. Moreover, IBM and other vendors are creating VGA or VGA compatible display adapter boards to use in older PCs, giving any PC user access to VGA resolution and colors. Although these adapters and the displays capable of supporting VGA adapters were initially more expensive than EGA display systems, the difference was not extreme and was expected to disappear in a short time. Although the market may decide otherwise, VGA is likely to be IBM's flagship display adapter for the foreseeable future.

Other Adapters and Displays

Both IBM and other vendors have produced display adapter systems with resolutions greater than those of VGA. No dominant standard has emerged in this area, however. Full-page display systems, which are the most advanced ultrahigh-resolution display systems, are discussed later in this chapter. Even todays best displays, however, fall short of the 2000 to 4000 pixels per inch (ppi) that the human eye can resolve on a 12 inch diameter display.

Macintosh Display Systems

When the Macintosh was first released, it was sold with a single display system—a built-in 9 inch diameter monochrome display system. In contrast, when the Macintosh II was developed, it came with *no* standard display system at all, although Apple offered some display systems that could work with it.

The Original Apple Macintosh Display System

When the Macintosh was built, the failure of the overpriced Lisa was uppermost in the minds of all Apple designers. Although a good display had to be built, its price had to be kept competitive.

Apple's solution was to design a small but ultra-crisp monochrome display system with black characters on a paper white background. This was a 9 inch diagonal display system with 512 pixels across and 342 pixels vertically, giving a horizontal pixel density of 72 pixels per inch and a vertical pixel density of 72 pixels per inch.

IBM's EGA system operates with an 11.25 inch diagonal viewing area that is 9 inches wide and 6.75 inches high. Its 640 by 350 pixel layout translates into a horizontal pixel density of 71 pixels per inch and a vertical pixel density of 52 pixels per inch. In other words, although the Macintosh screen is smaller, it has dense resolution.

The Macintosh screen shows information full size. Its 7.1 by 4.75 inch viewing area corresponds to a 7.1 by 4.75 inch printing area. This is helpful for desktop publishing and advanced word processing graphics applications, in which page layout is very important.

Although the original Macintosh did not offload any graphics work to coprocessors, its MC68000 microprocessor chips are said to be graphics-oriented. The system software's QuickDraw routines allow graphics images to be created very rapidly.

Display Systems for the Macintosh II

When the Macintosh II was created, Apple completely reversed its stand on display systems. In contrast to the original Macintosh, which was equipped with only one display system, the Macintosh II *did not come with any standard output at all.*

Instead, each program has the option of having 1, 2, 4, 8, 16, or 32 bits per pixel in its bit map. At the high end, this allows over 4 billion colors from an absolute palette representing more than 280 trillion colors. The Macintosh II does not, however, specify the number of pixels horizontally or vertically, nor does it specify the number of colors that can be supported by an adapter. Users can therefore change adapters without changing software at all. This brings an unprecedented degree of upward compatibility.

Another interesting feature of the display design is its ability to work with more than one display at a time. If the user has two displays, the desktop image (see Chapter 8) will be split over both displays. This happens even if one is a monochrome display and the other a color display.

When Apple introduced the Macintosh II in 1987, it did offer a color graphics display system with 640 by 480 resolution and 16 colors—exactly the same as were offered in the high-resolution mode of IBM's VGA adapter discussed earlier.

Flat Panel Displays

A number of displays now use technology different from the **CRT** technology pioneered on home TVs. These new technologies are being used to produce **flat panel** displays, which take up much less space than a traditional CRT display. This compactness is necessary for laptop computers. Flat panel displays also consume much less power than traditional CRTs—another important benefit for laptop computers.

The most popular choice today for flat panel displays is the **liquid crystal display (LCD),** which was pioneered on digital watches. It allows a flat panel design that uses exceptionally little power. LCDs are still expensive, however, and when they are made large enough to show a full display screen, their sensitivity to light and viewing angle becomes troublesome to users. According to one rumor, when a senior IBM executive was shown an early prototype of a laptop, he said "Turn it on." The chagrined technician replied "I already did." Although screen brightness and contrast can be increased by back lighting, this increased power drain shortens the time a machine can be used between chargings.

Other technologies can be used, including the Electroluminescent Display (ELD) and the plasma display. Although they offer much clearer pictures than LCD displays, they are even more expensive. They have therefore been relegated to niche markets. Furthermore, by the time they become economically attractive, advances in LCD technology that bring higher contrast and even color may make other technologies obsolete.

In the long run, LCD technology is likely to produce even higher resolution than CRTs. CRT resolution is improving very slowly, but LCD resolution is governed largely by the circuitry that controls individual spots on the screen, and the miniaturization of this circuitry is improving very rapidly. In the long run, LCD should bring the 300 pixel per inch resolution of laser page printers to everyone's personal computers.

Full-Page Display Systems

The wish lists of many users have long included **full-page display systems** that can show a full 8.5 by 11 inch sheet of paper on a single screen. Although full-page displays were produced in the early 1980s, they were incompatible with most application software. Lotus 1-2-3 would work on these screens, for example, but it used only the first 25 lines and 80 columns, leaving the rest of the screen blank. These displays were extremely expensive.

In 1985 and 1986, however, a fair number of products could be used with these displays. For example, CAD (computer-aided design), desktop publishing, and other graphics-intensive software needed large-screen displays to thrive, so their developers made them compatible with a number of large-screen displays. In addition, Lotus Development Corporation began to support several of these displays, for Lotus 1-2-3 and Symphony, in order to give their users a larger window on the world.

Full-page display systems typically have diagonal sizes of 15 inches to 19 inches and resolutions of around 1000 pixels horizontally and vertically. This requires display bandwidths of around 50 MHz—three times the 15 MHz to 16 MHz used in most PC displays. Because their market sizes are limited and their equipment pushes the state of the art, complete systems with adapters and displays cost $2,500 to $3,500 in 1986. These prices are falling rapidly, however. Some full-page display systems even cost under $1000, although they are quite limited today.

Users who are interested in full-page displays must consider three factors besides price: the number of programs that can work with the display system; whether the system is limited to a full page or can show more than a full page; and the degree of distortion, instability, and lack of contrast in the image on the screen. The word "degree" must be used here because at the time of this writing all full-page displays on the market have some image quality problems, some of them severe.

Projection Systems

For training purposes, many people commonly gather together in a room. Many training facilities now have **projection systems** to display images on a large screen, so that everyone in the room can share the information being presented. Some of these projection systems have even found their ways into corporate board rooms, so that the participants in a meeting can see real-time data retrievals, what-if analysis, and other types of on-the-spot computations; these meeting support systems are discussed in Chapter 17.

Image Quality

When selecting a projection system, image quality is crucial. Some projection systems were designed for broadcast television signals and only have a bandwidth of 4 MHz for pictures. For computers, a bandwidth of 15 MHz to 20 MHz is needed, as discussed earlier. If a projection system cannot support these bandwidths, there is no reason to consider it further.

Even among projection systems that do support 15 MHz to 20 MHz bandwidths, image quality varies remarkably. None is as clear as an ordinary CRT, but the best systems are far easier to read than the worst. Although price is important in a purchase decision, picture clarity is crucial, and organizations should be willing to pay a premium price to get it.

Brightness

A related concern is the brightness of the picture. Ideally, the screen should be perfectly readable with the room lights left on. Practically speaking, however, it is usually necessary to dim them, and for some systems, the lights must be turned out entirely, as they are for a slide presentation. As a result, note-taking is difficult in training sessions and in meetings as well. A lights-out projection system is not likely to be practical in either training or meeting support.

Monochrome and Color

Some projection systems are monochrome, whereas others offer color. Color is desirable, but many monochrome systems are both clearer and brighter, as well as less expensive. For word processing, analysis, data base, and many other applications, color is rather unimportant, and the added clarity and brightness of monochrome may tip the balance away from color.

When color is used by an application program—say, when a pie chart is produced by a spreadsheet program—the monochrome projection system has to map these colors into shades of its monochrome color. It is important to see a demonstration of how color images are mapped into monochrome shades and hatching patterns. If a pie chart or bar chart shows two adjacent areas with the same shading or hatching pattern, the system is not likely to be very useful in meeting support or in other graphics applications.

Room Preparation

When projection systems are used in training or meeting support, room modifications are often made. In many cases, the projection system is mounted in a fixed location, typically on the ceiling, where it is out of the way when not in use. Although portable systems are useful, the time needed to set them up and test them is troublesome. Frequently used projection systems are almost always mounted.

Few training programs and meetings are run with a projection system as the only visual aid. It is important to have a traditional overhead projector that can point at the screen, as well as a blackboard and a flip chart stand. It may be desirable to set the computer screen off to one side of the room, instead of making it central, but since most projectors have a narrow field of focus, placing it to the side of a room is not always workable.

A narrow field of focus also constrains room design. Because few projection systems can be used in wide and shallow rooms, they should only be placed in deep and narrow rooms or in rooms where seating can be limited to the projection system's field of focus. Some projection systems use curved screens to improve brightness, but these narrow the focus even further. It is often better to sacrifice brightness for a wider field of focus.

Inasmuch as few projection systems can work in full room light, a dimmer should be added to the room lights. This dimmer should be controllable from the speaker's position. Dimming may not be possible when fluorescent lights are used, so a major change in lighting may be needed. Finally, covers should be placed over windows in order to allow better control over lighting.

PRINTERS

Once a user specifies a basic system consisting of electronics, disk drives, and a display, the largest decision remaining is the choice of a printer. Office printers cost $200 to $6,000, and within this enormous price range is an enormous range of speeds, print quality levels, and graphics capabilities.

Printers are the most difficult family of peripherals to discuss because the decision of what printers to buy is normally done on an officewide basis, not on the basis of individual needs. Most offices have a mix of printers, with varying speeds and quality levels. Each time a new printer is selected, the purchase must be made in the context of existing equipment.

PC printers may be divided into three major categories.

Line Printers These printers print a whole line at a time. They are very fast, but they are too expensive to be used in most offices.

Character Printers These printers print one character at a time. They are slow but inexpensive.

Page Printers These printers use lasers or other optical technologies to create a page image by writing a series of scan lines, much as the image on a CRT set is made by drawing a series of scan lines. PC page printers are expensive and fast.

Solid Font Printers

We will begin our discussion of printing alternatives by looking at the kind of printer that most closely resembles the ordinary office typewriter. This is the solid font printer.

Golf Ball Printers

In typewriters, a die in the shape of the character to be printed is struck against a ribbon, which strikes the paper, leaving an impression on the paper. Printers that use fully formed character dies are called **solid font printers.**

The traditional "golf ball" element shown in Figure 7-13 places the character dies on the surface of a ball. Although this allows moderately fast operation, a ball element can only turn so fast, and golf ball printers are limited to about 15 characters per second. This speed, though fine for typewriters, is totally inadequate for office printing.

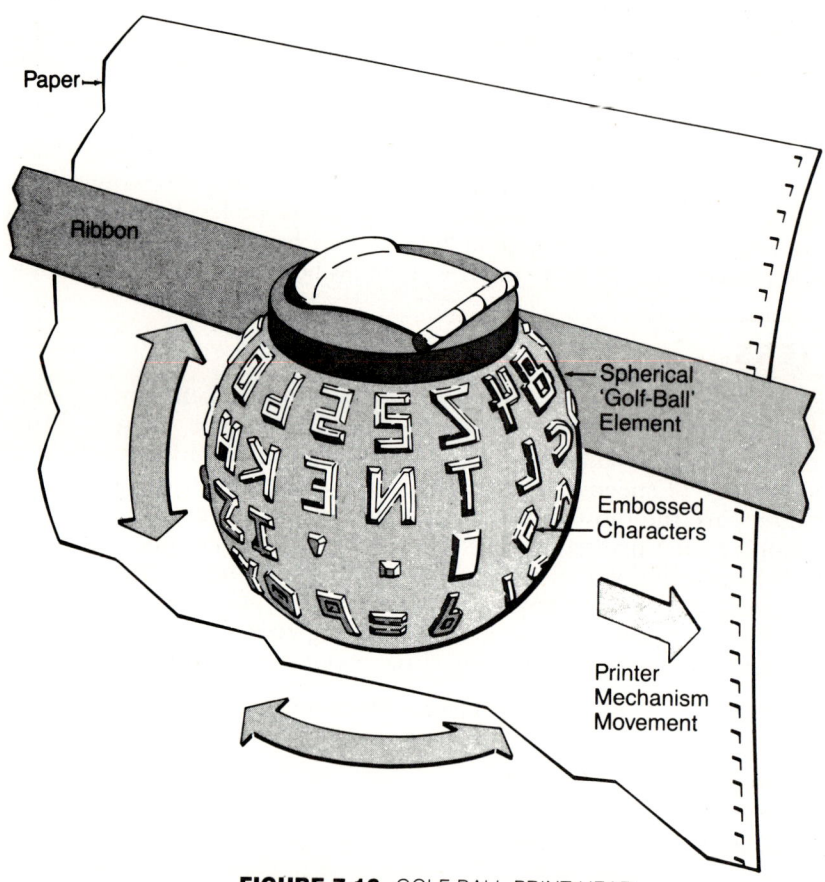

FIGURE 7-13 GOLF BALL PRINT HEAD

Daisywheel Printers

Most solid character computer printers place the dies at the end of short arms arranged around a central hub, as shown in Figure 7-14. These are called **daisywheel** printers because the rods and dies look like petals on a flower. Daisywheel elements can turn, start, and stop much faster than ball elements, giving speeds up to 100 characters per second, although 40 to 50 characters per second is typical of good office daisywheel printers. Even ordinary typewriters are beginning to use daisywheel printing elements.

Letter-Quality Printing

The most important feature of daisywheel printers is that daisies, like all other solid font printers, produce true **letter quality.** This means that the

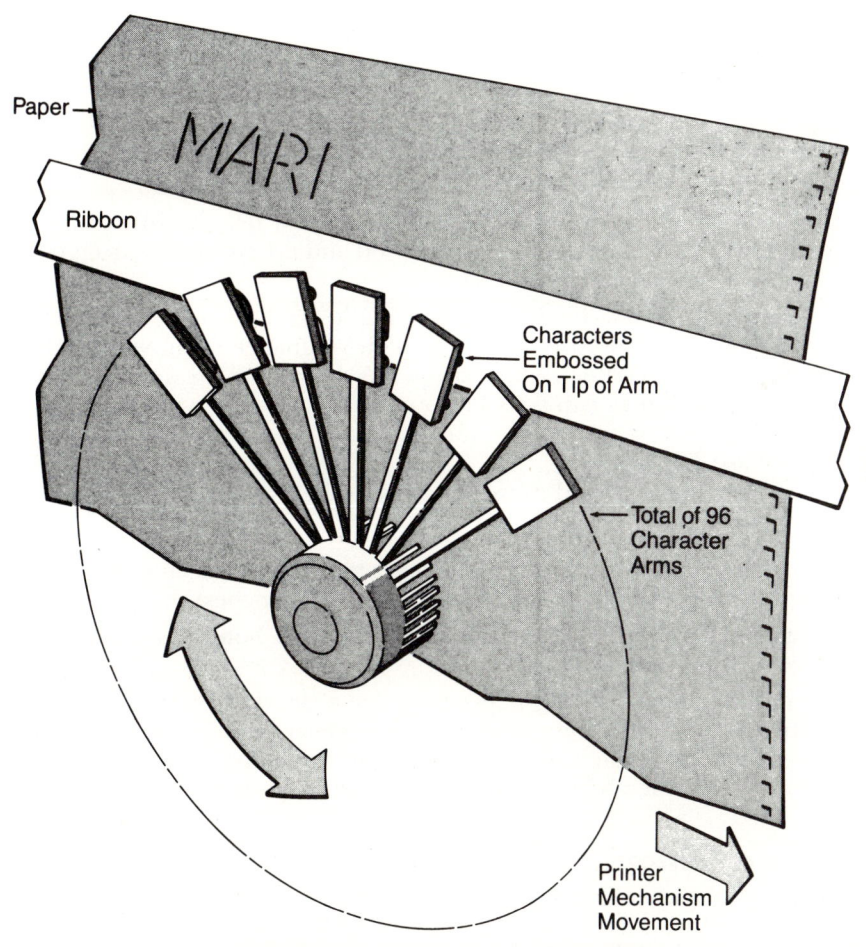

FIGURE 7-14 DAISYWHEEL PRINT HEAD

quality of a daisywheel printer is about the same as that of an ordinary typewriter. This is hardly surprising, inasmuch as the typewriter was the original solid font output device. Letter quality, also called **correspondence quality,** is critical in many applications, particularly when the output must go outside the firm.

An Inability to Handle Graphics

Because daisywheel printers have solid character dies, they cannot print individual dots and so cannot do graphics. Some programs are available to do graphics using the period die, but these tend to wear out the daisywheel element rapidly and to produce graphics very slowly. This absence of graphics is a major problem for many users.

Major Cost–Performance Categories

Daisywheel printers on the market today may be divided into three major cost–performance categories.

Occasional Printers These daisywheel printers are inexpensive, but they print only 10 to 15 characters per second and are good only for people who need to produce a few one- or two-page letters a day. These low-end daisies are fragile. Running one of these slow daisies many hours a day to make up for its slow speed would ruin the machine.

Office Printers These daisies are the ones most used in offices today. They print 30 to 60 characters per second and are sufficiently rugged to be used two or three hours a day.

Production Printers These high-end daisies run 60 to 100 characters per second. They are used mostly in high-volume environments such as word processing centers, where speed is essential and the machine has to be tough enough to run 6 to 12 hours a day.

Other Cost Factors

In addition to speed and durability, three other factors affect the cost of daisywheel printers.

1. A printer with a wide carriage (15 inches to 17 inches) is more expensive than a printer with a narrow carriage (11 to 14 inches).
2. Because daisywheel printers are noisy, a **sound hood** costing $300 or more is often purchased.
3. Because manually feeding paper to printers can destroy the user's productivity, it is also common to purchase **sheet feeders.** Sheet feeders start at $300 and can cost considerably more if they offer special features, such as the ability to feed two different kinds of paper.

Dot Matrix Printers

Although the daisywheel technology is simplest to understand, because it is an extension of ordinary typewriter technologies, it is not the most common printer used with PCs. That distinction falls to dot matrix printers.

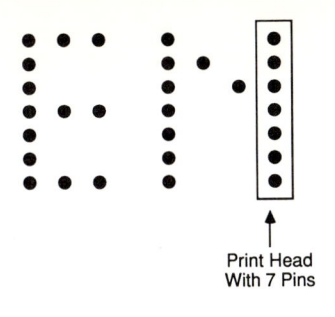

FIGURE 7-15 MECHANICAL DOT MATRIX PRINTING

Dot Matrix Printing Technology

As shown in Figure 7-15 a dot matrix printer has a **print head** with a number of vertical **pins.** As the print head moves across the page, the pins strike against a ribbon, leaving printed dots on the page.

Graphics

Figure 7-15 shows a text character being formed by the print head, but dot matrix printers, unlike daisywheel printers, are not limited to printing characters. The computer software can draw any pattern of dots on the page, and so daisywheel printers can do graphics as easily as text. In fact, they allow text documents with embedded graphics to be created.

Print Quality

The biggest factor in the cost of a dot matrix printer is its resolution, that is, the number of dots it can print horizontally or vertically. In general, dot matrix printers can be classified as **draft-quality** or **near letter-quality (NLQ)** printers.

Draft Printers These machines can only print at a resolution of 50 to 175 dots per inch horizontally or vertically. Their quality is usually acceptable for internal work but is too poor to distribute outside the work group. Their advantage over dot matrix printers with better quality is their much lower cost.

NLQ Printers Near letter-quality printers have a resolution of 200 to 250 dots per inch. Full letter quality requires a resolution of 300 dots per inch, but many NLQ printers are so good that the difference is not worth considering. They are more expensive than draft printers, but this cost penalty is disappearing.

The term "near letter quality" is frequently abused. Many printers with resolutions of only around 100 to 150 dots per inch bill themselves as being near letter quality, but in reality, they do not even approach it.

Denser Print Heads

Near letter-quality printing is achieved in two ways. The first is to increase the number of pins on the pin head. Until recently, most dot matrix printers had **9-pin** print heads, in which there was a single vertical column of nine pins. Figure 7-16 illustrates this arrangement.

- If there is one pass per row of characters, and if there are six lines of text per vertical inch, the vertical resolution is a mere 54 dots per inch (9 pins times 6 lines per inch).
- Some 9-pin dot matrix printers print each line of text in two passes. On the first pass, they print the top half of each character, and on the second pass, they print the bottom half. This doubles the vertical resolution to 108 dots per inch.

Many newer dot matrix printers use **24-pin** print heads, which have 24 pins. These pins are usually arranged in two columns of 12 pins each, as shown in Figure 7-17. The two columns are staggered vertically by a half pin, so that the second column fills in the spaces between pin marks from the first column. If each pass prints one row of text, and if there are six lines of text per vertical inch, the effective density is 144 dots per inch (24 times 6).

If two passes are made to print each row of text, with the first pass printing the top half of each letter and the second pass printing the bottom half, vertical resolution jumps to 288 dots per inch. Some higher density print heads have as few as 18 and as many as 32 pins, but "24-pin" printer has become the generic name for machines with more than 9 pins.

The 24-pin printers have two disadvantages, the first and most obvious one being that they cost more than 9-pin printers. This drawback will fade over time. The second problem is that they are much noisier than 9-pin printers. With twice as many pins hitting the paper each second, they, of course, make twice as much noise. Many offices that were able to get by without a sound hood when 9-pin printers were used have found that a sound hood is indispensable with 24-pin printers.

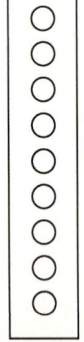

FIGURE 7-16 PRINT HEADS WITH 9 PINS AND 24 PINS

9-Pin Print Head (In-Line)

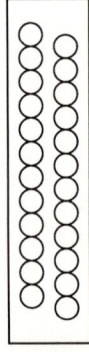

24-Pin Print Head (Staggered)

Multiple Pass Printing

A second way to increase printing quality has long been used by 9-pin printers and is still being used by 24-pin printers. This is to make multiple passes along each line of text, as shown in Figure 7-17. The first pass produces an image in normal resolution. The second pass is made with a slight offset—vertically or horizontally—effectively doubling the vertical or horizontal resolution. Additional passes can be used to improve resolution further. If the first pass was used to double horizontal resolution, the second pass is used to increase vertical resolution, and vice versa.

Near letter-quality printers have several modes. The fastest mode uses a single pass to print very quickly with draft quality, and the slowest mode uses multiple passes to print slowly but very well. Most near letter-quality printers have three to five modes with different speeds and quality, depending on the nature of the work to be done.

Limits on Printing Quality

Although increasing the number of pins and making multiple passes can greatly improve quality, three factors work against dot matrix printers when they attempt to produce full letter quality.

1. It is difficult to get the print head aligned perfectly, so that the dot spacing is not fully uniform. This decreases quality. In multiple pass mode, this imprecision is amplified by imprecision in overlapping the dots on separate passes.
2. The dots are large. Although the rated resolution of NLQ printers often exceeds 350 dots per inch, their large dots reduce the effective resolution to well under 300 dots per inch. In contrast, the page printers discussed later in this chapter have very small dots, giving an effective resolution close to their rated resolution.
3. Most dot matrix printers use cloth ribbons instead of the one-time carbon ribbons found on typewriters. As a result, even the best dot matrix printers fall a step below full letter quality.

The first manifestation of these differences from true letter quality is the graininess in the printed image. Even if the individual dots are not separable by the viewer's eye, it is clear that a dotting process was used to create individ-

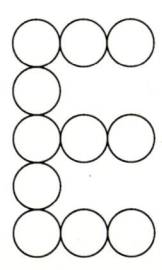

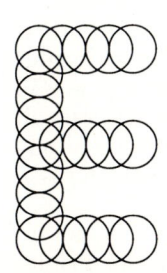

Single Pass   Multiple Passes

FIGURE 7-17 DOT MATRIX PRINTING WITH MULTIPLE PASSES

ual letters. When letters are rounded, for example, there are "jaggies" along the curves.

The second way the difference from true letter quality is felt is in font design. Typewriter and daisywheel fonts use many rounded surfaces because a curved die is as easy to produce as a die with straight lines. NLQ dot matrix fonts, however, tend to avoid curves as much as possible, in order to reduce the incidence of "jaggies." As a result, many NLQ fonts are less pleasing to the eye than typewriter fonts.

Other Dot Matrix Technologies

Although **mechanical dot matrix printers,** which have moving rods in their print heads, are the most popular form of dot matrix printers, mechanical printing is not the only dot matrix printing technology on the market. There are also ink jet printers and thermal printers.

Ink jet printers **Ink jet printers** spray droplets of ink directly at the paper. Ink jet printers equal mechanical dot matrix printers in speed, cost, graphics capability, and, unfortunately, quality. They are much quieter, however, and so no sound hood is needed.

Because of their quiet operation, ink jet printers have become very common for low-end printing needs. They have not been successful so far, however, in the near letter-quality market, which is the vanguard of dot matrix printing today. As a result, ink jet printing remains a secondary technology whose future is uncertain.

Thermal printers **Thermal printers,** like mechanical dot matrix printers, have a series of pins on their print heads. But instead of striking a ribbon into the paper to make impressions, thermal printers use heat. Early thermal printers produced images by burning spots onto special paper—a process that was messy, uneconomical, and lacking in print quality. Newer thermal printers use an entirely different approach. They melt ink off the ribbon, and this melted ink sticks to the paper behind it. This method produces NLQ printing that is superior to the quality of most mechanical NLQ printers. The printing speed of these machines is slow. They are aimed more at daisywheel printers than at mechanical dot matrix printers.

Cost Factors

Three factors dominate the costs of dot matrix printers: speed, printing quality, and use of a sound hood if one is needed. Several other factors must also be considered when comparing the prices of comparable machines.

The first of these is paper handling. Printers that can handle wider paper are more expensive than those handling 8.5 inch wide paper. In addition, tractor feeders for paper with sprocket holes along the sides are included in the prices of some systems but are extra-cost options in others. For low-end dot matrix printers, the price of a tractor feeder is a significant fraction of the total price.

The second factor affecting cost is emulation. Most dot matrix printers can emulate the traditional IBM Graphics Printer, an Epson MX-80 sold under the IBM name. This allows them to work with programs designed for the emulated printer. Some printers can emulate a wide range of other printers, and in some cases, emulation is done by adding extra-cost modules to the printer. If a printer will need to emulate a particular device, its ability to do so must be understood. The extra cost of this emulation, if any, must be factored into the purchase equation.

Page Printers

Page Printer Technology

Page printers are modified copiers. As shown in Figure 7-18, a copier has a light source. This used to be a fluorescent light, but today it is usually a laser or light-emitting diode (LED) array. This light source illuminates the document. Some of the reflected light from the document strikes the printing drum, creating an electrostatic image that is transferred to a sheet of paper.

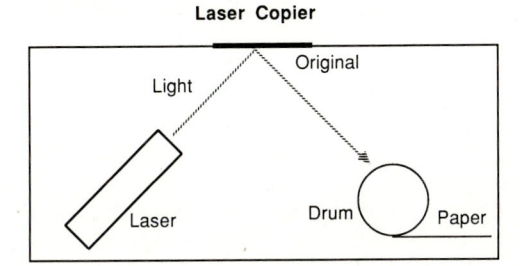

Page printers use the same basic technology, but, as shown in Figure 7-18, they aim their light source directly at the drum in order to form the electrostatic image directly. Because lasers and other new light sources can be aimed very accurately, very high resolution is possible.

Page printers are often called **laser printers** because most use lasers as their light sources. But **light-emitting diodes (LED)** and other light sources are likely to become increasingly popular. It therefore seems best not to use "laser printer" as a generic name for these machines.

Performance

Daisywheel printers have excellent quality but are slow and cannot do graphics. Dot matrix printers are fast and can do graphics, but their quality is not as good as that of a typewriter. Page printers offer the advantages of both.

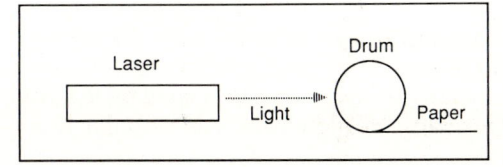

FIGURE 7-18 LASER COPIERS AND PAGE PRINTERS

- They can produce eight or more pages a minute.
- They can produce high-resolution graphics.
- They produce letter-quality text at 300 dots per inch and can produce text with multiple type fonts and sizes. Page printers produce output that looks far more like the output of a professional print shop than the output of a typewriter.
- They are as quiet as copiers.

Page printers fall into three major categories, based on printing speed.

1. Low-speed page printers produce 8 to 15 pages per minute when double-spaced text is being printed. They have a duty cycle of only about 3000 pages per month which comes to only 150 page per day. Running a low-speed page printer much beyond its rated capacity can permanently impair its printing quality. These are the most common page printers used in offices.
2. Medium-speed page printers produce 20 to 50 pages per minute and have duty cycles of 10,000 pages per month or more. These machines are beginning to move into individual offices, but they are still too expensive for most departments.
3. High-speed units produce 70 or more pages per minute and have the heavy duty cycles needed in the central printing operations where most are used.

Low-Speed Units

Because low-speed units are the most common page printers in offices today, we will divide them into finer categories.

Text plus page printers The least expensive page printers are **text plus** units that print text better than daisywheels but do little if any graphics. The original Hewlett-Packard Laserjet was a text plus page printer. Text plus units can print proportionally spaced fonts in such printshop type faces as Times Roman and Helvetica, so their output looks better than that of a daisywheel printer. They also print much faster than daisywheel printers and operate silently. Best of all, they are only a little more expensive than fast daisywheel printers with sheet feeders and sound hoods.

These units normally come with a few built in text fonts, plus the ability to add a few more, but they cannot be loaded with a wide range of fonts, because they lack the memory to store the fonts. This lack of memory also prevents them from printing graphics images well. A full page graphics image at 300 pixels per inch requires a megabyte of storage, and text plus units have far less than this. While some can produce partial page graphics at low resolutions, this is not satisfactory for most users of graphics applications.

Pixel graphics page printers **Pixel graphics** page printers have the memory that text plus units lack. This allows them to full page graphics at 300 pixels per inch. It also allows them to store many fonts, so that users will have a wide range of printing styles and character sizes. Hewlett-Packards' popular Laserjet Plus is a pixel graphics printer.

Pixel graphics printers cost a few hundred dollars more than text plus units, but are almost mandatory in today's increasingly graphics-oriented world. Many buyers of text plus printers find themselves spending several more hundred dollars in a few months to add the memory needed for graphics. They spend another few hundred dollars on extra fonts. In fact, they often spend more than they would have had they bought a pixel graphics printer in the first place.

Intelligent page printers Object graphics programs store their data as a set of objects to be painted on the screen or to be printed. With simple pixel graphics page printers, these programs must convert the object data into a pixel map. The PC is tied up during this conversion process. Then, the PC must download this 1 MB pixel map down to the page printer. Again, the PC is tied up, since most interfaces run at only a few tens of kilobits per second.

For simple graphics images with only a few objects, the delays are not too bad. But for images with many objects, including desktop publishing pages, engineering drawings, or even complex hand-drawn art, the delays caused by converting the object data into a pixel map and transmitting the pixel map to the printer can run to several minutes per page.

For heavy object graphics applications, users need **intelligent** page printers that can work directly with object graphics data. The PC does not have to convert the image into a pixel map, then transmit the dense pixel map to the printer. It merely transmits the object graphics data to the printer and lets the printer do the rest. This way, there is no conversion time, and object graphics data take only a fraction of the transmission time of the converted bit map. Apple's LaserWriter and LaserWriter Plus are intelligent page printers.

Intelligent page printers have roughly the processing power of a personal computer, so they cost $1000 to $2000 more than pixel graphics page printers. But these costs are falling, and for heavy graphics use, intelligent page printers are the only way to avoid massive delays in printing and PC tie-ups. Adding intelligence to a pixel graphics printer may be possible, but it usually costs a good deal more than it would cost to buy an intelligent version of the printer in the first place.

The dominant printer format for intelligent page printers is the PostScript page description language developed by Adobe. Much of the high cost of intelligent printers is due to royalties paid to Adobe. Several companies are now trying to clone PostScript, without using Adobe's implementation code. The competition that results is likely to press down the cost of PostScript boards.

A major advantage of PostScript is that output formatted for this page description language can also be sent to many photocomposition machines with resolutions of 1000 pixels per inch or more, giving true typeset quality. When these units are used, the page printer itself becomes a draft printer.

In the Macintosh world, a few intelligent page printers are starting to work with Macintosh's native screen painting routines, the QuickDraw ROM service programs discussed earlier in this chapter. They either support QuickDraw instead of PostScript or in addition to PostScript. QuickDraw support allows programs that use QuickDraw but not PostScript to print much more rapidly.

Features

All page printers of the same general type are not created equal. After selecting a general category of machines, a user must look at the specific features these units offer.

Print quality The most important feature is image quality. Most page printers produce output at 300 pixel per inch (ppi), but a growing number offer 400 ppi or 600 ppi resolution. For fine detail, higher resolution produces clearer images with less jaggedness in tight curves.

But even printers with the same nominal resolution may vary considerably in print quality. It is important to look at actual output, paying particular attention to the presence of stray dots of toner and seeing if black areas are really black or merely dark gray.

Speed Most office page printers are rated at about 6 pages of double-spaced text per minute, but some are rated at only 4 or 5, while others are rated at 8 to 10. Although vendor ratings are often inaccurate, real speed differences do exist, and users should test printers carefully with representative mixes of printing jobs. First, single-spaced and double-spaced text with a number of font changes should be printed and timed. Second, pixel graphics output should be printed and timed. Third, if the page printer is intelligent, representative pages should be output in PostScript or whatever format the intelligent printer supports.

Interfaces Speed is at least somewhat dependent on the type of interface used to connect the PC to the page printer. Early page printers used IBM's serial adapter discussed earlier in this chapter. This interface, usually running at 9600 bits per second, is barely adequate for moving text. For pixel graphics at 1 MB per page, transmission time would be more than 800 seconds. As a result, most page printers now support IBM parallel interfaces as well as serial interfaces. Users should be sure to use the faster parallel interface, and even the parallel interface is slow for transmitting 300 ppi graphics.

Some page printers now use custom-designed adapter boards that can transmit at the same speeds that video adapters use to refresh display screens. These printers are very fast, but there are no standards for video-speed adapter boards, and the costs of these units are high.

Fonts As discussed in Chapter 11, a font is a group of characters with the same design. The same design means having the same size, the same type face (such as Times Roman or Helvetica), and the same emphasis (such as normal, italic, boldface, underlined). Ideally, a page printer should offer many fonts. Unfortunately, most text plus printers support only a few and lack the memory to hold more. Pixel graphics printers and intelligent printers usually support a fair number of fonts.

All page printers come with a few **internal fonts** built into ROM and always available. To these can be added more fonts. One way to add fonts is to buy a ROM font cartridge that plugs into the front of the printer. These cartridges, however, only have a few fonts. Switching to a different set of fonts requires swapping font cartridges, and constant swapping is a poor idea, since the life spans of these cartridges are rated in terms of numbers of insertions.

A second way to add fonts is to download fonts from the PC's disk drives when the printer is initialized. This lengthens the time to initialize the printer, but the only limit on the number of fonts that can be supported is the printer's memory. A good mix of fonts will cost several hundred dollars in either cartridge or downloadable form.

Endurance As noted earlier, most page printers for offices are limited to about 150 pages per day. They are essentially low-volume copiers, and pushing them beyond their limit can permanently damage their printing quality. A few devices with greater endurance are beginning to reach the market. They can produce almost 1000 pages a day, but their price tags are double or triple that of standard page printers at the time of this writing. They are desirable primarily where PC networking is being done and where two or even three page printers are on the network.

Paper handling Most page printers are designed to handle 8½ in. by 11 in. paper or the similar A4 page size used in many other parts of the world. A few can handle paper that is slightly longer, say 14 in. Only a few can handle larger paper sizes.

Because page printers are very fast, there must be adequate paper bins, or the operator will have to tend the machine constantly while it is printing. High-capacity paper bins add significantly to the cost of a system and are only available on some printers.

Emulation Most page printers can emulate popular dot matrix printers and daisywheel printers. This allows them to be used by programs that lack specific printer drivers for these page printers. Some emulate only a few traditional printers, making them dangerous choices. Others emulate many. In all cases, it is important to test the quality of the particular emulations needed by an organization.

Because of the Hewlett-Packard laserjet family's popularity, many page printers offer Laserjet emulation. Unfortunately, many emulate only the very limited original Laserjet, not later siblings like the Laserjet Plus, which have much more capability. In addition, the quality of emulation is uneven from printer to printer. Finally, some printers do not emulate Hewlett-Packard's fonts, substituting their own fonts, which will give different results when printing.

Color A number of page printer vendors are now testing color versions of their machines. Although the first color models are likely to be out before this book is published, their costs are expected to be beyond the reach of most departments in the foreseeable future.

Plotters

For applications that require high-quality graphics output, users often turn to **plotters.** These devices draw with pens. On **flat bed plotters,** a robot arm moves the pen around on the paper, and on **moving bed plotters,** the paper is moved under a stationary pen.

When ultrahigh-quality charts are to be produced, plotters are almost always used.

- Pen drawing gives perfect straight lines, and many plotters have built-in capabilities to draw perfect circles or arcs of circles.
- Text also looks good on a plotter, although boldness and fancy fonts are not likely to be available or to look good if they are available.
- Plotters use several pens in order to draw multicolor output.

The price of a plotter depends heavily on its size. There are five popular sizes for office plotters.

1. A plotters can use paper up to 8.5 by 11 inches.
2. B plotters can use paper up to 11 by 17 inches.
3. C plotters can use paper up to 17 by 22 inches.
4. D plotters can use paper up to 24 by 36 inches.
5. E plotters can use paper up to 36 by 48 inches.

For most offices, the B size plotter is the best option. Images are seldom more than 11 by 17 inches, but they are occasionally larger than 8.5 by 11 inches. C, D, and E plotters are normally used in drafting offices and other places where engineering work is done.

Other factors that affect the cost of a plotter are speed, accuracy, types of pens that can be used, number of pens that can be used, and ability to emulate other popular plotters. Most plotters use fiber-tip pens, which give good quality and high speeds. Liquid ink pens offer the best quality, but they tend to be difficult to use; disposable liquid ink pens have removed some, but not all, of these use problems. Some plotters offer a choice of several types of pens.

Another consideration is how the plotter will work with the user's computer and software. For example, does a plotter work with a standard PC serial or parallel interface, or does it require a special-purpose interface that is not ordinarily found on a PC, for example, the IEEE GPIB electrical interface or the HPIB electrical interface created by Hewlett-Packard? Does it emulate the Hewlett-Packard Graphics Language, which is becoming a de facto standard for plotters, and does it emulate other graphics languages or popular plotters?

Color

Until recently, color output was not very important, and the only major printing technology for producing color was the multipen plotter. In the future, however, color output is likely to become popular.

Color is normally used by printing with the three primary colors for pigments, namely, yellow, magenta, and cyan. Combining two of these colors will produce the three secondary colors—green, orange, and purple. Leaving a spot on a piece of paper blank will produce white. More complex mixing will eventually produce a broad spectrum of colors, but for now, most color printers are limited to the three primary colors, three secondary colors, white, and sometimes black.

The biggest mechanical problem in color printers is getting precise overlap when colors are laid down. Normally, the three primary colors are laid down in three passes along a line or over an entire page. Unless paper handling is nearly perfect, there will be blurred rainbows around each point. To reduce overlap problems, many of today's color printers are limited to 200 pixels per inch or less. This resolution limitation will eventually be overcome.

Another problem has been color stability. Many systems produce bright colors, but these colors fade or change over time. When evaluating color printers, it is a good idea to take samples and let these sit for several weeks or even longer.

The most promising technology for color printing today is thermal transfer printing. As discussed earlier, thermal transfer printing melts ink off the ribbon and onto the paper. For color, multiple ribbons or a three-part ribbon with yellow, magenta, and cyan stripes must be used. Other color printers use mechanical dot matrix print heads with multipart ribbons, ink jet print heads that spray three colors of ink, and page printers with interchangeable ink drums or multiple ink drums. In general, low-quality color costs only a little more than monochrome printing for any given technology, and the results can be sufficiently impressive to overcome low resolution and other printing limitations.

On the negative side, color printing is much slower than monochrome printing, and relatively few firms have color copiers or are willing to pay for the widespread distribution of color copies. Thus, even if the cost of initial production is attractive, the time spent printing and the difficulty of making copies should cause users to think carefully before committing themselves to color.

For 35 mm slides, which are used in many meetings, special cameras allow a simpler approach to color. These cameras snap over a display screen and take pictures directly off the screen. This approach works well, but several problems can arise. First, there is often some distortion around the edges of the slide. Second, screen resolutions are sometimes marginal to begin with. Third, as with all cameras, user skill is important in picture taking.

Market Dynamics

Dot matrix printers have always dominated the market for PC printers. Their wide range of costs and capabilities should allow them to maintain this position through the foreseeable future.

Daisywheel printers are likely to fade somewhat in prominence. Daisies are being squeezed from both above and below. When printing quality is important, many users are already selecting page printers, and as page printer prices fall rapidly in the years ahead, the choice of page printers over daisies will be made more often. At the lower end, dot matrix printers will continue to offer speed, price, and graphics, while closing in ever more on daisywheel quality.

These market dynamics are reflected in International Data Corporation's forecasts for the installed base of PC printers in business from 1985 to 1990. (1)

- In 1985, mechanical dot matrix printers made up 74 percent of the installed base. In 1990, their share of the installed base will be virtually the same, 72 percent.
- Between 1985 and 1990, however, the daisywheel printer's share of the installed base is expected to fall from 19 percent to 14 percent. Its share of sales will fall even more steeply.
- Taking up the slack will be new printing technologies, particularly page printers, which will jump from 1 percent to 4 percent, thermal printers (including those like IBM's), which are forecast to grow from 3 percent to 5 percent, and ink jet printers, which are also forecast to grow from 3 percent of the installed base to 5 percent.

Although the number of page printers will remain comparatively small, their high unit cost will give them a disproportionate percentage of sales revenues. In terms of total spending, page printers will give daisywheel printers a good run for the second spot, particularly if improved technology further cuts into the remaining advantages of daisywheel printing technology.

All of these printers will share a much larger installed base in 1990 than they did in 1985. (1) In 1985, the installed base was 6.8 million printers in the United States. For 1990, International Data Corporation projects it to rise to 20.9 million. This is more than a threefold jump-a compound annual rate of growth of 25 percent.

This growth will be driven at least partly by falling costs. International Data Corporation (IDC), for example, has forecast that the price of low-end dot matrix printers with speeds of under 100 characters per second (cps) will fall from $310 in 1985 to only $169 in 1990. (2) In this same forecast, IDC projected that dot matrix printers running at 300 cpm or higher will fall from $2,288 in 1985 to only $1,137 in 1990. Heavy price declines will also occur in other printing technologies, especially among page printers.

INPUT DEVICES

Keyboards

The most common input device for users is the keyboard. The standard U.S. typewriter layout is called QWERTY because the first six letters on the top alphabetic row are Q-W-E-R-T-Y. This keyboard layout was conceived in the 1860s as a way to prevent jams on primitive early typewriters by **deliberately slowing the user.** To prevent jams, the most common letters were scattered around the keyboard. (As a side note, QWERTY was also set up so that "typewriter" could be typed by a salesman using just the top row of keys.) So today we are stuck with a keyboard standard that is very inefficient. Although you can buy optional keyboards with the more efficient ANSI standard Dvorak layout on many PCs, few people are willing to learn how to type all over.

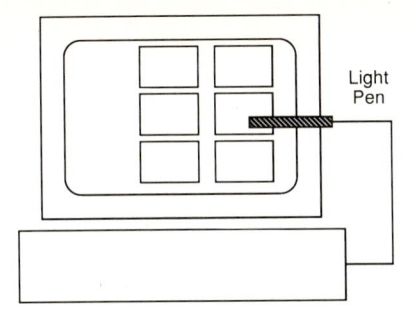

FIGURE 7-19 LIGHT PEN

Although the user has little choice over the arrangement of keys in most instances, the tactile feel of the keyboard is extremely important, especially for word processing work. In addition, for the IBM PC, a number of vendors offer add-on keyboards that separate the number pad and cursor keys or that are specially set up for specific programs such as word processing programs.

Pointing Devices

Instead of typing, it would be nice to be able just to point to what you want on the display screen. A number of pointing devices exist, and more and more software is being written to use them.

Light Pens

The oldest point device is a **light pen,** shown in Figure 7-19. The "pen" is actually an input device. The computer compares the time that light comes into the pen from the screen with the position of the scanning beam at that moment. This tells the computer where the light pen is pointing.

Touch Screens

The **touch screen** does away with the light pen, letting users touch the screen with their fingers (see Figure 7-20). A touch screen is very natural to use, but it does have two disadvantages. First, most touch screens do not allow the user to point to individual characters, but only to a "block" one or two characters on a side. This is not acceptable for many applications. Second, touching the screen creates smudge marks that reduce legibility. This can lead to eyestrain.

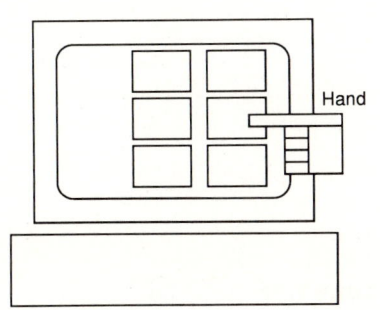

FIGURE 7-20 TOUCH SCREEN

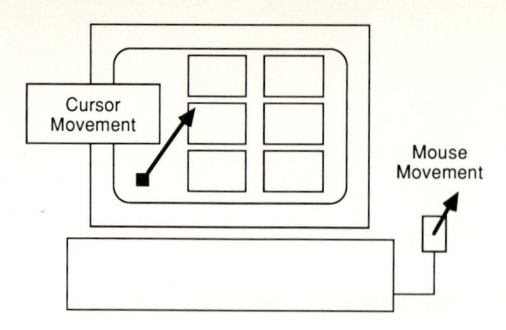

FIGURE 7-21 MOUSE

Mice

For constant pointing work, a device called a **mouse** seems to be the least tiring and most precise. As shown in Figure 7-21, when the mouse moves along on a table, the cursor on the screen moves accordingly. After a little practice, users have no trouble pointing to a single character all the way across the screen from the original cursor location. Because a quarter of all word processing keystrokes are cursor movements, it is hardly surprising that the mouse is becoming popular.

The mouse was popularized by the Apple Macintosh, and many people think it is a new invention. In reality, it was invented in 1962 by Dr. Douglas Engelbart at Stanford Research Institute. His programmers carried this idea with them when they moved to the Xerox Palo Alto Research Center (PARC), and, in turn, Xerox PARC "alumni" carried the mouse with them to Apple.

Input Tablet

Another pointing device is the **input tablet,** a rectangular surface with the same basic shape as the screen. As shown in Figure 7-22, the user can draw on this tablet, sometimes with fingers, sometimes with a special stylus, and the cursor moves accordingly on the screen.

Input tablets are excellent for freehand drawing. Most people find them much easier to draw with than a mouse. In addition, if a drawing is placed over the tablet, the user can trace it with a stylus.

Most tablets are only the size of a sheet of writing paper, but a few are much larger. Engineers often work with input tablets called **digitizers** that are

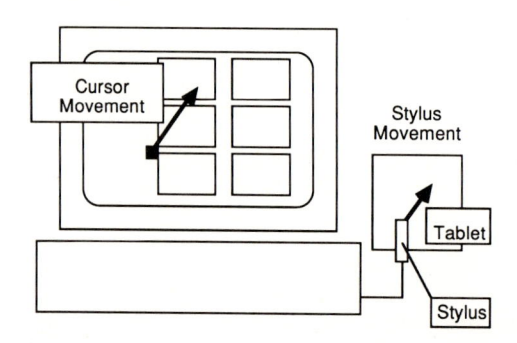

FIGURE 7-22 INPUT TABLET

the sizes of large tables. With high-precision pointing devices, the engineer can point to within a tenth of an inch. This allows large drawings to be entered into the computer (digitized).

While input tablets are much better than the mouse for free-hand drawing, they are harder to use to point to specific information on the screen—say to place the cursor between two characters in a sentence. The mouse and input tablet are complementary, not competitive.

Scanners

It would be nice to hand the computer a printed page and have it "read" the page into its memory, instead of having to retype text and redraw pictures. In fact, there are devices called **scanners** that can do this. There are two major categories of scanners: text scanners and graphics scanners. We are also beginning to see hybrid scanners that can combine text and graphics scanning, even on a single page.

Text Scanners

If a document consists entirely of text, it can be read into a computer through a text scanner. Text scanners use **optical character recognition (OCR)** technology. When a page is placed in a text scanner, the machine scans the document from left to right, top to bottom. Whenever it encounters characters, it compares them to known patterns. If it finds a match, it enters the ASCII code for that character into the input file. If it cannot find a match, it places a special symbol in that character's position. One or two dozen errors per page is typical. Input is relatively fast, taking three to five minutes per page.

After a document is scanned, the user goes over the file, filling in missing characters from context, by using a spelling checker or by looking at the original. Often, all three techniques are used, with spell checking catching most errors. Most of the errors are removed by reading the word in context, and the few remaining ones are cleared up by reading the original.

When OCR was first created, it had many disadvantages. Only special fonts could be read in, and even then, there were many errors to correct. Error correction after the initial reading sometimes took as long as typing the document through the keyboard would have taken. Today's text scanners, however, can read a variety of type fonts, have a low error rate, are compact in size, and are not prohibitively expensive. Unfortunately, many of these features are only available on text scanners costing over $10,000. PC units still have some limitations on the kinds of fonts they can handle. (For example, many units read standard typewriter fonts such as Courier but cannot read dot matrix fonts.)

Pattern recognition techniques that come from artificial intelligence are making text scanners much more flexible. Previously, a sample of the font containing standardized text had to be typed and then scanned, in order to train the text scanner. Now, most high-end machines need no pretraining, and many can even handle proportionally spaced and typeset documents. These capabilities will soon be common on PC units.

Most units also insert tabs in white spaces and put carriage returns at the ends of lines only where they seem to be needed. This allows word processors to handle their input easily. For highly formatted documents, the formatting abilities of current text scanners are still too rudimentary.

Graphics Scanners

Like text scanners, graphics scanners read a page as a series of scan lines, from left to right, top to bottom. They convert the pattern of light and dark images into pixel codes and store them in a computer file. Graphics Scanners work much as a facsimile device works; in fact, many graphics scanners use the Group 3 or Group 4 facsimile standards for representing data (see Chapter 17).

The data representation approach must do a great deal of compression. A full page of text scanned at 300 pixels per inch horizontally and vertically would take a full megabyte to store without data compression. Data compression decreases the amount of storage needed by as much as 75 percent, but even this requires as much as 12 KB per stored page, and data compression also requires extensive processing.

One of the most innovative graphics scanners is ThunderScan from Thunderware. This product has a read mechanism that takes the place of the print head in an Apple Imagewriter printer. The page to be scanned is placed in the printer, and the ThunderScan software running on a Macintosh runs the read head over its surface as if it were printing instead of reading. The pattern of light and dark is then digitized into the popular MacPaint format.

Most graphics scanners produce files that can be manipulated directly by graphics programs or that can be converted into the file formats of popular graphics programs. This allows the user to clean up the graphics file. (Shades of gray are often mishandled.) It also allows images to be input into the computer, modified, and then placed into other graphics images or combined with text. Because displays have comparatively low resolution (about 70 pixels per inch, instead of the 300 or so ppi of scanned image), editing images on screen can be difficult and can produce some damage.

Hybrid Scanners

Hybrid scanners combine text and graphics scanning. In general, these scanners require the page to be input twice—once for text and the second time for graphics images. In the near future, these hybrid scanners will probably dominate the market because of their versatility.

Hybrid scanners cost about $3000 in 1986. This cost usually came in the form of three separately priced components—the hardware of the scanning unit, an adapter expansion board, and software to run on the computer. Many scanners with base prices of well under $3000 in 1986 really came close to $3000 when all costs were included. A paper feeder is a worthwhile addition if it is not included in the base price; not all units have paper feeders, however. Prices are expected to fall very rapidly, and capabilities to advance very rapidly, so the future of hybrid scanners seems very bright.

Voice Technology

Personal computers are now capable of both voice output and voice input. Because voice output is easier and more mature, we will begin with output.

Voice Output

Voice output is called **speech synthesis.** Four major technologies are used in speech synthesis.

Message Recording The simplest approach is to record complete messages and then play them back. This is useful only if there is a limited number of possible messages.

Phoneme Generation Human speech consists of sound units called phonemes. Phoneme generation units play back appropriate combinations of phonemes. Speech quality is poor, but the low cost of this approach makes it widely used.

Predictive Coding Predictive coding is generally used to encode words. As each word is spoken, it is sampled every few milliseconds. The sample is then stored, taking up much less room than a full recording. A predictive coding algorithm (usually linear predictive coding) then creates the full word from the stored pattern. This technique produces good quality and is becoming popular despite its heavy processing needs compared to phoneme generation.

Waveform Coding Waveform coding uses techniques that are more complex than predictive coding to store information according to a mathematical model of speech. The results are lifelike speech, but the processing requirements are still beyond those of personal computers.

Speech synthesis can be used to allow programs to give verbal warnings and other information to users, but the most exciting use of speech synthesis is to convert computer text from a word processor into spoken English. Although this is being done mostly for the blind, it will have broad use in the future. Current systems do an amazingly good job most of the time, although they stumble over many phrases, especially foreign phrases. (A demonstration in Hawaii using a local telephone directory produced more amusement than conviction.)

Voice is not the only kind of sound produced by computers. Even early computers could produce music poorly. Newer units are beginning to use the **musical instrument digital interface (MIDI)** standard, whose bandwidth is an ample 31,250 bits per second. Although MIDI is used mostly on home computers, it provides a way to bring high-quality sound of all types to office computers.

Voice Input

Voice input is usually called **speech recognition.** In speech recognition, systems are classified along two dimensions.

- **Discrete speech** units require the speaker to pause after each word, whereas **continuous speech** units allow the speaker to talk normally.
- **Speaker-dependent** units require the unit to be "trained" to understand individual users. Training involves repeating a standard list of words.
- **Speaker independent** units can work with most users without prior training.

Most units on the market are discrete, speaker-dependent units. This limits their usefulness but allows voice recognition to be done with good accuracy over low-cost devices.

One important product dimension is the size of the unit's vocabulary. Most units can understand only about a hundred words, but the most expensive devices can understand about a thousand, and even moderate-cost units will soon have such vocabularies. Although a large vocabulary is generally good, systems with very large vocabularies often have to restrict users to perfectly discontinuous speech instead of the semicontinuous speech support on some units with smaller vocabularies. The number of errors tends to go up as the number of words in the vocabulary increases. Today, reasonably priced units are good mainly for such functions as giving commands in DOS or some other limited system, but as vocabularies improve, the number of applications using voice recognition should increase considerably.

Error rates are often quoted, but these should be taken with more than one grain of salt. Most quoted error rates are based on tests in perfectly quiet rooms and with trained, carefully selected speakers.

Speech recognition is sometimes confused with natural language input because the two are linked in many science fiction movies. They are entirely different, however. Speech recognition means that the system can understand individual spoken words. In contrast, natural language input means that the system also understands syntax and semantics. Although a speech recognition typewriter will allow people to "type" individual words, it will not allow the system to understand natural language commands.

CONCLUSION

The number of hardware options on personal computers is already mind-numbing. Yet the number of options in each category is growing rapidly, and major new categories of hardware options are appearing each year. The information center has no choice but to standardize options selectively. Each option to be standardized must be tested carefully for its interactions with other hardware and software options.

The best approach for the future is likely to be the development of "gamma test sites" within the company. In product development, alpha testing is done on the vendor's premises with prerelease products, whereas beta testing is done on a customer's premises, again with prerelease products. In gamma testing, a *released* product would be tested in the user's organization to understand its benefits, real costs, and problems. The information center's main role in product selection over the long term may well be to coordinate gamma testing and to ensure that zealous test groups that experience only one product do not push inappropriate standards on the corporation.

REVIEW QUESTIONS

1. Why does a PC bus need so many lines? Be specific about the roles various groups of bus lines perform.

2. What are the main dimensions along which different Intel microprocessors differ? What dimensions have increased the most over time? The least?

3. Why were early PCs limited to 64 KB and then 1 MB of internal memory?

4. Somebody says they want to add RAM to their system. What would you tell them? In your discussion, warn them about purchase mistakes they might make.

5. What are the major types of PC expansion boards?

6. Why are parallel and serial adapters important? What different roles do they play? Now that serial adapters are used by many peripherals, what problems do IBM PC users face? How do IBM and Macintosh serial and parallel adapters differ?

7. Why are some adapters so much more expensive than others?

8. What are your options for accelerating the speed at which your computer can process your data?

9. What are the power problems facing PC users? Which of these problems are inexpensive to avoid?

10. Why are there three tiers of memory, instead of just two?

11. Describe the classical way of laying out information on a floppy disk. How are things different for hard disks? For Macintosh disks? For optical disks? What problems does the optical disk recording format create?

12. What advantages do 3.5 inch diameter floppy disks have over 5.25 inch floppy disks?

13. What are the main reasons for using hard disks instead of floppy disks?

14. What are a hard disk user's main backup options? Which do you think is best? Distinguish between image and file-by-file backup, including their relative advantages and disadvantages. Which do you think is best?

15. What are the advantages of today's Bernoulli drives and optical disk drives? The disadvantages?

16. What are pixels? How is text created using pixel technology? Graphics images? What is resolution?

17. Explain what must be done to add gray scale or color to simple monochrome graphics. Why are these additions expensive?

18. Compare the relative advantages of pixel and object graphics. Under what conditions is each best?

19. Why do you think that graphics will be increasingly used in the future?

20. What are the major graphics standards and how do they relate to one another? Which are de facto standards, as opposed to official standards? Why are page description languages important, and why will they be difficult to standardize? Are these standards more oriented toward pixel or object graphics?

21. Is the distinction between text and graphics display systems in the display itself or in the adapter? Compare the strengths and weaknesses of IBM's line of display systems (including both the display and the adapter). Do the same for Macintosh display systems. What advantages do third-party display systems have?

22. What are the main problems today with flat panel displays? Full-page display? What tradeoffs do engineers have to make when designing flat panel displays?
23. Explain why solid font printers give very good quality, and assess the likelihood that they will disappear by the early 1990s.
24. What advantages do dot matrix printers have over daisywheel printers? What is their main disadvantage, and what steps are being taken to overcome it? Why are these steps likely to take dot matrix printing only so far? Why are there "lies, damn lies, and near letter-quality printing?"
25. What are the main technologies for doing dot matrix printing? What advantages does each have?
26. Some page printers are inexpensive, and others quite expensive. Explain what paying more can give an office and what disappointments may come from buying the lowest cost page printers.
27. What are the relative advantages of the mouse, the light pen, the touch screen, and the input tablet?
28. What are the basic types of scanners? What are the limitations of OCR units?
29. What are the differences between voice output, voice input, and natural language processing? Which of these are often confused by potential buyers? What are the main technologies for voice output? What are the main characteristics that separate voice recognition systems?

REFERENCES

1. "Microspots," *Computerworld,* October 14, 1985, p. 73.
2. LEDDY, MARY K., "Decline in Prices of Dot-Matrix Printers Expected to Continue," *PC Week,* February 18, 1986, pp. 111–114.

PERSONAL COMPUTER SOFTWARE TRENDS 8

A typewriter will always be a typewriter. A computer, however, can be made into a typewriter one minute, a calculator the next, and an artist's palette just a minute later—simply by changing its software.

This flexibility means that most older computers are literally better than new. Their owners have usually purchased additional programs and have replaced many of their original programs by newer versions of these programs or by better programs from other companies.

Software is evolving at least as rapidly as hardware. Better user interfaces, integration, artificial intelligence, and other important developments will make tomorrow's software far easier to use and far more powerful than today's programs. It is important for the information center to anticipate important changes in software technology in order to avoid being caught by surprise with an obsolete software strategy.

In this chapter, we will look at general software concepts, but we will emphasize system software, especially the computer's operating system. Given the dominance of IBM, our discussion of operating systems will focus on IBM's two PC operating systems, DOS and OS/2. We will also examine the operating system on the Apple Macintosh, which has set new standards for ease of use.

INTERNAL MEMORY CONCEPTS

During execution, a program must be in a computer's **internal memory,** which consists of both RAM and ROM. In this section, we will discuss two complementary ways of looking at how computers use internal memory. One is the address space view, which focuses on how programs share memory and interact with one another. The other is the layered view, which also focuses on interaction but adds the idea that one program may be regarded as being subordinate to others. Both views are equally correct, but they highlight somewhat different aspects of interaction, and both need to be mastered. After discussing these views separately, we will see how they are integrated through such processes as jump with return and lookup tables.

The Address Space View

Address Spaces

As discussed in Chapters 6 and 7, microprocessors have **address registers** whose sizes dictate the maximum amount of internal memory that can be addressed directly. Early PCs, such as the Apple II family up to the GS model, had 16-bit address registers that permitted an **address space** of only 64 KB. The Intel 8088 microprocessor used in the IBM PC had a larger address register that bumped the address space to 1 MB. The Intel 80286 used in the IBM PC AT and mid-range PS/2 models raised the address space to 16 MB, and the Intel 80386 used in high-end PS/2 models allows a virtually unlimited address space of 4 GB.

IBM's first operating system, DOS, was limited to a 1 MB address space, 384 KB of which was reserved for system use, leaving only 640 KB for user memory. IBM's advanced operating system, OS/2, raised the limit to 16 MB when it was introduced in 1987. Although DOS can work on both IBM PC and PS/2 products, OS/2 can only run on computers with 80286 or 80386 microprocessors, including most members of the PS/2 line, ATs, and one model of the XT line (the Model 286). OS/2 cannot work with 8088 or 8086 computers—or even the PS/2 Model 30—because their address registers cannot support 16 MB address spaces.

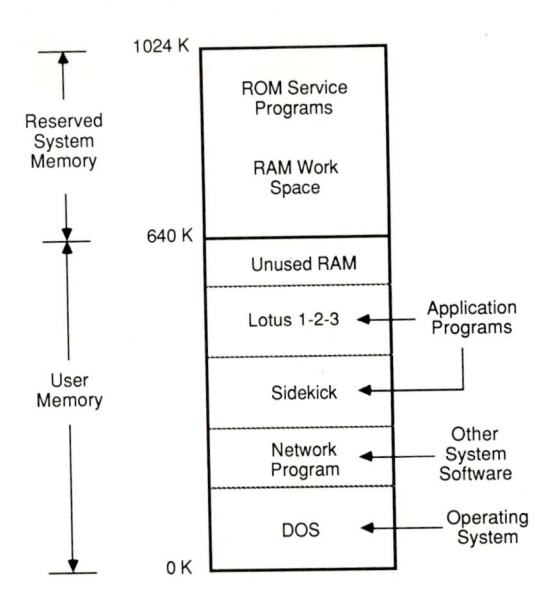

FIGURE 8-1 ADDRESS SPACE VIEW OF INTERNAL MEMORY

Memory Map

Figure 8-1 shows the internal organization of the address space under DOS. Although OS/2 uses a different organization, it employs the same general organizing principles (see Figure 8.2). This memory map views internal memory as a sequence of one-byte memory locations beginning at zero KB and extending to the largest address.

Note that the address space includes ROM as well as RAM. Although RAM and ROM are very different technologically, they are identical as far as the operating system is concerned, beyond the fact that write operations will not work with ROM addresses.

Reserved System Memory

As shown in Figure 8-1, IBM designers reserved 384 KB of the address space for system uses, leaving only 640 KB for user memory. System memory encompasses **ROM service programs,** including the diagnostic routine used whenever a PC is started as well as many service programs for handling communications with peripherals.

The reserved system memory also has RAM working memory for peripheral devices. About a third of the reserved space, 128 KB, for example, is used by display adapters to hold information to be painted on the display screen.

In most PCs, a good deal of reserved system memory lies unused. Some

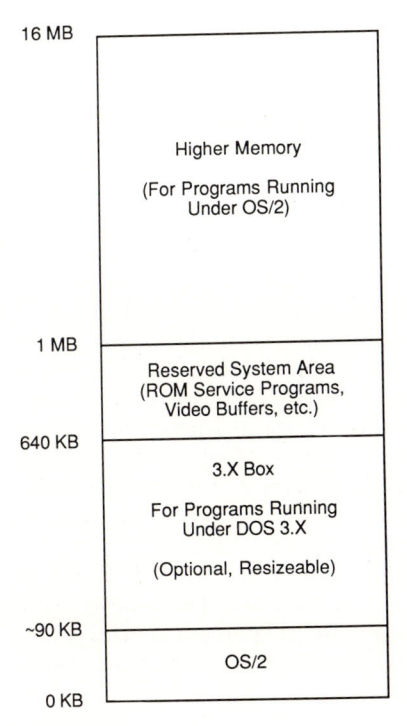

FIGURE 8-2 ADDRESS SPACE IN OPERATING SYSTEM/2

special software programs violate IBM's design rules and use these portions of system memory, but for most users, the unassigned portions of reserved system memory lie unused and inaccessible.

The Operating System

The memory used by the operating system is taken from user memory, rather than from reserved system memory, since operating systems are not part of the basic machine design. Although almost all IBM PC and compatible users run DOS, some use different operating systems, such as Unix.

The heart of DOS is COMMAND.COM, the program that controls the user interface when users type commands at DOS's > prompt. COMMAND.COM also executes a number of DOS commands directly, including COPY and ERASE. Finally, COMMAND.COM calls in other programs from disks as needed, including DOS commands such as FORMAT and application programs such as Lotus 1-2-3.

During the boot process, COMMAND.COM is loaded into RAM, along with two minor housekeeping programs, IBMBIOS.COM and IBMDOS.COM. These satellite programs handle such arcane technical details that they are not even shown when users list the files on disks.

These three DOS programs take up only part of the 40 KB or more required by different versions of DOS. There is also a working area to hold DOS programs that are normally kept on disk, such as FORMAT.COM. When these "external" programs are needed, they are loaded into the working area. When they are finished, their space is normally released for other programs. This general idea of creating suites of programs, with some being permanently internal and some kept external on disk, will be discussed more fully later in this chapter.

Other System Software

Although the operating system is the most important type of system software, it is not the only type. For example, if a user has a network program, this network program is also of system software, as shown in Figure 8-1.

Application Programs

Finally, the address space holds application programs, such as Lotus 1-2-3, dBASE III Plus, or WordPerfect. Typically, these application programs claim enough space when they are loaded for both their code and for the data they will use. Some claim only a fixed amount of memory for the program and data. They must go to disk when they have more data. Initial versions of Multimate used this approach, although some new versions of the popular word processor do not. Others claim as much memory as the address space can offer. This reduces disk swapping but limits the amount of data that can be handled. Lotus 1-2-3 uses this approach.

Although it is normal to have only a single application program in RAM, with the space being reused when a program terminates, DOS allows programs to stay resident in RAM after they terminate by giving a special termination command. Figure 8-1 illustrates this phenomenon, using a popular terminate-and-stay resident program, Sidekick.

Unused Space

Finally, there may be some unused space in internal memory that has not yet been claimed. DOS keeps track of this space so that it can use it as needed.

Actual Memory

Of course, not all PC running DOS have 640 KB of user memory installed. Some have only 256 KB, or even less. DOS keeps track of the computer's actual memory, allocating only what is really there.

The Layered View

The address space view of internal memory holds that all programs are merely locations within a single address space. This makes them peers able to call one another freely. Although this view is technologically correct, software designers usually take an equally correct but very different approach to programs. This view, the hierarchical (see Figure 8-3), shows that certain programs are subordinate to others.

The user always works with a single program that might be called the **primary program.** When the user first starts the computer, this is normally the operating system. When he or she starts an application program, it becomes the application program.

The primary program controls the user interface. For example, when a user loads Lotus 1-2-3, he or she sees the familiar worksheet area with its lettered columns and numbered rows, as well as a "control panel" to guide the user.

A good primary program will shield the user from the operations of lower level programs in the hierarchy. It will create and preserve the illusion that it is the only program that exists. The best primary programs create the

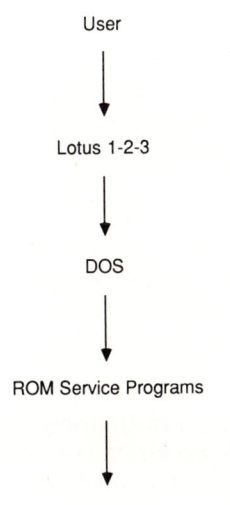

```
User
  ↓
Lotus 1-2-3
  ↓
DOS
  ↓
ROM Service Programs
  ↓
Hardware
```

FIGURE 8-3 LAYERED (HIERARCHICAL) VIEW OF SOFTWARE

illusion that the whole computer is nothing more than a "Lotus 1-2-3 machine" or a "WordPerfect machine."

Layered Calls

Beneath the illusion of the single program, the situation is far different. This can be illustrated by the things that take place when the user wants to load a data file.

First, the user gives a command to the application program that he or she wants to retrieve a file from disk. In Lotus, this command would be "File Retrieve." Then, the application program gives the user a list of files that may be retrieved. The user selects one, and that file is loaded.

For the actual file retrieval, the application program does only some of the work, calling on lower level programs to handle as many details as possible. To the operating system, for example, it will give commands to display a list of files and to do the actual retrieval. The operating system, in turn, will delegate as much work as possible to ROM service programs, which include basic disk handling routines.

Efficiency

The most important reason for layering is efficiency in software creation. The writer of an application program has enough to do without worrying about low-level details, such as how to list the files on a disk. Just as a good manager conserves his or her time by delegating simple tasks, good application programmers write as little code as possible by delegating work to lower level programs whenever feasible.

Consistency in User Interfaces

The Apple Macintosh illustrates another reason for delegation—the maintenance of a consistent user interface. As discussed later in this chapter, the interface of the Macintosh at the system level is powerful, yet extremely simple. Nearly all Macintosh application programs use this same basic interface at the application level. As a result, once Macintosh users learn some basic work approaches in one program, learning another program becomes very easy.

IBM is trying to foster a similar approach in the IBM world by creating standards for user interfaces. These standards will be discussed later in the chapter, in the section on IBM's Systems Application Architecture (SAA).

Combining the Two Views

Both views of internal memory operations—the address space view and the layered view—are equally correct. Linking them together are two concepts that deal with interactions among programs in internal memory, namely, jump with return and service program lookup tables.

Jump with Return

All memory locations in the computer's address space can be used to store program instructions. To execute an instruction, it is necessary only to place its address in the microprocessor's instruction register. The microprocessor will then execute it as the next instruction.

Before it executes the command, however, the microprocessor increments the instruction register by one, to point at the next memory location. When the microprocessor finishes executing the instruction, it loads the next instruction—the instruction whose address is in the address register. Therefore, the microprocessor normally executes program instructions sequentially.

The microprocessor's instruction repertoire also contains "jump" instructions that cause the microprocessor to begin executing instructions in another part of internal memory. Jump instructions do so by placing the address of the first instruction to be executed in the instruction register. This replaces the incremented value placed in the instruction register before the jump instruction is executed.

Jump instructions can transfer control to instructions within the same program, but they can jump to any address in the address space. They can therefore jump to another application program, to the operating system, or to ROM service programs. When jumping to another program, they can either jump to the first instruction in the called program or to an instruction in its middle.

Layering requires that, after a service has been provided by a lower level program, execution must return to the calling program, beginning with the instruction after the jump instruction. This is done through a special jump instruction called **jump with return.**

When a jump with return instruction is given, the contents of all registers in the microprocessor are saved in a special area of RAM so that the called program can use these registers without changing their original data. When a terminate command is reached in the called program, the saved registers are stored and the original program continues.

RAM-Resident Programs

Jump with return is even used by the operating system to run application programs. After loading the program into RAM, it jumps with return to the first instruction in the application program. When the application program gives a "terminate" command, the operating system regains control.

Normally, the application program's memory returns to a pool of available memory space after termination. As a result, only one application program is in RAM at any one time. But there is a special **terminate-and-stay-resident** command that tells the operating system not to reallocate the space. This command allows the program to terminate but still remain resident in RAM. Many application programs, such as Sidekick, do this. Even some operating system commands, notably MODE and GRAPHICS, terminate and stay resident.

Interrupt

In normal operation, programs pass control to others in a process like that of passing the gavel at a meeting. Each program determines its successor.

There are exceptions to this rule. Whenever a hardware device needs servicing, it places an **interrupt** signal on the bus. This happens, for example, every time a user strikes a key on the keyboard. Software can also generate interrupts, although less commonly. When the microprocessor receives an interrupt, it normally stops whatever program it is running and services the interrupt. It does a jump with return to a special **interrupt handler** program which handles the details of the servicing. When the interrupt program is finished, it terminates and control is restored to the calling program.

The interrupt handler relies on a special **service program lookup table** at the lowest 1.5 KB of user memory. As shown in Figure 8-4, the table has two columns. The first holds the interrupt number (all interrupt types have a different number), and the second holds the location of the program to service the interrupt.

If an interrupt servicing program is changed in order to add new features or to run more efficiently, the only thing that needs to be done is to change its address in the lookup table. This provides flexibility to designers and allows servicing programs to be changed without any change in peripherals, the bus, or interrupt-generating software. Both ROM service programs and the operating system have lookup tables; both set up their lookup tables when they are started.

Adding a Layer

If networks are to provide services that the standard operating system does not offer, it is necessary to add another layer of software, as shown in Figure 8-5. When application programs issue disk handling calls and other requests, the network system software intercepts the call. It handles dealings with remote disk drives by itself but passes on requests for local disk services to the operating system. This means that both the application program and the operating system can be ignorant of the network software. The application program merely issues calls in standard form, and the operating system only receives ordinary requests.

The network system software intercepts calls by placing the address of its own disk handling routines in the lookup table for the operating system. As a result, all disk handling calls are routed to it first.

Service	Memory Location
1	15,000
2	25,000
3	33,000

Note:

The service program lookup table gives the starting position of each service program.

If a new location is put in the "memory location," the program at that location will be executed when the service call is made.

FIGURE 8-4 SERVICE PROGRAM LOOKUP TABLE

```
User
  ↓
Lotus 1-2-3
  ↓
┌─────────────────┐
│ Network Program │
└─────────────────┘
  ↓
DOS
  ↓
ROM Service Programs
  ↓
Hardware
```

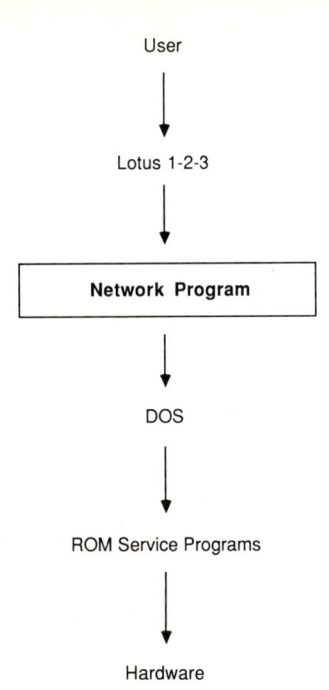

FIGURE 8-5 ADDING A LAYER OF SOFTWARE

Pop-Up Programs

Sidekick and many other programs that terminate and stay resident can be activated when the user is in another program, merely by hitting a special keystroke combination. These programs can do so because they place their own addresses in the lookup table entry dealing with keyboard interrupt. Thus, *each* keystroke is handled by the pop-up program. The pop-up program passes on keystrokes to the interrupt handling program—until Sidekick sees its activation command. Then it takes full control of the computer.

Conclusion

Over time, the management of internal memory has grown more complex under constant pressure from users and programmers to add layers of software to do specialized tasks. There is some hope that new operating systems will decrease the complexity of internal memory strategies or at least hide the complexity of these strategies from user organizations. But much simpler predictions have appeared and have too often failed to form a solid foundation for the training needs of information center staff members and power users. Even department managers, secretaries, and ordinary users must have at least a little training in this area. These same remarks hold for the next major set of software concepts to be discussed—those dealing with interactions between internal memory and external memory.

RESERVED MEMORY

As discussed in the text, 384 KB on the IBM PC are reserved for "system use," whereas the remaining 640 KB in the user's address space are available for user programs, including the operating system. This box takes a closer look at reserved memory.

In terms of the IBM Memory Map, it is useful to think of the 1 MB of internal memory as 16 **blocks** with 64 KB each. This gives 1024 KB or 1 MB. Memory reservations are defined in terms of these blocks. The first 10 blocks are available for user memory. The next six, referred to as A, B, C, D, E, and F, are reserved for system use. Note that user memory is in the lowest memory addresses, whereas the reserved area is at the top of the address space.

A This block is reserved for extended display memory. It is used by the display memory of IBM's EGA display adapter (see Chapter 7). Because Block A is at the edge of user memory, some compatibles that do not offer EGA support add this block to the memory available for user programs, bumping the available user RAM from 640 KB to 704 KB. Some compatibles use other reserved blocks in memory that are not widely used, in order to increase the amount of user RAM to nearly 800 KB. Application programs can write to this display memory in order to do very rapid screen refreshes and special effects, so compatibles must use this display memory the same way IBM does. The same is true for the standard display memory in Block B.

B This block is the memory area used by standard display adapters. It is divided into two subblocks, one used by the standard monochrome display adapter, and the other by the color graphics adapter. It is therefore possible to have both a monochrome display adapter and a color graphics adapter on the same system. Lotus 1-2-3, for example, allows a spreadsheet model to be displayed on the monochrome display and a graph to be displayed on a color display. It is even possible to add an Enhanced Color Display, since it uses memory block A.

C This block is reserved for ROM expansions. As new capabilities are added, additional ROM may be needed. If so, it is placed in this area. The IBM PC XT and the 3270 PC require additional ROM in this area.

D and E These two blocks are reserved for other uses. The PC jr. used these blocks for its ROM cartridges, which allowed programs to come on ROM, which is much faster than floppy disk. Use of two blocks, however, limited cartridge programs to only 128 KB. In the future, this area will be used for other purposes.

F This is the home of standard system ROM, including the ROM-BIOS (Basic Input/Output System) and ROM-BASIC (a very limited version of BASIC). Because many compatibles do not emulate ROM-BASIC, it is essential to use the proper version of disk BASIC when using compatibles.

Although IBM officially reserved 384 KB of the address space, it takes a small bite out of user memory. At the very bottom of user memory, a small 1.5 KB of RAM is reserved for the working space needed by various ROM programs, DOS, and BASIC. Most of this low-end memory is taken up by buffers and by lookup tables (see Figure 8-4).

> **ROM INTERRUPTS**
>
> When a program or device wishes to generate an interrupt, it generates a special interrupt signal on one of the control lines. For example, Interrupt 5 creates a print screen, Interrupt 16 calls for video services, Interrupt 19 is for disk services, Interrupt 20 is for serial port services, Interrupt 22 is for the keyboard interrupt, and Interrupt 23 is for parallel port services. There are a fair number of other interrupts which are widely used by application programs. For example, when a RAM-resident program monitors the keyboard, it really monitors Interrupt 22.
>
> Most interrupts provide more than one service. When they are called, they read the contents of a special register that gives the number of the service they will provide. For example, Service 0 of the disk services resets the drive and controller, whereas Service 1 reports the status of the drive, Service 2 reads one or more consecutive tracks into RAM, Service 3 writes several sectors, Service 4 verifies that a read or write operation has been performed properly (but does not check for errors in the resultant data), and Service 5 formats a single track.

INTERNAL AND EXTERNAL MEMORY

So far, we have looked at the behavior of software in internal memory. Now, we must broaden the picture and examine the relationship between programs in RAM and programs on external memory. For simplicity, disk memory will be assumed, but the picture is nearly the same for other kinds of external memory.

Why External Memory?

Internal memory is fast enough to keep up with the computer's processing circuits. All programs used must therefore be loaded into RAM for processing, and system service programs must be in ROM internal memory. Internal memory presents two problems, however. First, RAM is limited. Although most users have tens of megabytes of user programs and data files, most computers have less than a megabyte of RAM. Second, the RAM needed for user programs is **volatile.** If power is cut off, even for an instant, everything in RAM is erased.

As a result, computers have two basic tiers of memory. Internal memory provides fast processing, and external memory provides long-term storage. External memory is slow, but its cost per byte of storage is low, and its capacity is very high. In addition, external memory is nonvolatile, retaining its data unless the storage medium is damaged. As discussed in the previous chapter, there is a third tier of memory, archival memory, but we will ignore it here because it adds no new principles.

Copying

When a user *loads* a program or data file into RAM, it is **copied** into RAM. When a file is *saved,* in turn, the original is still in RAM, but now there is a new copy of the file on disk. Although this is a simple process, users often have trouble understanding the implication of copying. These implications must therefore be taught clearly.

1. Unless a program or data file in RAM is saved, the disk files will not be changed. Some programs save automatically; others do not.
2. On most computers, if you save a file and give it a name of a file already on the disk, that file already on disk is overwritten by the saved file.
3. Loading a program into RAM does not affect the original copy on disk. So if power is lost and the RAM versions of files are lost, nothing on disk is lost since the last save.
4. If a program is loaded entirely into RAM, the disk can be removed, and the RAM version will run without it. At the same time, as discussed below, some programs are "interactive," and their disk must be kept in the disk drive at least some of the time.

Although such implications are obvious to anyone who has worked in the field professionally, it is both difficult and critical for users to understand the interactions between RAM and disk and to understand the implication of these interactions.

Interactive Programs

The fourth item in the preceding list states that after a program is copied into RAM, the disk together with the program can be removed—unless the program is interactive, in which case the disk must be present at least some of the time.

Interactiveness has its roots in a common problem—that is, most programs today are too large to fit into RAM. As a result, they must be broken into pieces. The most common way to do this is to create a **core** or **internal program.** This core or internal program has the most commonly used functions of the original program, in order to minimize the number of disk accesses, because even hard disks are far slower than RAM.

As shown in Figure 8-6, this core or internal program reserves a certain amount of space, called an **overlay area.** The other parts of the original program, which are called **overlay** or **external** programs, are copied into this overlay area when they are needed. When an overlay call is made, the called program usually overwrites any overlay that is already there, although some core programs create overlay areas large enough to hold several overlay or external programs.

If users are familiar with an interactive program, they can remove their disks except when an overlay is needed. In addition, many programs are polite enough to ask the user to reinsert the original disk if it is needed. This is the norm on the Macintosh, but it is the exception on the IBM PC. Others only give cryptic error messages inviting the user to try the operation again with the proper disk in place.

Interactiveness can be more complex for data files. Some programs, such as Lotus 1-2-3, save only when the user gives a specific command. Other programs save data more or less constantly. Unless the user understands when and how a program saves, the user must keep the data disk in place constantly.

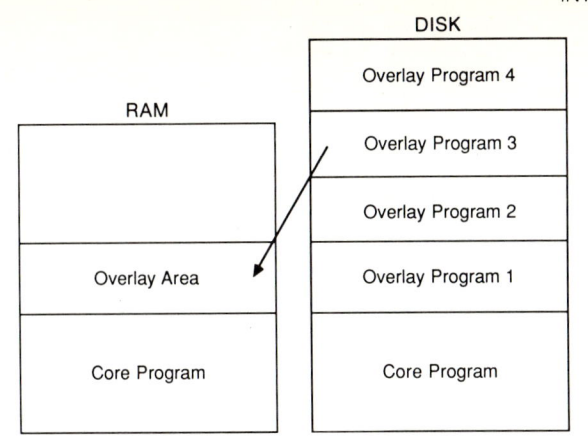

FIGURE 8-6 CORE PROGRAM AND OVERLAYS

Note: Overlay Program 3 has been brought into the overlay area.

Virtual Memory Operating Systems

The division of a large program into a core program and overlays is a general solution to the problem of programs being too large to fit into RAM, but the method does have weaknesses. Specifically, it requires that the program developer manage the overlay area explicitly.

Future PC operating systems should have the **virtual memory** capabilities now found on most host computers. In virtual memory, which is illustrated in Figure 8-7, the operating system automatically chops a program up into **pages** of something like 16 KB. It then loads pages into memory as needed, without the user's or program's awareness. When memory gets full, pages that have not been used for a while are erased in RAM (but not on disk).

Because everything is done by the operating system, the original programmer builds as big a program as he or she likes. There is no need to worry about the details, and so program development time is decreased.

FIGURE 8-7 VIRTUAL MEMORY

PERSONAL COMPUTER SOFTWARE TRENDS

The core/overlay approach can produce better performance during execution, however. The programmer that creates a core program and overlays can ensure that the most commonly used functions are always in RAM. Virtual memory cuts up programs at random. Key functions are not always kept in RAM, and contiguous parts of crucial sections may end up in different pages. The performance advantage or the core/overlay approach is not likely to be enough to prevent the rapid growth of virtual memory operating systems on PCs with sufficient processing speeds and disk access speeds—machines in the IBM PC AT class and beyond.

Bank Switching

As noted above, the number of bits in the address register of the microprocessor limits the address space a microprocessor can call *directly*. With *indirect* addressing, however, this "address space barrier" can be softened.

Figure 8-8 shows how indirect addressing works. This process is called **bank switching**. In **normal memory**—the memory that can be addressed directly—a transfer area is reserved. This is typically about 64 B. In higher memory, above the address space, programs and data files sit until needed. When a program or data file is needed, it is copied from higher memory to the transfer area and then executed in normal memory.

The whole program or data file is *not* transferred. The bank switching software, which is called in the user's startup batch file, automatically breaks programs up into pages, just as virtual memory operating systems do. But now the pages are stored in RAM instead of on disk. Each page is typically around 16 K. Only individual pages, not the entire program or data file, need

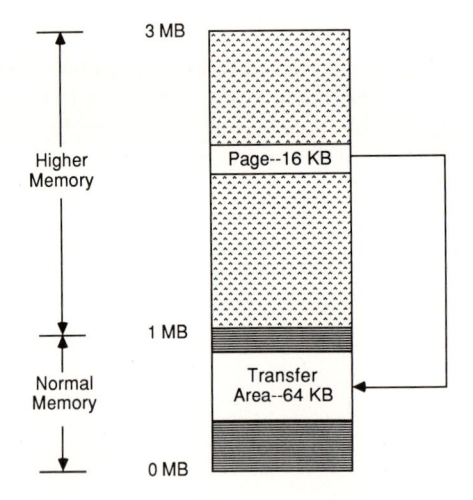

Note:
Only code in normal memory can be executed. Pages are copied to the transfer area of normal memory as needed.

FIGURE 8-8 BANK SWITCHING

to be copied to the transfer area. This is obviously the RAM counterpart of virtual memory.

One complication is that application programs must be written to work with bank switching software. IBM does not have a standard for bank switching, but Lotus, Intel, and Microsoft have produced **EMS,** the **Expanded Memory Specification.** A number of application programs have been rewritten to work with this standard, but many have not.

Bank switching is convenient because the programmer does not have to chop a program up into core programs and overlays, just as in virtual memory. Bank switching, however, is slower than direct addressing, sometimes considerably slower. As operating systems are rewritten to work with the larger address spaces possible with Intel 80286 and 80386 microprocessors, bank switching should fade in importance.

RAM Disks

RAM is 50 times faster than a floppy disk drive and 10 times faster than a hard disk drive. To get more speed from interactive programs, interactive data files, or both, many users buy special utility programs called **RAM disks.** These RAM disk programs set aside a portion of internal memory to act as a very fast floppy disk or hard disk, as illustrated in Figure 8-9.

In operation, a user's startup batch file calls this RAM disk program, tells the program how much room is to be allocated, and gives the drive a name, typically C: or D:. Programs, data files, or both are then copied by the startup batch file to the RAM disk. The startup batch file can even create multiple RAM disks, say one for data and another for programs.

Later, when a file on Drive C: or D: is accessed by another program, the file will be accessed from the RAM disk. The fact that the called drive exists in RAM instead of being a physical disk drive is completely transparent to the application program. Even operating system commands can be issued to the RAM disk.

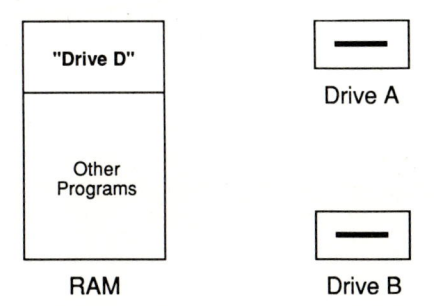

A RAM Disk program makes a section of RAM act like an ultrafast disk drive.

RAM Disks respond like any other disks to other programs.

FIGURE 8-9 RAM DISK

As noted above, low-end IBM PCs can only access 640 KB of memory. Even if such a machine has less than 1 MB of RAM, RAM disks are useful. If the machine has a memory board with 2 MB to 4 MB of RAM, however, RAM disks are even more attractive. With these boards, the first 1 MB can be used for normal operation, and memory above 1 MB can be used for RAM disks.

RAM disks do have one glaring weakness. If power is interrupted, everything on the RAM disk is lost immediately. It is important to copy files onto physical disks frequently. With the CMOS technology discussed in the previous chapters, RAM disks will gradually become more immune to power outages, but for the near future, RAM disks must be handled carefully.

SYSTEM SOFTWARE

General Considerations

The task of selecting personal computer standards does not stop at selecting hardware configurations. Selecting PC standards also requires that the information center select system software, especially an operating system. Most PCs can run more than one operating system, and even if a PC only runs a single operating system, new versions of the operating system with additional functions are likely to appear every year or so. At the time of each release, the information center must decide whether or not to upgrade. If the decision to upgrade is made, the information center must decide whether to upgrade all PCs or only some of them. In any case, a solid understanding of current and potential services provided by operating systems is essential.

Hardware and ROM Service Programs

When a computer is manufactured, it has circuits to implement its basic **instruction set**—the 200 or 300 basic commands it can obey. Although 200 or 300 instructions seems to be a large number, most of the commands do roughly the same things. For example, if the control unit has 10 registers, then there will be 10 commands for bringing a byte of data from a memory location to particular registers. There will be another dozen commands to send a byte from a register to a location in memory. There will even be more transfer commands to move data from one register to another.

Because of the limited nature of computer instruction sets, nearly all computers are sold with a set of **ROM service programs,** as noted earlier. These are programs in ROM that do common low-level tasks, such as checking to see if a disk drive is ready for access or accepting a stroke from the keyboard.

Operating Systems

Even these low-level ROM service programs, as we saw earlier, are too limited to perform such functions as store a file on disk. As a result, all personal computers are sold with a special program called an **operating system,** which handles a number of important housekeeping chores. First, the operating system provides a number of important services to application programs.

1. The operating system loads programs into RAM's empty spaces, runs the program, and handles program terminations.
2. The operating system handles the details of various input/output operations such as disk accesses and printing.
3. The operating system allocates resources among programs in multitasking environments (which are discussed later).

In addition to providing these services for application programs, operating systems do things directly to users. For example, a user can type a command to see a list of all files on a disk, to erase or rename a file, and to do many other housecleaning chores associated with running the computer. We will consider these services in more depth later in this chapter.

Selecting an Operating System
There are two general considerations in selecting an operating system. The first is the set of **services** it provides. To select an operating system, a company must decide which services are crucial and which are merely desirable or even relevant. When considering cooperating systems, the services provided by each relevant. When considering cooperating systems, the services provided by each must be identified and assessed in detail.

The second general consideration is the corpus of application programs that have been written to run with the operating system. An application program is designed to run with a particular operating system because when it saves files on disk and does many other low-level chores, it issues a call to an operating system service instead of including the code itself. As discussed earlier in this chapter, if a user tries to run a program on a different operating system, this different system will not recognize these service calls, and the program will malfunction. The selection of an operating system effectively determines the number of application programs available to the organization.

Because the application programs are critical for users, corporations almost always select operating systems primarily on the basis of the second consideration, the number of application programs that run with the operating system. It is rarely sensible to pick an advanced operating system with myriad functions but with few application programs.

As noted earlier, most operating systems are updated about once a year; organizations therefore need to make upgrade decisions after the operating system is first selected. Upgrades are expensive, in terms of both payments to the software producer and the labor costs of upgrading the many computers that exist in every firm. At each upgrade, then, costs must be balanced against the value of the additional functions provided with each upgrade.

Simple Operating Systems

A Historical View
The first PC operating systems appeared in the mid-1970s. Large firms such as Apple produced their own operating systems, but smaller firms selected a generic operating system, **CP/M,** which was produced by Digital Research Corporation. Digital Research rewrote CP/M to run on each com-

puter, but the services provided to application programs and to users were identical on all computers, with a few minor exceptions. Any program that could run on CP/M could run on virtually any CP/M computer.

CP/M was written for 8-bit microprocessors such as the Intel 8080 and the Zilog Z80. As discussed in Chapter 7, these machines had limited address spaces and could only support 64 KB of internal memory without bank switching and other tricks.

When Intel produced its next family of microprocessors, the 8086 and 8088, a new version of CP/M was needed, but Digital Research delayed its introduction of a new operating system. A hardware vendor, Seattle Computer, responded by producing its own operating system, which tried to be close in "feel" to CP/M. Microsoft Corporation later purchased this operating system and called it MS-DOS, for Microsoft Disk Operating System (meaning that it could handle floppy disk drives).

When IBM built its first PC in 1981, it decided to purchase an operating system instead of creating its own. It selected MS-DOS over Digital Research's new operating system, CP/M 86. Rather than sell it as MS-DOS, however, it sold it under the name **PC-DOS**. PC-DOS offers a few commands not found in MS-DOS, because of the special features found in the IBM hardware and service ROM. Otherwise, MS-DOS and PC-DOS are identical. We will refer to them both as **MS-DOS.**

The IBM PC can run other operating systems, including the Unix derivative Xenix from Microsoft. IBM even sells these other operating systems. From the beginning, however, almost all users have purchased MS-DOS with their computers, making MS-DOS the de facto standard on IBM PCs. Today, so many programs have been written for MS-DOS that other operating systems are used mostly in specialized applications.

The initial versions of MS-DOS, including MS-DOS 1.0 and MS-DOS 1.1, were very weak products. MS-DOS 2.0 greatly strengthened the program's capabilities and drew many features from Xenix, giving MS-DOS a slight Unix flavor without including the advanced features of Unix. In particular, Version 2.0 introduced hierarchical directory support and support for hard disks.

MS-DOS 2.1 was introduced to work with half-height floppy disks, because these half-height floppies are too slow to work with Version 2.0. A disk formatted in 2.0 will not work with half-weight floppies. Many corporations have standardized on Version 2.1.

MS-DOS 3.0 was created to support the features needed in PC networking, as well as to add many smaller features. Because 3.0 was bug-ridden, 3.1 became the standard in many corporations. MS-DOS 3.2 was introduced to add support for 3-½ inch floppy disks.

At the time this book is being written, an advanced version of MS-DOS is pending release. Designed for 80286 and 80386 microprocessors, this new version of DOS will provide many advanced features. Since the purpose of this section is to discuss simple operating systems, we will not describe the advanced features expected from the advanced DOS.

The Size Squeeze

The main problem facing operating system designers has always been memory. When CP/M was written, few computers had even 16 KB of memory, and the first versions of MS-DOS were implemented on machines with 64 KB or less of memory. This meant that the operating system needed to be kept as small as possible.

Even as internal memory became more ample, users were reluctant to purchase large operating systems because they wanted to use as much of the available RAM as possible for application programs and data. As a result, the pressure to keep operating systems small persisted even after RAM became more plentiful.

Operating system designers responded in two ways. The first was to break the operating system into pieces. An internal (core) program would always be kept in RAM, whereas external (overlay) programs were kept on disk and were called into RAM only as needed.

In the case of IBM PC, the internal part of MS-DOS consisted of three core programs. The first two are hidden programs that do not show up with the standard command that lists files. The third is COMMAND.COM, which serves both application programs and user commands. Parts of COMMAND.COM may be erased by an application program or data. As a result, when leaving an application program and returning to MS-DOS, a disk holding COMMAND.COM may have to be in the main drive.

Whenever a computer is **booted,** the internal parts of the operating system are loaded into RAM. These are then directly available to the user and application programs. External parts of MS-DOS are kept on disk, one file to a command. When an external program is called by the user or by an application program, a disk holding the external program being called must be in the main drive.

When an application program is first purchased, it has neither the internal nor external parts of DOS on it. The first step a user takes after purchasing a program is usually to create a **book disk,** which has the application program's files, the internal parts of DOS, and whatever external parts of DOS the user wishes to transfer to the boot disk. This is called a boot disk because, if the system is booted (started) while the disk is in the main drive, the disk has the information to complete the booting process, which includes the loading of MS-DOS's three internal files into RAM.

The second way that software designers have responded to space limitation pressures is to use very crude user interfaces. MS-DOS, for example, is command-driven, and the syntax of commands is not very easy to learn. For example, to copy a file from Drive B: to Drive A:, a user may have to type the following.

```
COPY B:\NEW\BUDGET.WKS A:\BACKUP\LASTBUD.BAK
```

Because MS-DOS is blind to upper and lower case, things do not have to be typed exclusively in capitals, as shown in the example. However, MS-DOS is absolutely rigid on spacing and almost every other aspect of command syntax.

As a result of this crudeness, operating systems place heavy learning burdens on users. To learn MS-DOS adequately takes about 4 hours; to learn it very well takes 12 to 16 hours of instruction.

Many new operating systems are far more attractive than MS-DOS, because they refuse to accept stringent memory limitations. We will look at these advanced operating systems later.

Disk Operations

Some operations work on entire disks. We will use examples from MS-DOS to illustrate basic disk handling operations.

The **FORMAT** command prepares a disk to receive data. A new disk can be thought of as a level but unpaved field. To turn it into a parking lot, you must first pave it. Then, you must draw lines to mark where cars can park. The FORMAT command does this to all new disks. Although it does not actually erase information, it destroys all pointers to it and effectively wipes out any data already there, "paving the disk clean." It then divides the disk up into sectors (see Chapter 7), like marking lines for parking spaces. It even puts barriers around defective sectors, just as a parking lot builder may put barriers around potholes.

In the same way as a parking lot builder may leave space for a guard post and a place to hold information on where each car is parked, FORMAT reserves part of the disk for DOS's use. The **directory** area holds general information about each file, including its name, size, and the date last modified. The **file allocation table** holds pointers to specific sectors.

The **DISKCOPY** command can copy the entire contents of one disk to another disk. **CHKDSK,** in turn, can check a disk for damage and other characteristics. **DISKCOMP** compares two disks thought to be identical and determines whether they are identical.

File Operations

Other MS-DOS operations work on individual files or groups of files.

COMP compares two disk files thought to be identical.

COPY copies one or more files, usually from one disk drive to another.

COPY CON: allows the user to create a file by typing the contents of the file on the keyboard.

DIR shows a list of all the files on a disk.

ERASE erases a disk file.

RENAME renames a disk file.

TYPE types the contents of a file on the display screen; special characters will show up as "garbage" on the screen, so TYPE is normally used only for the simple ASCII text files discussed later in this chapter.

MS-DOS Input/Output Operations

Most I/O operations are handled at the request of application programs, but users have control over some of what happens. For example, the **MODE** command is used to change default settings for I/O device handling. For example, the MODE command can be used to specify that if a monochrome and color monitor are attached, the color monitor should be used. It can also specify that output to a certain printer port, say LPT1 (parallel port #1) should be diverted to another, say COM1 (serial port #1).

MS-DOS DIRECTORIES

When MS-DOS formats a disk, it reserves about one percent of the available space for its own use. First, there is a single sector (512 bytes) that holds the **boot record,** which is used in the booting process but is really used to identify the disk as being formatted in MS-DOS, since even data disks have a boot record. The boot record is in the same sector on every disk formatted by MS-DOS.

In addition, there is the root directory, which has 32 bytes for each file on the disk. Eight are used for the file name and three for the extension. Other bytes are used for the date and time last modified, the file's size, the file's attributes (read-only access, etc.), and the location of the disk cluster holding the first bits of the file. Although file attributes are often used to provide security, it is important to keep in mind that a person with data snooping utilities, which are discussed in this chapter, can easily break security provided by attributes.

When a file is erased, the information in its root directory entry is not really erased. Instead, the first character of the name is changed to a special code that indicates that the entry is free to be reused. Thus, if a data snooping program changes the first character of the file name in the root directory, the file can be unerased.

If a user creates a hierarchical file structure on the disk, the directory organization on the disk becomes more complicated. In hierarchically organized disks, the root directory becomes only one of several directories on the disk. For each branching point in the hierarchy, there is a subdirectory with the same basic form as the root directory. When subdirectories appear, some of the entries in the root directories point to subdirectories rather than to individual files. Entries in the subdirectories can also point to further subdirectories. In other words, hierarchical file structures are handled by extending the root directory concept.

As just noted, the root directory holds the location of the file's starting cluster. What about subsequent clusters? The answer is that DOS also places a **file allocation table (FAT),** which has one entry for each cluster. The entry gives the location of the *next* cluster in the file. So the first cluster effectively points to the second, the second to the third, and so on.

If the disk is a boot disk, formatting will write additional system information onto the disk, most notably COMMAND.COM, which provides the user interface when users give MS-DOS commands directly, and two hidden files.

Hierarchical File Structure

DOS and virtually every other operating system that works with hard disks allow the user to create a **hierarchical file structure.** Instead of having hundreds of organized files, the user can organize files by categories. For instance, in Figure 8-10, all budgeting work is placed under the "Budget" category at the top of the hierarchy, and "Budget" is further subdivided into "Thisyear," and "Lastyear," each of which will hold several budget models and memos.

```
Root          Budget\          Thisyear\         Budget.DAT
Directory     Subdirectory     Subdirectory      File
                                                 
                                                 Progress.DAT
                                                 File

                               Lastyear\         Budget.BAK
                               Subdirectory      File

              Subdirectories                     Progress.BAK
                                                 File

                                                 Summary.DOC
                                                 File

              Report\          Jan-Rpt.DAT
              Subdirectory     File              Files

                               Feb-Rpt.DAT
                               File

                               Mar-Rpt.DAT
                               File
```

FIGURE 8-10 HIERARCHICAL FILE STRUCTURE

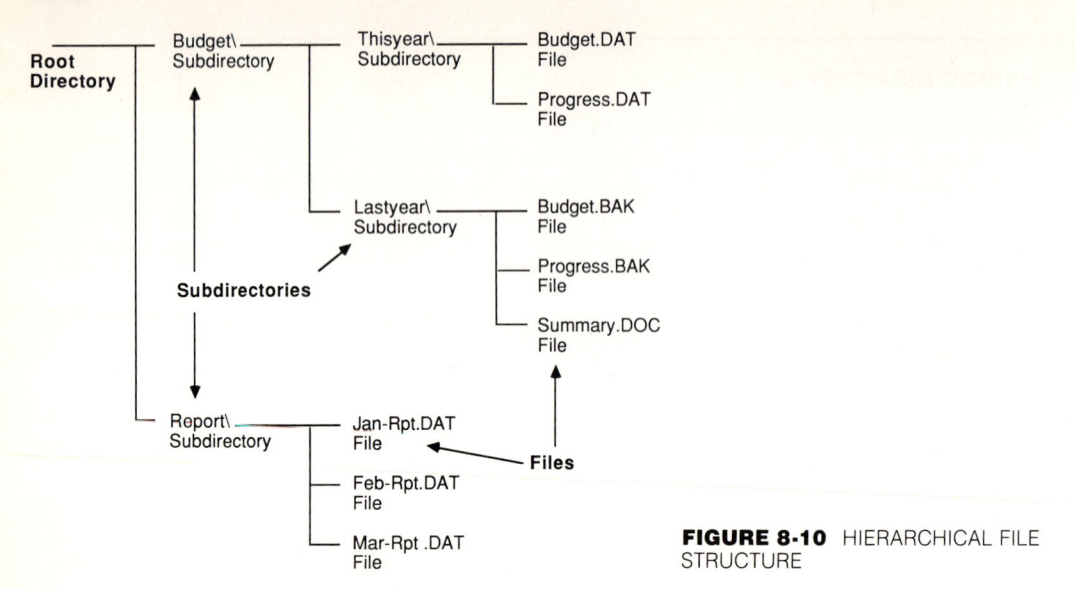

MS-DOS Batch Files

A user may have several repetitive MS-DOS tasks. For instance, the user may periodically archive all files that are more than a year old onto a floppy disk. This could require several copy and erase commands. It is possible to create a **batch file** called something like "archive" to do the work. The archive command, which will save the name ARCHIVE.BAT, can be called whenever archiving is needed. The command ARCHIVE will execute this batch file.

If the name of a batch file is AUTOEXEC.BAT, this batch file will be executed automatically whenever the system is booted. An AUTOEXEC.BAT file might, for example, look up the date and time from an internal clock and calendar, create a RAM disk called D:, copy the data files from the disk in Drive B: to Drive D:, and then load a word processing program from A:.

Multitasking and Multiuser Operating Systems

Basic operating systems served PC users well in the early years, when simple applications brought major new benefits and when microprocessor power was too limited for advanced operating system services. Today, however, the easy gains have already been mined, and newer microprocessors are capable of supporting advanced operating system services without "browning out."

Multitasking Operating Systems

Most PCs have **single tasking** operating systems, meaning that they can run only one program at a time. In contrast, most hosts have **multitasking** operating systems, also called **multiprogramming** operating systems, which can run several programs at the same time.

Of course, a computer's control unit can only process one instruction at a time. Multitasking means that if one program needs to wait, say because the printer's buffer is full and the printer cannot accept more characters at this time, then a second program will be executed until it needs to wait. At that point, the control unit returns to the original program or, if the first program is still waiting, to yet a third program.

With a multitasking operating system, a user can work on a memo with a word processing system while the computer is also doing a data base retrieval, repaginating another document, or logging into a remote computer to check on the user's electronic mail.

In the past, multitasking required so much processing power that multitasking operating systems on PCs ran too slowly. Now, however, new microprocessors, such as the Intel 80286 and the Intel 80386 have very fast cycle times (10 MHz to 20 MHz, instead of 4.77 MHz for the IBM PC's Intel 8088), plus the ability to move 16 or 32 bits at a time, instead of the 8 bits at a time moved by an Intel 8088. In addition to this increase in sheer horsepower, many new microprocessors have built-in circuitry to handle multitasking; handling these functions in hardware instead of software improves efficiency substantially.

As discussed in Chapter 7, the Intel 80286 and 80386 have two modes of operation. The first is an ordinary mode in which specialized circuitry for multitasking is unavailable; the microprocessors are simply faster 8088s. The second mode is the **protected** mode, in which the circuitry for multitasking is available. Versions of DOS through the 3.X series could only operate in the ordinary mode. By the time this book is published, an advanced version of MS-DOS capable of operating in protected mode should be available.

Multiuser Operating Systems

Some PC operating systems are **multiuser operating systems,** which allow several terminals to be attached to one PC. Each terminal user can then run a different program, as if he or she had a dedicated PC. The terminal users can even share multiuser data bases.

Multiuser operation is not the same thing as multitasking. Multitasking is the foundation on which multiuser operation is built, but not all multitasking operating systems are multiuser operating systems. Mulituser operation requires *additional* capabilities on top of the foundation laid by multitasking.

Unix

Unix, a sophisticated operating system developed by AT&T, offers such features as multitasking and multiuser processing, as well as a host of application development tools designed to improve the ability of programmers to develop sophisticated applications.

Unix has long been viewed as a ready-made solution to the need for an advanced operating system. It is available on a wide variety of minicomputers and microcomputers, and versions are even available for the IBM personal computers. Many vendors outside of AT&T are offering Unix on their own machines, and many government contracts specify Unix as the operating system, in order to avoid getting locked into a single vendor.

Unix also has problems. Although billed as a "universal operating system," the truth is that the many versions of Unix on the market today are only somewhat compatible. AT&T's System V is the basis for many Unices, but only AT&T produces System V. Microsoft's Xenix is moving toward compatibility with System V, but both Xenix and System V offer some special features. Many other Unix operating systems are compatible with other "standard Unices," including Berkley 4.2 Unix. Some are not compatible with anything. The situation has become sufficiently serious that the IEEE has created POSIX, a standard not for Unix itself but for calls to Unix operating systems. This means that a program can issue POSIX calls, which a special driver will translate into the calls for a particular Unix. Unfortunately, POSIX provides only a subset of System V capabilities.

Another problem is the size of Unix. Only hard disk machines with ample processing power can run Unix efficiently, and until recently, only a limited number of office PCs had hard disks. As a result, few organizations could switch over entirely to Unix. Furthermore, now that many PCs have hard disks, advanced MS-DOS promises to provide Unix-like functionality and reasonable compatibility with single-user MS-DOS versions.

The user interface is also a problem. The user interface is governed by the "shell" program, which interprets user commands, much like COMMAND.COM in MS-DOS or Finder on the Macintosh. Because the shell's user interface was born in the days of slow paper teletypewriters, shell commands are very terse and difficult to understand, making life difficult for most users. Although it is possible to create customized commands or to replace shell by an entirely different user interface program, this makes the user interface specific to a certain firm or even to an individual.

Unix's biggest problem is that few of the most popular end user application programs, such as Lotus 1-2-3, run on Unix. As a result, a firm that adopts Unix is locking itself out of the richest base of end user application software in existence—application software for MS-DOS environments. Although Unix end user software is no longer scant, it is still far beyond MS-DOS end user software. This problem of lack of software is so great that Unix is likely to remain a minority operating system for special uses.

In the final analysis, Unix is too oriented toward the needs of programmers. It has many elegant concepts, such as creating a single type of file structure and using it to describe data files, internal RAM memory, and I/O devices, but these features appeal far more to programmers than to users. In addition, Unix comes with an extensive library of application development tools—again, features that appeal to programmers rather than users. In addition, many advanced aspects of Unix that do appeal to users, including the ability to create hierarchical file structures, to automatically send the output of one program to another program as if they were sections of a pipe, and to redirect output from one device specified by the application program to another specified by the user have already been incorporated into MS-DOS.

Windowing Operating System

Traditionally, the program in operation completely filled the computer screen. During the late 1960s, however, several research groups produced operating systems that could divide the screen up into multiple windows, each holding different information. As shown in Figure 8-11, windows can overlap

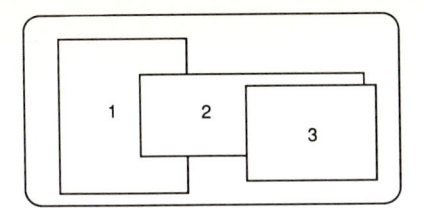

There are four overlapping windows. The fourth window is completely covered by one of the others, but it can be recovered.

FIGURE 8-11 WINDOWING

and even cover one another completely in many windowing systems, although some systems do not allow overlapping windows.

Windowing operating systems allow the user to see different information in different windows. As we will see later, this can range from viewing several parts of a single data file to viewing several different data files under the control of several different programs. It may even be possible to transfer information between windows. By providing multiple views of the world, windowing essentially gives the user multiple computers, which is consistent with the user's fragmented, often-interrupted working world.

To run in a windowing environment, some modification is usually necessary in application programs. For example, most programs assume that they have the entire screen to themselves, and quite a number of programs often bypass the operating system to talk to ROM service programs—a practice that can rarely be tolerated in windowing operation systems. The more complex the windowing environment is, the more modification is usually required. We will look at various degrees of complexity and sophistication in windowing environments, beginning with the simplest cases.

Single-Tasking Windowing

In **single-tasking windowing,** only a single program can run at a time, say a word processing program. Windows are then used to show different parts of the same document or, in more advanced programs, parts of two different documents. Many application programs already provide this kind of windowing, instead of leaving windowing up to the operation system.

Task-Switching Windowing

In **task-switching windowing,** different windows can have different programs. Only one window can be active at once, however. When that window is active, programs in other windows do not run.

An interesting example of task switching *without* windowing is the **Switcher** program for the Macintosh. Switcher allows several application programs and the desktop image to have *complete screens.* Conceptually, these screens are placed side by side around a cylinder. Each time the user touches a special icon, the screen pans one screen to the right or left. You can watch one program's screen roll off the display and another program's screen take its place.

Although task switching does not provide multitasking, that is, the simultaneous execution of several programs, task switching is extremely valuable. As noted above, users often switch back and forth between tasks in the course of their daily work, and task-switching windowing allows the computer to fit into the constant interruptions in the professional's day.

Multitasking Windowing

Multitasking windowing operating systems rise above the level of task switching to provide true simultaneous operation for two or more programs. With multitasking, a background program in one window can log into a remote computer to get the user's mail or execute a standardized report on a host data base management system, while the user is working with word processing in another window and a spreadsheet program in another window.

Copying Across Windows

Often, a user will want to copy information from one window to another, perhaps even to a window running a different application program. Copying is relatively easy to implement if only one program is running in all windows. This simplicity comes from the fact that the data file in each window will have the same file structure. If different windows hold different programs, however, different file structures will be involved. To allow copying across programs, windowing operating systems normally have standards for copying operations that application programs must obey if they are to be used as the sources or destinations for copies.

User-Friendly Operating Systems

During the 1960s and 1970s, Stanford Research Institute and the Xerox Palo Alto Research Center developed a series of computer systems that attempted to make computers easier to use. The mouse came out of this research stream, as did overlapping windowing, pop-down menus, and the use of icons. The Apple Macintosh brought these innovations into the heart of the commercial world, and we will use the Macintosh for examples.

The Initial Desktop

When the user first turns on the Macintosh, he or she sees the Macintosh **desktop** (shown in Figure 8-12). This image is called the desktop because, like a real desktop, it is a work space where things can be placed and work laid out.

- At the right side are three **icons** that represent objects or actions. The two disk icons (PROGRAM DISK and DATA DISK) represent the disks in the Macintosh's internal and external drives. The **trash icon** is for discarding files. The disk in the internal drive is shown in black, to indicate that it is "selected." Pointing to another icon and clicking the mouse button will cause it to be selected.

- At the top is a **menu bar** that has a number of choices. In Figure 8-12, the user has pointed to the "File" choice. This causes a **pop-down** submenu to appear. The option "Open" is being chosen in order to indicate that the user wants to open the selected icon.

The combination of icons and pop-down menus provides an extraordi-

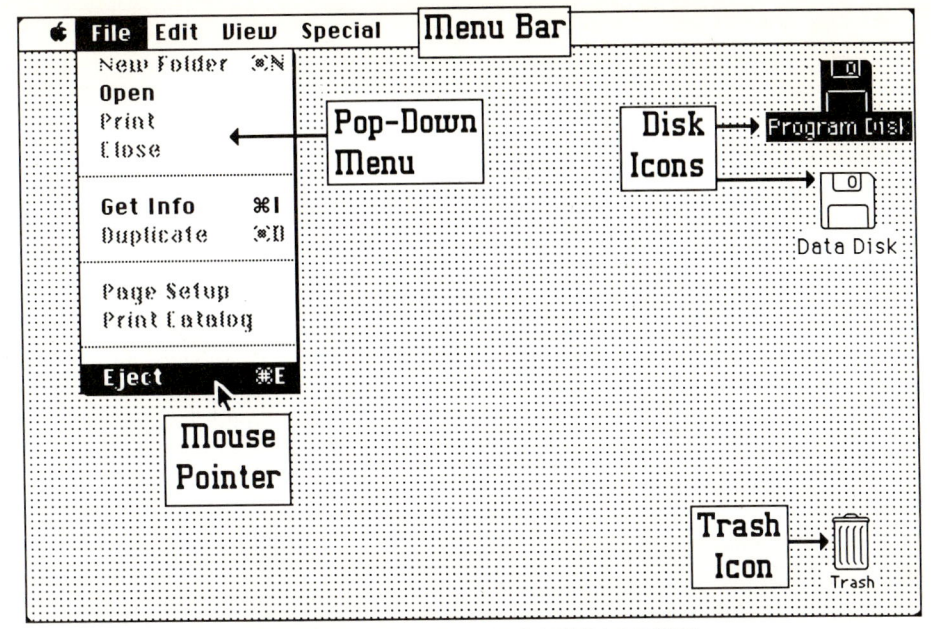

FIGURE 8-12 INITIAL MACINTOSH SCREEN

narily simple-to-use interface for both new and experienced users. In contrast to DOS, there is no command syntax to learn. (At the same time, experienced users are able to use a large number of tricks to speed their operations.)

Windows

Selecting "Open" causes a window to be opened to show the contents of the selected disk icon, as shown in Figure 8-13.

In the window, three icons appear. One is an icon for a *program file* (Word Processing), another is an icon for a *data file* (EUC), and the third is a *folder* icon (Letters) that can hold several data files, program files, or both. A folder can even hold other folders, giving a hierarchical file structure.

These icons can be selected and opened, just as the disk was. Selecting and opening different icons will give different results.

- Opening a program icon will cause the program to be started.
- Opening a data file icon will cause the program that created the data file to be found and to run on the data file.
- Opening a folder icon will cause a new window to be created, showing the contents of the folder.

Other actions allow common disk and file manipulation "commands" to be given.

- As indicated in Figure 8-14, if a disk file is dragged to another disk's icon (dragging it to another disk's open window will do the same thing),

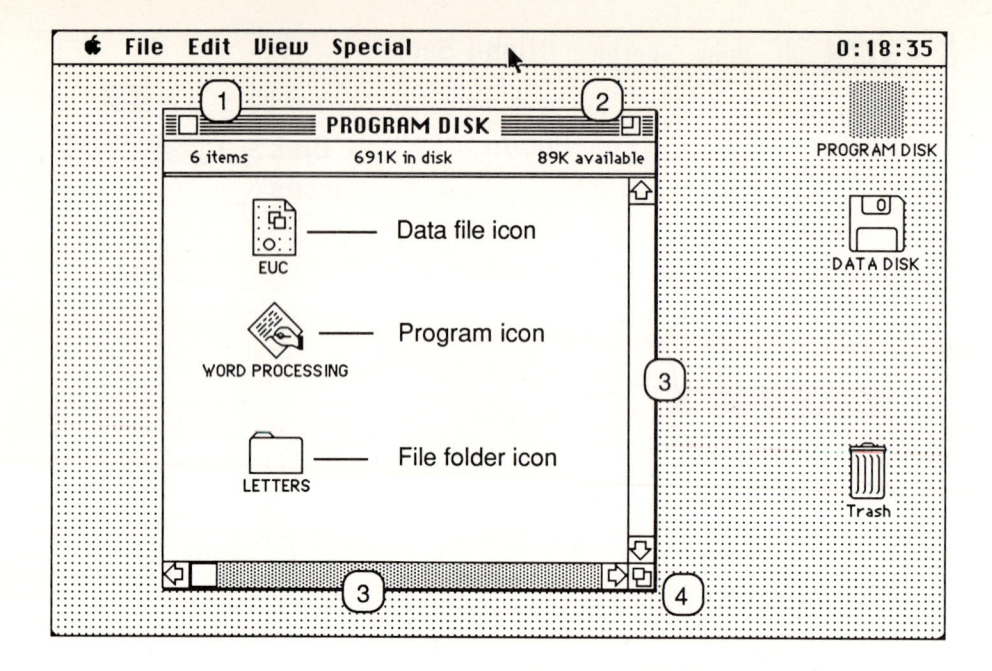

1   Close box -- to close window

2   Full screen box -- to expand window

3   Scroll bar -- to scroll window over underlying information space

4   Size box -- to make window larger or smaller

FIGURE 8-13 WINDOW SHOWING CONTENTS OF DISK

Macintosh copies the file to the other disk. If a file is already there with the same name, Macintosh asks for a confirmation that that file is to be replaced.

- As indicated in Figure 8-14, if a disk file is dragged to the trash icon, the file is erased. However, a file can be unerased later, simply by opening the trash icon and copying the file back. Not until the user selects "Empty Trash" from the "Special" menu is the file permanently erased and its disk space released for other uses.
- If one disk icon is dragged to another, this signals the Macintosh to copy the entire contents of the dragged disk to the other disk, erasing everything already there. Macintosh asks for a confirmation before actually doing the copying.

In the Macintosh environment, then, most ordinary operating system "commands" are done almost automatically. Even "formatting" is utterly sim-

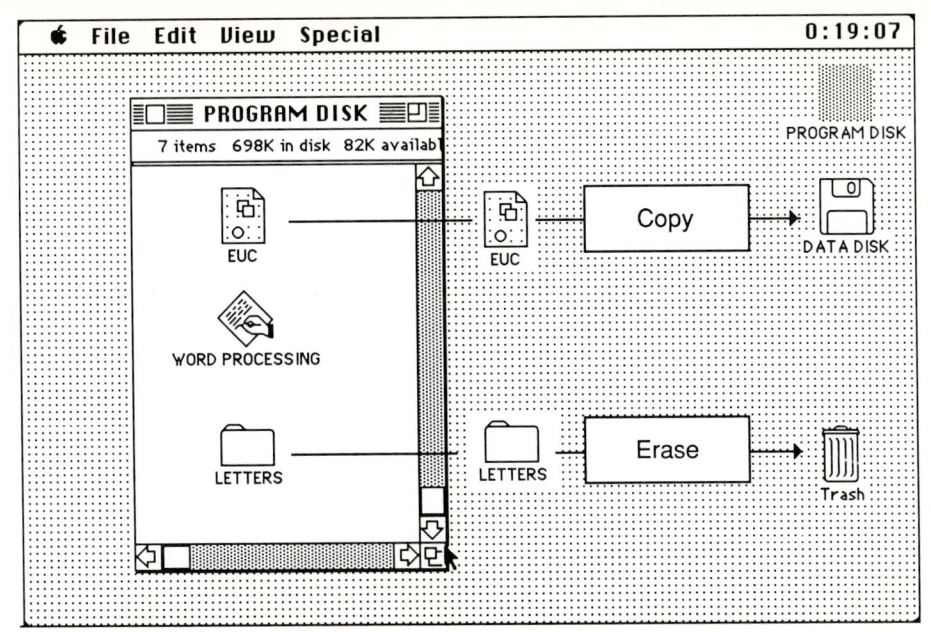

FIGURE 8-14 COPYING AND DISCARDING FILES BY DRAGGING ICONS

ple. If the user inserts a disk that has not been initialized, Macintosh opens a **dialog box** as shown in Figure 8-15. The user simply clicks on the Initialize choice. Such dialog boxes are common on the Macintosh.

Operating on Windows

Figure 8-13 shows a single window, but a user may have several active windows on the screen, showing the contents of different disks and folders and perhaps even running different application programs. Under these conditions, some housekeeping may need to be done on windows.

Only one window is active at any time. To operate on a window, the user first selects it by clicking anywhere inside of it. If other windows overlap it, the active window is placed in front of them, giving a clear and unrestricted view of the window. Once a window is selected, the user can move it around without changing size, alter its size, or simply close it.

In addition to moving the window around on the desktop, the user may have to move the window around over its **underlying information space.** As shown in Figure 8-16, the window may show only part of a document, spreadsheet, or contents of a disk file. The Macintosh allows the user to scroll up or down and pan left or right to see a different part of the underlying information.

The ways the Macintosh handles window operations quickly become second nature to users. These window operations are used not only at the desktop level, but also by all application programs that do not take up the entire screen. Even programs that take up the entire screen normally use the Macintosh's basic scrolling and panning operations.

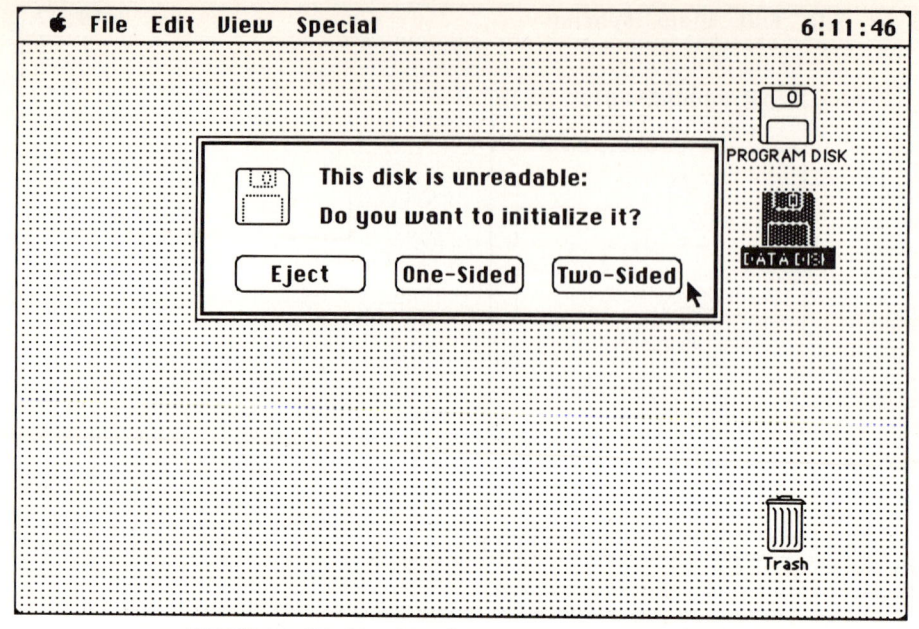

FIGURE 8-15 DIALOG BOX SIMPLIFIES INTERACTION

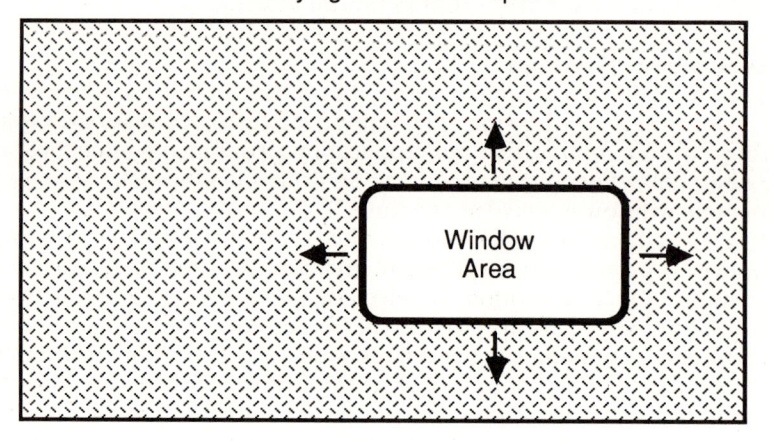

The window shows only a part of the underlying information space.

The window can be moved around on the information space.
(Or, the information space can be viewed as moving around under the window.)

FIGURE 8-16 WINDOW AND UNDERLYING INFORMATION SPACE

IBM's Operating System/2

In 1987, IBM announced its flagship operating system for the future, **Operating System/2** or **OS/2.** Although IBM will continue to support DOS, it will be putting most of its energies into OS/2.

Many aspects of OS/2 have excited prospective users. Its simplest version, called the **Standard Edition,** supports a 16 MB address space, virtual memory, windowing, advanced graphics, and many ease-of-use features. It also remains highly compatible with DOS—a development that many analysts had thought would be impossible. In addition, an optional **Extended Edition** provides extensive communications support and an integral data base management system.

Other aspects are less desirable but were expected. In terms of size, the Standard Edition requires 1.5 MB to 2 MB of RAM. RAM requirements for the Extended Edition have not been announced at the time of this writing. In terms of disk capacity, the Standard Edition requires 5 MB, as well as ample space for its working files. Extended Edition requires even more. In terms of price, the Standard Edition costs a hefty $325 and the Extended Edition $795. (A Standard Edition user can upgrade for $625.)

Other undesirable aspects of OS/2 were totally unexpected. By far the worst of these was the timing of releases. Although OS/2 was announced on April 2, 1987, the first deliveries of the Standard Edition would not take place for a year, and even then, windowing would be missing, and there would not even be enough graphics to do a pie chart. No schedule was given for adding these features, nor was a schedule given for the release of the Extended Version. IBM seemed to be trying to freeze the market by announcing far in advance of delivery, probably to hold off the Macintosh. Given the unexpectedly long development of OS/2 by Microsoft and IBM, who jointly developed the operating system, many users doubted that even the first version of OS/2 would be delivered on time.

Although Microsoft announced that it would introduce a variant of OS/2 for compatibles, it cautioned that the two would have only some things in common and it refused to release information about what aspects would exist in common. As a result, early application programmers could not design their code to separate common and specific matters. Therefore, even when compatibles get the operating system, it may take time for application software to appear.

On a positive note, OS/2 was designed under IBM's **Systems Application Architecture (SAA),** a set of programming specifications designed to let complying programs run on a wide variety of IBM computers. SAA will be discussed later in this chapter following a discussion of OS-2.

Memory Management

DOS was created as a single-tasking operating system limited to 640 KB of memory. OS/2 breaks those limits, but its ability to do so is based on the speed and special features of the Intel 80286 and 80386 microprocessors (see Chapter 7). As a result, it will not run on 8086 and 8088 machines—not even IBM's Personal System/2 Model 30. A user must have an AT or PS/2 above the Model 30 to run OS/2 and take advantage of improved memory management features.

A 16 MB address space OS/2 breaks the 640 KB limit of DOS by offering a full 16 MB address space. This is the maximum allowable on the 80286, but it falls far short of the 4 GB supported by the 80386. By the time OS/2 becomes popular, 1 Mbit and larger RAM chips should make 16 MB a tight fit. Perhaps the 16 MB limit will be expanded then, but its enshrinement in the basic standard is puzzling.

Virtual memory OS/2 takes advantage of special circuits on the 80286 and 80386 to offer virtual memory. Users of virtual memory need ample hard disk space for swap files.

Multitasking OS/2 supports full multitasking, including background and foreground processing and sophisticated interprocess communications features that allow several tasks to be integrated so that they look like a single program to the end user.

Other memory management features OS/2 has a number of other memory management features of interest to programmers. Among them are the ability to call OS/2 features from within application programs and the on-the-fly linking of programs to library modules on disk, so that modules used in several programs do not have to be loaded with each program.

Ease of Use

Taking cues from the Macintosh and various other modern operating systems, OS/2 incorporates a large number of ease-of-use features.

Operating systems ease of use IBM did a number of things to make OS/2 easy to use compared to DOS's cranky user interface. When the user boots OS/2, the > prompt of DOS can be replaced with a full-screen user interface complete with menu-based command selection. To prevent total culture shock for former DOS users, however, OS/2 uses many DOS command names. It also contains a tutorial for learning OS/2 and, perhaps best of all, meaningful error messages.

Presentation manager Ease-of-use functions in OS/2 go beyond basic improvements in the ways users give operating system commands. OS/2 also supports a **presentation manager** that offers a single set of functions for windows, graphics, and other features that govern what the user sees at *both* the system and application levels.

Windows in the Presentation Manager The Presentation Manager offers a rich set of windowing functions similar to those on the Macintosh. Windows can be sized, moved, and scrolled, and there is a clipboard for moving information across windows.

Graphics Also like the Macintosh, OS/2 offers a rich set of pixel and object graphics functions (see Chapter 7). A set of rapid redraw routines allows very fast screen changes, as do the QuickDraw routines in the Macintosh. In an advance over basic Macintosh graphics, OS/2 can transfer text without losing typeface, size, and other information. Not until the Macintosh II did this become standard in the Apple world. In addition, OS/2 comes with a standard set of fonts and the ability to handle downloaded fonts. Although these graphics capabilities are very rich, their delay until 1988—four years after Macintosh graphics burst onto the scene—reduces their impact.

Program selection As noted earlier, programs can be selected from a menu within OS/2. This same capability is available at the level of application programs.

Presentation interface OS/2's Presentation Manager also includes a device-independent interface for calls to displays, printers, and input devices such as mice. Device drivers can then translate the standard I/O calls into language-specific calls to the called device.

The Communications Manager

OS/2's Extended Edition offers a rich set of communications support tools. With these tools, a user can maintain concurrent communications with different host computers. He or she can, for example, work with a VAX computer via VT100 emulation and an asynchronous link while holding a 3270 session with an IBM host and exchanging a file over an IBM Token-Ring network via APPC/PC. Readers who are not familiar with these concepts may wish to read Chapters 13 through 15.

Link support At the lowest level, OS/2 can communicate over many kinds of communications links, including SDLC, the IBM Token-Ring Network, the IBM Personal Computer Network, and simple asynchronous links, including RS232C cables and ordinary telephone lines.

File transfer At a higher level, OS/2 supports a number of file transfer protocols, including IBM mainframe file transfer protocols, the 3270 PC File Transfer Program, and XModem—depending on what host it is using.

General protocols Over the appropriate links, OS/2 can communicate via a number of protocols, including simple asynchronous exchange, LU 2 (3270 data stream), and LU 6.2.

Program and user interfaces *Programs* can work with these communications features by giving calls to popular program interfaces, including IEEE 802.2 for LANs and APPC for direct communication with another application program on another machine (see Chapters 14 and 15). *Users* can work with communications tools directly via terminal emulation. OS/2 emulates 3270 terminals, and IBM 3101 terminals, which are TTYs (see Chapter 13).

Hosts supported OS/2 can provide communications services for connections with a wide variety of IBM computers, including System/370 mainframes, System 3X small business computers, Personal System/2's, Series/1 minicomputers, and the IBM Personal Computer RT workstations. Non-IBM computers are not supported directly, except through TTY and VT100 links.

Conclusion Overall, the communications functions of OS/2, which are found only in the Extended Edition, provide concurrent links, over a wide variety of conditions, with many types of IBM products. Its links to products from other vendors, however, are rudimentary.

Data Base Functions

Another important feature of the Extended Edition is data base management. By incorporating considerable DBMS power, OS/2's Extended Edition becomes a powerful tool for application development.

Data base functionality The embedded data base functions include a major subset of IBM's main relational DBMS for host computers, namely, **IBM Database 2 (DB2).** These functions include interactive schema definition tools, a form creation function for data input, tools to create menus, and even an embedded 4GL for creating procedures.

One important feature is the way updates will be handled. Updates are always temporary until a COMMIT command is given at the end. This greatly simplifies crash recovery.

Retrieval The embedded functions also include a subset of IBM's **Query Management Facility,** which supports brief queries via SQL (Structured Query Language), which is discussed in Chapter 16, and also supports the creation and saving of report formats for report generation.

Utilities The data base functions will include a number of utilities, including those to import and export data, to back up and restore data, to unload and reload individual files, to reorganize tables for efficiency, and to provide statistics.

Data base access via LANs These data base functions are designed to work over LANs without any reprogramming. This raises the possibility that OS/2's Extended Edition will be used heavily as server software.

IBM's Systems Application Architecture (SAA)

Digital Equipment Corporation's VAX line of computers ranges from personal computers to mainframes. All use the same systems software, so an application program written for one will run on all others. This makes it easy for application developers to create applications such as word processing, which must be able to run on many different sizes of computers.

People who want to develop such applications for IBM face a much harder task. IBM has several major lines of computers, including personal computers, System/36s, System/38s, and System/370s. Each uses a different operating system. In fact, the System/370 runs several different operating systems, including MVS, VM, and DOS. All of these operating systems are very different, so a vendor who wants to write a word processor to run on six IBM systems will have to write a half dozen programs. Although these programs may act the same to users, their internal code will be radically different, because each operating system requires very different calls for services. Even IBM has had a poor track record of developing applications that run on different computers in the IBM stable.

The Systems Application Architecture Approach

To bring some order to this chaos, IBM is developing a way to let programmers write programs that will run with any major member of the IBM line—without rewriting a single line of code. This approach is called **systems application architecture (SAA).** As shown in Figure 8-17, SAA will place a layer of software between applications and the system software of the computer being used, which may be a personal computer, System/36, System/38, or System/370.

SAA, then, is a set of specifications to be followed by program developers. These specifications define how calls are to be made to the SAA layer. They define what services can be called, how they should be called, and what results should be expected from each call. But SAA *does not* specify how the internal code should be written for programs that make calls to SAA. That is considered to be an implementation issue to be left to programmers. SAA only governs how a program looks to the SAA layer.

Common applications As shown in Figure 8-17, SAA has four major components. First, there are **common applications**—applications that comply with SAA by issuing their service calls in a standard way. These might be word processing programs, calendar management programs, spreadsheet programs, or any other programs that might be run on more than one machine.

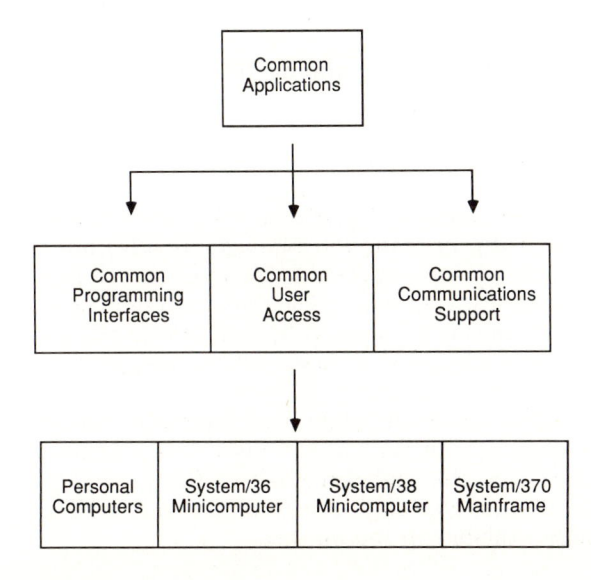

FIGURE 8-17 IBM'S SYSTEMS APPLICATION ARCHITECTURE

Common programming interfaces Second, there are **common programming interfaces,** which govern calls to application development utilities, including programming languages such as COBOL, FORTRAN, C, as well as calls to SQL and QMF (Query Management Facility) programs for data base queries (see Chapter 16), and IBM's GDDM product for graphics operations. Application programs will be able to call these and other utilities with confidence that the results of a call will be the same no matter what computer is being used.

Common user access Taking a cue from the Apple Macintosh, SAA will present a standardized set of user interface tools to application developers, so that all programs will run fairly similarly. If the program has windows, for example, the user will be able to manipulate these windows in ways learned by using other common applications. The **common user access** standards will include windowing, icon operations, mouse operations, and support for high-resolution color graphics display systems.

Common communications support Because most programs operate in a communications-rich world, SAA has standards for calls to IBM's major data communications services, including the IBM 3270 terminal data stream, SDLC, the IBM Token-Ring Network, SNA Distribution Services (asynchronous SNA), and even IBM's electronic mail standards, DIA and DCA. SAA will also include standardized calls to non-IBM data communications services, including TTY emulation, X.25, and Ethernet. These data communications approaches are discussed in Chapters 13 through 15, except for DIA and DCA, which are discussed in Chapter 17.

SAA and OS/2

Operating System/2 will be the first major implementation of SAA. As usual, IBM is confusing the situation by using different terminology in OS/2's implementation of SAA than it uses in its description of SAA.

For example, what IBM calls common program interfaces in its SAA documentation is called the **Applications Programming Interface** in OS/2. This will include calls to several popular programming languages. It will also include calls to the DBMS functions to be embedded in the Extended Version of OS/2. These functions are drawn from SQL and IBM's Query Management Facility (QMF).

In addition, SAA's common user access specification is called the **Presentation Manager** in OS/2. Although the Presentation Manager is still under development at the time of this writing, it is expected to look very much like Microsoft Windows, which itself derives from the Apple Macintosh interface.

Finally, SAA's common communications support becomes OS/2's **Communications Manager.** The Extended Version of OS/2 will be very rich in communications functions.

It is clear that IBM expects users who want to take advantage of common applications (that is, those that comply with SAA specifications) to purchase the Extended Version of OS/2. Given the high price tag of the Extended Version, a good deal of user resistance is expected, at least until a wide variety of common applications becomes available on the market.

SAA in Perspective

Analysts today are deeply divided in their assessment of SAA. Optimists see it as IBM's solution to its deep interconnection problems among its various computers. In their view, SAA will form a hard floor on which application programs may stand without worrying about underlying details.

Pessimists see SAA as a chance to keep wavering customers with IBM. They point out that complete SAA specifications are far off. They also point to IBM's poor record in the past with TopView and other "strategic" products that were later abandoned or left in limbo. At best, they say, SAA gives a single name to a hodge-podge of existing IBM practices and does not represent a well-conceived set of standards at all.

More pragmatically, there are concerns with timing, overhead, and generality. SAA will be released gradually over time, and if this process takes too long, SAA will become a dinosaur before it is ever developed. In terms of overhead, it is expected that SAA will add considerable processing overhead, and the potential amount of this overhead could make IBM's integration strategy a costly one. Finally, in terms of generality, there are questions over whether all IBM computers will be supported. Only IBM's personal computers, System/3X, and System/370 families are currently slated for SAA support. Although these are the most popular IBM machines, they are not its only machines.

Environments Versus Operating Systems

Advanced operating systems of all types begin with one enormous strike against them. To offer advanced features, they must be large, often a mega-

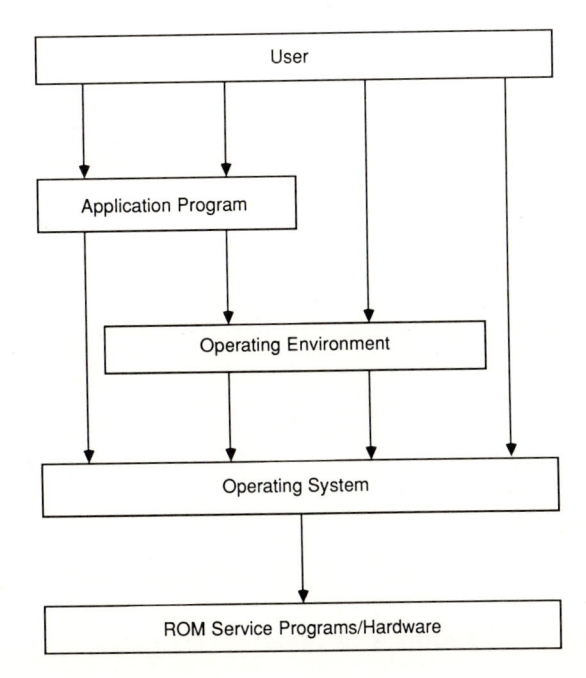

FIGURE 8-18 OPERATING ENVIRONMENT

byte or more. As a result, they will be unattractive to users with low-end personal computers.

One solution to the problem of different people needing different things is to use the principle of layering and to divide the operating system into two parts—a small core program that is basically the normal limited operating system, and an **environment** or **shell** that provides advanced functions. Figure 8-18 illustrates this process. Users could then elect to use the environment or not use the environment, depending on the size of their machine and their desire for advanced functions. Some programs, of course, might require the use of the shell.

Several shells now on the market offer ease-of-use features including IBM's TopView, Microsoft Windows, and GEM Desktop. Nearly all of these operating environments also support windowing with at least limited cut-and-paste among applications running in different windows. Many offer a grab bag of desk accessory programs such as pop-up calculators and notepads. (Desk accessories are discussed later in this chapter.) Finally, some offer multitasking and even multiuser capabilities.

Microsoft's advanced version of MS-DOS is expected to include the core part of Microsoft Windows. If it becomes popular, it will cast doubt on the future of operating system shells because it will offer a single "standard," and this will appeal to software developers.

Other System Software

Although the operating system is the most important piece of system software, it is not the only important one lying beneath the user's application software. In general, other types of system software are called **utilities**. They add capabilities that are not offered by the operating system.

Keyboard Enhancers

Under most conditions, the application program defines the meaning of all keys on the keyboard. **Keyboard enhancers** allow the user to attach his or her own meanings to one or more keys. As shown in Figure 8-19, the keyboard enhancer is a RAM-resident program that intercepts every keystroke. If the user has not defined a special meaning for the key, the keystroke is passed onto the application program. If the user has given a special definition to this key, then the keyboard enhancer executes the user's instructions for that key.

In the simplest cases, the user's special instructions consist of one or

Key typed	Keyboard enhancer sends
Alt-A	Alt-A
Alt-B	Alt-B
Alt-C	[Null]
Alt-D	/PPR[Enter]G
Alt-E	End User Computing

FIGURE 8-19 KEYBOARD ENHANCER

more keystrokes which the keyboard enhancer passes onto the application program. For example, suppose that the user constantly has to type "end user computing" while writing a document. She might assign "end user computing" to the keystroke combination <Alt><e>. Whenever "end user computing" must be typed, she simply types <Alt><e>. To the word processing program, it appears that the user is typing "end user computing."

Another use for playing back text is to "customize" the keyboard for consistency across a user's programs. For example, the "goto" key in Multimate is <F1>. In Lotus 1-2-3, it is <F5>. If a user constantly switches between the two programs but works mainly with Multimate, he or she might reassign <F1> in Lotus 1-2-3, which is normally 1-2-3's help key, to send the goto command (<F5>) to 1-2-3. If the user does not want to lose 1-2-3's online help, she could redefine <Shift><F1> to send <F1> (help) to 1-2-3. This would be a good choice for a Multimate user because <Shift><F1> is Multimate's help key. If the user works with many different application programs, each can be given its own keyboard enhancer profile, so that, for example, all programs would use <Shift><F1> for help. Redefining keys can also be useful if the application program has an awkward assignment for an important key.

An especially innovative way to use keyboard enhancers is to produce "training wheels" versions of packaged programs for users who are just learning them. This is done by assigning "null" text strings to keys that do advanced work, so nothing happens if these keys are struck. As a result, the user will be prevented from getting into trouble by accidentally hitting the wrong key. Later, the restrictions can be removed, either all at once or in logical groups as the user learns new features.

The assignment made to a key does not have to be simple text. It can also be a string of commands to the application program. For instance, a Lotus 1-2-3 user might want to save a program onto the disk in Drive B, replace this disk with its backup, save the file again on the backup, and then replace the backup with the original disk. The command keystrokes needed to do this could be recorded once, assigned to <Alt><s>, and then played back as often as desired by hitting <Alt><s>.

Most keyboard enhancers have their own control commands. These allow them to do such things as pause and prompt the user to take a certain action, for example, replace the disk in Drive B. Advanced keyboard enhancers can even accept input from the terminal for variable information, do if-then-else control over execution, and sometimes loop through steps several times. In other words, many keyboard enhancers are modest programming languages.

The most powerful keyboard enhancers allow the user to build full applications, including pop-down menus and even help screens. These applications can be employed by users who are not adept at using the underlying application program. These capabilities are similar in spirit and in operation to the Lotus 1-2-3 menu macro commands discussed in Chapter 9.

Keyboard enhancers should offer several ways to create assignments. In the **learn mode,** the user names the key to be given the assignment and then goes through the actions manually. These keystrokes are recorded and stored with the key. For more advanced uses, some keyboard enhancers offer full-screen text editors to create assignments or edit existing assignments. Some can even capture text off the screen, using the screen capture tools discussed later in this chapter, in the Integration section. Most can also import assignment files created for other keyboard enhancers that are especially popular, especially Prokey.

For editing, full-screen editors are desirable, but they are only one element needed in the editing mix. At a minimum, the user should be able to see a list of keys that have assignments, but this is not possible for all keyboard enhancers. In addition, some keyboard enhancers cannot use changes until they are completely restarted, so that the user cannot make changes on the fly, while using his or her application program.

Disk Managers

Although MS-DOS was created specifically to work with computers having disk drives, its disk handling features are quite limited. It has no way to unerase a deleted file, unformat a disk that was accidentally reformatted, or add security to user files. In addition, many of the capabilities it does have are too limited to be very useful. For example, although MS-DOS allows users to create hierarchical file structures, it is very weak at managing these hierarchical directories.

Disk managers add some of the capabilities that were left out of MS-DOS for reasons of space, Microsoft design philosophy, or simple development oversights. Different disk managers have different capabilities, but we will look at the general disk management capabilities that users are likely to need from one or more disk management programs.

First, **hard disk management** allows users to manage the tens of megabytes of memory capacity found on hard disks. Even a small hard disk may contain dozens of files, and large hard disks may contain hundreds. Moreover, the way MS-DOS manages its directory hierarchy, as just noted, is relatively crude. Hard disk organizers take over where MS-DOS leaves off, making the user's life much easier. They allow users to organize their files hierarchically, see the hierarchy on-screen, and move a file from one subdirectory to another by pointing to the file, giving the disk manager's move command, and then pointing to its destination subdirectory.

Many hard disk organizers include security functions to help the user ensure the confidentiality of files on the hard disk. These security functions range from simple systems that require passwords before a file can be accessed to complex functions that include true file encryption. A number of the weaker approaches are easily accessed by anyone sophisticated enough to use the next set of features, "data snooping."

In **data snooping,** the utility user can look at the bit contents of individual sectors on floppy disks and hard disks. This is useful in the fine repair of certain types of damage, but anyone who is familiar with these programs and with the way MS-DOS formats and uses data disks can defeat many kinds of protection systems. The Norton Utilities were the first major set of data snooping programs, but there are many on the market today.

Programs that can do data snooping can get around the two worst problems of MS-DOS, namely, accidental file deletions and accidental reformatting of disks. DOS has an erase command that, combined with "wild card" symbols, can erase a large number of files with a single command. MS-DOS does not offer an "unerase" command, so erasures are irreversible through MS-DOS. In addition, MS-DOS has no way of undoing a formatting operation. Many users have watched in horror as their hard disk totally reformats itself because they typed "Format" at the C> prompt, instead of "Format A:."

Many data managers offer detailed data snooping to reverse both kinds of damage, at least partially, and most offer specific high-level commands for unerasing and unreformatting. When MS-DOS "erases" a file, it does not physically erase it. It merely changes the first character of the file name in the directory entry to a special symbol that indicates that this directory location is free for new entries. Unerasing can be done by looking at a list of files and indicating what character should be changed in the name of the erased file. Reversing formatting is more complex, but at least partial reversal is possible because formatting, like erasing, destroys very little actual information.

Disk Copying Programs

Many programs are copy-protected to deter unauthorized copying. A number of programs such as PC Copy II attempt to circumvent these copy protection schemes, so that users can make backup copies of floppy disks, copy the program to run easily on a hard disk, or, most sadly, do pure and simple piracy.

Programming Language Compilers and Interpreters

Compilers and interpreters for programming languages such as BASIC, PASCAL, COBOL, and C are classified as system software. We will delay the discussion of these compilers and interpreters until Chapter 12, where they will be discussed in the context of other tools.

Integrated Utilities

The trend today is toward integrating several utilities into a single package. In some cases, there is a set of core functions to which extensions have been made. For example, many desk accessory programs and keyboard enhancers have the ability to run DOS commands without exiting from either the utility or the application program currently in use.

There is also a growing trend toward offering a single **core utility manager** program that is RAM-resident and can call any of several overlay utilities from the vendor of the core utility manager or from other vendors. In addition to offering a broad spectrum of tools, these core utility managers ensure that the user does not have to suffer through the wars that result when several RAM-resident programs all fight for control of the keyboard interrupt.

Among the services offered by integrated utilities of all types are the following.

- The ability to call application programs from menus.
- Desk accessory functions.
- The ability to give MS-DOS commands without leaving the utility or the application program.
- Keyboard enhancement functions.

- Management functions for hierarchical directories.
- Data snooping, unerasing, and reformatting.
- Copying copy-protected programs onto hard disks.

INTEGRATION

Most users have more than one application package, for example, Lotus 1-2-3 for spreadsheet analysis, Multimate for word processing, dBASE III for data management, and Crosstalk for terminal emulation.

A user's work on a single project often cuts across several of these packages. For instance, a user might retrieve data from dBASE III or a mainframe data base, analyze the data in Lotus 1-2-3, and finally write up the results in Multimate.

Ideally, information should move freely and automatically among applications. A data extract from dBASE III should flow nicely into a 1-2-3 worksheet, and tabular results from the analysis should pop right into a word processing document.

Things are rarely this easy, however, and users must resort to a number of "fixes" to move information among applications. We will discuss these approaches after looking at why they are necessary, namely, incompatibilities among data file formats.

Incompatible Data File Formats

Each program has its own way of storing data. Different programs usually have incompatible file formats, even if they are in the same general application category, such as word processing. Programs in different categories, such as word processing programs and spreadsheet programs, nearly always have data file formats that are deeply incompatible.

To see why incompatibilities exist, we will look at word processing file formats. At first glance, it would seem that word processing documents should consist only of letters, numbers, and punctuation symbols, which are all included in the ASCII character set (see Chapter 13) used by all popular word processing programs. But document files also include formatting codes to govern such items as left margins, boldface, font changes, and line spacing. To complicate matters further, many word processing programs offer very different features, and there is often no simple one-to-one correspondence between their formatting codes.

For other types of programs, there is not even a simple base design such as ASCII files. For spreadsheet programs, to give the most obvious example, there is no easy way to represent cells and their contents.

Integrated Software

The cleanest way to move information among several applications is to use **integrated software** packages such as Symphony, Framework, and Enable. These programs contain several modules—usually word processing, spreadsheet, data management, analytical graphics, and terminal emulation—and they can move data easily among these modules, with little or no damage.

The problem with integrated programs now on the market is that their individual modules are functionally inferior to stand-alone programs. Although Symphony understandably has a strong spreadsheet module, for example, its word processing module is weak, and its data management module is embryonic. As a result, few organizations are willing to settle on integrated systems as their main standards.

In general, integrated systems are used by individual staff analysts with one major need, say spreadsheet analysis, as well as modest needs in other areas. These analysts usually buy an integrated package that is very strong in their chief areas and see the lack of power in other functions as being less important than the easy integration they offer.

If these analysts turn their documents over to secretaries for editing, the integration problem appears all over again, because the secretaries probably use a different word processing system. Without secretarial support, analysts will waste a great deal of the time doing blue pencil editing, spell checking, and printing.

Desk Accessory Programs

As noted above, integrated programs seem to work best for the person with one dominant need and several smaller needs in other areas. Another way to serve those with one dominant need and several smaller needs is to provide them with **desk accessory programs.** These programs are RAM-resident programs that remain in RAM when not in use. These programs usually provide limited word processing, calculator functions, and appointment calendar, and perhaps a simple filing system. These systems are discussed in more detail in Chapter 12.

Many "integration" needs are really task-switching needs. As discussed earlier in the chapter, a user may want to interrupt a spreadsheet session to jot down a few notes, check on the time of a meeting later in the day, or look up a telephone number. Desk accessory programs provide painless task switching.

Desk accessory programs also provide limited cut and paste capabilities. For example, a table produced in a spreadsheet program can appear on the screen, be "cut out" by the desk accessory's word processing function, and be captured into the word processing function's file. Words can then be written around the table to produce a formal memo through the desk accessory. This is one example of "screen capture," a general technique for cutting and pasting that is discussed in more detail a little later.

A number of operating environments (discussed earlier in this chapter) include desk accessories, and the file formats used by these desk accessories may be readable by other programs. The best example is the Apple Macintosh operating system. As shown in Figure 8-20, the "apple" icon at the start of virtually every menu in Macintosh programs leads to a good set of desk accessories that are bundled with the system.

On the Macintosh, it is easy to install *new* desk accessories that are accessed just like the system's basic accessories. Figure 8-21 shows Creighton Development Inc.'s MacSpell+ added to the pop-down Apple menu. Another popular add-in is Dubl-Click Software's Dubl-Click Calculator, a customizable calculator designer that lets users build virtually any kind of calculator they

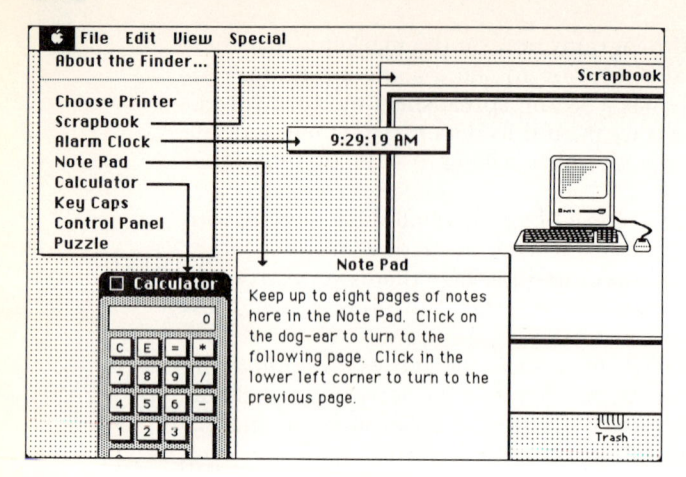

FIGURE 8-20 DESK ACCESSORIES UNDER THE APPLE MENU CHOICE

want, say one that has buttons for Fixed Cost, Unit Variable Cost, Units Sold, and Break Even Point.

The desk accessories' chief problems, of course, are their very limited functionality and the very limited ways in which they can cut and paste information.

MacSpell+™ is installed with the basic desk accessories.

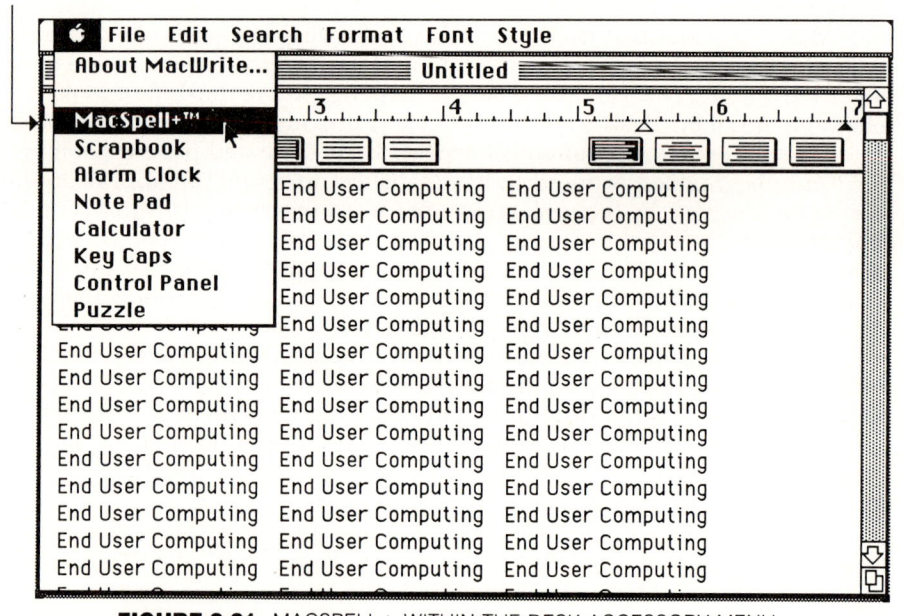

FIGURE 8-21 MACSPELL+ WITHIN THE DESK ACCESSORY MENU

Screen Capture

One general technique for doing limited cutting and pasting between applications is to use **screen capture**—capturing the information that an application places on the display screen.

Text Screen Capture

As noted in Chapter 7, simple text characters on an IBM PC or compatible are represented as 2-byte codes, with the first byte holding the ASCII code for character and the second byte holding the codes for such attributes as reverse video and blinking.

An area of RAM holds the information shown on the display. This area of RAM is character-mapped, meaning that there is one 2-byte location for each of the 2000 character positions on the screen.

Text screen capture programs, illustrated in Figure 8-22, permit the user to designate part or all of the screen. The relevant characters in the screen map are then transferred to a cut file as a series of ASCII characters. (The attribute byte is normally stripped off.) A carriage return is normally placed at the end of each line.

Text screen capture works well for text information that appears on a single display screen. If a table or other information appears on several display screens, several "snapshots" usually have to be taken and pasted together later. This can be a difficult process.

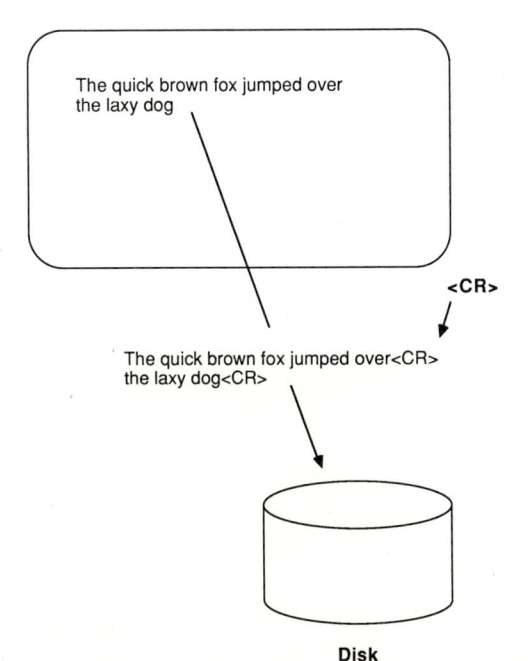

FIGURE 8-22 TEXT SCREEN CAPTURE

Graphics Screen Capture

A graphics display image also has a mapped area in RAM, as discussed in Chapter 7. **Graphics screen capture** programs clip out all or portions of this map and transfer it to another program. This allows users to do such things as create a pie chart in Lotus 1-2-3, view it on the display, clip out the image, and paste it into a file of a sophisticated pixel-oriented graphics program in order to improve the appearance of the graph.

Macintosh Screen Capture

The Macintosh is particularly rich in screen capture capabilities. For graphics, the key combination Command-Shift-3 captures the entire visible contents of a window into a MacPaint file, which is the lingua franca graphics file of the Macintosh.

Most programs also have Cut and Copy commands that capture portions of a screen and can capture text as easily as graphics. Because the entire operating system is oriented to graphics handling, nearly all word processing programs on the Macintosh and many other programs allow embedded graphics that have been imported through cut or copy operations. Cut and copy are so common that the Macintosh operating system offers a Scrapbook desk accessory that can store many cuts and copies for later pasting into one or more application files.

Dumb Terminal Screen Capture

As discussed in Chapter 13, PCs can emulate dumb TTY terminals when they deal with a host. This provides one more opportunity for screen capture. When the host communicates with the PC, say to show a report on-screen, the host sends the information as a series of ASCII text lines ending in carriage returns. Most TTY terminal emulation programs can capture these ASCII text lines in RAM, disk files, or both. Many programs, as discussed later, can import simple ASCII files.

Because there are carriage returns at the ends of all lines, it is difficult to work with documents transferred into word processing systems in this way. Placing a carriage return at the end of each line makes later editing nearly impossible, as discussed in the word processing section of Chapter 11. For tabular information, of course, there is no problem.

The advantage of screen capture in TTY terminal emulation (and in most other forms of terminal emulation as well) is that information that extends to more than one screen can be captured as easily as information on a single screen. This is rarely the case with simple text screen capture programs.

File Format Conversion

Although screen capture may be suitable for transferring small amounts of information, users often have to transfer entire files. This requires the file in the native format of the source program to be converted into a file in the native format of the destination program.

As shown in Figure 8-23, there are two basic ways to handle file conversion: direct file conversion and intermediate file conversion. In **direct file conversion,** information is converted directly from one program's native file format to another. Many programs, for example, can **import** Lotus 1-2-3,

Direct File Conversion

File Format for Program A ⟶ File Format for Program B

Intermediate File Conversion

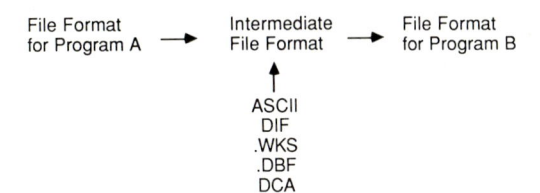

File Format for Program A ⟶ Intermediate File Format ⟶ File Format for Program B

↑
ASCII
DIF
.WKS
.DBF
DCA

FIGURE 8-23 DIRECT FILE CONVERSION AND INTERMEDIATE FILE CONVERSION

dBASE III, Multimate, or WordStar files directly, and quite a few can also **export** to these popular file formats. In **intermediate file conversion** neither of the two programs that need to communicate can understand the other's native file format, but both can work with a third or **intermediate file format.** The sending program exports to this intermediate file format, and the other imports the intermediate file.

In direct file conversion, there is only one step. Either one program imports another's file directly, or one program exports to the other's native file format. Intermediate file conversion requires two steps, doubling the amount of work to be done.

Direct file conversion produces little damage in translation because the one-to-one conversion allows the good handling of conversion problems. In contrast, intermediate file formats must serve the needs of many programs, so individual conversion problems cannot be addressed. In addition, two conversions double the damage that does occur. Overall, more damage occurs during conversion, and it may take quite a bit of time to undo the damage with the receiving program's editor.

For both direct and intermediate file conversion, there are two questions to ask: how much work must be done, and how much damage is created. Some programs do conversion within their main programs, do it easily, and do it quickly, whereas others require a separate program to be loaded, run, and then unloaded. Damage is minimized when programs that do the conversion are flexible and offer many options to handle such specific matters as tab settings in word processing and field and record delimiters in data management systems.

ASCII Files

As already mentioned, the simplest kind of intermediate file is the ASCII file. This file is nothing more than a stream of bytes, with each byte being drawn from the ASCII symbol code discussed in Chapter 13.

ASCII files have two basic formats, which are differentiated by whether a carriage return is placed at the end of each line. If a carriage return is placed at the end of each line, then the file will be printable without further modification. A common way to create such a file is to do a print command in the source program and to send the output to a disk **print file.** If no special printer formats are embedded in the file, a simple ASCII file with carriage returns at the end of each line will result.

As noted earlier, files that have carriage returns at the end of each line are difficult to edit. If a word is deleted from the middle of a line, for example, a short line will result, and there will be no way for a word processor to tell whether it should override the carriage return and move up characters from the next line or whether it should respect the carriage return because it is the end of a line in a table or marks the end of a paragraph.

When all line endings are marked, the normal end is a carriage return, which is interpreted as going to the left margin and moving one line down. But some programs that generate line-ended ASCII files terminate each line with a carriage return plus a line feed. An importing program must be sufficiently flexible to import either type of file correctly.

For data base file transfers, it is common to make each record (row) a line and to end the line with a carriage return or carriage return plus line feed. Within each record, there are two options for delimiting fields. The first option is to have **position-delimited** fields, that is, to give each field a constant length, so that a field always begins at the same character position within a record. The second option is to have **symbol-delimited** fields, in which a special symbol is placed between each field. If this symbol appears as data within a field, either this symbol is stripped out, damaging the file, or a special "escape character" is placed before the symbol to indicate that the symbol is not a field ending.

The problem with all forms of ASCII intermediate files is that they represent a lowest common denominator in expressiveness. Like pidgin, they fail to express many things, and a great deal is usually lost in translation. When word processing files are translated into ASCII, for example, tab stops and centering are replaced by spaces. Boldface and other text characteristics must be stripped out, and headers and footers must be removed to avoid confusion. ASCII's basic problem is that it is *too general* an intermediate file format. The only way it can be all things to all programs is to give up virtually all internal structure.

We will now turn to more sophisticated intermediate file formats. These result in translation with little or no damage because they have the rich internal structure to permit feature mapping during both export and import. The price they pay for this sophistication is a *loss of generality*. These sophisticated intermediate file formats are normally linked to specific application categories.

Spreadsheet File Formats

Lotus Worksheet Files

In the spreadsheet world, the dominance of Lotus 1-2-3 on IBM PCs and compatibles has led to its .WKS files becoming the main intermediate file format when text, numbers, formulas, and as much other information are transferred among spreadsheet programs.

The most extreme example of .WKS compatibility is presented by the 1-2-3 "clones" discussed in Chapter 9. These clones use the *same* file format as Lotus 1-2-3, so that even such advanced information as macros can be exchanged.

For other spreadsheet programs, which use different native file formats, something is always lost in the translation, especially if .WKS is used as an intermediate file format to transfer information between two other spreadsheet programs that use non-.WKS native formats. In these cases, something is lost during both export and import.

Although most spreadsheet programs can read .WKS files, not all can write them, and this limits their ability to transfer files. If a program claims either the ability to read and/or write Lotus worksheet files, the claim should be checked carefully. As noted above, some advanced features may not be readable or writable. In addition, different releases of 1-2-3 have different worksheet files formats. Although we have called these files .WKS files, .WKS is actually the file format of Releases 1 and 1A. The Release 2 family uses the compatible but extended .WK1 file format.

DIF Files

Software Arts, the creator of VisiCalc, created an intermediate file format for sending VisiCalc tables to other Software Arts programs, such as VisiPlot. It called this file format the **Data Interchange Format, DIF.**

In contrast to .WKS and .WK1 files, DIF files do not include formulas, macros, or other advanced information. When a DIF export is made, all formulas are converted to their current values. DIF, as its name suggest, deals only with data. Of course, this limit is important only for exchanging full spreadsheets between spreadsheet programs. It has proven no barrier to transfers to other programs.

Most word processing programs can read DIF files and convert them into tables. In the conversion, they normally set up tab stops, instead of just inserting spaces. This makes for very clean editability.

Most data base programs can both read and write DIF files. This capability allows them to send data to a spreadsheet program for inclusion in an analysis and to incorporate data from an analysis.

Even spreadsheet programs find it convenient to read as well as write DIF files. Although formulas are lost, many spreadsheet-to-spreadsheet transfers consist of data anyway, and reading is needed to get information from many data base programs.

Word Processing File Formats

The General Situation

In word processing, most programs can read or write directly to the native file formats of several other programs, eliminating the need for intermediate file processing in many cases. For competitive reasons, most programs can read far more formats than they are willing to write, in order to facilitate conversion to them rather than coexistence.

When two word processing programs cannot communicate directly, WordStar's file format is often used to build an intermediate file because WordStar is so broadly supported. In the future, most word processing programs are likely to support two file formats created expressly to handle intermediate file conversions. These are IBM's Document Content Architecture (DCA) and emerging international standards.

DCA

Many word processing programs are beginning to support IBM's **Document Content Architecture (DCA).** As discussed in Chapter 17, DCA's position is strengthened by IBM's market dominance, by its use in IBM word processing products on both PCs and hosts, and by its intrinsic merit. DCA is an advanced intermediate file format that produces exchanges with little damage. DCA is improving very rapidly, and its long-term prospects are excellent.

When transmission is to be done by data communications, DCA becomes even more important because a growing number of communications programs can transmit DCA files without damage, despite the fact that DCA files contain a number of special symbols that could be misinterpreted as command codes. Although other file formats are also supported by communication programs, DCA promises to be ever more popular.

International Standards

Internationally, ISO is developing sophisticated document architecture standards that will rival DCA and will even jump beyond it, into desktop publishing functionality. By 1990, these international standards should be in place.

Other Intermediate File Formats

Data Base

In the data base area, dBASE II and dBASE III have long dominated the high-end DBMS arena, whereas pfs:file has led the market at the low end of file management. Their native file formats are often used as intermediate file formats or in direct conversions.

Graphics

For graphics, the standards discussed in Chapter 7 for systems that draw with basic geometric objects such as polylines are useful for object-oriented graphics. In addition, Lotus 1-2-3 .PIC files can usually be read by analytical graphics programs.

For pixel-oriented graphics, no standards exist, but pixel-oriented graphics often works with screen-size images, so screen capture is workable. In the Macintosh world, MacPaint offers a de facto standard for full-page pixel-oriented graphics.

Windowing Environments

We will close this section by mentioning windowing environments, such as Microsoft Windows.

Windows and most other windowing environments offer cut and paste across windows running different programs. Although limited in functionality, these transfer capabilities are easy to use and should prove very popular.

ARTIFICIAL INTELLIGENCE

The Breakthrough of the 1980s

The term **artificial intelligence (AI)** was born in the 1950s. At the time, many believed that "giant brains," as computers were often called, could soon be taught to think like people. Progress in this area proved to be slow and difficult, however. During the 1970s, a great deal was written about the "death of artificial intelligence," and research funding grew slim. The 1980s brought two major innovations that revitalized the field. AI is now exploding into almost every aspect of business and nonbusiness software.

Limited But Important Problems

The first of these two breakthroughs was an emphasis on **limited** but **important** classes of problems.

- In the early days, AI had often focused on **limited and unimportant** problems, such as playing the game of checkers, in the hopes of finding general algorithms. Unfortunately, all it produced was the ability to play checkers.

- At the other extreme, AI often attacked **important and unlimited** problems, such as the translation of human languages. Unfortunately, these large problems are too rich and complex to handle well with either yesterday's or today's skills, and the results were often ludicrous. According to one popular story, "The spirit is willing, but the flesh is weak" was translated into Russian and then back into English. The double translation produced "The vodka is good, but the meat has spoiled." Although the story may be apocryphal, it illustrates the general failure of grand efforts.

The abandonment of both extremes led to the focus on (1) *limited* problems that could be understood and computerized with current AI tools yet are also (2) *important* in and of themselves. One example of this focus on limited but important problems is the use of AI for natural language command input in data base access, spreadsheet analysis, and other application packages. Although natural language understanding is beyond our capabilities at the level of entire human languages, the relatively few verbs and nouns within these applications allow sufficient natural language understanding for freeform command input.

The Knowledge-Based System Approach

The second major breakthrough of the 1980s was the refinement of a particular approach to programming AI applications. This was the creation of **knowledge-based systems.** Figure 8-24 shows the three components of a knowledge-based system.

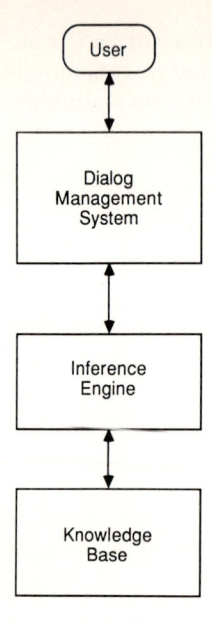

FIGURE 8-24 COMPONENTS OF A KNOWLEDGE-BASED SYSTEM

1. The knowledge base management system.
2. The inference engine.
3. The dialog management system.

We will now look at each of these three pieces, beginning with the heart of any knowledge-based system, the knowledge base.

The Knowledge Base

Overview

In knowledge-based systems, knowledge about the particular application is usually expressed as a body of **statements** such as the following.

- Fido is a dog.
- All dogs have hair.

These statements have three parts: a subject, a relationship, and an object. The subject ("Fido" and "All dogs" in the examples given above) and the object ("dog" and "hair") are entities that are related. The relationship ("is a" and "have") specifies the relationship between the two. As we will see later, this subject–relationship syntax is only one of several statement syntaxes used to express knowledge.

The statements in a system are called, collectively, its **knowledge base.** Figure 8-25 illustrates a simplified knowledge base with eight statements. This is, of course, a highly artificial example. In any real knowledge base, there will be 50 to several thousand statements.

Statements can be added to the knowledge base in any order, in a way reminiscent of relational data bases (see Chapter 10) or model statements in

Subject	Relationship	Object
Pat	is a	cat
Cats	have	fur
Bob	is a	dog
Dogs	have	hair
Peg	belongs to	Larry
Peg	is a	horse
Horses	have	4 feet
Horses	have	hair

FIGURE 8-25 KNOWLEDGE BASE

analysis programs such as Interactive Financial Planning System, IFPS (see Chapter 16). Thus, it is very easy to add or to delete statements from the knowledge base. In traditional programming languages, statements are embedded in an elaborate control structure, and adding or deleting "knowledge" from a program consists of making changes that may affect many other parts of the program and so must be very carefully considered.

The **knowledge base management system (KBMS)** manages the data base. It allows rules to be added, deleted, and edited, and better KBMSs can even check for consistency among rules.

Knowledge Representation: Semantic Networks

In Figure 8-25, knowledge is represented in a particular way—as a series of subject–relationship–object statements. This is only one way to represent knowledge, however. Classically, there are three major ways to represent knowledge, namely, the semantic network approach, the frames approach, and the rules approach.

The **semantic network** approach is illustrated in Figure 8-26. In this approach, concepts are represented by ellipses, and relationships by arcs. This is a very free-form way to represent many kinds of knowledge.

The subject–relationship–object syntax flows naturally from the semantic network approach. Each statement represents an arc (relationship), as well as the names of the two concepts being connected. Subject–relationship–object tables merely express the same information in tabular form, instead of as a networked graph.

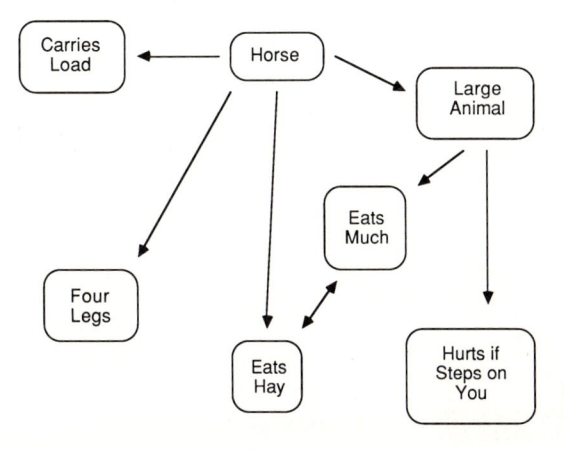

FIGURE 8-26 SEMANTIC NETWORK KNOWLEDGE BASE

In a semantic network, attributes can be inherited across two or more arcs in the network. If I know that Christmas comes in December and that most days in December are cold, I know that most Christmases are cold.

Knowledge Representation: Frames

Related to the semantic network approach is the frames approach. In this approach, several attributes are attached to major concepts. As shown in Figure 8-27, the concept "mammal" has such attributes as breastfeeds its young. The concept and its attributes are called **frames**.

Attributes can be inherited by lower level frames. For example, the frame "dog" comes under "mammal" because dogs are mammals. We therefore know that dogs breastfeed their young, despite the fact that the frame "dog" does not have this information repeated from the mammal frame. In a real sense, the frames approach is the semantic network approach with a hierarchical structure superimposed on it.

Knowledge Representation: Rules

Another popular way to represent knowledge is to use rules. **Rules** are if–then constructions such as the following.

```
IF the patient has a fever
    and an elevated blood count
    and abdominal pain
THEN there is a high likelihood of appendicitis.
```

Uncertainty and Inheritance

Things are simplest when knowledge is clear—for example, when we can say with certainty that all dogs have hair. However, little in life is com-

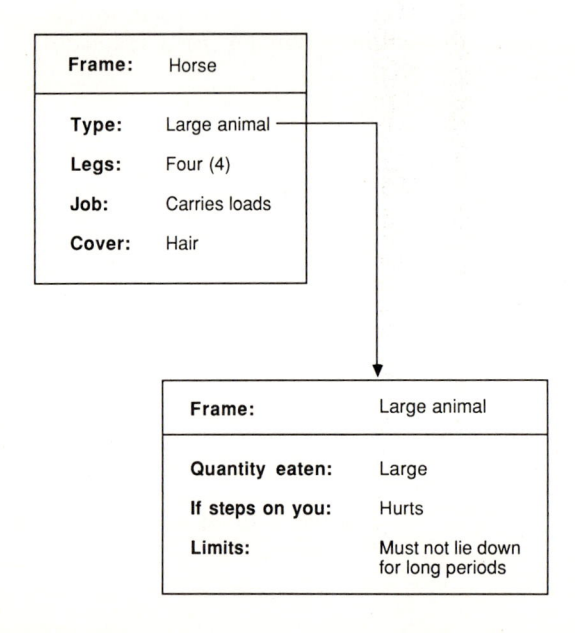

Frame:	Horse
Type:	Large animal
Legs:	Four (4)
Job:	Carries loads
Cover:	Hair

Frame:	Large animal
Quantity eaten:	Large
If steps on you:	Hurts
Limits:	Must not lie down for long periods

FIGURE 8-27 FRAMES KNOWLEDGE BASE

pletely certain. There are at least a few breeds of hairless dogs in the world. It is possible to attach probability estimates to knowledge statements, of course, but then how should *chains of probability* be computed? Beysian analysis offers one approach, but its validity for subjective probability assessment is not universally accepted. The representation of **uncertainty** is one of the central problems of knowledge base design.

Another difficult issue is **inheritance.** It is hard enough to decide whether a characteristic of A, which is related to B, is inherited by C, which is related to B. When many levels of connection exist, the validity of inheritance can become extremely tenuous. This tenuous nature of inheritance is compounded by uncertainty.

The Inference Engine

The Need for an Inference Engine

In a relational data base management system, three general actions can be taken on the data to produce results (see Chapter 10). These are select, project, and join. Although a few relational data base management systems require the user to work with only these three basic operations, as well as a few minor operations, most relational data base management systems allow users to make general statements, such as "Show the names of all customers with credit balances over $200." An internal module of the data base management system then finds a good series of selects, projects, and joins to carry out the request.

In statement-based analysis programs, such as IFPS, the model statements are really a set of simultaneous equations to be solved. A module within the program solves this set of simultaneous equations in a way that is hopefully efficient and effective.

In knowledge-based systems, a special module is also needed to turn user requests into manipulations of the knowledge base. This is called the **inference engine.** Although the user does not work directly with the inference engine, its efficiency and effectiveness are crucial.

Forward Chaining

Figure 8-28 illustrates one simple approach to inference in a knowledge base. It is called **forward chaining.** In this figure, a simple question is asked of our knowledge-based system, namely, "Does Peg have hair?"

In the first step to answering this question, we begin with Peg as our subject and look through the entire data base, statement by statement, finding all statements in which Peg is the subject. We would like to get "Peg has hair," but we do not immediately reach this ultimate goal. Instead, we get two statements.

1. Peg belongs to Larry.
2. Peg is a horse.

Now we make our second pass through the knowledge base, this time with Larry as our subject. This pass proves fruitless because Larry does not appear as a subject in any statement. In addition, we are looking for an "is a" relationship to ensure inheritance, not a "belongs to" relationship.

Subject	Relationship	Object
Pat	is a	cat
Cats	have	fur
Bob	is a	dog
Dogs	have	hair
Peg	belongs to	Larry
Peg	is a	horse
Horses	have	4 feet
Horses	have	hair

Does Peg have Hair? (Peg has hair)?

Pass 1 (Peg is the subject)

Peg	belongs to	Larry
Peg	**is a**	**horse**

Pass 2 (Larry is the subject)

Nothing

Pass 3 (Horse is the subject)

Horses	have	4 feet
Horses	**have**	**hair (QED)**

FIGURE 8-28 INFERENCE THROUGH FORWARD CHAINING

Now we make our third pass through the knowledge base, this time with "Horse" as our subject. The first statement we find is "Horses have four feet." This does not satisfy our request, but we may use the statement in another pass, say to find if having four feet means that the animal has hair. The second statement we find with horse as a subject is "Horses have hair." Since we already know that Peg is a horse, and we now know that horses have hair, we can conclude that Peg has hair.

Note that even this very simple query on our very small knowledge base produced two complete passes through the knowledge base and part of a third pass. In a real knowledge base with hundreds of rules, it may take dozens of passes to do forward chaining. This is why knowledge-based systems require a great deal of computer power.

Backward Chaining

Figure 8-29 illustrates **backward chaining,** another approach to inference. This illustration uses the same example, "Does Peg have hair?" In backward chaining, we begin with the object, "hair," and try to work backward to Peg. The figure demonstrates that backward chaining is also laborious.

Advanced Inference

Many advanced approaches to inference have been developed to speed the inference process as much as possible. Some of these approaches use a combination of forward and backward chaining. Others give each statement a value that reflects how often it has been used in successful solutions; these approaches use more successful statements first when they have several possi-

Subject	Relationship	Object
Pat	is a	cat
Cats	have	fur
Bob	is a	dog
Dogs	have	hair
Peg	belongs to	Larry
Peg	is a	horse
Horses	have	4 feet
Horses	have	hair

Does Peg have Hair? (Peg has hair)?

Pass 1 (Hair is the object)

| Dogs | have | hair |
| **Horses** | **have** | **hair** |

Pass 2 (Dog is the object)

| Bob | is a | dog |

Pass 3 (Horse is the object)

| **Peg** | **is a** | **horse (QED)** |

FIGURE 8-29 INFERENCE THROUGH BACKWARD CHAINING

bilities to check out. Fortunately, most details of advanced inference are hidden from the user.

The Dialog Management System

The **dialog management system** is the end user's main contact with the system. This system serves four major purposes.

- It allows the end user to express a query, such as "Does Peg have hair?"
- If the user asks, the dialog management system can provide a discussion of the reasoning it used to reach a particular conclusion. In the Peg's Hair example, the line of reasoning would be given as "Peg is a horse, and horses have hair, so Peg has hair."
- If the system needs knowledge that the user may have, it can ask the user for information. For example, it may ask the user how old Peg is, if this has a bearing on the solution to the problem, and if the knowledge is not already in the knowledge base.
- If the user asks why a particular piece of information is being requested, the dialog management system will explain the line of reasoning it is trying to establish.

Languages for Building AI Applications

LISP

For many years, the chief language for AI applications has been **LISP,** a powerful tool for doing many kinds of logical text processing. It is roughly at the level of FORTRAN or COBOL. In other words, it is a third-generation language.

LISP's structure allows nonconventional computer architectures to be used to speed up the processing of LISP programs by an order of magnitude or more. There are many special-purpose "LISP machines" on the market. Although they are not needed to run LISP, they are widely used because of the computational intensity of most AI problems.

PROLOG

Many AI builders are now turning to another language, **PROLOG (Programming in Logic),** which is a less general-purpose language than LISP but is more efficient at building knowledge-based systems. (LISP is not limited to knowledge-based systems, whereas these systems are PROLOG's forte.) Somewhere between a third- and fourth-generation language, most PROLOG compilers have suffered from a problem common to many new post-third-generation languages, namely, weaknesses in secondary tools such as logic debuggers to check for consistency among rules.

Shells

In time PROLOG will lose the weaknesses that are linked to its insufficient secondary tools. In the long run, however, it may lose out to higher level tools that are tied to even smaller problem domains but that are far more efficient in those domains.

For example, in expert systems, which are mentioned below and are discussed in Chapter 12, the attempt is made to capture the knowledge of human experts in diagnosis or other areas. **Expert system shells** can build expert systems far more efficiently and faster than either PROLOG or LISP. Since most knowledge-based systems fall into a few well-defined categories, it remains to be seen whether PROLOG will be used widely in the long run for system development.

In the past, most expert system shells were written in LISP or PROLOG, but there is a growing trend toward building shells in languages for which there are more compilers or interpreters on the market. The most notable example is **C,** which may be described as intermediate between an assembly language and a third-generation programming language.

Major Applications

Natural Language Input

One of the most rapidly growing areas of AI is **natural language input,** in which users can type commands in plain English and let the natural language input interface translate their sentences into the syntax needed by programs.

Natural language input is especially useful for features that a user does not use very often. For occasional users, most features fall into this category, but fewer do for expert users. Because natural language input frees users from having to memorize syntax, it can greatly improve ease of learning.

Expert Systems

As noted above, expert systems attempt to capture the expertise of some human expert. **Expert systems** are always available, never quit the organization, are patient when the same question is asked for the millionth time, and are often faster than a human expert. (This speed is crucial for real-time operations such as aircraft problem diagnosis in flight.)

Expert systems are discussed in Chapter 12. One of the biggest problems that will be mentioned in that chapter is the difficulty of eliciting information from human experts. This arduous process, called **knowledge engineering,** is a key research field in IS today.

Although advanced expert systems are very difficult to construct, a growing number of end users are building their own simple expert systems, for instance, to assess a loan application, to check a customer's credit when taking an order, or to help decide what financial ratios to look for when considering acquisitions.

Anticipatory Software

Today, most programs are rather stupid in their dealings with humans. A user would often like to say "Now graph it" after computing revenues over a two-year period. Although natural language input may be able to translate the command into a form that would ask the user what "it" meant, **anticipatory software** would go the next step and graph what the user had just finished doing. It might even select a chart form based on what the user normally does and what kind of chart seems best given the current data being graphed. Lotus Development Corporation's **HAL** adds anticipatory capabilities to Lotus 1-2-3 and Symphony. To do this, HAL's knowledge base has many statements based on common problems people have expressed and on common use patterns identified by HAL's developers.

CONCLUSION

In this chapter, we have discussed the complexities of PC software technology. We have focused on general principles and on system software rather than on application programs.

The first theme of this chapter was that users rarely deal with individual programs. Rather, they deal with suites of programs that are linked together by jump instructions. This networked approach allows layering, so that individual program designers can focus only on one small piece of the problem. Layering concepts surface over and over in discussions of application programs, network operating systems, and many other topics. We have already looked at layering, without calling it by that name, when we discussed IBM PC compatibles in Chapter 6, and again when we discussed device drivers and comprehensive graphics standards in Chapter 7. Layering is fundamental to the understanding of full program compatibility. In a real sense, understanding the concepts of layering and the reasons for layering is like learning the alphabet. There is no way to read about the field without mastering layering concepts.

The second major theme of this chapter was the management of interactions between internal and external memory. Whenever external memory becomes involved, its slow speed drags down the performance of user applications. Software designers have resorted to many approaches, from the simple use of overlays to such complex alternatives as virtual memory, to cope with the slow speed of disk as well as with the problem that internal memory is very limited, so that some ways must be found to bring parts of the program into internal memory while leaving other parts in external memory.

Afterward, we examined system software, beginning with operating systems ranging from simple operating systems such as early versions of MS-DOS to advanced operating systems that provide multitasking, multiuser operations, windowing, and user-friendly interaction. We also focused on some of the limitations that users may encounter when dealing with windowing and other advanced operating system features. After dealing with operating systems, we turned to system software utilities, including keyboard enhancers, disk managers, and integrated utility products.

The next major topic was integration, and we began with a discussion of differences among file formats and the problems caused by these differences. We then looked at a broad spectrum of ways to integrate information from the files created by different programs, from the simple expedient of buying integrated application software from a single vendor to highly complex approaches using complex file format conversion and intermediate file formats.

This chapter ended with a discussion of artificial intelligence, which is beginning to come of age and will affect virtually every aspect of PC software in the future. We focused on knowledge-based systems, which are the most common type of AI applications today.

REVIEW QUESTIONS

1. How does the use of software give computers a degree of flexibility enjoyed by no previous machines?
2. In a memory map, why do RAM and ROM share the same memory space? What determines the size of a PC's memory space? Why is only 640 KB of memory available to users of low-end IBM PCs, despite the fact that the 8088 microprocessor has an address space of 1 MB? Can only one program be in memory at a time?
3. What are the advantages of layering? What is a service set, and why are service sets important concepts in layering? What is the relationship between layering and device drivers? How does table lookup allow tailoring at the level of system software?
4. Why is jump with return necessary? How do interrupts provide jumping?
5. What practical problems do each of the following address, and how are they better or worse than other approaches to addressing these problems? Core programs and overlays. Virtual memory operating systems. Bank switching. RAM disks.
6. Explain the interactions between application programs, operating systems, and system ROM service programs.

7. Why do simple operating systems tend to have few features, and why are they difficult to use? What are the main features found in simple operating systems such as MS-DOS through its 3.X versions?
8. What is the differences between task-switching, multitasking, and multiuser operation?
9. Briefly, what are the strengths and weaknesses of Unix?
10. What are the advantages of windowing? What important features associated with windowing are not provided by most or all windowing systems?
11. What makes the Macintosh user interface so friendly?
12. State the two best aspects of IBM's Operating System/2 and its two worst aspects. Justify your answers.
13. Describe the key elements of SAA.
14. What are operating environments, and what is their advantage over an advanced operating system?
15. What are the main functions offered by the two largest classes of system software utilities, namely, keyboard enhancers and disk managers?
16. From the simplest to the most complex, what are a corporation's alternatives for providing integration? From the least to the most effective, what are a corporation's choices?
17. What are the relative strengths and weaknesses of ASCII files, DCA files, and Lotus .WKS files?
18. What were the breakthroughs that led to the AI explosion we are experiencing today?
19. What are the three components of a knowledge-based system? How does this differ from the organization of a BASIC program? A spreadsheet system? How is this similar to BASIC programs and spreadsheet systems?
20. What are the three most common ways to represent knowledge in the knowledge base? What are the strengths and weaknesses of each?
21. In terms of inference approaches, why do AI applications tend to require enormous processing power?
22. What are the relative strengths of LISP, PROLOG, and application-specific shells?
23. What are the major uses of AI in business software today? Which do you think you would want to experience first? Why?

9 ANALYTICAL MODELING ON PERSONAL COMPUTERS

Engineering is a quantitative discipline, but this was not the case in the 1960s. In those days, the slide rule was the engineer's main analysis tool, and most products were built with empirical design curves instead of analysis. Computers were used in only the most critical tasks.

During the late 1960s, a small number of engineers began to learn how to program. When they first arrived in corporations, they were generally viewed as curiosities, and many were actively discouraged from programming because programming would detract from their "real jobs."

In a short time, however, most engineers began to see that computers offered unprecedented capabilities for changing the very way they approached problems. The "young turks" who could write their own programs were producing far more useful results than their more experienced colleagues. The handwriting was on the wall, and engineers did not shrink from the challenge. In one organization, only three engineers in a unit of 200 could program in 1968; by 1970, a majority had taken a programming class.

Today, engineers who have moved into management are experiencing a feeling of deja vu. In the late 1970s, a few managers began to use VisiCalc on Apple II computers in order to perform analytical studies that were far beyond the powers of hand calculators. Not only was their analysis faster, but they also tested dozens of alternatives instead of just one or two alternatives. Their models often reached a level of sophistication and flexibility that would have been extremely difficult to achieve with traditional programming languages. Managers literally began walking into computer stores and asking for "VisiCalc and something to run it on." In less than five years, VisiCalc had passed away, but the new generation of tools it spawned was used daily by millions of managers.

We have yet to see the wholesale upgrading of managerial analysis that we have experienced in engineering, in part because management is more people-oriented than engineering. Yet when you talk to managers who have been using computers for a year or two, you usually find that they are doing much more careful analysis than they did before computers. Even they are usually surprised when, after reviewing their old reports, they see how many critical decisions were made with little supporting analysis.

Although analysis is not the most common use of personal computers overall, it is the most common application for managers and professionals. In addition, analysis has the greatest potential for changing the nature of managerial work, not just making it more efficient. In almost every industry, it is much harder to turn a profit or even survive today than it was five or ten years ago. Although good analysis tools alone will never make someone a good manager, it is hard to imagine a good manager approaching today's complex problems without doing a thorough analysis of alternatives.

ANALYTICAL MODELING TOOLS

Spreadsheet Analysis

During the late 1970s, an MBA student named Daniel Bricklin was growing tired and frustrated by the need to copy complex case analyses off the blackboard. It was even worse when the professor began to explore the impact of a strike or some other assumption by changing one or two numbers and then seeing how these changes trickled down to the proverbial "bottom line." And, of course, there were the inevitable arithmetic errors.

Bricklin asked a friend, Robert Frankston, if it would be possible to make a computer screen look like a blackboard. The blackboard would hold titles and numbers, and some of these numbers would be calculated. If one number changed, all the other numbers that depended on it would change automatically.

Frankston turned to his personal computer, an Apple II, and developed a program that would give the user a "visible calculator"—VisiCalc for short. VisiCalc created a large blackboard and drew columns and rows on it, emulating the "spreadsheets" used by accountants and finance specialists to keep their analyses neat. A sample spreadsheet screen is shown as Figure 9-1.

This spreadsheet contains text, numbers, and formulas. Text and numbers appear directly on the screen. For formulas, however, the results of the calculations appear instead of the formulas themselves. It is possible to look at underlying formulas, of course, but the normal way to view the spreadsheet is to look at results.

Because the spreadsheet imagery is so close to what users normally see with paper and pencil analysis, spreadsheet systems are far easier to learn than formal programming languages. Normal intuition works for the user.

Spreadsheet models also lend themselves well to alteration. Users often start with simple models and then add capabilities until their models are more complex than entry-level programmers would like to tackle. Best of all, using

```
E8: +C8-D8                                                                    |READY|

      _____A_____B_____C_____D_____E_____F_____G_____H__|
|1  |Spending Forecast                                         6   Month
|2  |
|3  |              6 Current month
|4  |
|5  |         Spending Spending Spending Forecast Percent
|6  |Division To Date  Forecast Budget   Overage  Overage
|7  |--------  --------  --------  --------  --------  --------
|8  |Tulsa        $463     $926    $900  |   $26|      3%
|9  |Redmond      $220     $440    $515     ($75)    -15%
|10 |Hong Kong    $175     $350    $215     $135      63%
|11 |Mexico Cty    $31      $62     $50      $12      24%
|12 |          --------  --------  --------  --------  --------
|13 |Total        $889   $1,778  $1,680      $98       6%
|14 |
|15 |
|16 |
|17 |
|18 |
|19 |
|20 |
```

FIGURE 9-1 A SCREEN IMAGE FROM A SPREADSHEET PROGRAM

the model enhances user's understanding of the problem, and it is far easier to extend the model in a spreadsheet system than if a formal programming language were used. In addition, because the users can do it by themselves, changes can be made immediately.

Other Analysis Tools

Although most users of personal computers begin with simple spreadsheet systems, many "power users" move on to more potent analysis tools, often on a mainframe computer. As discussed in Chapter 1, the most popular of these advanced tools are financial and statistical analysis programs, but all professions and managerial specialties seem to have their own special analysis needs and programs.

In this chapter, we will not look at analysis tools beyond spreadsheet systems. Instead we will discuss these tools in Chapter 16, which deals with host data and decision support applications. The most commonly used financial and statistical analysis tools today continue to be host-based, because hosts provide the processing power needed for their more sophisticated analysis procedures, because hosts provide easy access to existing corporate data bases and ample space for ad hoc data bases, and because host computers allow multiuser applications like corporate budgeting.

At the same time, it would be wrong to give readers the impression that advanced products are unavailable on personal computers. For relatively small data collections, some very good products are available on PCs and can benefit from ease-of-use features on PCs. For example, Figure 9-2 shows a typical screen from Brainpower's StatView on the Macintosh. StatView embraces almost all features of host-based statistics tools, including multivariate analysis, and its use of windowing allows users to explore their data flexibly and vividly. StatView graphs can even be transferred directly to documents, thanks to the inherent features of the Macintosh.

Another reason for deferring the discussion of advanced analysis tools until Chapter 16 is simple convenience. A strong trend for the future will be "integrated PC–host software," with software modules from the same vendor operating on both hosts and PCs. The user will do highly interactive work on the PC module, and heavier processing and filing on the host module. The PC and host software modules will be able to exchange information easily. It is more convenient to discuss this situation after introducing technical aspects of host applications.

Good Modeling Practice

Although analysis tools are becoming indispensable to corporations, they also create vexing problems for managers of end user computing. Spreadsheet models may be easy to build and expand, but unless the user–developer is very careful, undetected errors may lead to disastrous results.

In the early days of end user computing in engineering, there were

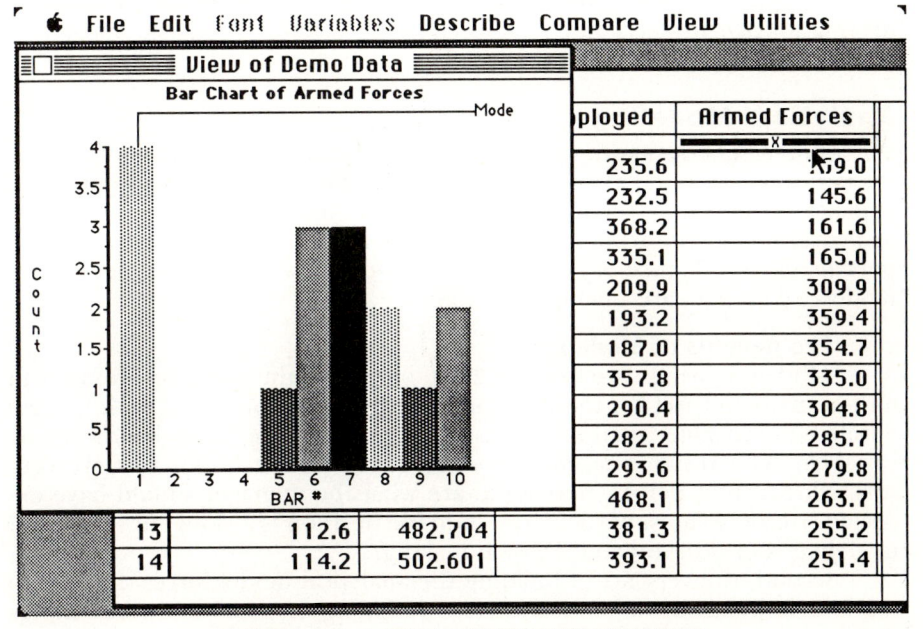

FIGURE 9-2 A SCREEN IMAGE FROM STATVIEW

ample horror stories. The real number of disasters was probably small, but engineers soon learned that they had to adopt the disciplines of "good programming practice" long advocated by professional programmers. New dogs had to learn old tricks.

Engineering management, in turn, had to learn to audit important models created by end users, just as it had to audit models created by professional programmers. This was especially important for models that related to critical decisions, that would be used by other people, or that would be used repeatedly over long periods of time.

Today, managers, general professionals, and secretaries are repeating the cycle. They will have to learn good modeling practice, and both IS and corporate management will have to develop suitable policies for auditing models or assuring good performance in other ways.

The problem is especially difficult for high-powered financial and statistical tools, because the proper use of these systems requires good understanding of sophisticated concepts. Unless someone knows the assumptions behind various statistical tests and financial calculations, he or she may create highly inappropriate analyses, and neither the person nor that person's audience is likely to realize it. The difficulties in auditing models built with sophisticated tools are so great that few organizations attempt it. Even simple spreadsheet models are rarely audited.

ANALYTICAL MODELING PRINCIPLES

The first job of a manager, whatever the second may be, is to understand the environment that he or she is managing. This is true both for ongoing management, such as working to keep a hotel's occupancy at its maximum, and for making long-term decisions, such as choosing whether or not to add a new product.

Analytical Modeling

When managers deal with decisions that can be at least partially quantified, the first step is to build an **analytical model** of the situation. For example, if a manager is deciding whether or not to open a new line of business, the analytical model will contain estimates for sales, prices, costs, and other important factors. Figure 9-3 is an example of such an analytical model; real models, of course, are far more complex.

The Benefits of Modeling

Modeling brings two benefits. First, of course, the numerical results can have a major impact on the decision. Managers can only deal with a small number of variables in their heads, whereas computers can handle many variables. As a result, analytical models often produce results that are very surprising at first but, in retrospect, are what the manager should have expected. In some cases, particularly when the decision is a close one, analytical modeling is critical to good decision making.

Second, the very act of building the analytical model forces the user to think logically about the decision, often revealing the need to include things that had been overlooked initially. An analytical model provides a structure

Category	Year 1	Year 2	Year 3
General Information			
Unit Sales	300	400	500
Revenues			
Unit Price	$10	$11	$9
Revenues	$3,000	$4,400	$4,500
Expenses			
Fixed Costs	$2,000	$2,000	$2,000
Unit Cost	$4	$3	$2
Variable Cost	$1,200	$1,200	$1,000
Expenses	$3,200	$3,200	$3,000
Income Before Tax	($200)	$1,200	$1,500

FIGURE 9-3 AN ANALYTICAL MODEL IN SPREADSHEET IMAGE

for the decision maker to think about the important facts and relationships that will have an impact on the decision. The very act of modeling, in other words, tends to force managers into more careful and detailed thinking and to produce not just a mathematical model, but also a structure for thinking about the situation being modeled.

The Dangers of Modeling

Although analytical modeling is important in business today, it is also dangerous. There is an old maxim in modeling "numbers drive out thinking." This means that when people see the results of a model, especially if the modeling is done on a computer, the "hard" figures pouring from the model tend to overwhelm softer qualitative arguments about problems such as customer good-will or impacts on relationships with suppliers. Analytical modeling must be viewed as only one of many inputs to the decision-making process.

Another problem with modeling occurs even for quantitative variables. This is the "drunk under the street light syndrome." There is an old story about a police officer who came upon a drunk staggering around under a street light. When the officer asked what was going on, the drunk said, "I'm looking for my keys." When the officer asked where the drunk had dropped the keys, the reply was "Back in the alley." When the officer asked why the drunk was looking under the street light instead of in the alley, the drunk replied, "Because this is where the light is." In modeling, certain quantitative variables will often be difficult or even impossible to quantify, and there is a tendency to leave them out of the model. As a result, a large fraction of all business models leave out important quantitative variables. This is another reason to treat analytical models as only one part of the decision-making process.

A third reason to be cautious about the output of analytical models is that many models contain subtle logical errors. This is especially true of large models, whose very size makes "debugging" difficult. One reason why managers need to learn about modeling is to be able to study a proposed model for possible errors.

Model Images

Figure 9-3 shows a simple analytical model, but the format of this figure is only one of several ways to represent this particular model. Ways of representing models are called "images." Here we will examine three common images for representing models—**spreadsheet, equations,** and **dependency images.**

Spreadsheet Image

As noted earlier, the spreadsheet is an accountant's or financial analyst's normal way of representing an analytical model. An analytical model in spreadsheet image is a table or group of tables with numbers. Some numbers are given, and others are calculated.

As noted earlier, the spreadsheet image shown in Figure 9-3 shows *results.* It shows such "bottom line" numbers as Income Before Tax. To a decision maker, the final numbers are the things that count, and the spreadsheet image of the analytical model contains all important numbers.

The fact that spreadsheet images do not show how each number was computed can cause problems, however. In analytical models of any size, there will always be questions about how certain numbers were computed, and the spreadsheet image does little to illuminate such problems.

Equations Image

Fortunately, the spreadsheet image is only one of several ways to represent analytical models. Another image, the **equations image**, focuses explicitly on formulas, giving up the showing of results entirely. Figure 9-4 casts our analytical model in equations image.

Dependency Image

Figure 9-4 illustrates the overall logic of the model, but it is sometimes difficult to trace exactly what variables are related to what other variables. To see where "Unit Sales" appears in equations, for instance, one would have to look through every single equation.

Figure 9-5 presents another image for representing analytical models, the **dependency image.** Like the equation image, the dependency image focuses on the logical structure of the model, instead of on results (which are

```
100   Columns                 Year 1, Year 2, Year 3
110   *General Information
120       Unit Sales          =300, 400, 500
130   *Revenues
140       Unit Price          = 10, 11, 9
150       Revenues            = Unit Sales * Unit Price
160   *Expenses
170       Fixed Costs         = 2000, 2000, 2000
180       Unit Cost           = 4, 3, 2
190       Variable Cost       = Unit Sales * Unit Cost
200       Expenses            = Fixed Costs + Variable Cost
210   *
220   Income Before Tax       = Revenues - Expenses
```

FIGURE 9-4 AN ANALYTICAL MODEL IN EQUATIONS IMAGE

```
100   Columns  Year 1, Year 2, Year 3
110   *General Information
120   Unit Sales = 300, 400, 500
130   *Revenues
140   Unit Price = 10, 11, 9

150 Revenues = Unit Sales * Unit Price

      120  Unit Sales = 300, 400, 500  160
      140  Unit Price = 10, 11, 9

160   *Expenses
170   Fixed Costs = 2000, 2000, 2000
```

FIGURE 9-5 AN ANALYTICAL MODEL IN DEPENDENCY IMAGE

shown best in the spreadsheet image). In contrast to the equation image, however, the dependency image shows, for each equation, the other equations that feed into it. In other words, it permits us to see the direction of relationships among variables—what variables in the analytical model are dependent on what other variables.

The dependency image shows all of the equations, just as the equations image does. The dependency image, however, is basically a debugging tool that allows the user or someone else to see the logical flow of the model. In many cases, errors can be spotted with a simple glance at an equation and the formulas that come under it. The equations image is still better for the common task of reading the general structure of the model. The extra information under each equation in the dependency image is distracting to the person interested in the overall flow of the model. Basically, the dependency image puts the model under a microscope and examines it in fine detail. Because of this microscopic focus, it is easy to lose the broad picture.

Images in Perspective

These three images for representing analytical models—*spreadsheet, equations,* and *dependency*—all have strengths and weaknesses, and a good analytical modeling program will support all three. This allows the decision maker to switch instantly from looking at bottom line results, to examining how a group of variables are computed, and then to examining what variables need to be studied to see how different conditions might affect a particular variable.

Building Analytical Models

Every analytical model is different, but five basic steps are needed to build any analytical model.

1. Understanding the problem
2. Identifying the variables in the model
3. Quantifying variables where possible
4. Specifying relationships among variables
5. Testing the model

Understanding the Problem

It is a truism that you must understand your problem before you can model it. It is also a truism that modeling something is often the only way to understand it. Both statements are correct. Understanding a problem often takes a spiral growth path. A model builder first tries to understand the problem as well as possible. Then, he or she models it to test their understanding as well as to gain insight. The modeler then changes the model and begins another cycle.

Even so, it is important to understand the problem as much as possible before beginning to model it, because models that are badly off base at the start will take endless iterations to get on track. Models that are built too hastily often have to be scrapped after several iterations because their underlying structure is so poor.

In small models, this cycle is so fast and changes are so small that little advance planning goes into the picture. The loops in the spiral have small diameters and are closely spaced. In contrast, for large problems a great deal more effort must go into understanding the problem before any construction or even design begins. What do various people want from the model, and what do they really need? What level of detail and accuracy is needed? With regard to conceptual matters, what theory or conceptual framework seems to fit the problem?

It is good practice to formally begin an analysis with a clear statement of goals, limitations, and initial conceptual understandings, and to circulate this statement to everyone involved. Later, every time a major change needs to be made on the basis of growing insight, the original statement should be amended formally.

In almost every case, the decision maker starts out trying to solve the wrong problem. For example, one bank began by asking how much it could charge customers to use automated teller machines. When this problem specification was made formally, one marketer remembered that the machines were purchased primarily to keep users out of the branch offices during peak hours. Charging would dilute their value in this area. After some discussion, the initial problem specification had to be amended substantially. It is important to realize the importance of "sweating" the initial problem specification.

Identifying the Variables

The second step in building a model is to list the variables that will go into it. It is usually possible to come up with a good list of major variables with little effort, for example, Revenues. Identifying all of the many variables that will go into a complex model will be very time consuming, however. Often, the list of variables coming out of Step 2 is tentative, and it is not uncommon to see variables added to the list throughout the model-building process.

In our analytical model, the most obvious variables were Revenues, Expenses, and Income Before Tax. Only a little more thought was needed, in this simple case, to break down Revenues and Expenses into their basic components: Unit Sales, Unit Price, Fixed Costs, Unit Variable Cost, and Variable Cost. For complex models, the job of identifying variables is far more time consuming and difficult.

Quantifying Variables

The third step in building a model is to quantify as many variables as possible. In some cases, hard numbers can be used. For instance, the number for Fixed Costs might represent a known corporate allocation of costs to the proposed project.

In other cases, numbers are merely informed guesses. Unit Sales represents such an informed guess. As we will see later, the modeler will have to see how different guesses would affect the bottom line.

Specifying Relationships Among Variables

Not all variables are defined by data. Many of them are defined by their relationships to other variables. Variable Cost, for instance, will be defined in terms of its relationships with Unit Variable Cost and Unit Sales.

In some cases, relationships will be obvious. For instance, it is clear that Income Before Tax = Revenues − Expenses. In other cases, it might be difficult to identify relationships at all or to specify them even after they are identified. For instance, there might be several competing ways to allocate corporate overhead to projects, each of which might have strengths and weaknesses for representing the realities of the situation.

Testing the Model

After some variables have been quantified and other variables have been defined by their relationships to other variables, the modeler has the ingredients to write down the analytical model. Even so, the model-building job is still not finished. The next step is to study the model for errors. Nearly every model of more than five or ten variables contains errors when it is first created. It is critical to test every model before using it to produce important results.

The first stage in testing a model is to look at its basic logic. Often, by reading the model through once or twice, the modeler can identify a number of errors and change them on the spot. Common sense will uncover a majority of all errors.

Just reading the model through will rarely catch all errors however. The modeler is too close to the model to have good perspective. Just as people who proofread their own documents often miss obvious errors because they tend to see what they think is there rather than what is really there, modelers often read past obvious errors. When possible, "proofing" a model for obvious errors should be done by someone other than the model builder.

The next step in testing a model is to use test data. Instead of using real data, the model builder uses round numbers such as 10, 100, or 1000. When round numbers are plugged into the model, many obvious errors are immediately visible. With real data, it may be difficult to detect an error.

The user also needs to get out a calculator and go through at least one full case (in our model, one time period), to be sure there are no subtle errors in the model. If the calculator and the computer produce different results, the cause of the discrepancy must be tracked down.

One of the earliest computers, the IBM-Aiken Mark I, used electromechanical relays to do computations. At one time, it was producing errors that could not be tracked down by the programmers. The problem was eventually traced not to the program but to one of the electromechanical relays. Somehow, a moth had flown into the relay and had been smashed when the relay closed. The moth was pulled out and the relay cleaned. Since that time, finding errors has been called "debugging."

Good Practice in Model Building

In computing, there are many rules about how to do things such as building analytical models. These rules are referred to as **good practice.** Although a modeler can get results without following the principles of good practice, these violations are likely to produce subtle problems and waste a great deal of time. Good practice is the compilation of painful experience, and violating good practice produces inefficiency and error. For large models, good practice is especially critical.

Designing Equations Properly

When building models, it is especially critical to design equations properly. The equations in Figure 9-4, for example, always have one of two forms. For each variable in each time period, the model specifies either a single number or does not contain any numbers at all. This is not an accident; it is a deliberate practice, following a rule called the **First Law of Modeling.** This law specifies that a variable should be defined in only one of two ways.

Either the variable is defined by a single number, or

It is defined by a formula not containing any numbers.

In the spreadsheet image, this law is applied to each cell, that is, each entry. For a model with equations image in which several time periods follow the equal sign, the law applies to each time period.

The First Law of Modeling reflects the fact that we know two different things. Either we have a value (number) for the variable, or we know how it is related to other variables.

To see why you must have either all numbers or no numbers to the right of the equal sign, Figure 9-6 recasts Figure 9-4 to violate the First Law of Modeling. It does so by putting the estimate for Unit Sales as a number in the

```
100    Columns  Year 1
110    *General Information
130    *Revenues
140        Unit Price = 10
150        Revenues = 300 * Unit Price
160    *Expenses
170        Fixed Costs = 2000
180        Unit Variable Cost = 4
190        Variable Cost = 300 * Unit Variable Cost
200        Expenses = Fixed Costs + Variable Cost
210    *
220    Income Before Tax = Revenues - Expenses
```

In a what if analysis that changes unit sales, the modeler may not know what to change or may change only one of the unit sales numbers (300).

To the right of every equal sign (or in every cell) there should be either

    1) all data or

    2) an arithmetic expression consisting only of variables and operations (and no data).

FIGURE 9-6 AN ANALYTICAL MODEL VIOLATING THE FIRST LAW OF MODELING

ANALYTICAL MODELING PRINCIPLES   **377**

two equations that reference Unit Sales. For simplicity, only one time period is shown.

Suppose that you are told that the estimate for Unit Sales has changed—that it is now 400. Here are some of the problems you would face with improper equations.

First, you would not know what to change. There is no longer anything in the model labeled "Unit Sales." Even in a simple model, it is easy to forget the details of the model's structure. In a complex model, finding an unlabeled variable is nearly impossible.

Second, there is danger that the variable will appear in more than one place, as Unit Sales does in this example. If you made only one of the two changes, all results would be in error. To avoid making such an error, you would have to examine every single statement in the model.

The **Second Law of Modeling** is that information must never be repeated in a model. If data or relationships are repeated, an interrogation may change only one of the two equations or cells in which information is repeated. Figure 9-7 gives an example of this problem.

Here, the variable Unit Sales is defined as 300 twice, once in Line 120 as Unit Sales and again in Line 170 as Units Sold. This repetition is extremely dangerous because it creates a logical time bomb in the model. Later, if someone is told to change Unit Sales to 400, the person may look down the model, find Unit Sales in Line 120, and change the equation to Unit Sales = 400. They probably would not think to look for another statement defining Unit Sales and so would not change Line 170. As a result, Expenses and Income Before Tax would not be computed correctly.

Following the Second Law of Modeling would have eliminated the problem. The user could not have created the two statements defining Unit Sales.

Although the twin rules for proper equation design will eliminate many bad modeling practices, they are not foolproof. The basic idea is to make the structure of the model mirror reality, so that if Unit Cost is a single reality, there will be only one variable to represent it. Unfortunately, implementing

```
100    Columns Year 1
110    *General Information
120        Unit Sales = 300
130    *Revenues
140        Unit Price = 10
150        Revenues = Unit Sales * Unit Price
160    *Expenses
170        Units Sold = 300
180        Fixed Costs = 2000
190        Unit Variable Cost = 4
200        Variable Cost = Units Sold * Unit Variable Cost
210        Expenses = Fixed Costs + Variable Cost
220    *
230    Income Before Tax = Revenues - Expenses
```

Never repeat data. Here, unit sales information is given in line 120 and is also given in line 170. In a what if analysis, the modeler may change one and forget to change the other.

FIGURE 9-7 AN ANALYTICAL MODEL VIOLATING THE SECOND LAW OF MODELING

the basic rule that the structure of the model should mirror reality is difficult to use directly, so the two laws of modeling are useful as a way to teach good design.

Hierarchical Design

In Figures 9-3 and 9-4, which illustrate our simple analytical model in spreadsheet and equations image, the rows and equations are not organized at random. Rather, they are organized in a way that maximizes readability and error identification. Although the model would have worked if the rows and equations had not been laid out in an orderly way, it would have taken far longer to develop and test the model, and the modeler could have missed several errors.

In both figures, the model is arranged hierarchically, with sections and subsections. At the top level, there are:

General Information

Revenues

Expenses

Income Before Tax

In a complex model, each section is likely to have several subsections. For instance, Expenses can be broken down into Fixed and Variable Costs. There will be several levels of subsections in complex models.

Hierarchical design makes the model easy to understand; you can look at a model and understand it very quickly. Hierarchical design also makes the model easy to test. For example, you can test the model by plugging simple round numbers into Revenues and Expenses and then see whether income before tax is computed properly. This process can then be repeated at lower levels, in order to test the revenue and expense equations with round numbers for the major revenue and expense categories.

Modular Design

In conventional programming, modular design is another important design principle. In **modular design,** there are two goals.

1. The program should be divided into a number of self-contained units called **modules,** each of which should contain one logical piece of code.
2. Each module should have only one entry point and one exit point. The entry point should accept a few specified values from other modules and should output a few specified values to other modules.

If modularization is followed rigorously, each module can be tested independently, and any change in a module will produce predictable changes for other modules. Without modularization, a large model will have such complex interrelationships among variables that errors will be almost impossible to detect and diagnose, and changes in one place may produce unforeseen changes in other places.

Strict modularization may be impossible to implement completely in analytical modeling, but general principles do carry over. First, the overall

ANALYTICAL MODELING PRINCIPLES

Model Area of Worksheet

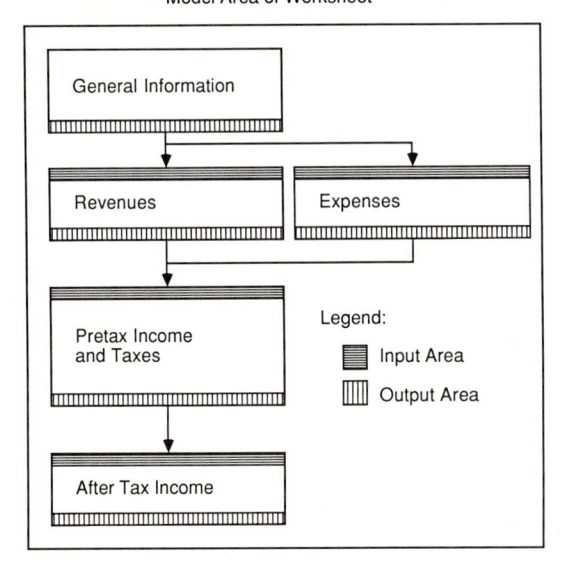

[Diagram showing modules: General Information → Revenues and Expenses → Pretax Income and Taxes → After Tax Income. Legend: Input Area, Output Area.]

Each table should be a module forming one logical unit.

Interactions among tables should be minimized.

Interactions should be limited to well-defined transfer areas for input and output.

FIGURE 9-8 MODULAR MODEL STRUCTURE

model should be subdivided into tables, each of which expresses one logical unit. Figure 9-8 illustrates this approach.

Second, each module should have one well-defined input area and one output area. The input areas will contain data coming from another table module. The cells in the input area should contain nothing but cell references to output areas in other modules. All outputs, in turn, should be placed in a specific well-defined output area, even if this means repeating results in the body of the module by means of cell references.

Documentation

Without documentation, a model's limitations and logic will be lost if the developer leaves or even if the developer stays and forgets these limitations and the model's detailed logic after a few months. Even one-page models need to be documented to answer subsequent questions about the analysis.

Documentation begins within the model itself. A few lines of text can be added to explain everything that is not self-apparent.

In addition, variables should be named clearly in order to help people read the model. Spreadsheet programs normally allow cells and larger areas to be "named," so that cell formulas can look like "Overtime Hours + Regular Hours" instead of "F37 + Q13." The first expression is far more readable than the second.

Some add-on programs allow information about a cell to be attached as a note. The first product to do this for Lotus 1-2-3 was Note-It. In Note-It, the user can point to a cell, ask for information, and see a paragraph of explanation.

Some firms now require every spreadsheet model to have several distinct areas, as shown in Figure 9-9. Each area is assigned a standardized name so that, for example, the area of the spreadsheet named "DOCUMENT" will always contain documentation.

The documentation section should also be standardized. The mandatory information should include the following topics.

Model name and version (if applicable)

Modeler

Date developed

Person responsible currently

Equipment requirements for using the model

Cautions and limitations

Purpose

Discussion of the model's logic

How to use the model

A good discussion of the model's logic is important because few people can even understand their own models after being away from them a few weeks. Anything in the model that is at all "tricky" should be explained thoroughly.

Instruction on how to use the model should also be included because the original builder and user may not be the only users in the future.

Construction and Testing

Construction and testing were discussed earlier, but when hierarchical design and modularization are used, a few new wrinkles are added.

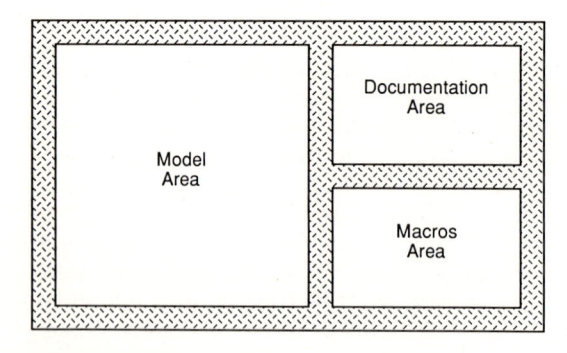

There should be mandatory areas for the model's logic, documentation, and macros. These areas should be given standard names.

FIGURE 9-9 STANDARDIZED WORKSHEET LAYOUT

ANALYTICAL MODELING PRINCIPLES

If hierarchical design is used, it is good to begin with a top-level skeleton for the model, as shown in Figure 9-10. Numbers can be plugged in for testing purposes, and the overall logic can be settled. Afterward, the internal logic of each top-level piece can be added and tested. For example, the Expenses information can be added and tested to be sure that is produces the right answer for Expenses on line 6.

Starting from the top in construction and testing gives the modeler confidence that overall design is good, so that attention can be shifted to subsections. It also tends to catch gross problems in the model's overall logic before a great deal of time is lost developing pieces that will not fit together in the end.

Modular design adds one more piece to the picture. As noted earlier, the input area of a table should refer to output areas of other tables. For internal testing, however, round numbers can be typed into the input areas. The modeler can then go through a few simple test cases by hand, checking the results in the output area. After testing, the test numbers can be replaced by the original cell references.

```
B7: +B5-B6                                                              |READY|


        A         B         C         D         E       F       G       H
|1  |Income Projection      Tax Rate      0.4
|2  |
|3  |
|4  |           Year 1    Year 2    Year 3    Total
|5  |Revenues   1000      1500      2000      4500
|6  |Expenses    900      1100      1300      3300
|7  |Profit BT  | 100|     400       700      1200
|8  |Tax          40       160       280       480
|9  |Profit AT    60       240       420       720
|10 |Cum. PAT     60       300       720       720
|11 |
|12 |
```

A skeleton consists of only top-level information (revenues, expenses, and so on).

The skeleton is tested with round numbers (1000, 900, etc.) to be sure the overall logic is correct.

After this high-level logic testing, revenue and expense details are added. Each block of added cells is tested using round numbers.

FIGURE 9-10 CONSTRUCTION AND TESTING WITH SKELETONS

Interrogation

Building the model and generating numerical results is only the beginning of the modeler's work. The next step is **interrogation.** Interrogation is making changes in the original or **base model,** in order to make various kinds of predictions and to study various aspects of the mode. We will look at four kinds of interrogation: what if analysis, sensitivity analysis, how can analysis, and how best analysis. Before we consider individual forms of interrogation, however, we need to cover one basic concept that lies at the heart of all forms of interrogation. This is the difference between independent and dependent variables.

Independent and Dependent Variables

In any model, some variables depend on other variables. Figure 9-5 shows dependency relationships in our model. If an equation has equations under it, the variable it specifies is dependent on the variables specified by the equations under it. When any pair of variables is related, one is the **dependent variable** and the other is the **independent variable.** Not surprisingly, the variable whose value depends on the other is the dependent variable.

The following illustration may be helpful in understanding the difference between dependent and independent variables. Consider this highly simplified model:

```
50 Price of Corn = 10
60 Amount of Corn = 10000
70 Cost of Corn = Price of Corn * Amount of Corn
80 Other Costs = 55000
90 Total Cost = Cost of Corn + Other Costs
```

In this model, some variables are unrelated. For example, Other Costs are unrelated to the Price of Corn and to the Amount of Corn. Other variables are definitely related in an independent–dependent relationship. The following table shows these relationships.

INDEPENDENT VARIABLE	DEPENDENT VARIABLE
Price of Corn	Cost of Corn
Price of Corn	Total Cost
Amount of Corn	Cost of Corn
Amount of Corn	Total Cost
Other Costs	Total Cost
Cost of Corn	Total Cost

In this table, note that some relationships are direct, for instance, the first entry—the relationship between the Price of Corn and the Cost of Corn. Here the independent–dependent relationship is immediately obvious.

Other relationships are indirect. For instance, in the second entry, Price of Corn and Total Cost are indirectly related, through Cost of Corn. Here the relationship is Price of Corn → Cost of Corn → Total Cost. The independent–dependent relationship between Price of Corn and Total Cost still exists. The relationship is one between pairs of variables, regardless of whether the relationship is direct or indirect.

A computed and therefore dependent variable can also be an independent variable for other variables. In the last entry of the table, Cost of Corn and Total Cost are related with Cost of Corn as the independent variable. No variable is independent or dependent in the abstract. Independence and dependence can only be talked about in reference to a *specific pair* of variables. In some pairings, a variable will be the independent variable. In others, it will be the dependent variable, and in yet others, it will be unrelated.

What If Analysis

The base model represents the modeler's best estimate of what things will be like in the future. In most cases, however, one can build alternative scenarios for the future. For instance, the base model may assume that there will be no strike, but management may ask, *what if* a strike does occur.

Asking what if questions like this one requires the modeler to change one or more independent variables. In this case, the wage rate might go up, hours of work would go down, sales would go down, and fixed costs would probably decline somewhat, although in a complicated way. Then changes would be observed in dependent variables, most notably profit after tax. In other words:

> In **what if analysis,** the user changes one or more independent variables, in accordance with a possible change in the condition of the world, and then observes changes in one or more dependent variables.

The following illustration may be helpful in understanding the concept of what if analysis. Consider the following simplified model.

```
50 Price of Corn = 10
60 Amount of Corn = 10000
70 Cost of Corn = Price of Corn * Amount of Corn
80 Other Costs = 55000
90 Total Cost = Cost of Corn + Other Costs
```

For this model, there are four possible what if analyses.

1. Change the Price of Corn, for example, to reflect an expected price increase, and assess the impact on the Cost of Corn and Total Cost.
2. Change the Amount of Corn, for example, to reflect an expected business volume increase, and assess the impact on the Cost of Corn and Total Cost.
3. Change both the Price of Corn and the Amount of Corn, to assess the impact on the Cost of Corn and Total Cost.
4. Change Other Costs, for example, to reflect the impact of a probable wage hike, to assess the impact on Cost of Corn and Total Cost.

We can also consider what if analysis in terms of the income statement model we used earlier in this chapter to discuss model images and the two laws of modeling. In the model, we might need to do a what if analysis to understand what would happen if Unit Sales rose 100 units per year in response to the opening of foreign markets. We would plug these numbers into our model, and the computer would tell us how our Revenues, Expenses, and Income Before Tax would change as a result.

Of course, we could do these calculations without a computer, but before computers, what if analysis was extremely difficult to execute. Even with our little model, it would take 15 minutes to do and check the calculations. With "real-world" models, manual what if analysis is rarely feasible, beyond perhaps a "best case," "worst case," and "optimistic case" set of calculations.

As a result, even when manual models were built, users rarely took the time to "sweat" their decisions by doing a solid group of what if analyses to probe the consequences of various decisions and events outside their control. As a result, when reality later diverged from predictions, as a result of these decisions and events, decision makers were unprepared and could not react swiftly. Now that computers are used heavily by decision makers, there seems to be a growing tendency to think through major decisions in far greater detail and to prepare realistic contingency plans to deal with likely problems.

Sensitivity Analysis

Sensitivity analysis is a cousin of what if analysis. In sensitivity analysis, the user almost always changes just *one* independent variable and observes the changes the model predicts for one or more dependent variables.

Sensitivity analysis differs from what if analysis in two fundamental ways.

- First, although what if analysis can change one or more independent variables, sensitivity analysis almost always changes just one independent variable.
- Second, they differ in motive. In what if analysis, the change from the base model is effected to reflect a specific change in the condition of the world—a strike, the opening of a foreign market, the closing down of a service organization, or the entry of a new competitor. In contrast, in sensitivity analysis changes are made in the face of imprecisions in measuring independent variables. Different values are tried in order to see how these imprecisions will translate into uncertainties in predicting dependent variables.

For examples, we can again turn to our simplified "Corn model."

```
50 Price of Corn = 10
60 Amount of Corn = 10000
70 Cost of Corn = Price of Corn * Amount of Corn
80 Other Costs = 55000
90 Total Cost = Cost of Corn + Other Costs
```

In this model, our biggest uncertainties are likely to come in the Price of

Corn. A sensitivity analysis would vary the Price of Corn by small amounts around its most likely value, $10, and then see the impact on dependent variables. Such a sensitivity analysis would result in a table like the following one.

PRICE OF CORN	COST OF CORN	TOTAL COST
8	80000	135000
9	90000	145000
10	100000	155000
11	110000	165000
12	120000	175000

In this case, we could have done this analysis in our heads, because each dollar change in the Price of Corn corresponds to a $10,000 difference in both Cost of Corn and Total Cost. In real analyses, of course, sensitivity analysis is much more difficult to do.

We can give another example, this time from our Income Before Tax model. For example, suppose that the Unit Sales estimate for the first year, namely, 300 units in the model we have been illustrating, has an uncertainty of plus or minus 10 percent. In this case, the user might do a sensitivity analysis in which three values are plugged into the model. The first would be the base model's 300; the second would be a "low estimate" of 270; and the third a "high estimate" of 330. The user would then present three projections for income before tax to senior management. From this example, we can define sensitivity analysis formally:

> In **sensitivity analysis,** the user changes (usually) one independent variable, in accordance with uncertainties in the estimation of this variable, and then observes changes in one or more dependent variables.

How Can (Goal-Seeking) Analysis

In both what if and sensitivity analysis, the user changes *independent variables* and observes the effects on *dependent variables*. **How can** analysis does the opposite. In how can analysis, the user specifies a value for one *dependent variable* and changes the value of one *independent variable* until the target value is reached for the dependent variable. For instance, in the Income Before Tax example we have been using, the user might specify a target for Income Before Tax of $1000 and stipulate that Unit Sales should be changed to achieve that target. In effect, how can analysis asks "how can we achieve a certain target?"

In how can analysis, only *one* independent variable is changed. In practice, a computer program solves the problem by iteration, changing values of the one independent variable until the dependent variable reaches the target value. If the base model gives a projection above the target value, the program might cut the value of the independent variable in half. Dependent on the results, it might cut it in half again or split the difference between the first trial value and the base model value. Some computer programs limit the number of iterations, either by specifying a maximum number of iterations or an acceptable difference between the calculated value for the dependent variable and the target value for the dependent variables.

The independent variable does not have to be defined by data, such as Unit Sales. It can also be a dependent variable itself, calculated from other variables. In other words, if the target variable is Expenses, the user may specify the variable to be changed as Unit Sales, Fixed Costs, Unit Cost, or Variable Cost (which itself depends on Unit Sales and Unit Variable Cost).

We will again give an example from our Corn model.

```
50 Price of Corn = 10
60 Amount of Corn = 10000
70 Cost of Corn = Price of Corn * Amount of Corn
80 Other Costs = 55000
90 Total Cost = Cost of Corn + Other Costs
```

Here, we might have a target for total costs. For example, we might want to keep our total cost under $175,000. In this case, we would set the target variable to Total Cost and its value at $175,000. We would then set the Price of Corn as the variable to be changed to meet our goal for Total Cost. The program would then tell us that Price of Corn would have to be 12.

> In **how can analysis,** the user sets a target value for a single dependent variable and then requires the program to change a single dependent variable until the target value is achieved for the dependent variable.

How can analysis is needed in many practical situations. In a labor dispute, for instance, management might want to know the wage rate that will just produce a certain minimum performance level measured in terms of income, return on investment, or some other performance measure.

How Best (Optimization) Analysis

In how can analysis, a target value is set for a single dependent variable, and a single independent variable is modified until the target value is achieved. In **how best** analysis, the user specifies *one or more* dependent variables. Instead of specifying target values, the user specifies a desire to maximize or minimize the values of these dependent variables. Instead of specifying a single independent variable, the user may specify *one or more* independent variables to be changed, in addition to certain constraints (such as "capacity may not exceed the maximum capacity of the factory"). The user then asks the program to optimize the dependent variables by changing independent variables, subject to the given constraints.

How best analysis is also called **optimization.** Few general-purpose analysis programs are capable of doing optimization, but optimization is sometimes available as an optional module on high-end analysis programs.

We will again give an example from our Corn model, to which we have added some information about wheat.

```
20 Price of Wheat = 7
30 Amount of Wheat = 6000
40 Cost of Wheat = Price of Wheat * Amount of Wheat
50 Price of Corn = 10
60 Amount of Corn = 4000
70 Cost of Corn = Price of Corn * Amount of Corn
80 Other Costs = 55000
90 Total Cost = Cost of Wheat + Cost of Corn + Other Costs
```

Here, wheat and corn are at least partial substitutes, with one unit of corn substituting for one unit of wheat. Suppose that they are substitutes as long as corn is at least 15 percent of the total (perhaps to reflect nutritional requirements) and as long as at least 2000 units of corn are purchased (perhaps to reflect a long-term contract).

A how best analysis would find the optimum mix of wheat and corn. To do so, it would need the following.

1. The base model
2. The constraints (10000 total units, 15 percent corn, and 2000 units of corn)
3. An optimization goal (minimize total cost)

The program would eventually find that 2000 units of corn and 8000 units of wheat will minimize the Total Cost at $131,000.

> In **how best analysis,** the user specifies one or more dependent variable to be optimized, subject to constraints, by changing one or more independent variables.

Interrogation in Perspective

So far, we have only looked at the four basic types of interrogation in isolation. Many interrogations combine two or more basic types of interrogations, however. For example, suppose that a decision maker wants to raise corn prices but realizes that revenues will decrease somewhat as prices go up. In this case, the decision maker might ask what corn price will give a 20 percent return on investment if Unit Sales fall by 10 percent. To do this, the decision maker would specify that Unit Sales will fall by 20 percent (what if analysis) and then specify that a target ROI of 20 must be obtained by changing the price of corn (how can analysis). Many advanced statistical tools can do interrogations that combine two basic forms of interrogation.

Another important matter is how easy interrogation is to do. In some programs, such as Lotus 1-2-3, users must change their base models and then restore them later if they want to get back to the originals. In other programs, such as the Interactive Financial Planning System (IFPS) discussed in Chapter 16, the base model is never changed; instead, a temporary model is generated automatically. Other ease-of-use features of IFPS are the easy specification of interrogations and the automatic numbering and labeling of interrogations if several are done in a series.

Richness in interrogation functions and ease of use when employing these functions are critical in high-end analysis tools designed for specialists in modeling and analysis, who will spend much of their days "sweating" the model after it is created. Low-end users are more likely to want smaller systems with fewer functions. On the rare occasions when they must do sensitivity or goal-seeking analyses, what if analysis will see them through. Several what if analyses will give a sensitivity output, and by trying several values in the variable to be adjusted in a how can analysis, the user can find the value that meets the target.

SPREADSHEET CAPABILITIES: LOTUS 1-2-3

To help the reader understand the capabilities of spreadsheet programs, we will examine a specific program within this category, Lotus 1-2-3 by Lotus Development Corporation. Lotus 1-2-3 is the leading spreadsheet program for personal computers; in fact, it is the most widely used personal computer program of any type. Releases 1 and 1A were introduced in 1983, and in 1985, Release 2 of 1-2-3 added many new capabilities. Although other spreadsheet programs offer some features that 1-2-3 does not, 1-2-3 gives a very good picture of the features found in today's successors to VisiCalc.

Basic Capabilities

As the name 1-2-3 suggests, this product has three basic sets of capabilities. The first is **spreadsheet analysis.** Lotus 1-2-3 is a very powerful spreadsheet program and would have sold very well if this had been its only function.

The second set of capabilities, **graphics**, is less well developed, but Lotus was the first taste of graphics for most users in the PC world. Although 1-2-3 is not a professional graphics tool, it is at least a talented amateur.

The third set of capabilities is called **"database"** handling, but even the name is misleading because only single tables are handled, not multifile data bases (see Chapter 10). This table handling is the least developed of 1-2-3's capabilities.

There is actually a fourth set of capabilities in 1-2-3: an embedded programming language called **"macros."** Macros automate repetitive work and make 1-2-3's most cumbersome operations far easier to use.

Because 1-2-3 embodies more than just spreadsheet functionality, it is often classified as an integrated program along with Symphony and Framework (see Chapter 12), but 1-2-3 would best be called a "spreadsheet plus" program, because spreadsheet modeling is its only strong feature.

We will now look at some of the specific ways 1-2-3 implements its spreadsheet, graphics, data management, and macros capabilities.

Model Building

Figure 9-11 shows a simple spreadsheet model in Lotus 1-2-3. The lower part of the screen shows the worksheet area, where the model itself is displayed. This worksheet area shows eight columns, labeled A through H, plus 20 rows labeled 1 through 20.

The intersection of a column with a row defines a **cell.** For instance, the

B8: +B6-B7

```
|       A         B        C        D        E       F  |
|1  |THREE-YEAR BUDGET
|2  |JOHN KERR                    0.433  Tax Rate
|3  |
|4  |
|5  |            Year 1   Year 2   Year 4   Total
|6  |Revenues    113428   129648   186754   429830
|7  |Expenses    110860   117094   128769   356723
|8  |Profit BT|   2568|    12554    57985    73107
|9  |Tax         1111.944 5435.882 25107.50 31655.33
|10 |Profit AT1456.056 7118.118 32877.49 41451.66
|11 |
|12_|
```

The cursor is in cell B8 (profit before tax for Year 1).

Cell B8 contains the formula +B6-B67.

Other cells contain numbers or labels (text).

FIGURE 9-11 A SIMPLE BUDGET MODEL

cell in the upper left-hand corner is called A1, whereas the cell in the lower right-hand corner is cell H20.

Cell B8 is highlighted to show that it is the "current cell"—the cell holding the cursor. As shown in Figure 9-11, this cell holds Income Before Tax for the first quarter (2568). Obviously, this figure is calculated. It is the first-year Revenues (Cell B6) minus first-year Expenses (Cell B7), but 1-2-3 shows the **result** of the calculation on the screen in Cell B8, not the formula to do the calculation.

To see the formula itself, look at the line at the very top of the screen. This line always shows the cell holding the cursor, in this case Cell 8, followed by the contents of the cell. In this case, the contents are +B6−B7. The initial plus is there to tell 1-2-3 that this is a formula, not a title to explain numbers on the spreadsheet.

Lotus 1-2-3 models, then, consist of cells containing (1) text, (2) numbers, or (3) formulas. Text and numbers are displayed in their cells, whereas the results of formulas, instead of the formulas themselves, are displayed in the worksheet area of the screen.

This spreadsheet image is natural and easy to comprehend for managers and professionals. In addition, because models are always expanded incrementally, by putting simple formulas in individual cells, managers quickly build models that would take hours or even days to produce in conventional programming languages such as BASIC.

Even the mechanics of entering text, numbers, and formulas is simple. The user cursors to the cell, types the entry, and then cursors to another cell. In formulas, for example, +B6−B7, the user does not even have to type B6 or B7. The user can simply point to these cells with cursor keys or a mouse.

The Underlying Worksheet

The eight columns and 20 rows shown in Figure 9-11 are sufficient for small models, but for larger models, the 160 cells shown on the screen are totally inadequate.

The worksheet area on the screen in Figure 9-11 merely shows the upper left-hand corner of a very large worksheet. The full Lotus 1-2-3 worksheet has 256 columns, so to see the whole worksheet, the user would need a screen 32 times wider than normal. The worksheet is also extremely "tall." Release 1A supports 2048 rows, whereas Release 2 supports 8192 rows.

No computer has enough internal memory to hold full 1-2-3 worksheets (1-2-3 keeps the entire spreadsheet in internal memory), but computers with ample memory can hold complex analyses consisting of several tables linked together. A corporate budget, for instance, might hold several departmental budgets, as well as a consolidation area that totals their individual numbers.

The worksheet area on the display screen, then, is merely a window on the entire worksheet. Although it begins in the upper left-hand corner of the worksheet, the worksheet display area can be moved to any other part of the worksheet as the user commands.

Improving the Model's Appearance

Although the model in Figure 9-11 contains the desired results, it is something of an eyesore. Figure 9-12 shows the same model after 1-2-3's capabilities for cosmetic surgery have been called into play. A user would be much more comfortable handing a printout of this new model to his or her boss than the original model.

Four improvements were made in the original model's appearance. First, all numbers were **formatted.** Formatting puts commas between thousands places if desired, and it adds dollar signs, percentage signs, and other special symbols, as the user specifies. It also limits the number of decimal points displayed, although it does not round off the underlying number stored in the cell.

Second, the text in some cells was adjusted. Lotus 1-2-3 normally prints all text flush left in its cell. For headings on numerical columns, however, it is better to display the information flush right in the cell, and this was done in Figure 9-12. Lotus 1-2-3 can also center information in a cell.

The third change made in the model was to adjust column widths. Lotus 1-2-3 makes each column nine characters wide. For Figure 9-12, however one command was given to make all columns a little wider, and another command was given to make the first column much wider, in order to display less cryptic row titles. Release 2 of 1-2-3 allows the user to change a column's width to zero, effectively hiding it from view.

When a model is printed, it is generally printed exactly as displayed, with all improvements in appearance. The user may override this, however, and

B9: +B7-B8 |READY|

```
     |        A          B          C          D          E       F   |
    |1 |THREE-YEAR BUDGET
    |2 |JOHN KERR                                    43% Tax Rate
    |3 |
    |4 |
    |5 |                  Year 1     Year 2     Year 4     Total
    |6 |Revenues        $113,428   $129,648   $186,754   $429,830
    |7 |Expenses        $110,860   $117,094   $128,769   $356,723
    |8 |Profit Before Tax| $2,568|   $12,554    $57,985    $73,107
    |9 |Tax               $1,112     $5,436    $25,108    $31,655
    |10|Profit After Tax  $1,456     $7,118    $32,877    $41,452
    |11|
```

The widths of individual columns have been adjusted.

Numbers have commas, dollar signs, percent signs, and a fixed number of decimal points.

Labels (text) are left-justified, right-justified, or centered in their cells.

FIGURE 9-12 MAKING THE BUDGET MODEL LOOK MORE ATTRACTIVE

print the contents of cells exactly as they exist, including unrounded numbers and full formulas.

The top line of the control panel shows the fourth aspect of 1-2-3's ability to improve the appearance of models. The contents of B8 are shown as +YR1 Revenues −YR1 Expenses. Lotus 1-2-3 allows users to name individual cells and larger areas. If a named cell or area is used in a formula, its name is shown instead of its column/row designation.

As discussed earlier in the chapter, the importance of cell naming extends beyond mere appearance into good modeling practice. Lotus 1-2-3 models that only use column/row intersections are notoriously difficult to read. This is especially true of large complex models, but it is even true of small models if the reviewer is not the original model builder or even if the reviewer is the original model builder and is returning to the model several months after it has been built. Cell naming not only saves time when models are reviewed, but it also greatly reduces 1-2-3's tendency to produce models with subtle hidden errors.

Extending the Model's Logic

Models often start simply and grow as the user's understanding of the situation grows. New information sometimes requires the model to be extended.

ANALYTICAL MODELING ON PERSONAL COMPUTERS

The very process of building the model often gives the user new insights that suggest extensions to the model.

Figure 9-13 shows our initial model in the process of being expanded. A column for percentage of revenue figures has already been added, as have several rows to give details for computing the revenues and other rows. Two other lines (6 and 18) have been added to set off sections of the model. When 1-2-3 adds rows or columns, it automatically adjusts existing formulas, for instance, changing the Income Before Tax formula from +B6−B7 to +B9−B14. When the revenue details are added later, the Year 1 Revenues cell, which is now B9, will have to be changed. Its original value, simply a

```
B16: +B9-B14                                                       |READY|


         A               B           C           D           E          F
|1  |THREE-YEAR BUDGET
|2  |JOHN KERR                                   43% Tax Rate
|3  |
|4  |                                                            Pct. of
|5  |                  Year 1      Year 2      Year 4      Total    Revenues
|6  |                 ----------------------------------------------
|7  |Units             1,100       1,323       1,987       4,410
|8  |Unit Price         $103         $98         $94         $97
|9  |Revenues       $113,428    $129,648    $186,754    $429,830     100.0%
|10 |
|11 |
|12 |
|13 |
|14 |Expenses       $110,860    $117,094    $128,769    $356,723      83.0%
|15 |              ----------
|16 |Profit Before Tax| $2,568|   $12,554     $57,985     $73,107      17.0%
|17 |Tax              $1,112      $5,436     $25,108     $31,655       7.4%
|18 |              ==================================================
|19 |Profit After Tax  $1,456     $7,118     $32,877     $41,452       9.6%
|20 |
```

A percent of revenues column has been added.

Rows have been inserted to hold revenue details, perhaps revenues by product line.

Rows with dashed and double-dashed lines have been added.

FIGURE 9-13 THE BUDGET MODEL BEING EXPANDED

number value, will be replaced by a formula, based on the details to be added in lines 10 through 13.

What If Analysis

Anyone who has ever prepared a budget knows that input numbers—in our case, revenues and expenses—are subject to constant change. Figure 9-14 shows the budget model we have been using as an example. The structural changes begun earlier have now been completed. In addition, the entry for Tax Rate (cell D2) has been changed from 0.433 to 49 percent, in order to reflect new information or to test the impact of an increased tax rate. The numbers that depend on Tax Rate—Taxes and Net Income—have changed. In 1-2-3 and other spreadsheet programs, these changes take place automatically and virtually instantly.

Lotus 1-2-3 also has an extension to basic what if analysis called **data table** analysis. As shown in Figure 9-15, the user can create a table in another part of the worksheet, in this case columns G, H, and I.

The first column contains a series of "what if" values for the variable to be studied, in this case Tax Rate. These values range from 40 percent to 50 percent.

D2: (P0) 0.49 READY

	A	B	C	D	E	F	
1	THREE-YEAR BUDGET						
2	JOHN KERR			49%	Tax Rate <-- Changed assumption		
3							
4						Pct. of	
5		Year 1	Year 2	Year 4	Total	Revenues	
6		----------	----------	----------	----------	----------	
7	Units	1,100	1,323	1,987	4,410		
8	Unit Price	$103	$98	$94	$97		
9	Revenues	$113,428	$129,648	$186,754	$429,830	100.0%	
10							
11	Per Unit	$50	$47	$42	$45		
12	Variable	$55,000	$62,178	$83,443	$200,621	46.7%	
13	Fixed	$55,860	$54,916	$45,326	$156,102	36.3%	
14	Expenses	$110,860	$117,094	$128,769	$356,723	83.0%	
15							
16	Profit Before Tax	$2,568	$12,554	$57,985	$73,107	17.0%	
17	Tax	$1,258	$6,151	$28,413	$35,822	8.3%	<-- Results
18		==========	==========	==========	==========		
19	Profit After Tax	$1,310	$6,403	$29,572	$37,285	8.7%	<-- Results
20							

The user has changed the tax rate from 43% to 49%. The program automatically recalculates the spreadsheet model, changing all numbers that are affected by the change in tax rate.

FIGURE 9-14 A SIMPLE "WHAT IF" ANALYSIS

H4: +E19

	G	H	I
1		Total Profit	PAT as %
2	Tax Rate	After Tax	or Revenues
3			
4		$41,452	9.64% <-- +E19/E9
5	40%	$43,864	10.21%
6	41%	$43,133	10.03%
7	42%	$42,402	9.86%
8	43%	$41,671	9.69%
9	44%	$40,940	9.52%
10	45%	$40,209	9.35%
11	46%	$39,478	9.18%
12	47%	$38,747	9.01%
13	48%	$38,016	8.84%
14	49%	$37,285	8.67%
15	50%	$36,554	8.50%
16			

A Data Table allows many tax rate values to be tried.

The program calculates changes in total profit after tax (cell E19).

The program also calculates changes in PAT as a percent of revenues (+E19/E9).

FIGURE 9-15 A SENSITIVITY ANALYSIS USING A DATA TABLE

At the top of the next two columns, the user places formulas depending on Tax Rate. In this case, the column H heading holds +E19, the Net Income in the total column, whereas the column I heading holds +E19/E16, which gives Net Income as a percentage of Income Before tax.

Lotus 1-2-3 automatically fills in the rest of the data table when the user gives the **data table** command. This produces a sensitivity analysis that would take a long time if each of the ten what if analyses had to be computed separately. In addition, there is no need to write down the results of many individual what if analyses.

Analytical Graphics

One of the most endearing features of 1-2-3 to early users was its graphics capabilities. For the first time, large numbers of managers were able to produce graphs of their results. Releases 1 and 1A offered pie charts, two kinds of bar charts, and two kinds of line charts. Release 2 added an exploding pie chart and other improvements.

If the user has a color graphics display, he or she can view the graph as often as necessary during its construction. The user can specify some aspects of the graph, see the results, and then change these choices or go on to add new aspects. If the user has both a monochrome and color graphics display, both the spreadsheet and graph can be displayed simultaneously. Even users of monochrome displays can see graphs in progress if they buy a monochrome graphics board such as the Hercules monochrome graphics board (Chapter 7).

Lotus 1-2-3 cannot print graphs directly. The user must leave 1-2-3, insert a second program disk (on a floppy disk system), and then print the graph already created in 1-2-3. This is an awkward and unpleasant process.

Lotus 1-2-3 graphs are reasonably attractive, even on dot matrix printers, and on plotters, they are far better. Even so, 1-2-3 is behind the state of the art in graphics. Even other spreadsheet programs offer such enhancements as three-dimensional graphs, and dedicated graphics programs such as Chartmaster can do far more.

Lotus 1-2-3 users often read their graph files (called PIC files) into comprehensive graphics programs such as Chartmaster and then process their graphs further.

Some graphics programs can leave a module resident in RAM after the user leaves them. If Lotus 1-2-3 is subsequently entered, this module can take a "snapshot" of a graphics screen produced in 1-2-3. The user can view a graph and, if it looks right, capture its image. This captured graph can then be dressed up using a dedicated graphics program's full functionality.

Built-in Computational Functions

Some kinds of calculations, such as square roots, are difficult to do. Others, such as the net present value of an investment, are easy to calculate but time consuming. Lotus 1-2-3 has built-in functions to do common operations. These are called @-functions because they all begin with the character @. Releases 1 and 1A had many computational @-functions. Release 2 added more computational @-functions, including multiple regression. Release 2 also offered a rich set of string manipulation @-functions.

Financial @-Functions

Lotus 1-2-3 is widely known for its financial @-functions. To evaluate investments, it offers @NPV to compute net present value and @IRR to compute internal rate of return. It can also compute annuity payments and find the present and future values of annuities. Release 2 adds the ability to handle the number of periods or rate needed for an investment to reach a certain value, as well as depreciation using double declining balance or sum of the year digits.

Although @-functions take the drudgery out of computations, they are dangerous if the user does not understand the theory of financial discounting and the mechanics of how 1-2-3 does calculations. For example, Lotus 1-2-3 treats the first year as Year 1, but many investment analysts treat the first year as Year 0 for discounting purposes. If a firm's cost of capital is high, the impact is significant, and the user must adjust for it.

Statistical @-Functions

Lotus 1-2-3 offers a number of statistical @-functions, including @COUNT, @SUM @AVG, and @VAR. These perform their calculations on a range of cells.

Again, the user must be aware of exactly what these functions do. For instance, variance and standard deviations use N in the denominator instead of N − 1. This is appropriate if there are data for everyone in a population. If a sample is taken, however, N − 1 must be the divisor and 1-2-3 calculations must be adjusted.

All statistical @-functions ignore blank cells but treat cells with labels as containing zero. Moreover, a cell containing only spaces is a label, not an empty cell. Users must be very careful of label cells and cells that appear to be blank.

If data tables are used (these are discussed later in this chapter), a new set of statistical @-functions comes into play, including a @DSUM and @DAVG. These do their computations only on certain rows in a data table. For instance, a user might want to know the average salary of female employees in the marketing department.

The multiple regression @-function of release 2 takes 1-2-3 into a whole new world of functionality. Multiple regression is not even available in many simple statistical packages. As more such advanced tools appear in spreadsheet programs, these programs will assume even wider importance.

@IF

The @IF function has three parameters: (1) a test, (2) a value if the test is true, and (3) a value if the test is false. The following @IF function computes the absolute value of a difference between the value in cell C10 and the number 27.

```
@IF (C10-27 > 0, C10-27, 27-C10)
```

This essentially says:

```
IF C10-27 > 0
   Then C10-27
   Else 27-C10
```

Table Lookup @-Functions

The last @-functions we will discuss are 1-2-3's table lookup functions. @LOOKUP is a vertical lookup function, and @HLOOKUP is a horizontal lookup function.

Many calculations can only be defined as table lookup procedures, a good example of which may be income tax tables. As shown in Figure 9-16, a user can look down the table's first column until he or she finds his or her income bracket, then move over one or more columns depending on filing status. The user then places the number in the appropriate line of the income tax form.

@VLOOKUP does exactly that. This @-function has three parameters:

A6: (C0) @VLOOKUP(A5,B9..D15,A4)

```
|      A         B        C        D        E   |
|1  |Vertical Lookup Example
|2  |
|3  |_____2 Filing Status
|4  |_____2|Offset (Number of columns to look horizontally)
|5  |_$32,000|Taxable Income (Value to look up)
|6  |__$8,100|Tax to be paid (Value looked up)
|7  |
|8  |          Income    Alone   Jointly
|9  |         | $5,000      $0       $0|  <-- Lookup
|10 |         |$10,000  $1,000     $900|      Table
|11 |         |$20,000  $3,000   $2,700|
|12 |         |$30,000  $9,000   $8,100|
|13 |         |$40,000 $27,000  $24,300|
|14 |         |$50,000 $35,000  $31,500|
|15 |         |$60,000 $45,000  $40,500|
|16 |
```

Given taxable income $32,000 (A6), @VLOOKUP goes to the lookup table (B9..D15).

It goes down the first column of the table (B) until it finds a value equal to or greater than $32,000. This is $30,000 on Line 12.

It then moves over 2 columns--the number of columns dictated by the offset (A4). This takes it to cell D12.

@VLOOKUP then takes on the value found there: $8,100.

FIGURE 9-16 A TABLE LOOKUP USING THE @VLOOKUP FUNCTION

(1) the area where the table is to be found, (2) the value to be looked up in the first column, and (3) the number of columns to move to the right to find the correct value.

As in all @-functions, specific implementation must be understood. If the value to be looked up is exactly equal to a value in the first column, the action is obvious. If the value to be looked up falls between two values, however, @VLOOKUP will *drop back to the lower value and then do the lookup*. If the value to be looked up is larger than the last value in the first column of the table, @VLOOKUP will drop back to the table's highest value. If the value to be looked up is smaller than the first value in the table, @VLOOKUP will place @ERR in the cell, indicating an error.

As a result, @VLOOKUP will behave totally unexpectedly if the table values in the first column are not arranged in ascending order from top to bottom.

Logical and String Handling @-Functions

Release 1A introduced several logical tests of conditions, for instance, the ability to test whether a certain cell held NA or ERR. Release 2 expanded these logical possibilities, including the ability to compare strings of text as well as just values.

String handling, ignored in Release 1A, came into its own in Release 2. It is even possible to replace certain characters in a cell's string with another set of characters, just using an @-function.

Data File Tables

A rectangular area on a worksheet can be made to resemble a simple flat file (Chapter 10). As shown in Figure 9-17, a flat file has several rows, one for each individual (Brown, Andrews, etc.). Each column, in turn, holds information about a single attribute (name, age, income).

Lotus 1-2-3 is adept at sorting such data file tables as shown in Figure

Before (unsorted on any category):

	A	B	C
1			
2	NAME	AGE	INCOME
3	Brown	24	$21,840
4	Andrews	17	$18,321
5	Grimm	33	$43,872
6	Liu	50	$33,184
7	Ochoa	21	$23,560
8	Braun	33	$33,123

After (sorted by age in descending order):

	A	B	C
1			
2	NAME	AGE	INCOME
3	Liu	50	$33,184
4	Grimm	33	$43,872
5	Braun	33	$33,123
6	Brown	24	$21,840
7	Ochoa	21	$23,560
8	Andrews	17	$18,321

FIGURE 9-17 A "DATABASE" TABLE BEFORE AND AFTER SORTING

9-17. It can even sort on two columns, say, Lastname and then Firstname if both are on the table. Lotus 1-2-3 will sort first on the primary key, Lastname. If there is a tie on the primary key for two or more records, 1-2-3 will then sort these ties on the basis of the secondary key, Firstname.

To do more than this is somewhat difficult, but a perservering user can learn to find specific records based on Boolean conditions (Age >30 and Income >20000). The user can also extract a subtable with only selected columns and rows from the first. The columns do not even have to be in the same order found in the initial table. Surveys show that 1-2-3, despite its weaknesses, is one of the most popular data management tools for PC users.

Lotus Development Corporation has enhanced the data handling capabilities of 1-2-3. First, it sells an integrated package Symphony (see Chapter 12) which is somewhat richer in data handling capabilities than 1-2-3. Second, it sells a report generator, 1-2-3 Report Writer, which can reach into a 1-2-3 or Symphony worksheet and generate a report or mailing labels from a data file table.

For heavy processing, many 1-2-3 users export their data tables as DIF files (Chapter 8). Most file and data base management programs can import these DIF files, and some DBMSs can import Lotus 1-2-3 worksheet files directly.

Keys, Menus, and Macros

We have not discussed the details of how 1-2-3 can be commanded to do all of the actions covered to this point; a full book would be needed to do that. It is necessary, however, to have an overview of the three ways 1-2-3 commands can be given: from the keyboard, from menus, and through macros.

The Keyboard

Lotus 1-2-3 was designed for the IBM PC and uses the PC's keyboard extensively. The cursor keys on the right side of the keyboard are used for virtually all navigation of the worksheet, and the strategically placed "+", "−", "*", and "/" keys are used to create formulas. The Backspace, Esc, and Del keys are used in editing.

On the left side of the keyboard, 1-2-3 makes frequent use of function keys. For instance, F5 is the "Go to" key, taking the user to a specific cell. F1 gives help, F2 takes the user into the EDIT mode and out again, F3 shows names of cells and areas, and so on.

Lotus 1-2-3 even uses the misplaced "/" command near the right-hand little finger. This key calls the Main Menu discussed later. The Alt key, in turn, allows the user to execute any of 26 user-defined macro programs, from Alt-A through Alt-Z.

Menus

For less frequent commands, 1-2-3 provide a multitier menu of command choices. When the user hits the "/" key, a **Main Menu** appears, as shown in Figure 9-18.

Note, in this figure, that the top of the line control panel still shows the current cell and its contents. On the right-hand side of this line, however, the mode indicator has changed to MENU.

```
A1:                                                                |MENU|
|Worksheet| Range  Copy  Move  File  Print  Graph  Data  Quit
Global, Insert, Delete, Column-Width, Erase, Titles, Window, Status


     A       B       C       D       E       F       G       H
|1 |_____|
|2 |
|3 |
|4 |
|5 |
|6 |
|7 |
|8 |
|9 |
|10|
```

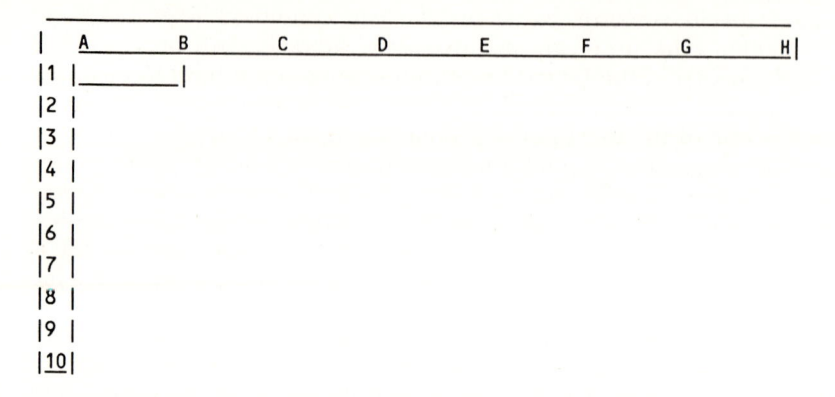

The user brings up the main menu by typing a slash (/).

The user selects a choice either by typing the first character of the choice (R for Range) or by cursoring to the choice and hitting enter.

Most choices have subchoices.

FIGURE 9-18 THE MAIN MENU IN LOTUS 1-2-3

The second line shows the Main Menu choices, from Worksheet to Quit. The first choice, Worksheet, is highlighted initially. The left and right cursor key move the highlighting to other choices.

The third line gives further information about the highlighted choice. In the case of Worksheet, the third line shows the submenu of choices that will appear if Worksheet is selected. In other cases, some general descriptive information is available.

To select a choice, the user can cursor to it and hit Enter, but it is faster to use the second approach, just typing the first character of the choice. Most users memorize frequent keystroke series, such as "/WCS20Enter," to give the command Worksheet Column-Width set 20 Enter. This sets the width of a column to 20.

If the user hits Esc, 1-2-3 backs up one step in the menu selection. Hitting Esc repeatedly will take the user out of MENU mode. The Ctrl-Break combination will do this immediately.

Macros

As noted earlier, a user may utilize certain keystroke combinations repeatedly. To set column width to 20, for instance, the user cursors to the column and types "/WCS20<Enter>".

It is also possible to do something else, namely (1) enter the keystrokes required to execute the column width change in a cell, (2) then name the cell, and (3) later execute these keystrokes by hitting only two keys. The keystrokes in the cell essentially form a program that can be executed as often as desired. Instead of calling these keystrokes a program, however, 1-2-3 refers to them as a "macro."

Any combination of keystrokes can be put in a cell. If there are too many keystrokes to fit easily in the cell, the user can continue onto the cell below and to cells below that. When 1-2-3 runs out of keystrokes, it always continues to the next cell down, until it runs into a blank cell.

The first cell in the macro must be given a name from \A to \Z. In other words, there are 26 possible names for macros on any worksheet. If it is named \S, then Alt-S will activate the macro that begins there.

Lotus 1-2-3 has certain commands, called /**X commands,** that can only be used in macros. These /X commands, which begin with /X followed by other information, turn macros into programs, providing IF/THEN/ELSE, LOOPING, INPUT, and other control structures.

There is even the /XM command, which lets users create their own customized menus. As shown in Figure 9-19, the custom menu resembles the regular menu. The user can cursor among choices, seeing different information on the third line of the control panel. There can even be several levels of submenus.

```
A1:                                                              |CMD MENU|
BROWSE  FIND1  REPORT  CLEAR  OTHER
Browse by Last name, Nickname, or Social Security Number


   |     A           B                C         D    E       F        G      H|
|1  |           |                           |          |               |
|2  |ID Number  |First Name, Middle         |First Name|Last Name      |
|3  |           |                           |          |               |
|4  |-----------|---------------------------|----------|---------------|
|5  |575-48-2564|Henry Eric                 |Hank      |Fujita         |
|6  |298-49-0022|Jessica L.                 |Jessica   |Siu            |
|7  |576-25-4756|Robert A.                  |Robert    |Lee            |
|8  |455-92-3036|Steven I.                  |Steve     |Keown          |
|9  |576-99-1764|Anna V.                    |Anna      |Ikehara        |
|10 |566-26-5047|Donna J.                   |Donna     |Young          |
```

Users can create their own menus by means of macro programs.

The normal actions that can be done on the Main Menu of the program can be done on the macro menu.

FIGURE 9-19 A USER-CREATED MENU BUILT WITH A MACRO

ANALYTICAL MODELING ON PERSONAL COMPUTERS

	O	P	Q R S T U
1	\G	GRAPHICS MACRO	TO BUILD ROUGH GRAPH OF REVENUES, EXPENSES
2		{Home}	Go to cell A1
3		{Goto}I1~	Put modified budget in place
4		/G	Go the the graphing menu
5		RG	Reset Graph Settings
6		TB	Type = Bar Chart
7		XPeriod~	The Horizontal Axis is the range Period
8		ARevenues~	The A Range is Revenues
9		BExpenses~	The B Range is Expenses
10		O	Go to the options submenu
11		TFOne Year Budget~	Title = One Year Budget
12		TYBudgeted Figures~	Y axis title = Budgeted Figures
13		LARevenues~	Legend for A Range is "Revenues"
14		LBExpenses~	Legend for B Range is "Expenses"
15		Q	Quit the options submenu
16		V	View the graph onscreen
17			

Each macro cell consists of a small and logically complete set of steps.

Next to each macro statement is an English description of what the steps in the cell do.

FIGURE 9-20 A CLEARLY WRITTEN MACRO

The only real problem with macros is their terseness. If someone reads a macro that says /WGCS20~ (~ indicates Enter), can he or she really read what it does? Even small macros are extremely hard to debug, and it is easy for unintended operations to do extreme damage to the worksheet.

During development, macros must be tested carefully, with frequent backups of the spreadsheet. The macro developer also needs to learn how to execute the macro one step at a time during testing.

Because most macros will need to be changed later or at least audited, it is very important to set up macros for readability, with only a few keystrokes on each line and good marginal documentation. Figure 9-20 shows a clean, simple macro with adequate documentation.

Although macros are powerful, they can become unguided missiles doing great harm. In addition, their lack of easy readability can lead to the existence of uncaught errors and macros that are too unreadable to alter with time.

SELECTING SPREADSHEET SOFTWARE

Spreadsheet analysis is a core software need, and nearly every firm of any size has already selected its basic spreadsheet software. As indicated earlier, a majority of all firms have standardized on Lotus 1-2-3. Quite a few, however, have standardized on other programs, and many others support more than one spreadsheet package to a greater or lesser degree.

Lotus 1-2-3 Alternatives

Direct Competitors

A number of products have attempted to compete head on with Lotus 1-2-3, but to date, none has been very successful. Because Lotus has not kept 1-2-3 at the forefront of the spreadsheet market, companies continue trying to beat 1-2-3, hoping that theirs will be the product that finally dethrones 1-2-3, just as 1-2-3 once dethroned VisiCalc when the product virtually owned the spreadsheet world.

After Lotus 1-2-3, the two most popular choices on IBM PCs and compatibles seem to be Multiplan and SuperCalc. Multiplan was designed to run on 8-bit machines. As a consequence, it runs on virtually every computer in existence, giving it a universality not enjoyed even by Lotus 1-2-3. In addition, Multiplan can link spreadsheets on different disk files. SuperCalc tries to compete directly with 1-2-3, giving better functionality in individual features. VisiCalc, the early leader, is no longer in production, and the number of organizations using VisiCalc is likely to decline.

A new generation of spreadsheet products is beginning to appear to challenge Lotus 1-2-3, Multiplan, and SuperCalc. Among the most promising is Microsoft's Excel, which was first introduced on the Macintosh and was later moved to the IBM PC. As shown in Figure 9-21, Excel can show multiple

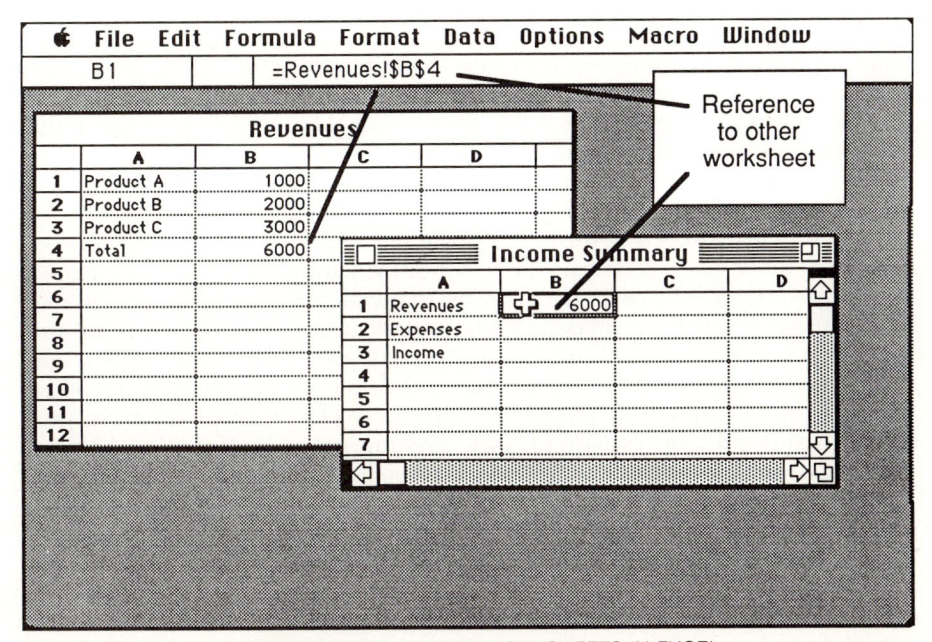

FIGURE 9-21 LINKED WORKSHEETS IN EXCEL

worksheets on the screen and can link the worksheets together. For example, the Revenues worksheet totals revenues for three products in cell B4, and the Income Summary worksheet copies this total into its Revenues cell through the formula "=Revenues!B4."

Many companies offer spreadsheet programs for mainframe computers (see Chapter 16). In general, host spreadsheet programs have lower functionality and a more rigid user interface than PC users have come to expect.

In most cases, companies are not likely to switch from their current spreadsheet systems to programs of comparable functionality. Few 1-2-3 users have switched to Multiplan, for instance. Although more Multiplan and SuperCalc users have switched to 1-2-3, they have done this more to take advantage of infrastructure considerations, such as training, than because of functionality itself.

Other Products

Although competition is rather static among traditional products, many new products are trying to bite into the spreadsheet world, and these products offer new choices for microcomputer managers. In most cases, they will live alongside 1-2-3 or whatever spreadsheet program is now in existence, but some firms are replacing their current offerings entirely with new products.

Not surprisingly, most new entrants take direct aim at Lotus 1-2-3. This is the "product to beat" if any significant level of market share is to be obtained. In general, new entries are following three different strategies to cut into firms using 1-2-3.

The first approach is to offer added functionality in certain specific areas in order to appeal to power users who have outgrown 1-2-3's capabilities. For example, Javelin and IFPS/Personal are really spreadsheet financial analysis packages but are sold as competitors to 1-2-3. (For further information about financial analysis systems, see Chapter 16.) While lacking 1-2-3's generality, they offer much higher functionality than 1-2-3 in financial analysis, which has always been an important 1-2-3 application. Many firms now see Lotus 1-2-3 as a general-purpose analysis program that works well in certain cases but must be able to work with more specialized analysis tools for people doing specialized tasks such as financial analysis or statistics.

Another approach is to make a product that works exactly like 1-2-3, looking as much like 1-2-3 as possible without violating copyright laws. Paperback Software's VP Planner is currently the leader among "clone builders." These low-cost clones are making a big impact in price-conscious institutions that do not need to depend on Lotus Development Corporation's good customer support. When Lotus discontinued Release 1A following its introduction of Release 2, many corporations switched to clones simply to make purchases that would be consistent with existing releases of 1-2-3. Another advantage of these clones is that they often provide richer features than Release 1A of 1-2-3, especially graphics. VP Planner, for example, prints graphics without requiring the user to leave the main program. It also supports three-dimensional modeling, so that the top "sheet" on the screen can be a consolidation of data from several departments on underlying sheets in the third dimension.

A final approach is to offer an integrated product that offers more than

1-2-3 while still being compatible with 1-2-3 data files. Enable is currently the class example of compatible integrated products, but newer entries are beginning to include spreadsheet modules that are virtually 1-2-3 clones. Lotus Development Corporation's Symphony is the leading example of integrated products that allow users to trade up from 1-2-3.

Selecting Add-On Programs

Once a spreadsheet is purchased, this is not the end of things. In many cases, corporations continue to buy products that enhance the functionality of their spreadsheet programs. Not surprisingly, most add-ons are directed to the one to two million people who already use 1-2-3 and whose number is growing constantly.

Generally, these are in the form of **templates**—models whose logic is complete and which just need data. For instance, an expense report template may only require the user to type in essential information on spending. All calculations will be done automatically. Many templates include macros and even macro menus.

In addition to templates, users can buy RAM-resident utilities to extend the capabilities of 1-2-3. These products sit in RAM until called by hitting a particular keystroke combination. They then "pop up" on the screen to do things that 1-2-3 cannot do by itself or can only do awkwardly. 1-2-3 Report Writer, mentioned earlier, was developed outside of Lotus Development Corporation. Other useful add-on programs are Sideways, which prints output sideways on the paper; the Spreadsheet Auditor, which prints out cell formulas in row/column form and checks for some errors; and Note-It, which allows notes to be attached to individual cells, for example, to explain the origin of an estimate. Also worthy of mention are utilities that extend 1-2-3's limited interrogation capabilities. Goal Solutions, by Enfin Software, allows the user to do how can analysis (goal seeking).

Lotus itself seems to be trying to build revenues by selling many add-ons instead of incorporating these into upgrades. 1-2-3 Report Writer is one example. Another is HAL, which allows users to type commands in English and also performs a number of tasks not possible in 1-2-3 itself, for example, linking cells in two different worksheet files.

Many users resent having to pay a great deal of extra money to buy large numbers of add-ons, arguing that Release 2 of 1-2-3 should have incorporated most or all of the capabilities provided by add-ons. It is true that users will have to pay a great deal of extra money if they buy a half dozen or so add-on products. Other users like the ability to buy add-ons from several different sources, so that they can choose among several alternatives for auditing capabilities, sideways printing, how can analysis, and other capabilities.

Lotus Development Corporation seems intent on sustaining the practice of using add-ons to improve its basic product. In 1986, it released the Lotus Developer Toolkit to integrate add-ons more smoothly with Release 2 of 1-2-3. This tool has allowed the creation of integrated word processing programs, SQL-oriented data management programs, and other useful programs. Unless some competitor provides an attractively priced product offering a wide variety of add-on features in one basic package, it will be difficult to compete with the 1-2-3 environment.

SUPPORTING SPREADSHEET USERS

Training

Spreadsheet programs are easy for users to appreciate. In about five minutes, a teacher can show a spreadsheet with a budget model, including the steps needed to enter the model. In another five minutes, students can work a simple exercise to enter formulas using cell references. As dessert, the teacher can show a simple what if analysis that anyone who has ever done a budget can readily appreciate.

The only problem with this kind of introduction is that it gives the impression that spreadsheet systems are easy to master. The reality, of course, is that below the surface of this simple introductory example lie level after level of detail. What are "ranges," and how are they entered? What should be done if the model gets too large for the screen or printer? In the end, the simple spreadsheet image degenerates into numerous details to be mastered.

To learn the basics of Lotus 1-2-3 takes about six hours of classroom instruction, and another two to four hours of hands-on exercises after the class ends. To learn advanced applications such as graphics and the full printing capabilities of the system will take about two hours per advanced application, and it takes at least a day to teach macros and two days to teach it well. Corporations must require computer users to commit themselves to these time and cost investments.

Few corporations have to teach the mechanics of spreadsheet programs, especially if they use Lotus 1-2-3. In most parts of the country, there are at least three or four private and public organizations that teach Lotus 1-2-3, and in quite a number of areas, there are dozens of training organizations. For in-house training, there are videotapes and CAI programs, as discussed in Chapter 5.

Teaching Simple Good Practice

Although most training sources are good at teaching the mechanics of spreadsheet programs, quite a few do a poor job of teaching even the simplest elements of good modeling practice that every user needs to know. Unless an outside vendor teaches good practice, the information center will have to offer a supplemental class.

One important problem that must be tackled in training is not letting users "cheat" by doing things the hard way in order to avoid learning techniques that will eventually save them time or reduce the chances of error. For example, users should be taught not to work out the whole model on paper and then just go to the machine to do the mechanics of entering it. Rather, they should build their models interactively. In general, care needs to be taken to be sure that users do not develop a training wheels mentality that will ultimately cripple their use.

Support for Larger Models

For larger models, several types of support are needed beyond the kind of support needed by people who only build small models. First, more tool training is needed because building large models requires a good grasp of the system. Advanced viewing and printing knowledge is needed, and in general, users must to be as efficient as possible.

Second, the firm needs to established policies on good modeling practice, and it must train users in the process and details of such practice. The methods discussed at the beginning of this chapter must be taught using examples. Along with setting policies and training users in these policies, the information center staff may have to conduct model audits to ensure compliance with good practice techniques.

Third, for larger models, a good deal of live assistance is likely to be required. The information center staff may well be advised to go through the basic model development steps with the user, both to ensure compliance with policies and to provide the user with the benefits of the information center staff's experience with such products.

Fourth, for large projects that are likely to be beyond the abilities of the intended user to create, the information center staff may become involved in model building, using either its own staff and chargeback procedures or an outside contractor. It may not be worth the user's time to learn spreadsheet technique and good practice well enough to do a one-time job.

As in every aspect of end user computing, it is critical to realize that end user projects vary enormously in scope, and firms need to have separate support strategies for projects of both small and large scope.

CONCLUSION

Analysis is one of the most important tools available to managers and professionals. The analysis market today is dominated by general-purpose spreadsheet tools, particularly Lotus 1-2-3. Many organizations once standardized on 1-2-3 and considered the matter closed. Now, however, new products, 1-2-3 "clones," and numerous add-on products for 1-2-3 users have made the market extremely complex. In addition, Lotus 1-2-3 is an aging product, whose complex ways of printing ranges and graphs and other limitations have made it rather vulnerable, although no one has yet been able to exploit this vulnerability. Although the spreadsheet market is fairly stable today, product selection still requires time and is likely to require much more time in the future.

Now that basic software skills are common in spreadsheeting, the information center can push users above the level of mechanical use in order to consider the many issues raised under the banner of "good practice." Now that many models are large and crucial to decision making, the strong tendency of Lotus 1-2-3 and other spreadsheet modeling programs to produce models that are nearly unreadable and unauditable is probably leading to some very bad modeling and some bad decisions as a result. Until better software becomes available, training in good practice will be critical, and for important models, auditing may also be required.

REVIEW QUESTIONS

1. Summarize the benefits and dangers of doing analytical modeling on computers.
2. Summarize the relative advantages and disadvantages of the spreadsheet, equations, and dependency images of analytical modeling. For

each, give a specific example of conditions under which the image is best. Create your own small model and express it in all three images.

3. What are the five steps involved in building an analytical model? Which step do you think is the hardest for end users without formal IS training? Which do you think is most often done too hastily by users?

4. What is the First Law of Modeling? Make up your own example of a model violating the First Law of Modeling. Why do problems associated with the First Law only appear during what if analysis and other forms of interrogation?

5. What is the Second Law of Modeling? Make up your own example of a model violating the Second Law of Modeling. Why do problems associated with the Second Law only appear during what if analysis and other forms of interrogation?

6. What are the advantages of hierarchical design? Modular design? How does modular design in spreadsheet systems differ from modular design in general?

7. Critique the standardized spreadsheet layout shown in Figure 9-9 and the details in the text. What should be added? Left out?

8. What are the advantages of construction and testing with skeletons?

9. Can a variable be both an independent and a dependent variable?

10. What are the differences between what if and sensitivity analysis? What if and how can analysis? How can and optimization?

11. Summarize the things that Lotus 1-2-3 does to make models look attractive. What more could be done to make models look more attractive on screen? On paper?

12. How does 1-2-3 do simple what if analysis? How does the data table function improve what if analysis? Why do you think data table analysis is not used by most 1-2-3 modelers? How can you do how can analysis in 1-2-3?

13. What is a macro? Argue that all 1-2-3 users should use macros. Argue that all use of macros should be forbidden. What can be done to reduce the dangers of macros?

14. List the major categories of alternatives to Lotus 1-2-3. List some major types of add-ons to 1-2-3. Which type of add-on would be most useful to you? Why?

15. What kinds of support do you think should be provided for projects to build large models?

DATA MANAGEMENT ON PERSONAL COMPUTERS 10

Data management is one of today's fastest growing applications on personal computers. This chapter will discuss data management in general, setting the stage for both PC data management and for data management on host computers, which is discussed in Chapter 16.

INTRODUCTION

Data

Traditional data processing applications are characterized by massive collections of structured data. For example, a manufacturer may have thousands of parts in its inventory of components. Its inventory system would have to store information about each part in a highly structured way, as shown in Figure 10-1.

The table shown in Figure 10-1 is called a **data file.** A data file holds information about one kind of thing, in this case, parts on hand. Other data files on the manufacturer's computer hold information about other kinds of things: suppliers, job applicants, invoices, orders, and medical plans, to name just a few. The kind of thing about which data is stored is called the data file's **entity.** There will be a separate data file for each entity.

Collections of related data files are called **data bases.** For our manufacturer, for example, there might be an inventory data base holding information about parts on hand, vendors, and purchases, as shown in Figure 10-2. Although any good-sized firm will have dozens or even hundreds of data files, it will usually have only a small number of data bases.

Data processing has long handled its files and data bases on host computers. Chapter 13 discusses the process of downloading data from corporate

OnHand		
PartNo	Qty	UnitCost
2386	287	$10
5640	39	$218
5912	4,289	$43
6281	320	$97
7194	15	$12

FIGURE 10-1 A DATA FILE FOR PARTS ON HAND

data to personal computers for subsequent processing. Chapter 16 examines host-based data retrieval and application development tools.

More recently, data management tools on personal computers have joined host tools. Tens of thousands of end users now use their PCs to develop personal and departmental applications. Even on stand-alone PCs, which can only be used by a single person at a time, data management has become extremely popular. With networking, data management on personal computers has begun to compete with minicomputer data management. (This development is discussed in Chapter 12.)

Later in this chapter, we will discuss data file and data base concepts in more detail, getting into the fine knowledge that users and information center staff members need to master to work effectively with either PC data management tools or data management tools on host computers.

Data Management Tools

Third-Generation Languages

Until recently, information systems (IS) departments developed nearly all of their data applications with third-generation languages. COBOL, which

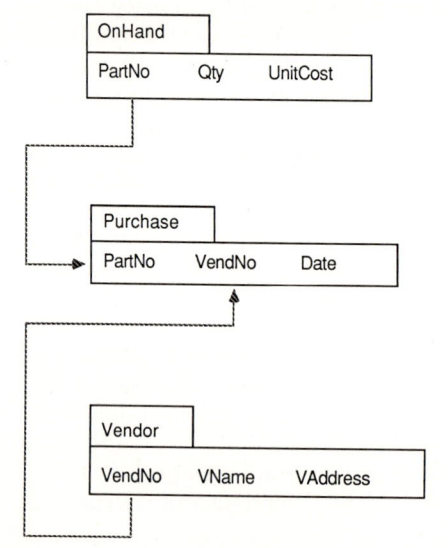

FIGURE 10-2 AN INVENTORY DATA BASE

is oriented toward data file processing, is by far the most widely used language for developing DP applications.

COBOL and other third-generation languages are tedious to use because they are **procedural languages.** Users of procedural languages must specify, in detail, the procedure to be done on each piece of information in the data file, in order to accomplish a specific job. For example, if the purpose of the program is to print the part number and quantity on hand of every part whose unit cost is over $100, the programmers must tell the program to get information for the first part, test whether its price is more than $100, and, if so, print two pieces of information—part number and quantity on hand—on the basis of a format specified in detail by the programmer. The programmer must also tell the program to repeat this procedure on subsequent parts, stopping at the last part. If the output should be sorted, for example, in increasing order of quantity on hand, the complexity of the programmer's job is multiplied. Even this simple job would take hours to do in COBOL.

Special-Purpose Fourth-Generation Tools

During the 1970s, software vendors began to sell tools to automate several of the most common data application development tasks, such as generating reports. These tools were called **fourth-generation** tools because they were much easier to use than third-generation languages such as COBOL, just as third-generation tools were easier to use than second-generation tools (assembly language). For example, to print the report discussed above, the user of a fourth-generation tool might only have to type the following.

```
PRINT PartNo, Qty
  FROM OnHand
  WHERE UnitCost > 100
  SORT BY Qty
```

This kind of tool is called **nonprocedural** because the user does not specify the procedure to be performed on each and every record. Instead of describing *how* to do the job, the user merely specifies *what* should be done—namely, that two columns of output should be printed, that these two columns should be PartNo and Qty, that only information on only certain parts should be printed, and that the output should be sorted in increasing order on the basis of quantity on hand.

The problem with most of the fourth-generation tools developed in the 1970s was that they were special-purpose programs that could only do one task. Some could automate the creation of reports, whereas others could sort existing files, and others could do other specific tasks. As a result, an IS department might have to stock a dozen or more of these special-purpose fourth-generation tools.

Data Management Systems

Although special-purpose data management tools are still being sold and purchased, many corporations are now looking beyond special-purpose tools. They are beginning to buy general-purpose **data management systems** that combine the functions previously found in many individual tools and can handle virtually all aspects of developing a data application. With a good comprehensive data management system, a firm could conceivably stop COBOL programming entirely, doing everything within the data management system.

Figure 10-3 illustrates the major components found in data management systems.

- The heart of the system is the **data management module,** which manages the physical storage of the data. This module shields all other modules from the details of how the data are stored physically. Other modules merely refer to the logical structure of the data base.
- Another critical module is the **schema definition module.** This module allows the application developer to define the **schema** (logical structure) of the data base. Once the schema is developed, the data can also be called by other applications, which refer to the schema to understand how the data are stored.
- The **data entry and editing module,** as its name suggests, allows data to be entered into the system and to be changed later, either to correct errors or to update the system in response to changes in the real world.
- The **retrieval** module that allows users to retrieve specific information from the data base, for instance, a particular person's last name or a list of everyone with a certain job skill.
- The **application development module** allows developers to create customized applications, such as an applicant tracking application in a

```
Schema
Definition      ─┐
Module           │
                 │
Data Entry       │
and Editing     ─┤
Module           │
                 │
Retrieval        │
Module          ─┤
                 │         Data
Application      │       Management ── Data
Development     ─┤         Module
Module           │
                 │
External         │
Interactions   ─┤
Module           │
                 │
Administrative   │
Module          ─┘
```

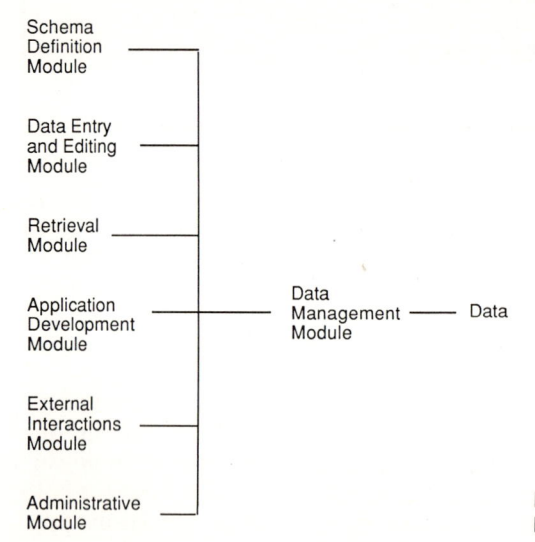

FIGURE 10-3 COMPONENTS OF A DATA MANAGEMENT SYSTEM

human resources department. Users of these customized applications might be given a series of menus from which they must select choices. Users of the customized applications developed through this module would be shielded from the complexity of the data management system.

- The **external interactions module** allows the data management system to interact with the outside world by importing data from other programs, exporting data to other programs, or executing commands issued by an external program.

- Finally, the **administrative module** allows someone to control the entire system. This person might be in charge of security, planning, and billing. For PC systems, the administrator role is usually small, although critical data bases do require careful administration, and networking will soon enlarge the need for administrative attention in PC data management systems. For data management systems on host computers, the data administrator role is extremely important and complex.

Limitations on Fourth-Generation Tools on Hosts

Today's host-based fourth-generation tools are still not strong enough to displace COBOL in most companies for large data processing applications. Their worst problem is that their DP applications run too slowly because the code they produce to run these applications is less efficient than a good COBOL programmer could produce. As these systems begin to approach the efficiency of an average COBOL programmer, and as computer costs fall, so that running efficiency will be less important than programmer productivity, fourth-generation tools should dominate the scene, just as third-generation languages eventually surpassed second-generation (assembly language) languages despite running less efficiently. For now, however, the efficiency gap between third- and fourth-generation products is too large for major production systems in corporate data processing.

The second problem with today's fourth-generation tools is their lack of flexibility. Although COBOL is difficult to use when setting up a report, the programmer has absolute control over the format of the output. In fourth-generation tools, this is not the case. Although most reporting functions offer users a number of options as to how the output will be formatted, there are many things users cannot control. The same lack of flexibility exists in other data management system functions.

For corporate data processing applications, this relative inefficiency and lack of flexibility are major problems and have relegated both special-purpose tools and comprehensive data management systems to secondary roles. Although these tools are good enough to handle small and infrequently run applications, in the eyes of most IS departments they are still not adequate for central DP applications.

Personal Computer Products

For end users on personal computers, neither inefficiency nor lack of flexibility is the problem it is for host DP developers. First, most PC applications are relatively small, so running efficiency is usually not critical to acceptability. Second, end users in general are more than willing to lose some flexibility in order to avoid learning a formal programming language. Although some end users do learn formal programming languages, as discussed in Chapter 12, most end users limit themselves to fourth-generation tools on PCs. In fact, most eschew special-purpose tools and turn directly to data management systems.

Categories of PC Data Management Systems

PC Versus Host Tools

When talking about data management tools, a number of distinctions need to be drawn among products on the market. We will limit the discussion to PC tools; categories of host data management systems are discussed in Chapter 16. Before leaving host tools, however, we should say that, in general, host-based data management tools have several advantages over PC tools.

- Most host tools have more functionality than PC products and are often superior for complex applications.
- Most host tools allow multiuser applications to be built, so that several users can access the system from different locations, perhaps simultaneously and perhaps one at a time. PC networking is only beginning to bring multiuser operation to the PC world.
- Because they run on large computers, host tools can tap the immense processing power of these machines for large jobs—although this advantage disappears on a heavily loaded computer.

On the negative side, most host tools are difficult to use today. Even the most powerful PC tools, such as dBASE III Plus and R:BASE System V, are at least somewhat easier to use than typical host products. In addition, although virtually no host product can be called really easy to use, low-end PC products such as Q&A and pfs:file are quite easy to learn and use for simple tasks.

If the user is primarily a PC user for other tasks, such as writing reports and doing analysis, PC data tools are more likely than host tools to be able to exchange data easily with the user's other PC tools.

Stand-Alone Versus Networked PC Products

Until recently, most personal computers were stand-alone machines, and data management products were single-user systems. Now that networking is becoming popular, many networked data management products for PCs are being introduced, and many former stand-alone data tools are being extended to network operation.

At the time of this writing, however, existing networked products are only beginning to have all of the features they need for efficient and effective operation. Many provide only the crudest protection if two users try to update the same file at the same time. Many offer little security. Few are good at recovering from crashes without doing extensive damage to the data they contain. Chapter 12 discusses the security offered in various kinds of multiuser data management systems on personal computers.

File Management Systems

Within the data management family, a hierarchy of three kinds of products exists: file management systems, low-end data base management systems, and high-end data base management systems. On the lowest rung of the hierarchy, **file management systems** can operate only on individual files. If the information needed is in several different files, file management systems offer little or no help.

Typical file management systems are designed for novice users. They are menu-driven with few ways to work quickly, and they offer relatively few features. Most offer no embedded programming language at all. The most popular file management systems today on IBM PCs and compatibles are the pfs: series and Q&A. Both are extremely easy to learn and use, although their one-file limitation excludes them from a large number of applications. On the Macintosh, a wide variety of easy-to-use file management tools is available.

High-End Data Base Management Systems (DBMSs)

At the other end of the hierarchy is the high-end **data base management system** or **DBMS**. As the name implies, these systems work with entire multi-file data bases, not just with individual files. This is only the beginning of what these programs offer.

High-end DBMSs are loaded with special tools for developing customized applications. Exemplified by dBASE III Plus and R:BASE System V, these products are, in many ways, primarily application development tools. One could even argue that they are application development tools with associated DBMSs, since their full high-end power is accessible only when users master at least a little programming.

In this chapter, we will focus on high-end DBMS because these are the tools many end users will eventually trade up to and because these require the greatest amounts of support. In any organization, however, more users are likely to be using file management systems than high-end DBMSs.

Mid-Range DBMSs

Mid-range DBMSs work with full data bases instead of individual files but offer fewer features than high-end DBMSs. Most importantly, mid-range DBMSs do not have sophisticated application development tools. So far, mid-range products have fared badly on the market, being squeezed out by products at the two extremes. In the rest of this chapter, when we refer to "DBMSs," we will mean high-end DBMSs.

Data Management Products Embedded in Other Programs

To this point, we have discussed programs written specifically for data management, but data management features are also available as parts of programs in other categories.

The most notable example is Lotus 1-2-3, which offers "database" capabilities (really only crude file management) based loosely on IBM's Query by

Example approach. This capability in 1-2-3 is extremely difficult to use, but the extreme popularity of Lotus 1-2-3 means that a large number of people who do file management—perhaps even the majority—do it in Lotus 1-2-3 instead of another program. In addition, Lotus Development Corporation now offers a program called 1-2-3 Report Writer, supplements 1-2-3 data management functions. 1-2-3 Report writer can generate neatly formatted management reports, mailing labels, and forms from data in standard 1-2-3 spreadsheets.

Many word processing programs also offer embedded data management products for automated mailing control. Data management functions are also being offered in programs for graphics, project management, decision support, and general utility operation. In all but a handful of cases, these are file management tools instead of DBMSs.

In integrated programs such as Symphony, Framework, and Enable, there is almost always a file management module. In a few cases, true DBMS capabilities are provided, although usually at a level well below high-end DBMS products.

The Market

Figure 10-4 shows a market projection for all data management software. The importance of multifunction products (chiefly Lotus 1-2-3) and programs for other purposes that include data management functions are very clear from this picture. Because most products not designed for data management are used primarily for other purposes, however, their importance may be overstated. In addition, in the realm of DBMS service, the strongest players are dedicated data management products.

Steps in Developing Data Applications

As shown in Figure 10-5, developing a data application requires that the developer take a number of steps. Each step builds on the ones before it.

The first step, of course, is to identify user needs. The output from this section should be a detailed description of needs with some priority assignments. This output should appear on paper instead of being merely verbal.

For existing applications, even if they are only being done manually, needs identification should be accurate. For applications that are completely new, identification will be more tentative and incomplete. In general, for well-defined situations, the steps in Figure 10-5 should be sequential. For novel

	1984	1990
Multifunction (includes 1-2-3)	32%	30%
Word processing	22%	14%
Pure data management	20%	14%
Other	26%	42%

Source: Whyte (1985)

FIGURE 10-4 SALES OF PERSONAL COMPUTER DATA MANAGEMENT SYSTEMS

1. Identify user needs.
2. Develop a data model (schema).
3. Enter the data model (schema).
4. Enter and edit the data.
5. Retrieve information.
6. Develop customized applications.
7. Develop ongoing work systems.

FIGURE 10-5 STEPS IN DEVELOPING DATA APPLICATIONS

situations, there will be extensive backtracking to earlier steps, as discussed in Chapter 2.

The second step is to develop a **data model** or **schema** that specifies what data should be in what files. For file management systems, which deal only with a single file, data modeling is limited to deciding what types of information to keep. For data base management systems, data modeling must be taken to the additional step of deciding how to divide up the information into multiple files. This step is extremely difficult, for reasons that should be apparent later.

The third step is to enter the data model or schema into the computer. The fourth step is to enter data into the model and correct any errors. The fifth step is to retrieve information from the data management system.

The sixth step, which is optional, is to develop customized applications. This involves creating a program that will be executed to do predefined tasks. Several tools are available for creating customized applications. Later in this chapter, we will look at two of these tools—fourth-generation languages and application generators.

The seventh and final step is developing ongoing work systems that involve not only the computer, but also procedures followed by the people who use the system. The most obvious need in the ongoing work system is to keep the data in the system backed up.

After examining data concepts in more detail, we will discuss each of these seven steps. Most of our examples will be drawn from dBASE III Plus, the DBMS of Ashton-Tate that dominates the PC DBMS market today.

DATA CONCEPTS

As discussed earlier, there are two basic levels of data collection, namely, the individual data file and the larger data base. We will begin with the concepts needed to describe data files, first, because data files are conceptually similar to data bases, and, second, because data bases are really collections of data files. Therefore, all of the concepts introduced in the section on data files will carry over to the discussion of data bases.

Data Files

Figure 10-6 illustrates the basic unit of data storage on computers—the **data file.** This data file, named EmplMast, is an employee master file, giving basic

EmplMast File

EmplId	Lastnm	Firstnm	DeptID	Rating	StartSal	StartDat	Exempt?
2547	Browne	Mary	Mkt	3.8	$20,050	3/17/85	T
3759	Gomes	Harold	Mkt	4.2	$33,800	11/21/85	T
3981	Solari	Martha	Fin	4.0	$23,500	3/7/86	T
4025	Hirata	Steven	Acctg	3.4	$20,000	4/19/86	T
4238	Browne	Charles	Mkt	4.5	$41,500	6/27/86	T
4310	Robinson	Claire	Acctg	4.4	$18,500	6/28/86	T
4311	Ochoa	Roberto	Acctg	3.8	$20,010	6/28/86	T
4876	Cheung	May Ling	Fin	3.9	$19,800	10/5/86	T
4881	Belinski	Kevin	Mkt	4.8	$10,230	10/5/86	F
5004	Ibrahim	Ibrahim	Fin	4.1	$31,700	1/5/87	T
5125	Sullivan	Mary	Mkt	4.1	$20,060	2/8/87	T
5278	Stein	Hava	Mkt	3.9	$32,800	5/16/87	T
5279	Akana	Lehua	Acctg	4.5	$23,600	5/16/87	T
5681	Krug	Gustav	Acctg	3.2	$19,700	11/4/87	T
5693	Pascua	Jennifer	Acctg	3.9	$11,200	11/4/87	T
5840	Brown	Pat	Mkt	3.1	$23,700	1/20/88	T
5891	Anderson	Kaisa	Fin	4.6	$11,040	2/19/88	T

Record   Field   Value

FIGURE 10-6 DATA FILE IN TABLE IMAGE

information about each employee, including ID number, last name, first name, department, performance rating, starting salary, starting date, and whether or not the person is exempt from union classifications. To keep examples simple, information is shown for only a few people. Any file this small could be handled on paper instead of on a computer, but imagine what would happen if the file contained information about several hundred or even thousands of people. For such large files, the kinds of operations discussed throughout this chapter make a data management system a necessity, not a luxury.

The Table Image

Figure 10-6 shows the data file as a table, in which there is a row for each contact. Columns, in turn, show contact **attributes,** such as ID number and last name. In formal terminology, our file has the following components.

- The **file** is the complete collection of information about *all employees.* In the table image, the file is the *entire table.*
- A **record** holds information about *one particular employee.* In the table image, the record is a *row.* In this example, the row of information about Charles Browne is a record.
- A **field** contains information about *one attribute.* In the table image, a field is a *column.* In our sample data file, DeptID is a field.
- A **value** is an entry *in one field for one record.* In the Charles Browne record, the entry for start date (6/27/86) is a value.

Data Files: The Form Image

Although the **table image** shown in Figure 10-6 is broadly useful for representing data files, another image is also popular. This is the **form image,**

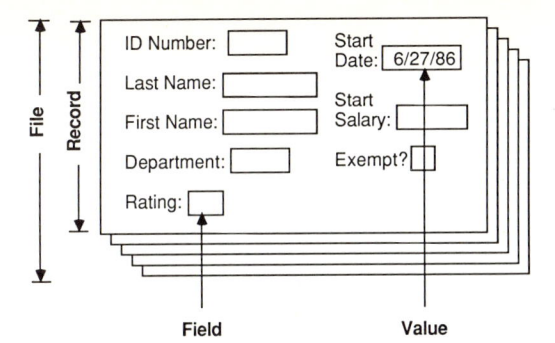

FIGURE 10-7 DATA FILE IN FORM IMAGE

which reflects the fact that information about individuals is often collected on individual forms, as shown in Figure 10-7. The form image looks very different from the table image, but the two are structurally identical.

- The **file** is the complete collection of information about *all employees.* In the form image, the file is the *collection of all individual forms.*
- A **record** holds information about *one particular employee.* In the form image, the record is an *individual form.*
- A **field** contains information about *one attribute.* In the form image, a field is a *space to be filled in on a form.* In this example, the space for Lastnm is a field.
- A **value** is an entry *in one field for one record.* In the form image, *each entry in a space to be filled in is a value.*

The table and form images hold exactly the same information and can be described with the same basic terminology of values, fields, records, and files. Yet each has particular advantages in different situations. The table image is useful if you want to look at many records at one time. You can quickly find the field you want to search on and then look down the field until you get to the record you want. The form image is useful if you want to look at each record in some depth. The layout of the form should be designed to draw the eye to key information, and the meaning of each field is clearly labeled. Most data management programs can alternate between the table and form image, thus allowing users to work with the most natural representation of their problem at a particular time.

Repeating Fields

In the preceding discussion, it was tacitly assumed that for each record, there would be only one value in a field. A person, for example, would have only one last name or customer ID number. In many cases, however, a field in a record will have more than one value. A person can have more than one telephone number, more than one job skill, more than one department, and so on. Fields that can have more than one value for an individual are called **repeating fields.**

There are two basic ways to represent repeating fields, as shown in Figure 10-8. The first method is to show multiple values within a single field.

Fixed-Length Records

EmplID	JobCode	Skills
2547	S10	TA, RN, BQ
5004	M3	TA
5840	E6	BQ, LT

Variable-Length Records

EmplID	JobCode	Skills		
2547	S10	TA	RN	BQ
5004	M3	TA		
5840	E6	BQ	LT	

FIGURE 10-8 REPRESENTING REPEATING FIELDS

In the table image used in this figure, some records have multiple values in the job skills column. In the form image, there will be more than one entry in a space to be filled out. This gives **fixed length records.**

The second representation creates a separate field for each value. This yields **variable length records,** because not everyone is likely to have the same number of values for any particular repeating field. Some people will have only one telephone number or a few job skills, whereas others will have two telephones and many job skills.

Basic Relational Data Base Concepts

As discussed earlier, a data file is only one unit of data storage. A larger unit is the data base, which is a collection of related files. To understand data bases, the end user needs to master a number of concepts beyond those introduced in the preceding section on data files.

The Need for Data Base Processing

Until recently, most data management systems worked only with individual data files. Most programming languages such as COBOL also worked primarily with single files. This one-file-at-a-time limitation is fine for some purposes, but many applications require the user to work with more than one data file at a time.

For example, suppose that you want to know who Mr. Lee's manager is. As shown in Figure 10-9, the information is likely to be stored in several files. You will have to look up Lee's ID number in the employee Master file and then go to the Employee–Department file to look up the department associated with Lee's ID number. Finally, given the name of that department, you will have to go to the Department–Manager file and look up the name of the department's manager.

This task can be done in COBOL or a data management system that deals only with individual files, but searching through three files is likely to be

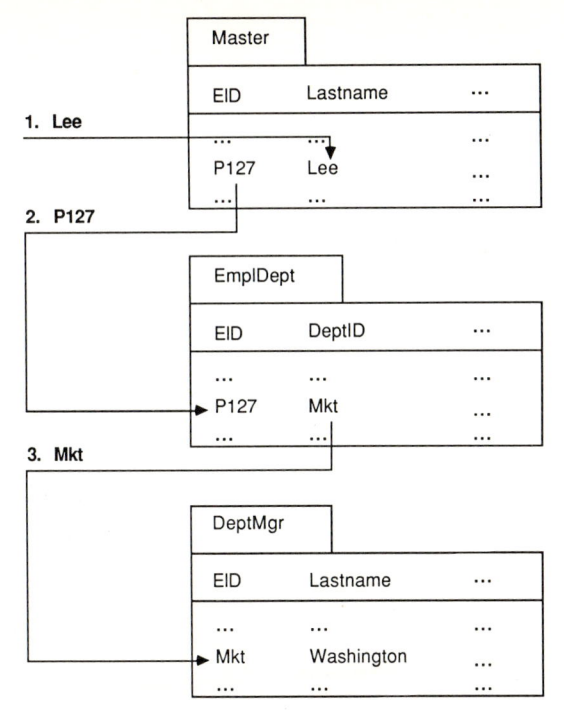

```
                  Master
                  ┌─────────────────────────┐
                  │ EID      Lastname    ··· │
1. Lee            │ ···      ···         ··· │
                  │ P127     Lee         ··· │
                  │ ···      ···         ··· │
2. P127           └─────────────────────────┘

                  EmplDept
                  ┌─────────────────────────┐
                  │ EID      DeptID      ··· │
                  │ ···      ···         ··· │
                  │ P127     Mkt         ··· │
                  │ ···      ···         ··· │
3. Mkt            └─────────────────────────┘

                  DeptMgr
                  ┌─────────────────────────┐
                  │ EID      Lastname    ··· │
                  │ ···      ···         ··· │
                  │ Mkt      Washington  ··· │
                  │ ···      ···         ··· │
                  └─────────────────────────┘
```

FIGURE 10-9 A DATA BASE LOOKUP

extremely time consuming. It is desirable to have a **data base management system** or **DBMS**—a data management system that deals with whole **data bases.** A data base management system can pull information from multiple files.

Network Data Bases

Every DBMS needs a method of representing files and the relationships between files. There are two widely used approaches to organizing data: **network organization** and **relational organization.** We will look at the older network organization first.

Figure 10-10 shows a data base with a network organization. As shown in this figure, each record has one or more links to other records in the data base. These links point to related records in different files.

The earliest host DBMSs used network organization because it is the simplest data organization to implement. Moreover, it is very efficient because links are "hard wired" into the system. Operations that jump from record to record via links are extremely fast.

If a link has not been set up, however, it may be difficult or even impossible to do operations that jump from record to record. Although it might seem that *all possible* links could be built into the system, in actual practice it is usually impossible to identify all possible relationships among records.

For clerical transaction processing needs, links almost always exist because needs are easy to identify and because a failure to implement a link used

```
Master
EID         Lastname      Salary      Skills
P127        Lee           Link        Link
...         ...           ...         ...
```

```
Skills
SkilCode    Level
BN          3
FR          1
...         ...
```

```
Salary
BaseRate    Bonus
$29,425     $3,780
...         ...
```

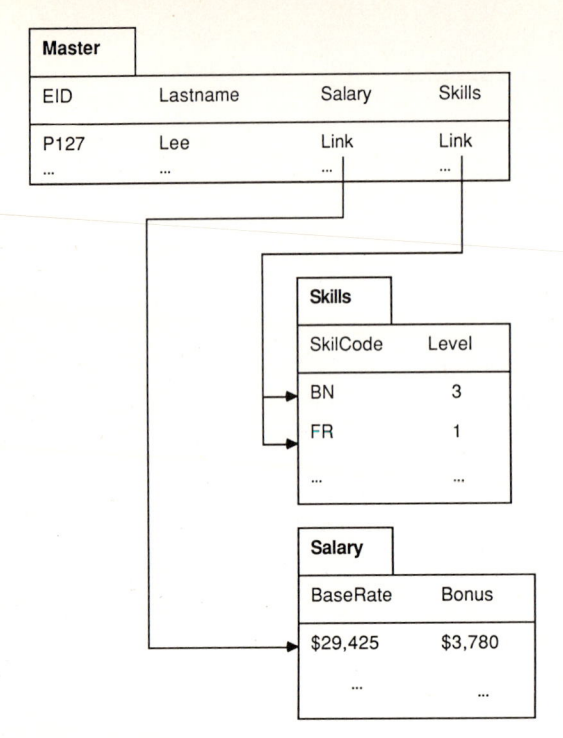

FIGURE 10-10 NETWORK ORGANIZATION OF DATA

day in and day out by clerical workers will soon be discovered and rectified. Managerial and professional needs, however, tend to take unexpected turns. Nearly every major managerial problem requires new paths through the data base. As a result, network organizations tend to be fine for production clerical transaction processing, but they are too inflexible for managerial needs.

For host production work, the network organization is still extremely popular, and there are many classes of products, ranging from simple products that require records to be arranged in a strict hierarchy to powerful products that allow complex webs of links to be defined. In the PC world, however, the network organization has never been popular. Its benefit of running efficiently is not extremely important for most PC applications, which tend to be small. Moreover, its inflexibility is often intolerable in end user environments, where actions that were not even identified when the system was designed are commonplace.

Relational DBMS Terminology

Figure 10-11 illustrates another data organization, the **relational organization.** As the figure shows, the relational approach seems to deal with a number of table image flat files. From the standpoint of both terminology and substance, matters are not quite that simple, however.

From the standpoint of terminology, the relational organization has a peculiar terminology that reflects its origins in mathematical theory. As a result of these origins, it tends to use mathematical jargon in place of standard data file terminology.

DATA CONCEPTS

Master Relation

EID	Lastname	...
P127	Lee	...
...	...	...

Skills Relation

EID	SkilCode	Level
P127	BN	3
...	...	...
P127	FR	1
...	...	

Salary Relation

EID	BaseRate	Bonus
P127	$29,425	$3,780
...	...	...

FIGURE 10-11 RELATIONAL ORGANIZATION OF DATA

In the relational approach, the word "file" disappears from the vocabulary. Instead, the tables are now called **relations.** Although this seems to be just an annoying switch of jargon, trading one term for another, it is useful to have a different name for tables in the relational theory because there are certain restrictions on relations that you do not find on ordinary files, as we will see later.

Another change in terminology is to use the term **attribute** instead of "field." Because fields do hold information about attributes, this should cause little confusion.

Rows are generally referred to simply as rows or records. In the original mathematical theory, rows were called "n-tuples," but this strange piece of jargon is almost unnecessarlly ignored.

Normalization

From the standpoint of substance, relations are tabular in form, but not every tabular file can be called a relation. The relational theory places several restrictions on the organization of tables. In the relational terminology, relations that comply with these restrictions are said to be "normalized." Normalization is a complex topic, which cannot be covered here in depth. However, we will briefly describe the first normal form.

In the first normal form, usually written as INF, two restrictions are placed on relation. The first is that there may not be duplicate rows in the table. This restriction might seem to be unnecessary because users would rarely, if ever, put duplicate rows in a relation, except by accident. Certain file extraction operations, however, can create extracted relations with duplicate rows, so a question to ask after every major extraction is whether duplicate rows can result.

The second restriction of the first normal form is that there may not be repeating fields. In Figure 10-8, repeating fields were shown for a simple job skills file. The last field, Skills, could have multiple entries, either by placing several skills in a single field or by having variable length records with multiple skills fields. To put such files into first normal form, the user must break the relation into two other relations, as shown in Figure 10-12.

- Both of these relations have the same primary key as the original relation, namely, Empl-ID.
- The first derived relation, EmplMain, has all of the fields except for the last repeating field.
- The second relation has the repeating field, Skills, but this time there are no multiple values. For each record in the original file, there is one record in the Skills relation for each employee–job skill pair. In this relation, a rating field has been added to indicate the employee's rating in that job skill.

If a person has three job skills, there will be three records in the Skills relation. On the other hand, if a person has no job skills listed, there will be no entries for this person in the skills relation.

Decomposition into two INF relations brings certain benefits. Every time an employee adds a job skill, a separate record is entered in the Skills relation.

Unnormalized File

JobSkils File

Empl-ID	Location	Skills
3759	Seattle	CK
5278	Omaha	RM, PF, CK, LN
5861	Miami	BA, LN
...	...	...

**Normalized Relations
(First Normal Form)**

EmplMain

EmplID	Location
3759	Seattle
5278	Omaha
5861	Miami
...	...

Skills

EmplID	Skill
3759	CK
5278	RM
5278	PF
5278	CK
5278	LN
5861	BA
5861	LN
...	...

FIGURE 10-12 PUTTING A FILE IN FIRST NORMAL FORM

This is usually faster than editing the contents of an existing record, as would have to be done in the original Orig file.

On the other hand, if you need to find the names of everyone who is a cook, you may have to join the two relations together to produce a single large relation. (Joining is discussed later in the chapter.) This is likely to take quite a bit of time on the computer.

Because of this time penalty, many DBMSs that bill themselves as relational allow the user to "cheat" by building repeating fields. These DBMSs then allow the user to search for string matches anywhere inside the record. For example, if you had the designation CK for cook, you would ask the DBMS to list all records in the original unnormalized file for which the Skill field contains the string "CK."

Normalization beyond the first normal form becomes progressively more difficult, and there are at least five main normal forms, each adding more restrictions on relations. Because of this difficulty, many end users fail to normalize their data bases, a situation that can produce problems.

An approach called Entity-Relationship Modeling, which is discussed later in this chapter, provides a way for even neophyte users to build data bases with normalized relations. In a landmark study, Jarvenpaa and Machesky (3) compared Entity-Relationship Modeling with direct normalization by following rules. They found that using Entity-Relationship Modeling produced more complete models and produced these models faster. In their comments at the conference presentation, Machesky added that few of the relations produced by direct development were properly normalized. Given these factors, we will not discuss normalization further. For a full discussion of normalization, Date (2) is a good reference.

The Future Is Likely to Be Relational

We have spent far more time on the relational data organization than on the network organization. Network organizations are very fast because each link field points precisely to another record (or at least to its primary key). In comparison, the relational approach uses a more leisurely process to finding relationships among records. As a result, network organizations produce much faster processing than relational organizations. Network organizations pay a steep price for speed, however: loss of flexibility. Network organizations are **only fast** if a retrieval goes along preestablished retrieval paths represented by the links. Because establishing and maintaining links is time consuming and expensive, most data base administrators tend to establish links only where they are needed for frequent inquiries. This means that links are established primarily for clerical processing needs.

End user inquiries, as noted earlier, tend to cut across file boundaries in new and unforeseen ways. As a result, these inquiries tend to get little support when network organizations are used for a data base and its processing. The relational approach, though slower for clerical applications, is completely flexible and can readily be used readily for any managerial search, whether foreseen or unforeseen. The question of what data base organization an enterprise should adopt, then, is a matter of tradeoffs between clerical needs and managerial needs.

Today, the stark performance versus flexibility tradeoff between the two forms of organization is beginning to ease somewhat. Many systems have an underlying network structure but also present a relational interface to managers. These systems can process unforeseen managerial searches, although less efficiently than they can process clerical inquiries.

On host computers, network data bases are holding on, but on personal computers, the relational approach has already won the war. It is hard to find nonrelational DBMSs on personal computers today. As a result, we will only look at relational DBMSs in this chapter. Chapter 16 returns to the network theme slightly, but does not present a full discussion of the network data organization, which now is almost universally seen as "the wave of the past."

Relational Algebra

Initially, the most appealing aspect of the relational approach was that the mathematical theory developed by Codd (1) demonstrated that only a handful of operations were needed to do almost anything the user desired. For older hierarchical and network data base organizations, there was no corresponding theory.

File Extraction: Select and Project

Codd, who developed the original relational theory, identified two powerful operators, Select and Project, that copy a relation to a new relation but copy only part of the original relation. In effect, these two operations make extract files.

Select copies the records in the original relation to the target relation, but it only copies certain rows. Boolean logic is used to limit the records copied. You could, for example, copy only rows with people in a particular department, such as Accounting. Select copies all attributes (fields) in each record.

Project also copies the records in the original relation to the target relation, but this time only specified *attributes* are copied for each record. All rows are copied, so Project results in a new relation with all rows but only certain columns from the original.

Select never results in duplicate rows, but Project may. For example, suppose you have a relation with two fields, Class ID and section number. If you did a Project, copying only Class ID and not section number, all classes with multiple sections would result in duplicate rows. As a result, the full relational Project command always goes through the target relation after the copy and carefully removes all duplicate rows, since duplicate records are not permitted under the relational theory.

In practice, most DBMSs combine Select and Project into a single command that copies a relation but copies both specified rows and specified columns. These DBMSs do so because it is normally simpler for the person to do both actions in a single command.

Many DBMS vendors become sloppy about their terminology. Microrim's R:BASE System V, for example, uses Project for the combined copy command and uses Select for something else entirely. When a user approaches a DBMS, he or she must understand its terminology very carefully.

Another concern with current DBMSs is that many fail to remove duplicates after a Project. As a result, the user may have to approach every project as a two-step process: (1) copy only selected columns, which may result in duplicates; and (2) give the "remove duplicate rows" command available in most DBMSs.

Join

Sometimes, you need to combine the information on two relations into one larger relation. For such needs, Codd was able to prove the effectiveness of one method of doing this on relations. This method is the **join.**

It is probably best to illustrate join with an example. Suppose you have the following two relations that you want to join:

```
              Location Relation
              Empl-ID    City

              =======    =====

                 1        NY
                 2        LA
                 4        NY
                 5        CHI


              Skill Relation

              Empl-ID    Skill

              =======    =====

                 1        CK
                 1        PR
                 3        BF
                 4        CK
```

The first relation lists the location of each employee, and the second the job skills of each employee. For a join to be possible, the two relations must have a field covering a common "domain." Because Empl-ID does this, a join is possible.

In a join, a new relation is created; we will call it Location-Skill. To create records for this new relation, you begin with the first record in the Location relation, employee #1 in New York. For this record, you look at every single record in the Skill relation. If the employee ID is 1, a combined record is made of the two records. Otherwise, nothing is done. For the first record in the Location relation, two records are produced, as shown below.

```
          Location-Skill Relation

   Empl-ID      City          Skill

   =======      ====          =====
      1          NY            CK
      1          NY            PR
```

When the second record in the Location relation is compared against records in the Skills relation, no records result at all because no job skills are recorded for employee #2.

The third record in the Location relation does generate another row for the joined relation because there is information about employee #4 in one record of the skills data base. This record extends the joined relation to the following.

```
          Location-Skill Relation

   Empl-ID      City          Skill

   =======      ====          =====
      1          NY            CK
      1          NY            PR
      4          NY            CK
```

The last row in the Location relation also fails to yield additional rows for the Location-Skill relation.

Although the join produced few records, it did tell us that there are two cooks (CK) in New York City. Without the join, it would have been very difficult to have seen this pattern.

In the full relational theory, the only common operations are Join, Project, and Select. If the information is in two or more relations, a series of joins are done until all of the desired fields are in one relation. One Project and one

Select are then done to produce a relation that answers a specific query. This relation is then displayed to the asker.

At first, it seems disconcerting that some employees will not appear in the joined relation at all. After some reflection, however, it seems reasonable that if you want to locate people with specific job skills in specific areas, it will not help you to know about people for whom you do not have relevant information.

Join, Project, and Select, then, can combine information and pare it down until exactly the information a user needs obtained. There are a few other relational operators that would be learned by a serious user in a system that was based primarily on relational algebra, but these three are the main ones.

Relational Calculus

In his seminal article, Codd also mentioned the possibility of relational calculus, which would stand alongside relational algebra. In an algebra, you have a small set of operators (+, −, etc.) that you apply in sequence to produce a desired result. In a calculus, however, you specify the result you want to see instead of worrying about how to produce the result. If you write the integral of x**2 dx, you are merely saying that you want to produce the result somehow. This, of course, is the essence of nonprocedural computing—you give the desired result and then let the program figure out how to produce it. *Although relational algebra has received a great deal of popular press, it is relational calculus that users really want and use.*

For example, suppose that a user has a bank customer master file and wants to know the full names of all customers living in New York. In IBM's SQL relational calculus tool for retrieving data, a user would write the following.

```
SELECT      Firstnm, MI, Lastnm
FROM        CustMast
WHERE       State = "New York"
ORDER BY    Lastnm, Firstnm
```

Here, the user is telling SQL to look at the CustMast relation and print the fields firstname, middle initial, and last name (in that order). The user is also telling SQL to show data only from records with the value "New York" in the State field and to sort the output alphabetically by name.

Several things make this example different from the algebraic select.

First, and most importantly, the SQL select does not create a new relation. It merely lists information on the screen. In addition, it embraces both the row selection of the algebraic Select and the column selection algebraic Project.

In fact, as the following example shows, SQL can even embrace a join operation in which two relations, Location and Skills, are to be joined on the employee ID, which is called Empl in Location and ID in Skills.

```
SELECT      City, Skill
FROM        Location, Skills
WHERE       Empl=ID
ORDER BY City
```

Although relational calculus lacks the mathematical elegance of relational algebra and requires the user to learn the specific relational calculus commands of a particular query system, a single relational calculus command can do the work of several relational operations and not worry the user with details of what series of operations is needed to do the job. As a result, relational calculus is used in practice far more than relational algebra, even in systems where both are present.

NEEDS IDENTIFICATION AND DATA MODELING

Now that we have looked at the major concepts in data file and data base design, we are ready to return to Figure 10-5, our step-by-step guide for developing a data application. In this section, we will concentrate on the first two steps in this figure: analyzing needs and developing a data model (data base schema).

In the development of a data model, we will use a specific approach, **Entity-Relationship (ER) Modeling.** A study by Jarvenpaa and Machesky (3) found that when students used ER Modeling, instead of developing relations directly, they were faster and more successful. In addition, almost no students who went directly to relations did proper normalization. The problem used for examples is a modification of the problem discussed by Jarvenpaa and Machesky. (3)

Needs Identification

The first step in the development process is to identify user needs and to turn them into specific requirements. There is nothing mechanical at all about this phase, and the only basic principle is to keep digging well beyond the time when people agree that all requirements have been specified. Spending extra time at this step usually results in large savings later.

The General Situation

It is good to begin with a general understanding of the situation. In our example, we will be designing a system to keep track of journal articles. Articles will be retrievable by author, title word, or topic. The topics will be assigned by the user. In real-world situations, the situation is usually far more complex.

Design Rules

Next, the designer must specify **design rules** that characterize the specifics of the design. In our example, the design rules shown in Figure 10-13 would be given.

Output Requirements

After the design rules have been specified, the next stage will be to determine output requirements. To a very large extent, output requirements dictate the kinds of information that must be stored. For our example, the following output requirements might be stated.

1. A list of articles, including Article ID, Title, Authors, Address, Publication Date, and Topics.
2. A list of topics and the articles classified under these topics, including Article ID, Title, and Authors.
3. A list of journals and articles, including Journal ID, Journal Name, Publisher, Call Number, Article ID, and Article Title.

Design Rules

An author may write several articles, and articles can be multiply authored.

An article may be assigned several topics, and many articles may have the same topic.

A journal will publish many articles, but an article will appear in only one journal.

An author will have only one address.

Candidate Entities

Address
Author
Article
Topic
Journal

FIGURE 10-13 DESIGN RULES AND CANDIDATE ENTITIES

4. A list of articles and authors, including Article ID, Title, Author ID, and Names.

It is a good idea to lay out sample reports in visual form, using dummy data. Users seem to find it easier to critique concrete layouts and simple statements of output requirements like those shown above.

A Managerial Focus

A constant danger in the needs identification stage is a tendency to focus on clerical considerations instead of managerial considerations. Clerical considerations are easy to identify and specify. To identify managerial considerations, however, the analyst must ask the user to completely rethink how an activity should be managed. This is extremely difficult, even when the analyst is also the managerial user. Furthermore, even when managerial needs are identified, they can be difficult to specify in detail.

New Versus Existing Application

It is generally said that all-new applications are harder to design than modifications to existing applications. With existing applications, users have better insight into needs and often have specific requirements for changes. Many of their insights, in fact, will already have been added to the existing application over time. For new applications, users often have a hard time articulating their needs and tend to underestimate the amount of detail needed.

Existing applications, however, do present one problem that new applications lack: existing applications tend to channel users' thinking in certain directions. "What is" tends to be confused with "what is possible," especially if the existing system is manual. In a sense, existing applications can be *too well* specified already. A good analyst must work to unfreeze current thinking when applications already exist.

Entity Identification

Once needs are understood, the next step is to identify the major focal points of data storage, which are called **entities.** Entities are people, places, things, ideas, or events about which data are collected. In the example we have been using, candidate entities might be the following.

- Address (of an author)
- Article
- Journal
- Topic
- Author

The reader may realize that address is not really an entity but is only an attribute of the author entity. We will include this error, however, to illustrate how such mistakes can be caught.

Later in the data modeling process, several pieces of information will be collected for each entity. For articles, publication date is an obvious example. Pieces of information about entities are called **attributes.**

During the entity identification, the analyst sits down and creates a list of entities, often with users sitting at the same table. It is very easy to overlook minor entities, for example, Journal in the problem we are using.

It is also easy to mistake an attribute for an entity and vice versa. For example, author Address—an attribute—might be mistaken for an entity, as in our candidate list. On the other hand, Journal—an entity—might be mistaken for an attribute of Article.

The rule for distinguishing entities from attributes is that *entities have attributes, whereas attributes do not have other attributes.* Author Address, for example, has no attributes in our application, so it is an attribute. Publication, however, may have at least one attribute, its publisher, so it is an entity.

Whether something is an attribute or entity depends on the design rules. In our example, no information is to be kept about the author address, except the address itself; it is therefore an attribute. Other design rules could require other information to be kept about each address, for example, whether the address is permanent or temporary. In this case, author address would be an entity.

Designing Entity-Relationship Diagrams

Once entities have been identified, the next step is to identify relationships among the entities. This is done through **Entity-Relationship (ER)** diagrams like the one shown in Figure 10-14. In an ER diagram, each entity is shown as a "bubble" (rectangle with rounded corners).

Some entities are directly related, and others are not. For entities that are directly related, an arrow is drawn between the two.

One-to-One Relationships

The arrow between Author and Address is one-directional and ends in a single arrow head. This means that Address depends on Author—if you tell me the author, I should be able to tell you the Address. The fact that the arrow points one way means that, in my design, if you tell me an address, I will not be expected to give the author as a basic part of the data model. The fact that it ends in a single arrow means that it is a **one-to-one** relationship. In the design rules, it was assumed that an author should have only one address.

One-to-Many Relationships

There is a single-directional arrow with two heads between Journal and Article. This indicates a one-way relationship that is **one to many**—given one journal, there may be many articles. In a one-to-many relationship, there may be zero, one, or several entities on the many side.

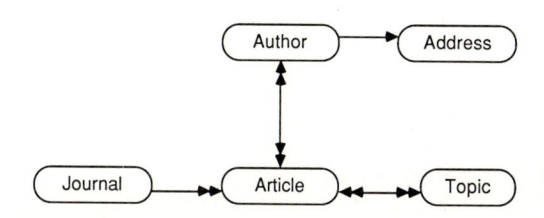

FIGURE 10-14 PRELIMINARY ENTITY-RELATIONSHIP (ER) DIAGRAM

Many-to-Many Relationships

There are two-way arrows between Author and Article and between Article and Topic. Each of these arrows has double heads at both ends. This type of relationship is called **many-to-many.** The first of these two-way arrows reflects the fact that one author may have several articles. The second reflects the fact that an article may have multiple topics and that a topic may be assigned to several articles.

In all cases, relationships are determined by the application specification embodied in the design rules. For example, an author may have multiple addresses, but one of the design rules in Figure 10-13 explicitly chooses to ignore this possibility. When reality and design rules clash, the design rules should be reviewed. In many cases, however, the design rule will be kept because of the way the data base is expected to be used.

Refining the ER Diagram

Figure 10-14 is a preliminary ER diagram. As we will now see, it has two problems, which are corrected in Figure 10-15, the refined ER diagram.

Removing One-to-One Relationships

First, the publisher's Address entity has been removed. Address is an attribute of the publisher, not an entity in its own right. Most preliminary ER diagrams will have at least one attribute that must be removed. The best giveaway of an attribute's presence is a one-to-one relationship (arrow with a single head). The bubble at the head is an attribute of the entity at the root.

Converting Many-to-Many Relationships

Another refinement is the creation of two new entities: Author-Article between Author and Article, and Article-Topic between Article and Topic. This changes the two many-to-many relationships into four one-to many relationships.

In the final picture, *all* entity relationships are one-to-many relationships. Once this condition is reached, the ER Modeling stage is finished.

Well, almost finished. Because ER Modeling is rather difficult, it is a good idea to scrutinize the final model closely and, if possible, to have others who know ER Modeling critique it.

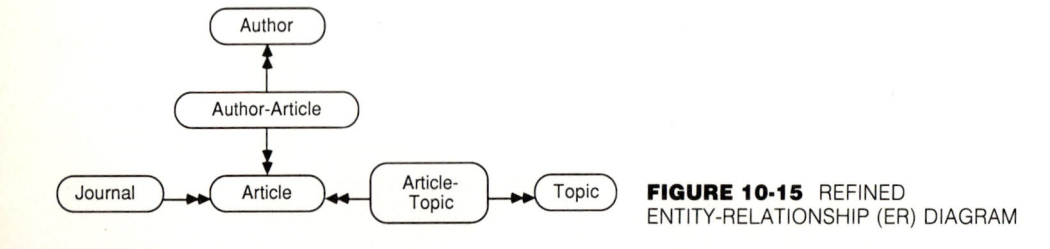

FIGURE 10-15 REFINED ENTITY-RELATIONSHIP (ER) DIAGRAM

Creating Primary Keys

The next step is to create a primary key for each entity. The **primary key** is a field whose value is used to store records. For example, in personal telephone books, information is stored by last name, so last name is the primary key.

A little reflection will show that primary key field value must be filled in for every record. Otherwise, there would be no way to store the record. How could the telephone company, for example, print information about a person in the telephone book, if it did not know that person's name?

The primary key field value must also be *unique*. Otherwise, two records might be stored in the same location. In the telephone system, telephone number acts as a primary key. Imagine the chaos that would result if several other people had the same telephone number you did.

Natural Primary Keys

Things are simplest when each entity has a natural primary key—a unique identifier found in everyday life. Social security numbers are often used, although their use raises serious policy issues. For the telephone company's subscriber data base, telephone number is a natural primary key.

In our example, Topic will always exist and be unique, and so it would be a good primary key. Journal name would also seem to be a good natural primary key, since all journals have a name and never have identical names.

For most entities, however, there is no obvious natural key. In the case of author, for example, name is not always unique. More subtly, two articles may have the same name, a fact that someone who is not familiar with journal articles may easily overlook. Although it is uncommon for two articles to have the same name, it is by no means rare.

Artificial IDs as Primary Keys

If there are no natural primary keys, one solution is to create an **artificial ID.** New employees in a corporation, for instance, are usually given artificial employee IDs. In our example, we would need artificial IDs for author and article.

Although artificial primary keys can be used in all cases, they should not be used if a natural primary key exists. They tend to be hard to remember, and even if the original intent is to use them for storage purposes only and not for retrieval, updating, and other purposes, there is the danger that they will become more IDs for everyone to memorize.

Sequence Number Primary Keys

One form of artificial primary key is so important that it requires separate mention. This is **sequence number.** When sequence numbers are used as primary keys, a unique serial sequence number is assigned to each record at the time it is added to the data base.

Sometimes, as in the case of dBASE III, this sequence number can be used in commands. Other DBMSs hide these sequence numbers from users.

Sequence numbers represent a natural and painless form of primary key. In fact, if they are hidden from the user, they relieve both the schema designer and the user from having to worry about the very concept of primary keys.

In some systems, sequence numbering is permanent. This is critical in things such as transaction processing systems in which auditing is critical. In other DBMSs, renumbering occurs after deletions and/or sorts. If sequence numbering changes are undesirable, and if the DBMS allows them, then a separate absolute sequence number field should be created in order to prevent accidents that would effectively destroy most or all important references.

Avoiding Meaningful Keys

Another attraction of sequence numbers is that they are meaningless. Designers of artificial IDs tend to build meaning into them. For example, a ship traveling from Honolulu to Seattle on December 12 might have the ID number HONSEA1213. This is intuitively attractive, but it tends to lead to disaster over the long run.

What if the ship is rerouted during the trip? Then the "meaningful" ID number will be misleading. If it is changed, say to HONLA1213, then this may cause confusion among people whose earlier reports fail to show a HONLA1213 cruise but did show a HONSEA1213 sailing that seems to have been swallowed up by the sea.

Matters are even worse when the basis for building meaningful keys changes. For an example, suppose a company has six major product lines (A through F) and several hundred products in each category. Then keys may vary from A001 to F999. If the company changed its way of categorizing products, every last record would have to be changed. The amount of work needed to make the change might be extreme.

Even for natural keys, change can lead to confusion. Although we have said that journal name would be a good natural primary key, a journal may change its name from time to time, and this can cause problems.

Multifield Primary Keys

One alternative to artificial primary keys occurs for some but not all entities. This is the multifield primary key. For example, even if neither Author name nor Institution name is unique, it is extremely unlikely that two people at the same institution will have the same name. Therefore, the two-field combination Author name-Institution name will be a good primary key. To give another example, for many data bases, an entity consisting of people can do well with a multifield primary key consisting of last name, first name, and middle initials.

Even when multifield primary keys can be used, not all DBMSs support them, so the possibility may be valueless. It is important to understand the data base management system that will be used before selecting final primary keys.

There is one situation in which a multifield primary key is always used. This is when artificial entities are created in ER Modeling to resolve a many-to-many relationship into two one-to-many relationships. For example, the many-to-many relationship discussed later between Author and Article is resolved by creating an Author-Article entity. This relation has a two-field primary key field: the primary key of Author (AuthID); and the primary key of Article (ArtID). For artificial entities, no other primary key should be created if the DBMS can support two-field primary keys.

NEEDS IDENTIFICATION AND DATA MODELING   437

Setting Up Relational Tables

Once one-to-many relationships have been specified and primary keys have been established, the next step is to set up relational tables. Each one-to-many relationship requires two tables. We will use the example of the Journal-Article relationship, in which Article is at the "many" end.

First comes the table for the entity at the "one" end of the arrow, in this case, Journal. As shown in Figure 10-16, the Journal table has its primary key field as its first column. For other columns, attributes will be added later. (Publisher is one possible attribute; call number in the library is another.)

Next comes the table for the "many" end of the arrow, in this case the Article. As shown in Figure 10-16, the first column contains the primary key for the Article relation, namely, ArtID, but another column must be specified for "many tables." Another column *must* hold the primary key of the "one" entity, Journal. Journal name is not part of the primary key, but if it is left out, there will be no way to link queries that cut across the Journal and Article tables. So specifying the primary key of the "one" entity as an attribute in the schema of the "many" table as an attribute is extremely important.

Adding Attributes

The next step is to fill out each relational table by adding columns for the entity's attributes. The needs and requirements in the very first stage should identify all attributes, but the experience gained during the design stage may suggest new attributes.

For most attributes, it will be obvious in what table to place them. Author Address, for example, clearly belongs in the Author Relation. Confusion tends to arise, however, when many-to-many relationships have been broken into two one-to-many relationships by creating an artificial entity. In our example, the many-to-many relationship between author and article required

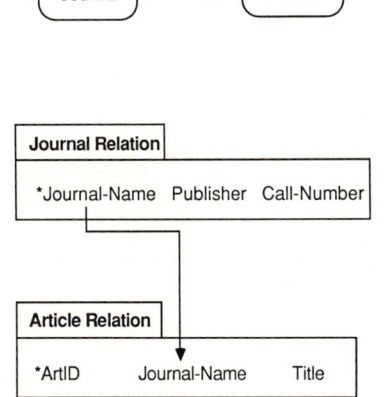

FIGURE 10-16 CONVERTING ONE-TO-MANY RELATIONSHIPS INTO RELATIONS

*Primary Key

the creation of an Author-Article entity, which led to an Author-Article relation.

Suppose that our example required us to keep data on whether or not an author was the primary (first) author. Should this attribute be added to the Author or Author-Article table? To answer such conflicts, the question to ask is "Does the attribute (Primary) depend on the Author primary key or the primary key of Author-Article (Author ID-Article ID)?"

In our case, the answer is that primary authorship is specific to both a particular author and a particular article. In contrast, an author may be primary on one article and not primary on another, so primary authorship is not a characteristic of Author. The Primary column, if it existed, would be added to the Author-Article table.

Assigning Attribute Types

As discussed earlier in this chapter, when a data base schema is entered into the computer, a "type" must be specified for each attribute. This type designation governs how entries will be stored and, as a result, what kinds of data can be entered. In the remainder of the discussion on adding attributes, we will focus on the various attribute types commonly found in DBMSs.

Text

Text is usually stored in the ASCII code, although IBM's similar but incompatible EBCDIC code is often used. Both codes have a separate one-byte symbol for each character. So "Good morning" would require 12 characters. (Yes, the space in the middle is stored explicitly as a character.) Chapter 13 discusses these codes in more detail.

Integer Numbers

As we turn from text to numbers we note that the simplest kind of number is the **integer.** An integer is an odd or even whole number, for example, "0," "10," and "−376." No decimal points are allowed.

Positive integers are stored as simple binary numbers. So one is 1, three is 11, and eight is 1000. Negative integers are usually sorted in "two's complement" form.

Some programs limit integers to two bytes. This gives two to the sixteenth power numbers, about 64,000, and a range from about +32,000 to −32,000. Other programs use four bytes, giving two to the sixty-fourth power—a virtually unlimited range.

Integers are simple to represent, but division causes problems because only whole numbers can be represented. Dividing 5 by 3 gives 1, not 1⅔. This process is called truncation. Integer representation should therefore be used only if whole numbers will appear and if either division is not meaningful or truncation in division is acceptable.

Real Numbers

Real numbers are not constrained to being whole numbers. They may contain decimal points, and there is no truncation in division (although there is rounding error at the least significant digit).

Real numbers are stored in the binary equivalent of scientific notation. Normally, one bit is used to represent sign (positive or negative); another 16 to 32 bits are used to represent the number; and 8 bits or so to represent the power of two (like power of 10 in scientific notation).

Some programs offer **double precision** real numbers. Although a normal real number takes about four bytes of storage, a double precision real number requires about eight. It uses most or all of the extra bits to give more precision to the number that will be raised to a power of two. This reduces rounding error when high-precision analysis is done.

Binary Coded Decimal (BCD) Numbers

Real numbers have one inherent problem. They are stored as binary decimals, not base 10 decimals. In base 10, many simple fractions such as two-thirds cannot be represented accurately. They are always rounded at some point. In base 2 arithmetic, many simple decimal (base 10) numbers, for example, 0.13, must be rounded in base 2. Calculations that should give zero when two quantities are divided often fail to do so because of this rounding error.

Some advanced DBMSs offer a way to store base 10 numbers in their original form. This approach is called **binary coded decimal (BCD)** because each decimal digit is encoded as a 4-bit binary number. (Four bits can encode 16 symbols—enough for the 10 digits of base 10.) For example, the number 10,365 would require two and a half bytes. In groups of four bits, these bytes would be 0001 (1), 0000 (0), 0011 (3), 0110 (6), and 0101 (5).

Special software is then needed for BCD calculations. This software tends to run much more slowly than base two integer and real arithmetic software, but its ability to avoid precision errors in dollars and cents makes it widely used in financial calculations done in dollars and cents.

Logical Fields

Some fields hold true/false information, such as "Is there a credit warning for this customer?" For **logical** fields, the data management system also has the ability to check whether data in a field are true or false. Most data management systems support logical typed data, but some do not.

Date and Time Fields

Most data management systems have field types for date, and many also have one for time. Each, unfortunately, has a different way of entering date and time information.

In the United States and some other countries, the month is written first; a typical date value would be 12-25-89, that is, Christmas 1989. In many other parts of the world, the order is day-month-year, as in 25-12-89. For days smaller than 12, one must know which approach is being taken. For example, 1-3-89 means January 3, 1989, but in many parts of the world it means 1 March 1989. Some U.S.-developed data management systems allow only the month-day-year format, and this can be an important purchasing consideration in multinational corporations. Many DBMSs offer several formats for storing date information.

Special Field Types

Most data management systems support **special field types** beyond those already discussed. The most common of these is the **dollar type,** which uses two decimal places, commas between the thousands places, and a dollar sign. Multinational corporations will need other currency types. Some data management systems allow users to define their own special data types.

Documenting the Schema

The last step in design is to document the schema. As shown in Figure 10-17, this can be done with a simple table showing a list of relations and the fields they contain, including each field's type and length, and also showing whether or not the field is a primary or secondary key. If possible, a narrative description should also be attached to each field and to each relation, because field names tend to be rather cryptic.

The table shown as Figure 10-17 also gives the number of bytes per record in different relations. For example, the first relation listed, Author, has 34 bytes per record. This is useful in estimating the sizes of complete data bases. The user simply estimates the number of records per relation and multiplies this times the number of bytes per record. So if there are likely to be 1,000 records, the Author relation will need 34,000 bytes of storage.

This estimation process must be done for all relations. This will allow the total number of data bytes in the data base to be estimated. In addition to these data bytes, most DBMSs also have overhead storage needs. These needs

Relation	Field name	Type	Length	Key?
Author	AuthID	Integer	4	Primary
	Name	Text	15	Secondary
	Institut	Text	15	
			34	
AuthArt	AuthID	Integer	4	Primary
	ArtID	Integer	4	Primary
	Primary?	Logical	1	
			9	
Article	ArtID	Integer	4	Primary
	Title	Text	15	Secondary
	JourName	Text	15	
			34	
ArtTopic	ArtID	Integer	4	Primary
	Topic	Text	10	Primary
	Main?	Logical	1	
			15	
Topic	Topic	Text	10	Primary
	Category	Text	10	
			20	
ArtJour	ArtID	Integer	4	Primary
	JourName	Text	15	Primary
	Volume	Integer	3	
	Number	Integer	2	
	FrstPage	Integer	3	
	LstPage	Integer	3	
			30	
Journal	Journal-Name	Text	15	Primary
	Publisher	Text	15	
	CallNumb	Text	10	Secondary
			40	

FIGURE 10-17 THE FINAL DATA BASE SCHEMA

typically run less than 30 percent of the data bytes. So if the estimated number of data bytes in all relations combined is 100,000, then about 130,000 total bytes of storage will be needed to hold the data base.

For large files, the calculation of storage requirements is critical. Even moderately large data bases can exceed the storage capacity of a floppy disk, and many exceed the capacities of 10 MB and 20 MB hard disks. A size estimation is needed to determine if the application can be done on a particular computer.

SETTING UP THE DATA BASE

After the data model has been defined down to the level of individual fields and their characteristics, the next steps in Figure 10-5 prepare the data base for ongoing use. These steps are as follows:

1. Enter the schema into the computer (and establish index files if desired).
2. Enter the data into the computer.
3. Edit the data to correct any errors.

Entering the Schema

In the data modeling step, the schema was designed down to the level of individual fields and their characteristics. Before anything else can be done, the user has to enter this schema into the computer. We will discuss how this is done, using dBASE III Plus in most of our examples.

In the examples, we will use the EmplMast data file shown as Figure 10-6. Because this file is at least in first normal form, we will treat it as a relation. The same process used with EmplMast, however, could be used with the relations identified in the preceding section on data modeling.

dBASE III Plus

When a user first enters dBASE III Plus, he or she is given the menu shown in Figure 10-18. Although dBASE II was exclusively command-driven, and although dBASE III used a menu mode as a supplement to command input, dBASE III Plus is primarily menu-driven. Experienced users can bypass the menus to give commands, but this is the exception rather than the rule.

The menu layout draws from both Lotus 1-2-3 and the Macintosh. As in Lotus 1-2-3, there is a horizontal menu at the top of the screen; below this menu line is a large open space to show information. As on the Macintosh, however, the dBASE III Plus menu uses pop-up submenus that appear to give further choices, instead of merely using a second horizontal line to show choices. In fact, dBASE III Plus is very free with its use of pop-up menus. As we will see later, they can pop up anywhere in the working area below the single-line menu bar, not just under a main menu choice, as on the Macintosh.

Initially, the cursor is on "Set Up." This choice is used to select a "Database file" for use, quit the program, and do other frequent tasks.

As the cursor is moved to the right using cursor arrows, other menu choices are highlighted. For example, "Create" is used to create the data base

```
|Set up| Create  Update  Position  Retrieve  Organize Modify Tools |10:07am|
|               |                        |
| Database file |                        |
|---------------------------------------|
|               |                        |
| Format for Screen                      |
| Query         |                        |
|---------------------------------------|
|               |                        |
| Catalog       |                        |
| View          |                        |
|---------------------------------------|
|  Quit dBASE III PLUS                  |


|    ASSIST         |   <A:>   |              | Opt: 1/6   |            |
      {On-Screen Directions Shown Here}
                         Select a databse file.
```

The top row has the Main Menu, which is a pop-down menu.

The Setup option has been selected. Suboptions are shown in a pop-down menu.

Database file is highlighted. This choice allows the user to specify the database file to be used.

The actual dBASE III PLUS screen is not exactly as shown.

FIGURE 10-18 INITIAL SCREEN IN dBASE III PLUS

schema, formats for reports, and formats for mailing labels, as well as other definitional work. When the cursor is moved to "Create," the pop-up menu for "Set Up" disappears, and a pop-up menu for "Create" takes its place, as on a Macintosh.

Creating a Data Base by Giving Its Schema

If the user selects "Create" and the subchoice "Database file," he or she is shown the file definition screen shown as Figure 10-19. This screen allows the user to define the data base file schema by filling in a form.

For each record, there is a single line with four spaces to be filled in. The user first types a field name and then hits "Enter." This takes the user to the Type space.

The type is automatically set to "Character," the most common choice. As shown in Figure 10-19, the user has just entered the field name "Salary"

SETTING UP THE DATA BASE   **443**

```
                                    Bytes remaining:    3962

|CURSOR    <-- -->   |   INSERT         |   DELETE         | Up a field             |
| Char:    <-  ->    | Char:   Ins      | Char:   Del      | Down a field           |
| Word:   Home End   | Field:  ^N       | Word:   ^Y       | Exit/Save         ^End |
| Pan:     ^<-  ^->  | Help:   F1       | Field:  ^U       | Abort:            Esc  |


       Field Name      Type      Width    Dec        Field Name   Type   Width  Dec
       ================================               ==============================

   1   EMPLID          Numeric      4       0
   2   LASTNM          Character    9
   3   FIRSTNM         Character    9
   4   DEPTID          Character    5
   5   RATING          Numeric      3       1
   6 | SALARY     |  |Character |  |__|   |__|




|CREATE          | <B:> | PERFORM         | Field: 8/8        |       | Caps|
                  Press SPACE to change the field type.
        Character fields contain character information of a specified length.
```

To define a file, the user fills out a form.

The bottom line of the screen gives information about the current space being filled in.

The actual dBASE III PLUS screen is not exactly as shown.

FIGURE 10-19 FILE DEFINITION SCREEN

and has moved to the "type" space. The note at the bottom of the screen tells the user to "Press SPACE to change the type of field." If the user repeatedly hits the space bar, the choice for type will toggle to numeric, date, logical, and back to character. These four are the only field types supported by dBASE III Plus. For faster entry, the user can also type the first character to the field type.

For character and numeric fields, the user must enter the width for the field, that is, the number of characters to be stored for each entry in that field. If the type is numeric, the user must also specify how many decimal places should be used.

The user enters field information until all fields are defined. If he or she makes mistakes along the way, a powerful array of full-screen editing operations are shown in the menu at the top of the page.

Note that dBASE III Plus requires the user to define all files separately, instead of entering a full data base schema. Later, we will see that users can effectively define data bases "on the fly" by opening whatever group of files he or she chooses. These opened files then constitute a data base, and multifile operations can be done on them.

Another popular PC DBMS, R:BASE System V, takes a very different approach to defining data base schemas. In R:BASE, the schema definition is done for an entire data base. The user first gives a name for the whole data base and then enters the definitions of individual relations and their fields. If the user enters a field name previously defined in another relation within the data base, R:BASE automatically enters the previously defined type and length. By defining whole data bases instead of individual files, R:BASE gives cohesiveness to the data base and prevents the awkwardness that dBASE III Plus users encounter when using operations on multiple files. In addition, the R:BASE approach ensures that a field used in several relations is defined consistently in each one.

Entering Data

After the schema has been defined, the next step is to enter data. In dBASE III Plus, hitting "Control-End" at the finish of the schema creation phase not only saves the schema; it also asks the user if he or she wants to begin entering records. Otherwise, the user can add data later, using the "Append" choice under the main menu's "Update" choice. In either case, the user is taken to the data entry screen shown as Figure 10-20.

The data entry screen resembles the schema creation screen. Specifically, it, too, has a menu at the top; many of the menu choices are the same as for the schema creation screen; and below the menu are areas to be filled in using full-screen data entry and editing.

In Figure 10-20, the user has already entered some information for the first record ("Record No. 1" is shown at the top of the screen). The user has already entered Mary Browne's ID number, last name, first name, department, and performance rating. The user will continue entering her starting salary, starting date, and whether or not she is exempt from union regulations.

In the menu shown at the top of the screen, there are numerous keys for detailed editing. With these options, a user can alter data previously entered—not only in this record but in previous records as well. One of these operations, PgDn, allows the user to add a narrative memo to the record. Effectively, this is a fifth field type within dBASE III Plus. Hitting F1 toggles this menu off and on.

Editing Data and Changing File Structures

Basic Choices

After the data have been entered, the user may want to edit data, reorganize data, or change the schema of the data base. The main menu in dBASE

SETTING UP THE DATA BASE **445**

```
|CURSOR <-- -->   |        UP    DOWN  | DELETE        | Insert Mode: Ins  |
|Char:   <-  ->   | Field:              | Char:   Del   | Exit/Save:  ^End  |
|Word:  Home End  | Page:  PgUp  PgDn   | Field:  ^Y    | Abort:      Esc   |
|_____ | Help:  F1           | Record: ^U    | Memo:      ^Home  |
```

```
              ____
EMPLID    |2547|____
LASTNM    |Browne  |
FIRSTNM   |Mary ___|
DEPTID    |Mkt _|
RATING    |3.8|_____
STARTSAL  |     . _|
STARTDAT  | / / |
EXEMPT    |?|
```

```
|CREATE        |<B:> | PERFORM        |Rec:  None   |     |   Caps|
```

The user has full-screen editing capabilities and may change previously entered data or even previously entered records.

The actual dBASE III PLUS screen is not exactly as shown.

FIGURE 10-20 DATA ENTRY SCREEN

III Plus offers four sets of functions for modifying information: Update, Modify, Organize, and Tools.

"Update" is used for working with records. With Update, the user can perform the following tasks.

- Add records to the end of the file.
- Browse through existing data in either table or form image.
- Mark records for deletion, unmark them, and finally do the deletion.
- Do global replacements, for example, change all references to a corporation's name when it changes its name.

"Modify" is used to change things built under the "Create" choice, as well as a number of other useful things. This choice can change the data base schema, for instance, delete a field from records or change a field width. Some of these changes cause problems if data have already been entered, although they cause fewer problems than they did in earlier versions of dBASE.

"Organize" is used to change the organization of data in the file. The user can sort the records in the file, create an index (discussed later), or create a copy of the file with selected records and fields from the original.

Finally, "Tools" is used to do general file handling. It can copy whole files for backup, it can erase or rename data base files, and it can also be used to import data from existing data files created by other programs and to export data into the formats used by other programs.

Indexing a File

One operation under "Organize" is somewhat complex from a theoretical viewpoint. This is the creation of an index. Every major DBMS has a similar operation, and indexing must be learned because it can affect the speeds of retrieval and data entry enormously.

To illustrate indexing, we will return to Figure 10-6, our EmplMast file. Suppose we want to retrieve information for all people with the last name "Browne." As shown in the table, two people have this last name. With this small file, we can easily pick out both records.

In a large computerized file, however, the situation would not be so easy. The program would have to look at every single record's Lastnm field and select those records where the Lastnm value was "Browne." In a large file, looking at every single record would be very time consuming. This kind of search is called an **exhaustive search,** both because it exhausts all possibilities and because it is exhausting to the computer in terms of machine resources. An exhaustive search would take a great deal of time on a large file.

To speed retrievals, most DBMSs allow the user to speed access on the basis of frequently used fields by building secondary files called **index files.** As shown in Figure 10-21, an index file has two fields. The first holds values of the field that was indexed, in this case Lastnm. The second has the record numbers of all records that have that last name.

In our index file, the Lastnm field becomes a *primary key field*. Because accesses to primary key fields are always very rapid, the system can jump directly to the Browne record in the index file and see that Browne appears in record numbers one and five. The system can then jump directly to record numbers one and five, again with fast primary key field jumps. So instead of an exhaustive search of all 17 records, the use of an index cuts the number of

LNIndex

Lastnm	EmplID
Akana	5279
Anderson	5891
Belinski	4881
Brown	5840
Browne	2547, 4238
Cheung	4876
...	...

FIGURE 10-21 AN INDEX FILE

record accesses to three. This is moderately helpful in small files, but in extremely large files, the gains are enormous.

As noted earlier, dBASE III Plus allows users to create indices by going to the "Organize" choice at the main menu and then selecting the "Index" subchoice. Later, when the user opens the file through the "Database file" choice of the "Set Up" submenu, he or she has the option of specifying an index file. If the user does specify an index file, then that index file will be attached to the data file, and the data file will appear to be sorted on the basis of the index file's primary key field. Any access involving that field will automatically be done through the index.

dBASE III Plus allows several indices to be built for any given file, but only one of these can be used at any time. To switch indices, the user must give another Use command with a different index file.

Other DBMSs are somewhat more flexible than dBASE III Plus. For example, R:BASE System V allows users to specify several fields as **key fields** during the schema definition phase. These are not primary key fields, because a file can have only one primary key field. Rather, these are **secondary key fields**—fields for which indices have been built.

It would be nice if all data base management systems used the same terminology to refer to the indexing process, but some speak of indexing and others speak of creating secondary key fields. To complicate matters further, many programs, including R:BASE System V, that hide the existence of the sequence number primary key from users call their secondary key fields "key fields," as just noted.

In systems that allow multiple index files to be built, it would be tempting to make *all* fields into secondary key fields by creating index files for them. Although this would speed retrievals, it would slow data entry speed dramatically, as the following example will illustrate.

Suppose that we did not index any fields in our EmplMast file. Then every time we added a record, we would only have to update a single file, EmplMast. Now suppose that we indexed all eight fields in the file. This time, every record added would require *nine* files to be updated—the EmplMast file itself and the eight index files. Because index files are sorted, updating them is a more complex task than appending a record to their ends. Even on a PC AT-class machine, updating nine large files would take a long time.

There are ways to get around this sluggishness in data entry. For example all the data could be put in without any index files and index files could be added later. This would also be time consuming, and the index files would have to be removed and added again each time more data were added. The best advice is to create secondary key field index files only for fields that are *frequently used* in either retrievals of specific records or in sorting output.

Retrieving Information

After the data base has been created and filled with data, the next step is to begin using the data base. Generally, this involves retrieving information, often in summarized form.

Query Languages and Report Generators

Most DBMSs provide two very different ways of retrieving information:

DATA MANAGEMENT ON PERSONAL COMPUTERS

query languages and report generators. **Query languages** allow quick retrieval of information. Most queries can be done with a single sentence containing several clauses, such as the following.

```
PRINT Lastnm, Firstnm, DeptID
  FROM EmplMast
  WHERE Rating < 4.0 AND StartDat > 1/1/86
  SORT BY Rating
```

In the section on relational calculus earlier in this chapter, a similar query was shown. In both cases, the queries specify what fields will be printed, what records will be printed, and how output is to be sorted. No other formatting is done, and although some calculations can be performed in many systems, these calculations are usually simple.

In contrast, **report generators** are used when formatting must be controlled in fine detail and when more extensive calculations need to be done. Figure 10-22 shows output from a report generator. Note that there is free-

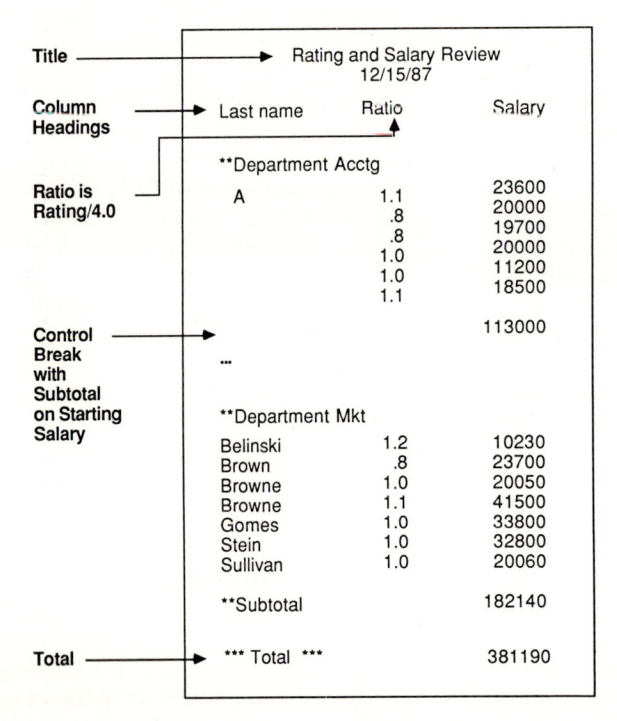

	Rating and Salary Review	
	12/15/87	
Last name	Ratio	Salary
Department Acctg		
A	1.1	23600
	.8	20000
	.8	19700
	1.0	20000
	1.0	11200
	1.1	18500
		113000
...		
Department Mkt		
Belinski	1.2	10230
Brown	.8	23700
Browne	1.0	20050
Browne	1.1	41500
Gomes	1.0	33800
Stein	1.0	32800
Sullivan	1.0	20060
**Subtotal		182140
*** Total ***		381190

Labels: Title; Column Headings; Ratio is Rating/4.0; Control Break with Subtotal on Starting Salary; Total

FIGURE 10-22 A SAMPLE REPORT

form titling at the top, that column names have long English names instead of using cryptic field names, that one column (ratio) is calculated by dividing the rating by 4.0 (the company's average rating), and that starting salary is subtotaled by department and totaled for the entire table.

In summary, query languages are good for quick and dirty output, whereas report generators allow complex reports to be created. Depending on what the user wants to accomplish, he or she will find one of these two tools suitable for most retrieval needs.

Query Languages

We will illustrate query languages using dBASE III Plus. Although this program can do queries through its main menu, as we will see later, power users often do queries in command mode. To get to command mode from the menu, the user hits "Escape" when at the main menu. The user then gets a simple dot (period) prompt, dBASE III Plus's normal prompt. To return to the menu, the user can type "Assist" at the prompt.

In dBASE III Plus, the query language function consists primarily of the DISPLAY command. This command has a number of clauses.

```
DISPLAY scope
    FIELDS expression list
    FOR/WHILE condition
    TO PRINT
    OFF
```

The **scope** parameter refers to the location of the record pointer. dBASE III Plus always points to a single record, and operations can change this pointer. If no scope clause is given, the query will retrieve only the current record—the record at the pointer. In most cases, the scope parameter is given as ALL, so that the query will be done on all records. Other common scope parameters are RECORD n, where n is a record number, and NEXT, which shows the record after the current record and moves the pointer to that record.

The scope parameter should not be confused with the **FOR/WHILE** clause. The scope parameter sets a basic range of records for searching. FOR/WHILE is used to filter records within that range, to specify which ones should be displayed. If FOR is used, all records passing the filtering condition will be displayed. If WHILE is used instead, records will be displayed until one fails to pass the filter condition.

dBASE III Plus has a large number of filtering conditions. The six basic comparisons can be used (less than, less than or equal to, equal, not equal, greater than or equal to, or greater than). These comparisons can be used to compare a field's value with a number, a text string, or even the value of another field in the same record. Filter conditions can be strung together using AND, OR, and NOT, and parentheses can be used to control the order in which AND, OR, and NOT are applied. dBASE III Plus also has several other ways of filtering records in both FOR and WHILE.

FOR and WHILE conditions can also be used in another dBASE III Plus command, SET FILTER TO. After this command is given, only records that pass the filter are used in *any* command. It is as if an extract file had been created that only contained the records passing the filter.

The **expression list** can consist of field names or of mathematical expressions. It can, for example, be Lastnm, Firstnm, Rating/4.0, StartSal − $20000. In other words, although query languages are not rich in computational abilities, most can do at least limited calculations.

Users often want to do queries that span information from multiple files. Suppose, for instance, that a user wanted to use two files. One is Empl, with fields ID, Lastnm, and Firstnm, and the other is Progress, with fields ID, Quota, and Sales. The user might want a single report giving Firstnm, Lastnm, Quota, and Sales.

In some PC DBMSs, query languages can only retrieve data from individual files. In R:BASE System V, for example, the user must combine two relations into a single larger relation and then do the query on the combined relation. This is obviously time consuming and awkward.

Other query languages on PC DBMSs can extract data from multiple files. dBASE III Plus can do this, but the process is awkward.

- The user would first give the command USE Progress INDEX ID to open the Progress file and index it on the field that the two files have in common, namely, ID.
- Each open file has a work area number. For our example, suppose the number is five.
- The user would then say "USE Empl" without indexing it. The user now has Empl as his or her current file, as well as PROGRESS in work area five.
- The user next gives the command SET RELATION TO ID in 5 to link the current file, Empl, to Progress in work area five. Giving just SET RELATION followed by nothing would be used later to unlink the files.
- The user would then give the query by putting the following in the expression list: ID, Firstnm, Lastnm, Progress->Quota, Progress->Sales.

In addition to showing lists of records, most PC DBMS query languages can perform calculations. For example, dBASE III Plus can do averages, counts, and sums, whereas R:BASE System V can do more, including simple frequency distributions. Given the growing importance of statistical calculations in many business organizations, it is surprising that most existing query languages do so little statistical work.

In this section, we have skimmed lightly over query languages. The reason is that the American National Standards Institute has specified a particular query language as a national standard. This is SQL, originally developed by IBM. More importantly, many vendors are now making SQL their

SETTING UP THE DATA BASE **451**

query languages within their DBMSs. In the not too distant future, dBASE III Plus and other programs are likely to adopt SQL, and although they may support their original query languages, these vendor-specific query languages are likely to fall into disuse. Because SQL first emerged in the host computer environment and is still used most heavily there, we will defer the detailed discussion of query languages until Chapter 16.

Before leaving query languages, we should note that dBASE III Plus's normal menu allows queries to be done entirely by selecting menu choices and by typing in variable information, such as a number to be used in a filtering condition. The menu does this by giving the user a number of pop-up menus that allow the user to select the scope, filtering conditions, and fields to be printed. Figure 10-23 shows a DISPLAY being specified interactively.

```
Set Up  Create Update Position |Retrieve| Organize Modify Tools | 10:28:31 am |
| EMPLID    |            | List    |                              |
| LASTNM    |            | Display | | Execute the command       |
| FIRSTNM   |            | Report  | | Specify scope             |
| DEPTID    |            | Label   | | Construct a field list    |
| RATING    |            | Sum     | | Build a search condition  |
| STARTSAL  |            | Average | | Build a scope condition   |
| STARTDAT  |            | Count   |
| EXEMPT    |


              | Field Name         Type      Width   Decimal |
              |_____|
              | PERFORM->EMPLID    Numeric    4       0     |
              |_____|




Command:  DISPLAY ALL SUPPLIER, PREFERRED, RATING, DATE
|ASSIST         | <B:> | PERFORM            | Rec: 3/3    |        | Caps|
  {On-Screen Directions Shown Here}
              Specify which fields to include in this retrieval.
```

A Series of Pop-up menus allow the user to define the column interactively.

The actual dBASE III PLUS screen is not exactly as shown.

FIGURE 10-23 SPECIFYING A DISPLAY INTERACTIVELY

Report Generators

The creation of a report is an involved process We will discuss how dBASE III Plus handles this problem through the "Report" subchoice of "Create."

After prompting the user for a name to be given to the report form (format), the dBASE III Plus presents the initial report definition screen shown as Figure 10-24. This screen allows the user to specify several important aspects of the report.

Options Allows the user to specify global aspects of the report, including page title, page width, left and right margins, lines per page, and

```
|Options  |    Groups        Columns       Locate      Exit   |10:34:13 am |
| Page title                        |
| Page width (positions)    80      |
| Left margin                8      |
| Right margin               0      |
| Lines per page            58      |
| Double space report       No      |
| Page eject before printing Yes    |
| Page eject after printing  No     |
| Plain page                 No     |


    ___Report Format_____
    |>>>>>>>> - - - - - - - - - - - - - - - - - - - - - - - - - - - |
    |                                                               |
    |                                                               |
    |                                                               |
    |_____|
    |                                                               |
    |_____|


| Create Report  | <B:> | B:PROBLEMS.FRM      |Opt:  1/9    |      | Caps|
    {On-Screen Directions Shown Here}
Enter up to four lines of text to be displayed at the top of each report page.
```

Reports can be defined simply by selecting menu choices and filling in forms.

The actual dBASE III PLUS screen is not exactly as shown.

FIGURE 10-24 INITIAL REPORT SPECIFICATION SCREEN

SETTING UP THE DATA BASE **453**

whether there should be page ejects before and after printing. This choice is highlighted initially, as shown in the figure. The program supplies reasonable defaults that the user can accept simply by not changing them.

Groups Allows the user to do control breaks. In Figure 10-22, there was a control break after each department's data. A subtotal was provided for starting salaries.

Columns Allows the user to define the content of individual columns.

Locate Lets the user change the definition of a specific column.

Exit Ends the report specification process.

When the user specifies a column, as shown in Figure 10-25, he or she is shown a pop-up submenu that asks him or her to specify the following.

```
Options          Groups       | Columns |         Locate       Exit  |10:36:50 am|
                             | Contents           Rating / 4.0                   |
                             | Heading                                           |
                             | Width              5                              |
                             | Decimal places     2                              |
                             | Total this column  No                             |
                             |_____|


                                        _____
                                       |                                     |
                                       |                                     |
                                       | Relative                            |
    __Report Format__                  | Performance                         |
   |>>>>>>>>                           .--------------------------------------|
   |                                                                         |
   |                                                                         |
   |_____|
   |         ############.##                                                 |
   |_____|


    _____
   | CREATE REPORT   | <B:> | B:PROBLEMS.FRM      | Column: 1     |   Caps |
                Enter column heading.  Exit - Ctrl-End.
   Enter up to four lines of text to display above the indicated column.
```

Column contents can consist of field names or more complex expressions.

The actual dBASE III PLUS screen is not exactly as shown.

    FIGURE 10-25 DEFINING A REPORT COLUMN

Contents Specifies the content of the field, which is is either a field name or a calculation. In this case, the calculation is "Rating/4.0."

Heading Allows the user to create a heading for the column. This column heading may be up to four lines long and may be as long as the user desires. In Figure 10-25, the user has selected "Heading" from the submenu, and a pop-up box shows a column heading being entered. Its name is "Relative Performance."

Width Allows the user to specify how wide the column should be.

Decimal places Allows the user to specify the number of decimal places.

Total Allows the user to decide whether the column should be totaled Subtotals will be produced at control breaks.

Creating Custom Applications

Some users of a data base will have very limited needs. For these people it is often desirable to create custom applications, so that they will not have to master the full complexity of the DBMS to get their work done. Most PC DBMSs have **application development tools** for producing customized applications.

A Customized Application

Suppose that someone working with our EmplMast file has three simple needs: he or she has to look up records about people in the file, either by employee ID, last name, or department. This person should have a simple application that does the following.

- The user should be presented with a simple menu, like the one shown as Figure 10-26. This menu asks whether records should be looked up on the basis of employee ID number, last name, or department. The user types a 1, 2, or 3 to select a choice.
- In each case, the screen clears, and the user is asked to type an employee ID number, last name, or department, depending on what choice was selected.
- Finally, the application displays all records with the specified employee ID number, last name, or department.

```
Search on ...

    1. Employee ID
    2. Last name
    3. Department




Please enter your choice:
```

FIGURE 10-26 A MENU FOR A CUSTOM APPLICATION

Fourth-Generation Language (4GL)

One way to satisfy this need is to use the DBMS's embedded **fourth-generation language (4GL)** if the DBMS has one. A 4GL is a *statement-based* language, that is, a language whose programs are created by writing statements, as is done in assembly language, BASIC, COBOL, and other traditional programming languages. Like traditional languages, it has a full control structure for jumping, if-then-else constructions, and other basic operations. In addition, like other languages, it has functions for handling input and output.

What makes it different from third-generation languages is that its statements can include most or all of the fourth-generation commands available within the DBMS to command-level users. In dBASE III Plus, for example, a program can include a DISPLAY command, a FILE EXTRACTION command, or even a command to print a report according to a predefined report form. This capability of introducing fourth-generation functions within the program allows small programs to do tasks that would take large and complex programs in third-generation languages such as COBOL.

Figure 10-27 shows the program that would be needed to build our sample application using dBASE III Plus's embedded fourth-generation language. Most of this program is similar in style and complexity to programs

```
@4,30 SAY "Search on ..."
@8,30 SAY "1.  Employee ID"
@10,30 SAY "2.  Last name"
@12,30 SAY "3.  Department"
WAIT "Please enter your choice:  " TO Choice
CLEAR
DO CASE
   CASE Choice = "1"
      USE EmplMast INDEX IDIndex
      ACCEPT "Please enter the ID number:"  TO ID
      CLEAR
      DISPLAY ALL for EmplID = ID OFF
   CASE Choice = "2"
      USE EmplMast INDEX LNindex
      ACCEPT "Please enter the last name:"  TO LN
      CLEAR
      DISPLAY ALL for Lastnm = LN OFF
   CASE Choice = "3"
      USE EmplMast INDEX DPTIndex
      ACCEPT "Please enter the department ID:"  TO DP
      CLEAR
      DISPLAY ALL for DeptID = DP OFF
   OTHERWISE
      CLEAR
      @15,20 SAY "Incorrect Choice.  Please Start Over."
ENDCASE
```

FIGURE 10-27 A FOURTH-GENERATION LANGUAGE PROGRAM

written in third-generation languages for full-screen interface applications. But the DISPLAY commands within this program would take dozens of lines of COBOL or BASIC programs to replace. Again, it is the ability of embedded 4GLs to use commands of the DBMS as statements that gives them their power.

Application Generators

Although 4GLs are powerful, the fact that they are statement-based means that the user must memorize rather complex syntax. An alternative for creating customized applications is an **applications generator.** With an applications generator, the user does not write statements of code. Instead, his or her interaction with the computer consists of (1) selecting options from a menu, and (2) filling in forms.

Figure 10-28 shows the main menu of dBASE III Plus's applications generator. This is a sister program to dBASE III Plus and can be loaded from within the main dBASE III Plus program.

```
|                         dBASE III PLUS                          |
|                    APPLICATIONS GENERATOR MENU                  |
|                                                                 |
|                                                                 |
|                    1.  CREATE DATABASE                          |
|                    2.  CREATE SCREEN FORM                       |
|                    3.  CREATE REPORT FORM                       |
|                    4.  CREATE LABEL FORM                        |
|                    5.  SET APPLICATION COLOR                    |
|                    6.  AUTOMATIC APPLICATION GENERATOR          |
|                    7.  RUN APPLICATION                          |
|                    8.  ADVANCED APPLICATION GENERATOR           |
|                    9.  MODIFY APPLICATION CODE                  |
|                                                                 |
|                    0.  EXIT                                     |
|                                                                 |
|                                 select                          |
|_____|

| Command         | <C:>     |          |          |     |     |
```

By selecting menu choices and filling out forms, the user can create menu-driven applications.

The actual dBASE III PLUS screen is not exactly as shown.

FIGURE 10-28 APPLICATIONS GENERATOR MENU IN dBASE III PLUS

SETTING UP THE DATA BASE **457**

The Applications Generator allows the user to do a number of individually useful tasks such as creating a data base schema, building report forms, defining mailing label forms, and producing custom data entry screens. Figure 10-29 shows the user building a custom data entry screen within Applications Generator. The user can lay out the form on the screen as if the screen were a blackboard, and can erase fields or move them around to other places on the screen.

Applications Generator also allows the user to build custom applications. He or she can use the simple automatic application generation choice or the more powerful and complex application generation. These tools allow the user to step through a process and have the application generator remember the steps along the way. When necessary, they present the user with forms to specify information, such as what columns will appear in a report. They also

```
 Set Up            |Modify|              Options          Exit    |06:37:44 pm|


 Employee ID number: |9999|

          Last name: |XXXXXXXX|    First name: |XXXXXXXX|



         Department: |XXXXX|
             Rating: |9.9|
    Starting Salary: |99999.99|
      Starting Date: |XX/XX/XX|


 Exempt from union regulations? |?|



 |CREATE SCREEN    | <C:> |ACCOUNTS       |Row 17, Col 27  |      |     |
   Enter text.  <----| to drag field or window corner under cursor. F10 for menu.
                        Screen field definition blackboard
```

The developer can lay out a data entry screen interactively.

The actual dBASE III PLUS screen is not exactly as shown.
FIGURE 10-29 DEFINING A CUSTOM DATA ENTRY SCREEN

allow a menu to be built for a custom application to access the processes that the applications generator has memorized. Without writing a single statement of code, the user can create a custom application. Of course, the user can modify the code created by Applications Generator by selecting the "Modify Application Code" choice.

Figure 10-30 shows a custom application developed to work with the EmplMast file. Note that, in addition to the three retrieval applications specified earlier, the developer has included several general choices for entering, updating, and viewing information. He has done this because it is easy to do with Applications Generator.

Merging the Two Tools

Although some PC DBMSs offer only a 4GL or an applications generator, most offer both. More importantly, the two are related; in most cases, the

```
|--------------------------------------------------------------|
|                  EMPLOYEE MASTER FILE MENU                   |
|--------------------------------------------------------------|
|                                                              |
|              1.  ADD INFORMATION                             |
|              2.  CHANGE INFORMATION                          |
|              3.  REMOVE INFORMATION                          |
|              4.  REVIEW INFORMATION                          |
|              5.  RETRIEVE BY EMPLOYEE ID                     |
|              6.  RETRIEVE BY LAST NAME                       |
|              7.  RETRIEVE BY DEPARTMENT                      |
|                                                              |
|              0.  EXIT                                        |
|                                                              |
|--------------------------------------------------------------|


|Command          |<C:>    |          |          |     |    |
COMMAND:   <E>xit, <R>edo, <S>ave
```

This menu was developed by the dBASE III Plus Applications Generator.

The actual dBASE III PLUS screen is not exactly as shown.

FIGURE 10-30 MENU FOR THE GENERATED APPLICATION

applications generator creates a program in the fourth-generation language embedded in the system. We have already seen that dBASE III Plus does this.

This use of the 4GL by the applications generator is important, because while applications generators are easier to use than 4GLs, they are also less flexible. To some degree, they are like fifth-generation tools (not using the AI concept of fifth generation); they offer greater ease of use than 4GLs while taking away flexibility. If the applications generator does not create 4GL code, there will be no way around this loss of flexibility. If the applications generator does create 4GL code, then the application builder can work primarily in the applications generator to "rough out" the code and then turn to the 4GL to fine-tune the process.

THE ROLE OF THE INFORMATION CENTER

Throughout this chapter, we have discussed what PC users need to know to create data bases, retrieve data, or build custom applications. This last section reviews and summarizes the kinds of support, training, and direction that users are likely to need from the information center staff.

Overall, support is needed in three main areas. The first area is concepts and terminology. Using a DBMS requires end users to master quite a number of new ideas and some particular jargon. Most users need significant training to develop the knowledge required in these areas.

The second area is learning how to use specific software packages such as dBASE III Plus or R:BASE System V. DBMS packages are considerably harder to learn than spreadsheet or word processing programs because they tend to have more functionality and because they sometimes use outdated user interfaces.

The third area is data administration. Many users find themselves managing a significant fraction of their department's critical data. If they must learn data administration from experience, the learning process can prove costly to their work units.

Concepts and Terminology

Spreadsheet programs and word processing programs draw their concepts and terminology from everyday experience. Users can use their intuition to understand columns, rows, margins, and pages. Even new terms such as cells and ruler lines fit well into the user's basic intuitive framework.

This is not the case with data bases or even individual data files. Because terminology needs to span a large number of office activities, each with its own terminology, DBMS designers resort to general abstract terminology. In some cases, a strong mathematical heritage adds additional layers of jargon, as in the case of relational data bases.

It would be nice if we could teach users simpler terms, such as table, column, and row, but these would tend to limit users to certain views of data bases. More practically, every DBMS on the market uses specific jargon, so there is no practical way to shield hands-on users from the need to master jargon.

Basic Concepts

Every user needs to master the basic elements of data base organization, including data base, data file, record, field, and value. Moreover, users should be able to recognize those concepts in both table image and form image representations. Experience has shown that between a half hour to an hour of teaching is needed to convey these ideas, including exercises to help users develop their ability to label elements in table image and form image representations.

Key Fields and Index Files

Key fields and index files can be taught in two ways. One method tells users that if a field is labeled a key, something called an index will be built, and that this will speed retrieval and sorted output while increasing data entry time and storage space requirements. This "black box" characterization is then followed by an exercise to see if users can discern which fields should be made keys and which should not. About fifteen minutes of teaching time is needed, most of it in the exercise.

The second method opens the black box and shows how index files work. This will help users understand why indexing affects performance the way it does. A detailed example will take around ten minutes to develop.

Relational DBMSs

Because relational data organization is now the norm in PC DBMSs, most teachers spend little time, if any, on the network data organization or its subclass, the hierarchical organization.

Teaching relational terminology presents real problems, because basic data base concepts are normally taught first, and relational terminology gives new names to previously learned concepts. (Relation and attribute replace the file and field.) The only solution to this unhappy situation seems to be repetition—using relational terms over and over, in many different examples. If an organization has standardized on one particular DBMS package, some relational terminology may be abridged if the user is not likely to run into it. In addition, more esoteric aspects of relational terminology, including "domains" and "n-tuples," are rarely taught.

Similarly, it is not clear that the theoretical concepts of Select and Project should be taught abstractly in any form, because most DBMSs have a combined operation (in dBASE III Plus, COPY) for the two separate relational algebra operations. In addition, most DBMS packages use Select, Project, or both terms, in nonstandard ways. (Both dBASE III Plus and R:BASE System V use SELECT in a nonstandard way, for example.)

Join is worth teaching abstractly, because most DBMSs follow it closely, but even here, DBMS-specific details must be handled. Other ways of combining files—Intersect, Union, and Subtract—are not likely to be taught abstractly, since many popular packages do not support them at all, and others that do (notably R:BASE System V) support them in ways very different from the way relational theory dictates.

In general, although relational algebra is neat and appealing to teachers, most DBMS designers virtually ignore it in favor of relational calculus.

Teaching Specific Packages

Teaching DBMS packages tends to be harder than teaching spreadsheet packages, first, because DBMS user interfaces tend to lag behind spreadsheet interfaces. Most DBMS interfaces are command-driven, perhaps with good reason but nevertheless making them harder to learn. Although most are beginning to add menu overlays or have already done so, quite a few retain a strong flavor of command-driven interaction, especially in their embedded programming languages.

Second, DBMS users have to master a large number of basic operations and concepts to even begin using a DBMS. Look at the complexity of dBASE III Plus's DISPLAY command, for instance, and this is only one complex command that even casual users need to master. In contrast, a user can begin building good spreadsheets after an hour or two of instruction.

The usual way to teach DBMSs is to begin with a simple exercise in which the user builds a very small data base schema, enters and edits data, and does a simple query. Then, each basic operation can be taught again, in much more depth.

In teaching specific programs, a considerable amount must be taught before the user can begin doing solo problems. Sample problems involving a simple "get in, do these steps, and get out" exercise can be taught quickly and can be effective if good assistance will be nearby when a user does the exercise. For anything larger or for solo activity, a good deal of overhead must be taught. In a command-based system, does upper versus lower case matter, for instance, and how are continuation lines indicated on long commands? How does a user get help or other assistance?

We have put off the discussion of Boolean logic until now. Although Boolean logic is a general concept, there is little point in teaching it abstractly. Every DBMS has specific notation and other limitations on the expressions a user can give. In virtually every command in a DBMS, there is something like dBASE III Plus's FOR/WHERE clause, which allows users to select certain records on the basis of field values.

The first thing to teach is that there are six and only six ways to compare two values. A number of word exercises can be done, using a model data base, to turn verbal descriptions into valid queries. When to use the equal sign should be emphasized in examples (for instance, "age is at least 24"). If the DBMS to be used employs <> as its symbol for "not equal," it is good to point out that not equal means either less than or greater then, hence the <> symbol.

After the user has worked several simple comparison examples, the Boolean AND and OR conditions can be introduced. Although this can be done with Venn diagrams, it is usually faster to explain simply that AND means that both must be true and that OR means that either must be true. Then several examples can be given to clarify the concepts.

Next, multiple AND/OR conditions can be introduced, with a heavy complement of word problems emphasizing the importance of order of applying AND and OR. If possible, parenthesis should be introduced to simplify the user's life, for instance, to clarify the meanings of such expressions as (Age > 30 or Income > 30000) and Sex = F.

The Boolean NOT condition is probably best put off to last, when the user is comfortable with simpler cases. Many users have considerable trouble with NOT logic's reversal of the following term's meaning.

Teaching Programming

Although the DBMS's embedded programming language is, strictly speaking, an integral part of the DBMS, it is almost always taught as a separate module, after the user has mastered individual commands for all functions. There is no point getting into programming until the user has mastered basic commands. In addition, many users build their own data bases and generate output without touching the programming language.

If possible, the user should first be taught to use his or her DBMS's embedded application generator. Many customization needs can be met entirely with these aids, and users should realize the advantages of trying to solve problems using application generators instead of writing programs in the embedded 4GL. Advanced users, however, will want to learn the 4GL.

The teacher must cover the general concepts to be taught for all programming applications, including design, modularization, structured logic, documentation, testing, user feedback, and other broad concerns. These must be introduced in any DBMS programming course.

DBMS 4GLs tend to be much easier to learn than third-generation languages such as BASIC, PASCAL, and COBOL. They are not much simpler if you count the total number of concepts to be mastered, but users already know most commands from their previous command-level use of the DBMS. As a result, only control flow, input/output, and a few other functions need to be taught.

It is good to begin with a simple program consisting of three to ten basic commands that would normally be given by hand but would be tedious to type time after time. The user can then enter these in the program editor, name them, run them, and have the immediate feedback of seeing their commands and output race across the screen.

Now that the user has executed a series of keystrokes, the concept of **metcommands** that modify the basic flow should be introduced. These metacommands are used only in programming. Only after the user has had one or two of these high feedback experiences should metacommands that hide command typing and output be introduced. This will preserve feedback in the initial run or two and also show the user the advantage of being able to hide "messy detail" from the command user.

Next, simple input and output can be added to allow the program to talk with the user about the commands being executed and what is happening. Control logic should be introduced gradually, beginning with the simplest case in the DBMS being taught (usually either IF/THEN/ELSE or Looping). Then, more advanced control structures can be taught.

Support in Application Building

For concepts, basic package use skills, and programming, the basic type of support needed is training. For the design and implementation of applications, however, extensive one-on-one consulting or at least group workshops are needed.

Chapter 5 described the "workshop" approach in which a group of people building different applications are brought together and coached through a series of application development steps with individual and group feedback at each stage. This approach seems especially useful for DBMS applications.

In addition to the standard modules discussed in Chapter 5, a number of DBMS-specific workshop modules are needed. For instance, needs assessment is especially difficult to teach and lends itself well to a workshop format. After a module introducing the concepts and methods of needs assessment, the participants go back to their organizations and build their assessments. At the next class, their assessments are critiqued and refinements suggested.

The next step—designing the data base schema, including normalization—also benefits from the human touch. After a module demonstrating the process of data modeling and warning about such things as repeating fields and the need to define the entity of each relation carefully, the participants would draft a schema. At the next class session or even before, the teacher would go over the schema carefully with each individual. It may be that the participant will not worry about normalization but will leave the degree of normalization to the teacher's discretion.

Building procedures for security, data collection, data entry, data updating, and other processes also benefits from outside criticism and suggestions. The price of errors is too high in many cases to allow learn-as-you-go procedure development.

Although all such procedures can be performed individually, the workshop approach may be more efficient, and each participant will benefit from the errors and insights of other participants.

CONCLUSION

Most users begin with simple applications—typically spreadsheet analysis or word processing. If they move into data applications cautiously, by adopting a simple file management system, learning only a query language, or using the embedded file management tools in spreadsheet and word processing programs, they should not have too much difficulty. However, when they move into the world of data base management systems (DBMSs), they suddenly find themselves dealing with an entirely new level of complexity.

First, the few and intuitive concepts of word processing and spreadsheet analysis are replaced by a large number of difficult concepts whose names have no use in the ordinary office (relations, entities, etc.). Not only are the names strange, but many of the operations they represent require considerable study to understand.

Second, DBMSs have much higher functionality than spreadsheet and word processing programs, making them difficult to learn. This functionality barrier to learning is compounded by the fact that many data management programs have old-fashioned user interfaces or the remnants of old interfaces that have been plastered over with menu front-ends.

Third, the process of creating a data application is long and conceptually difficult. Using Entity-Relationship Modeling or some other technique, the user must organize data into files (relations). This is a very subtle skill that requires considerable training.

Fourth, once a person's or department's data are placed on a computer, a whole new set of administrative details must be worked out. In some cases, the administrative problems are new to most office workers. For example, few office workers back up their paper documents because file drawers do not catch fire every year or so, whereas hard disks do fail with some regularity. In other cases, traditional problems are magnified. Although confidential information in paper files has always been protected, someone reading through a paper file is very conspicuous. Someone accessing the data through a PC keyboard may not be very obvious, especially in a networked environment.

Therefore, there is a great need for training and support. Training must be very extensive, and heavy support must be provided throughout the entire application development life cycle. The workshop approach discussed in Chapter 5, in which groups of people building different applications meet regularly for training, critiquing, and information sharing, is especially attractive for DBMS applications.

REVIEW QUESTIONS

1. What are the relative advantages and disadvantages of the following for working with data: third-generation languages, special-purpose fourth-generation tools, and data management systems?

2. What are the major modules in a data management system? For each module, list two or three commands in dBASE III Plus (discussed later in this chapter).

3. What are the relative advantages of PC data management tools versus host tools? Stand-alone versus Networked PC products? File management systems versus DBMSs? Stand-alone data management tools versus embedded data handling capabilities in other programs? What kinds of tools are used most heavily by end users? How do you think this will change in the future?

4. Make up your own data base. What are its entities? Draw one data file in table and form image. In each case, identify the file, a record, a field, and a value. If this data base were relational, what would correspond to a relation? An attribute?

5. What are the major ways of handling repeating fields? Include a discussion of and your own examples of fixed-length records, variable-length records, and normalization (discussed later in this chapter).

6. What are the relative advantages of the network organization of data and the relational organization of data? Which organization do you think will win out in the end? Why?

7. The information you need is in two related files. What three relational operations are you likely to have to do to get the information you need? In what order would you perform them?

8. What is the difference between relational algebra and relational calculus? What is the advantage of each? Which do you think will be used most widely in the future? Why?
9. What are the seven steps in developing a data application? What are the steps in needs identification and data modeling? Briefly characterize what is done in each step in data modeling and how that step lays the groundwork for later steps.
10. In building the preliminary ER diagram, what are the three kinds of relationships? Make up two examples of each.
11. When refining the ER diagram, what do you do with each kind of relationship? How do you build relations from the final ER diagram, and what do you use as a primary key field for each?
12. What are the main ways to create primary keys? What are the advantages and disadvantages of each?
13. A teacher wishes to keep track of the students who have taken each of his classes. Go through the steps in needs identification and data modeling and finish with a complete schema for the teacher's data base.
14. What are the main general kinds of attribute types? What are the advantages and disadvantages of each?
15. Contrast the way dBASE III Plus and R:BASE System V define the data base schema. Contrast the way they handle indexing. What are the advantages and disadvantages of their different approaches to indexing? What is the difference between a primary and secondary key?
16. What are the differences between query languages and report generators? What are their relative advantages? Under what conditions would you use each?
17. What are the differences between 4GLs and applications generators? What are their relative advantages? Under what conditions would you use each? How do they work together in some DBMSs?
18. What are the three areas in which support is needed from the information center by DBMS users?

REFERENCES

1. CODD, E. F., "A Relational Model of Data for Large Shared Data Banks," *Communications of the ACM,* June 1970.
2. DATE, C. J., *An Introduction to Database Systems,* second edition, Addison-Wesley Publishing Company, 1977.
3. JARVENPAA, SIRKKA L., AND MACHESKY, JEFFRY J., "End User Learning Behavior in Data Analysis and Data Modeling Tools," *Proceedings of the Seventh International Conference on Information Systems,* December 15–17, 1987, pp. 152–167.
4. WHYTE, CHRISTINE, "A Sense of Balance," *PC World,* December 1985, pp. 286–295.

11 COMMUNICATION APPLICATIONS ON PERSONAL COMPUTERS

There is a fundamental distinction between communications (with an "s") and communication (without an "s").

- **Communications** refers to transmission systems, for example data communications networks.
- **Communication** refers to person-to-person interactions, whether face to face or "mediated" by electronics or simple paper.

This chapter looks at the main communication applications found on personal computers. It begins with word processing, which is the most popular kind of communication program. In fact, word processing is the most popular application program of any kind on personal computers. As discussed in Chapter 1, managers and professionals spend a quarter of their working days reading and writing, and secretaries spend most of their days supporting this written communication, so the popularity of word processing is hardly surprising.

The chapter then turns to conceptual graphics. In contrast to **analytical graphics,** which summarizes data in the form of pie charts, bar charts, and other numerical charts, **conceptual graphics** is designed to communicate a concept or relationships among concepts. An organization chart is an example of conceptual graphics. In this book, all but a handful of the figures are examples of conceptual graphics.

Word processing and conceptual graphics were traditionally handled by separate programs, but the two are now coming together in single programs. At the simplest level, many word processing programs can now import analytical and conceptual graphics images and merge them with text. At a more sophisticated level, **desktop publishing** programs provide the ability to mix text and graphics in complex page layout formats like those found in newspapers, magazines, and books.

This chapter begins with word processing; it then moves on to conceptual graphics (analytical graphics are treated in Chapter 16); and ends with a discussion of desktop publishing and possible trends beyond desktop publishing.

WORD PROCESSING

A Historical Perspective

Before the PC explosion, word processing was available only on dedicated word processing systems. These machines were so expensive that they could only be used by typists in specialized word processing centers, where equipment could be used eight or more hours a day. As a result, the functions offered on these dedicated systems were oriented toward the needs of production typists.

When PCs arrived, they offered a lower cost alternative to dedicated word processing, but there was a price to pay for this lower cost: lower capabilities. Early PC word processing programs were much more limited than the software on dedicated word processing systems. Another problem was that PC software continued to focus on the needs of secretaries.

Since those early days, the situation has changed enormously. First, the most sophisticated PC programs began to approach and in many ways even surpass the functionality of dedicated word processing systems. Because numerous managers and professionals were using PCs for word processing by that time, it made less and less sense for secretaries to continue using incompatible dedicated word processing systems. As a result, dedicated word processing systems began to fade in importance.

Another trend has been a shift in focus from secretarial support to author support, by the addition of features that help authors during the creation phase of word processing. Although most word processing programs continue to focus on secretarial support, a growing number try to build a competitive advantage by emphasizing managerial and professional functionality.

Types of Word Processing Software

In analysis, a single program dominates the market, Lotus 1-2-3, and its competitors have roughly the same level of functionality. In word processing, however, no program has achieved comparable dominance, and there is a broad spectrum of functionality among programs with significant market shares.

Text Editors

The simplest programs are **text editors.** In text editors, users *must* type a carriage return at the end of each line, as they do when typing a typewriter. This example illustrates the process.

```
Now is the time for all men<CR>
to come to the aid of their<CR>
country.<CR>
```

This works fine during the initial typing, but typing a carriage return at the end of each line makes subsequent editing difficult. Suppose someone adds "good" before men, in the first line. This will make the first line too long, requiring another carriage return to be entered.

```
Now is the time for all good <CR>
men <CR>
to come to the aid of their <CR>
country. <CR>
```

Now, however, the second line is too short, consisting of only a single word, "men." To fix this, the third line would have to be moved up to the end of the second, and then the new second line would have to be broken in the correct place. This process would have to continue to other lines in the paragraph. In other words, placing a carriage return at the end of each line makes subsequent editing very difficult.

In word processing systems other than text editors, the user only types carriage returns where they are absolutely needed—for instance, at the end of each paragraph or at the end of each line in a table. Within paragraphs, the user never types a carriage return. Instead, the computer automatically breaks each line within the paragraph, making this break at a word ending or by inserting a hyphen. This automatic process is called **word wrap** and is illustrated in the following example. Notice the lack of carriage returns at the ends of lines within the paragraph.

```
Now is the time for all men
to come to the aid of their
country. <CR>
```

Now, suppose the user inserts "good" before men. With word wrap, the system merely adds the word and rewraps the paragraph automatically.

```
Now is the time for all good
men to come to the aid of
their country. <CR>
```

Word wrap, then, is essential for editing. Without it, there is no way for the program to know whether a carriage return at the end of a line can be overridden, as in the example we have been using, or whether the carriage return is necessary, say, because it marks the end of a paragraph or the end of a line in a table.

Why, then, do text editors avoid word wrap? The answer is that text editors are not designed for documents. Rather, they are intended for creating computer programs, which are line-oriented. In computer programs, *all* line endings are normally important, so word wrap would be superfluous.

Because text editors are not designed for documents, they are not considered to be true word processors at all by most people. We will follow that practice, not viewing text editors as word processors in the rest of this chapter. We have introduced them for only two reasons: (1) to warn that some text programs are not designed for document creation, and (2) to introduce word wrap, one of the most critical concepts in word processing.

Personal Programs

A number of users feel that they are too busy to learn a complex word processing program and that they have no need for the full range of functions found in standard word processing programs. For these "light" users, a number of **personal** word processing programs have been created which allow simple document creation, editing, and printing.

After the user has created and printed the document, there are two options: to mail it out "as is," or to give the disk and a marked-up copy of the printed document to the secretary, for advanced manipulation with a fuller word processing program. Because this second option is important, personal word processing programs used in the corporation should be compatible with the corporation's standard word processing programs.

Personal programs should not be confused with early word processing programs, which also had low functionality. In contrast to those early programs, modern personal programs have much better user interfaces, and the choice of which functions to include is made on the basis of our modern understanding of user needs—not simply on an inability to produce higher functionality or a lack of understanding about what is possible.

Although personal programs are often purchased as stand-alone products, the word processing modules in most integrated products such as Symphony, Framework, and Enable are basically personal word processing programs.

Standard Word Processing Programs

The most popular word processing programs are more powerful than personal programs but are less sophisticated than the most powerful programs on the market. Because of their popularity, we will call them **standard** word processing programs. Common examples are DisplayWrite, MultiMate, and WordStar.

Standard word processing programs are the workhorses of corporate word processing today, but their future is in doubt. The higher functionality of more advanced programs is beginning to attract more and more corporations, and although newer versions of standard programs have added a great deal of functionality, many additions are clumsy and slow, having an air of ad hoc add-ons instead of deep integration into the basic design.

Advanced Word Processing Programs

Standard word processing programs try to strike a balance between the needs of simple users and users who want a great deal of power. In contrast, advanced programs cater directly to the needs of sophisticated users.

For simple users, either extensive training must be done or a simpler word processor must be selected. A simpler word processor must be able to export files to the advanced program for heavier editing. Importing files from the advanced program may not be possible because advanced formatting codes are not likely to be translatable to the simpler program.

Some of the functionality of advanced programs is aimed at secretaries. The objective of these enhancements over standard programs is to meet the functionality of today's best dedicated word processors, which have surpassed the secretarial functionality of standard word processing programs.

Other functions are aimed at supporting authors during the initial composition stage. This was not a concern when word processing was only a secretarial tool, but now that word processing is used heavily by managers and professionals, author aids are receiving a great deal of attention.

Advanced programs offer many tools for both secretaries and authors. Some are balanced in their emphasis, a good example being WordPerfect. Other programs lean slightly more toward secretarial tools (SAMNA Word) or authoring tools (Microsoft Word).

Many producers of standard programs compete with advanced programs by offering advanced versions of their standard programs. Ashton-Tate's MultiMate Advantage is a good example.

Desktop Publishing Programs

In the past, word processing has had only one high-quality output device, the daisywheel printer. Daisywheel printing normally means a single type size and type face, except through the laborious process of changing the entire typing element. It also means the absence of graphics and slow speed.

Now, however, users can buy more flexible, high-quality output devices, most notably laser printers and, to a lesser extent, near letter-quality dot matrix printers. These devices can print text in different sizes, fonts, and styles (concepts discussed later in this chapter). They can also mix graphics with text.

To take advantage of these new output alternatives and the graphics capabilities of newer office personal computers, a number of software vendors have produced **desktop publishing** programs, that allow the user to approach the layout capabilities needed in newspapers, magazines, and sophisticated newsletters. Multiple text columns, headline boxes, think lines to mark off areas, the insertion of graphics, and similar capabilities have brought massive improvements in layout functionality. Desktop publishing programs are discussed at the end of this chapter.

Seeking Compatibility

When PCs first entered the scene, the issue was what single word processing program to select to balance the needs of secretaries and authors. Today, the situation is very different. Many companies are now replacing their initial word processing software standards with more sophisticated programs. Some firms have switched standards twice or even three times.

Another difference today is that many firms have given up on having a single word processing standard. Instead, they have one basic standard for general word processing, either a standard or an advanced program. They may also support both a personal program standard and a desktop publishing standard. Some even support a separate standard for scientific and engineering departments, which have specialized needs.

Standard Programs

As discussed earlier, standard programs have more functionality than personal programs but less functionality than advanced programs. They are the most common word programs today.

Basic Menu Operations

When most standard programs are started, they present the user with a menu of basic choices. Figure 11-1 illustrates the basic menu in MultiMate, a typical standard program. In this menu, the first two choices begin document creation and editing.

- The next three choices deal with printing. They allow the user to print a document; do other printing operations such as kill a job already printing or change printer defaults; and do a mass mailing in which a standard letter is merged with a file containing variable information.
- Choices 6 and 7 are for less frequent operations, for instance, to allow the user to customize the system to his or her normal working practices.
- The eighth choice allows the user to spell check a document, that is, proofread the document to find possible spelling errors.
- The last choice returns the user to the operating system.

Text Entry

Once the user has created a document or selected a document to be edited, he or she is ready to type new text. If the document is a new one, the user begins typing. If the document already existed, the user can go to the end and begin typing new material.

```
         MultiMate
         Version 3.30

    1) Edit an Old Document
    2) Create a New Document

    3) Print Document Utility
    4) Printer Control Utilities
    5) Merge Print Utility

    6) Document Handling Utilities
    7) Other Utilities
    8) Spell Check a Document
    9) Return to DOS

       DESIRED FUNCTION: ▪

Enter the number of the function; press RETURN
Hold down Shift and press F1 for HELP menu
              S:↑ N:↓
```

FIGURE 11-1 INITIAL MULTIMATE SCREEN

Typing on a word processor is very much like typing on a correcting electric typewriter. The user types, and the text appears on the screen. If the user realizes that he or she has made an error (about 90 percent of all typing errors are realized when they occur), the user can backspace to the error. Backspacing usually erases all text to the point of the error. As discussed earlier, the user does not type carriage returns at the end of each line within a paragraph. The system automatically breaks each line at a reasonable point.

Formatting

During the typing the user has considerable control over the layout or format of the document.

- **Normal tabbing** is possible, moving the cursor to the next tab stop and beginning typing again at that point.
- **Decimal tabbing** is used to type columns of numbers, as in a table. Hitting decimal tab moves the cursor to the next tab stop, but now the decimal point is locked at that tab stop. If the user types 99.5%, for example, the decimal point is locked at the tab stop. The "99" is placed in the two spaces before the tab stop, whereas the ".5%" is placed in the two following spaces. This is the normal way to line up columns of numbers in a table.
- **Centering** centers one or more lines of text, so that the user does not have to waste time counting out spacing when typing a centered line.
- **Paragraph indenting** indents an entire paragraph, so that bullet points and other matter can be set off from the main text.

Text Characteristics

In addition to controlling the layout of the text in general, the user can normally control the appearance of text. With a daisywheel printer, the user has comparatively little control, other than underlining and some form of boldface. With a laser or dot matrix printer, however, the user can control several text characteristics, as shown in Figure 11-2.

Typeface and emphasis First, the user can control the **typeface**—the design of the individual letters. For documents, the user might use Times Roman, which has a businesslike style that is easy to read in long blocks. For overheads, the user might choose Helvetica, which has a boxy style that stands out well when there is only a little text on a page. For special effects, the user might choose other typefaces that are elegant, eye-catching, or have other desired visual impacts.

Typefaces fall into two categories. First, there are **serif** typefaces, whose characters have many small lines (serifs); for example, an "h" has small horizontal lines at its feet and at its top. The typeface in this book is a serif typeface, and this is not surprising. Most book and document typefaces use serifs, because it is believed that serifs make it easier for the eye to recognize individual characters and to move smoothly through large blocks of text. **Sans serif** typefaces, in contrast, lack these small marks, making them "cleaner" in appearance. Sans serif typefaces are normally used in overheads, signs, and other brief materials.

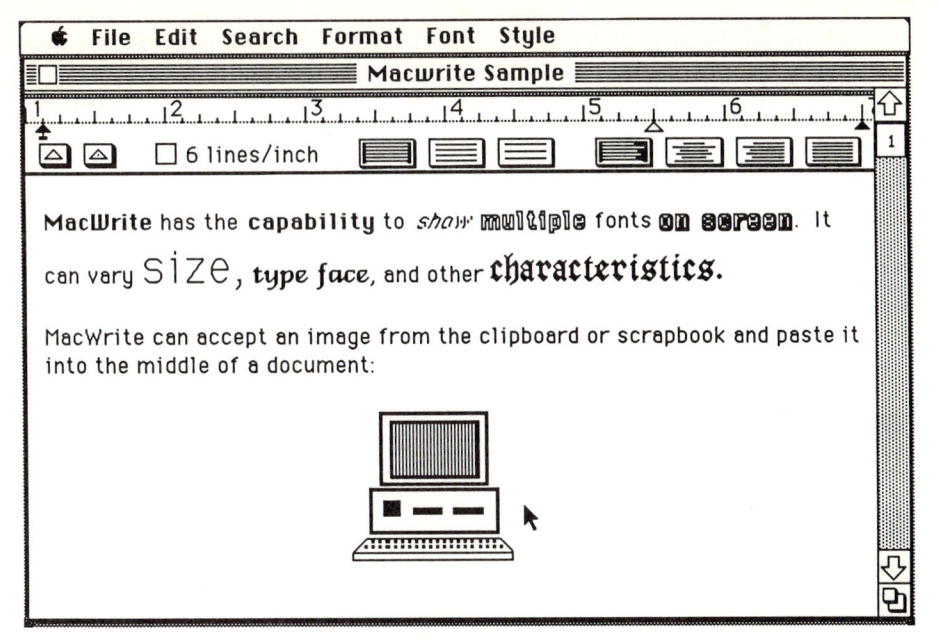

FIGURE 11-2 MULTIPLE TEXT CHARACTERISTICS AND EMBEDDED GRAPHICS

Many word processing systems also allow the control of **emphasis,** including boldface printing, italic printing, underlining, shadowing, and other variations from the basic design of the typeface.

Character sizes (height) Size is another important text characteristic. Typesetters normally use **picas** and **points** to specify size. There are six picas to the inch, and there are 12 points to the pica, giving 72 points to the inch.

Type **sizes** (heights) are almost always measured in points. Since normal printing gives six lines to the inch, a typical character normally occupies 12 points of vertical space. But point sizes can vary from about 8 to 36 points in printed material and can extend to 48 points or more in overheads and signs.

The most advanced word processing systems follow more exacting typographical practice by specifying *two* heights when they define type. First, they specify the height of the characters themselves, as measured from the tops of ascenders on tall characters, such as "f," to the bottoms of descenders in characters that go below the line, such as "y." Second, they specify the **leading** (pronounced "ledding"), which is the space between the descenders on one line and the ascenders on the following line. For normal printing, 10-point text with 2 points of leading are used. In simple word processors, this is simply called "12 point" type.

Width The second dimension of size is width. Width is not independent of height. Once height is specified, width is governed by the typeface and emphasis.

Although widths are normally measured in picas by typographers, most word processing programs use a different measure called **pitch.** Pitch is the number of characters per inch. Normal typewriters use "pica" type, which is a 10-pitch type (10 characters per inch horizontally). Elite typewriters use 12 pitch. Many printers have a condensed mode that gives around 16 pitch.

Pitch is useful for fixed-spaced typefaces, in which every character is printed with the same amount of space. However, some typefaces use **proportional spacing,** in which wide characters, such as "W" use more space than narrow characters, such as "i." For these typefaces, it can be difficult to estimate the number of characters that will be printed on a line.

Just as type height is divided into character height and leading in advanced word processing programs, character width in proportionally spaced typefaces is divided into two parts in advanced word processing program. First, there is the inherent width of each letter, with a "W" being wider than an "i." Then, there is spacing between adjacent pairs of letters. Most word processing programs put the same space between each letter pairs. Some, however, provide **kerning,** in which spacing is defined for each possible pair of letters. This produces spacing that is more pleasant to the eye.

Font Now that we have discussed the text characteristics commonly encountered by users, we are finally able to talk about the most misunderstood term in typography, **font.** Font, which is derived from "fountain," is a collection of characters in the same typeface, emphasis, and height. So bold 10-point Helvetica is a different font than italic 10-point Helvetica or bold 12-point Helvetica. Often, font is erroneously equated with typeface, but font also embraces the notions of emphasis and height.

Note that font specifies the actual characters that may be used. Some fonts with the same typeface, emphasis, and height have different numbers of characters. One may be very basic, while another may include special characters used in non-English languages and yet another may offer many math symbols.

Justification

Although it is important to control the design of individual characters, it is also important to control the positioning of lines of text on the page. Under the general heading of **justification,** there are four ways to position lines of text on a page.

- **Flush left**—all lines start at the left margin; the right edge of the text block is kept ragged. This is the normal way of doing printing.
- **Flush right**—all lines end exactly at the right margin; in this unusual positioning approach, the left edge of the text block is left ragged.
- **Justified** (sometimes called **fully justified**)—both the left and right edges of the text block are set flush with their margins. This is often done in books, magazines, and newspapers.
- **Centered**—the text is centered between the left and right margins.

Many users turn to full justification because it seems to give a professional look, but full justification leaves unsightly gaps between words unless the word processing system has proportional spacing and hyphenation and perhaps automatic kerning as well. These gaps between words harm readability to a substantial degree, and full justification should be avoided unless it can be done properly.

Figure 11-3 illustrates the basic components of a simple printed page. More complex page layout concepts will be discussed in later sections on advanced word processing programs and desktop publishing.

- The **body** of the document has the text of the document. This is the heart of the printed page.
- Along the four edges are the left, right, top, and bottom **margins,** where there is no text at all. This is called white space.
- **Headers** and **footers** lie just above and below the body of the document, within the left and right margins. The headers and footers contain information that repeats on each page, for instance, chapter titles. Special symbols in headers or footers usually allow the automatic numbering of pages.

Word processors must be able to control the size of margins and the size and contents of headers and footers. Word processors must also be able to specify the size of the page because not all printing is done on 8-½ by 11 inch paper.

In word processing, there is no standard way to specify page size, and left, top, and bottom margin at one time. To set the right margin, as well as some other information, however, most systems use the same approach—a **format line,** also called a **ruler line.** Figure 11-4 shows a typical format line.

- **Line spacing** controls whether the typing will be printed in single spacing, one and a half spacing, double spacing, triple spacing, or some other spacing between lines. In Figure 11-4, the "2" specifies double spacing.
- **Tab stops** are also set this way. There are often two different tab symbols: one for regular tabs, and another for decimal tabs.
- Finally, there is the **right margin.**

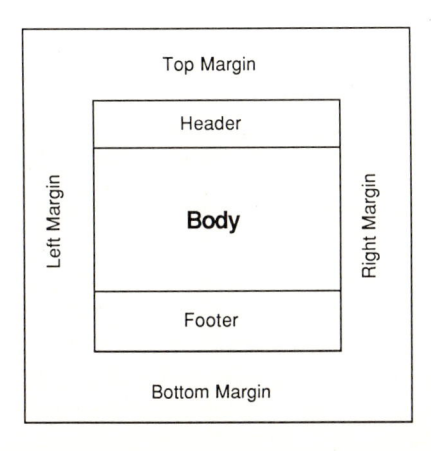

FIGURE 11-3 COMPONENTS OF A SIMPLE PRINTED PAGE

```
|2--->---->-------------------------<
      ↑    ↑                        ↑
      │    │ Tab stop
      │    └ Double spacing
      └ Right margin
```

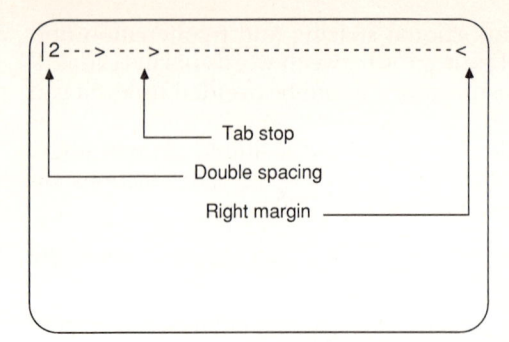

FIGURE 11-4 A FORMAT LINE IN WORD PROCESSING

When the user first creates a document, a format line automatically appears at the top of the screen. If the user does not want the standard settings, he or she can change them.

Later, the user may want to change the settings for part of the document. For instance, to enter a table, a user may have to change from double to single spacing and will almost certainly have to change tab stops. To do so, the user inserts a new format line and sets it as needed.

Editing

Composition and editing have always been viewed as two distinct phases. When authors do their initial composition online, however, the dividing line between the two phases disappears. Authors often pour over a difficult paragraph many times before going on, rewording phrases and sentences until the paragraph communicates its idea properly.

To assist authors and secretaries, word processing systems offer a variety of simple and advanced editing functions. Two of the simplest functions, insert and overstrike, allow the user to type new text in the middle of existing text.

- **Insert** inserts one or more characters at the point of the cursor, moving text following the cursor to the right, in order to make room for the inserted text. If the cursor comes between the C and D in "ABCDEF" and the user types "XX," the text becomes "ABCXXDEF."

- **Overstrike** lets what the user types replace characters already there. If the cursor comes between the C and D in "ABCDEF" and the user types "XX," the text becomes "ABCXXF." Many word processors have a key that toggles back and forth between insert and overstrike modes.

Equally important are functions to allow users to delete information already in the document.

- **Character delete** deletes the character above the cursor and moves the following text over to cover the gap. If the character delete key is held down, successive characters drop into the "black hole" over the cursor.

- **Block delete** allows the user to preview a deletion before it is done. In the first step, the user marks a block of text to be deleted, as shown in

Figure 11-5. After confirming visually that this is what should be deleted, the user gives the Delete command.

Block delete is usually only one of several **block operations** offered to users.

- **Block move** deletes the text but stores it in a special buffer. The user can then go to another part of the document, insert a cursor, and have the deleted text inserted at that point. Some programs allow the material in the buffer to be inserted in several different places.
- **Block copy** is similar to block move, except that the original material is not deleted.
- **External copy** allows the material in the buffer to be inserted in another document. External copy is particularly attractive if the word processing system allows two documents to be shown in different windows.

Printing

In the printing phase, the user cannot merely type "print" and have everything be automatic. Printing is a complex operation in which the user must specify many things.

- Paper size, top margin, bottom margin, left margin, pitch, and lines per inch.

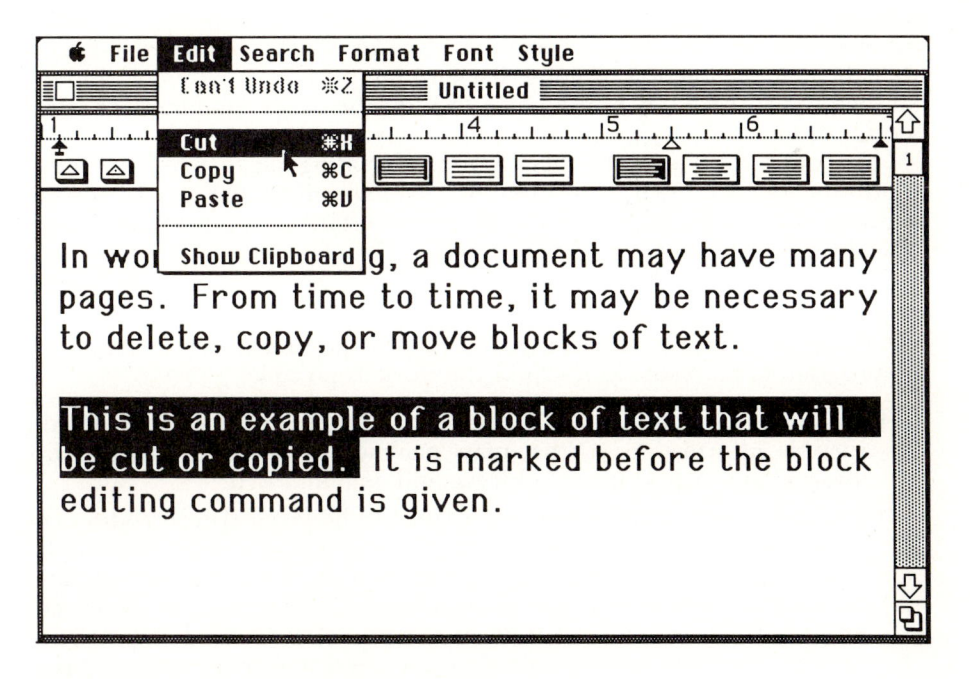

Note: This example is taken from MacDraw.

FIGURE 11-5 BLOCK EDITING

- The printer to be used. (Many programs have generalized output that must be converted to the codes of a particular printer through the use of a special conversion program.)
- What pages should be printed. (A printing job does not always start with the first page or end at the last.)
- Whether continuous forms or cut sheets of paper are to be used. (For cut sheets, the printer must be told to pause after each page, so that the user can insert a new page.)
- How many copies should be printed.
- In some cases, whether draft of final quality printing is desired.

A good word processing program will have a large number of printing options, but to avoid overloading the user with choices, it will provide defaults for all major settings. These defaults are in effect unless the user changes them. The user should be able to override these defaults at printing time and should also be able to modify the system defaults, in order to provide defaults in line with the user's normal working conditions.

After printing has begun, the user should be able to kill the printing, cause it to pause, or restart it after a pause. This will avoid the printing of output that the user realizes is wrong. It also allows the user to have the system pause so that new paper can be inserted.

Printing can be done either in the foreground or the background. In **foreground printing,** the user cannot work on the computer while a job is printing. The printing program takes over the machine completely. In **background printing,** the user can begin creating or editing another document while the first document is printing. Background printing is extremely important because foreground printing can lock up the user's computer for long periods of time.

In background printing, there is often a **printing queue,** that is, a group of printing jobs waiting for execution. If queuing is done, the user should be able to modify the queue by killing a job before it starts printing or modify the order in which documents will be printed.

Automated Operations

If the user has repetitive tasks, it should be possible to use functions of the program to automate as much of the work as possible.

- **Mail merge** functions allow form letters to be created and merged with variable information, so that mass mailing can be done with specific information such as name, address, and amount owed.
- **Prestored text recall** allows text strings to be given special codes. To create standardized documents such as contracts, the user can simply type the codes for standard paragraphs and have the system generate the contract or at least a draft to be edited to produce the final contract. Prestored text can also be used in general typing for salutations and closings, often-repeated technical phrases, and similar repetitive typing.
- **Embedded programming languages** allow users to automate a complex series of commands. The simplest ones merely record the keystrokes

made by the users and play them back verbatim. In contrast to prestored text playback, techniques specify command keystrokes as well as text keystrokes. More sophisticated embedded programming languages allow the program to pause for variable text entry, loop through a series of commands, or execute alternative blocks of commands on the basis of an IF/THEN/ELSE/ construction.

Import and Export

As discussed in Chapter 8, most word processing programs can input ASCII files. During importation, however, the program must guess what line endings should be word wrapped and which lines should be terminated in carriage returns. Extensive damage can result.

Little damage will result if spreadsheet or database data are imported either in the DIF file format (see Chapter 8) or in the native file formats of popular spreadsheet or data base programs.

For text, most programs can import word processing files from the native formats of popular word processing programs, but damage may occur because of differences in capabilities.

The cleanest text importing occurs when the IBM DCA standard (see Chapter 8) or an international text standard is used (see Chapter 17). A growing number of word processing programs can import files in these formats, and the importing tends to be very clean.

Most word processing programs can export files as simple ASCII files. For competitive reasons, however, few will export files into the native file formats of other popular word processing programs. A growing number can export files in the DCA format, so DCA is becoming a *lingua franca* for word processing. Eventually, international standards should supersede DCA, but international standards are still in the embryonic stage.

Advanced Formatting

Formatting is one of the key areas in which most advanced word processing programs excel. Advanced formatting is important to secretaries, who have a hard time dealing with such problems as multiple text columns on a page if they have only a standard word processor. Advanced formatting is also important to the many authors who take great pains with layout in order to maximize the communication impact of their documents.

Table Layout

Typing tabular materials is one of the biggest headaches for secretaries. Before the actual typing begins, the secretary must find the longest entry in each column and then add these lengths to decide how many spaces to put between columns.

The best word processing programs have table setup tools that ask the secretary for the number of columns and then instruct the secretary to type the longest entry in each column. The programs then insert a format line with appropriate tab settings.

Even standard word processing programs have the ability to do horizontal totals on rows of numbers and vertical totals on columns of numbers. Most also allow users to delete a whole column or move a column between two other columns. These capabilities are called **column math** and **column editing.**

Advanced WYSIWYG

In an ideal word processor, the text is displayed on the screen exactly as it will appear when printed. This is known as **WYSIWYG**—What You See Is What You Get. Standard word processors offer only limited WYSIWYG. They generally make only two guarantees.

- Lines end on the screen where they will end during printing.
- Pages end on the screen where they will end during printing.

Even this limited WYSIWYG is useful. It allows a great deal of editing to be done without constantly reprinting the document to check its layout. Some word processing programs use so many embedded formatting codes that these two minimal aspects of WYSIWYG are violated. These word processing programs cause endless problems if layout is important to the author.

Advanced programs with high-resolution graphics screens can provide much truer WYSIWYG than standard programs. Figure 11-2 illustrates such a program. When multiple type faces, sizes, pitches, and emphases are used, or when proportional spacing is used, advanced WYSIWYG is very important.

Multiple Columns

Newspapers, magazines, and other publications are generally printed with multiple text columns on each page. These are called **snaked text columns** because one column "snakes over" to the top of the next.

Another type of text column is the **bound text column** in which the user can jump horizontally across columns. For example, in a computer manual, there may be entries in the first column for each command name, with a corresponding description of command in the second text column. In contrast to a simple table, the text in the second column may go on for several lines. When creating such text, the user will type the entire entry for the first column, hit a special key, and then type the entire entry for the second column. The program will then line them up correctly. These columns are

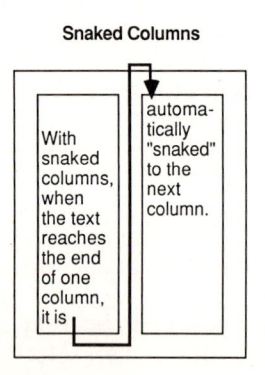

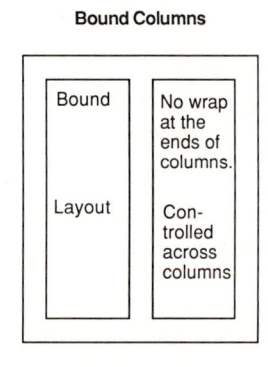

FIGURE 11-6 MULTIPLE TEXT COLUMNS

called "bound" because text does not spill over the bottom of the first column into the second column, as it does with snaked columns.

It is important to have both snaked and bound columns (see Figure 11-6). Snaked columns are needed for most kinds of multicolumn narrative prose, but there are many occasions when information in adjacent columns must match up precisely, for example, in manuals, teaching materials, and even simple table layout. For these applications, bound columns are crucial.

Style Sheets

In many corporations and departments, there are standards for creating certain types of documents. For example, consider the first page of a proposal. The company may have a **style sheet** specifying tabbing, centering, font, emphasis, and other layout characteristics.

Some advanced word processing programs allow standard style sheets to be defined. When beginning the first page of a proposal, the user can invoke the appropriate style sheet and begin typing, knowing that the standard layout will be followed exactly and that he or she will not have to stop constantly to change text styles and other settings.

Page Description Languages

The advent of very high-resolution output devices, especially the laser printer, has brought strong responses from software vendors.

One response has been the creation of **page description languages** (see Chapter 7) that require application software to encode text characteristics and other layout matters in a standard way. These page description languages then do the best job possible to match these formatting codes to the characteristics of the output device selected by the user. On a laser printer, for example, letters can be drawn with higher resolution than can be shown on the screen. Geometric images can also be printed with higher resolution than the display screen can show. The most popular page description language is PostScript.

Usually, the end user never sees the page description language. All interactions take place between the application program and the page description language. Some advanced users, however, use page description languages directly.

Graphics

Until recently, the only way to include graphics in a document was to leave several blank lines where the figure should go and paste the figure onto the printed output.

The blank lines were not usually inserted until the final printing because any editing done after inserting the blank lines could throw them across page boundaries. Unfortunately, few "final printings" are completely final, and even minor changes can force the user to look at every figure's space.

Some newer word processing programs allow a figure marker code to be inserted, telling how many blank lines to leave. If editing pushes half the figure over a page boundary, these programs do not split the blank lines across the pages. Instead, they put the figure entirely on one page or another, flowing the text around the figure to avoid leaving extra blank lines in the document. This is called **text flow**. It is rare but highly desirable.

More advanced programs even allow an entire graphics figure to be inserted into the body of the text, as shown in Figure 11-2. This produces a high degree of WYSIWYG. Many programs that do so, however, lack automatic text flow capabilities, spoiling much of the value of embedded graphics.

Author Aids

Other enhanced functions in advanced word processing programs are author aids, which are designed to help authors during the creation phase of document preparation.

Outlining

A number of programs allow authors to begin by creating an outline of their documents, then change the outline until it is satisfactory, and finally fill in the outline with text. Although any word processor can do basic outlining, special features are needed to move whole branches around easily and to allow users to telescope their view to see all levels or only some levels.

Outlining began with Stanford Research Institute's NLS in 1964, but it was rediscovered in the PC world by ThinkTank by Living Videotex. PC outlining programs were originally stand-alone programs, but these functions are now being added to several advanced word processing programs.

Revision Aids

After an author creates a first draft, he or she needs to proofread the document for typographical, spelling, grammar, and stylistic errors, and then revise the document to communicate better.

Spelling checkers scan the document for typographical and spelling errors. These programs work by comparing each word to a dictionary, so if a user types "grown" instead of "brown," no error will be detected. These programs do not completely eliminate proofreading. Spelling checking functions vary remarkably in speed and in the number of user-specific words (such as "EUC") that can be added to their basic dictionary.

Most spelling checkers are run on a document after a draft is completed. Some, however, allow the user to spell check a single word or a portion of a document. This flexibility is more important to authors than to secretaries. Some even spell check each word as the user types. These, however, can break the flow of thought.

Once a word is highlighted as a potential misspelling, the user is normally given a list of possible corrections. The user can then choose one of these, make his or her own change, add the word to the dictionary, or just leave it alone and go on to the next highlighted word.

Some advanced programs also offer a **thesaurus,** which give synonyms and antonyms. This is also an author-oriented aid, allowing the writer to avoid repetition and select the most precise word to express a particular thought.

Some advanced programs even offer limited **grammar checking,** to catch obvious grammatical errors and **style checking** to suggest stylistic changes—such as avoiding pompous terms, for instance, "utilize," and to change passive voice to active voice.

Some advanced programs offer **readability analysis** that rate the readability of a document or section by scholastic grade levels. Originally created because many states have laws governing the readability of insurance and other financial contracts, these functions can now flag troublesome documents or sections in a document.

Other Useful Features

If a document has many numbered footnotes, references, figures, or tables, numbering them can be a major chore. In addition, they may have to be renumbered after edits have been made. A number of advanced programs can do this numbering or renumbering automatically, although this is usually done in batch mode instead of on the fly.

A related set of needs is the creation of tables of contents and indices. Some programs provide automatic section numbering along with the automatic generation of tables of contents. The automatic generation of an index is another advanced feature.

Word Processing in Perspective

Word processing is not only better than it was when it first came to personal computers. It is also more diverse, ranging from personal programs and standard programs to advanced programs and desktop publishing. Many firms have tried to cope with this diversity by providing several standards in different functionality categories. To do so without a clear process for exchanging files quickly and easily, however, is to risk creating a Tower of Babel in which managers with personal programs have to do all of their own fine editing, simply because the secretary's word processing program cannot read their data files.

High-end programs, including advanced word processing programs and desktop publishing programs, raise new issues in user training. Informal training that consists of merely learning from other users or reading tutorials was never satisfactory for standard word processing programs. For high-end programs, informal learning will leave the user with a crippled understanding that will effectively negate the value of advanced features. In addition, high-end programs allow users to impose stylistic elements on their text and page layouts. In most cases, users are ill-equipped to deal with these style issues adequately. Training for high-end programs must involve such "good practice" issues as page layout and the effective use of changes in text characteristics.

CONCEPTUAL GRAPHICS

Basic Distinctions

Analytical Versus Conceptual Graphics

As noted in Chapter 1 and at the start of this chapter, there is a fundamental distinction between analytical graphics and conceptual graphics.

- **Analytical graphics** is used to summarize patterns in large collections of

numbers. Analytical graphics includes pie charts, bar charts, line charts, and other ways of representing data.
- **Conceptual graphics** is used to represent *concepts and relationships among concepts.* In this book and most others, virtually all figures are examples of conceptual graphics.

Initially, analytical graphics was the only common form of graphics in personal computing. Lotus 1-2-3 and other spreadsheet programs popularized analytical graphics in the early 1980s. Even if a user did not have a graphics display, he or she could still create a chart in 1-2-3 and print it on a dot matrix printer. Although it was convenient to be able to preview a chart on-screen, it was not essential, and even low-resolution CGA display systems (see Chapter 7) were good enough for previewing.

For conceptual graphics, on-screen viewing is absolutely necessary for work of any complexity, and high-resolution display systems are needed to create conceptual graphs with multiple elements. It was several years before high-resolution displays became sufficiently inexpensive for most people to use; therefore, conceptual graphics did not begin to grow until long after analytical graphics.

Normal Versus Presentation Quality

When graphics applications first appeared, the dot matrix printer was the only viable option for output. Rather quickly, however, some vendors began to produce output devices with much higher quality. Pen plotters with multiple colors (see Chapter 7), cameras that could take pictures of displays and produce 35 mm slides, and several other devices produced output so good that a new term, **presentation quality,** was coined to describe their output. The name implied that their output was good enough for formal presentations to senior management or outside clients.

Today, the term "presentation quality" is becoming less and less meaningful as the range of output devices broadens. Laser printers, phototypesetting machines, and other ultrahigh-quality output devices are raising the top end, and, at the low end, there are debates over whether output devices originally called presentation quality still merit that name. In the long run, "presentation quality" is likely to become a meaningless term, but, at least for now, the distinction between normal quality and presentation quality is still a valuable one.

Pixel Versus Object Graphics Software

A conceptual image may consist of two kinds of shapes.

- **Objects** are basic geometric shapes, such as lines, arrows, circles, and rectangles. Each object can be represented with a few simple parameters such as point of origin and a radius. In addition, lines and outlines have thicknesses, and enclosed spaces can have color and shading.
- **Pixel images** are drawn from individual pixels (see Chapter 7) and are not restricted to simple geometric forms. They can do any free-hand

drawing, including wavy lines drawn by pencils or paint brushes. Pixel images are described by the locations of all their pixels.

Advantages of Pixel Graphics Software

The main advantage of pixel graphics software is its ability to draw freeform images while retaining the ability to draw such elementary shapes as lines and squares. Pixel graphics software is general-purpose software.

A second advantage of pixel graphics software is that the user can edit individual pixels, achieving very fine editing. The precision provided by pixel editing is unmatched in object graphics programs, although most object graphics programs have a limited "closeup" mode for drawing very small objects.

Advantages of Object Graphics Software

As discussed in Chapter 7, object graphics software uses a great deal less memory than pixel graphics software. A circle can be represented with only a few bytes of internal memory or disk storage, and even complex figures usually need less than 5 KB of memory. In contrast, a pixel graphics page of comparable complexity will require 15 KB to 50 KB.

A second advantage of object graphics software is that the individual objects such as circles do not lose their identity by being turned into separate bits. As a result, a circle can be manipulated after it is created. It can be moved, expanded, or filled in with some pattern—even if it overlaps another object. This is impossible to do in pixel graphics software. In pixel graphics software, once a shape overlaps other shapes there is no way to manipulate it, except by manipulating individual bits. In addition, object graphics programs allow related elements to be **grouped** so that they can be manipulated as a single unit. If a car is drawn as a collection of grouped elements, then the car can be moved around or even shrunk or expanded.

The third and by far the biggest advantage of objects graphics software makes itself felt during printing. Object graphics programs can take advantage of the full resolution of the output device because they can map basic objects into whatever resolution the printer supports. So a conceptual graphics page printed on a laser page printer will be dramatically better than a conceptual graphics image printed on a dot matrix printer. As output technology improves further, object graphics images will continue to improve. For pixel graphics software, however, output usually looks only slightly better on laser page printers than it does on dot matrix printers.

Hybrid Programs

Overall, pixel graphics software gives freedom of expression and pixel-by-pixel editing, whereas object graphics software is better at almost everything else. A few software vendors are beginning to produce programs that combine the best of both worlds. These hybrid programs provide two sets of tools—one for object drawing and another for pixel drawing. The first of these tools was Superpaint on the Macintosh, but it will be followed by many others. These **hybrid pixel—object graphics** programs are likely to dominate the market in the future.

> **MACPAINT AND MACWRITE: TWO CLOSEUPS**
>
> Conceptual graphics is one of the newest and least understood computer applications. To help the reader understand the implications of conceptual graphics and the difference between pixel graphics programs and object graphics programs, we will take a closeup look at the first major pixel and object graphics programs, MacPaint and MacDraw on the Macintosh.

MacPaint, a Pixel Graphics Software Program

MacPaint is the classic example of pixel graphics software. MacPaint was bundled with every Macintosh when that computer was first introduced, and this practice continued until the introduction of the Macintosh Plus. Today, there are many pixel graphics programs for the Macintosh and the IBM PC and compatibles. Although most offer improvements over MacPaint, MacPaint illustrates the basic principles found in nearly all pixel graphics programs.

The Initial Screen

Figure 11-7 illustrates the initial screen in MacPaint. Five areas of the screen are marked in this figure.

1. The **tool palette** offers 20 tools for creating or modifying images. The paint brush, shown in reverse video, is the default selection. Other tools can be selected by moving the mouse pointer to the proper tool icon and clicking the mouse button.

2. The **line width palette** selects the width of lines and outlines for enclosed figures such as boxes and ellipses. The selected line width is marked with a check mark.

3. The **pattern palette** has 38 patterns for filling in enclosed areas. At the far left of the pattern palette is a large box showing the "current pattern." Initially, this is a solid black pattern.

4. The **drawing window** is the user's drawing area. Although the entire **canvas** is a normal-size sheet of paper, the drawing window shows only about a quarter of the canvas at any time. The drawing window can be moved to show and work on other parts of the canvas.

5. The **menu bar** has pop-down menus to specify how text will be represented and to make other important choices.

Figure 10-7, by the way, was created with MacPaint. First, a "snapshot" was made of the screen, by hitting <Command><Shift><3>. This combination caused a pixel screen image of any normal Macintosh window to be saved on the internal disk as a MacPaint canvas. Then, the saved image was modified to add explanatory text. The title, numbers, and notes were created with the text tool, and lines were drawn with the line tool. The arrows were drawn

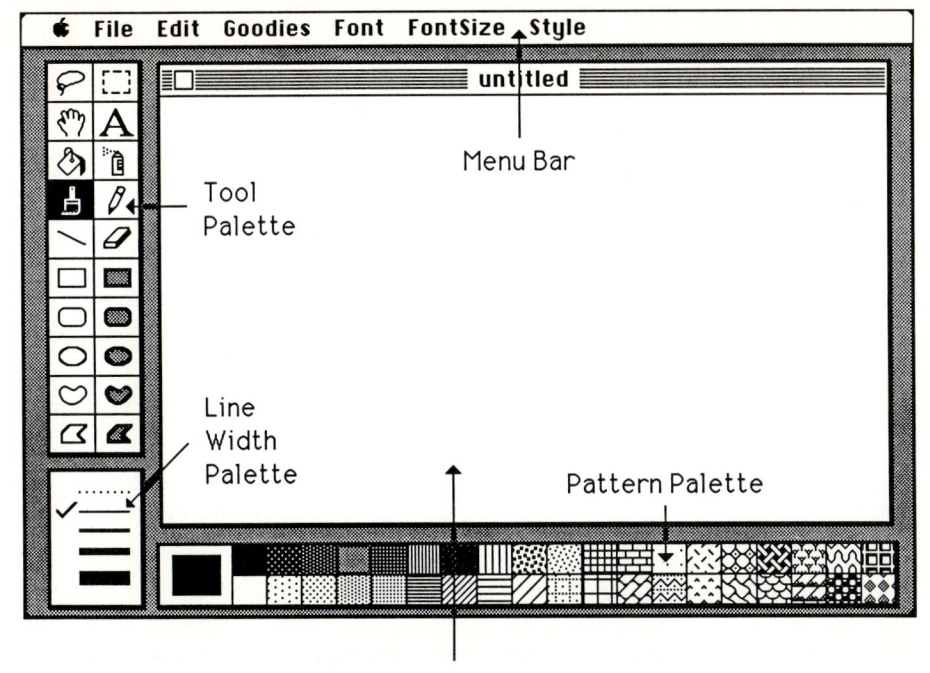

CONCEPTUAL GRAPHICS **487**

FIGURE 11-7 INITIAL SCREEN IN MACPAINT

with a pixel editing capability called "Fat Bits," which is discussed later in this chapter.

The Text Tool

Although MacPaint is geared toward the creation of visual images instead of text, its text tool is rich. The user may select a number of text attributes through the menu. (These characteristics were described earlier in the chapter and are only summarized here.)

- **Font** selects the type face.
- **Fontsize** sets the height of the letters. As discussed earlier, in the word processing section, height is measured in "points," with 72 points to the inch.
- **Style** involves two considerations. One is whether the text should be right justified, centered, or left justified, relative to the location of the cursor. The other is whether the text will be plain (standard) or whether it will be shown enboldened, italicized, underlined, outlined, or shadowed.

The text tool is not a full word processing tool. If multiple lines are typed, there is only single spacing. In addition, there is no word wrap. If the user types beyond the right edge of the drawing window, the text is lost; if a user types below the bottom edge of the drawing window, the text is lost. Several other limitations apply, for instance, the fact that one cannot change the size or style of a single word in the midst of typing.

Free-Form Drawing Tools

MacPaint has a number of free-form drawing tools.

- The **paint brush** paints a swath of paint whose width is governed by the line width palette. The paint brush is the default tool upon entering MacPaint, a fact that testifies to its importance.
- The **pencil** draws a curved line one pixel wide.
- The **spray paint** tool sprays "paint" on the surface in a spattered pattern. It is primarily used for shading and other special effects.

These free-form tools allow creative expression and permit almost any picture to be drawn. The primary limitation is the user's skill in moving the mouse.

Shape-Drawing Tools

Many drawings need rectangles, squares, circles, lines, and other shapes that can be drawn by shape-drawing tools. MacPaint can draw these objects, but only as collections of pixels. In contrast to the shapes drawn in object graphics programs, however, these shapes look no better on high-resolution printers than they do on-screen.

MacPaint offers a number of shape drawing tools. In all of them, the user selects a starting point (for example, the upper left-hand corner of a rectangle), and then selects an ending point (the opposite corner of the rectangle). MacPaint dynamically enlarges the object as the user moves to the ending point. When the ending point is reached, the figure is locked in.

- The **line** is a single line connecting the starting and ending points. If the <Shift> key is held down, the line is restricted to the horizontal, vertical, or 45 degree direction.
- The **box** (rectangle) is painted with an outline thickness governed by the line width palette. There are two box tools: the empty box is not filled in; and the filled box is filled with the current pattern in the pattern palette. Holding down the shift key restricts the box to being a square.
- The **oval** (ellipse) is also painted with an outline thickness governed by the line width palette. There are two oval tools: the open oval and the filled oval. Holding down <Shift> restricts the oval to being a circle.
- The **free-form curve** allows a free-form curve to be painted, as with a paint brush tool. However, if the filled free-form curve tool is selected, any enclosed area will be filled with the current pattern.
- The **polygon** tool draws a series of straight-line segments. Each time the user clicks the mouse, the current straight-line segment is locked in and another segment begins from the click point. If the filled polygon tool is selected, any enclosed area is filled with the current pattern.

CONCEPTUAL GRAPHICS **489**

Layout Tools

The drawing window normally shows about one-quarter of the full canvas. The **grabber** tool (which looks like a hand) allows the drawing window to be moved. The grabber effectively grabs the canvas and slides it around under the drawing window, so that a different part of the canvas shows.

The grabber is fine when you only need to shift the canvas a little bit under the drawing window, but for larger movement, the user selects **show page** from the "Goodies" menu. As shown in Figure 11-8, the user then sees the entire page (canvas) in reduced size. The current position of the drawing window is shown. In "Show Page," the user can take two actions.

- If the cursor is placed in the drawing window and dragged, the position of the drawing window is moved to another location on the canvas.
- If the cursor is placed anywhere else on the canvas and dragged, all images are dragged around on the canvas in the same direction. This allows the user to center the images on the canvas.

"Show Page" shows the entire canvas and the drawing window. The drawing window can be shifted. The entire image on the canvas can also be shifted.

FIGURE 11-8 FULL PAGE IN MACPAINT

Although "Show Page" gives a reduced picture of the entire canvas, at the other extreme **fat bits** blow up a very small section of the canvas. As shown in Figure 11-9, "Fat Bits" shows individual pixels. This allows the very fine editing needed to clean up pictures, for example, to make sure that a line running into a second line stops exactly at the second line. In addition, small arrows and other small designs can be created in fat bits. Most tools work in Fat Bits. The most commonly used tool, the pencil, changes individual pixels from black to white or white to black.

Editing Tools

"Fat Bits" is both a layout tool and an editing tool for very fine changes. MacPaint offers many other editing tools beginning with the **Undo** option under the edit menu. If the user creates a paint brush stroke, rectangle, or any other one-action image, the Undo command erases it. This allows the user to experiment with the assurance that things that do not work out can be easily erased. Undo also undoes most subsequent editing actions.

Most other editing actions require the user first to select the part of the canvas to be edited. There are two tools for making this selection.

- The **selection rectangle** allows the user to draw a box selecting a rectangular area.

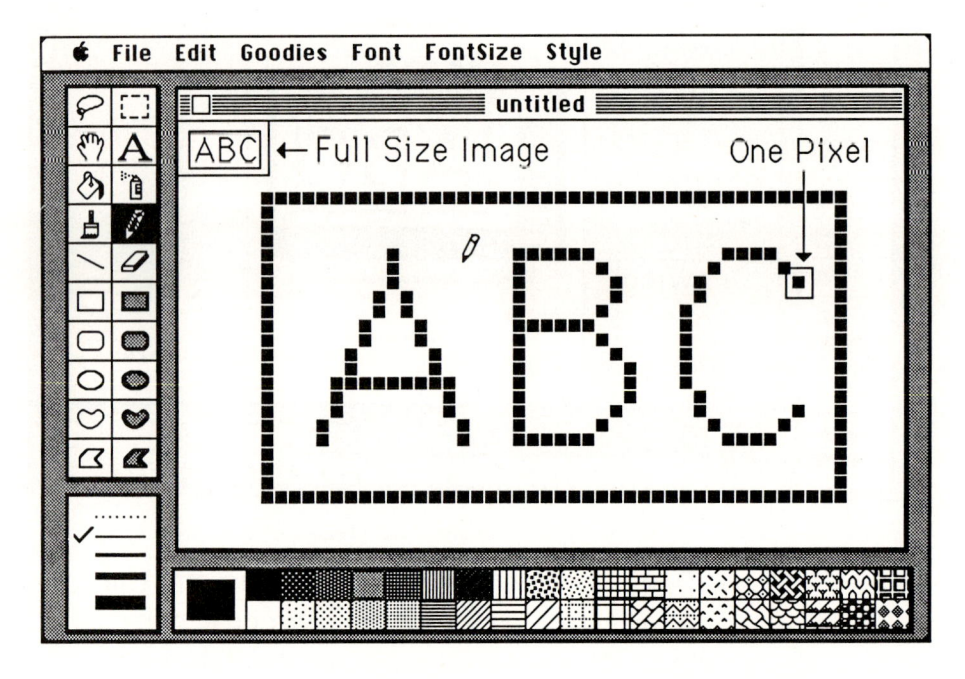

In "Fat Bits," individual pixels can be edited.
FIGURE 11-9 FAT BITS

- The **lasso** allows the user to draw a closed loop. When the user lets up on the mouse button, the lasso "tightens up" until it just encloses any irregular image of dark pixels against a white background. This allows an object to be picked up very precisely, without any background.

Once a section of the canvas has been selected, it can be edited in several ways. First, if the user moves the cursor into the selected area and then drags the cursor, the image will move. This allows the user to reposition the image to another location.

If the user holds down the **Option** key while moving the cursor, the original image is left in place, and a copy is moved to the new location. This allows the user, say, to create one picture of a terminal and make many copies to illustrate a system with many terminals.

From the Edit menu, a user can also **cut** or **copy** the selected area. Both create a copy of the area in the Macintosh **clipboard** file, but cut deletes the original while copy leaves the original intact. Once the image is in the clipboard file, it can be **pasted** in another location. Because pasting does not destroy the contents of the clipboard file, the image can be pasted many times. A related command, **clear,** is like cut but does not copy the image into the clipboard file.

It is even possible to save the current MacPaint file, open a second file, and paste the image stored in the clipboard into the second image. It is even possible to leave MacPaint, enter another program, for example, MacWrite, and paste the image into a MacWrite document.

The clipboard file can hold only a single image, but the Macintosh's **scrapbook** file can have many MacPaint images pasted into it. This allows many images to be transferred among Macintosh programs.

If the selection is done through the selection rectangle, a number of other editing operations come into play. To give just one example, the image can be rotated through successive 90 degree angles or even flipped end for end, horizontally or vertically.

Add-On Products

MacPaint was such a stunning product that it created a subindustry of add-on products for MacPaint users.

The most common products have been **clip art** disks containing dozens for pre-drawn MacPaint images. These allow even people with comparatively little drawing skills to produce nice-looking output. Clip art products are produced by a number of companies. Figure 11-10 shows a typical clip art page.

In addition to clip art, a number of companies provide software products that extend the capabilities of MacPaint. An example is T/Maker's Click Art Effects, which can rotate images by any number of degrees instead of just 90 degrees, among other effects. Many newer pixel graphics programs now incorporate such advanced effects as part of their basic functions.

Conclusion

Overall, MacPaint offers a versatile and powerful set of functions to help users create excellent free-form graphics. Newer pixel graphics programs

FIGURE 11-10 A CLIP ART PAGE

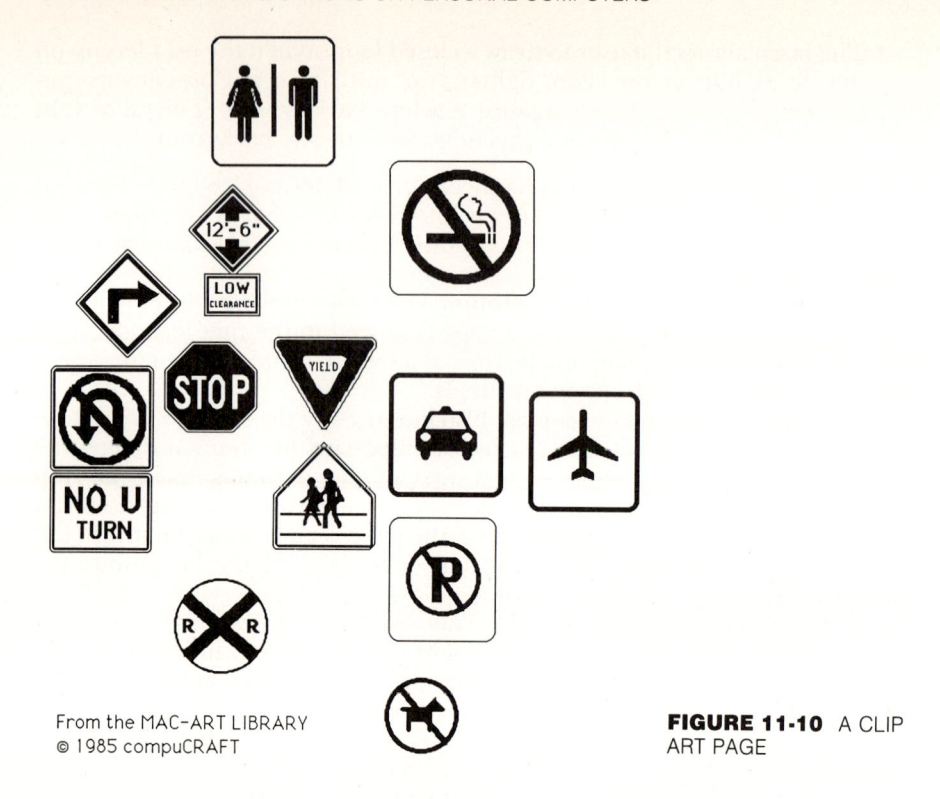

From the MAC-ART LIBRARY
© 1985 compuCRAFT

have gone far beyond MacPaint, although few introduce major new principles for pixel graphics. The only critical limitation of MacPaint, which is shared by most other pixel graphics programs, is that MacPaint cannot use the very high-resolution laser output devices effectively to improve the quality of its images.

MacDraw, an Object Graphics Program

When Apple developed MacPaint, it also developed an object graphics program, MacDraw. Because MacDraw was not packaged with every Macintosh sold, it did not become as popular as MacPaint, but many MacPaint users soon "graduated" to MacDraw, especially after Apple introduced the LaserWriter printer, which could produce high-resolution output from MacDraw files. Many users found that a high percentage of their graphics needs could be handled by an object-oriented program.

The Initial Screen

Figure 11-11 shows a basic screen in MacDraw. This figure is a few steps beyond the initial image that the user first sees upon entering MacDraw. A few objects have already been drawn, showing how objects can overlap. One object, a box, is marked with dots; these are used to move or resize the object, as discussed below.

CONCEPTUAL GRAPHICS **493**

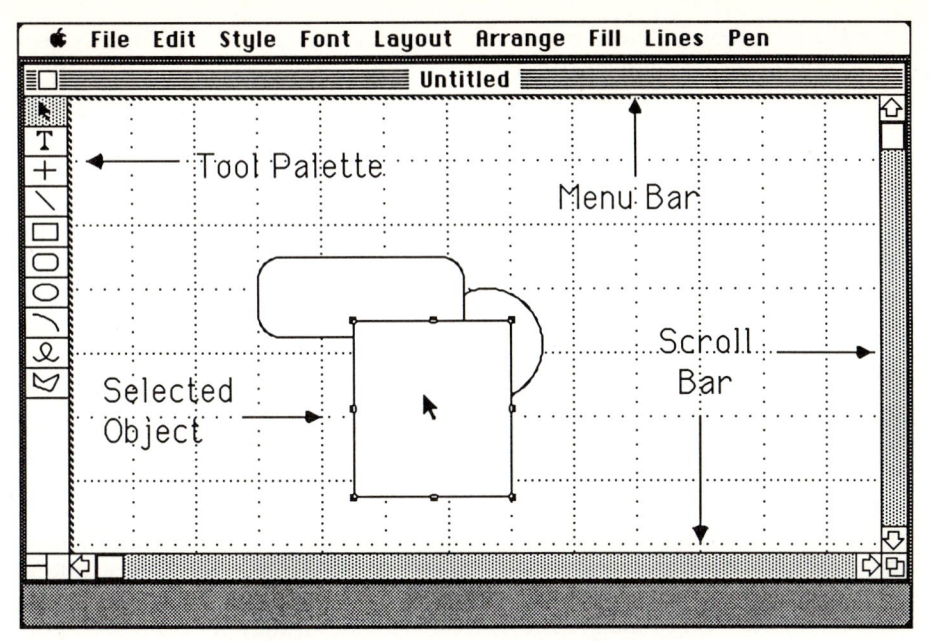

FIGURE 11-11 A BASIC SCREEN IN MACDRAW

On the left side of the screen in a **tool palette.** This palette is smaller than the tool palette in MacPaint. First, MacDraw offers fewer tools than MacPaint. Second, there is no distinction between such things as filled objects and empty objects. Objects that can be filled are filled by the "Fill" menu choice.

At the bottom and right edges of the screen are **scroll bars.** These are standard window scroll bars for Macintosh windows, and any user familiar with the Macintosh will immediately know how to move the drawing window around on the underlying full-page canvas.

Object Drawing Tools

MacDraw has all the basic object drawing tools of MacPaint, including the line, the box, the rounded box, the oval, and the polygon made from straight lines. In addition, it has a curved line (the third object from the bottom), whose curvature can be adjusted after its two end points have been set.

Although these are by and large the same object tools found in Mac-Paint, they are much more flexible in MacDraw. First, although a new object is automatically placed over existing objects, the "Arrange" menu selection allows the user to place a new object behind older objects. In other words, the user has control over what object overlaps what other objects.

As shown in Figure 11-11, any object can be **selected** after it is created. The selection tool is the arrow tool at the top of the tool palette. Once a tool is selected, it can be acted on in three basic ways.

- If the cursor is placed inside the dots marking the object's limits, dragging the mouse moves the object to another location.
- If the cursor is placed on one of the dots, dragging the cursor will change the size of the box in that direction.
- Third, after selection, the user can use the "Edit" menu choice to (1) cut it, (2) copy it, (3) clear it (erase it without placing it in the clipboard), (4) duplicate it, or (5) paste it in another location. Clearing can also be done simply by hitting backspace. If an object is duplicated and moved horizontally or vertically, duplicating it again places another copy an equal interval beyond the first.

The line tool is particularly interesting. The "Lines" menu choice not only controls the width of the line; it also allows the user to add an arrow or arrows pointing to the starting point, the ending point, both, or (in the default) neither.

Because MacDraw lacks anything like "Fat Bits" in MacPaint, MacDraw needs a different way to be sure that objects that should just meet actually do so, without one going slightly past another or not quite up to another. This is accomplished through the grid lines shown as dots in the drawing window. Unless alignment to the grid is turned off (through the "Arrange" menu choice), objects tend to snap to the nearest grid lines if they are close to it. This allows very precise positioning.

Free-Form Drawing Tools

MacDraw, being object-oriented, is poor at free-form drawing. It has only one free-form tool, the **free-form line** that is the second tool from the bottom. This tool draws a free-form line whose width is determined by the "Lines" menu choice.

In contrast to pixel images created with free-form tools in MacPaint through the paintbrush and pencil tools, the free-form tool in MacDraw actually creates an object. The object never loses its identity. It can always be selected and acted on by other tools, even if it overlaps other objects.

MacDraw has nothing like the spray paint tool to do shading, but the "Fill" menu choice allows the user to shade an enclosed area with any pattern. This can be effective with both object tools and free-form drawing tools.

The Text Tool

The text tool has all of the basic options found in MacPaint, including the choice of font, size, left/center/right justification, and special characteristics such as underlining and italics, but these are only the start of MacDraw's text drawing functions.

The text tool in MacDraw is much closer to being a true word processor that is the comparable tool in MacPaint. The user can set line spacing at single spacing, 1½ spacing, and double spacing. Because text is often used for titles and captions, the user can even specify that everything will be in upper case, lower case, or capitalized as a title. In addition, because each text item is an object, the text can be moved around on the canvas and even resized.

Finally, like all objects, text objects can be printed with very high resolution in MacDraw. Although MacPaint text looks grainy on laser printers,

MacDraw can use the full resolution of laser printers to produce text of outstanding quality.

Layout Tools

Because page layout is so important, MacDraw has a rich set of options under the "Layout" menu choice. The "Show Rulers" subchoice allows the user to display rulers along the top and left edges of the drawing window. As the cursor is moved around on the canvas, small markers move along the rulers, so the user can always tell the exact position of the cursor on the canvas to within a fraction of an inch. These rulers can be turned off and on again at will, and it is even possible to build customized rulers.

The "Reduce" suboption allows the user to see a reduced image of the canvas through the drawing window, so that more of the canvas shows. There is also a "Reduce to fit" option that shows the entire canvas at once. These seem to be extensions of the MacPaint "Show Page," but in MacDraw, almost all tools continue to work, so that full-canvas editing is possible. Once some degree of reduction has been made, the "Enlarge" and "Normal Size" options appear.

Newer object graphics programs such as GEM Draw even allow the user to enlarge from the basic image, giving several degrees of close-up capability roughly comparable to Fat Bits in MacPaint. Although MacDraw does not support flexible enlargement, the "File" menu choice allows the user to specify reductions in printing size when the page is printed.

MacDraw also allows users to specify aspects of the page other than reduction. Normally, a MacDraw image is output on a vertical sheet of 8½ by 11 inch paper. Under the "File" menu option, however, the user can specify European A4 paper and even sideways printing. The user can also specify larger page sizes, so that an object can be enlarged to print on several standard sheets of paper that can be taped together to produce a poster-size image.

Arrangement Functions

Objects can be arranged separately by choosing the selection tool and then manipulating the object with cursor movements or options under the "Edit" menu choice. The "layout" menu choice provides ways to arrange several objects together.

Earlier, we described the "Send to back" option that sends an object behind others. "Layout" also allows an object to be sent to the front, and it permits the user to paste from the clipboard either in front of other objects or behind other objects. In addition, it allows an object to be rotated left (counterclockwise), rotated right, flipped horizontally, or flipped vertically.

The user can group several objects by selecting the first and then selecting others while holding down the Shift key at each mouse click. Once several objects are selected, they are "grouped," so that in the future they can be moved, flipped, and generally acted upon as a single option. MacDraw remembers their individuality, however, and allows a grouped object to be ungrouped later.

Finally, "Arrange" allows items to be locked on the canvas so that they cannot be moved (unlocking later is possible), and several selected objects can be aligned to either the grid or other objects. Alignment to other objects allows several objects (for example, boxes in an organization chart) to be aligned vertically or horizontally for a uniform look.

Conclusion

Although MacDraw lacks the ability to produce free-form objects easily, figures that consist of text, lines, arrows, boxes, and ovals can be produced much more powerfully in MacDraw. In addition, these objects can be output using the full resolution of high-resolution output devices such as laser printers, or even ultrahigh photocomposition output devices.

DESKTOP PUBLISHING

Beyond Word Processing

The Limitations of Word Processing Programs

The first word processing programs followed the model of typewriter output, with each page consisting of a series of lines of straight text. Furthermore, the text on a page typically had only one font, style, and size.

In those early systems, graphics was not handled at all. If a user wanted to insert a half-page figure, he or she had to leave an appropriate number of blank lines in an appropriate place, then print the document and manually paste a picture onto the printed sheet. This was tedious, of course. In addition, even the smallest edits tended to move the blank space enough to straddle a page boundary. So after every edit, every graphics space in the document had to be examined and readjusted if necessary.

As discussed earlier in this chapter, many newer word processors have become much more ambitious. With page printers (see Chapter 7), almost all word processors can handle multifont, multisize, multistyle, and proportionally spaced text, giving a level of quality that looks close to typeset. Although these capabilities had been used occasionally with dot matrix printers, the low quality of dot matrix printers produced unattractive output.

Some newer word processors can also handle embedded graphics images. These images are normally imported from graphics programs—either those from the word processing vendor or third parties. In the best of these systems, whenever text is changed, the words **reflow** around the graphics figures, so that no manual repositioning is needed. This automatic reflow, however, is far from universal.

Page Layout

Although these changes have brought startling advances, even today's best word processors are still weak in the critical area of **page layout,** in which text, graphics, and demarcation objects are laid out in specific areas of each page. Extensive page layout capabilities are needed to bring computers into the world of newspapers, magazines, books, excellent technical documentation, and even corporate newsletters.

The only way to produce such complex documents when PCs first came out was to create the document in a word processing program, embed endless numbers of "format codes" such as .LM15.TR12 (for left margin 15 and Times Roman 12 point text), and then ship the document to a typesetting service to get a printed proof to guide the next round of editing changes. This process was obviously cumbersome, slow, and generally unsatisfactory.

Beginning in 1985, new PC programs began tackling the page layout problem aggressively, by showing users the page layout on-screen, exactly as it would look when printed. These programs allowed interactive editing, so that the results of changes could be seen immediately. Paul Brainerd of the Aldus Corporation coined the term **desktop publishing** to describe these programs in 1986, when his company introduced the first major program in this arena, PageMaker.

Desktop publishing programs first appeared for the graphics-oriented Macintosh with its fast microprocessor, but they soon began to appear for high-end IBM PCs as well. Desktop publishing quickly generated more excitement than the PC industry had seen since its earliest days. Although no one could precisely tie down a definition of this new field, everybody wanted to jump into it with both feet.

Desktop Publishing Versus Word Processing

From what we have seen so far, it follows that desktop publishing is differentiated from traditional word processing in four ways. These four distinctions serve to define desktop publishing.

1. Desktop publishing programs offer extremely sophisticated page layout features. The screen becomes a paste-up board, on which the user can lay out columns, headlines, ruler lines, and other page characteristics.
2. Desktop publishing programs can import text from a variety of word processing programs. After importing the text, they can change the characteristics of the text and its alignment.
3. Desktop publishing programs can import graphics images from a variety of graphics programs. After importing the graphics, they can at least crop the image and may be able to do more active processing.
4. Desktop publishing programs can print their work on high-quality output devices.

Desktop Publishing Software

A desktop publishing system has several major components. The first is the desktop publishing program itself, such as PageMaker, Ventura Publisher, or ReadySetGo. These programs cost $200 to $7000 and vary greatly in page layout sophistication, maximum document size, processing speed, and other important characteristics.

The Computer

The second component of a desktop publishing system is the computer. Because of the intensive processing done by desktop publishing software, a Macintosh or IBM PC AT class machine is an absolute minimum, and even these machines are somewhat underpowered for the task.

On an IBM PC, either a Hercules Graphics Board and a monochrome monitor or an enhanced graphics adapter and an enhanced color display (see Chapter 7) are absolute requirements. Large-screen displays that let the user see a full page of text in full size (Chapter 7) are highly desirable but too expensive for most users. Even for the Macintosh, large-screen displays that show an entire page of text are highly desirable additions to the Macintosh's graphics capabilities.

The Printer

The third piece of technology is the page printer, which is usually a laser printer. As noted in Chapter 7 and earlier in this chapter, desktop publishing requires a page printer with built-in page description language hardware that can take image information from the PC and flesh it out to make maximum use of its screen resolution. Without page description language hardware (and software) built into the printer, desktop publishing systems slow to a crawl because of the heavy burdens placed on the PC, and a great deal of image quality is usually lost as well.

For high-quality printing, users can send their final documents to a typesetting service for printing on 1000 ppi by 1000 ppi typesetting machines that not only give high resolution but also much darker images than most page printers. These are the same machines that professional publishing companies use.

The Future

In today's entry-level desktop publishing systems, the biggest disappointment for most users is speed. Layout processing is extremely complex, so a very fast processor is needed to give adequate speed. In addition, a full page of text can have a megabyte of pixel codes. Therefore, graphics processing requires vast memory, as well as extensive processing power to manipulate these pixels. Even with good software, an AT–Macintosh class processor, and a page printer with a built-in page description language processor, a desktop publishing system takes far longer to print each page than a conventional word processor. As Intel 80386-based PCs and Motorola MC68020-based PCs become more popular, many of these speed problems will be dispelled, but for the many users who cringe at the cost of desktop publishing on even today's PCs, acceptable processing speeds may still be several years away.

If a company wants to move beyond PCs, a number of vendors have desktop photocomposition systems that use more expensive computers, large-screen displays, and more sophisticated software than PC-based systems. As the cost differential becomes smaller between these systems and PC desktop publishing systems, high-end user choices should abound.

Page Layout

Basic Elements

Figure 11-12 shows the basic elements of a laid-out page. As shown in this figure, which illustrates page layout in ReadySetGo, a laid-out page consists of several types of **blocks,** each holding a different kind of information.

DESKTOP PUBLISHING **499**

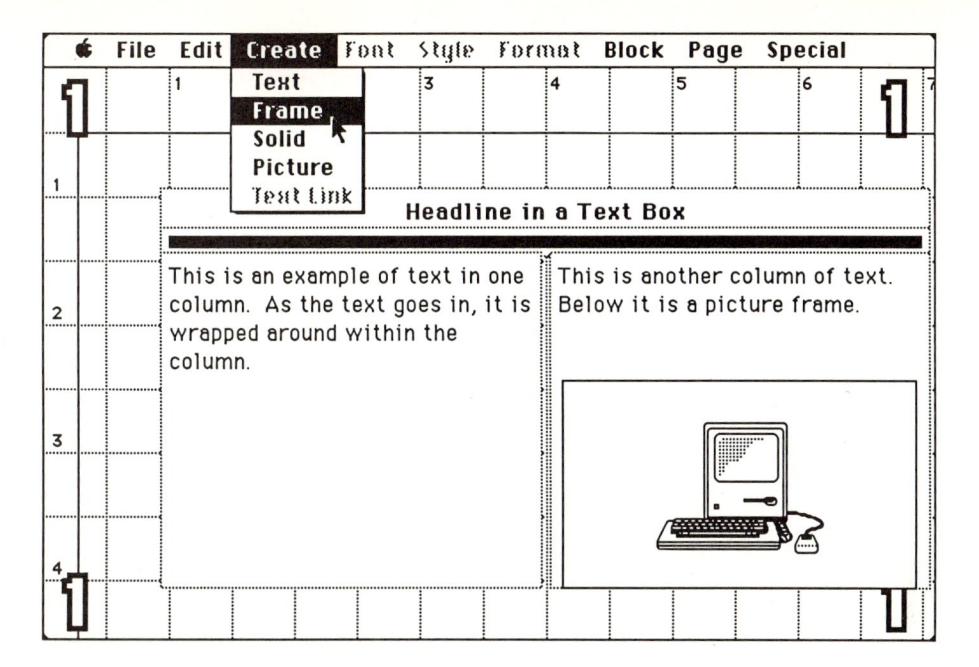

Note: This example is taken from Ready,Set,Go.

FIGURE 11-12 A LAID-OUT PAGE

Text Blocks Hold lines of text, essentially like minipages in a classical word processor.

Graphics Blocks Hold images that are normally created in other programs and then "pasted" into the graphics block. As noted earlier, when text is changed, it should reflow around the graphics block.

Emphasis Blocks Set off graphics and text. The solid dark line beneath the title in Figure 11-12 is an emphasis block. Another use of an emphasis block is placing a dark frame around important information on the page in order to draw attention to this information.

If a graphics block is added to a text block that already has text, the text should **reflow** around the graphics block. There are several levels of reflow in desktop publishing programs.

- At the simplest level, the user has to do the reflow manually.
- At the next level, reflow is automatic, but only if the graphics block is exactly as wide as the text block
- At the next level, reflow is automatic even if the graphics block is narrower than the text block, so that some short lines of text are produced in the reflow.

- At the most sophisticated level, reflow is automatic even if the figure is irregularly shaped, so that short lines of text are produced and these short lines will have different lengths.

In Figure 11-12, the blocks do not overlap; they fit against one another like floor tiles. However, overlapping blocks can be implemented. If the overlapping is opaque, then the underlying text must reflow around the overlaying block, as just discussed. If the overlapping image is transparent, the underlying block will show through, thereby permitting text to be superimposed on a light background image for added visual effect.

Because block layout is so important, the precise positioning of boxes has received considerable attention. Like most page layout programs, ReadySetGo allows the user to use the mouse to drag the box around or change its size dynamically. In addition, as shown in Figure 11-13, ReadySetGo's Block Modify option allows the user to specify the exact placement and dimensions desired for each block. If block dimensions are changed after text has been entered, the text should reflow after each change. In some systems, placement can be expressed in decimal inches. In others, it is necessary to use typesetting measurements, including points (1/72 of an inch) and picas (12 points).

If the user does not have a large-screen display, a way must be found to preview an entire page without printing it each time. As shown in Figure 11-14, full-page previews in ReadySetGo cannot show individual characters,

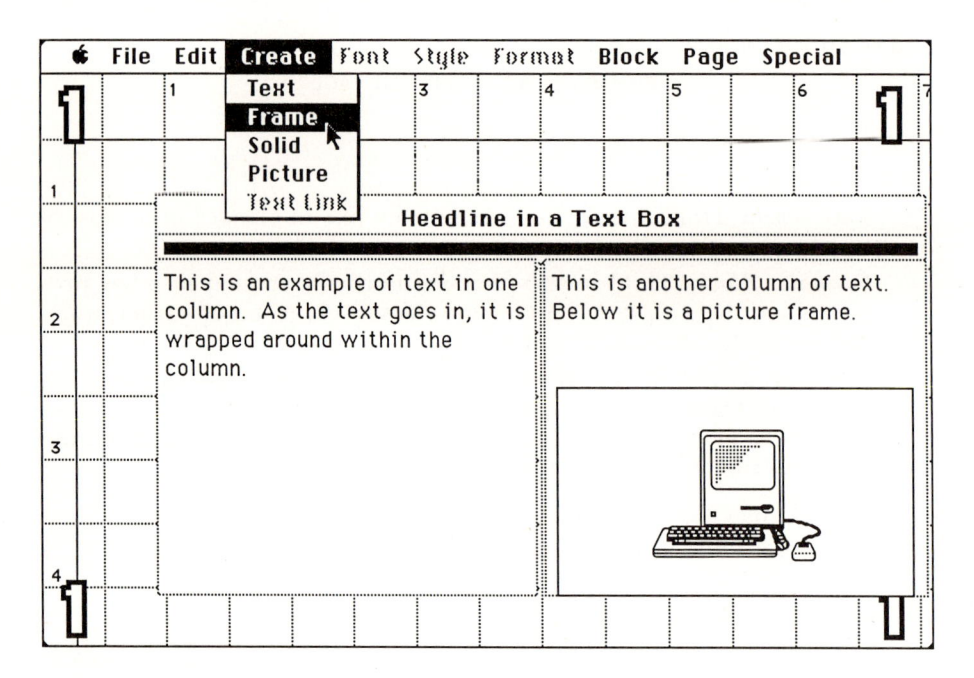

Note: This example is taken from Ready,Set,Go.

FIGURE 11-13 PRECISELY POSITIONING A BLOCK

DESKTOP PUBLISHING   **501**

Displaying a Full Page

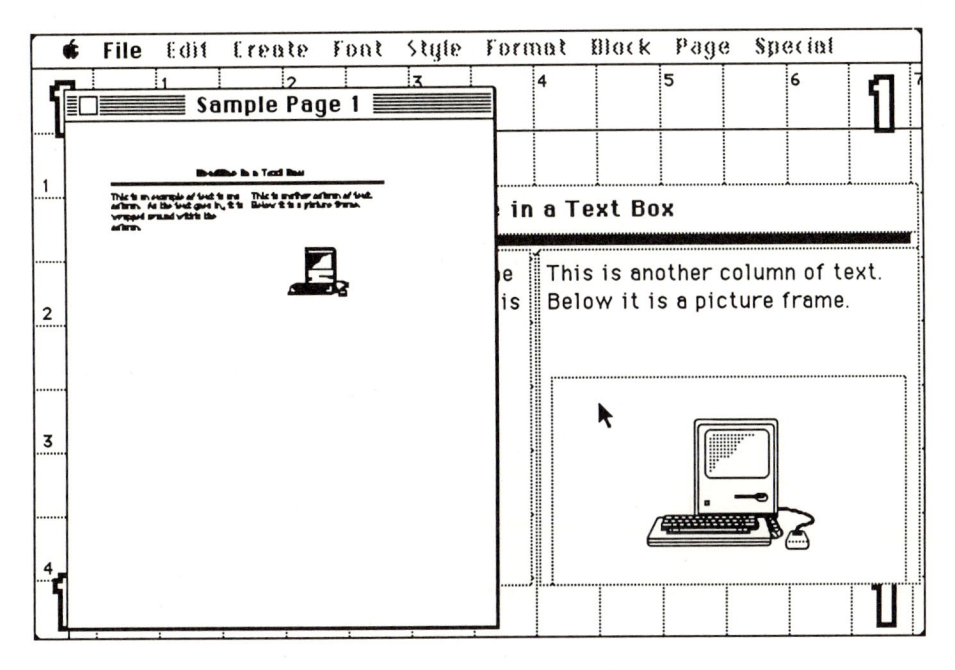

Note: This example is taken from Ready,Set,Go.

FIGURE 11-14 DISPLAYING A FULL PAGE

but they can show the visual effectiveness of the current layout. The replacement of characters by unreadable blocks or symbols is called "Greeking," a term coined when a user reportedly said "It's Greek to me."

Some desktop publishing programs can show the page in several sizes, from full-page miniaturization to 200 percent or 300 percent enlargement. Some cannot do any editing in nonstandard size views, but others support most or all of their editing tools in these views.

Another consideration in WYSIWYG (What You See Is What You Get) representation is whether text fonts are represented accurately on the screen or whether a generic font is used for all characters. In one sense, it is much better to see the real font on screen. In another, programs that use generic fonts operate much faster, and this is an important consideration for heavy users.

The figures we have shown so far are destined for printing on 81/2 by 11 inch paper, but desktop publishing programs should be able to work with multiple paper sizes, including the A4 page used heavily in Europe. They should also be able to print in **portrait** orientation (vertical) or **landscape** orientation (sideways).

So far, we have only looked at the layout of individual pages, but a document has many pages, each of which can have a different page layout. One approach in formatting multiple pages is to use a layout duplication command that duplicates the layout of a page already in the document. The user can then make the additional changes needed on a particular page, such as adding a graphics image. A better approach is to define **page sets**—groups of pages with the same layout, except perhaps for the addition of a few added elements on each page. This allows a single layout format change to affect all pages in the set, without having to go back and change individual page formats.

The most sophisticated desktop publishing programs have **style sheets,** which specify standard layout information for the entire document and/or individual sections, such as headings or normal text. As noted earlier in the chapter, style sheets specify not only page layout, but also text fonts, standard elements such as logos, and other standard settings that will form defaults for major types of text in the document. Furthermore, if the style sheet is changed, the document will change automatically to reflect the changes in the style sheet. In addition to simplifying life when a user lays out a complex document, it provides standardization within an organization.

One last word on multipage documents is in order. Most desktop publishing programs are useful only for small jobs of a few pages. Few handle chapter-length publications, and even fewer handle book-length publications.

Text Creation and Importation

Most desktop publishing programs have word processing features, but these features are usually minimal. They are good enough for one- or two-page documents and for editing text that has previously been imported from other word processing programs, but virtually all desktop programs depend on importation for the basic text of large documents. Desktop publishing programs are not designed to be stand-alone programs. They rely on both imported text and, as we will see later, imported graphics.

As discussed in Chapter 8, simple ASCII text files are the easiest to import, but this process loses the embedded formatting codes that are needed to govern text layout within a text block. To avoid such damage, most desktop publishing programs can import files directly from the most popular word processing programs that run on the computer. On the Macintosh, this includes MacWrite, Microsoft Word, and other popular programs. On IBM PCs, a typical list includes WordStar, MultiMate, WordPerfect, DisplayWrite, and Microsoft Word. Except for advanced formatting features, the importation is usually tedious but low in damage.

Importing, however, is not a perfect solution. If the user could create text directly within the context of its ultimate layout, he or she might write very differently, taking advantage of page positioning.

Some word processing vendors are beginning to attack desktop publishing by adding page layout features to their basic programs. Most top-end word processing programs already support multifont page printer text, limited multiple column, printing, and at least simple graphics importation. Adding even modest page layout gives any current user at least minimal desktop publishing capabilities. It remains to be seen whether these extended word processing systems will be sufficiently competitive to hold their own against full desktop publishing programs, with more and better features.

Importation involves a good deal more than merely pasting the text into place. During importation, it is critical to retain such features as boldface, and it is desirable to keep as much internal formatting knowledge as possible from the original document. Some desktop programs strip out most or all character and layout formatting when they import.

After text is imported, it often needs to be adjusted to fit. This is done primarily by changing the vertical spacing between characters and the vertical spacing between lines. As noted earlier, spacing between characters is called **kerning,** and there must be a table specifying the spacing between each pair of characters. Spacing between lines is called **leading.** Leading is easiest to adjust to make things fit. Some systems even have automatic **vertical justification,** which adjusts leading so that the material will fit and will have the same spacing between all lines.

The best desktop publishing programs have features found in only the best word processors, including automatic hyphenation on imported text, headers, footers, automatic figure numbering, automatic footnote numbering, automatic section numbering, and automatic index generation. In contrast, the worst systems do not even number pages automatically.

After many desktop publishing programs import text, the text in the desktop publishing program is no longer linked to the original document. Other desktop publishing programs retain the main document, and the only way to make edits in the laid-out text is to make the changes in the original document, using an editing window that opens to let the user edit the original. The best desktop publishing programs are set up so that edits can be done in either the original or the laid-out text, with changes to one being reflected in changes to the other.

Some systems import text only into individual blocks, truncating any text that does not fit. Most systems, however, automatically cause the text to flow to the "next" block if it overflows the boundaries of one block. The best systems allow the user to specify what block to use next if there is an overflow; in newspapers and other publications, the text at the bottom of a column may have to flow to the middle of another page.

Graphics Creation and Importation

Most desktop publishing programs can do limited graphics creation, including rectangles, rounded rectangles, ovals, lines, and text within graphics images. They can usually provide different line thicknesses and styles for lines and enclosed figures, and they can usually fill areas with various patterns. In other words, they have primitive object graphics.

These capabilities are very limited, and just as desktop publishing programs depend on importation for their text, they depend on importation for most or all of their graphics. Importation is especially useful for entering clip art—portfolios of professionally drawn images. Their internal graphics capabilities are useful mostly for editing imported images.

On the Macintosh, MacPaint and MacDraw were the original standards for pixel and object graphics, respectively, and almost all Macintosh desktop publishing systems can import their files. Other graphics program files are often imported as well. On the IBM PC, desktop publishing programs must be able to import a wide variety of graphics file formats, ranging from Lotus 1-2-3.PIC files to the files produced by a wide variety of pixel and object programs for analytical and conceptual graphics. In addition, the growing use of scanners for input (see Chapter 7) means that scanner images should be supported. Finally, the program should have a basic graphics screen capture utility for capturing images that cannot be drawn in through direct file importation.

On both the Macintosh and the IBM PC, an alternative to full file importation is the use of screen capture, in which the quarter million or so pixels on the screen are placed in a simple memory map, usually with one bit per pixel (see Chapter 8). As discussed in Chapters 7 and 8, however, screen resolution—in terms of dots per inch—is only a fraction of page printer resolution, so screen capture produces a grainy image.

As VDI and NAPLPS standards become more widely used (see Chapter 7), the problem of embedded graphics should be reduced. These may take years to become popular, however, and, as noted in Chapter 7, they are suitable only for object graphics, not for pixel graphics.

In operation, a user of a desktop program normally begins to import an image by creating a picture block, as shown in Figure 11-12. This block determines the size of the image on the page.

The next step is to select the image file to be imported. This process varies from simple when MacPaint images are imported on the Macintosh to complex when unusual formats are imported on an IBM PC.

The third step is to rework the image to fit the image block. This may involve expanding or shrinking the image, cropping only part of it, and then editing it with the desktop publishing program's internal graphics capabilities. Editing may involve rotating the figure through 90 degree increments or reversing black and white. In addition, it may be desirable to set off a graphics image with a box or with lines at its top and bottom.

Editing

Although most desktop publishing systems are good at page layout, importing text, and importing graphics, editing is the litmus test that separates good systems from the bad systems. Editing often takes the lion's share of the user's time. All can do editing, but the best are much better at the task than the worst.

The basic question is what happens after the user makes a change, say, to edit text or change the size of one or more columns. In the best systems, reflow takes place automatically, so that text flows properly around graphics images and across block boundaries in the appropriate way. Some systems are much more automatic than others.

It is desirable to keep the original word processing text and the text in the desktop publishing program consistent. The best systems allow edits to be made in either and then make the appropriate edits in the other. The next best do the editing in the word processing original and then effectively reimport the text. The worst do not change the word processing original.

Another issue is whether editing can be done in reduced or expanded views, or whether the user must constantly return to the normal size view every time he or she wants to do an edit. It is very desirable to be able to perform edits in all views of the file.

The Future

Desktop publishing is changing so rapidly that predicting its future is extremely hazardous. Nonetheless, few predictions can be made with some confidence.

First a new generation of hardware is needed to give desktop publishing adequate speed. Today, operators waste a great deal of time staring at their frozen displays while output is laboriously processed and printed. Processing is very intense, and the 1 MB required of each page has thus far discouraged multipage print spooling—which would be problematic anyway at today's processing speeds. Even simple edits and reflows often produce slow-motion work that stymies the productivity of operators.

Second, desktop software will produce large performance gains by improving features. Even the earliest systems could do good block layout, text importation, graphics importation, and printing, but many of these core features were hard to use and required excessive manual work. Moreover, even such critical matters as reflow were originally viewed as options to be added later.

Third, a good software package does not make users into layout specialists. Page design is an art in which few people really excel. Although dazzle will be good enough for a little while, training and artificial intelligence-aided design will be needed in the future. One shorter term solution is to use style sheets developed by layout professionals, although most specialists would argue that the layout design can only be set after all of the text and graphics are available, so that alternatives can be tried to see the best layout.

The fourth and last point is that today's distinction between work processing, graphics, and desktop publishing features is artificial. It would be ideal to have single **multimedia communication programs** that would combine all of these features with voice annotation and perhaps even video. At the very least, paper-oriented multimedia programs that eliminate importing are highly desirable. To be successful, however, these integrated programs would have to offer high functionality in each feature as well as high synergy among features, excellent ease of use, and easy importing from other programs. These goals will not be easy to achieve.

CONCLUSION

The written word has long been a staple of business communication. Word processing was one of the earliest uses of personal computers and remains among the most important. Today's PC-based word processing systems are almost perfectly equal in features to the best dedicated word processing systems, and the growing ability of PC-based word processing systems to work with other PC software makes PC word processing even more attractive.

It is difficult to come up with a good set of standards for PC word processing. No one product dominates the market, and not all users want sophisticated programs. Many firms now support two or three word processors, and solving the resultant incompatibility problems has become something of a nightmare.

The graphics explosion was initially felt in face-to-face presentations, where analytical graphics dazzled participants. Now, conceptual graphics is beginning to do for concepts what analytical graphics did for numbers. Conceptual object graphics is particularly important because this type of graphics can make full use of the high-printing resolution offered by today's page printers. Furthermore, both analytical and conceptual graphics are beginning to show up within word processing, and documents that combine both text and graphics are no longer rare.

Today, desktop publishing systems are again upping the ante in written communication. PC users can now produce publications with page layout features previously found only in professionally produced publications. Page printers with built-in page description language capabilities are able to turn these desktop publishing screen images into high-impact visual output.

The next step in the process will be multimedia document processing, in which text and graphics are combined with voice annotation and perhaps even some video characteristics. Given the fact that today's desktop publishing programs already need much more processing speed than today's PCs can provide, however, multimedia document processing may have to wait for at least one more generation of technology—although multimedia processing is becoming available on host-based office automation systems, as discussed in Chapter 17.

As functionality increases, training requirements also increase. Many standard word processing programs were implemented with little or no formal training. With advanced word processing programs and desktop publishing programs, formal training is an absolute requirement. An advanced word processing program probably requires 12 to 15 hours of training, spread over several modules. Desktop publishing programs probably need a good deal more training. Only part of this training for advanced communication software involves using the product. The training must also include "good practice" education, so that users will understand the elements of good page layout and the effective use of multiple fonts and embedded graphics.

REVIEW QUESTIONS

1. What is the difference between "communication" and "communications?"
2. What are the major types of word processing software? What capabilities are added at each step of the hierarchy? Which type do you think will be used most widely in corporations three years from now? Why do you think that?
3. Briefly describe the following: decimal tabbing, font, emphasis, size, pitch, proportional spacing, kerning, right justification, full justification, header, format line, overstrike, and insert.
4. What is the difference between character delete and block delete?
5. Briefly describe the following: background printing, mail merge, prestored text recall, embedded programming languages, import, and export.
6. What are the major types of advanced formatting? Which would you say is most important? Why? What is the difference between bound and snaked columns?

7. What are the major types of author aids? Which would you say is most important? Why? Can you think of an author aid that is missing from the list?
8. What is the difference between analytical and conceptual graphics? What does "presentation quality" mean, and why will this term grow ever less meaningful in the future?
9. What is the difference between object and pixel graphics? What are the advantages of each? Is it possible to have the best of both worlds?
10. What are the main tools in MacPaint's tools? When MacPaint's rectangle tool draws a box, is this object graphics? Which tool would you say would be the most useful? The least useful? Why? What other capability in MacPaint would you say would be the most useful? Why? What one feature would you add to MacPaint if possible? What is "clip art?"
11. What are the main tools in MacDraw's tools? When MacDraw's rectangle tool draws a box, is this object graphics? Which tool would you say would be the most useful? The least useful? Why? What other capability in MacDraw would you say would be the most useful? Why? What one feature would you add to MacDraw if possible?
12. What hardware and software are needed to constitute a desktop publishing system with adequate performance?
13. Describe the layout of a page in desktop publishing. What is reflow and when is it important? List the main features desired in text importation and in graphics importation.
14. What are the training implications of advanced word processing systems and desktop publishing systems?

12 OTHER PERSONAL COMPUTER APPLICATIONS

The final chapter on PC applications is a potpourri of applications and application tools. Each is small in size but may be critically important to many individual end users. The topics covered include the following.

- Online services for information retrieval, electronic mail, and transaction services.
- PC networking services that turn the bare hardware of networking into a working environment for its users.
- Integrated programs that combine word processing, spreadsheet, data management, analytical graphics, communications, and sometimes other tools.
- Desktop accessories that provide a collection of useful tools with low functionality but high ease of use and also have the attraction of always being available at the press of one or two keys.
- Programming languages, which are not commonly used but are very important to many "power users."
- Project management systems for complex activities with numerous tightly woven subtasks and with tight time requirements.
- Business applications, such as accounting, payroll, and billing, for small firms that do not have larger computers or that have small isolated applications resembling operational systems in content.
- Vertical applications, which aim at very specific applications, such as loan appraisal.
- Expert systems, which codify an expert's knowledge in a specific problem domain.

ONLINE SERVICES

Much of the information that a manager or professional needs is sitting on his or her PC or on a corporate host. Other data, as well as a number of interesting services, can only be obtained from commercial **online services** that reside on time-shared hosts owned by outside organizations.

The Industry

Commercial online services offer a wide array of information and processing services, but four service offerings dominate the industry today.

- **Basic retrieval services** allow a user to move through a tree-structured system of menus to reach widely used types of information, such as weather forecasts and stock market quotes.
- **Sophisticated retrieval services** allow the user to do more sophisticated searches involving Boolean queries applied to large data bases containing high-value data for limited audiences, such as freight rate data for shippers.
- **Electronic mail** allows users to send messages to one another. These messages are delivered to "mailboxes," and users are notified of new mail whenever they log into the online service computer.
- **Transaction services** allow the user to execute complete transactions, such as buying stock or making airline reservations.

Some online services, including MCI Communications and Dialog, specialize in one of these four areas. Specialization, they feel, can give them a better focus for product development, user support, and marketing. Their services tend to be rather fully developed.

Others, including CompuServe and The Source, try to be electronic supermarkets, offering a broad spectrum of services. Breadth, they feel, gives them a critical mass of services accessible through a single gateway menu. Although individual services tend to be less well developed than they are in online services that specialize in them, users only need to master one set of interaction skills.

Online services differ from computer **service bureaus,** which provide *processing power* for firms that do not have their own computers. These service bureaus provide everything from accounting for small firms to car ordering for automobile dealers. Although online services resemble other forms of end user computing, service bureau offerings usually resemble operational systems. A few service bureaus are moving into online services, but this represents a second line of business, not just an extension of their service bureau offerings.

Not all online services are healthy and experiencing explosive growth. The truth is that, although online services form a multibillion dollar market, growth is only moderate, and few companies are profitable at all. The use of online services will be an important PC application, but it is not showing signs of becoming a dominant application.

Basic Information Retrieval

Basic information retrieval aims at simple and low-cost access to widely needed information. To keep things simple and costs low, the user is not allowed to do sophisticated queries that traverse large data files. Instead, as noted above, the user typically moves through a series of simple menus until the desired information is reached. During normal business hours, costs tend to run $10 to $30 per connect hour, but after hours these services are made available for a few dollars an hour.

Basic information retrieval services aim at information that appeals to broad groups of people: weather conditions in different cities, currency conversion rates, stock market prices, and other "reference data," because, by appealing to broad audiences, they can spread their data collection costs over large numbers of users, furthering the goal of keeping costs low.

Although basic information retrieval services are constrained to simple searches, the creative use of menus and simple commands (which provide menu bypass) can give them considerable power. The Official Airlines Guide, Electronic Edition, for instance, allows the user to type commands to specify desired departure times and see what flights and connections can be used to get the user to his or her destination. Along with each flight will be information about type of aircraft, meals, and fares.

Advanced Information Retrieval

In contrast to basic information retrieval services, advanced information retrieval services allow users to search large data bases with sophisticated Boolean queries (see Chapter 10). Their cost tends to range from $50 per connect hour to $200 per connect hour.

Because of the high costs and sophisticated features of advanced services, most accesses are not made by end users directly but by trained "chauffeurs" who work with the user to formulate a request and then do a series of queries on the system to try to get what the user needs. These chauffeurs can work very efficiently because they know the software, major index terms, and numerous tricks to make efficient searches. Chauffeured access began in libraries, and most chauffeured accesses continue to be done by reference librarians.

When *documents* are being sought, there is a critical distinction between citation services and full-text retrieval services. **Citation** services merely give citations to documents, whereas **full-text retrieval** services provide the full text of the document on screen or in printed form. Full-text services are obviously better, but the high cost of storage for full text has limited their popularity.

Not all advanced information retrieval services limit themselves to queries. When data are being retrieved, a considerable amount of processing may be done. Freight rate data bases, for example, may compute the lowest cost way to route a particular shipment or help users assess the best place to locate a warehouse.

Many advanced information retrieval services are aimed at particular groups. Freight rate data bases, of course, are aimed at distribution departments. Other data bases, such as LEXIS, are oriented toward lawyers who are working in areas where case law is exploding.

Electronic Mail

If many people use the same time-shared computer, why not let them send messages to one another? In the mid-1960s, even the earliest time-shared computers had "mailbox services," and when networks began to proliferate in the mid-1970s, multihost electronic mail delivery became possible.

Most electronic mail systems today can deliver a message for only two or three times the cost of postage, and this includes composition and reception costs. However, a lack of standards for interconnection between different vendors has forced many users to log into two or more services each day, and such inconvenience has made market growth extremely disappointing. Now that electronic mail standards are beginning to proliferate (see Chapter 17), this situation may change. Other problems will continue to be present, including the fact that most communication is intracompany. Therefore, when electronic mail begins to grow, it will probably grow most rapidly on corporate hosts, not on online services.

Most electronic mail systems are **electronic message systems** that deliver brief messages from one user to the mailboxes of other users named in a distribution list. Their ability to send documents is too limited to justify the full title of "electronic mail" (see Chapter 17). Some are **computer conferencing systems,** also called **bulletin board services,** which allow users to post messages to a general work area that many other users can read.

Transaction Services

Transaction services allow users to make purchases online. For example, the Official Airlines Guide, Electronic Edition, mentioned earlier not only allows users to select an itinerary, but it also enables them to book reservations and pay by credit card if the proper arrangements have been made in advance.

Electronic shopping will be extremely useful for catalog searches for supplies and many other kinds of goods. Future services may even allow the user to check for the availability of goods in stock and to check when an order has been shipped.

Reaching Online Services

An online service vendor must buy or lease a host and then find the right software and data to appeal to users. The most important technical matter, however, is building a communications path between the host and the user.

Public Data Networks

As discussed in Chapters 14 and 15, public data networks are common carriers like telephone companies. Instead of carrying sounds, however, public data networks carry digital information. Their error rates are very low, and by allowing many users to share transmission lines, they provide transmission costs far below those which users could achieve with simple long distance calls.

Nearly every online service is attached to the two biggest public data networks, Telenet and TYMNET. Many are also connected to smaller networks as well, and a few online services belonging to large service bureaus have their own networks. Most also allow users to call in with direct dial lines or WATS lines, but this is rarely done because the cost of doing so is too high—except if the user is in an isolated area, far from the node of a public data network.

Because nearly all online services use Telenet and TYMNET, these two networks (and to a lesser extent, other networks) have become electronic supermarkets that give individual users access to literally hundreds of data bases and other services on dozens of online services.

Modems

Although public data networks transmit all information digitally, the terminal or PC user reaches the network's local node in his or her city via a telephone call. This means that the user needs a modem (see Chapter 13) as well as a terminal or PC. Most networks support both the 103 and 212A modems, and many are beginning to support the faster V.22 *bis* modems as well.

Terminal Emulation and Videotex

As discussed in Chapter 13, virtually all online services support a simple kind of terminal called a TTY (teletypewriter). If a user has a personal computer instead of a terminal, he or she can buy a serial board and a communications program to emulate a TTY—that is, act just like a TTY.

Commercial online services support TTYs precisely because the TTY is widely available, and this gives them access to the broadest possible market. Even simple home computers usually have optional hardware and software to let them act like TTYs, and dozens of communications programs are available for office PCs.

The TTY is an extremely limited terminal, however, and some analysts feel that the industry will not jell until more sophisticated terminals are available. Generically, sophisticated terminals that provide two-way interaction, graphics, and color are called **Videotex** terminals.

Although Videotex has been available since the mid-1970s in some countries, it has suffered from a lack of standards. The earliest system was the British Prestel system, which divided the screen into a group of rectangular boxes. Inside each rectangle could be either a text character or a colored box. Because this approach combined alphanumeric information with graphics that resembled mosaic tiles, it was called an **alphamosaic** system.

Later, Canada developed a more sophisticated approach, in which the simple mosaic tiles of Prestel were replaced by geometric shapes such as circles, arcs, lines, and boxes. Commands to draw individual shapes were sent down to terminals, which would draw them on the screen. This **alphageometric** approach produced far better images, although it cost too much initially.

During the 1980s, AT&T led the development of a new alphageometric standard that built on the Canadian efforts. This was **NAPLPS**—the North American Presentation-Level Protocol Standard. Discussed briefly in Chapter 7, NAPLPS is emerging as the main Videotex standard and may achieve full international standards status in the near future.

Dedicated NAPLPS terminals and attachments to home televisions can be purchased, but most NAPLPS terminals are likely to be home or office computers with added expansion boards and software. Even home computers can give adequate performance, and office PCs give excellent performance at higher screen resolutions than home TVs.

Unfortunately, Videotex is emerging very slowly. The weak performance of the general online services market, despite the presence of many TTY terminals, has dampened enthusiasm for developing sophisticated Videotex services that cost far more to create and load with information and yet have no large base of terminals in existence. Some vendors, however, feel that the higher quality of Videotex images will help the industry turn the corner. They are moving forward, and by 1990, Videotex should finally have the chance to prove itself.

Communications Programs

As discussed in Chapter 13, logging into a remote computer is a long process. The user must set communication parameters on his or her terminal or PC, dial the number of the public data network's local node, identify his or her terminal type to the node, give the address of the host to be reached, and finally log into the host. Most communications programs go far beyond terminal emulation. Nearly all can automate the process of reaching and even logging into the host.

Most popular communications programs can work with any online service, but a few online services offer their own communications programs. These make getting to the service extremely simple, and many offer such advanced services as the ability to compose an electronic message at the PC, so that the user can minimize the amount of costly time spent online. Of course, vendor-specific communications programs tend to lock the user into a particular online service.

Managing the Use of Online Services

Few organizations have comprehensive policies for managing online services, in part because this category is so diverse. In several areas, however, management direction can be extremely beneficial.

Assessing Competing Services

In several key areas, such as electronic mail and multiservice vendors such as CompuServe and The Source, there will be a sufficiently large number of potential users in the firm that an assessment is likely to prove valuable, although few firms fully standardize on one particular vendor.

Ease of use can be rated, including the ease of accessing a particular alternative from various sites in the company. The services available on each can also be compared. The biggest problem, however, is how to compare costs because the cost structures of different services tend to be quite different.

Many services have a monthly charge per organization and account, as well as a transmission charge that may depend on traffic, a use charge per connect hour, a CPU intensiveness surcharge, and a charge for each kilobyte of storage. Some of these charges may vary by the user's transmission speed.

To compare costs, the information center must get a full rate structure from each firm and then compare the costs of representative sessions on each of the services. Even after careful consideration, the results may be disappointing because the conclusions may be extremely sensitive to the assumptions made about representative sessions.

Although these cost analyses may not allow the organization to show that one system is clearly superior to another, they will help give users a reasonable picture of what various systems will cost.

The one service that almost certainly does need to be standardized is electronic mail, since it is extremely desirable to have everyone in the organization using the same service. Inasmuch as this gets into the broader area of office automation standards, we will defer discussion of electronic mail standards until Chapter 17.

Supporting Basic Services

Although basic information retrieval services, electronic mail services, and transaction services are simple enough (by design) for individuals to learn, the information center staff should become familiar with a number of the most popular services. Not only do questions invariably arise from users, but also if something does go wrong, it may have to be traced to the user's equipment, to the public data network, or to the vendor, and this requires familiarity with individual services.

Training and promotion are also needed. Classes to help users learn how to use their terminals, public data networks, and specific services help orient the user to this new and unfamiliar world. In addition, by helping the user understand how to avoid wasting money while the clock is ticking away online, these classes can probably pay for themselves several times over.

Another area of support is the setting up of user PCs for terminal emulation and building macros to help users reach remote computers. If possible, macros for such items as uploading prepared outgoing mail, downloading incoming mail, and returning to local mode to look through the mail will not only save users a great deal of time but also slash costs.

Macros do raise one policy question, however. Most communications programs allow the user not only to access the system, but also to log on automatically and even call a particular service and give commands within that service. As discussed in Chapter 13, automated log-in almost always requires the user to insert his or her secret password into the macro, and anyone who steals or copies that person's communications program can get access to that person's data files. Many organizations flatly prohibit the inclusion of passwords and require two macros to be created—one to take the user up to log-in and the other to continue after log-in. There should also be a clear policy that the user is responsible if unauthorized use occurs because of improperly secured passwords.

Supporting Sophisticated Information Retrieval Services

As discussed earlier, sophisticated information retrieval services usually require chauffeured access, usually by a reference librarian. Reference librarians must be highly trained if they are to be efficient, and this almost always means taking a course from the online service vendor, often at the vendor's site.

Some advanced systems, such as freight rate data banks or legal information services, will be used almost exclusively within a single department. In these cases, the expertise to use the service well must be developed within the user department, and it must also be maintained despite staff turnover. This requires careful policy making at the department level.

PC NETWORKING SERVICES

Online services link PCs with external host services. Later, in Chapter 13, we will read about services that link PCs to corporate hosts. PCs also need to talk directly to one another, in order to share peripherals and information.

Networking Basics

The Main Components

Figure 12-1 illustrates a typical personal computer network. This network has several components.

- **User PCs** are the machines that sit on the desks of ordinary office workers. They are also called **workstations,** although that term is often reserved for high-performance engineering workstations (see Chapter 6).
- **Servers** provide the services for which users buy PC networks.
- **Internal hardware and software** consist of expansion boards and various kinds of network software inside the user PCs and servers.
- **External hardware and software** consist of the cabling, wiring concentrators, and (sometimes) switches that link user PCs and servers.

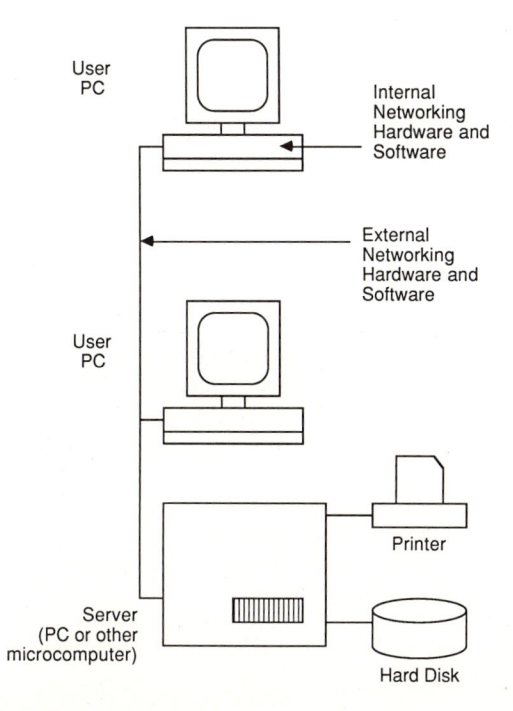

FIGURE 12-1 COMPONENTS OF A PERSONAL COMPUTER NETWORK

Chapters 13 and 14 discuss these components in more detail. For example, those chapters discuss the three categories of servers.

- **Nondedicated PC Servers** are personal computers that can be used as PCs while performing their server functions. If these machines are heavily loaded, of course, both their server and user PC performance will suffer badly.
- **Dedicated PC Servers** are personal computers that *cannot* be used as user PCs while performing their server functions.
- **Non-PC Servers** are special-purpose microcomputers whose designs are optimized for their server role. Although most PC servers must be limited to three to six machines if performance is to be kept up, most non-PC Servers can serve 10 to 30 users.

Why PC Networks?

There are several reasons for buying PC networks. The most important is **information sharing**—being able to move files around easily for editing by secretaries or distribution to their ultimate audiences. Without networking, floppy disks must be hand-carried from PC to PC. This approach, called "sneakernet," breaks down as the volume of PC use increases and as the speed at which an office works increases as a result of PC support.

A second benefit is **time savings.** If a special printer is needed, for instance, there is no need to hand-carry disks to a PC attached to the printer. In addition, such jobs as maintaining printer paper supplies, backing up hard disks, and maintaining retrievable tape archives of old files can be delegated to secretaries, so that these maintenance chores do not waste the time of managers and professionals.

A third reason for networking is **multivendor integration,** for instance, to connect IBM PCs and Apple Macintoshes within a single department. Multivendor integration is possible, but it must be part of a broader integration strategy involving the careful selection of application software, as discussed in Chapter 8.

A fourth reason for networking is cost savings due to **hardware sharing.** As discussed in Chapter 6, however, the high cost of networking hardware and software eats up most of the cost savings attributable to hardware sharing. Although networking costs are falling, the costs of hardware are also decreasing rapidly.

Taken together, these benefits are impressive, but, as discussed in Chapters 14 and 15, installing even a small PC network is a major undertaking requiring specialized technical knowledge. What is more, after the network is installed, a good deal of labor must be devoted to low-level network management and high-level planning.

Perhaps the worst problem with networks is diagnosing the inevitable problems that occur. If a network works in an undesirable way, it is very difficult to tell if the problem lies with the network's hardware, the networking software, the server, the user PCs, the application software, or a failure to follow instructions for doing certain tasks. Given normal salaries and overhead costs (see Chapter 6), most network problems cost hundreds of dollars to fix. Diagnosis ends up being far more expensive than networking hardware and software.

Diagnosis can be especially frustrating if the problem arises from slight incompatibilities in IBM PC clones or from undocumented incompatibilities between networking software and the user's application programs. Many application programs cannot work with specific networkings, and the decision to use a specific network is usually a decision to give up some of the user organization's current applications software or third-party utility software. Very few organizations can simply add a network and go on working the way they always did apart from doing more device, file, and software sharing.

Printer Services

Printer services allow application programs on user PCs to send their output to printers attached to servers. This is especially valuable when an office has one or two high-cost printers, such as page printers, or specialized devices such as plotters or 35 mm slide producers. Printers are discussed in Chapter 7.

At a minimum, the **printer server** software must **automatically redirect** printing to the server when an application program gives a print command. When the user turns on his or her PC, a command in the AUTOEXEC.BAT (see Chapter 8) file should connect the user's PC to the network automatically and establish how print output should be directed. To application programs, it should seem that there are several printers attached to the PC, with no distinction as to which are local and which are reached via the network.

Another minimum requirement is that printing jobs must be **queued** at the server if the server is already doing another print job. Users should be given the ability to change the order of jobs on the queue if properly authorized. Other controls, such as the ability to print multiple copies or the ability to redirect the output to another printer if it was originally sent to the wrong printer, should also be provided. Of course, the size of the possible print queue should be ample.

It is highly desirable for the server to do **printer control code conversion** without user intervention, so that a print file created for one printer can be translated into the format needed by another printer. This is rarely provided today, but it is critical that the server should at least not strip out printer control codes as some early server programs did, so that most features of the printer are effectively disabled.

It is likely that the department's main high-performance printers will be located near the secretary, so that support workers can change paper, ribbons, and toner, burst fan fold paper, put queued output in appropriate "out trays," and do other low-level chores. However, individual workers are still likely to have low-performance printers for small convenience printing chores.

Communications Service

Communications services link user PCs to the world beyond the PC network—principally host computers and larger local area networks. At a minimum, a **communications service** should allow several PCs to **modem share**—share a single high-speed modem, so that the organization does not need a modem per PC. Communications servers should also be able to do TTY, ANSI, and host-specific **terminal emulation** (see Chapter 13) without adding any hardware or software to the user PCs. In addition, they should be able to provide **access macros** to simplify connection, as well as **file transfer protocols** such as XMODEM, Kermit, X.PC, and MNP (see Chapter 13). Also useful is the ability to provide **gateways** (see Chapter 14) to various local area networks and public data networks.

If the secretary is properly trained, he or she can set up macros for specific needs, do occasional diagnostics on the modem, and even do individual file transfers.

Disk and File Sharing Services

Basic Concepts

Disk and file sharing services are the heart of PC networking's ability to support information sharing, because information sharing normally consists of sharing files on the same disk or transferring disk files from one user to another.

When assessing a network, there is a critical distinction to be made between disk service and file service.

- In **disk service,** the server's disk is merely divided into volumes, as discussed below. Access is only controlled at the volume level, not at the level of individual files.
- In **file service,** the server software controls access to individual files. This not only increases security, but also assures that two users will not update a file at the same time.

The server can allow both data files and program files to be shared. Some programs, however, cannot be legally run from a server, whereas others require site licenses. As noted below, only some data base programs support concurrent multiuser access to data bases on the server. Finally, each network has a different network operating system, and because application software must be specially written to work with each network operating system, the kinds of application programs that will run on any particular network and how *well* they run on a particular PC network must be assessed very carefully.

Volume Sharing

As shown in Figure 12-2, some network operating systems divide a disk into several **volumes,** giving each individual a single volume, just as if he or she had a dedicated hard disk of the volume's capacity. This effectively gives everyone a hard disk, but it does little to aid sharing beyond the simple expedient of giving several people access to the same volume.

Volume sharing by several users is dangerous, as the following example will show. Suppose a shared volume holds a Lotus 1-2-3 data file. User A loads the file into his computer's RAM and begins changing it. In the meanwhile, User B loads the file into her RAM and works at it. User A then gives a SAVE command, putting his revised version on the disk. User B then gives her

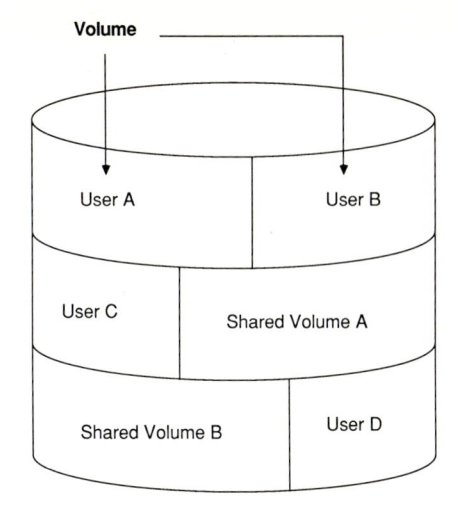

FIGURE 12-2 DIVIDING A HARD DISK'S CAPACITY

SAVE command, putting her revised version on the disk and wiping out all of User A's changes. Especially if some PCs are physically out of sight of one another, volume sharing is a poor way to share files.

Sharing at Three Levels

Better network operating systems permit **file sharing,** in which the system always know when a file is being worked on. Through a process called **file locking,** it gives a "file busy" signal to anyone trying to retrieve the file, thus preventing update anomalies.

Some network operating systems also provide **record locking** in record-structured data files and data bases (see Chapter 10). This approach allows several people to work on the file simultaneously. Only when two users try to refer to the same record is one locked out. This is extremely useful in small data base management systems because it allows several people to be inputting data while one person is doing queries.

If several people can work simultaneously on a file, this is called **concurrency.** Although all networks are **multiuser** environments, not all support concurrency or even the less potent capabilities of file locking. In a multiuser data base environment, record locking is absolutely necessary.

Some network operating systems offer a third level of locking, **field locking.** At this level, individual fields in a record (see Chapter 10) can be locked to prevent simultaneous access.

In addition to preventing simultaneous access, locking usually provides *security*. File-locking systems can attach passwords to files, whereas record-locking systems can provide password security at the record level and field-locking systems can provide password security at the field level. A manager, for instance, may only be allowed to look at information in a master personnel file for people in his or her department and in fact only at nonsensitive fields within his or her employees' records.

In many network operating systems, a skilled computer user can easily bypass security. In some systems, for example, a special bit in a file's directory record is set to "flag" the presence of a lock. Almost any commercial data-snooping program (see Chapter 8) can bypass this type of security. Encryption and other heavier measures may be needed if sophisticated users pose a potential security threat.

Programs such as DBMSs may implement the security offered by the network operating system but many DBMSs ignore network operating system security and either provide no security or implement their own security controls. Security controls imposed only by application programs tend to be fairly easy to bypass at the operating system level, although this is not always true. In addition, if a particular application program somehow bypasses network operating system security, it can accidentally damage a locked file or even damage files protected by the network operating system.

Networked DBMS Programs

Although many network operating systems now provide record locking, there is still a shortage of good application packages that can take advantage of these capabilities. Unlike printer and communications services, record-locking services cannot be used directly by users at the operating system level. The record-locking services require application programs tailored to record locking in general and to the specific implementation of record locking on a particular network operating system.

Managing Shared Disks

The most obvious management task raised by shared disks is backup. The disk should be backed up every night or on some other fixed schedule. Each night's backup should probably go on a separate tape, so that if a problem is not detected for several days, it will still be possible to make a full recovery.

As discussed in Chapter 7, image backup units save information sector by sector and can only restore an entire hard disk, not individual sectors. In contrast, file-by-file drives store information file by file and can restore individual files. If an organization adopts a file-by-file drive, the secretary must learn how to restore individual files. It is quite likely that most restorations will have nothing to do with disk failures but will stem from accidental file erasures or editing changes that provide unwise in hindsight. Host operators restore lost files constantly, and office secretaries, too, will probably find themselves doing many restorations because of human error, rather than mechanical error.

As discussed in Chapter 7, many backup units offer *both* image and file-by-file backup. Unless the corporation has a policy mandating file-by-file backup, many departments may be drawn by the faster speed of image backup, perhaps not even realizing the capabilities they are missing and the added dangers they are incurring.

With a large hard disk, the secretary is also likely to be the disk manager, allocating capacity and keeping track of what volumes belong to whom. Within a volume, the secretary may organize files into a hierarchy if users so desire. The secretary may also maintain a retention schedule and keep track of files reaching review date. To save managerial and professional time, the secretary will also do the deletes and reorganize directories as desired by the managers and professionals.

Finally, the secretary is likely to do preventative maintenance on the hard disk, conducting periodic diagnostic checks. For example, it is necessary to reformat the disk periodically and reload all files one at a time, in order to detect new bad sectors as well as to reorder the disk.

Electronic Mail

Most networks provide electronic mail as part of their basic offering. Generally, this means electronic messaging, but a few offer group meeting scheduling and perhaps computer conferencing (also called bulletin board services). Although electronic mail is an application program and not part of the network operating system, it is often bundled with the network operating system.

The problem with PC electronic mail systems is that they are not likely to be compatible with future corporate-wide electronic mail systems. Although they often prove valuable within a department that has implemented PC networking, a conversion to a corporate system will be required at some time in the future.

Managing a Networked Environment

A PC network always needs a great deal of management. Printers, hard disks, and individual files all require a good deal of planning and mundane maintenance. These can be delegated to secretaries in many cases.

The secretary will also need to become proficient in the networks' **network management program,** which is used to add users and resources, delete them, and change various profiles. The network management program does considerable diagnostics when problems occur and when routine maintenance is implemented. It should also be able to show how intensively various resources on the network are being used, in order to help with capacity planning.

Some network management programs provide considerable security. These usually begin with passwords at the server, volume, and file level. Many systems can also do file encryption. Few if any, however, have the more intensive security capabilities found on host computers (as discussed in Chapter 13). The bottom line is that network security programs are oriented toward keeping casual snoopers out but not dedicated hackers.

Not all chores can be safely delegated to a secretary or other support staff member. Although low-level details can be handled by support workers, such higher level concerns as capacity planning, security planning, and disk organization at least need to be reviewed by the office head.

INTEGRATED PROGRAMS AND DESK ACCESSORY PROGRAMS

Integrated programs package a number of functions into a single program or at least a suite of core programs and overlays that act almost like a single program to the user. The most common functions packaged in these integrated programs are:

Spreadsheet analysis
Word processing

File management (and occasionally data base management)

Analytical graphics

Terminal emulation

An embedded programming language to automate common procedures.

Integrated packages entered the market with a flurry of excitement in 1984 and 1985, but their initial sales were extremely disappointing. Subsequently, their sales have grown slowly but steadily, and integrated programs now represent an important application area, although far less important than many had at first expected.

The general problem of integration was discussed at the end of Chapter 8. That discussion focused on file importing and exporting, as well as other roads to integration, notably operating environments that allow stand-alone packages to exchange data more easily and RAM-resident desk accessory programs, which provide low-level integrated functionality to work with a stand-alone application program. In this section, we will focus only on fully integrated programs and desk accessory programs.

Why Integrated Programs?

There are several reasons why users will want to work with a single integrated program rather than a group of separate stand-alone programs.

Cost

The first reason is cost. An integrated program is expensive, listing for $400 to $700, but this is still considerably cheaper than a suite of stand-alone programs to do the functions embedded in the integrated programs.

Integrative Applications

A second reason is the ability to work with applications that span the functionalities of individual packages. A manager may wish to download data from a corporate data base, extract a subfile with only the rows needed for an analysis, load the data into a spreadsheet for analysis, graph the results, and write a report to communicate the findings.

With separate stand-alone packages, endless importing and exporting would need to be done. Even where this is easy, it is always time consuming. The user must set up the importing program or subfunction, specify conditions for format conversion during importing, and then wait for several minutes for the importing to be done. Furthermore, "damage" may occur during the importing, requiring the user to spend even more time editing the imported file before using it.

As shown in Figure 12-3, integrated programs such as Enable, Framework, and Symphony allow the user to divide the screen into a number of windows. A separate functional module can be viewed in each window, although without multitasking only a single window's function can be working at any given moment. This provides a first step in integration, allowing the user to see information in two different applications.

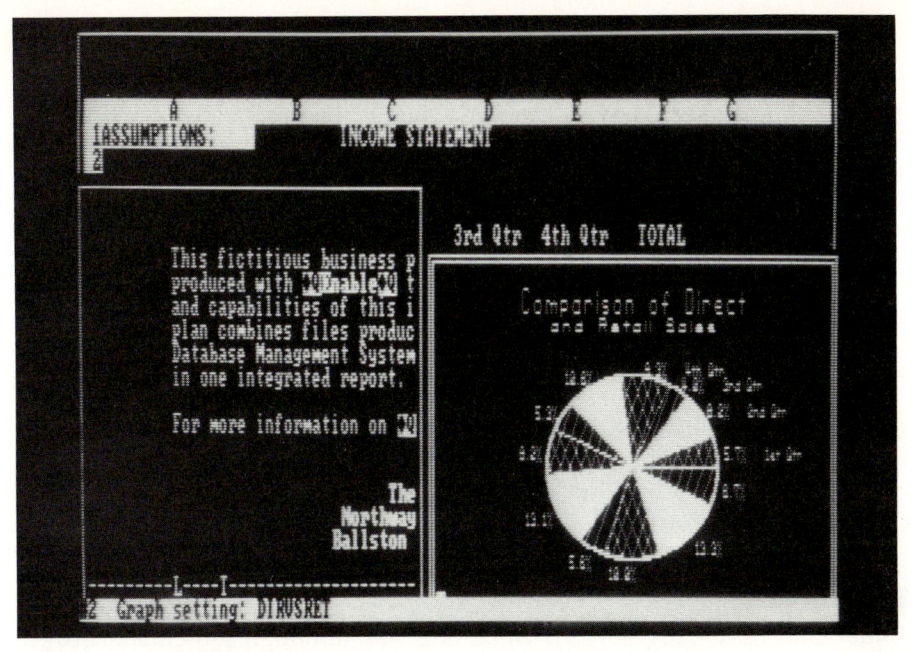

FIGURE 12-3 WINDOWING IN AN INTEGRATED PROGRAM

The next step uses the integrated program's **cut and paste** functions to move information between applications. These cut and paste functions occur at the window level, and so they are available in all individual functions.

Ease of Learning
A major problem with learning several stand-alone application programs is that each uses different interaction styles. Even for programs that consciously mimic a popular application style, such as Lotus 1-2-3 horizontal menu lines, there are enough individual differences to cause learning dissonance. Where interaction styles and the use of keyboard keys are radically different, learning is even more difficult. By offering a single interaction style, it is hoped, integrated programs will improve learning time and make the learning of additional functions more attractive to users.

The Emergence of Integrated Programs
In the 8-bit world of the 1970s, computer programs were limited to 64 KB. In this small space, it was difficult to implement even a single function, so little thought was given to integrated programs. The only nod to integration came in the form of program families that consisted of several stand-alone programs that offered a consistent user interface and had a common intermediate file format such as the DIF file format created by Software Arts (see Chapter 8). The most famous of these families is the pfs: family of personal productivity and business applications.

When the IBM PC first appeared in August 1981, it came standard with only 16 KB of RAM, but all but the earliest units could hold 256 KB of RAM on the mother board. In a bold move, Lotus Development Corporation released 1-2-3 in early 1983 with an "enormous" requirement for 192 KB of RAM, which was very expensive at the time.

Lotus 1-2-3 was basically a very advanced spreadsheet program, with a macro facility to automate common applications. As its name suggested, however, it offered two other application functions. The first of these was an analytical graphics capability that was the first introduction to computer graphics for nearly all PC users. The second was initially touted as word processing, but this capability was so poor that it was quickly forgotten, and the third capability became what Lotus called "data base" but was really only an underdeveloped group of file management commands.

Everyone expected that the next step would be to package more functionality into a single program. In 1984 and 1985, Lotus Development Corporation offered Symphony, Ashton-Tate offered Framework, and several other companies entered the fray. The integrated program with all normal core functions had arrived.

Problems

Initial sales were extremely disappointing, and although subsequent growth has been steady, integrated programs have come nowhere near to dominating the market.

Incompatibility with Existing Standards

The most crucial reason for the faltering of integrated products was their incompatibility with existing software standards. When 1-2-3 arrived, few if any companies had graphics software standards and not very many had data management standards. Lotus 1-2-3 succeeded not so much because of its integration, but because it displaced VisiCalc and did not interfere with existing standards.

By the time integrated programs arrived, however, most companies had firm standards in at least spreadsheet, word processing, and file or data base management. Many had standards in analytical graphics and terminal emulation as well.

Despite this standards-intensive environment, the first generation of integrated programs could only import files from popular programs if they could work with them at all. As a result, user companies either had to scrap their existing stand-alone standards and switch entirely to Symphony, Framework, or another integrated program—or, they could discard compatibility and allow two standards to coexist.

Few companies scrapped their existing standards because the quality of functions in integrated programs was far less than was available in stand-alone products. Few modules in integrated programs would have won a simple competition against existing corporate functions that existed when they emerged. In addition, 1985 also represented a quantum leap in stand-alone word processing and data base functionality.

As time went on, quite a few corporations accepted a second standard for users who had intense needs for integration. This occurred mostly in staff departments such as finance. However, because lack of integration still caused problems for managerial-secretarial cooperation and even raised problems in many cases for people using spreadsheet or data base programs from the same vendor as the integrated program vendor, the second standard solution was not adopted in every corporation.

Hardware Concerns

Just as 1-2-3 needed to set a new standard for hardware configurations, integrated programs had to break the standard configuration of 256 KB and two floppy disk drives. The new standard would be 512 KB to 640 KB of RAM and a hard disk of at least 10 MB capacity. Although a few integrated programs can run with 256 KB of RAM and floppy disks, performance usually degrades dramatically, and floppy shuffling quickly becomes unbearable. If an integrated system vendor "recommends" 512 KB and a hard disk, this recommendation is virtually mandatory.

Although organizations have been moving toward this new standard, many will not move the bulk of their installed equipment base to this new standard until the end of the 1980s. As a result, wholesale conversion to integrated programs has been slowed even further.

Learning Problems

Although integrated programs were expected to be easy to learn, difficulty of learning became a major criticism of early systems. Part of the problem has been the simple fact that it takes users a long time to learn five or six stand-alone packages. Therefore, even if there were strong economies of learning with integrated packages, learning time would still be extensive. Nor did integrated program vendors make it easy for users to start with one application and then move gradually to others by means of a well-laid-out training program that allowed them to start anywhere.

Beyond this, the very windowing tools and other concepts needed to create integration imposed some learning friction on users. The initial functional module of an integrated program would be significantly harder to learn than a stand-alone program of similar functionality, even if later learning for other modules would be improved. Generality often translates into an increased number of keystrokes for individual functions, so that a person doing mostly spreadsheet work will find the core 90 percent of his or her daily work becoming slightly more, not less, difficult.

Limited Attractiveness

Although all users need integration to some extent, not all feel the need very strongly. As illustrated in Table 12-1, (2) some users, such as salespeople and retail property managers, feel a very strong need for integration, but many users do not, including analyst/researchers and systems analysts/programmers. So far, the penetration of integrated programs has been strong only in departments where many workers have a strong need for integration. Unfortunately, in order to serve these narrow markets well, integrated program vendors will have to build bridges to basic corporate programs in individual areas.

TABLE 12-1
THE IMPORTANCE OF INTEGRATION

USER JOB	PERCENT*
Salesperson	78.0%
Retail property manager	77.5%
Accountant/bookkeeper	72%
Administrator/clerk	62.5%
Business executive/manager	58.8%
Lawyer/paralegal	55.5%
Doctor/dentist/pharmacist	54.1%
Writer/editor/reporter	51.1%
Engineer/scientist/architect	50.2%
Analyst/researcher	35.7%
Systems analyst/programmer	35.3%

* Percent responding that integration is either "very important" or "somewhat important."
SOURCE: D. Nucci (Ref. 2)

Managing Integrated Programs

The first step in managing integrated programs involves a choice of general strategy between (1) wholesale conversion (highly unlikely), (2) accepting a second standard for common functions, or (3) taking a wait-and-see approach.

For companies willing to accept a second standard, a survey should be conducted to identify departments with strong need for integrated packages. Within these departments, it should be determined if a core need more important than other needs exists. Most integrated programs are still strongest in a single area, for instance, Symphony in spreadsheet and Framework in word processing. Selecting a package that best suits core needs may be highly advantageous.

The next step is to see how each candidate package works with existing standards in the firm for stand-alone functions. It is important to conduct actual import and export tests, because there can be remarkable differences among the speed, ease of use, and competence of importing and exporting capabilities.

Third, how are training and support to be provided? For popular packages, training may be contracted out, but for ongoing support, at least two information center staffers must learn the selected package exhaustively. A learning time roughly equal to that of five stand-alone packages must be budgeted.

Although integrated packages are beginning to have a large enough market share to make it hard to take a complete wait-and-see attitude, many organizations feel that at this point controlled experimentation is more viable than creating a full second standard.

Desk Accessory Programs

In 1984 and 1985, many analysts assumed that integrated software would soon dominate the market. When this failed to happen, large numbers of users turned to **desktop accessories,** which add limited functionality to a user's basic program.

Desktop accessory programs are RAM-resident programs that use the "terminate and stay resident" capabilities discussed in Chapter 8. This allows them to monitor the keyboard interrupts, so that when a user types a key, the desk accessory considers whether the keystroke is destined for it and, if not, passes it onto the application program.

These desk accessory programs usually provide a simple calculator, a notepad, a telephone directory (perhaps linked to an autodialer), an appointment calendar, and perhaps more complex functions such as a small spreadsheet program, a limited file management system, and access to DOS commands.

Suppose a user is working with WordPerfect, a word processing program. At some point, the user needs to calculate a number. He or she hits the "Alt" and "Ctrl" keys simultaneously, and the desk accessory's menu of functions appears. The user selects "calculator," and a small calculator appears. Using the calculator-style section of the PC keyboard, the user does the calculation and hits the "capture" key. He or she then hits escape and the calculator disappears, returning the user to WordPerfect. As its last act, the desk accessory types the calculated value into the word processing document, just as if the user were typing it from the keyboard.

Next, the user realizes that he or she should include a table from the document in a memo. He or she brings the table onto the display and again calls up the desk accessory program, this time selecting "notepad."

When the notepad appears, the user selects "screen capture" from a menu of function key operations. The notepad disappears, and the user employs the cursor to mark the upper left and lower right corners of the table. Hitting the capture key again causes the designated text to be copied into the notepad. The user then writes text around the table and hits the "print" key to print it on his or her printer. The user then returns to WordPerfect.

Later, the user is interrupted by a telephone call. He or she pops up the notepad and takes notes during the call. Afterward, the user calls up the desk accessory's online telephone book, selects the boss's telephone number, and has the system dial the number. He or she then discusses the call that came in earlier, using the notes as a memory jogger.

The boss suggests a detailed meeting to follow up. The user and boss call up their appointment calendars, find a free time, and schedule the meeting. The desk accessory can later print a revised schedule for the week.

Desk accessories, as this scenario indicates, provide limited but always-available functionality for task switching, as well as limited cut-and-paste screen capture integration. (See Chapter 8 for a discussion of screen capture integration.)

The desk accessories that are now on the market are rather limited. Most offer only a few of the dozen or so possible functions, so that buying one desk accessory instead of another is a matter of giving up some features to gain others.

This situation will change as "boutique" desk accessory programs become more popular. These contain a **manager** program that always remains RAM resident, as well as a number of **application modules** selected by the user. The application modules are usually swapped in from disk when needed. The Macintosh has always offered this capability, providing basic desk accessories but allowing users to drop application modules individually and add third-party application modules as well, such as spelling checker programs. Several IBM PC software developers have subsequently adopted this approach.

As discussed in Chapter 8, operating environments usually include both desktop accessories and a manager for adding or dropping desk accessories. If operating environments become popular, they will represent a focal point for the development of application modules.

As functionality increases, so do the sizes of desk accessory programs. Some have become too RAM-hungry for many users. Others, which bring modules in from disk as needed, are less RAM-ravenous but require a hard disk for adequate storage and speed.

LESS COMMON APPLICATIONS

We have now looked at the most common personal computing applications found in organizations, but a number of less common applications also need to be standardized and managed.

Programming Languages

Most users start as command-level users, giving individual commands. Many go beyond this, stringing together series of commands using the embedded programming languages found in most packages. Only some go beyond this stage to work with formal programming languages such as BASIC, but enough make this step to require most information centers to support at least one end user programming language on PCs.

The extent of end user programming was probed in a 1985 readership survey by *PC Magazine*. (1) Of those responding to its survey, only 4 percent labeled themselves professional programmers, but a surprising 60 percent said they programmed in a formal programming language. Although this figure is inflated by *PC Magazine's* readership expertise and self-selection biases in answering the questionnaire, it does indicate that formal programming languages are used significantly.

Readers who answered that they programmed were then asked what languages they used. The following are the percentages of programmers using particular languages. (Totals exceed 100 percent, because some use more than one language.)

    87%—BASIC

    38%—Assembly Language

30%—Pascal

21%—C

8%—COBOL

Of the languages on this list, BASIC and Pascal are aimed at end users. In fact, BASIC was created in 1964 precisely for nontechnical students at Dartmouth University. C and COBOL are designed for people who are developing commercial packages, and they are not likely to be supported by information centers. Assembly language is the most complex of all; although it may be appropriate for some end user purposes, it is rarely supported.

In the microcomputer world, BASIC was the first language converted to run on these small machines. This gave it momentum. When IBM packaged an advanced BASIC created by Microsoft with virtually all of its PCs, and when Microsoft offered versions of this BASIC interpreter on other PCs, BASIC's predominance in the PC world was assured.

BASIC was originally a very crude language, but today's BASICs are quite powerful. In particular, they have specialized tools for building full-screen interfaces within their basic features, and programmer utilities are often available for such things as screen generation. There are even "hooks" to the level of individual memory locations.

BASIC is an interpreted product, which makes it easy for users to change programs, but programs run slowly once they are created. IBM offers an extremely advanced compiler that costs around $500 but supports such advanced features as ISAM file structures. Microsoft, in turn, offers a compiler at about $100 that does less but is sufficient for most needs. Both products have run-time modules or can create .EXE files that can run alone.

The Microsoft/IBM BASIC is not highly structured, but a number of BASIC interpreters do offer structured programming. For example, True BASIC, which was created by the team that originally built BASIC, conforms closely to drafts of the proposed ANSI standard for BASIC that includes structured programming.

For small jobs, there is Better BASIC, which has an editor environment that makes it look like an interpreter. Better BASIC, however, is really a very fast compiler that immediately produces compiled code after each change. Although syntactically nearly identical to Microsoft BASIC, Better BASIC also supports structured programming.

During the late 1970s and early 1980s, Pascal was touted as the better language to use. It was inherently structured and produced readable, maintainable code. In addition, its compiled programs, run swiftly. Powerful Pascals were very slow to emerge, and lack of standards for portability was also a serious problem. Pascal might have degenerated into a small niche market, but Borland International produced its low-priced Turbo Pascal, thereby reviving the language's popularity for very small jobs.

In assembly language, there is again a Microsoft/IBM connection. IBM markets Microsoft's assembler. For some jobs, assembly language may be ideal, but there is also immense potential for wasting large amounts of time. End users who want to use assembly language should be required to justify their use of assembly language.

Project Management

Project management is a common problem for managers. A variety of project management systems exist to serve different levels of needs.

The simplest project management systems merely allow the user to enter activities and see the time needed to complete the entire project.

The next level of programs lets the user begin to manage a project. As tasks are accomplished, the real results are entered, so that updating can be accomplished. More importantly, programs above the basic level can do **load leveling.** If a particular critical resource is oversubscribed at a particular time, the system will readjust tasks somewhat to keep the load on this resource within its stated bounds.

The most advanced systems can manage the *multiple* projects that must take place in any particular office. Load leveling can cut across multiple projects, for instance.

Few project management systems can do the whole job of managing a project-oriented department, including keeping detailed budgeting information, analyzing how well particular projects kept to time and budget, and so on. Few, in addition, do what if analysis of scheduling alternatives. These high-level refinements will have to come with time.

The biggest problem with project management systems, however, is not in the software but in the failure of most departments to adopt the general discipline needed to manage projects effectively. Unless the department already has adopted the rigors of project management discipline or is willing to do so, purchasing project management software is not likely to be very fruitful.

Business Applications

Accounting, payroll, billing, and other "business applications" are usually relegated to the world of operational systems. In smaller organizations, however, the information center may find its role less clear. This is particularly true when a firm has many small subsidiaries, or in gray areas such as property management in real estate, where the application is difficult to categorize on the basis of size as either end user computing or as an operational system.

In all of these cases, the system development process greatly resembles the traditional systems development process created for data processing (see Chapter 2). The one difference is that business applications on PCs or networks of PCs may be built around a full data base. Few minicomputers even support DBMSs, and in the larger world of mainframe operational systems, the transition to DBMSs have been very slow.

Vertical Software

Vertical software is created to handle a specific application, for instance, stock portfolio tracking or home mortgage closing computations. They are rich in specific functionality but, of course, apply to only a single application.

Functionality is the main purchase consideration, of course, but another important consideration is maintainability. Some applications are only sold in **object code,** which means that they have been compiled from humanly readable **source code** into an undecipherable machine language version called

object code. Such programs cannot be changed by the buyer. At the other extreme, many applications are macro-driven Lotus 1-2-3 templates (pre-created spreadsheet models) that any moderately experienced 1-2-3 user can modify.

Even if modification is possible, however, it may not be desirable. If the vendor releases a series of progressively better update versions, all modifications will have to be redone every time an update is purchased. This may be time consuming. Modification may also invalidate warranties that come with the application and may also invalidate customer service telephone assistance contracts.

Vertical applications vary from simple Lotus 1-2-3 templates produced by one end user for another to sophisticated real estate property management programs that take up millions of bytes of code and tens of millions of bytes of hard disk data storage.

For commercial packages, referrals are usually the best sources of information. Demo versions are not always available and are often too limited to reveal serious problems. Moreover, many problems are not discovered until after six months or a year of use. If local referrals are not available, the user may find it difficult to get on-site support, because the vendor is not active in the area or because the local dealer is inexperienced with the product.

Expert Systems

DEFT System

IBM uses an **expert system** to help it test its mainframe disk drives before shipping these drives to customers. (3) At each site, the individual components are built and tested, and then assembled into complete disk drives. The last step in the process is "final test," in which the complete unit is tested. It is in this last step that IBM uses its expert system DEFT, which stands for Diagnostic Expert—Final Test.

By the time the drives reach the final test, most of the easy problems have been ironed out. Therefore, final test usually deals with problems that require a high level of expertise to solve. This makes final test an ideal environment for using an expert system.

DEFT was built chiefly to reduce costs. IBM estimates that the system is saving $5 million to $8 million per year. In addition, DEFT is always available 24 hours a day, with help and full diagnostics available. Assistance is therefore even available after the main testing experts have gone home. Another stream of benefits comes from the training of new technicians and from letting new technicians turn to the system first, so that they will take up less of the senior technicians' valuable time.

In order to test DEFT, a six-month evaluation was done during which 658 product bugs were identified. Of these, 353 were small problems that could be solved without expert help, and of the remaining 305 difficult cases, an impressive 94 percent were solved on the first try using DEFT.

Expert systems are no longer science fiction. DEFT is only one of many examples now in existence in which expert systems have proven their abilities to handle difficult tasks and save time and money. As computer hardware and expert system development tools mature, expert system development may become a major application in end user computing.

What Are Expert Systems?

As the DEFT example indicates, expert systems are applications that attempt to solve problems that would normally require considerable expertise. Applications simple enough to solve without the use of a computer or with the help of a simple spreadsheet model or program do not rate as expert systems.

A second part of a definition for expert systems would add that expert systems use knowledge-based approaches from artificial intelligence, which are discussed in Chapter 8. Instead of the developer writing a traditional program, he or she develops if–then rules to describe what should be done and what each piece of knowledge implies. This approach allows the use of **heuristics**—rules of thumb that exist even where precise algorithmic approaches are lacking. DEFT has 1426 separate heuristic rules. (3) As discussed in Chapter 8, these rules constitute a "knowledge base" that is searched by an "inference engine" to find the implications of testing results.

In operation, the ultimate user interacts with the expert system by answering a series of questions about the subject. Figure 12-4 (4) illustrates an interaction in which a physician works with MYCIN, a system for diagnosing bacteremia (an infection involving bacteria in the blood) meningitis.

MYCIN begins by asking for four pieces of information about the patient—name, age, sex, and race. All are essential to any diagnosis, so they are asked at the onset of the session.

1. Please enter information about the patient.

Name	Age	Sex	Race
Sally	42 years	Female	Caucasian

The physician enters the information and MYCIN continues.

2. Are there any positive cultures obtained from SALLY?
   No

3. Are there any pending cultures of SALLY?
   Yes

4. Site: date   stain   method of collection
            collected: examined?   (urine, sputum only)
   CSF   3 June 75   Yes

5. Stain of smear: morph:
   (type NONE if no organism was seen on the smear)
   None

FIGURE 12-4 A SESSION WITH AN EXPERT SYSTEM   *(continued)*

The second piece of information that MYCIN wants concerns the availability of cultures with positive readings. Rather than attempting to deduce the results of tests, MYCIN allows the physician to state what is known. In this case the physician does not have any positive cultures, and so MYCIN probes further (question 3), asking whether this patient has pending cultures. The patient does—and so MYCIN provides headings for the physician, who enters CSF to indicate that a cerebrospinal fluid culture has been taken but that no organism has yet been seen. MYCIN is unable to reach conclusions from laboratory findings, but, like the physician, MYCIN continues to ask questions. Eventually, MYCIN reaches this:

13. Has SALLY recently had symptoms of persistent headache or other abnormal neurologic symptoms (dizziness, lethargy, etc.)?
    Yes

14. Has SALLY recently had objective evidence of abnormal neurologic signs (nuchal rigidity, coma, seizures, etc.) documented by physician observation or examination?
    Yes

    The CSF cultures will be considered to be associated with MENINGITIS.

    MYCIN's questions 13 and 14 show a more traditional approach to the diagnosis by symptoms, and after receiving the answer to question 14, MYCIN reports its first conclusion: The CSF infection is likely to be meningitis. MYCIN then begins another line of reasoning aimed at identifying the particular organisms responsible for the meningitis infection. Further questions lead to the following:

34. Is the meningitis a hospital-acquired infection?
    No

35. Is SALLY's clinical history consistent with EPIGLOTTITIS?
    No

36. Is SALLY's clinical history consistent wit OTITIS-MEDIA?
    No

37. Has the patient ever been to an area that is endemic for coccidiomycoses?
    Unknown

38. Is SALLY a burn patient?
    Why

When asked whether the patient is a burn victim (question 38), the physician responds by typing WHY. MYCIN responds by restating its understanding of "why" in this context, and then explains what the information will be used for. To explain, MYCIN displays the particular heuristic rule it was considering, Rule 578, and explains how the requested information would be useful.

[i.e. WHY is it important to determine whether SALLY has been seriously burned?]

(continued)

[4.0]
    This will aid in determining the organisms (other than those seen on cultures or smears) which might be causing the infection.
    It has already been established that
    [4.1]   the infection which requires therapy is meningitis, and
    [4.2]   organisms were not seen on the stain of the pending csf culture (CULTURE-1), and
    [4.3]   the type of the infection may be bacterial
Therefore
    [4.4]   SALLY has been seriously burned
then
    there is suggestive evidence that Pseudomonas aeruginosa is one of the organisms (other than those seen on cultures or smears) which might be causing the infection [RULE578]

[back to question 38 . . .]

How 4.3

The physician is curious about how MYCIN was able to conclude that the type of infection is bacterial. "HOW 4.3" is a request to explain how MYCIN established clause [4.3] of the rule it is considering. MYCIN responds with its understanding of the question, and then reports the rules it used in determining this fact. The physician can press for greater detail by asking HOW 4.5 to track down what heuristic Rule 500 is and how it was confirmed. By repeatedly asking HOW, the physician can backtrack right to the beginning of the consultation.

Notice that MYCIN has four rules that support the likelihood that the infection is bacterial, and one rule that suggests (certainty factor of 17) that the infection is not bacterial. MYCIN is considering both possibilities. Momentarily, it is following up on the more probable one.

[i.e. HOW was it established that the type of the infection may be bacterial?]

The following rules concluded about: the likelihood that the type of the infection may be bacterial

	Rule	Yes	No
[4.5]	RULE500	(.4)	
[4.6]	RULE501		(.17)
[4.7]	RULE502	(.1)	
[4.8]	RULE524	(.42)	
[4.9]	RULE504	(.28)	

    Thus, it has been established that the type of the infection may be bacterial.

We rejoin MYCIN several questions later as it reports its conclusions about the culprit organisms, and then turns to the final phase of its consultation, the prescription of a set of antibiotics. MYCIN checks for known allergies (question 43), for other characteristics that relate to the use of particular medications, and then for the patient's weight.

(continued)

My therapy recommendations will be designed to treat for organisms that either are very likely or, although less likely, would have a significant effect on therapy selection if they were present. It is important to cover for the following probable infection(s) and associated organism(s):

INFECTION-1 is MENINGITIS

+ ITEM-1 MYCOBACTERIUM-TB [from clinical evidence only]
+   COCCIDIOIDES [from clinical evidence only]
+   CRYPTOCOCCUS [from clinical evidence only]

43. Does SALLY have a clinically significant allergic reaction to any antimicrobial agent?
    No

44. Is SALLY pregnant or breast feeding?
    No

45. Do you have reason to suspect that SALLY may have impaired renal functions?
    No

46. SALLY's weight in kilograms (or number POUNDS):
    51.3

From these 46 questions MYCIN makes a prescription (REC-1), explains its reasoning, and proposes additional tests and procedures.

[REC-1] My preferred therapy recommendation is as follows: Give the following in combination:

  1. ETHAMBUTAL
     Dose: 1.28 g (13.0 100mg-tablets) q24h PO for 60 days
            [calculated on basis of 25 mg/kg]
            then 770 mg (7.5 100 mg-tablets) q24h PO
            [calculated on basis of 15 mg/kg]
     [The dose should be modified in renal failure. I can adjust the dose only if a creatinine clearance or a serum creatinine is obtained.]
     Comments: Periodic vision screening tests are recommended for optic neuritis.
  2. INH
     Dose: 513 mg (5.0 100mg-tablets) q24h PO
            [calculated on basis of 10 mg/kg]
  3. RIFAMPIN
     Dose: 600 mg PO q24h
     Comments: Administer dose on an empty stomach.

Although I suspect that fungus may be a possible pathogen, in the absence of definitive evidence I will not recommend antifungal therapy at this time. Please obtain samples for fungal, TB, and viral cultures, cytology, VDRL (blood and CSF), cryptococcal antigen (blood and CSF), viral titers (blood and CSF). An infectious disease consult may be advisable.

(continued)

> MYCIN's explanations, although quite useful, are limited to a review of its reasoning process and a display of its knowledge. MYCIN cannot justify or explain the rules themselves, nor can it define the terms it is using. That is, the physician cannot ask WHY RULES78 or WHAT IS PSEUDOMONAS AERUGINOSA. Rules contain the knowledge gleaned from an expert.
>
> It is assumed that the terms MYCIN uses and the answers it requests are familiar to the physicians using the program. Knowledge systems like MYCIN must be carefully tailored to match characteristics of their user communities. The knowledge engineers who built MYCIN were responsible for making sure that terms such as "culture," "staining," and "Mycobacterium-TB" would be familiar terms to MYCIN's users.

FIGURE 12-4 (concluded)

In general, the user takes a passive role, providing the information requested or saying "unknown." In interaction 38, however, the user takes a more active role, asking why a particular question is being asked. The user, noting a conclusion that does not seem warranted, asks how MYCIN established finding 4.3, that the type of infection may be bacterial. MYCIN responds with rule numbers to support its conclusions.

Expert System Shells

Although it is possible to build expert systems using PROLOG, LISP, or other AI-oriented programming languages (see Chapter 8), most expert systems are built with **expert system shells,** which provide high-level tools for application development and use.

The first consideration in selecting an expert system is whether the problem can be handled on a personal computer or whether it is so large that it must be handled on a mainframe-based shell. Whatever the precise limit, it is true that the largest applications require mainframe power to run. IBM's DEFT, for example, with more than 1000 rules, was built using IBM's Expert Systems Environment (ESE) shell on a mainframe computer. (3)

A second consideration is the functionality of the shell. Like other fourth-generation products, expert system shells must be feature-rich to avoid frustrating developers who need to do particular tasks and find that the system cannot handle them.

The editor must allow the developer to add and drop rules easily. It should also provide a list of rules when asked, preferably including relationships among the rules. Because the display of relationships is so complex, a variety of tools for windowing, tracing logic flows, and other diagnostics should be provided. It should also be able to test new rules for consistency with old rules because human expertise is often inconsistent and contradictory.

The inference engine should be able to handle probability, not just solid facts. Much of human knowledge consists of likelihoods rather than certainties. A user should therefore be able to add a probability to a statement, and the system should be able to handle the multiplication of probabilities. This is a ticklish subject, because the most common way to multiply probabilities is the use of Beysean analysis, whose validity in ordinary human situations has been criticized. Therefore, even at a theoretical level, probability is difficult to handle.

For advanced professional expert system developers, an important consideration may be the ability to control the search strategy used by the inference engine, for example, the ability to blend depth forward and backward chaining (see Chapter 8) and the ability to control whether the program searches deeply down individual branches of the search tree (depth-first searching) or looks at all branches to a small depth before going deeply down any branch (breadth-first searching). Today not many expert system developers can make use of these capabilities.

Another consideration is the kind of tasks handled by the shell. Most shells are oriented toward diagnosis, planning, or both. If the user's needs fall into one of these two areas, product selection will be easy. If the user has other kinds of application, however, it may be difficult to find a good shell, and the range of shells from which to choose will be somewhat limited. Harmon and King (4) identify a large number of potential types of tasks for expert systems, including interpretation, prediction, diagnosis, design, planning, monitoring, debugging, repair, instruction, and control.

For ultimate users, a major consideration is how easy it is to interact with the system. If the application asks a question, the user should be able to ask why the question is being asked, and the expert system should be able to explain its lines of reasoning. In addition, when the system reaches a conclusion, the user should be able to ask for and receive a detailed explanation of the logic used to reach the conclusion.

Ease of learning is also important. As in most fourth-generation products, expert system shells tend to be oriented either toward the sophisticated needs of professional programmers or toward the simpler needs of end user developers. The most sophisticated packages require intense formal training, but for most users, including IS professionals, development products need to be simple enough that they can be learned from tutorials and manuals, because there are not enough users of most products to justify holding training programs in many cities.

A final consideration is whether the expert system development tool is a stand-alone product or whether it can be linked to other programs, including data base management systems that can *extend* the expert system's power and word processing programs and other application programs that can *use* its power to act more intelligently to their users. Today, most expert system shells are stand-alone products, but this is likely to be just a passing phase, just as graphics began in stand-alone products and then spread through almost every application category.

Development

Although expert systems can be developed by trained IS professionals, the growing expertise of end users will probably lead to end user development becoming the dominant way to develop expert systems in the long run. The DEFT system, for example, was 99 percent coded by two senior technicians, (3) and there are many other examples of user-developed expert systems.

Whether IS professionals or end users develop the applications, however, a number of development issues need to be addressed carefully. The first of these is the process of codifying the expert's knowledge. This codification process is called **knowledge engineering.** Knowledge engineering is difficult because many experts find it hard to express their knowledge explicitly. When an IS professional develops the system, he or she must cope with foreign terminology and somehow elicit the information from the ultimate expert. If the ultimate expert develops the application, these problems are reduced, but many people find it hard to be sufficiently introspective without an external analyst.

Eliciting rules is only the beginning. The next crucial stage is testing. Because the results can be highly unpredictable when many independent rules are thrown into the knowledge base, it is dangerous to use a system without first testing it by giving it problems in parallel with a human expert and testing their agreement. In the early stages of an expert system's life, its behavior is likely to be bizarre, but as it matures, its behavior tends to become more reasonable and consistent.

Perspective

Today, expert systems are still in their infancy. Although we can cite some examples of clear victories using expert systems, we still have little understanding of the limits of expert systems, the kinds of functions that are most important to users, or how to do elicitation or testing. Corporations that move forward should proceed cautiously, but the potential benefits of expert systems are so great and these applications are so fascinating that experimentation should be widespread in the very near future.

REVIEW QUESTIONS

1. List the four major services offered by commercial online services. What are the differences between basic and sophisticated information retrieval services? Between citation and full-text retrieval services for documents? What do you need to reach an online service? Which of the four major services do you think you would use the most? The least?

2. What are the prospects for videotex? Define alphamosaic, alphageometric, NAPLPS, and TTY.

3. Why are the costs of using an online service difficult to define?

4. What support problems are raised by sophisticated retrieval services? How does this challenge the No Programming Dogma?

5. What are the four components of a personal computer network? What are the three main kinds of servers, and what are the advantages and disadvantages of each? What are the reasons for implementing a PC network?

6. What are the main services offered by servers? What are the desirable features to have in each? What is the difference between disk and file service? What are the three levels at which locking may be done to ensure safe multiuser access to information?

7. What management problems does PC networking create?
8. What is the difference between an integrated program and a desk accessory? What are the most common functions in integrated programs? What are the advantages of integrated programs? Why has their growth been so slow? In what sense is a desk accessory program a substitute for an integrated program? In what sense is it not?
9. Why do you think end users learn to program in a programming language? What are the primary target markets for BASIC, assembly language, Pascal, C, and COBOL? Why is it true to say that BASIC is interpreted? Why is it not true?
10. What are the levels of functionality in project management programs? What is the biggest problem with project management systems?
11. What are business applications? What is vertical software?
12. What is an expert system? Name advantages of expert systems. What control does a user have during interaction with an expert system? What are the qualities to look for in a development tool? Why is each important? What is knowledge engineering?

REFERENCES

1. DICKINSON, JOHN, "Programming Makes Sense for Business," *PC Magazine,* October 29, 1985, pp. 109–114.
2. DiNUCCI, DARCEY, "Environmental Impact," *PC World,* December 1985, pp. 224–231.
3. GOLDBERG, EDDY, "Vendor Uses Expert System to Assemble, Test DASD Units," *Computerworld,* November 17, 1986, pp. 14–15.
4. HARMON, PAUL, AND KING, DAVID, "Expert Systems," John Wiley & Sons, 1985.

13 WORKING WITH HOST COMPUTERS

In the next three chapters, we will look at the information center's role in communications. In communications, the information center will rarely have the power to make decisions on its own. Either it will be one voice in a larger committee that makes the decision, or it will be an advocate for end users in decisions made by a central telecommunications department.

Despite this subordinate status, the information center cannot just sit back and let others make decisions. End users have different needs than clerical workers and other communications users in the firm. Sometimes, in fact, end user needs are in conflict with other needs. In data communications, the information center needs to be a strong and knowledgeable advocate for end users.

To be an effective advocate, the information center staff must develop a great deal of technical expertise. Data communications is a complex field, and it is changing so rapidly that even specialists sometimes feel like throwing up their hands in dismay. In addition, few scholastic MIS programs in the past have included data communications courses, and as a result, many information centers professionals have never had a full course on the subject. In this chapter and the next, we will survey what the information center needs to know about data communications to work effectively with other parts of the corporate IS group.

Broadly speaking, the field of data communications has two parts. The first is **workstation–host communications. Hosts** are multiuser computers, including mainframes, minicomputers, and even multiuser microcomputers. **Workstations** are devices on users' desks, including terminals and personal computers. Workstation–host communications is the dominant form of data communications in organizations today. It is the focus of this chapter.

The second main part of data communications is **networking.** In networking, there is a central transmission system to which many devices are attached—terminals, hosts, and personal computers. The network can connect any attached device to any other, just as the telephone network can connect any telephone to any other telephone. In contrast, workstation–host communications can only connect a host with its own workstations.

But the any-to-any transmission service provided by networks is still only one step toward effective data communications. A network only transmits streams of bits among the devices attached to it. There is no guarantee that the receiver will be able to make any sense out of what the sender transmits. In a multivendor environment, effective communications requires comprehensive standards, including standards for the transmission system, standards for the attached computers, and standards for application programs. Unfortunately, the needed standards for effective communications are still in the process of evolving. As as result, the use of networking is quite limited today. Networking and comprehensive standards are discussed theoretically in Chapter 14. Chapter 15 discusses networking products.

The personal computer will eventually participate in networking on an equal status with host computers. Today, however, PC communications is very limited. First, PCs can work with hosts through the process of **terminal emulation,** which is effective for simple applications but uses only a fraction of the personal computer's power. Second, a few PCs can be linked with one another through **personal computer networking,** providing a department-sized work unit with limited connectivity. This chapter discusses PC terminal emulation. Chapters 14 and 15 discuss PC networking.

BASIC ISSUES

Linking Workstations to Hosts

When linking workstations—terminals or PCs—to hosts, there is one fundamental rule: The Host Calls the Shots. Technologically, terminals have always been mere appendages to the central host, and the kinds of terminals purchased and the kinds of transmission links used to connect terminals to hosts have always been dictated by the design of the host.

As noted above, when PCs are linked to hosts, it is usually done through **terminal emulation,** in which the PC is given special hardware and software to emulate a terminal acceptable to the host. In emulation, the PC mimics a terminal so completely that the host literally cannot tell that it is dealing with a PC instead of a terminal. Terminal emulation is merely a "technical fix," not a solution designed from scratch, and PCs that work with the hosts through terminal emulation inherit the subjugated status long held by terminals. More sophisticated ways to link PCs with hosts are discussed in Chapters 14 and 15, but in most firms today, terminal emulation is the norm.

If an end user is to be able to work with a host, the information center must ensure that four separate requirements are satisfied, as shown in Figure 13-1.

WORKING WITH HOST COMPUTERS

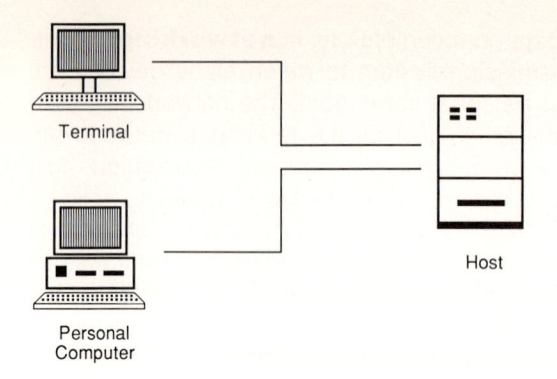

Requirements

A terminal acceptable to the host or a personal computer emulating such a terminal.

A transmission facility between the workstation and the host.

The information needed must be on the host, together with the application software needed to process it.

Access permission and arrangements with the host authority.

FIGURE 13-1 WORKSTATION–HOST COMMUNICATIONS

1. Users must have either **terminals** acceptable to the host or else **PCs** with special hardware and software to let the PCs emulate a terminal acceptable to the host.
2. There must be a **transmission facility** between the workstation and the host. This transmission facility may be anything from a direct cable connection to a complex network. It may be the same as the facility supplied to clerical users of operational systems, but it may be different.
3. Appropriate **end user application software** must be supplied on the host so that the user can work on the host with reasonable ease. It does little good to reach a host if there is no software there to help the end user work.
4. Finally, **access arrangements** must be provided to govern how the end user can use the host without causing damage and how the end user's departments will pay for the resources used.

In this chapter, we will look at terminals, terminal emulation, transmission facilities, and access arrangements. Application software will be discussed in Chapters 16 and 17.

Transmission Speed

The concept of speed runs throughout the next five chapters, so we will examine it before proceeding.

Bits Per Second

Transmission speed is measured in **bits per second** or **bps.** For high speeds, the standard metric conventions are used.

- 20,000 bits per second is 20 kilobits per second or 20 kbps.
- 2 million bps is 2 megabits per second or 2 Mbps.
- 2,000,000,000 bps is 2 gigabits per second or 2 Gbps. Because this is the U.S. billion and not the European billion, giga is the preferred prefix.

Note that the standard international metric prefix for kilo is "k" rather than "K." In computer memory, kilobytes are written as KB to indicate that 1024 is the unit of measurement, rather than 1000. Most communications books and journals use "kbps," but the abbreviation "Kbps" for 1000 bps is becoming fairly common, owing to the large number of computer specialists in the field.

Bits Per Second and Baud Rate

Another point of confusion is the difference between bps and **baud rate.** Baud rate is the number of times the transmission line changes per second. So if there are two voltage levels, corresponding to 0 and 1, the baud rate is exactly the same as bps.

Above 300 bps, however, most transmission schemes carry several bits of information per line change. For example, suppose there are four voltage levels, corresponding to 00, 01, 10, and 11. Now, every time the line changes, two bits of information are transmitted. So the baud rate is half of the transmission speed in bps.

Unfortunately, it is easier to say "baud" than "bits per second" or even "bps." As a result, "baud" is frequently used where "bps" is meant. But baud rate and bps are almost never the same on modern transmission systems. The popular 212A modem, for example, is a 1200 bps, 600 baud modem.

Duration and Noise

"Transmission speed" does not refer to velocity, in the sense of a car's speed. Instead, it refers to the duration of each bit. For example, a transmission speed of 300 bps means that each bit is 1/300th of a second long, or about 3 milliseconds. At 10 Mbps, each bit's duration is only 1/10th of a microsecond.

Shorter duration means more costly equipment. It is harder to detect changes reliably if they occur every 0.1 microseconds than it is if they occur every 3333 microseconds. In addition, at faster speeds, more complex signalling techniques are needed to transmit messages on most transmission lines. When transmitting over an ordinary telephone line, for example, 9600 bps is much more expensive to sustain than 1200 bps or even 2400 bps.

Shorter duration also means higher error rates. All transmission lines have **noise,** that is, spurious signals. This noise is random and comes in the form of short peaks and valleys of various sizes and durations. Most of these peaks and valleys are very short, say, a few microseconds. At 1200 bps, the 3333 microsecond duration of each bit causes most of the microsecond peaks and valleys to average out. At 10 Mbps, however, many more peaks and valleys are a whole bit long and may change a 1 to a 0 or a 0 to a 1. Higher speeds require lines with lower noise, sophisticated error detection and correction, or both.

Throughput

If you are told that a transmission system's speed is 10 Mbps, it would be logical to assume that a 10 million bit document could be transmitted in one second. In practice, however, it will take much longer to transmit the document. A transmission system's **throughput**—the number of user data bits sent per second—is always less than the system's rated speed. Sometimes, the throughput is less than half of the system's rated speed.

One reason why throughput is less than the rated speed is that user data are not sent back to back, with no space between them. As discussed later, transmission always requires spaces between at least some characters, as well as the sending of supervisory messages to control the transmission flow.

Another reason why throughput is less than the rated line speed is that many users may share a transmission line with other users. Even the largest superhighway can have traffic jams when too many cars use it at the same time.

TERMINALS

We will first discuss terminals, PC terminal emulation, and protocol converters. We begin with these topics for two reasons: (1) the terminal or PC will be the user's daily contact point with the broader world; and (2) terminal equipment is a good place to introduce a number of basic communications concepts, such as asynchronous and synchronous communications. These concepts will carry over to the discussions of transmission links, PC and host software beyond terminal emulation, and other technological matters.

The first item a user must have is either a terminal acceptable to the host or a PC that emulates a terminal acceptable to the host. There are two basic kinds of terminals that end users are likely to encounter or emulate with their PCs. The first is the **TTY,** a popular terminal accepted by many host computers. The second kind is the **host-specific terminal,** which can work only with a single family of hosts—for instance, the IBM "3270" terminals, which work only with IBM mainframe computers.

TTY Terminals

The simplest kind of terminal is called a **TTY,** which stems from its original name, "teletypewriter." Because the TTY has been around so long and is so simple, most of its features are de facto standards, although a number of important features are not standardized. Many hosts can talk to a TTY, and that is why we discuss it first.

Dumb Terminals

A TTY is a **dumb** terminal. This means that it cannot process information beyond the work needed to exchange characters with the host and "type"

TERMINALS **545**

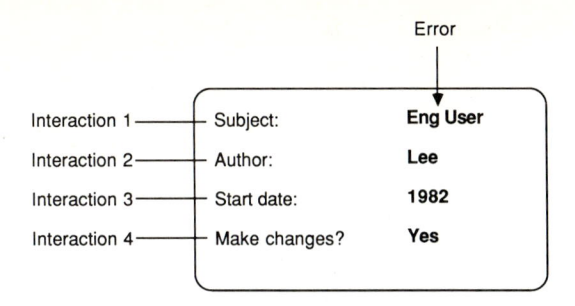

```
                              Error
                                ↓
     Interaction 1 ——— Subject:      Eng User
     Interaction 2 ——— Author:       Lee
     Interaction 3 ——— Start date:   1982
     Interaction 4 ——— Make changes? Yes
```

Editing can only be done on the current line (in this case, Interaction 4).

The user cannot cursor to the error in Interaction 1 and make changes.   **FIGURE 13-2** DUMB TERMINALS

characters on the display screen. Every last bit of information manipulation is done at the host. Whatever the user types is sent directly to the host, perhaps after being painted on the TTY's display. Whatever the host sends is routed to the display screen.

As shown in Figure 13-2, a TTY user can only edit the line currently being typed. If a mistake has been made on an earlier line, the user cannot simply "cursor up" to the error and edit the mistake.

Although this lack of power gives low performance, it does allow us to predict exactly what a TTY will do. If we send it information, that information will be shown on the screen. If someone types on it, whatever is typed will pass directly to the host. Unless there is a malfunction, nothing else will happen. This predictability makes it very easy for a host to work with a TTY.

ASCII

When Morse invented the telegraph, he had to invent a code for the alphabet, numbers, and other special symbols. Today, the Morse code is dead in data communications, although it is still used for person-to-person communication. Primacy has passed to another code, **ASCII,** and ASCII is the code used on TTYs. As shown in Figure 13-3, ASCII has seven data bits, so it can encode two to the seventh power or 128 possible symbols.

As shown in Figure 13-3, ASCII codes fall into two major categories. First, there are **information codes,** which convey the user's message. Letters of the alphabet, digits, and punctuation marks are the main information codes.

Other codes are **supervisory codes,** which control the flow of information. For example, Device Control No. 3 (Control-S) is often used to tell the other device to stop sending temporarily, whereas Device Control No. 1 (Control-Q) is often used to tell the other device to resume transmission.

Although ASCII is rich in supervisory codes, there is no standard way of using these codes in data communications. As a result, ASCII requires each host designer to make a number of ad hoc decisions about how supervisory codes will be used on that host, for example, whether to use Device Control 3

Information Codes

Capital letters	A	1000001
Lower case letters	a	1100001
Digits	1	0110001
Punctuation	!	0100001
Math symbols	<	0111100
Alternative character set	Shift out*	0001110

Supervisory Codes

Message formatting	Start of header	0000001
Terminal control	Carriage return	0001101
Transmission control	Device Control 3*	0010011

Notes:

ASCII has 7 data bits (128 possible symbols).

*Shift Out gives an alternative meaning to each symbol that follows the Shift Out code.

**Device Control C (Control-S) is normally used to request the other device to stop sending. It is also called XOFF.

FIGURE 13-3 ASCII CHARACTER CODE

to tell the terminal to pause. Some of these codes must be understood by the terminal user or added as parameters to PC terminal emulation programs. In other words, ASCII's lack of standardized supervisory codes places a learning burden on users, considerably diluting the TTY's claim to simplicity. TTY simplicity comes only at the level of technology. Hosts that work with TTYs work with almost any TTY on the market, but this does not mean that users will have a simple time setting up their particular TTY, which often comes with several switches to be configured.

Error Detection through Parity

In ASCII transmission, eight bits are actually sent per character. The eighth bit is a **parity** bit, which is used for error checking. Figure 13-4 illustrates the use of the parity bit. In **odd parity,** the parity bit is set so that the total number of ones in the seven data bits and the parity bit is an odd number. In **even parity,** the parity bit is set so that the total number of ones in the eight bits is zero.

Parity is used to detect errors. If one bit has been changed accidentally, the computer will find that the parity for that character is incorrect. Many

Character	A	a
ASCII code	1000001	1100001
Number of 1's	2	3
Odd or even	Even	Odd
Even parity	10000010	11000011
Odd parity	10000011	11000010

Parity bit

FIGURE 13-4 PARITY IN ASCII

errors are multibit errors, which change many bits instead of just one. Of course, parity is blind to an even number of errors. As a result, parity is rarely used today for error checking. In practice, parity is often "off," which means that the computer does not look at the parity bit.

Asynchronous Transmission

When TTYs transmit characters, they send them **asynchronously,** that is, one character at a time, with spaces between the characters—very much like commuters driving to work in their individual cars. Figure 13-5 illustrates asynchronous communications.

When no data are being sent, the transmission line is kept in the "zero" state, meaning that it is kept in the voltage level normally associated with a zero. Many ASCII characters start with zeros, however, so how can the detector in the receiving device know when a character starts? In other words, how can it tell the difference between "00111111" and "11111100?" To solve this problem, asynchronous transmission precedes each character with a **start bit**—a single "one." This causes an unambiguous line change in order to tell the detector that a new character is starting. Just to make sure, each character is also ended by a **stop bit,** another "one." (The Baudot code used primarily in Telex uses a stop bit that is 1.4 bits long.)

Asynchronous transmission is very inefficient. To transmit a single 7-bit ASCII information code, "asynch" transmission must also send a start bit, a stop bit, and a parity bit. These three bits represent an "overhead" of 37 percent (3/7). In addition, there must be spaces between each character sent. On a 1200 bps transmission line, asynchronous communications will have a hard time moving even 600 information bits per second.

The RS232C Electrical Interface

The terminal must have a physical and electrical "interface" to the outside world. This interface includes a connector plug of a specific shape as well as electrical signals of specific voltages. The TTY uses an interface originally developed to link a terminal to a device that will be discussed later, a modem.

This interface, **RS232C,** has 25 pins, as shown in Figure 13-6. Only three of these pins are used for data transmission.

- Pin 2 is for transmission *from* the terminal *to* the host.
- Pin 3 is for transmission in the opposite direction—*from* the host *to* the terminal
- Pin 7 is a signal ground, which creates a neutral voltage to allow the voltages associated with ones and zeros on other pins to be interpreted correctly.

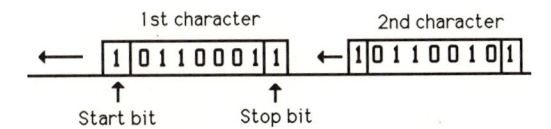

FIGURE 13-5 ASYNCHRONOUS TRANSMISSION

WORKING WITH HOST COMPUTERS

FIGURE 13-6 RS232C INTERFACE

25-Pin Connector (DB25)

Commonly used

Pin	Use
2	Terminal transmission to modem
3	Modem transmission to terminal
7	Signal ground to give a reference voltage
4	Terminal issues "Request to Send"
5	Modem gives "Clear to Send"
6	Modem gives "Data Set (modem) Ready"
8	"Data Carrier Detect"
20	Terminal gives OK to send ("Data Terminal Ready")

Limit

19,200 bits per second (19.2 kbps)

50 feet maximum distance to receiver or amplifier

Other pins are used to signal various conditions in the other devices and to provide an electrical ground to reduce shock hazards. The military has a similar standard, called MIL-STD-188C, which uses lower voltages to reduce radiation and therefore detectability. Internationally, the CCITT (International Consultative Committee on Telephone and Telegraphy) has the V.24 standard which is compatible with RS232C in the sense that there is a one-to-one matching of key pins, but V.24 connectors cannot be used to replace RS232C connectors without a translating device.

We will not get into the technical details of RS232C, but we will discuss its performance. Designed many years ago when speeds were much lower, RS232C can only transfer information between the terminal and outside world at 19,200 bps, that is, 19.2 kbps. Even if a terminal is connected with the host via a transmission line that can send more than a million bps, the RS232C interface places an absolute speed restriction on transmissions. It is a funnel at a feast.

In addition, RS232C is designed only to transmit its signal 50 feet. After 50 feet, there must either be the host computer or a device to amplify the signal. Note that the terminal does *not* have to be within 50 feet of a host; it merely needs to be within 50 feet of a modem, local area network port, or some other communications device that will amplify the signal and pass it on.

Speed

There is no standard transmission speed for TTYs. Most TTYs can transmit at several speeds, in order to deal with the demands of different hosts. Popular speeds are 300 bps, 1200 bps, 2400 bps, 4800 bps, and 9600 bps. Few TTYs can reach the 19.2 kbps speed limit of RS232C.

Duplex and Echoing

Most TTY terminals have a switch that specifies half-duplex or full-duplex transmission. In **half-duplex** transmission, both the terminal and host can transmit, but they must take turns. Transmission can occur in only one direction at a time. Once one side "grabs" the circuit, there is no way to interrupt it. Half-duplex operation was once the only common way to communicate.

Now, most circuits allow simultaneous two-way transmission which is normally done by assigning different signalling frequencies to the terminal and host. Because sounds at different frequencies do not mix together, the terminal and host can transmit simultaneously without their signals interfering. If the host supports simultaneous two-way transmission, this is called **full-duplex** operation.

In half-duplex operation, whatever the user types is both sent to the host and printed on the display, as shown in Figure 13-7. This is called **local echoing.**.

In full-duplex operation, only the host can paint characters on the TTY screen. This means that whatever the user types goes to the host and is then sent to the TTY's display by the host. This curious practice is called **remote echo.**

There are two reasons for doing remote echo. The first is to keep the user interface clean. Because both the user and the host can send simultaneously, local echo would often mix outgoing and incoming information on the screen, resulting in incomprehensible garble.

The second reason is that this approach provides limited error checking, because it allows the user to see errors on the screen. If what appears on the

Local Echo (Half-Duplex Operation)

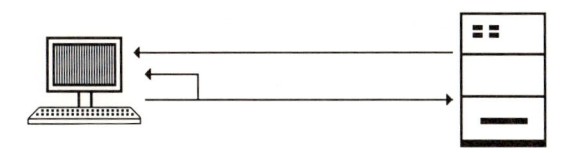

Characters sent to the host are echoed locally to the terminal screen as well as sent to the host computer.

Remote Echo (Full-Duplex Operation)

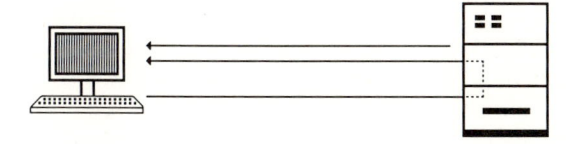

Characters sent to the host are echoed to the terminal screen by the host computer

FIGURE 13-7 LOCAL AND REMOTE ECHO

screen is not what the user typed or thought he or she had typed, then either there was an error in transmission or a typographical error occurred. Most transmission problems are obvious because they produce a large amount of "garbage" on the screen.

ANSI Terminals
A large number of minicomputers support Digital Equipment Corporation terminals, usually DEC's VT52 and VT100 terminals. The American National Standards Institute (ANSI) has produced a terminal standard based on the DEC VT100. These are usually referred to as **ANSI terminals.**

ANSI terminals are variants of the TTY terminal. They are asynchronous ASCII RS232C machines. What makes them special is their use of certain ASCII control codes to do cursor movements and erasures on the screen. This makes it easy for host software designers to build full-screen interfaces.

Although ANSI terminals are widely used in the minicomputer world, few mainframes work with these terminals. Because of this limited utility, we will not look at ANSI terminals further.

Host-Specific Terminals
Because of the limitations of TTYs, most computer vendors have developed their own standard terminals that communicate faster, communicate with a precisely defined and extensive set of supervisory codes, and catch errors more reliably. The most widely used host-specific terminals are those of the IBM **3270 terminal** family.

Smart Terminals
Many host-specific terminals, including 3270s, are **smart,** meaning that they have enough internal processing power to do full-screen editing as shown in Figure 13-8. These editing features fall far short of those needed in full word processing, but they are enough for filling out forms painted on the screen.

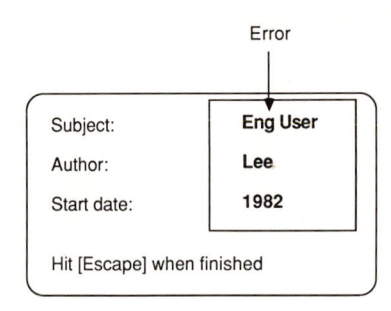

```
                         Error
                           ↓
   Subject:       Eng User
   Author:        Lee
   Start date:    1982

   Hit [Escape] when finished
```

Smart terminals provide full-screen editing.
The user may cursor back to fields already filled in and make edits.

FIGURE 13-8 SMART (EDITING) TERMINALS

Smart terminals can offload a good deal of work from the host. The host only deals with a smart terminal occasionally, whereas it may be interrupted every time a dumb terminal user hits a key.

For users, smart terminals provide the quick and consistent response times desirable in editing operations.

For application developers, smart terminals make it easy to design attractive full-screen interfaces that let users check off options in boxes instead of having to answer a long series of individual questions.

EBCDIC

IBM hosts do not use the popular ASCII character code discussed earlier. Instead, IBM uses its own character code, EBCDIC (the Extended Binary-Coded Decimal Information Code).

EBCDIC is an 8-bit code, giving it twice as many symbols as ASCII. As a result, there is no one-to-one correspondence between ASCII and EBCDIC. This lack of correspondence between ASCII and EBCDIC is very important in 3270 terminal emulation on PCs, since all personal computers use ASCII, including IBM's own personal computers. One of the reasons that 3270 terminal emulation is so expensive is the difficulty of translating back and forth between ASCII transmissions from the PC and EBCDIC transmissions from the personal computer.

Synchronous Transmission

For many host-specific terminals, including 3270s, communications between terminal and host takes place **synchronously.** As shown in Figure 13-9, the data characters to be sent are packed together in a group, with absolutely no space between them. This group of characters is called a **frame,** or, in the case of packet switching (see Chapter 14), a **packet.**

Just as moving many people by train is more efficient than sending them in separate cars, synchronous transmission is more efficient than asynchronous transmission and is used whenever very high transmission speeds are needed.

Instead of asynchronous communications' start bits and stop bits that mark the beginning and end of each character, synchronous communications only uses a single **start flag,** to mark the beginning of each frame, and a single **stop flag,** to mark the end of each frame. Both flags are usually one byte long. Because there will be many characters in the frame, these two bytes represent a very small amount of overhead.

Instead of parity bits for each character, synchronous transmission uses an **error detection field** that has a number computed from the entire content of the message. This error detection field can catch most of the multibit errors that commonly occur in transmission facilities.

Instead of single-character ASCII supervisory codes, there is a multibyte **control field** that specifies what is to be done with the frame when it arrives. It is even possible to send a frame without any data in the data field, if only supervisory commands need to be sent to the other device. This is done, for example, to tell the other device that an error has been detected.

Furthermore, synchronous protocols are designed for environments in which several devices share a single line. In such cases, the frame has an

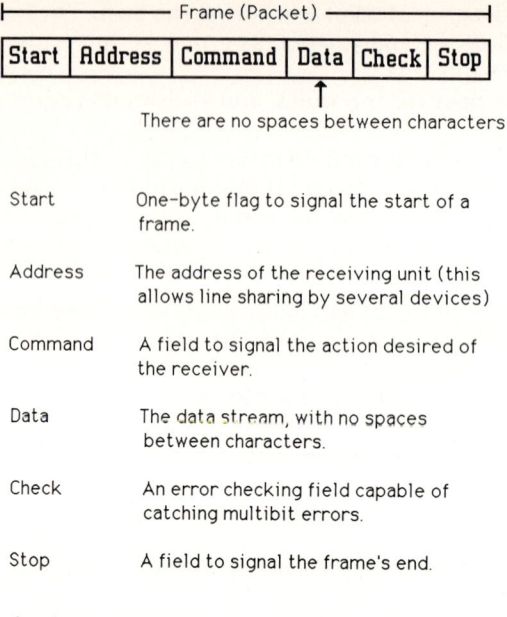

```
|-------- Frame (Packet) --------|
| Start | Address | Command | Data | Check | Stop |
                              ↑
         There are no spaces between characters
```

Start	One-byte flag to signal the start of a frame.
Address	The address of the receiving unit (this allows line sharing by several devices)
Command	A field to signal the action desired of the receiver.
Data	The data stream, with no spaces between characters.
Check	An error checking field capable of catching multibit errors.
Stop	A field to signal the frame's end.

Synchronous transmission has little overhead per character and a well-defined instruction set of commands for the command field.

FIGURE 13-9 SYNCHRONOUS TRANSMISSION

address field to indicate what device should interpret this frame. In packet switching, there may even be a sequence field, to number the packets as they are sent out, in order to make it easier to resort them into the proper order when they arrive. (In some forms of packet switching, packets may arrive out of order.)

In designing the synchronous protocol, a great deal of care is taken in deciding what supervisory functions must be provided. Synchronous transmission thus has a well-defined transmission control capability that frees the user from worrying about many details. At the start of a session, the host may even query the terminal to determine its speed and other information; it can then adjust to the terminal's limitations without troubling the user.

For its mainframe computer family, IBM has *two* synchronous protocols: bisynchronous and SDLC. The **bisynchronous** communication protocol is the older of the two. In operation, the host and terminal carry on a series of transactions each time a frame is sent.

1. The host first asks the terminal if it has anything to send.
2. If the terminal does have something to send, it sends a frame and then waits for the host to acknowledge it (ACK) or refuse it (NAK) if an error has been detected.
3. If the host acknowledges the frame, the next frame is sent. If a NAK is received, however, the terminal retransmits the last frame.

Waiting for a reply is necessary because "bisynch" operates in half-duplex mode. As a result, the host cannot interrupt the terminal during a transmission. This means that the only way for the host to tell the terminal when an error has occurred is to require the terminal to wait before sending another frame.

Another limitation of bisynch is that it is **character-oriented** or **byte-oriented.** This means that the information contained in the body of the document must consist of one-byte characters. This restriction was placed on bisynch because it was designed to carry EBCDIC characters, the text code the IBM mainframes use instead of ASCII.

The problem with character-oriented synchronous transmission schemes is that they restrict the kinds of information that can be sent. Many types of data, for example, pixel graphics information (see Chapter 7), do not contain an even number of bytes, and some of the patterns they do send are used in byte-oriented protocols as supervisory codes. Word processing programs, in particular, are notorious for using supervisory codes; they use them to represent formatting information.

The newer IBM synchronous protocol is **SDLC.** This is part of a broader IBM standards architecture, Systems Network Architecture, which is discussed in the next chapter. Even when considered alone, however, SDLC is impressive. First, it works on full-duplex lines, so that both of the two devices communicating can transmit at once. If the other device is a terminal, the host can interrupt it easily. Both devices are hosts, there may be multiple conversations among applications on the two hosts, and these multiple conversations can flow in both directions at once, like cars on a divided highway.

Second, SDLC's data field is **bit-oriented,** meaning that it is not divided into characters during the transmission. It can contain ASCII, EBCDIC (an IBM character code), or graphic information, as well as things that the communications system would normally recognize as a control field, start flag, or stop flag. (To prevent confusion, information that would be interpreted as part of the control process is preceded by an "escape sequence"—a special code stating that the following information is not to be taken as control information.)

Internationally, the CCITT and ISO (International Organization for Standardization) have produced an official standard for synchronous communications (see Chapter 14). This standard is called **HDLC** (high-level data link control) by the ISO and **LAP** (link access protocol) by the CCITT, but it is the same standard. Speaking more precisely, there is a family of HDLC/LAP standards, each offering somewhat different features. Thus, even when international synchronous standards are used, two devices will be able to communicate only if they are using the same *specific* HDLC/LAP standard.

Host-Specific Interfaces

Many host-specific terminals use the RS232C interface, limiting transmission speeds to 19.2 kbps. Other terminals, however, use interfaces that support a much higher transmission speed.

The Electrical Industries Association, which produced RS232C, has also produced a higher speed standard. In contrast to RS232C, which specifies both pin layout and electrical characteristics, the new standard is really two standards—the RS449 standard for pin layout and the RS422A standard for electrical signalling. RS449/422A can transmit at 10 Mbps at 10 meters and up to 100 kbps at 100 meters.

RS449/422A was developed too late to have a strong impact. IBM's mainframe communications strategy required it to provide speeds of up to 2 Mbps to its terminals. This "3270" transmission system, discussed later in this chapter, is now used by a number of other computer vendors. Other computer companies, including Wang Laboratories, have developed their own high-speed interfaces.

Line Sharing

TTYs assume that they have a single line to the host and that this line is not shared by any other devices. Later, will see how a process called multiplexing will allow several TTYs to share a single line, but multiplexing does this without the TTYs' knowledge and imposes nothing on TTY design and operation.

In contrast, many host-specific terminals, including 3270s are designed explicitly for **line sharing,** in which several terminals and printers share a single communications channel to the host. This requires more complex electronics in the terminal, but by allowing channels to be shared, it reduces transmission costs.

As shown in Figure 13-10, there are two popular methods for line sharing. The first is to place a **cluster controller** at the end of the line. The cluster controller merges host-bound traffic from several terminals onto the channel and routes incoming host messages to the proper terminals.

The second method is also illustrated in Figure 13-10. This is the use of a **multidrop line,** in which terminals are attached at several places along the line

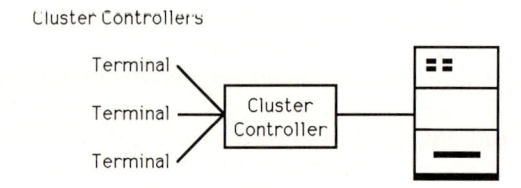

Cluster Controllers

All terminals are attached to a cluster controller at the end of a transmission line.

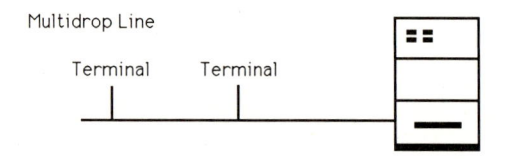

Multidrop Line

Terminals may be located anywhere along the transmission line.

FIGURE 13-10 LINE SHARING

rather than just at the end. Instead of there being a single cluster controller, there must be a controller at each device. These controllers are normally built right into the terminals.

Older communications systems tend to use cluster controllers for line sharing because controller electronics were too expensive to spread around to individual terminals. In addition, cluster controllers tend to be easier to design than multidrop line controllers. Today, controller electronics are much less expensive, so both forms of line sharing are used frequently to handle host-specific terminals.

Color and Graphics

Because the TTY is based on the ASCII character set, it is limited to text. But host-specific terminals, including some members of the IBM 3270 family, provide graphics, typically in color. For many applications, color and graphics provide a much richer working environment than simple monochrome text.

The 3270 Terminal "Standard"

A number of companies have produced 3270-compatible terminals of varying degrees of compatibility. Some firms have also programmed their hosts to work with 3270 terminals so that they can take advantage of the large installed base of such machines in the typical firm. As we will see later, however, "3270" is a broad family of products, and so claims of 3270 compatibility need to be tested carefully.

TTYs versus 3270 Terminals: In Perspective

We have discussed the individual features that separate TTYs from the popular IBM 3270 terminal family. We will now try to boil these differences down to a few general factors.

The chief advantage of 3270 terminals is their high performance—including transmission speed, full-screen editing, color, and graphics. In serious corporate data processing, high performance is extremely important. It is also very desirable in end user computing. On the down side, 3270 terminals are far more expensive than TTYs, and 3270 terminal emulation is much more expensive than TTY emulation. Another problem is that 3270 terminals only work with IBM mainframes and a few other computers. Not even IBM minicomputers, including the System/36 and System/38, work with 3270 terminals.

The chief advantages of TTYs, in contrast, are their low cost and the fact that they work with many different hosts. Even hosts that require specific terminals, such as 3270s, can work with TTYs through protocol conversion, which is discussed later in this chapter. But the TTY is strictly a lowest common denominator. Its slow speed, dumb editing, and its lack of graphics and color limit the ability of users to work effectively.

PC TERMINAL EMULATION

Users who already have personal computers do not want to have terminals on their desks as well. Instead, they want their PCs to be able to act like terminals. This requires PC **terminal emulation.** Terminal emulation means that the PC looks and acts to the host *exactly* like the terminal it mimics. The host literally cannot tell that it is dealing with a PC instead of a terminal. Anything users can do at terminals they can do equally well at PCs emulating those terminals.

Another reason for terminal emulation is that users may want to use the data they are receiving from the host—for example, monthly sales reports—in documents, data bases, or models they are creating on their personal computers. Because terminal emulation brings information to their PCs, they can capture this incoming information and convert it into the form required by their PC application programs.

Approaches to Terminal Emulation

Terminal emulation requires both hardware and software. The hardware comes on an "expansion board" which fits into an "expansion slot" inside the system unit. Chapters 6 and 7 discuss the general concept of expansion boards and expansion slots.

Software is also needed to manage the expansion board and to get the entire PC to function as a unit and act like a terminal. This "communications program" also provides a number of services beyond terminal emulation. We will examine these advanced services a little later. For now, we will concentrate on basic terminal emulation.

TTY Emulation

The TTY is the simplest kind of terminal, and it is the cheapest to emulate. The only hardware needed is a **serial adapter board,** which converts between parallel bus traffic and serial traffic with the outside world. The serial adapter board has an RS232C interface to the outside world.

A serial adapter board is a generic board that is used by several types of peripherals, including modems, mice (see Chapter 7), and many printers. These boards are relatively simple and cheap, costing only $25 to $80, depending on the computer. Most multifunction boards (Chapter 7) contain at least one serial adapter circuit that combines all of the functions of a single-function serial adapter board; this makes the cost of serial output even lower.

Because serial boards are available for virtually every PC, including most of the cheapest home computers, TTY emulation is almost universally possible. You can buy a serial board directly from almost every computer vendor, and third-party serial boards are available for most popular PCs.

You also need software, a **communications program.** This software implements terminal emulation, allowing your PC to act like a terminal. This is quite easy to do, and it is hard to buy a software package that is weak in terminal emulation. As discussed later in this chapter, however, most communications programs offer many other features, and there is wide variation in the features provided and in the quality of these features.

Typically, communications packages are produced by software houses that do not provide hardware. This means that users can buy their computers, serial adapter boards, and communications packages from three different companies. Users can expect to pay $50 to $350 for their communications programs, with price having little relation to features. Most programs fall into the $150 to $200 price range.

Emulating Host-Specific Terminals

To emulate a host-specific terminal, a user again needs an expansion board and software, but the comparison ends there.

One big difference is that the cost of this hardware and software tends to be much higher than the cost of the hardware and software to emulate a TTY. The reason for this high cost is that the emulation kit may have to do such complex things as translating between ASCII and EBCDIC and handling synchronous communications. Emulating an IBM 3270 series terminal, for instance, will cost $800 to $1000 in hardware and software.

Instead of using a general-purpose serial adapter board, the emulation of host-specific terminals usually requires a custom-designed adapter board. This board is purchased with matched communications programs from a single vendor, as a complete kit.

Host-specific terminal emulation kits are available for nearly all hosts, but for hosts with large market shares, there will be a greater variety of kits from which to choose and a greater number of terminal models for which kits are available. (Most generic types of terminals, for instance, IBM 3270 series terminals, come in a variety of models with special features that may be needed by different programs.)

Protocol Converters

Suppose your host requires a host-specific terminal but you have a large installed base of TTYs and PCs that emulate TTYs. Is there any way to get your host to speak to your incompatible TTYs and PCs? There is, and it is a simple solution. You buy a device to do translation between the host and terminals, and you place this device between the two, as shown in Figure 13-11.

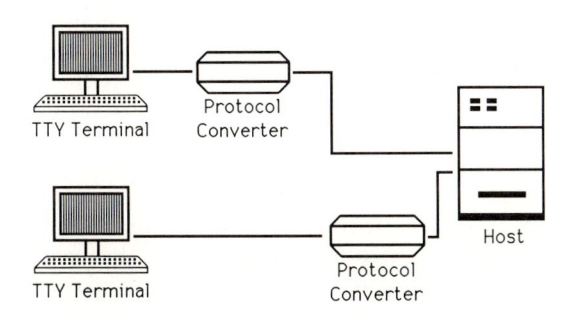

The protocol converter converts the TTY's transmissions into those a host-specific terminal would send.

The protocol converter converts the host's transmissions into those the TTY can understand.

The protocol converter can be located either near the terminal or near the host.

FIGURE 13-11 PROTOCOL CONVERTERS

The translator has a name. It is called a **protocol converter,** and it is sometimes referred to as a **black box.** For popular hosts, protocol converters are widely available. They are also available in less abundance for less popular hosts and in even less abundance for translating between hosts and terminals other than TTYs.

Figure 13-11 shows two popular locations for the protocol converter. One is right after the terminal, making the terminal and protocol converter serve as a single unit to the outside world. This approach requires a protocol converter for each terminal, although several terminals in an office cluster might be able to share a single unit. The second approach is to put the protocol converter at a dial-in port at the host, where it can be shared by many terminals.

Putting the black box by the terminal is best when you already have a large installed base of host-specific cabling (which will be discussed later in this chapter). Your protocol converter can then link directly into this cabling system. Placing the protocol converter near the host, in turn, is ideal when you have many TTYs that can dial in and that only use the host occasionally. The cost of the protocol converter will be spread over all of the terminals dialing in.

Communications Programs

We have already looked at communications programs briefly. A **communications program** works with the serial adapter board or host-specific adapter board to make the PC emulate a terminal. Communications programs also provide a number of other services that allow users to work more effectively and efficiently with their hosts.

Making the User's Life Easier

One of the biggest problems in using a host is the highly technical and arcane knowledge the user often needs to attach to a host computer (speed, duplex, and so on). Although the user can memorize a series of commands and settings, it would be nicer if most or all of the commands and setup work could be automated. Most communications programs for PCs do exactly that. We will illustrate the automation of user interactions using Smartcom II, the communications program sold by Hayes Microcomputer Products to work especially with its intelligent modems.

At the start of a session with Smartcom II, the user is taken automatically to the main menu shown as Figure 13-12. This menu shows a number of choices that can be selected by hitting the appropriate number on the keyboard. If a menu choice is not meaningful at a given time, an asterisk replaces its number in order to signify that it cannot be chosen.

In Figure 13-12, the user has already typed a "1" to begin communications with a host. The system has asked if the user wants to originate or answer. Since originate is the default choice, hitting <Enter> begins the origination process.

The program then needs to know what computer to contact. As shown in Figure 13-12, Smartcom II presents a menu of choices, using the letters of the alphabet from A through Z. The choices shown were set up with the software when it was sold. Because choice B has been set as the default, hitting

PC TERMINAL EMULATION 559

```
    Smartcom II              Hayes Microcomputer Products, Inc.

1. Begin Communication    *. Receive File        7. Change Printer Status  (OFF)
2. Edit Set               *. Send File           *. Select Remote Access   (OFF)
3. Select File Command    6. Change Configuration 9. Display Disk Directory (OFF)
A,B - Change Drive                                0. End Communication/Program

                          Press F2 For Help
Enter Selection: 1        O(riginate, A(nswer, D(ata: O
Enter Label: B

Communication Directory:

  A - CompuServe Direct       J - OAG EE Telenet       S - CompuServe Datapac
 |B - CompuServe Telenet    | K - OAG EE Tymnet        T - DJN/R Datapac
  C - CompuServe Tymnet       L - OAG EE UNINET        U - KNOWLEDGE INDEX Data
  D - DJN/R Telenet           M - THE SOURCE Direct    V - OAG EE Datapac
  E - DJN/R Tymnet            N - THE SOURCE Telenet   W - THE SOURCE Datapac
```

FIGURE 13-12 SELECTING A HOST AND NETWORK IN SMARTCOM II

another <Enter> selects CompuServe as the service to be used and selects Telenet as the network to be used to reach CompuServe.

As shown in Figure 13-13, the screen then clears, except for some indications at the bottom that several function keys are active and can be used to return the user to the main menu, copy all information from the host onto a disk file or printer, execute a macro (string of instructions), or send a break signal to the host. Then, the program automatically dials the number for Telenet and automatically advances through the dialog for the network and the host. It gives the network address it wishes to reach, logs into the computer, and takes the user right into the electronic mail system.

The last parts of the dialog represent a highly controversial use of automatic login. Note that the program itself gives two secret passwords as the user logs into the system. This means that anyone who steals or copies the disk has free access to the user's electronic mail files. In some applications, this may not be a problem, but many organizations have rules that prohibit secret passwords from being executed as part of login macros or any other macros.

If the user in our example were to be under such rules, his or her login macro would end after typing the initial account code. The user would then answer the next three queries. Afterward, the user would type commands or hit <F5> to start another macro.

It is very hard to enforce rules against including passwords in login macros, especially since many users now have their programs run in the background while they are doing something else with their computers interactively. Background jobs are very difficult to execute unless everything is completely automatic.

In this example, a user who has little sophistication or little desire to

```
TELENET
808 10V

TERMINAL=D1

@c 202202

202 202 CONNECTED

User ID: 4011012,7765776
Password:
Address ? PANKO
Code ?
InfoPlex 1E(233) -- Ready at 07:07 HST 06-Jan-86 on T10QEI
 1 Messages pending




.................................................<CompuServe Telenet>--

    Menu: F1      Print: F3     Disk: F4     Macro: F5      Break: F6
```

FIGURE 13-13 AN AUTOMATED DIAL-UP, LOGIN, AND PROGRAM INITIATION SEQUENCE

learn complex login operations has been able to reach a host computer with only a few keystrokes. After booting the system, our user has merely typed <1> <Enter> <Enter>. Even adding nonautomatic passwords would add little to the complexity. Simply put, if the communications program is set up properly by the information center, the magic incantations needed to connect a terminal or PC to a computer are kept at arm's length from the user.

To set up a Smartcom II disk, the information center staff may need to do research on each host computer. This research may need to be very detailed for TTY emulation—for instance, does the host use the ASCII code for Device Control 3 (DC3) to indicate to a terminal that it should stop communicating? For host-specific terminals, the research tends to be less, because the terminal and host were designed to work together.

In any case, the question of how easy it will be to establish a PC–host connection will depend neither on technology nor on the knowledge of the end user. Rather, it will depend on the amount of help given by the information center.

The Need for Data Transfer

Often, the user goes to a mainframe to get data for a PC analysis program. It would be nice to "download" the mainframe data in a way the PC could use directly, instead of rekeying the data from a printout.

Data can also flow the other way. The user may enter or process data on the PC and then "upload" it to the host. In electronic mail, for instance, the user may compose a message at the PC and then submit it at high speed to the host's electronic mail program.

Screen Capture

Most communications packages have a feature that copies the text destined for the PC screen to a section of internal memory, to a disk file, or both.

In most cases, the host inserts a carriage return at the end of each display line. This is fine if the user wants to "clip" a screen image such as an on-screen report and put it into another document. For other purposes, principally full document transfers, a carriage return at the end of each line makes subsequent editing very difficult.

All the characters sent from the host are ASCII characters (or EBCDIC characters translated into ASCII.) As a result, any application program that can read an ASCII file can read the captured information. Many application programs can **convert** an ASCII file into their native file formats. A few application programs, notably line-oriented text editors, can read ASCII files directly.

Although conversion is a workable way to get a captured file into another program's file structure, it usually takes several minutes to convert a file, even if the file conversion code is within the target system's main program. Often, however, the conversion program comes on a separate disk, adding another five minutes or so to the conversion process.

The converted file often has a good deal of "damage" that needs to be repaired. This repair can be extremely time consuming. In general, conversion tends to be faster than retyping a file, though not always.

Uploading ASCII Disk Files

If you have an ASCII file on disk, you may want to send it to the host. The simplest method to do so, within the disguise of terminal emulation, is to pretend that the characters are really coming from the keyboard. This is what most communications programs do. Because data can be uploaded much faster this way than any human could type, this mode is sometimes called the "demon typist" mode. The typing disguise even allows a user to mix commands and data. If the user has an electronic mail program on the host, a **batch file** can log the user into the computer, enter the electronic mail, start a message entry process, "type" the text, give the SEND command, and finally log out.

Uploading can also be used to upload information for storage on the host's disk memory. Because host disks are backed up faithfully, this provides insurance against lost information. To store an ASCII file on the host, the user would use a batch file to declare that the following data is the file to be saved, using whatever commands a terminal user would use to save a file. Many hosts cannot store any files that are not in the ASCII format, and IBM hosts may even require the data to be in EBCDIC form.

Nulls and XON/XOFF

Terminal–host communication was traditionally set up on the assumption that people are rather slow typists. Not even the best typist, after all, can type the 100+ characters per second supported at the fastest modem speeds.

When the user is uploading a file, then, he or she may outrun the host's ability to accept characters.

As noted earlier, many hosts support an **XON/XOFF** protocol to tell attached devices to stop transmitting or to start again. The XOFF signal, which tells the device to pause, is the ASCII Device Code 3 or DC3 (0010011). This is often implemented as <Control> <S>. The XON signal, which tells the device it may resume transmitting, is the ASCII Device Code 1 or DC1 (0010001). This is often implemented as <Control> <Q>.

Some hosts respect these two signals when they are transmitting *to* a peripheral. When a host is sending more than a terminal's screen can hold, <Control> <S> often stops the screen scrolling and <Control> <Q> often resumes it.

Many communications programs can support XON/XOFF, but it is not a universal solution to overloading the host because not all hosts support it. If the host does not support XON/XOFF and cannot keep up with the data uploading, it is necessary to use **nulls,** which are nothing but time delays. Null (or Nul) is ASCII code 0000000. Most communications packages allow the user to specify a number of nulls to be sent after every line and perhaps even after every character. Other communications packages merely let the user specify the lengths of delays directly, without referring to the use of nulls.

File Transfer Protocols

Most communications programs also have a feature that will upload and download files more automatically, doing error correction during the transfer.

In contrast to the techniques discussed so far, the implementation of specific file transfer protocols requires special software on the host. To the host's operating system, the PC is still disguised as a terminal, but the higher level file transfer program knows that it is dealing with a PC.

Obviously, the PC and host programs must use the same protocol. The most popular early file transfer protocol on early PCs was the public domain XMODEM protocol. XMODEM assumes that data consisted of bytes. This allows it to carry ASCII, which has one byte per character, and also permits some other kinds of files to be transferred.

Newer protocols such as Microrim's MNP (Microcom Network Protocol), X.PC (a variant of the X.25 protocol discussed later in Chapter 14), and X.25 itself are **bit-oriented.** Bit-oriented protocols can transfer files even if the file does not consist of bytes. For graphics-oriented applications, and for nearly all Macintosh applications, bit-oriented file transfer protocols are mandatory.

Although ASCII uses only seven data bits, reserving the last bit of its byte for parity, the IBM PC and many other PCs dispense with parity and offer 256 characters instead of ASCII's 128. These extra characters are often used for formatting in word processing programs, and they are also used in many other programs. As noted earlier, character-oriented transfer approaches cannot transmit characters beyond the basic ASCII set, either because they insist on using the parity bit for their own purposes or because they use the extra metacharacters for their own purposes. Many communications programs even strip out many normal ASCII characters used in supervisory signalling. These supervisory codes are also used in many PC programs to hold formatting and other information. Bit-oriented protocols have no problem with aberrations from the ASCII character set.

X.25 is more than a file transfer protocol. It is a general protocol for device–network communications. In addition, because X.25 was defined to connect hosts, which often have several software packages talking to several other software packages on another host, X.25 allows a PC to be linked simultaneously to several software programs on several different computers. X.25 and several newer PC-oriented protocols will gradually bring PCs into the complete data communications world.

Although we are focusing on PC–host communications in this chapter, most communications programs can also be used for PC–PC file transfer. In fact, many are better at PC–PC transfers than PC–host file transfers. In PC–PC transfers, bit-oriented protocols are particularly important.

Downloading with Format Conversion

If the host-based software knows what the PC user will do with a data file after it is received, it may be able to convert the file into the native format used by a specific application program on the user's PC. The most commonly supported target file formats are the Lotus 1-2-3 file format and the dBASE III file format. In addition, some host-based packages can download data in widely used formats that are not native to a particular program but that can be converted by PC programs with less damage than ASCII files. The most common generic format supported is the DIF file format (see Chapter 8), which is designed for tabular information. Other data-oriented formats also receive support, and there is also growing support for IBM's DCA format (see Chapter 17) that is used for word processing. At the time of this writing, file transfer with format conversion is available mostly within the integrated host data application development and decision support packages discussed in Chapter 16.

File Transfer in PC–Host Sister Programs

Many programs originally created for host computers, for example, IFPS and SAS, now come in PC versions. In a few cases, for example, Multi-Mate, PC software has been transported to hosts.

If sister programs are running on the host and PC, file transfer between the two is usually very clean, taking place with zero damage or conversion overhead. This transfer may even be invisible to the end user.

Micro–Mainframe Links

In everything we have discussed so far, the user has to know a good deal to make things work. Even simple screen capture requires a good deal of skill, and careful training is needed by anyone who wants to transfer files between PCs and hosts.

A number of products try to hide most or all of this complexity from users. Generically, these are called **micro–mainframe links.** With these programs, the PC and host blend into a single integrated system whose features are accessed by menus and other simple interactions.

For example, a micro–mainframe user might choose to see a list of all data bases available to him or her. Some of these might be on the PC, others on the mainframe. After selecting a data base, the user could then ask for certain information. If the data base is on the PC, the query would be handled locally. Otherwise, the query would be performed on the host. In either case, the results would appear on the screen in exactly the same way.

Micro–mainframe links sound very attractive, but there are two things that limit them today: functionality and cost. In terms of functionality, most micro–mainframe links are limited to a few tasks, such as office automation, data base handling, or numerical analysis. A few micro–mainframe links combine several of these tasks, but these highly integrated systems are generally weaker in each of these tasks than products that focus on a single area.

Most micro–mainframe links cost $250 to $500 per PC, plus $25,000 to $75,000 for the software on the host. These high costs, coupled with the limited functionality of micro–mainframe links, have slowed the adoption of these tools, but nearly everybody expects highly functional, highly integrated, and attractively priced micro–mainframe links to be part of nearly every end user's experience in the years ahead. When that happens, users will joke about the "bad old days" of Smartcom II and today's other state-of-the-art communications programs.

THE TRANSMISSION FACILITY

Thus far, we have looked at terminals and how to get personal computers to emulate terminals. Users also need transmission facilities to connect their terminals or PCs with their hosts. We will now consider progressively more complex ways to link terminals and PCs to host computers. In order of increasing complexity, we will discuss:

- Linking TTYs to hosts via the ordinary telephone system and bypass technologies.
- Linking TTYs to hosts directly with wires (over short distances).
- Using multiplexers to let several terminals share one transmission link.
- Linking IBM 3270 terminals to IBM mainframes.
- Linking terminals via complex more complex systems.

In the next chapter, we will examine even more sophisticated ways to link terminals to hosts. These methods involve networking, which offers communications service far beyond terminal–host communications.

Because terminal–host communications is only a subset of network service, we will not discuss the use of networks in this chapter. For an individual user who needs to connect to a host, however, a network is often the best alternative for terminal–host transmission.

Linking a TTY via Modems and the Telephone System

The simplest transmission facility is the ordinary telephone that sits right on the desk of almost every end user. This desktop telephone can dial virtually every other telephone in the world. It should be possible to let the terminal and host communicate by telephone, and, in fact, it is—provided the host has a dial-in port.

Modems

You will need some extra hardware to send data by telephone. Specifically, you will need a device called a **modem.** As shown in Figure 13-14, a modem translates between the digital (abrupt) voltage pulses used by computers and the analog (smoothly changing) signals carried by the telephone system.

Computers and terminals are digital devices that transmit signals that change abruptly between two states (1 and 0), which are usually represented by two voltage levels. If two computers are connected by a direct wire, they can send these pulses easily. However, the telephone system was designed for voice, which changes smoothly. The telephone system can *only* carry such smooth changing waves. Although its wires are capable of carrying digital signals, special devices called "loading coils" at the end of your wire to the telephone company's local office trap out everything except smoothly changing signals in the range of frequencies found in voice, specifically between 300 Hz (cycles per second) and 3300 Hz. Digital voltage pulses cannot pass through these loading coils.

When a device sends a digital signal, the modem translates it into an analog signal; this is called modulation. At the other end, the modem retranslates the signal into digital; this is called demodulation. Hence the name "modem."

Modems do nothing more than translation. For example, they do not perform error detection and correction to cope with line errors. Although some of the intelligent modems discussed later actually do advanced things, basic modems do not. A modem is a translation box, and to do more, you must buy one with advanced features or use other hardware and software.

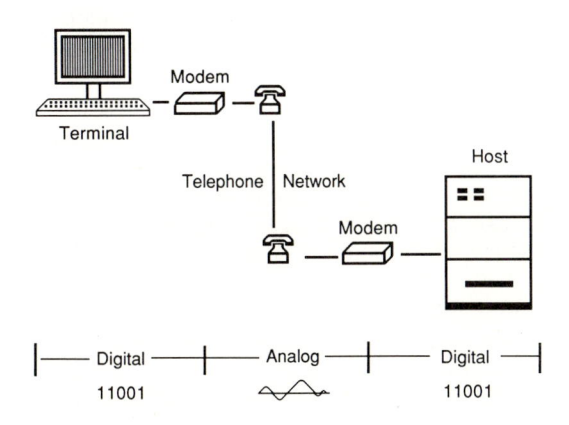

Modems translate between the digital signals used by computers and the analog signals used by the telephone network.

FIGURE 13-14 USING THE TELEPHONE SYSTEM AND MODEMS

Modem Standards

The two modems at the ends of the transmission facility must be able to understand one another. Fortunately, modems are well standardized, and if organizations stick to modems that obey these standards, they should be able to buy modems from several different vendors with only occasional compatibility problems. In this section, we will look only at modems for the normal public switched telephone network.

Specialized modems are available for leased lines and other transmission services discussed later in this chapter. We will not discuss these specialized modems, however, because they are so specialized that information centers rarely encounter them. Because prices for leased lines are falling rapidly (especially for high-speed leased lines), the information center will eventually have to develop an understanding of modems for analog leased lines as well as for digital interactions between terminals and digital leased lines.

In the United States, standards for low-speed modems were originally set by the Bell System. For 300 bps transmission, the Bell Model 103 modem was the most popular Bell modem, and for 1200 bps transmission, the Bell Model 212A was the most popular. The 212A can also talk to 103s, at 300 bps.

When competition was introduced in the U.S. modem market in the 1970s, most vendors produced products that were 103 compatible or 212A compatible. Today, 212A compatible modems dominate the market for dial-up modems, but a very large installed base of the slower 103 compatibles remains.

As noted at the start of this chapter, it is common practice to call 212A modems "1200 baud" modems, but as noted earlier in this chapter, bits per second and baud rate are different for such high-speed signalling. A 212A modem is really a 1200 bps/600 baud product. At higher speeds, there is even less relationship between bps and baud rate.

In Europe, many countries require the use of 1200 bps modems that follow a different standard, the CCITT's V.22 standard. As discussed in the next chapter, the CCITT is the main international standards body for telecommunications. V.22 and 212A modems are similar and can usually communicate, but there are occasional problems getting the two to work together.

For higher speeds, modem standards set by the CCITT are used in the United States. The CCITT's **V.22** *bis* standard governs 2400 bps transmission over dial-up lines. V.22 *bis* modems cost only a little more than 212A modems and are becoming very popular. When some V.22 *bis* modems slow down to 1200 bps, however, they often use the V.22 CCITT standard instead of the popular 212A standard. Such modems should be purchased only with caution.

The **V.32** standard governs 9600 bps transmission over telephone lines. V.32 modems are still very expensive because their ultrasophisticated modulation approach requires very high-density chips.

Not all modems on the market fit one of these four standards, but if you do buy a modem fitting one of them, it can almost certainly communicate with another modem in its class, even if the other modem comes from another vendor. Two modems from the same manufacturer, however, may offer valuable advanced functions beyond the basic standard, including "intelligence."

Intelligent Modems

Some modems have considerable internal processing power. These **intelligent modems** are like miniature CPUs. They have internal functions for such things as diagnostics, and they also have a command set that application programs can call. For example, in the most popular intelligent modem—the Hayes Smartmodem 1200—one command instructs the modem to "lift the receiver," in order to get a line tone. Another tells it to dial a certain number. Communications software in a personal computer can issue commands to the modem to do whatever is needed at a particular moment.

Although these actions seem easy, they require a good deal of processing. When a number is dialed, for instance, how should failures to answer or busy signals be handled? The Hayes Smartmodem 1200 can handle such problems, using delay times set in its registers. These delay times can be changed by the application program. In general, intelligent modems make life much easier for the application program developer, allowing the writer of application programs to shield the user from many calling complexities without having to write extensive (and sometimes nearly impossible) code in the application program.

Because of the Hayes Smartmodem 1200's popularity, many other modem vendors offer compatible modems. Compatibles are also on the market for Hayes' newer product, the Smartmodem 2400, which is a V.22 *bis* modem. Software that works with the Smartmodem 1200 and Smartmodem 2400, which have slightly different instruction sets, should also be able to work with these compatibles.

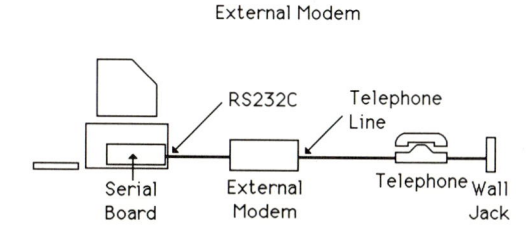

External and Internal Modems

An external modem is outside the terminal or PC, as shown in Figure 13-15. The terminal or PC must have a serial board with an RS232C interface.

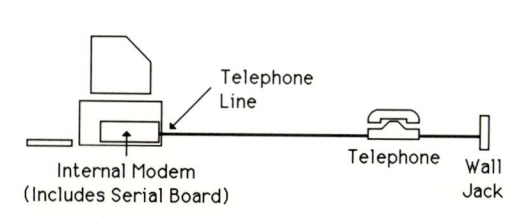

FIGURE 13-15 INTERNAL AND EXTERNAL MODEMS

(As noted earlier, RS232C was originally developed for device–modem connections.) The modem and device are linked by an RS232C cable.

Internal modems sit inside the terminal or PC, as shown in Figure 13-15. Sometimes internal modems are as standard features, and other times you must buy the modem as an expansion board. (Modem expansion boards for PCs are usually equippped with built-in serial board electronics, so you do not have to buy a separate serial board.) It may even be possible to buy a multi-function board (see Chapter 7) that has an internal modem as one of its functions. Because an internal modem is already connected to the device, there is no need for an RS232C device–modem interface. A simple telephone wire comes out of the device, and this wire can be plugged into a standard telephone jack.

One obvious advantage of internal modems is that they do not take up more space on desks already crowded with hardware. Another advantage is that they are less expensive than external modems, first, because they do not have to be enclosed in cases (which are surprisingly expensive) and, second, because they eliminate the need to buy a separate serial adapter board.

External modems also have advantages. First, they have lights on their front panels to indicate what they are doing and to signal errors. Second, many PCs do not have free expansion slots or the extra electrical power to support board modems. External modems use common serial adapter circuits, which are often available, and they are powered by a separate electrical cord.

Callback Modems

One of the biggest problems raised by end user access to host is **authentication**—ensuring that the user is the person he or she claims to be. Passwords are often used for authentication, but these can be guessed or stolen by hackers or dishonest employees.

One way to improve authentication is to use **callback modems** that associate a particular telephone number with each password. When a user dials into a callback modem, the modem does not connect the user to the host immediately. Instead, it asks the user for a password. When it receives an authorized password, it hangs up. The user also hangs up and puts his or her modem in receive mode. The callback modem then calls a number stored in its memory. If the user is at the right telephone, the callback modem will connect to the user's modem and then pass the user to the host.

Linking TTYS to Hosts Directly

Although the telephone system is always available, it may be cheaper to connect the terminal or PC directly to the host with wiring or cabling that runs entirely within a customer's premises.

RS232C Cables and Null Modems

If a TTY is near a host, you can run an RS232C cable between the terminal and host, but there are severe distance limitations when you use an RS232C cable. The RS232C interface was designed for a maximum distance between devices of only 50 feet. In practice, you can often extend this to 100 feet or even 200 feet, but that is about all. Direct RS232C cabling is normally limited to connections within a single room.

Even if you are close enough to the host to use an RS232C cable, you still have problems to face. As shown in Figure 13-16, the RS232C standard assumes that you are communicating between a computer device (data terminal equipment or DTE) and a modem (data communications equipment or DCE).

Both computers and terminals are DTEs. Both transmit on Pin 2 and both listen on Pin 3. If you just connect them with a standard RS232C cable, neither will hear the other's signals.

To solve this problem, you need a device called a **null modem** or, more accurately, a **modem eliminator.** A null modem is not a modem at all; rather, it eliminates a modem. Its only purpose is to let two DTEs communicate directly with one another.

As shown in Figure 13-16, the null modem crosses lines 2 and 3, so that the two devices can hear one another. Line 7 is a "signal ground"—a reference voltage level that is needed to interpret the signal voltages on lines 2 and 3. Line 7 is connected straight across.

The RS232C standard requires the DTE to refrain from sending unless several lines coming from the modem signal that the modem is ready to receive. The most commonly used lines for this are 5, 6, and 8. One way to handle these incompatibilities is shown in Figure 13-16: turn the terminal's own "Data Terminal Ready" signal on line 20 back onto the modem's OK to send lines, 5, 6, and 8. The same is done for the host. When this procedure is followed, both devices literally give themselves permission to send. Of course, the host and terminal cannot tell each other to stop sending, but the transmission can proceed.

The RS232C standard contains 25 pins, but few devices use more than the pins shown in Figure 13-16. Connecting a host and terminal with a mo-

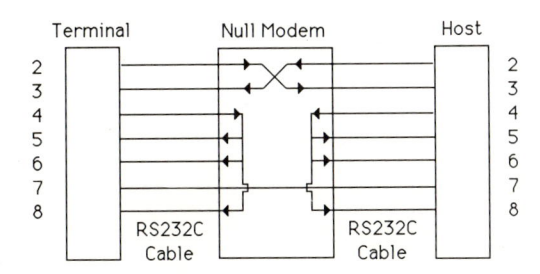

Pin	Use
2	Terminal (host) transmits
3	Terminal (host) listens
7	Signal ground to give a common zero level
4	Terminal (host) gives "Request to Send"
5	Terminal (host) gets "Clear to Send"
6	Terminal (host) gets "Data Set Ready"
8	Terminal (host) gets "Data Carrier Detect"

FIGURE 13-16 NULL MODEM CORRECTS PIN MISMATCHES

dem eliminator generally requires you to know in advance what parts of the RS232C standard each device obeys and requires the other device to obey. There are several "generic" null modems like the one shown in Figure 13-16, and matters are simplified if these can be used. If they do not work, however, considerable knowledge of RS232C will be needed.

Line Drivers

Line drivers get around the 50 foot distance limitation of RS232C. Simplifying things only a little, a line driver merely boosts the signal levels on an RS232C line, keeping the signal in digital form. This amplified signal can travel farther than 50 feet, but line drivers are still useful only over very short distances.

Short-Haul Modems

A cleaner solution for linking two RS232C devices within a limited area is the **short-haul modem** which transmits its signal over a twisted wire pair. This twisted pair is usually owned by the user organization.

In contrast to line drivers, short-haul modems modulate the signal into analog for transmission and demodulate it at the other end. This means that the short-haul modem can pass through PBXs, loading coils at the telephone local office, and other impediments that restrict traffic to analog transmission. Because the transmission is taking place only over a limited distance, however, short-haul modems can be built much less expensively than full modems designed to work well even when the terminal and host are thousands of miles apart. Short-haul modems have no standards. Because of this lack of standards, the short-haul modems at the two ends of the line almost always come from the same vendor.

Using Multiplexers

It is common for several TTY terminals and PCs in an office to need to work with a single host. If the office is far from the host, it is best to purchase one leased line and have the devices all share that single line. Even if direct dial service is used, line sharing is desirable. As shown in Figure 13-17, a **multiplexer** allows several terminals to share a single telephone line to the host. There is a multiplexer or **mux** at both the host end and the terminal end.

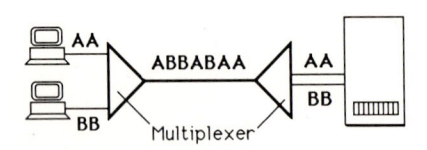

The multiplexer merges traffic to and from several user devices and sends this traffic over a single line.

Neither the terminals nor the host know that there is a multiplexor. Its operation is completely transparent.

FIGURE 13-17 MULTIPLEXING

As shown in the figure, each terminal is associated with a particular host port. Each terminal thinks that it has a direct line to its port, and the host thinks there is a direct line from the port to the terminal. As a result, multiplexing is transparent to both the terminal and host. Multiplexers can always be installed without needing to change anything else in the communication systems.

Multiplexers can also be used for local communications by means of direct wiring or cabling. It is expensive to lay wiring or cabling, even on the customer's premises. Multiplexing allows several terminals to share a single wire or cable.

Multiplexing does not eliminate the need for modems when analog transmission lines are used. In Figure 13-17, there still needs to be a modem between each multiplexer and the transmission facility. Although some multiplexers have built-in modems, most do not; this allows the user to select the best modem for the transmission line.

Fixed Allocation Multiplexers

The simplest multiplexers merely divide up the transmission line's capacity into chunks, allocating one chunk to each terminal. If a transmission line has a total capacity of 9600 bps, for example, it can be subdivided to give eight terminals 1200 bps capacity each.

The 1200 bps capacity in this example is guaranteed to each terminal; other terminals cannot encroach on its allocated capacity. On the other hand, no terminal can send faster than 1200 bps, even if none of the other terminals is using its allocations on the 9600 bps. This is obviously wasteful.

One way to allocate capacity in a fixed way is **time division multiplexing** or **TDM.** In TDM, each second is divided into many time slices. If eight terminals share the line, each gets every eighth slice. TDM is a simple protocol to implement, but the multiplexer must have a buffer so that the characters that a terminal sends outside of its time slice can be stored until that terminal's transmission window appears again.

A second approach to fixed allocation multiplexing is **frequency division multiplexing** or **FDM.** In FDM, each terminal's data are sent at a separate frequency. Signals at different frequencies do not interfere with one another, but each signal spreads somewhat outside of its **base frequency** or **carrier frequency,** and the faster the signal in bits per second, the greater the spread will be. This spreading limits the speed of each terminal because their signals must not cross.

Time division multiplexing is essentially a digital technique, and there is no need to convert digital computer signals when TDM is used, unless an analog transmission facility is used. In contrast, frequency division multiplexing, is an analog technique. Digital computer systems must be translated into analog before transmission and must be reconverted to digital at the other end. Devices that do so, as noted earlier, are called modems. In FDM, modems are always needed, and only analog transmission facilities can be used.

Statistical Multiplexers

In contrast to fixed allocation multiplexers, which give each terminal a fixed transmission speed regardless of how much the line is used, **statistical multiplexers** allocate line speed on the basis of need.

Terminal–host transmission tends to be highly "bursty," with long silences between transmissions and bursts that may average 20,000 bits (one display screen). With statistical multiplexing, the mux allocates line capacity according to need on a moment-by-moment basis, so eight terminals can enjoy much better than 1200 bps throughput on a 9600 bps line. Or, more terminals can be placed onto each line. Statistical multiplexers, of course, will give uneven service if you overload the line with too many terminals or if there are "peak load" periods for terminal use during the day.

Linking 3270 Terminals to Hosts

Many host-specific terminals, as discussed earlier in this chapter, are designed to use line sharing, either through cluster controllers or multidrop line techniques. Multiplexing brings line sharing to the TTY world, without requiring the redesign of either terminals or hosts. So far, we have looked only at the telephone system, direct connection via RS232C, and multiplexing. In the host-specific world, however, realities are far more complex. For many high-performance hosts, host-specific transmission schemes are needed as well as host-specific terminals. We will look briefly at the most common situation found in large corporations—linking a terminal or PC to an IBM mainframe computer.

IBM Mainframes and the 3270 Terminal Family

In the 1960s, IBM developed the System 360 family of mainframe computers. All of these computers were compatible, which means that they all had the same instruction set. In the 1970s, the System 370 line replaced the System 360s but retained the same instruction set. Today, System 360 instruction set compatibility is embodied in three product lines, all of which are compatible but differ in size.

The 9300 series machines—the smallest, overlapping the minicomputer range.

The 4300 series machines—medium-size machines.

The 3080/3090 series machines—the largest.

These machines require a family of host-specific terminals known as **3270 terminals,** although none actually has the product number "3270." This family includes several major types, most notably the 3278, 3279, 3178, and 3179. Note that more recent "3270" terminals begin with "31" because IBM ran out of four-digit numbers starting with "32."

To complicate matters further, each major type comes in a number of models. To buy a "3270 terminal" for a particular IBM mainframe is not easy. Even worse, some specific software packages require specific models.

Local Cabling for IBM 3270 Communications

Figure 13-18 shows local cabling options for IBM 3270 communications. IBM's 3270 series terminals do not connect to the host directly. Instead, they must be connected to a **local cluster controller,** which is in turn connected to the host. These cluster controllers offload most terminal management functions from the mainframe. They also have the processing power needed to

THE TRANSMISSION FACILITY

make 3270 series terminals, which are inherently dumb terminals, act as smart terminals.

The most common cluster controllers are the local 3174 and local 3274 cluster controllers. Both machines perform the same basic functions, but the 3174 is newer and offers many additional functions, including those needed to attach to the IBM Token-Ring Network discussed in Chapter 15. A 3174 can even act as a protocol converter, so that TTYs can be attached to it.

These local cluster controllers are **channel-attached** to the mainframe, meaning that they are attached directly to the computer's bus. In personal computer terminology, these machines are adapters.

Channel attachment means that local cluster controllers can move information at bus speeds—tens of millions of instructions per second. Although they serve up to 64 devices—3270 series terminals and 3287 printers—they can give each device service at 2 Mbps.

Channel attachment has one strong drawback: the local cluster controller must be located within about 100 feet of the host. Thus, the devices attached to the controller must be connected by long cables, often several thousand feet, thereby imposing heavy cabling requirements on the organization. In response, many organizations use multiplexers to let several remote devices share a single cable. This reduces the speed going to each device, but this loss is important only for advanced applications.

If a company has many TTY terminals, it can buy a 7171 protocol converter from IBM. This protocol converter is channel-attached to the mainframe's bus, but terminal–7171 interactions are still limited to the 19.2 kbps speed limit of the RS232C interface on TTYs. As noted above, a 3174 cluster controller is also capable of doing protocol conversion for TTYs. As 3174s become more widely used, the 7171 is likely to fade in importance.

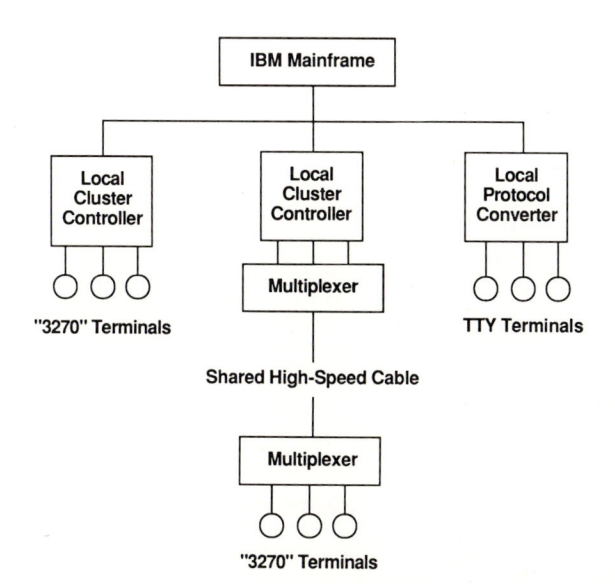

FIGURE 13-18 LOCAL COMMUNICATIONS FOR IBM MAINFRAMES

WORKING WITH HOST COMPUTERS

TTY terminals can also be handled by using third-party protocol converters. These can be placed at the terminal, allowing standard 3270 communications cabling to be used, or just in front of the cluster controller.

Long Distance 3270 Communications

For long distances, it is impossible to run cabling to every device. Devices may be thousands of miles away, and even if they are relatively nearby, they may lie outside the area in which the organization has the right of way to lay cable.

For long distance 3270 communications, the local cluster controller is replaced as the cluster controller by the **remote cluster controller.** Figure 13-19 illustrates this change.

Even though they have the same general model numbers (most commonly 3174 and 3274), local and remote cluster controllers are very different products.

- First, remote units handle fewer devices, typically 16 or fewer.
- Second and more importantly, remote units are attached to the host via communications facilities that may run at under 9600 bps. Even if faster lines are used, it is rare to find a transmission speed over 64 kbps, and this speed must be shared by all of the attached devices.

A remote office, then, will have a remote terminal cluster controller, a number of 3270 series terminals, one or more 3287 printers, a transmission circuit back to the host computer, and a modem if analog lines are used.

At the host end, there is a **communications controller.** This is a front end processor that offloads the work of handling remote cluster controllers

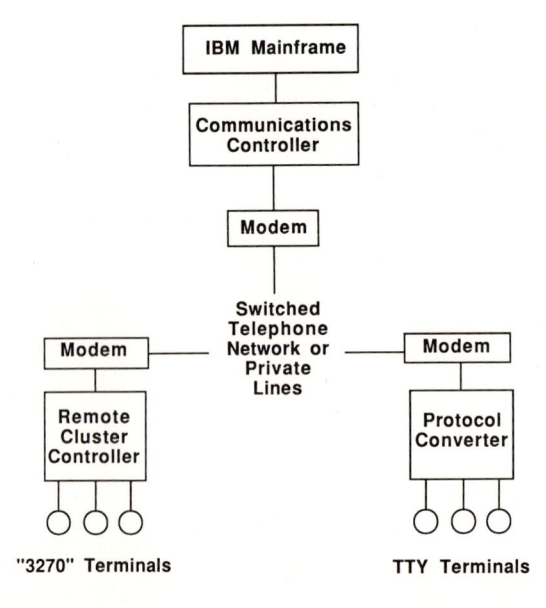

FIGURE 13-19 LONG DISTANCE COMMUNICATIONS FOR IBM MAINFRAMES

from the mainframe. Typical model numbers are 3720, 3725 and 3705 (an older unit).

If an organization has several mainframes, their communications controllers can be connected by transmission circuits. This arrangement will allow the communications controllers to act as switches, so that a terminal connected to one communications controller can be connected to the host attached to another communications controller.

Personal Computer 3270 Emulation

A number of companies now sell **3270 emulation** kits consisting of expansion boards and communications software. (PC emulation was discussed earlier in this chapter.)

As we have just seen, there is no such thing as a "3270." Instead, there is a large family of products that normally begin with the digits "32" but increasingly do not (3178 terminals and 3174 cluster controllers, for example). As a result, every "3270" emulation kit emulates a *specific* product in the 3270 family. A user must decide the specific kind of product he or she needs in order to select the right product.

The products emulated most frequently are terminals. If a 3270 cabling system already exists in an office, terminal emulation will be very attractive. However, the user still needs to select the specific 3270 model and submodel required by the specific host, operating system, and application software that he or she needs to use. Competing 3270 terminal emulation kits from different vendors tend to be loaded with features, so selecting the best emulation kit has only begun when the specific terminal to be emulated has been selected.

Terminal emulation kits are attractive if host cabling already goes to an office, but what if the office is remote or is located in an uncabled office near the host? In these cases, another type of kit is available, the **remote cluster controller emulation kit.** On a single board and with a single program, this kit emulates *both* a remote 3174 or 3274 as well as a terminal in the 3270 family.

This allows a single PC to work from a remote office without adding the cost of a full 3174 or 3274 to serve this single machine. In addition, most of these kits drive a simple PC printer, allowing it to look to the host like an expensive 3287 printer. Again, the specific terminal emulated and the specific features offered must be assessed critically.

Linking Terminals via More Complex Systems

If many remote terminals are to be attached to a host, long distance transmission costs will take a large bite from the corporate budget, unless some way is found to let user devices share communications lines as efficiently as possible. With many terminals, it is not enough to use multiplexers to keep line costs near their potential minimum. A complex and formal communications system must be developed.

Overview

A detailed description of such systems is not an appropriate topic for this book because, unlike modem and multiplexer procurement, which may fall into the hands of end user support personnel, the development of complex and formal networks is the domain of communications specialists. We will look at a few superficial features of such networks in order to show the communications environments in which many end users will live.

As shown in Figure 13-20, at the heart of any complex communications systems is the use of high-speed backbone **trunks** to carry the data from many terminals.

Telephone companies offer **private lines,** also called **leased lines,** which give a point-to-point connection for a flat monthly fee. Even over **voice-grade** private lines, which only carry signals between 300 Hz and 3300 Hz, you can transmit 9600 bps or even a little faster using special modems. You can do this because a private line always gives you a fixed circuit between two points, which can be **conditioned** to reduce noise and distortion.

Telephone companies offer higher speed private lines, typical speeds being 64 kbps and 1.544 Mbps. The faster lines are called T-1 lines. In some other parts of the world, T-1 lines have speeds of 2.048 Mbps. Most of these higher speed lines are digital, so their error rates are low, and modems can be eliminated. (The devices attached to these lines must still know how to work with the specific digital protocols used on these lines.) In the past, these high-speed lines were prohibitively expensive, but their prices have plummeted with the advent of competition, and they may soon be used even for office-to-office communications.

Suppliers

Until recently, telephone service was a near monopoly. In a particular area, service was provided by the local telephone company, officially called the

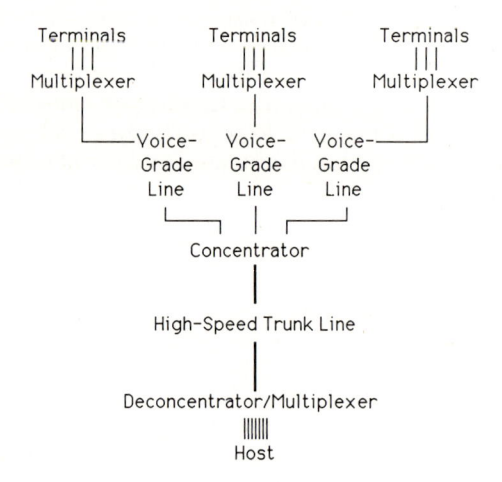

```
 Terminals        Terminals        Terminals
   |||              |||              |||
 Multiplexer     Multiplexer      Multiplexer
     |               |                |
     └──── Voice-   Voice-    Voice-──┘
           Grade    Grade     Grade
           Line     Line      Line
             └──────┬──────────┘
                    |
               Concentrator
                    |
            High-Speed Trunk Line
                    |
         Deconcentrator/Multiplexer
                 ||||||
                  Host
```

Multiplexers allow several devices to share one voice-grade line.

Concentrators allow several voice-grade line to share one high-speed trunk line.

FIGURE 13-20 COMPLEX COMMUNICATIONS SYSTEM

local operating company. For long distance service outside the jurisdictions of these companies, American Telephone and Telegraph (AT&T) had a complete monopoly.

In recent years, court decisions have broken this monopoly. First, long distance carriers besides AT&T were given permission to handle long distance calling, and local operating companies were required to give each customer a choice over that customer's default long distance carrier.

AT&T was broken apart, and its local operating companies were set up as separate companies. To implement this change, the Federal Communications Commission subdivided the country into many **LATAs**—Local Access and Transport Areas. It replaced the term "local service" with **intra-LATA** service, and it replaced the term "long-distance service" with **inter-LATA** service. AT&T's former local operating companies were forced to comply with these changes, as were the local operating companies of another giant, GT&E.

Now, competition is beginning to affect even intra-LATA service companies. Microwave carriers, cable television companies, and other carriers are beginning to provide intra-LATA service, and satellite carriers provide inter-LATA service without the need to work with a local carrier at all.

Multiplexing and Concentration

To use long distance lines efficiently, terminals must be connected to lower speed leased lines directly or via multiplexing, as shown in Figure 13-20. These lower speed lines are attached to higher speed lines through **concentrators.** Concentrators do such advanced functions as data compression to increase the throughput on each high-speed trunk line.

In some cases, minicomputers at each remote site are used to do as much local processing as possible and to manage the interface between that site and the network. Furthermore, "the host" may be a collection of hosts that work together to provide service. In many areas, particularly office automation and access to corporate data bases, a terminal user's normal path to the software they need will take them through two or even more computers.

Now that we have looked at terminal alternatives, PC terminal emulation, and a variety of nonnetworked transmission facilities, we are ready to turn from technology issues to management concerns.

Microwave Bypass

For transmission within a city, the simplest way to bypass the local telephone company is to install **microwave** equipment. Microwave is a radio system that operates at high frequencies, typically 4 to 6 GHz. At these frequencies, signals travel in straight lines, and antenna dishes are highly directional. This means that the sender and receiver must either be within line or sight or must be able to use a repeater that has line-of-sight access to both units.

Microwave is a proven and relatively inexpensive technology, but in most large cities, line-of-sight is difficult to obtain, and it may be difficult to get an operating permit for the microwave system, because of potential interference with other microwave units at similar frequencies. Most large cities are already crowded with microwave systems. If this were not enough, many building owners in large metropolitan areas refuse to permit roof-top antennas.

For shorter distances, laser transmission systems are attractive. Because lasers use light, instead of electromagnetic radiation at regulated frequencies, no permit is needed to install laser transmission systems. But this does not eliminate the need for providing line-of-sight access. In addition, laser signals attenuate more than microwave signals in rainstorms.

Optical Fiber Bypass

Optical fiber (discussed in Chapter 14) provides ultra-high transmission speeds, small cable size, ultra-low error rates, and virtual immunity from electromagnetic interference. As a result, many organizations now use optical fiber to connect their sites. But optical fiber requires a right-of-way permit, since it must be laid physically from location to location. These permits are difficult to obtain in crowded areas, so optical fiber bypass tends to be limited to sites within a customer premises, such as a research park or a university campus.

Satellite Bypass Systems

Among the most promising bypass technologies is the communication satellite. As shown in Figure 13-21, satellite users can place antennas on the roofs of their buildings and communicate across cities or even continents without involving a single LATA authority.

To keep costs low, most companies purchase **very small aperature terminals (VSATs).** These use reception dishes whose diameters are only three or four feet. These dishes are inexpensive and do not crowd the increasingly scarce real estate of building roofs.

As shown in Figure 13-21, VSAT systems usually have a single powerful hub station. This allows the use of inexpensive low-power equipment at user sites. Transmissions from one low-power user station to another must be delivered in two steps. First, the sender transmits the message to the hub station. Second, the hub transmits the signal to the intended receiver. This "double hop" can result in significant delays, because the communications satellite is 22,300 miles above the earth. Even at the speed of light, it takes a

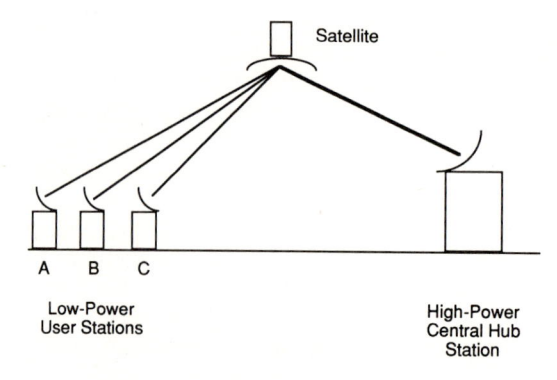

FIGURE 13-21 VERY SMALL APERATURE TERMINAL (VSAT) SATELLITE NETWORK

quarter of a second for a signal to go up and then come back down. With a double hop, the delay between sending and receiving is a half second.

The earliest communications satellites used **C band** frequencies, namely 4–6 GHz. C band equipment was inexpensive, because this is the frequency band long used by terrestrial (earth-bound) microwave. Unfortunately, C-band requires fairly large dishes, because signals at this "low" frequency spread rapidly. Another problem is interference with terrestrial microwave signals, particularly in large metropolitan areas. Although satellite dishes point upward, they still pick up many stray terrestrial signals.

Although a few VSAT systems use the C band, most use the **K band** at 12–14 MHz. At these higher frequencies, there is less signal spreading, so dishes can be very small. In addition, there is no interference from terrestrial microwave. In recent years, K band technology has fallen dramatically in price. In addition, K band satellites have added the power needed to transmit effectively despite rainstorms, which strongly attenuate signals at K frequencies.

Satellites and station equipment were extremely expensive in the 1970s and the early 1980s. Today, however, channels prices are very attractive, and station prices are falling rapidly. Direct satellite transmission must be considered seriously for intercity transmission, and it may even be competitive for cross-town transmission, given the high costs of terrestrial rights-of-way and the scarceness of microwave frequencies in high-populated areas.

SUPPORT AND CONTROL

Chapters 3 and 4 discussed the important policy issues that are created when large numbers of end users begin to access corporate hosts. Authorization, chargeback, data integrity, security, privacy, and other issues were mentioned in those chapters. Here, we will look at the technical side of security, discussing the host software needed to implement effective security.

Security Software

Security is a growing problem for all host administrators, not just on hosts used by end users. In many firms, however, the rapid growth of end user computing has intensified security concerns and brought access problems into focus. As a result, the explosive growth of end user computing has prompted many firms to buy special security packages to bolster the limited security features found in the computer's basic operating system. We will look at a few of the features found in one security package, Goal Systems' ALERT/CICS.

Access Limitations

There are two basic forms of access limitations in ALERT/CICS. The first is **temporal limitation,** which involves restricting access to certain time periods. Outside of open time periods, access to the resource is forbidden.

The second form of limitation is **degree of control** over resources once access is given. **Read-only access** allows information to be seen but not changed. **Read-Write access** allows the information to be viewed.

Multilevel Control

ALERT/CICS essentially places a series of gates between users and resources. At the highest level, ALERT imposes temporal and degree of control limitations on key **system resources,** including programs and data. In data files, degree of control limitations can be imposed down to the level of individual fields.

At the next gate, ALERT/ICS imposes temporal and degree of control limitations on terminals. Even if a program is available at a particular time, it may not be available to a particular terminal. In many situations, it pays to restrict access to a department's programs and data to terminals within the department. Callback modems, discussed earlier, allow security systems to control even dial-in terminals and PCs.

The third gate is limitations on individual users. Even if a user works at an approved terminal with an approved program at a particular time, that user may *not* have access at that time or to a particular degree of control.

Security Administrator Features

ALERT/CICS provides a number of features to support the security administrator. At the mundane but time-consuming level, ALERT/CICS helps the security administrator build the access profile for the hundreds of users, terminals, programs, data files, and other resources under the administrator's jurisdiction. ALERT/CICS, for example, allows the administrator to copy a profile from one terminal to another and then make only the changes required. ALERT/CICS also allows the administrator to change profiles in real time, so that changes can be made rapidly and temporary changes can be made as needed.

The last feature we will discuss is violation reporting. Security software does nothing if it merely sits idly while a user makes attempt after attempt to breach the system. ALERT/CICS provides periodic batch reports, real-time monitoring at a terminal, and host alerting at a terminal if a key resource seems to be under attack.

Organizational and Planning Issues

The personal computer no longer lives in splendid isolation. It can now reach out to host computers to use Software and data on the host and to capture data for downloading to the PC.

The technology of PC–host communications is still very crude, however. It requires a good deal of technical expertise to set up a link between a PC and a host. Once this link has been set up, the communications software on the PC allows much of the complexity to be hidden from the user.

It will probably be necessary, for some time at least, for the central information center staff to set things up for users, including installing terminal emulation boards and modems and setting up communications software profiles to let individual users work with hosts as automatically as possible. If this is done, the user's life in using host software should be fairly easy.

The next step—getting the software on the host to work with the software on the PC—is a very big one. (Host software that works well with PC software is discussed in Chapters 16 and 17.) All of this software is costly, and adding the software needed for smooth and effective end user access to hosts will represent an investment of at least $50,000 and may require an investment many times that high. As a result, good user access to hosts represents a serious chicken-and-egg problem. Without good access, user growth will be stunted, and the user base may remain too small to support the host access needed to attract many end users.

Resource allocation becomes a major problem as soon as many end users begin to use the host. User queries and other work tend to gobble up resources at a prodigious rate because user work tends to cut across traditional file boundaries and to pour over thousands of records at a time. It must be possible to partition individual users in order to fight degradation for other end users and production users. In addition, an effective chargeback scheme must be adopted, and users must be trained in ways that will let them work more efficiently. Not only is there no free lunch; in access control and support, there isn't even a reasonably priced lunch.

CONCLUSION

For most information centers, terminal–host and PC–host communications is the first step into the world of data communications. Although there are many other steps to take, as discussed in the next chapter, host communications by itself is a major learning challenge. To master host communications, the information center needs to absorb a good deal of technical data communications knowledge.

In this chapter, we have discussed PC–host communications as something that can be done today well. Other writers argue that the "micro-mainframe link" is still several years away. Actually, both views are correct. At the level of terminal emulation, which has been the focus of this chapter, good solutions are at hand, and these solutions are getting better. PC users can work with host application software as easily as terminal users, and with good service from the information center, users can do their work with a minimum of technical knowledge.

At higher levels, however, things are far less satisfactory. What we need is not just the ability to work with a remote host as a terminal, so that application software on the host can be accessed. At higher levels, we also need application software on the PC and the host that work together as a smoothly functioning team, so that users are buffered from as many technical details as possible. As discussed in Chapter 16, tools to meld PC and host software together are available, but they are still rare, expensive, and limited. PC–host communication today is still a tool for users with either simple needs or a pioneering spirit. Fortunately, quite a few of these users seem to be around.

REVIEW QUESTIONS

1. Describe the role of the information center in setting corporate data processing standards. In enforcing and supporting these standards.
2. What are the four requirements for terminal–host and PC–host communications?

3. How would you abbreviate 33,300 bits per second, 33,300,000 bits per second, and 33,300,000,000 bits per second? Do "bits per second" and "baud" mean the same thing?

4. Why is transmission speed not velocity? Why is it more expensive to communicate at higher speeds? Why is noise more of a problem at higher speeds? What is throughput, and why is it always lower than a transmission system's rated speed in bits per second?

5. What are the relative advantages of TTYs and host-specific terminals?

6. What are the relative advantages of dumb and smart terminals to users? To the host computer?

7. I have the ASCII code 0001111. What is the parity bit for odd parity? For even parity? What is wrong with parity as an error-checking approach?

8. What are the relative advantages of asynchronous and synchronous communications?

9. What are the problems associated with byte-oriented or character-oriented synchronous transmission? How does bit-oriented synchronous transmission reduce or remove these problems? Contrast bisynch, SDLC, and HDLC.

10. What kinds of line sharing are used in host-specific terminals? How does multiplexing add line sharing when TTYs are used?

11. What problems would appear if remote echo were used in half-duplex transmission? What problems would appear if local echo were used in full-duplex transmission? What is wrong if, when you type, nothing you type appears on the screen? What is wrong if, when you type, everything you type appears twice on the screen?

12. Why does terminal emulation always allow PCs to work with hosts? Why cannot most hosts deal with PCs directly? In terminal emulation, does the PC have to look like a terminal to software above the level of the host operating system? Why or why not?

13. What do you need to emulate a TTY, a host-specific terminal? For each, where would you buy the individual components?

14. List the main features offered in many communications programs. Within the list is data downloading. Describe the types of data downloading in order of *decreasing* desirability to end users. Which features require no special software on the host? Which do require special software on the host?

15. What does a protocol converter do? What are the advantages of placing the protocol converter right at the user's PC? At a dial-in port?

16. Why is the ordinary telephone system (the public switched telephone network) attractive as a transmission facility for terminal–host communications? Why is it *not* attractive?

17. Why is a modem needed? Do ordinary modems do error detection? For dial-up service, what are the commonly used modem standards for 300 bps, 1200 bps, 2400 bps, and 9600 bps? (There are two for 1200 bps.) If I have a 212A modem and the other side has a 103 modem, can we communicate automatically?

18. Why is it helpful to have an intelligent modem? Which is less expensive—an internal modem or an external modem? Why? What are the other relative ad-

vantages of internal and external modems? What happens when a user dials into a callback modem? Why does it provide security?

19. When is direct TTY–host connection with RS232C cables likely to be useful? How can the 50 foot distance limitation of RS232C be extended somewhat?

20. What specific problems do null modems address? (Refer to specific pins.) What is often lost by using a null modem? Why are short-haul modems used? How are they different from the modems used on the public switched telephone network?

21. Why is it important that multiplexing be transparent to both the host and the terminal or PC? Does multiplexing eliminate the need for modems? What are the advantages and disadvantages of fixed-allocation multiplexers and statistical multiplexers? How is multiplexing different from line sharing on host-specific terminals?

22. Do any IBM terminals have the model number "3270"? What do people mean by the term "3270 terminal"? For local communications, do 3270 series terminals connect directly to the host? What speeds can be available to 3270 series terminals in local communications? Is an IBM local cluster controller usually nearer to its terminals or its host?

23. What two devices stand between the terminal and the host in IBM long distance communications? What is the role of each? Contrast local and remote IBM cluster controllers, in terms of numbers of terminals handled and the speeds available to each terminal. In "3270 emulation" on personal computers, what are the relative advantages of emulating 3270 series terminals versus remote cluster controllers?

24. Why do you need to shop carefully for kits that allow PCs to emulate 3270 series terminals?

25. In terms of whom you can talk to, what are the differences between the ordinary public switched telephone network dial-up service and private line services (also called leased line services)? Contrast voice-grade and T-1 private lines, in terms of speed and analog versus digital signalling.

26. Does AT&T have a monopoly over long distance service? Does the local operating company still have a monopoly over local service? Define LATA, intra-LATA service, and inter-LATA service. Define local bypass and describe the advantages of popular local bypass technologies.

27. In security software, what are temporal limitation and degree of control? At what levels can temporal limitation and degrees of control be implemented? What features of security software are important for security administrators?

14 NETWORKING AND COMPREHENSIVE COMMUNICATIONS STANDARDS

Organizations today are struggling to cope with exploding communications needs.

- First, organizations have worked to develop good terminal–host and PC–host communications. Chapter 13 covered this effort.
- Second, organizations are beginning to install **data communications networks,** which can link large numbers computers. This chapter surveys the technical principles behind networking. Chapter 15 discusses the practical concerns involved in purchasing and installing networks.
- The third step will be to develop comprehensive standards for data communications. These standards will allow programs on computers from different vendors to work together smoothly. The last part of this chapter looks at comprehensive standards.

INTRODUCTION

Basic Concepts

Point-to-Point Communications Versus Networks

Data communications today is done mostly on a point-to-point basis. When a workstation is added to a host, a circuit has to be established for the workstation–host link. When a workstation is moved, the original circuit has to be disconnected and a new link has to be installed.

Point-to-point transmission is now beginning to break down. First, the number of devices that need to communicate is growing rapidly. Second, and more importantly, many of the new devices are personal computers. PCs need to talk to one another as well as to hosts. If 100 terminals are purchased, only 100 terminal—host links need to be established. If 100 PCs are purchased, however, they may all need to communicate with one another, so 4500 interconnections might be required. That would be impossible, with point-to-point communications, both economically and in terms of such practical matters as duct space.

This connectivity explosion was faced in voice communications more than 100 years ago. The answer then was to drop point-to-point wiring in favor of a comprehensive network of switches and transmission lines. This voice network was very expensive to install initially, but the cost to add or drop a device was very low.

Many organizations are now doing the same thing in data communications—dropping point-to-point transmission and installing data communications networks.

Networking Elements

Figure 14-1 shows the basic elements found in data communications networks.

The network has **transmission lines** that can connect every device to every other device.

Some networks, but not all, have switches to connect transmission lines.

Devices are attached to the network via controllers, which are like adapters in personal computers. Not merely wall plugs, controllers are active electronic devices.

Among the devices attached to the network are hosts, terminals, personal computers, and even printers.

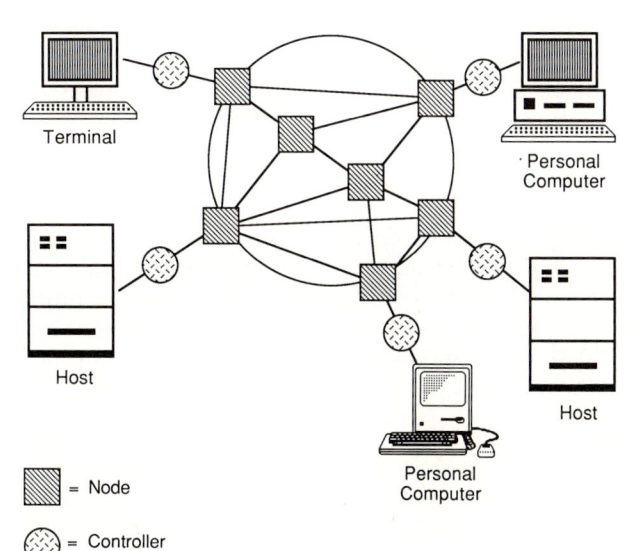

FIGURE 14-1 DATA COMMUNICATIONS NETWORK

Controllers connect user devices to the network. Not just cables, controllers are active devices that include hardware and software.

Once a device is connected to a network, its user simply gives the address of another device, and the network makes the connection. The user does not have to worry about the internal design of the network. The network is just a plug in the wall. To the people who have to maintain the network, of course, the situation is far more complex. As shown in Figure 14-1, a network is complex system of **switches** and **transmission lines.** User organizations must understand the technology so that they can make purchases intelligently and maintain the network after it is installed.

Often-Overlooked Considerations

The Need for Comprehensive Standards

Networks alone do not guarantee that any program on any machine can talk to any program on any other machine. Just as the highway system does not guarantee smooth relationships between mail order houses and their customers, data communications networks are merely information highways and do not guarantee compatibility among the computers using the network nor the software running on these computers.

Because total compatibility is what organizations need from data communications, networking is only a first step toward building a full data communications system. To achieve the broad goal of compatibility, organizations need to adopt comprehensive data communications standards ranging from the shapes of lowly wall plugs to such high-level issues as how their electronic mail programs will acknowledge receipt of a message. A number of organizations are now developing the comprehensive data communications standards that organizations will need to build on the foundations laid by data communications networks.

The Importance of Moving Data Quickly

Networks designed for the future cannot be planned on the basis of yesterday's applications. As shown in Figure 13-2, traditional applications could get by at fairly low speeds. New and emerging applications require much higher transmission speeds, and these speeds must be supported by tomorrow's networks.

Traditional speeds of 1200 bits per second were fine for conversational computing with its bursts of 100 or so characters. When applications transmit screens, exchange documents, download programs, and send graphics screens, however, speed requirements rise astronomically. Document exchange and program downloading are already very important, and graphics is expected to grow explosively.

PC Networking Needs

In the past, data communications products have focused on transmission, leaving service software to the domain of computers. As discussed in Chapter 12, PC networking requires the presence of server software, not merely transmission service. This software allows expensive peripherals to be

INTRODUCTION

	Modem 1200 bps	ISDN/PBX 64 kbps	LAN 1 Mbps
Traditional Applications			
TTY interaction (100 characters)	1 sec	--	--
Smart terminal interaction (1000 characters)	8 sec	--	--
Transitional Applications			
10-page document transfer (15,000 characters)	2 min	2 sec	--
Emergent Applications			
IBM EGA screen (128 kB)	14 min	16 sec	1 sec
10-page Macpaint document (300 KB)	42 min	47 sec	3 sec
Program downloading (360 KB floppy disk)	50 min	1 min	4 sec

FIGURE 14-2 THE NEED FOR SPEED

shared, information to be shared, and multiuser application software to be executed.

Because personal computers will be major clients of all data communications networks, any network must be evaluated on the basis of the PC server software it provides or to which it gives access.

Because the quality of server software varies enormously, check lists of functions provided are not enough to guide selection.

Another factor in PC networking is the number of application packages that can run on the network software, which acts as an extension to the PC's operating system. Application programs must be written for or adapted to work with the network program.

PC Networks, LANs, and Wide Area Networks

There are three basic categories of networks: personal computer networks, local area networks, and wide area networks. These represent three very different sets of purchase, implementation, and maintenance concerns.

Personal Computer Networks

Personal computer networks are aimed at supporting small numbers of personal computers. Most PC networking products are limited to about a hundred PCs, and few PC networks approach anything like that limit. PC networks are normally used to link a few PCs within a single department.

Most PC networks can transmit only a half million bits per second to 10 million bits per second. Because there are relatively few devices sharing the network's bandwidth, there is no immediate need for much higher speeds. At today's costs, the adapters and software to run at higher speeds would raise

PC networking costs too much to be attractive. Over time, however, higher speeds are likely to be common.

As noted earlier, personal computer networking requires the presence of good server software. No PC network is just a transmission system. Every PC network must have good server software and a large base of compatible application software.

It is possible to distinguish between "PC networks" and "PC networking." PC networks are specific products for short distance communications and services. **PC networking** refers to the services provided. In this context, it can be provided by products other than PC networks. For example, PC networking can be provided by the local area networks described in the next section. It can even be provided on host computers, as discussed later in the next chapter.

Local Area Networks

Local area networks (LANs) are larger than PC networks. They can link hundreds or thousands of devices within a building or group of buildings. They are, in effect, local superhighways for data.

Over short distances, transmission speed is cheap to provide, and most LANs can transmit data very rapidly—although if too many devices share the data highway, traffic slowdowns can severely reduce service to any individual device. This is just like a rush-hour traffic jam that grinds movement on a superhighway to a near standstill. Any claim about speeds must be tempered with warnings about traffic jams.

Because LANs normally sit within a single customer's premises, it is up to the customer to make the purchase, do the engineering, and maintain the system. Even if these are contracted out, the customer still needs to manage the contracts. LANs almost always require a quantum jump in data communications staffing.

Many LANS are high-speed LANs, which can transmit data between 10 million bits per second to about 400 million bits per second. High-speed LANS generally use coaxial cable or optical fiber as their transmission medium, although some use twisted pair telephone wire—either the normal kind used in telephone service or special shielded wire to reduce loss.

Short distance data communications can also be supported by some of the private branch exchanges (PBXs) that many firms are already installing to handle their telephone traffic. Some PBXs, but by no means all, have features that make them attractive for data communications as well as voice communications. These **data PBXs** come in two basic grades of service. Many are limited to speeds of 19.2 kbps to 64 kbps, but some can move data at 2 Mbps or more.

Wide Area Networks

If a company wants to transmit data among many sites scattered around the country or around the world, it might build its own wide area network. Most companies, however, use commercial **public data networks (PDNs)** that transmit data on a common carrier basis. These public data networks can move information between virtually any two cities in industrialized countries, and some support international data exchanges as well. Unless a company's internal transmission volume is enormous or it has only two or three sites, PDNs such as Telenet and TYMNET are the most attractive way to transmit data at low error levels.

Switched Versus Nonswitched Networks

Another fundamental distinction among networks is whether they are switched or nonswitched. **Nonswitched** networking, as shown in Figure 14-3, require all devices to share a single transmission link. As a result, *every device can hear everything transmitted by every other device.*

Figure 14-3 also shows **switched** networking, in which one or more switches are used to create one-to-one transmission circuits between callers. *Only the two callers in the circuit hear what is said.*

In general, switched networking is used in wide area networks, because the scattered nature of the devices on such networks allows switched operation to use comparatively few miles of transmission lines for the number of possible connections that can be established.

For short distance networking, however, the density of devices is great enough that switching's ability to economize on transmission lines begins to fall behind another factor—switching's vulnerability to single equipment failures. If a switch fails, literally thousands of devices may be left without communications. In nonswitched networks, most failures involve only one device or at most a few devices.

Controllers

In Chapters 6 and 7, we saw that personal computers deal with the outside world via *adapters,* which are also called *controllers.* Adapters allow the computer's control unit in the CPU to give simple generalized commands. The adapter or controller then handles the details of dealing with the peripheral to carry out these commands from the control unit. To computers, networks are treated as "mere peripherals," and the intricate details of dealing with a network are delegated to controllers.

In communications, the term "controller" is used more commonly than "adapter." We will follow that practice in most parts of this chapter and the

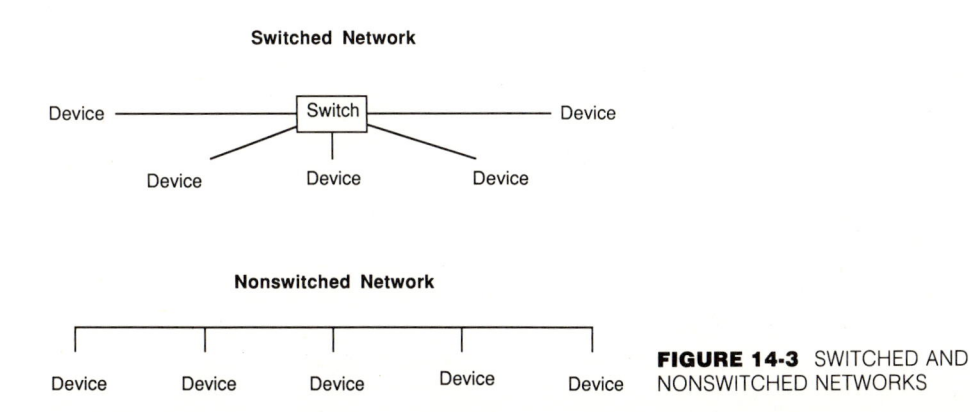

FIGURE 14-3 SWITCHED AND NONSWITCHED NETWORKS

next, reserving the term "adapter" primarily for personal computer networking, where it is still frequently used.

A controller has two requirements. First, it needs hardware to process as much information as possible in each clock cycle. In personal computer networks, it is common to find controller boards that have faster microprocessors than the PC's CPU.

Second, a controller needs software. Software is changed more easily than hardware, so implementing at least some functions in software gives flexibility. In addition, many functions are so complex that it would be horrendously expensive to implement them in hardware. For both of these reasons, all designers handle some functions with software. This hardware is normally implemented as an extension of the computer's basic operating system.

As shown in Figure 14-4, controllers fall into two major categories, internal and external. **Internal controllers** are built on expansion boards and are attached directly to the CPU's bus. (This bus attachment is often called **channel attachment** by communications specialists.) Bus attachment allows network exchanges at bus speeds—millions of bits per second.

External controllers sit outside the device to be attached. Inside the device is a simpler controller, such as a serial controller with an RS232C interface. External controllers are, in effect, extensions of the network's wiring. They are frequently mounted on walls, ready to have devices plugged into them. As we will discuss later, transmission speeds are limited to the speed supported by the interface between the device and the external controller.

Standards

Although physical systems are critical and highly visible, networking also involves a second concern, **standards.** Just as two people need to speak the same

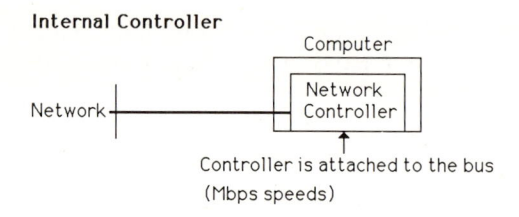

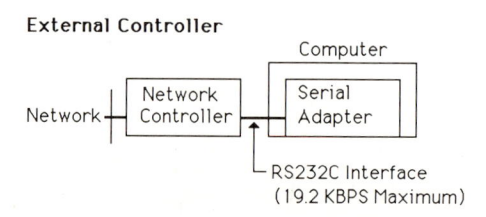

FIGURE 14-4 INTERNAL AND EXTERNAL CONTROLLERS

INTRODUCTION

language if they are to communicate effectively, two entities that need to communicate need to obey standardized ways of communicating.

Protocols

In communications, standards do not affect the internal design of a system—only the way it acts toward the outside world. If a system behaves correctly when it deals with other devices, it meets the demands of standards. This external nature of standards gives designers considerable flexibility in internal software design while still providing for interworking between devices.

More specifically, standards specify the **protocol** between two devices. In diplomatic circles, the protocol is the exact sequence of actions that each party takes in certain circumstances, say when meeting a visiting dignitary. One side does something in a ritualized way, and the other side responds with another set of ritualized actions.

In communications, protocols are also defined in terms of commands and responses. Each party has a certain set of commands it can give to the other party at any given moment. The other party has a set of possible answers to each command. This closed nature of interactions allows each side to design its interface unambiguously.

Layered Approaches to Standardization

As shown in Figure 14-5, standards must succeed in three major tasks for user programs on different machines to be able to work together.

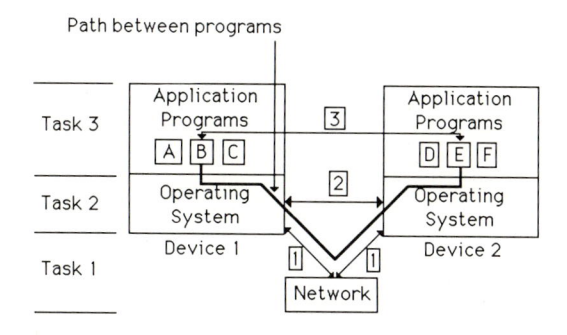

Task 1 -- Exchange data with the network, including routing information and error checking.

Task 2 -- Exchange data between the operating systems of the two machines and route data to the right application program.

Task 3 -- Exchange data meaningfully between two application programs.

FIGURE 14-5 THE THREE BASIC STANDARDS TASKS

- First, **transmission-level** standards must permit interactions between the device and the network. These standards take place at the level of hardware and operating system software.
- Second, **system software-level** standards must ensure that data can (1) be exchanged between the system software of the two machines, and (2) be routed to the appropriate application software packages.
- Third, **application-level** standards must ensure compatibility among the user programs that ultimately need to work together. It does little good if you have connected two electronic mail programs that cannot understand one another.

We can view transmission-level, system software-level, and application-level standards as forming three **layers,** with transmission standards forming a foundation, system software standards building on top of transmission-level standards, and application-level standards building on top of system software-level standards.

In this layering approach, each lower level provides certain services to upper levels, freeing standards builders from the need to worry about standards at lower levels. For instance, once transmission standards are established, standards-builders can create system software standards without having to worry about how the transmission is being done. If everything is going right, in fact, the system software standard will be exactly the same whether transmission is done by personal computer network, local area network, or international data network. The designers of application-level standards, in turn, can concentrate on building standards for interactions between user programs, confident that all lower level concerns are taken care of and that their standard will work regardless of whether one application program is working on an IBM host computer and another is working on a Wang computer.

This process of dividing a large problem into layers is familiar from traditional computer software. Beginning in the 1950s, it became common practice to build operating systems to shield application programmers from the details of how the computer's hardware operates (see Chapter 8). Layering carries this principle to the data communications world.

To avoid confusion later, we will continue to use the term "tasks" for transmission, system software, and application standards, instead of calling these layers. The reason for retaining the term "tasks" is that "layers" normally refers to the specific layering schemes used in international standards making. As discussed later in this chapter, the CCITT and ISO have divided the standardization problem into seven layers. They have done so by dividing the transmission task into three layers (physical, data link, and network), the system software task into two layers (transport and session), and the application task into two layers (presentation and application). IBM has also developed a specific layering scheme for its SNA approach to dividing up standards tasks. SNA is also discussed later in this chapter.

In the past, data communications standards tended to be limited to transmission concerns. To see an analogous situation, the telephone system provides low-level standards for voice communications, allowing you to connect your telephone to the network and issue commands to the network (specifically, telling it what number is desired). If the number you call is in Japan, low-level standards will not be nearly enough. If a man answers "Hai," You may think that he is saying "hello," when he is really saying "Yes?"

Today, however, the trend is toward building comprehensive standards that embrace all three tasks. In other words, we are moving rapidly toward an environment in which any user program will be able to work with any other program, regardless of the kinds of machines they are running on and the transmission facility being used. We will look at these comprehensive standards later in this chapter.

Bridges and Gateways

An organization is likely to have several networks. At a minimum, its local networks will have to be connected to its wide area networks. Within a local area, a firm may have several LANs and PC networks instead of just one.

When two networks that are designed to the same standard are connected—for instance, two LANs that use the 802.3 standard discussed later—the connection hardware and software is called a **bridge** (see Figure 14-6).

When an organization needs to connect two networks designed to different standards—for example, an 802.3 LAN to an 802.4 LAN or an X.25 public data network—the connection hardware and software is called a **gateway.**

Gateways are essentially protocol converters. As one might suspect, gateways are far more difficult to build than bridges. Because two networks designed to different standards may offer slightly different services, something is often lost in the translation.

BASIC TECHNOLOGICAL CONCEPTS

Now that we have looked at networking in general, we are ready to move to the technology of networking.

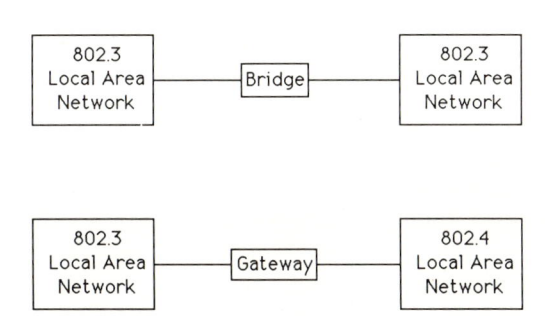

Bridges connect networks with the same standards.

Gateways connect networks with different standards.

FIGURE 14-6 BRIDGES AND GATEWAYS

Transmission Media

A network uses a transmission medium, usually wire, coaxial cable, or optical fiber. In local area networks, the choice of medium is crucial. In wide area networks, the choice is hidden from the user.

Attenuation, Noise, Distortion, and Interference

Different media have different **attenuation rates**—the rate at which signals fade with distance. As signals fade, they get closer to the random **noise** on the line, and error rates rise. Attenuation is usually highest at higher frequencies. A signal will become more and more distorted as attenuation increases, because its high frequency components will be eroded. Sharp-edged ones and zeros become rounded and indistinct as high-frequency components erode.

There is a tradeoff between transmission speed and attenuation rates. If the signal changes more frequently (corresponding to higher speeds in bits per second), the signal will have a higher average frequency. At 300 bits per second, the line will change around 300 times per second, giving a frequency of around 300 Hz. At 19.2 kbps, the frequency of the signal will be around 19,000 Hz. As noted above, high frequencies attenuate more rapidly than lower frequencies, so higher transmission rates mean higher losses.

Another concern is **interference.** Media typically radiate their signal into the outside world, causing interference that garbles the data being transmitted. Media also act as antennas, picking up outside interference and transmitting it as spurious signals.

Twisted Pair Wire

The simplest transmission medium is a **wire pair.** (Two wires are needed to complete an electrical circuit. The wire pair is usually twisted, which, for obscure technical reasons, reduces interference with other wire pairs. Even with this precaution, however, interference problems are high. Attenuation is also high. Although wire pairs are sometimes **shielded** with a jacket to reduce interference and attenuation, wire is inherently a low-speed high-interference medium.

Twisted pair wiring does have two very important advantages, however, and these are often critical, especially in PC networking products. First, wire is much cheaper to buy and install than any other medium, and cost-performance tradeoffs are often important in short distance networking. Second, it may be possible to use existing telephone wires for at least some needs, reducing costs even further. Over short enough distances, high speeds can be maintained with acceptable losses and interference and at a fraction of the cost of more expensive media.

Cable

For higher speeds and lower interference, many local networks use **coaxial cable,** usually called just **cable.** As shown in Figure 14-7, a cable's two conductors are a central wire and a concentric tube. The two conductors are separated by insulation, and there is usually additional insulation around the outer conductor. Because of this arrangement of the conductors, signals tend to be trapped inside the tube, resulting in low attenuation and little interference. Even at speeds of millions of bits per second, signals can travel thousands of feet and still be fully intelligible.

Cable is a mature technology. Cable and cable amplifiers have been used since the 1940s in cable television, or CATV, to bring television signals into the home. Many cable-based networks use standard CATV cable sizes.

Optical Fiber

The champagne of transmission media is **optical fiber.** Optical fiber uses light signals traveling down a long glass tube. The glass fiber is so pure that a fiber window 500 miles thick would be as transparent as an ordinary plate glass window.

If the signal begins to spread out toward the outer wall during transmission, it is artfully refracted back toward the center. Optical fiber has very low loss, and speeds of several hundred million bits per second are possible over distances of many miles. Furthermore, optical fiber is virtually interference-free. In the future, it is likely to be the principal networking medium, but for now at least, cable is the principal medium for LANs. Optical fiber is used, if at all, mostly as a "backbone" link to connect several cable-based segments of a LAN.

Switched Networks

Now we will look at switched networks, which are used predominantly for wide area communications. One reason for beginning with switched networks

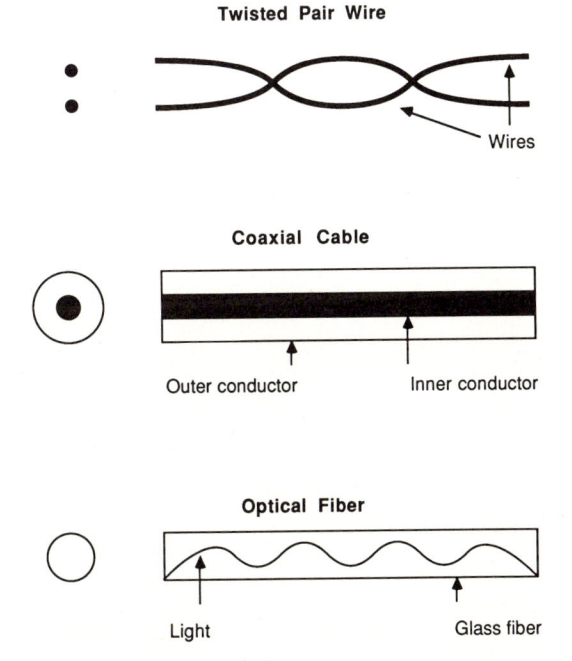

FIGURE 14-7 COMMON TRANSMISSION MEDIA

is to introduce the concept of "packet switching." Packetization is used in virtually all networks today, whether or not switching is employed.

Circuit Switching and Fast Circuit Switching

The public switched telephone networking uses **circuit switching,** in which a path between two devices is established at the time of connection and is maintained until the two telephones are hung up. Figure 14-8 illustrates circuit switching.

Data communications tends to be bursty, with long silences between bursts, but circuit switching maintains the line connection during the silences. As a result, circuit switching is wasteful of line capacity, and bills run high when circuit-switched networks like the telephone network are used for long distance data communications.

One way to get around the problem of burstiness is **fast circuit switching,** in which the two devices are disconnected and the path broken at the end of each burst. Traditional dialing methods are too slow to make this approach feasible, but newer connection technologies promise to make fast circuit switching attractive. For the present, however, fast circuit switching is only a theoretical notion and does not affect market choices.

Message Switching and Packet Switching

The telegraph system has long used another type of switching, **message switching,** which is also known as **store-and-forward** transmission.

As shown in Figure 14-9, whole messages are loaded into the network, which routes them to their destinations. If a transmission link is busy, the message is stored temporarily at the switch, hence the name "store-and-forward." A good message-switched transmission system packs its line efficiently.

One long-known problem with message switching is that message lengths vary tremendously. This makes it difficult to pack the network as efficiently as possible. In the 1960s, Paul Baran proposed breaking messages

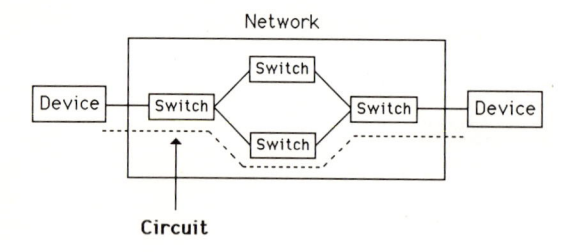

A circuit is established at the start of the call and is maintained until the end of the call.

Price normally does not fall if little use is made of the line.

FIGURE 14-8 CIRCUIT SWITCHING

BASIC TECHNOLOGICAL CONCEPTS

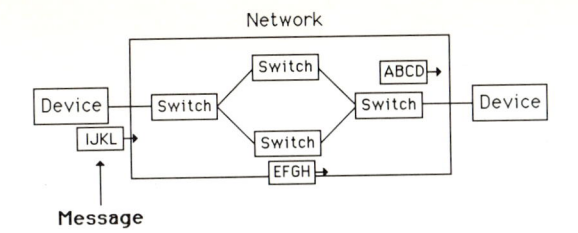

Each message is sent independently and is routed separately.

Price is based heavily on the number of bits sent.

The network's transmission lines are used efficiently.

FIGURE 14-9 MESSAGE SWITCHING

into tiny **packets,** then sending the packets as individual messages and reassembling them at the opposite end. Although **packet switching** is more complex than simple message switching, its statistical advantages are so great that packet switching is used today in nearly all data networks. Figure 14-10 illustrates packet switching.

Virtual-Circuit and Datagram Service

One of the most critical design choices in data networks is how much to do within the network and how much to require the device to do. Two basic

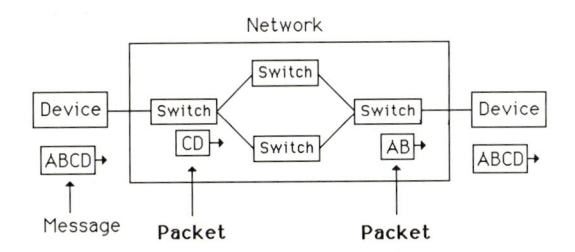

Each message is divided into numerous packets.

These packets are routed, then reassebled.

Small packets flow more efficiently than long messages.

Virtual-circuit service--all packets follow the same route and arrive in order.

Datagram service--packets are routed dynamically and may arrive out of order.

FIGURE 14-10 PACKET SWITCHING

design positions have resulted under packet switching—virtual-circuit service and datagram service.

Virtual-circuit packet switching does nearly everything for the devices. At each node-to-node transmission (see Figure 14-10), the network does error correction. It also makes sure that packets arrive in the same order they go out.

In **datagram** service, little or no internal error correction is done, and packets often arrive out of order. Typically, packet ordering is handled at the controller and is transparent to the user's device, but this is not always the case. Error detection and correction are almost always left to the user.

Where low error rates are very desirable, virtual-circuit service is highly desirable. Each error check takes a few milliseconds, however, and so in some real-time applications, such as voice, datagram service is necessary to prevent delays. Except in special cases, virtual-circuit versus datagram service is not a major selection criterion.

Switching Topologies

Some switched networks have only a single switch, but many have several switches. The way switches and transmission lines are connected is called the **topology** or **layout** of the network.

The simplest wiring layout for a switched network is the **simple switched** layout, shown in Figure 14-11. Each device has a direct and unshared line to the central switch, which can connect any pairs of devices. For obvious reasons, this is also called the **star** layout.

A more complex variation on the star theme is the **hierarchical switched** layout, shown in Figure 14-12. Here, subswitches allow several devices to share the message switch.

In a simple star network, the failure of the central switch brings the entire network to a standstill. In hierarchical switched networks, a subswitch failure knocks out all of its connected devices, but the entire network is not taken down.

Figure 14-13 shows another kind of topology, the **peer switched layout.** Here, again there are many switches, but now they are peers instead of masters and slaves. A message entering the net is routed to its destination by

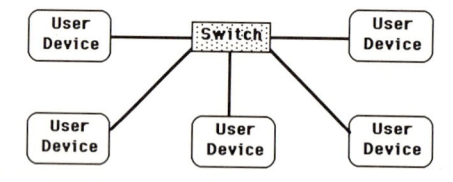

The central switch routes communications between each pair of devices that wants to communicate.

If the switch fails, no device can talk to any other.

FIGURE 14-11 SIMPLE SWITCHED (STAR) LAYOUT

BASIC TECHNOLOGICAL CONCEPTS

FIGURE 14-12 HIERARCHICAL SWITCHED LAYOUT

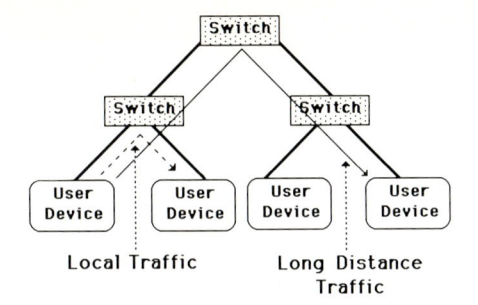

Local traffic is switched by the immediate switch.

Long distance traffic passes through two or more layers of switches.

negotiation between the peer nodes. If one node fails, there are usually enough transmission links among the nodes to route traffic around the failed node automatically. Wide area networks offered by common carriers are peer switched networks.

Nonswitched Baseband Networks

Now that we have looked at layout alternatives for switched networks, we will discuss layouts for nonswitched networks, beginning with nonswitched "baseband" networks. After examining baseband networks, we proceed to layout alternatives for nonswitched "broadband" networks.

Baseband Versus Broadband

Nonswitched networks fall into two basic categories, baseband and broadband. In **baseband** networks, the controller injects the signal into the

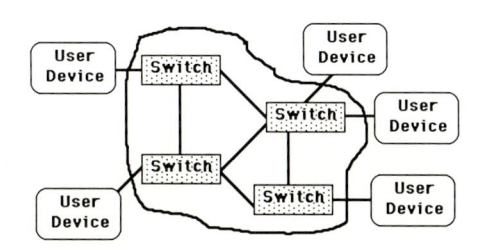

FIGURE 14-13 PEER SWITCHED LAYOUT

Each user device is attached to a node (switch).

The network has several switches that act as peers (there is no central control.)

Routing of messages is done by peer-to-peer decision making.

transmission medium, and the signal propagates in both directions along the medium. If two controllers inject their signals at the same time, the two signals will be jumbled together, and the receivers will not be able to pick out the signals intended for them. In baseband, devices must take turns.

In **broadband** networks, a number of channels (like television channels) are established. Each channel has its own upper and lower frequency limits, and there is no overlap among the different channels. Because signals at different frequencies do not interfere with one another, several signals can be transmitted simultaneously at different channels on a broadband network. The controller at the user device **modulates** the outgoing signal onto one of these channels. The receiving unit listens on that channel and **modulates** the incoming message.

Nonswitched networking seems to resemble frequency division multiplexing (FDM; see Chapter 13), but there is a critical difference. In FDM, each device has its own dedicated frequency; in nonswitched broadband networks, each frequency channel is shared by many devices. In other words, it is like having several baseband networks operating in different channels.

Bus Layouts

In a computer's central processing unit, all circuits communicate via a single high-speed party line called the bus (see Chapter 6). In **bus networks**, the transmission medium also acts like a high-speed party line, on which every device can hear everything said by every other device, as shown in Figure 14-14.

A variation on this theme is the **segmented bus** shown in Figure 14-15. Here, several busses are connected, and the connectors act as repeaters, so what a device sends is transmitted to every other device, even devices on other cable segments. Logically, a segmented bus acts to its devices like a simple bus.

In the segmented bus network shown in Figure 14-15, there is a central **backbone bus** that can carry information at high speed and with low losses. It is not necessary to have a backbone bus in segmented bus networks, but there

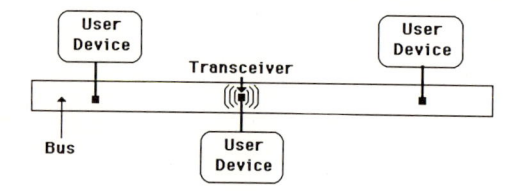

When a user's device transmits, every other device on the bus can hear the transmission.

Each device ignores messages addressed to others.

Discipline is necessary to avoid simultaneous sending.

If one device fails, other devices can communicate normally.

FIGURE 14-14 BUS LAYOUT

BASIC TECHNOLOGICAL CONCEPTS   601

FIGURE 14-15 SEGMENTED BUS LAYOUT

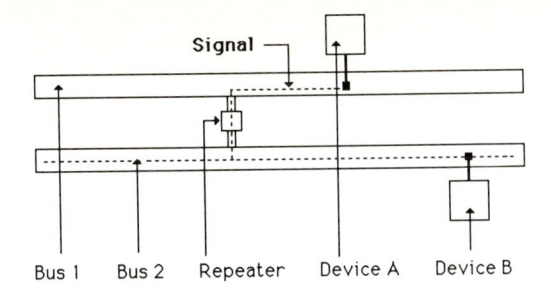

Repeaters retransmit signals from one bus segment to every other bus segment.

Every device can hear every other device on every other bus—there is one logical bus.

are advantages to this approach. The backbone bus can use an extra thick cable or even optical fiber for very low loss. Segments attached to the bus can use thin cable, which is easier to lay in buildings, because thin cable's higher losses are acceptable over the short distances covered on the noncentral segments.

Another way segmented bus networks appear is through the interconnection of several formerly separate networks. If several similar small bus networks are created, they can be melded into a single larger network with repeaters and transmission lines.

Bus networks usually fail gracefully. If a controller fails, one device is knocked out, but the rest of the network goes on happily. Only if the cable is cut do real problems occur. Such an occurrence is rare, however, and in a segmented bus, a damaged segment can be isolated merely by turning off its repeater.

Ring Topologies

A ring network is shown in Figure 14-16. Note that each device transmits only to the device next to it and that transmission occurs only in one direction—clockwise or counterclockwise. Messages must be passed around the network, node to node, until the message reaches its destination.

The ring is a series of broken segments linking the nodes. Each controller stops each bit coming into it, then regenerates the bit and sends it to the next mode. If a *single* controller fails, the entire network fails, which is in sharp contrast to bus networks.

Such catastrophic failures can be avoided. As shown in Figure 14-16, a failed node can be bypassed by putting a shunt across its lines, so that the signal bypasses the node. This can be done either manually or automatically. Although downed nodes can be bypassed automatically, the process may take a few seconds to accomplish in software. In personal computer networks,

FIGURE 14-16 SIMPLE RING LAYOUT

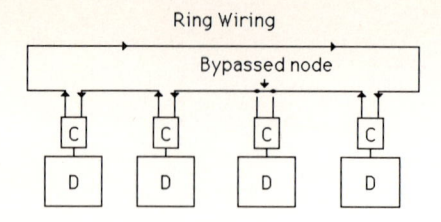

Ring Wiring
Bypassed node

C = controller

D = device attached to the network

Signals pass in one direction around the ring

Each controller captures each bit, then regenerates it instead of just passing it through

A single controller failure would break the network, so controllers can be bypassed manually or automatically

then, powering down a PC without first giving the command to bypass its connection point will produce a noticeable outage in the network.

All nodes are usually connected by cable to a single wiring concentrator. This makes the network look like a star, but no switching is involved, and the defining characteristic of ring networks—passing in one direction with regeneration—remains intact. In theory, rings could be as large as desired, but physically large ring networks are difficult to engineer. As a result, it is normal to build several small rings and link them together with a bridge, as shown in Figure 14-17. The bridge may even connect individual rings operating at different speeds.

At even larger scales, it is common to use a backbone transmission facility to link several bridges, (1) as shown in Figure 14-18. This backbone transmission facility can be a broadband network, a high-speed central ring, or any other kind of network.

Nonswitched Broadband Networks

Most nonswitched broadband networks use standard cable television technology, even using the same cable thickness used in commercial CATV. We will look first at traditional CATV and then at the modifications needed to handle cable.

CATV

Figure 14-19 illustrates a typical CATV system. Signals captured by an antenna or generated on a tape recorder are fed into the **head end,** which broadcasts the signals along several **trunks.**

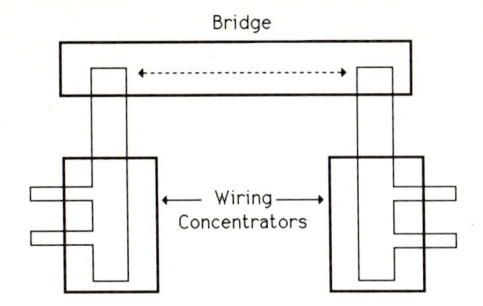

Ring networks must be kept small to prevent electrical distortion problems.

A bridge can connect several small ring networks.

In addition to passing signals between rings, a bridge can do speed conversion and other conversions.

FIGURE 14-17 USING A BRIDGE TO CONNECT SMALL RING NETWORKS

Along the way, **splitters** divide the signal onto several **subtrunks** that use thinner cable. Finally comes the **drop line**—a very thin cable, which **taps** into the subtrunk and carries the signal to the home television.

Figure 14-19 also shows amplifiers. These are analog amplifiers that typically amplify signals from 50 MHz to 300 MHz. Placed every half mile or so, amplifiers allow CATV signals to be delivered over tens of miles.

Dual-Cable Broadband Networks

Figure 14-20 shows a cable system used for data communications. This is a **dual-cable** network, with one cable for outbound signals and the other for incoming signals. For simplicity, splitting and amplifiers are not shown, although they do exist on real dual-cable networks.

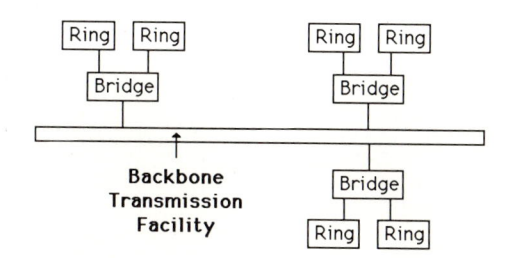

Several bridges can be connected by a backbone transmission facility.

The backbone transmission facility can be a broadband network or a high-speed ring network.

FIGURE 14-18 USING A BACKBONE TO CONNECT RING BRIDGES

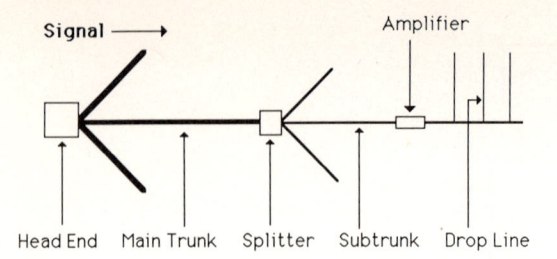

604 NETWORKING AND COMPREHENSIVE COMMUNICATIONS STANDARDS

The signal propagates from the head end, down several main trunks, subtrunks, and, eventually, drop lines to individual homes.

There may be several levels of splitters and subtrunks.

Amplifiers periodically boost the amplitude of the signal (and of noise).

FIGURE 14-19 CATV SYSTEM

The head end merely takes the signals on the incoming cable and rebroadcasts them on the outgoing cable. For this reason, it is usually called a **transverter**.

Of course, there must be two drop lines to each device controller—one to the outbound cable to receive signals and the other to the inbound cable for transmission.

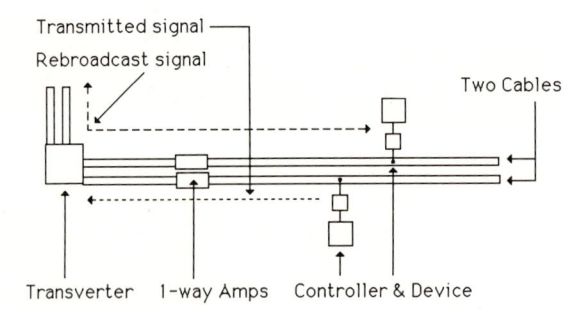

Signal is transmitted up on one cable.

The transverter rebroadcasts the signal on the other cable and sends the signal down to all receivers.

The signal is rebroadcast on all trunks, so all devices hear each transmission. Logically, the network is a bus.

FIGURE 14-20 DUAL-CABLE BROADBAND LAN

Single-Cable Broadband Networks

It is also possible to use a single cable in broadband networks, as shown in Figure 14-21. This requires **two-way amplifiers,** which transmit signals below some frequency in one direction and signals above some frequency in another direction. The transverter now converts incoming signals to the appropriate outgoing frequency.

Because single-cable networks must divide their channel capacity between upstream and downstream transmission, they have only half the capacity of dual-cable networks. In addition, the two-way amplifiers required in single-cable networks are nonstandard and so are rather expensive. In compensation, laying a single cable tends to be easier than laying two cables. Most broadband LAN vendors support both dual-cable and single-cable operation.

Engineering Broadband Networks

Large broadband networks can be built in two phases. In the first phase, the standard CATV cabling can be laid. This is often done by a cable television company operating in the area. Cabling does not have to be laid by the electronics vendor because the cabling is completely standard.

In the next phase, an engineering study is conducted to predict signal strengths along the network's cabling plant. Signal strengths at any point depend on distance from the last upstream amplifier. Each controller must be adjusted for signal strength at its location.

Very small broadband networks, however, do not have to be custom engineered. If cable is purchased in standard lengths and distances are kept under radii of about 1000 feet, pre-engineered kits can be used. As a result, broadband technology can be used in personal computer networking. IBM's original IBM Personal Computer Network used this approach.

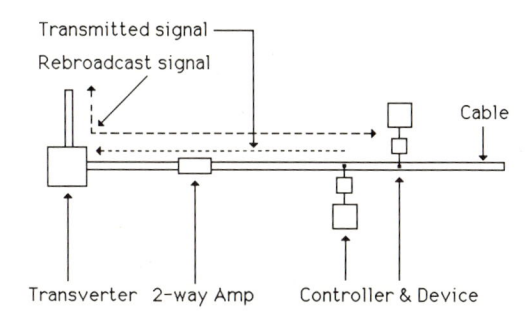

Signal is transmitted up the cable on one frequency.

The transverter rebroadcasts the signal on another frequency and sends the signal down to receivers.

The signal is rebroadcast onto all trunks, so all devices hear each transmission. Logically, the network is a bus.

FIGURE 14-21 SINGLE-CABLE BROADBAND LAN

Access Methods for Line Sharing

In nonswitched networks, many devices must send or receive over the same length of cable, wire, or optical fiber. To prevent chaos, some discipline must be imposed on when a particular device can transmit. The way this discipline is imposed is called the nonswitched network's **access method.** In switched networks, there is no access method because any line sharing within the network is invisible to the controller at the user device.

On baseband networks, the **access method** used to enforce line sharing is used for all devices. In broadband networks, different frequency channels may use different access methods.

Polling

Perhaps the simplest access method is **polling,** in which a master unit asks each device in turn if it has something to send and gives it permission to transmit if it does have anything to send. Polling is simple to implement and adequate if there are only a few devices to control. If the number of devices becomes large, however, polling is a very time-consuming and inefficient discipline.

Time and Frequency Division Multiplexing

Time division multiplexing and frequency division multiplexing (discussed in Chapter 13) are general line sharing disciplines. Without some central controller, the only way to use time division and frequency division multiple access is to employ a fixed allocation technique (see multiplexing in Chapter 13), and this is very inefficient.

CSMA/CD

One of the most popular forms of line sharing is **carrier sense multiple access with collision detection, CSMA/CD.** Although this technique has a long name, it is eminently simple. As shown in Figure 14-22, all devices are

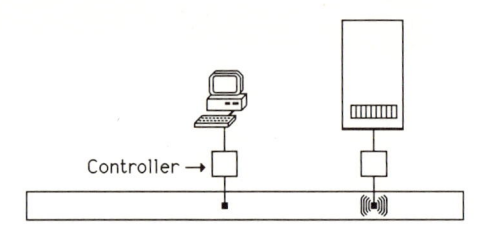

The controller always listens for transmissions (senses the carrier).

It transmits only when it hears no other traffic.

If it hears traffic when it is transmitting (detects a collision), it stops transmitting for a randomly selected period of time.

FIGURE 14-22 CARRIER SENSE MULTIPLE ACCESS WITH COLLISION DETECTION (CSMA/CD)

connected to a common bus and so can hear one another. Each device constantly listens to traffic on the bus. (This is known as "sensing the carrier.")

Deciding when a device may transmit is very elementary. A device sends only when the line is free, thereby preventing it from "jamming" an ongoing conversation by injecting its signals into the baseband network or into its channel of a broadband network.

Two devices can begin transmitting simultaneously. This requires each device to listen as it sends ("collision detection"). As in a human conversation, both devices back off when a collision occurs and one of them takes over the line. A different delay time is built into each device to prevent two devices from getting into an endless round of backing off and then colliding again.

Statistically, CSMA/CD has two problems. First, as traffic grows, CSMA/CD becomes relatively inefficient. Because this technique cannot fill a line to near its theoretical capacity, CSMA/CD networks should not be loaded heavily.

The second problem is related to the first: a CSMA/CD network can make no guarantees for the maximum time it will take to deliver a message. If the network is heavily loaded, delays can be extensive. In certain applications, such as factory automation, this situation is intolerable. In most office applications, however, it serves as only a minor nuisance resulting in occasional performance degradation.

Token Passing

Another line sharing technique used in local networks is **token passing,** in which a special packet called the **token** circulates constantly (see Figure 14-23). If the token is marked "free" when it arrives at a device, that device

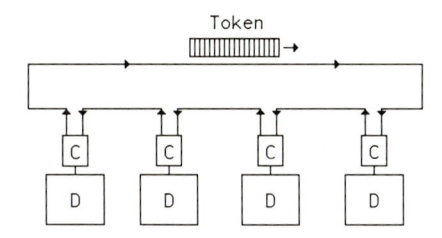

A special packet called a token circulates continuously around the ring.

If a controller has something to send when it receives the token, it changes the token to another pattern, the connector, and attaches its message.

Token passing can also be done on bus networks.

In token passing, there is a guaranteed maximum delivery time for information to be sent.

Token passing throughput falls off gradually as traffic nears the limit of the channel.

FIGURE 14-23 TOKEN PASSING ON A SIMPLE RING

can transmit. It does so by marking the token as "busy" and then appending its packet to the token. A token marked busy is called a connector.

In contrast to CSMA/CD, token passing networks can guarantee a maximum delay for the transmission of a packet, and it can pack a line much closer to capacity than CSMA/CD. In addition, although CSMA/CD is a good discipline for bus topologies, token passing can be used on either a bus or a ring topology.

The tradeoff which token passing makes for this performance is high complexity. Token passing is more difficult and expensive to implement than CSMA/CD, but as component prices fall and as the installed base of devices grows, the high cost of developing software can be amortized over many devices.

STANDARDS

Now that we have looked at networking theory, we will turn to the specific standards used to build communications systems today. Data communications standards are still in an early stage of development, and not all systems follow even those standards already on the books. However, nearly every corporation's strategic plan for data communications calls for future systems to follow specific standards.

Standards Basics

Some information on standards was introduced at the beginning of the chapter. We will now examine those early points in more depth.

The Protocol View

As noted at the start of this chapter, data communications standards do not govern the internal design of any computer system. They merely govern how the system acts toward other systems.

Specifically, standards define **protocols**—detailed descriptions of what each party may say and do under particular circumstances. Under any set of conditions, one party has a limited set of commands it can send to the other, and the other device has a limited repertoire of responses it can give in return. A protocol is like a computer's instruction set; it provides a limited repertoire of well-defined actions that must be performed in sequence to do a particular job.

A particular transaction between two devices may require a prolonged series of commands and responses to be exchanged. For instance, to initiate a conversation, the two devices may need to negotiate which optional features in the standard they will use. These long series of exchanges emphasize that protocols may extend beyond a single command-response exchange.

The precise formulation of a protocol is a complex business with interactions represented by state diagrams and other design paraphernalia, but these are mere details for representing limited command-and-response protocols.

The Players

Internationally, computer standards have traditionally been set by the International Organization for Standardization **(ISO).** Communications standards, in contrast, have traditionally been set by the International Consultative Committee on Telephony and Telegraphy **(CCITT).** Data communications spans both fields, and the ISO and CCITT have been working closely to create standards for data communications.

Often, standards are first proposed by other standards bodies and then submitted to ISO and the CCITT for international ratification. For example, the U.S. Institute of Electrical and Electronics Engineers' 802 Standards Committee has been the main definer of local area networking standards, as discussed later in this chapter.

Because international standardization often moves slowly, computer vendors build their own data communications standards. IBM, for instance, has a standards architecture called Systems Network Architeture (SNA), which is discussed later in this chapter. Because of IBM's market strength and the maturity of its standards compared to international standards, many other vendors have adopted SNA for their products. Earlier, most vendors developed proprietary standards, but most have now moved toward ISO/CCITT standards, SNA, or in some cases both.

Layering

As noted at the start of this chapter, three basic standards tasks must be completed. As shown in Figure 14-5, these come at the levels of (1) transmission, (2) the system software layer, and (3) applications.

To review and expand on what was said earlier about these tasks, transmission standards govern interactions between a device and the data communications network it uses. This includes signalling between the device and the network and specifically includes commands to tell the network where messages are to be sent. When transmission standards are successful, the situation is exactly like having a direct wire connection between the two machines.

The system software task, like the application layer above it, is concerned with interactions between the two devices that wish to communicate, instead of between these devices and the network. For this reason, system software and application standards are called **end-to-end** standards.

The purpose of system software standards is to let application software on one machine exchange files and commands with the application software on the other machine. When system software standards are successful, two application programs can exchange information as easily as if they were on the same machine.

At the highest level, the two application programs, whose interworking is the ultimate goal of the system, must be compatible. For instance, if they are both electronic mail systems, they should be able to exchange messages. When application standards are successful, the users of the application program should be served as easily as if they were sharing the same program on the same machine.

For two application processes to communicate, they need to be standards for all three basic tasks. To add a bit of complexity, standards agencies often create more than one standard to serve a particular task. These different standards are likely to be deeply incompatible. So it is not enough for both systems to use standards for all three tasks. They must use the *same* set of standards for *each task*.

ISO/CCITT Reference Model for Open Systems Interconnection

When data communications standards were first set, there was no overall plan for standards setting. If a standard was needed in a particular area, it was created with little regard for other standards. As a result, standards often overlapped, and many areas had no standards at all.

Overview

During the 1970s, ISO and CCITT worked to remedy this hit-or-miss situation by creating an overall plan or framework for setting standards. Their joint effort resulted in the **Reference Model for Open Systems Interconnection,** a comprehensive framework for standards setting. It is also called the **OSI framework** or simply **OSI.**

OSI is not a standard in itself but is rather a framework for setting standards, just as the general architecture of a house merely specifies what rooms need to be created and how they will fit together. Once this framework was put in place, however, the ISO and the CCITT could begin to develop standards for the specific need identified in the framework.

The OSI architecture is shown as Figure 14-24. As the figure shows, OSI is a variant of the simple tasks model shown earlier as Figure 14-5. Because of the detail needed in standards setting, each of the three basic tasks was subdivided into smaller layers. The transmission task was divided into the physical, data link, and network layers, the system software task into the transport and session layers, and the application task into presentation and application layers. This gave OSI seven layers.

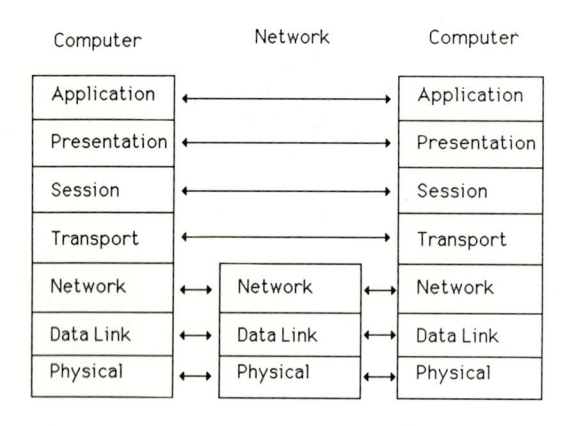

The bottom three layers deal with interactions between each computer and the network.

The top four layers deal with interactions between software on the two computers. These are called end-to-end layers.

FIGURE 14-24 REFERENCE MODEL FOR OPEN SYSTEMS INTERCONNECTION (OSI)

The Physical Layer
The physical layer has standards for physical and electrical connections between the device and the network. The RS232C interface discussed in Chapter 13 is essentially a physical layer standard, although it was never accepted as an official international standard. Because RS232C was created long before OSI, some aspects of its signalling take it a little into the next higher layer.

The Data Link Layer
The data link layer is concerned with the packaging of messages as they travel along a single physical link, such as a single length of wire or a non-switched network containing many devices. The synchronous packaging methods discussed in Chapter 13 are data link standards.

The Network Layer
The network layer governs how individual packets will be routed through the network. Addressing, route-setup, and congestion control are all important network layer standardization concerns. Nonswitched networks do not require network layer standards, since they have only a single link. Data link layer standards are sufficient for their needs.

The Transport Layer
The lowest three layers all deal with the interface between each device and the network—our basic transmission task. The fourth layer deals with the way the two computers will act jointly to pass messages between them. It is a machine-to-machine protocol, as opposed to the machine-to-network protocols that characterize the lowest three layers of the OSI framework. Whether half-duplex or full-duplex transmission will be used between machines, for example, is determined by standards at this layer. The two systems also have to be able to tell the other to stop sending if their buffers become full. Some error detection and correction may also be done at this level, if the underlying network is error-prone.

The Session Layer
Only one transport layer connection must be established when two machines begin to communicate, but in many cases, several application programs on one machine will need to communicate with several application programs on another. A separate **session** must be established and maintained between *each* pair of communicating application programs. Thus, whereas two machines will have only one transport connection, they may have several session connections.

Session layer standards permit each application program to talk to another as if they were the only programs running on their respective machines. The transport layer essentially multiplexes several sessions. If the transport layer is like a mailroom on another machine, the session layer is like the interoffice mail service that collects outgoing packages from individual offices at one end and distributes them to individual offices at the other end.

The Presentation Layer

Application programs have to make some assumptions about file structure, screen size, formatting codes in word processors, page layout codes in desktop publishing systems, and other things that have to do with the presentation of information. The presentation layer creates general standards for such information. Because a presentation layer standard may be used by several different higher level application standards, a distinct presentation layer was created. Presentation layer standards include the NAPLPS standard for videotex mentioned in Chapter 12. The document structure standards discussed in Chapter 17 also fall into the presentation layer.

The Application Layer

The application layer is concerned with making sure that both application programs can talk to one another. In the electronic mail standards discussed in Chapter 17, for instance, standards govern both message delivery and the structure of individual messages (for instance, To:, From:, and Date: fields).

Among the emerging Level 7 standards is the **File Transfer, Access, and Management (FTAM),** a file transfer protocol being developed by ISO. Another is the draft standard for **Electronic Document Interchange (EDI).** This standard, being developed by the CCITT, will be used for the exchange of standard forms, such as invoices and orders, among different corporations.

The X.25 and X.75 Standards

Now that we have examined the overall OSI architecture, we can begin talking about major individual standards that have been developed within the overall framework. We will begin with the oldest and most widespread international standards for data communications, the X.25 and X.75 standards for **public data networks,** which are common carrier wide area networks that use packet switching and peer switched layouts.

During the mid-1970s, the CCITT developed the **X.25** standard to link devices to public data networks. Like RS232C, X.25 only governs the **interface** between a device and the network, not the internal structure of the network. The internals of the network, in fact, are completely unknown to X.25.

As shown in Figure 14-25 hosts are attached to public data networks by the full X.25 standard. This permits them to submit packets to the network, receive packets from the network, and give and receive routing information. The X.25 software on the host can be a major consumer of CPU cycles, so the host often offloads the X.25 communications work to a front end processor.

The host is attached to a switching node, which converts the X.25 communications into details which the network can understand. When the node accepts a packet, it routes it to another switching node on the network, which in turn routes it to another node. This routing continues until the packet reaches the switching node attached to the target host, at which time the packet is delivered to that host by the local network node.

FIGURE 14-25 CONNECTIONS TO PACKET-SWITCHED DATA NETWORKS

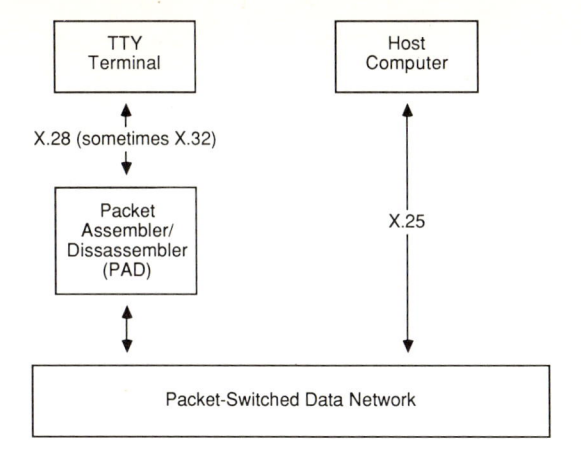

Hosts can be connected directly, using the X.25 standard.

TTY Terminals can be connected via PADs.

Other terminals can be connected via their hosts.

Terminal users have two options for reaching the network. First, if their terminal is attached to a host that is in turn connected to the network, terminal users are generally able to **reach through** the host to the network. In other words, a user attached to a host can use the network to use another host. This means that the user only needs to connect physically to one host. It may even be possible to reach through that second host to reach a terminal or PC attached to the second host. It is not uncommon for two people using terminals attached to different hosts to lock their displays so that they can type back and forth, seeing what the other types, in order to solve problems.

The second option is to use one of the **packet assembly/disassembly devices (PADs)** available on most public data networks. PAD nodes act the same way as ordinary nodes in their dealings with the network, but instead of requiring terminals to speak X.25, they allow terminals and PCs to dial in as TTYs (see Chapter 13). PAD nodes then provide the X.25 functionality needed to provide all the services that would be available to a terminal reaching the network via its host, including packet assembly and disassembly and error checking within the network (but not on the telephone link between the terminal and the PAD). The standard for linking nonintelligent TTY terminals to the PAD is called X.28. There is also a standard (X.32) for linking terminals synchronously to the PAD over dial-up lines. This standard is new and is not widely used, but it may replace X.28 eventually.

As public data networks began to proliferate in the 1970s, a standard became necessary to link X.25 networks, so that hosts on different networks could exchange data, and so that a terminal user connected to a PAD could reach hosts on multiple networks. To fill this need, the X.75 standard was created (see Figure 14-26).

X.25 was created before the OSI architecture was developed, but it is still possible to speak about X.25 in terms of layering, because X.25 served as the initial model for the kinds of functionality found in the three lowest levels of the OSI architecture—what we have called transmission-level standards. X.25 covers *all three* of the lowest OSI standards—physical, data link, and network. It is not simply a third layer standard.

When X.75 was proposed, it created some problems for layering purists because it was clearly higher than X.25, and yet lower than transport layer standards. As a compromise, X.25 is usually drawn as taking up all of OSI Layers 1 and 2 and only part of Layer 3, whereas X.75 takes up the rest of Layer 3, as shown in Figure 14-27.

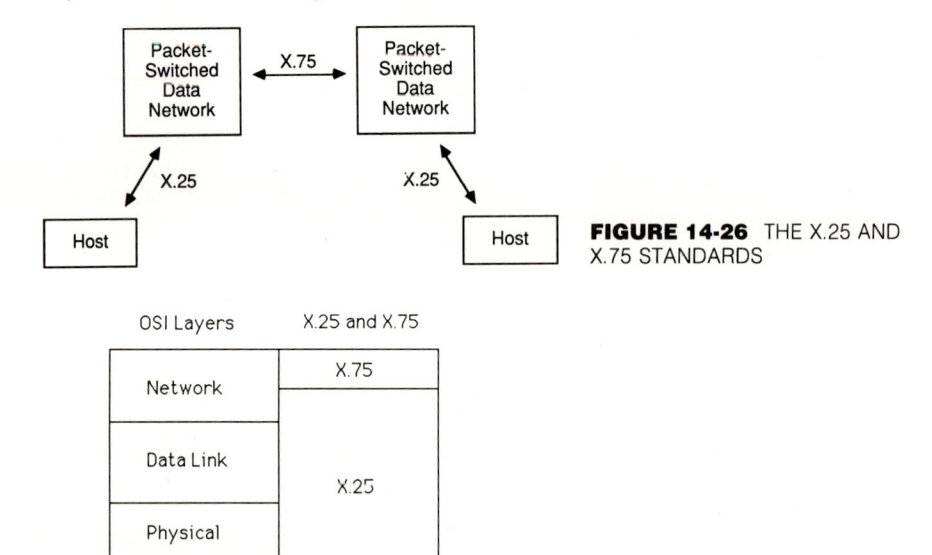

FIGURE 14-26 THE X.25 AND X.75 STANDARDS

X.25 is not a third layer standard. Instead, it covers the bottom two layers and part of the third

X.75 covers the top half of the third layer

FIGURE 14-27 X.25, X.75, AND THE OSI FRAMEWORK

ISDN Standards

Although the telephone system began as a purely analog system, its internals have grown more and more digital over time. In many areas, the **local loop** that connects the customer premises to the telephone company's local office is the last vestige of analog technology.

Because of these shifts, the CCITT is developing standards for a completely digital switched service, the **integrated services digital network, ISDN**. As ISDN services are phased in over the next 20 years, X.25 networks are likely to disappear. Even if companies like Telenet and TYMNET prosper, they will probably survive by converting themselves into ISDN carriers.

The heart of the ISDN service is the 64 kbps **B Channel**. In 1972, the CCITT standardized voice digitization at 64 kbps (8000 samples per second with a one-byte code per sample). A "B channel" can also be used for data, and its hefty 64 kbps speed is more than ample for most terminal-host applications.

Most users will not receive a single B channel. Instead, they will receive what the CCITT calls **basic service**. Basic service consists of *two* B channels as well as a 16 kbps control channel called a D channel. As a result, basic service is also called **2B + D**.

The user's two B channels can be linked simultaneously to two different destinations. For example, a basic service user in Seattle will be able to talk with someone in Toledo while the user's terminal is linked to a host computer in Phoenix.

As discussed earlier in this chapter, 64 kbps will be ample for many terminal-host applications, but for graphics and PC networking, 64 kbps is not fast enough. The CCITT has not addressed this issue, but one solution is to give users one of the faster ISDN services beyond Basic Service, for instance, the H_{10} service, which will be 1.544 Mbps in the United States and 2.048 Mbps in Europe. Because ISDN is a switched service, this high-channel capacity is not shared. A 1.544 Mbps nonshared service should be ample for most foreseeable user needs.

IEEE 802 Local Area Networking Standards

The X.25 standards lets computers link to wide area networks. There is a different set of standards for local area networks because LANs use different transmission and switching technologies.

LAN standards are emerging not from ISO or the CCITT, but rather from the U.S.-based Institute of Electrical and Electronic Engineers. The IEEE 802 Standards Committee has been developing a coherent set of LAN standards, which are being supported by most vendors and which are being ratified as formal international standards by the CCITT and ISO.

The Overall Framework

As shown in Figure 14-28, the 802 standards follow the Open Systems Interconnection framework, specifically serving the bottom two layers of the architecture. Because LANs are usually nonswitched networks and so have only a single link, there is no need for third-layer standards, which deals with routing through a network with multiple links.

Instead of settling on a single topology and a single access method, the 802 Standards Committee decided to create standards for several different topology/access method combinations. Although failure to create a single standard has brought the 802 Standards Committee a great deal of criticism, each of the three major low-level standards (802.3, 802.4, and 802.5) is better suited to particular circumstances than the other two.

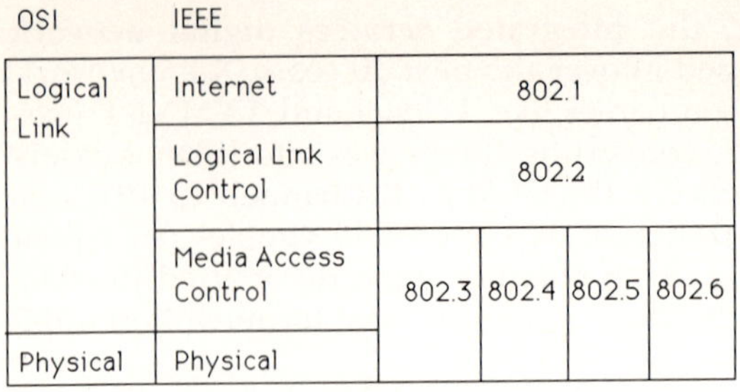

OSI	IEEE				
Logical Link	Internet	802.1			
	Logical Link Control	802.2			
	Media Access Control	802.3	802.4	802.5	802.6
Physical	Physical				

Media Access Control/Physical Signaling
    802.3 -- CSMA/CD Bus (Ethernet/Starlan)
    802.4 -- Token Bus (Factory LANs)
    802.5 -- Token Ring (IBM-sponsored)
    802.6 -- Metropolitan Area Network

Logical and Link Control (for all MAC/Physical)
    802.2 -- Used with all access methods

Internet Transmission Standard:
    802.1 -- For transmissions that cross networks

FIGURE 14-28 IEEE 802 LOCAL AREA NETWORKING STANDARDS

    The committee did create a single standard for part of Layer 2, the Data Link layer. This same 802.2 standard is to be used in all LANs regardless of their layout or access method. Technically speaking, the part of Level 2 that is taken up by 802.2 is called the **Link Layer Control** sublayer, whereas the lowest part of Layer 2, which is specific to topology and access method is called the **Media Access Control** sublayer.

    The committee divided Layer 2 into *three* sublayers, not just two, and it originally reserved the 802.1 standard number to designate a general description of the 802 standards. When the standardization work was well underway, however, it was realized that a standard was needed to connect the multiple LANs that are likely to exist at any site. As a result, 802.1 was converted into a standard for internetting 802 LANs, just as X.75 is an internetting standard for X.25 wide area networks. Just as X.75 is viewed as a higher sublayer of Layer 3, 802.1 is viewed as a higher sublayer of Layer 2.

    Because layering hides lower level details from standards at higher levels, the 802.1 standard will be able to interconnect any LANs that follow 802.2—even if they use different access methods and topologies. Some of the interconnected LANs may even use nonstandard access methods and topologies, as long as they use 802.2.

    Layering's ability to hide lower level details extends to even higher layers. Transport layer software can work to connect the system software on two machines regardless of what low-level 802 standards are used. With regard to X.25, transport layer software can connect the system software of two machines regardless of whether 802, X.25, or any future transmission-level standards are used for transmission.

802.3: CSMA/CD Bus Networks

The 802.3 standard designates a bus architecture and a specific CSMA/CD access method, which is a slightly modified version of the Ethernet design developed by Xerox, Intel, and DEC.

The first version of 802.3 to emerge was a baseband service with a speed of 10 Mbps. A broadband version is currently in development. Because 802.3 is a variant of Ethernet, which was already well defined, 802.3 emerged very early, and only IBM's refusal to support it kept 802.3 from becoming dominant.

Because 802.3 uses the CSMA/CD access method, there is no maximum delivery delay when the network is heavily loaded. As a result, 802.3 cannot be used in factory automation, where real-time equipment control makes it mandatory to have a strict upper bound on delays.

At the present time, 802.3 has only been defined for baseband bus networks. It is likely to be extended to run on broadband networks.

More recently, a variant of the original standard has been undergoing ratification within the IEEE. Just as the original 802.3 standard was based on a commercial product, Ethernet, this new alternative is based on AT&T's StarLan network. StarLan uses the same CSMA/CD access method as the original standard, but StarLan is cheaper, because it uses twisted pair telephone wires, which are far less expensive than Ethernet's cables. This cost savings may not be useful to many users, however, because the use of twisted pair wires requires the network to operate at low speeds. StarLan's speed is a mere 1 Mbps, restricting it to PC networking. Once StarLan is ratified, buyers of 802.3 products will have to be very careful to select the alternative that is best for them and to make sure that all equipment is compatible with the alternative selected.

802.4: Token Bus LANs

Because of CSMA/CD's potential delay problems, General Motors and other manufacturing users promoted a token bus standard, which took shape as 802.4.

Token bus was deemed more suitable for factory use than token ring, because the failure of a single node will bring the entire network down, at least for the milliseconds or seconds needed for automatic recovery to take place. The bus networks' superior robustness to single-device failures makes them mandatory for manufacturing's real-time equipment handling needs.

802.4 is defined only for broadband networks.

802.5: Token-Ring LANs

When the 802 Standards Committee first began its work, IBM submitted a rather fully specified standard for a Token-Ring Network. Because 802.4 had taken the industrial market, IBM's token-ring design, which became 802.5, had to battle 802.3 for the office market.

Technically, 802.5 behaves better than 802.3 when the network is heavily loaded. But without IBM's sponsorship of the more expensive 802.5 standard and without IBM's refusal to support 802.3, there probably would not have been both an 802.3 and 802.5 standard.

TCP/IP

While OSI is still in the painful process of early development, another set of standards for multivendor systems has achieved a fair degree of maturity and acceptance in the U.S. Federal government, in the U.S. military, and in universities. This is **TCP/IP**, the **Transmission Control Protocol** and the **Internet Protocol**.

TCP is analogous to X.25, while IP is analogous to X.75. TCP covers OSI's Layers 1 and 2, plus the bottom half of Layer 3. IP covers the top of Layer 3. But while TCP/IP covers the same layers as X.25/X.75, there is little similarity at the detailed level. TCP/IP and OSI protocols are different in both philosophy and in implementation, and while there are commercially available gateways between the two worlds, translation is difficult.

When users speak of TCP/IP, they usually mean more than TCP and IP alone. They usually mean a whole collection of standards that have emerged in the military community for such higher level functions as file transfer. TCP/IP is really a full working environment that accomplishes much of what the 7-layer OSI standards will do in the future.

Few people expect TCP/IP use to grow, because all of its biggest users now plan to move to the OSI environment. But information centers in organizations that deal with TCP/IP can expect to go through a period of confusion during the transition from TCP/IP to OSI.

IBM's Systems Network Architecture

Although OSI promises to be the lingua franca of communications in the future, its slow development has required most vendors to build their own communications architectures to guide product development. One of these architectures, IBM's SNA, is now so well established that it will probably survive indefinitely as a parallel standards environment to OSI.

Overview

Until the mid-1970s, IBM had no general architecture to guide the design of its own products. Instead, IBM had a variety of designs for batch file transfer (2780 and 3780), terminal-host communications on its mainframe system (bisynchronous), and other needs.

In 1974, IBM introduced its **Systems Network Architecture (SNA)** to guide the design of all future systems. Like the later OSI architecture SNA is a seven-layer architecture. The layers in the two architectures do not match, however, and so translating between the OSI and SNA world is not just a matter of building seven protocol converters. Any representation of OSI/SNA layer matchups can only be approximate, because the two are built on rather different philosophies. It is therefore impossible to talk about the precise relationships between their levels.

In the mid-1970s, SNA was master/slave-oriented, capable of connecting a host with its many terminals and with slave-distributed processors. Today, however, SNA is becoming fully distributed, so that it can embrace horizontal communications among mainframes, small hosts, and even PCs in addition to terminal-host and small host to large host communications.

Although SNA is IBM's direction for the future, its software is extremely resource consumptive, and many firms, including most smaller firms, have deferred adopting SNA. These organizations still use traditional bisynchronous communications to link their terminals and mainframes. Even firms that have adopted SNA generally may adopt only some of its features.

APPC

A major goal of standards is to allow two application programs to exchange information as easily as if they were on the same machine. In the original versions of SNA, one of the two application programs had to be on the host. Recently, however, IBM has introduced its **Advanced Program to Program Communications (APPC)** approach, which will let SNA support communications between any two application programs anywhere on the network, whether these programs are on mainframes, small business computers, personal computers, or any combination of these machines.

Figure 14-29 illustrates a typical situation in an SNA communications system. In this figure, one mainframe runs a program called the **System Services Control Point.** This program controls all traffic in the communications system, including what device can communicate with what other device. The figure also has another mainframe, communications controllers, and cluster controllers attached to several 3270 series terminals and 3287 printers.

In SNA terminology, a network consists of **network addressable units, NAUs,** which can be addressed by other units. There are three kinds of network addressable units.

1. **Physical units (PUs)** are major hardware components in the system. For example, PU 2 designates a terminal cluster controller, PU 4 designates a communications controller, and PU 5 a mainframe.

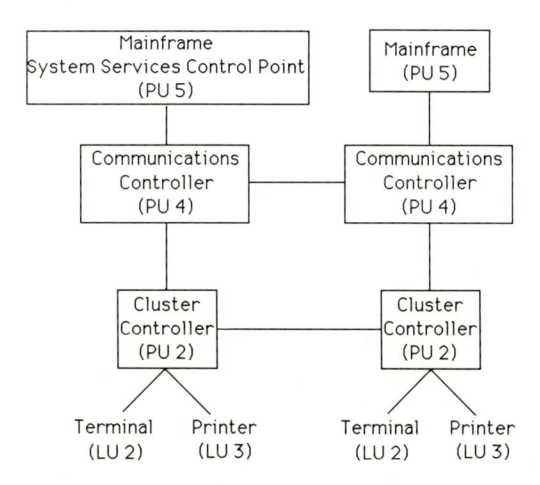

The system consists of network addressable units (NAUs) that can be addressed by name. The NAUs include the system services control point, physical units (PUs), and logical units (LUs). LU 6 designates program-to-program exchanges.

FIGURE 14-29 SNA COMMUNICATIONS SYSTEM

2. Some physical units are associated with multiple logical units (LUs). For example, a terminal cluster controller can serve several 3270 series terminals (LU 2) and several 3287 printers (LU 3).
3. The System Services Control Point is an NAU. There is only one System Services Control Point per SNA network.

As noted above, SNA was originally a master-slave protocol. Mainframe LUs, which were programs, had to initiate conversations with terminal LUs and maintained control over the conversation. Furthermore, all sessions between logical units were set up and monitored by a single program on the mainframe, the System Services Control Point.

In 1978, IBM developed a new logical unit, LU 6, which allowed two mainframes to establish direct communications between application packages. The first version of LU 6 only allowed a single session to be established, connecting a single program on one machine with a single program on the other machine. Version LU 6.1 soon extended the protocol so that multiple sessions could be established between two hosts. All LU 6.1 sessions, however, were still under the control of the System Services Control Point.

The rise of PCs, departmental computers, and other forms of distributed processing motivated IBM to extend the LU 6.1 standard to allow peer-to-peer sessions between programs on any two devices in the network. This extended protocol, **LU 6.2,** even removed control from the System Services Control Point, giving true peer control.

To make LU 6.2 useful, however, a change needed to be made in the architecture of terminal cluster controllers (LU 2s). Because cluster controllers were originally designed to link directly to communications controllers or mainframes, LU 2 specified only a single link to the outside world. This link could be shared by several terminal and printer data streams, but the basic design did not allow a cluster controller to be linked directly to several others of its kind, to minicomputers, or to multiple hosts. This kind of multiple linkage was needed for true peer processing, so a new design, **PU 2.1,** was created to permit new 3174 cluster controllers to maintain several links, each to a different physical unit.

Both PU 2.1 and LU 6.2 must be implemented to provide peer interaction. They were therefore given the combined name of **Advanced Program to Program Communications, APPC.**

In 1985, IBM brought personal computers into the APPC world via the IBM Token-Ring Network discussed in the next chapter. This network provided an APPC program interface **APPC/PC,** which allowed PC application programs to engage in peer-to-peer communications with application programs on other PCs or on hosts. Now APPC can also link a wide variety of mainframes and smaller computers, such as System 38s.

Because APPC is available only on hosts under SNA, because APPC also requires host networks to have new high-end terminal cluster controllers, and because application software capable of using APPC will take some time to proliferate, APPC is a standard whose full force will not be felt until the 1990s.

As APPC does become implemented more widely, it will make PCs full partners in the computer communications world. No longer will "fixes" like terminal emulation be needed. PC application programs will be able to talk to peers on other machines without having the slightest idea of what form of low-level communications is being used to make the link.

The Prospects for SNA

Over time, SNA is likely to be the internal standard for many firms, whereas OSI is likely to be the dominant architecture for interfirm communications. This means that firms using SNA will have to build links to the outside world via gateways, which, as noted earlier, are protocol converters that allow dissimilar networks to exchange information. If OSI continues to develop as slowly as it has, however, SNA may take the lead in interfirm communications as well.

Although a two-framework world seems the most likely outcome, many user organizations are working strongly to develop an all-OSI architecture quickly, viewing SNA as only a stop-gap framework to be completely replaced over time. For example, General Motors and other manufacturers are developing an OSI-based set of standards called the **manufacturing application protocol (MAP).** MAP uses OSI layering and chooses *specific* international standards at each layer. (Recall that the CCITT and ISO often provide multiple standards at each layer. Therefore, unless specific standards are specified at each layer, there is still no guarantee that two programs will be able to work together.) Boeing is leading another user push, notably the quest to develop a **Technical and Office Protocol (TOP)** for office work, including computer-aided design (CAD).

CONCLUSION

Networking—even personal computer networking—requires an organization to absorb a great deal of technical information. Yet networking is only part of the job of developing comprehensive standards for data communications.

Today the networking and standards pictures are in such flux that information centers and the broader information systems department would like to wait for things to settle down. Unfortunately, few can afford this luxury. They are besieged by demands from users, and their own strategic plans call for the rapid implementation of advanced data communications in order to avoid simple paralysis. There seems to be no way to avoid the hiring of a real data communications staff or at least the heavy retraining of the existing information center and information systems staff members.

REVIEW QUESTIONS

1. Why is point-to-point communications attractive for terminal-host communications but not for PC–PC communications? Why is data communications traffic expected to grow explosively during the next few years? What applications cannot be handled well at 1200 bps? 64 kbps? If a company begins today to plan for a large network, how long will it be before users can begin receiving benefits?

2. What are the three sizes of networks? How do they differ in scope and implementation problems? In PC networks, why is server software so critical? What are the main types of PC server software?
3. What is the difference between switched and nonswitched networks? Under what conditions will each be more economical?
4. In what sense is a data communications network a "mere peripheral" from the point of view of a PC? What are the advantages of internal controllers? External controllers?
5. Do standards govern the internal design of computer hardware and software? If not, what do they govern? What is a protocol, and why are standards specified in terms of protocols?
6. Name the three major standards tasks. What does each do? What is layering, and why is it important? How is it similar to layering within PC software (see Chapter 8)? Networks were traditionally concerned with transmission-level standards. Why is this transmission-level focus no longer sufficient?
7. What is the difference between a bridge and a gateway? Which do you think would be harder to design?
8. Why is noise more of a problem at higher speeds than at lower speeds? Why do we say that interference works in two directions? What are the advantages and disadvantages of twisted pair wire, coaxial cable, and optical fiber?
9. Why is circuit switching expensive for long distance data communications? Why is message switching fairly inexpensive for long distance data communications? Why is packet switching even less expensive? What are the technical differences between virtual-circuit and datagram service? What are the advantages and disadvantages of each?
10. Why is the simple switched network called the star layout? Why use a hierarchical switched layout instead of a simple switched layout? Why use a peer switched layout instead of a hierarchical switched layout?
11. Why can broadband networks carry more traffic than baseband networks?
12. Why are bus networks inherently more reliable than ring networks? How do ring designers get around these problems? Why are segmented bus layouts used?
13. Why are bridges used in ring networks? Why are backbone facilities used to connect bridges?
14. In broadband networks, why is the head end called a transverter? Why is a typical broadband system really a bus network? What are the advantages and disadvantages of single-cable and dual-cable broadband networks?
15. Why are access methods needed on nonswitched networks? Why are time division multiplexing, frequeny division multiplexing, and polling not good as access methods? In CSMA/CD, what does "CS" stand for? "CD?" What are the statistical problems of CSMA/CD compared to those associated with token passing access methods? What price does token passing pay to get around these problems?
16. What are the roles of ISO, CCITT, IEEE, and IBM in standards settings?
17. What standards problems existed before OSI?

18. Nonswitched networks do not need a network layer standard. Why?
19. The transport and session layers are part of the system software standards task. What different jobs do the transport and session layers do within the system software task?
20. Why is there a presentation layer separate from the application layer?
21. What types of networks use the X.25 standard? Does a terminal using an X.25 network have to conform to the X.25 standard? Why was the X.25. standard created? Why is it not viewed as merely a third layer standard?
22. What advantages will the ISDN standard give to data users? What is ISDN's "basic service," and why may it not be good enough for many applications?
23. Why did the IEEE 802 Standards Committee create standards for multiple layouts and access methods? Are the differences among these choices apparent to higher level processes such as system software-level standards or application standards?
24. In the 802 standards, what are the three sublayers of the second OSI layer? What is the job of each? Under what conditions will 802.4 be used? What are the relative strengths of 802.3 and 802.5?
25. SNA originally had a master-slave orientation. How has APPC changed this? What two upgrades are needed to implement APPC within SNA? What are the possible future roles for SNA?

REFERENCES

1. DIXON, R. C., STROLE, N. C., AND MARKOV, V. D., "A Token-Ring Network for Local Data Communications," *IBM Systems Journal,* Vol. 22, Nos. 1 and 2, 1983, pp. 47–62.

15 NETWORKING PRODUCTS

The last chapter surveyed the technology of networking. In this chapter, we will turn to more pragmatic concerns—the kinds of choices offered in the marketplace.

We will not look at wide area networking—either public data networks (PDNs) or internal corporate networks for long distance communications. The selection of a PDN is so heavily dominated by such factors as cost, where the network reaches geographically, and what hosts are already connected to it that it is difficult to say much about selecting a PDN in ways that are not highly specific to particular organizations. Internal wide area corporate networks, in turn, are so complex that information centers rarely have major input in their design, except through statements about end user computing in the overall strategic IS plan.

Instead, we will focus on PC networks and LANs. Because these networks are normally purchased and operated by end user organizations, it is important to know what to look for. Information centers tend to be heavily involved with these purchases because the wrong short distance network, selected only for the needs of operational systems, could strangle the future effectiveness of end user computing.

PURCHASING PITFALLS

Before examining individual types of networks, we will begin with short distance networking in general. Specifically, we will begin by focusing on the most common pitfalls that face potential buyers of PC networks and LANs.

A large number of myths, exaggerated expectations, and simple misunderstandings have grown up around PC networks and LANs. User organizations are partially to blame for this situation because they are so thin in data communications expertise that they often misunderstand what is being sold. Vendors are also to blame because they tend to use such standard terms as "synchronous" in ways that are very different from the standard definitions users have learned in communications classes. After we have surveyed the major myths surrounding short distance networking, we will discuss some specific kinds of networking products offered in the marketplace.

The Any-to-Any Myth

Many buyers believe that networks can link almost any device to any other. This conjures up visions of linking Wang hosts to IBM and Burroughs hosts, Apple IIs to IBM PCs. As noted in Chapter 14, however, the reality is much less exciting. Networks connect devices in the same way that the telephone system can link people in different countries. There is no guarantee that they will speak the same language, not to mention that they will have comparable business practices.

Nobody expects the telephone to translate voices—it is merely a transmission system. A network is also a transmission system, handling the bottom two or three layers of the OSI architecture. It will not translate between the operating systems differences among devices (Wang to Digital Equipment Corporation). Nor will it translate between incompatible applications, even if both are operating on computers from the same company. Unless two systems are compatible all the way through applications software, the ability of networking to connect many devices is meaningless.

Asynchronous and Synchronous Support

Many networks advertise "both asynchronous and synchronous transmission." From Chapter 13, these two alternatives seem to be all-inclusive, but when networking vendors use these terms, they mean something specific and, in the case of synchronous communications, something much less than the term usually connotes.

"**Asynchronous**" usually means asynchronous communications via an RS232C interface. This, at least, is pretty much what one would expect. RS232C limits transmission speeds to 19.2 kbps, but the asynchronous communication speed supported on a network is usually even slower—only 1200 bps to 9600 bps.

"**Synchronous**" however, means something very specific—synchronous communications for **IBM mainframe computers.** No other synchronous schemes need apply.

Furthermore, IBM has *two* synchronous schemes for its mainframes. First, there is the older **bisynchronous** communications protocol, which is used when a firm has not adopted IBM's Systems Network Architecture. Second, there is IBM's **synchronous data link control, SDLC**, which runs under SNA. It is important to ask whether a short distance network supports both.

Even more specifically, it is important to ask what devices a network supports. As discussed in Chapter 13, the "**3270**" architecture involves a number of devices. Most LANs can connect 3270 series terminals to cluster controllers, but some cannot link remote cluster controllers to communications controllers. None connects local terminal cluster controllers or communications controllers to the IBM mainframe, because these are channel-attached to the mainframe. With links going directly into the bus, they must be physically co-located with the host.

Even if 3270 series terminals are connected, you must understand what speeds are supported. IBM cabling can provide 2 Mbps to each terminal, but many networks support speeds of only 64 kbps or even less. In other words, going to a "high-speed" network can actually *slow* the terminal-host link.

What if you have a non-IBM host? Then you must either have a host that can emulate the appropriate parts of the IBM synchronous communications system or you must revert to the snail-paced asynchronous RS232C link. If you revert to RS232C, you may need to buy a protocol converter to place between the host and the network. Burroughs, for example, requires this because of its vendor-specific "poll select" protocol. This costs money, diluting the economic savings touted for the network. It may also degrade performance if the protocol conversion is not perfect.

Wang is a particular problem because it uses a 4.25 Mbps channel to talk to its terminal and frequently swamps multikilobyte pages with its intelligent terminals. To put Wang systems on an asynch RS232C link is ludicrous. Unfortunately, Wang's closed architecture has not allowed most LAN vendors to support Wang hosts and terminals.

Sometimes the limited support provided by networks forces companies to support parallel transmission systems for its Wang units and other non-IBM high-speed systems. This can utterly destroy the economic advantages of networking.

Controller Limitations

The limitations that emerge when external controllers are added to a network were discussed earlier, in the section on internal and external controllers. Because a misunderstanding of controller limitations is a major stumbling block for many buyers, however, we should repeat a few main points from that discussion.

A controller has three functions.

- First, it is a miniature transmitter and receiver that injects signals into the network and receives incoming signals. This usually requires it to listen for signals directed specifically to it.
- Second, the controller implements the specific access method used by the network, such as IEEE 802.3, 802.4, or 802.5. This can be a complex operation.
- Third, the controller must work with the device attached to the network, transferring messages when possible and buffering messages when exchange is delayed.

As shown in Figure 14-4, it is common to have **external controllers**. These devices are mounted on the cable and either lay on the floor or, if the cable is run through a wall, are connected to wall outlets.

The outlet, of course, must have a specific electrical interface. As noted earlier, RS232C and IBM's 3270 interfaces are the most commonly provided, but even 3270 interfaces are not always offered. Without a 3270 interface, it matters little that a network can move bits at a million bits per second or more because the 3270 series terminal will have to be connected via an RS232C port, and these ports are limited to 19.2 kbps.

Some networks provide an RS449 physical interface, with either the RS422A or RS423A electrical interface (see Chapter 13). RS422A supports very high speeds—up to 10 Mbps, but few devices support RS449 and RS422A or RS423A. In addition, some (e.g., the Macintosh) that do support RS449/RS422A use the 9-pin secondary connector for RS449, instead of the 37-pin primary connector used on most external controllers that support RS449.

The RS232C limitation is bad enough for terminal-to-host communications, but for PC-to-PC communications, it is a total disaster. As noted at the beginning of Chapter 14, such common PC networking tasks as transferring documents, downloading programs, and transferring graphics screens can take several minutes or even hours, and this is unacceptable. These excruciating delays are probably *understated* by a factor of two to eight because few networks support a full 19.2 kbps through their RS232C ports; many support only 2400 bps to 9600 bps. To put it briefly, PC networking makes no sense if external controllers are used, since emulating 3270 communications is too expensive to do on each PC.

The only way to handle PC networking is to use **internal controllers.** As discussed earlier, internal controllers are expansion boards placed inside PCs. Because internal controllers are thus connected directly to the PC's bus, they can transfer information into and out of the PC at bus speeds—2 Mbps or faster. With buffering, even faster burst transmissions over the network are possible.

Because expansion boards are *always* tailored to specific PCs, it is not enough to know whether a network offers PC controllers. You must know whether your network has internal controllers for your *particular* PCs.

As you would expect because of IBM's dominance in the PC arena, many networks have internal controllers for IBM PCs. Many, however, offer no internal controllers for PCs at all. Others, for example, Wangnet, at the time of this writing, offer internal controllers for some PCs but not for IBM PCs. So it is *not* a safe bet that internal controllers will be available for IBM PCs.

For non-IBM PCs, internal controllers are often unavailable. Even among IBM PC "compatibles," the picture is mixed because many PCs labeled as compatible cannot take internal controllers designed for the IBM PC. In general, the highly complex communications boards used in communications test the real limits of compatibility. Many compatibles that function perfectly with less complex expansion boards fail to work properly with networking boards or even host-specific terminal emulation boards.

Because of the overwhelming importance of personal computers in end user computing, the information center staff must do everything in its power to keep out networks that do not offer internal controllers for the PCs used in their firms.

Channel Speed Limitations

The broadband systems discussed later typically have 200 Mbps to 400 Mbps of channel capacity, but broadband systems divide this immense bandwidth into many channels, each having only a fraction of the bandwidth. Many networks have very narrow channels available to many applications, only 2400 bps to 9600 bps.

Wideband channels may be available on broadband networks, but the use of these channels requires internal (bus-attached) controllers on the host, and these may not be available for many hosts.

For PCs, these wideband channels may or may not be available in the sense that inexpensive internal controllers may not be available or the channels may be point-to-point channels instead of the many-to-many channels needed in personal computer networking.

Channel capacity can also be a problem for 3270 series terminal-host transmission. As noted earlier, local cluster controllers can communicate with their 3270 series terminals at 2 Mbps, but many networks provide much slower terminal-controller links, often below 64 kbps. This produces no degradation for some applications, but for other applications, low speeds are debilitating.

Low "3270" speeds can also cause problems when a PC emulating a 3270 series terminal wishes to exchange a large file with the host—although some terminal emulation hardware itself has limited speed.

PC Networking Needs

Initially, personal computer networking was a specialized field, the domain of dedicated PC networking. Companies now realize that they cannot have separate networks—one to link their PCs and another to link other devices. Many LAN vendors now offer PC networking.

Networking first emerged to link terminals to hosts. In such cases, application software was entirely a matter for the host and totally outside the scope of network vendors.

PC networking is entirely different. As noted earlier, there is not much point linking PCs together unless someone provides a great deal of service software for all PCs on the network. On PC networks, service software is the whole key to success.

Service software runs on computers called **servers.** In some cases, the server is a special-purpose microcomputer, and in other cases, a regular PC is the server. In the second case, it may or may not be usable as a PC while it is acting as a server. If PCs are linked to a host, the service software may run on the host.

As noted in Chapters 12 and 14, there are tremendous differences in service software quality, even for such simple services as disk and printer sharing. At higher levels, including file sharing and multiuser DBMS availability, service software differences are even greater. When considering a PC network, the evaluation of software should take far more time than the evaluation of hardware.

Network Management

Although not a pitfall per se, an important purchase concern is network management. Whenever devices are added or dropped from the network, or whenever the service profile of a device must be changed, a network administrator must update tables on servers and devices. Is network management software available to handle these chores and handle them easily?

Is there diagnostic software (and hardware) available to check the network periodically for minor malfunctions and to find the problem when a major malfunction occurs? Without good diagnostics and recovery, using a network can be a maddening experience. One large Army hospital suffered constant problems for months until a specialist was called in and discovered that its amplifiers were too weak, causing devices that could not hear incoming signals to conclude that the network had gone down. Because these devices were programmed to shut themselves off in case of network failure, low signals caused devices to "drop out" of the network constantly. Although the problem was obvious in retrospect (most problems are), the software that came with the network was unable to diagnose the problem.

Good network management also means performance reporting in order to give advance notice when more capacity will be needed, to warn of unusual patterns that could spell trouble, and to provide chargeback on large networks.

Another part of network management is security. Does the network support the National Bureau of Standards' Data Encryption Standard (DES) standard or some other encryption scheme? Can a device be limited to connecting only to specified other devices? If it is possible to enter the network via outside telecommunications, or if some directly attached terminals could be abused, are there good security measures, including warnings to the network manager if there are unusual patterns such as many log-in failures or a terminal linking to other than its usual host? Of course, security tends to make life harder for users, so security should be appropriate to expected security risks.

Pitfalls in Perspective

Today's networks often do much less than buyers assume they will. These limitations can be so severe that networking is not yet a viable choice for many applications. If you are considering a network, be especially sure you know exactly what each vendor offers. The Romans coined the phrase "let the buyer beware." Modern networking technology has perfected the concept.

PERSONAL COMPUTER NETWORKS

Personal computer networks are the smallest data communications networks that an organization can implement, but this does not mean that they are easy to implement. PC networking requires a quantum leap in technical expertise for most organizations that have not dealt with networking before. It is all too easy to be dazzled by hardware and performance considerations, to the detriment of skepticism when viewing the all-critical server and network management software that comes with these networks.

IBM Personal Computer Networking

IBM has already introduced two personal computer networks, which are head-to-head competitors. To people who view IBM as a monolith guided by clear strategic planning, this diversity seems confusing. The reality, however, is that IBM almost always produces competing products in major areas of its business. In a Darwinian view of planning, IBM often fosters competition among its product development units, letting the market decide which products will succeed. This confuses the market, but it usually prevents IBM from making disastrous moves by putting all of its eggs into one basket.

The IBM Personal Computer Network

IBM's first PC networking product was the **IBM Personal Computer Network (PCN).** Concerned by the slow progress made toward networking by other corporate units, the Entry Systems Division responsible for the IBM PC turned to the Sytek Corporation for a joint development project to produce a simple personal computer network.

As noted in the previous chapter, small broadband networks can be pre-engineered at the factory. Sytek took this approach to engineering the PC network. Although this choice of moving to pre-engineered cable lengths and limited distances produced some problems, the benefits it brought for ease of use were considerable.

Two design choices by Sytek seriously compromised the usefulness of the IBM Personal Computer Network.

- First, Sytek used its own proprietary CSMA/CD access method instead of adopting IEEE 802 standards. As a result, potential buyers were concerned about locking themselves into a nonstandard technology for networking their PCs. It would not even be easy to build gateways between individual PC networks and full corporate LANs, thanks to this use of nonstandard technology.

- Second, Sytek chose to use Intel's 82586 communications controller chip on its network controller board. This chip could only move information at 2 Mbps, which is somewhat slow for PC networking if more than a dozen or so devices are using the network.

Although many organizations bought a few of the original PC networks for experimentation, few large firms adopted it broadly. When IBM introduced its Token-Ring Network in 1985, the IBM Personal Computer Network's luster grew even dimmer.

The IBM Token-Ring Network for Personal Computers

As discussed earlier, IBM has long championed token ring networking (IBM spells it "token-ring") and the IEEE 802.5 standard in particular. In the early 1980s, IBM announced plans to produce a full 802.5 LAN. Its first 802.5 product, however, was not a full LAN. Instead, it was a personal computer network, the **IBM Personal Computer Token-Ring Network, TRN.** This network has since been integrated with broader TRN products, but we will look at the TRN's PC networking in isolation in this section, discussing the broader TRN later in this chapter, in the context of full local area networking.

From the very beginning, IBM signalled that its IBM Token-Ring Network for personal computers would be a strategic product. It announced that the TRN would one day embrace all IBM products both large and small, and it priced the product aggressively. In addition, it built the network to conform to the IEEE 802 standards discussed earlier, as well as the European ECMA 89 standard. This conformance to standards creates the open environment needed to encourage rapid growth.

To further encourage competition, IBM used standard commercially available chips, including the TMS 80 communications controller chip sold by Texas Instrument. IBM did use proprietary ROM programs on the adapter card, but these programs have been successfully cloned without violating copyright.

The Token-Ring Network Adapter Board

IBM's PC adapter card uses the Texas Instruments TMS 80 chip, as just noted. This chip can move information at 4 Mbps—twice the speed of the original IBM Personal Computer Network.

One of the adapter cards in every PC Token-Ring Network must be designated as the Ring Interface Adapter, which is capable of regenerating the token if it is lost, perform time-out controls and link fault detection, and do general error checking. If the card designated as the Ring Interface Adapter fails, another automatically takes up the role.

Cabling for the Token-Ring Network

The TRN supports two basic cable technologies. Using standard twisted pair telephone wire, the network can support up to 72 devices, with a maximum distance of 2000 feet between the farthest devices. Using IBM's more expensive data grade cabling, the network can support up to 260 personal computers and can reach over larger distances.

As shown in Figure 15-1, the TRN uses wiring concentrators called **multiple access units.** Although electronically inert, multiple access units connect the devices into a ring layout. The devices can be up to 200 feet from the multiple access unit.

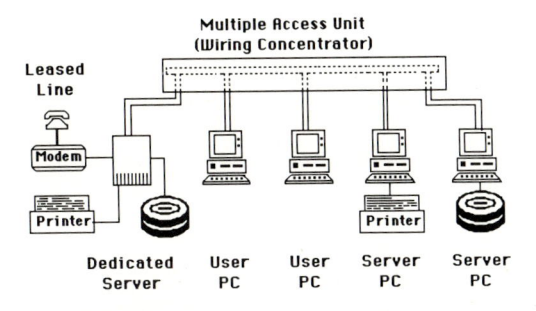

Requirements:

Wiring and wiring concentrator

Network controller expansion board in each PC

Network software for each PC

Additional network software for servers

Network management software

Application software that can be used on the net

FIGURE 15-1 IBM PERSONAL COMPUTER TOKEN-RING NETWORK

A single multiple access unit can connect up to eight devices into a ring. By linking up to nine multiple access units together, a user organization can create a TRN with up to 72 devices.

In practice, however, fewer than 72 devices are likely to be connected. First, it is important to leave room for growth. Second, some multiple access units may be in areas where only one or two PCs are in use.

Software for the Token-Ring Network

The network adapter card contains a certain amount of ROM code to offload work from the user's software. On the TRN, two ROM options are possible.

The first ROM option is the **NETBIOS** ROM originally developed for the IBM Personal Computer Network. Because both networks use the same NETBIOS ROM, program calls to ROM will work equally well on both boards. On the Personal Computer Network the NETBIOS ROM was mandatory; on the TRN, it is an option.

The second ROM option is the ROM needed to implement the Advanced Program-to-Program communications (APPC) protocol discussed in Chapter 14. Billed as **APPC/PC** on the IBM Token-Ring Network, the protocol allows PC programs to communicate as peers with programs on IBM mainframes and smaller products such as the System 38.

On a network adapter card for the TRN, a user may have the NETBIOS ROM, the APPC/PC ROM, or both. It is even possible, in principle, for a multitasking PC to be carrying on simultaneous sessions over the NETBIOS and APPC/PC ROM.

Two other pieces of system software are needed to complete the picture. First, users must have a copy of DOS 3.1 or higher. DOS 3.0 would work in theory, but the 3.0 version had technical problems. DOS 3.1 has special commands needed to work with networking.

Second, the user must have the **IBM Network Program.** This program provides the network series needed by users and application programs. Different versions of the IBM Network Program are needed for server PCs and user (nonserver) PCs.

As shown in Figure 15-2, the IBM Network Program sits on top of DOS, intercepting program calls before DOS gets to them. This frees the network program from the limitations of DOS, allowing such advanced services as file locking and even record locking.

In theory, the Network Program, DOS, and the adapter ROM are the only pieces of system software needed. In reality, however, users also need a network management program to manage the network efficiently, as well as a variety of advanced server utilities that go beyond the basic services offered in the Network Program. These options are priced separately and can add significantly to the cost of the network.

The users also need application programs designed for the network program, ROM, or both. Although some programs can be used on the network without modification, many copy-protected programs do not. It is always necessary to buy special versions of programs that allow concurrent access to data, for example, concurrent multiuser DBMSs.

As shown in Figure 15-2, users can give commands to their application

```
User            User            User
 |               |               |
Application     |              Application
Program         |              Program
 |           IBM Network         |
IBM Network   Program          IBM Network
Program         |              Program
 |             DOS               |
DOS                             DOS
 |              |                |
Network ROM   Network ROM    Network ROM
On Adapter    On Adapter     On Adapter
```

Users can work with an application program or directly with the IBM Network Program.

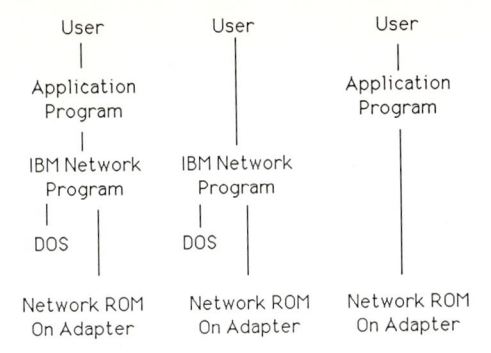

Application programs can work with the IBM Network Program or directly with IBM's Network ROM on the adapter board.

Because the IBM Network Program sits on top of DOS, application programs that use it are not restricted by DOS limitations.

FIGURE 15-2 THE IBM NETWORK PROGRAM AND IBM'S NETWORK ROM

programs or to the IBM Network Program directly, for instance, to log into the network when the computer is first turned on. Application programs, in turn, can talk either to the IBM Network Program or directly to the adapter ROM.

Microsoft, which produces MS-DOS, of which the IBM PC-DOS is a variant, also sells a variant of the IBM Network Program for some non-IBM computers, most notably IBM compatibles.

Other Dedicated PC Networks

Although LANS and host-based PC networking offer alternatives to dedicated PC networks, dedicated networks are still extremely important, allowing small work units to get into networking in comparatively simple ways. We have already looked in some detail at the IBM approach to dedicated PC networks. We will now quickly survey at a few other dedicated networks in order to give just a taste of the diversity that exists.

Token-Ring Network Compatibles

Whenever IBM develops a product, other vendors usually rush to produce compatible products. IBM has not made this difficult in PC networking. It uses standard off the shelf chips, and, as noted earlier, it has allowed Microsoft to sell its version of the Network Program. Although few compatibles appeared for the original Personal Computer Network, the compatibles market really heated up when the Token-Ring Network was announced.

When IBM developed the Token-Ring Network, it went out of its way to open the doors to vendors who could build compatible equipment. IBM even worked actively with some of the existing PC networking vendors to help them develop compatible products because IBM is more interested in promoting 802.5 networking than in selling these low-cost boards and server programs. Texas Instruments made its controller chip generally available, so there was in effect no real barrier to entry. A supplier had to design an adapter board, using most of the IBM adapter board's chips, and then develop a compatible set of ROM programs.

Although compatibles are just beginning to enter the market at the time of this writing, they are taking the familiar route of offering superior features at a slightly lower price, although IBM's aggressive pricing on the Token-Ring Network will make it difficult to compete heavily on price.

Many compatible vendors have long offered PC networks based on different technologies. For instance, 3Com has been a major supplier of 803.3/803.2 networks. These vendors are attempting to keep their existing user base by offering smooth gateways to link new 802.5/802.3 nets with existing networks with different technical bases.

Novell Netware

Although IBM originally offered only a single network operating system, its Network Program, customer complaints about the limitations of the Network Program caused IBM to add an alternative, the Netware network operating system of Novell.

Novell originally developed Netware for its proprietary network products, but the program received such good reviews that Novell adapted Netware to work on most other personal computer networks. Taking a cue from MS-DOS, Novell attempted to make Netware the "standard" network operating system for PC networking. It was largely successful with this effort until the IBM PC networks appeared with the Network Program, and many application programs have been written to run with Netware.

Because IBM did not choose Netware as its main network operating system, the product's future is in question compared to the Network Program. Nevertheless, users do have the choice of Novell Netware and IBM Network Program (also known as Microsoft Networks). The basic issue in the selection seems to be one of power versus simplicity. The Network Program is substantially easier to install and manage, whereas Netware gives more power.

3Com Etherseries

As noted earlier, IEEE 802.3 is a variant of the Ethernet network developed primarily by Xerox, with assistance from Intel and Digital Equipment Corporation. A number of companies now produce Ethernet or IEEE 802.3 networks. One of the largest is 3Com.

3Com originally developed its products for minicomputers and high-cost personal workstations such as the Xerox 8010 star. 3Com, however, also offers a compatible network, Etherseries, tailored to the IBM PC. In addition to controller boards, this product used thin cable connected to each controller board's external connection via a simple T connector, which screws onto the back of the adapter board as simply as screwing a coaxial CATV cable onto a home VCR.

The 3Com Etherseries board is about 25 percent more expensive than the boards for the IBM Personal Computer Network and the IBM Token-

Ring Network. Probably the main reason for this high cost is speed. Etherseries boards move information at 10 Mbps instead of PCN's 2 Mbps and the TRN's 4 Mbps. Given the bus speeds of personal computers, this added speed will not translate into a factor of two and a half to five in real transmission speed, but it does mean that the network will not produce traffic jams when loads are high.

3Com offers a dedicated network server (the 3Server) that acts as a file server, printer server, communications server, and processor for electronic mail. A good deal of multiuser software has already been announced for this Motorola 68000 microprocessor-based server. IBM PC XT's and AT's can also be used as servers.

3Com and other 802.3 networks are likely to be most attractive in environments with 802.3 large-scale LANs or where throughput problems are very large. Their future, however, is in doubt nearly everywhere.

Microsoft's MS-NET and LAN Manager
Microsoft and IBM have worked together to produce DOS and OS/2, and Microsoft has traditionally made co-developed products available to other computer vendors. For example, PC-DOS for the IBM PC was made available as MS-DOS for other computers.

IBM and Microsoft have also worked together to produce IBM's networking products. When IBM and Microsoft introduced IBM's first networking solution, which consisted of PC-DOS 3.X and the IBM Network Program, Microsoft introduced MS-DOS 3.X and a product comparable to the IBM Network Program, MS-NET.

Neither the IBM Network Program nor MS-NET was rated highly by the marketplace, and Microsoft, rather than wait for IBM to move, produced its own successor to the IBM Network Program and MS-NET. This is the Microsoft LAN Manager. Microsoft was able to make this strategy work in windowing operating environments, so that its Microsoft Windows products has virtually eliminated IBM's TopView from even IBM's planning.

Several companies have announced support for the Microsoft LAN Manager. Absent from this list is IBM, which is adopting its usual wait-and-see attitude. In an added bit of confusion, IBM has its own product called LAN Manager. The IBM LAN Manager is a network management module rather than a full network operating system like the Microsoft LAN Manager, but the naming confusion is unfortunate.

RS232C PC Networks
Most PC networks use sophisticated network adapter cards. A small number, however, use simple RS232C serial boards that are already on many PCs and that can be purchased for less than a hundred dollars.

Because of the law of conservation of difficulty, the use of a cheaper board means that the network software must do more work. This in turn means that network servers will not be able to support as many user PCs as a PC network based on a more complex adapter board.

Another problem is the low performance of the RS232C interface. RS232C is limited by design to 19.2 kbps, and although most RS232C networks can move data somewhat faster than this design limit and over more than the 50 foot distance design limit of RS232C, they are still comparative slowpokes. In addition, because RS232C cables use unshielded wires, these networks are quite susceptible to noise.

RS232 networks adapt to this situation by limiting the services they offer, the sophistication of these services, and the number of devices they can serve. RS232C networks are essentially quick-and-dirty implementations for offices that have only a handful of computers and for whom ease of installation and low cost are the deciding factors.

Macintosh Networks

When Apple built the Macintosh, it gave it RS449/RS422A interfaces. As discussed in Chapter 14, these interfaces can handle megabit per second data exchange speeds, although software can rarely approach such throughput.

The first step that Apple took to exploit its high-speed serial port was to introduce a cabling system called AppleTalk. A typical AppleTalk kit sells for only $50. It contains a two-meter cable that can plug directly into two serial ports. This allows the cable to link a single Macintosh with a printer (such as a laser page printer) or to link two Macintoshes. Apple also sells longer AppleTalk cables.

The kit also contains two connectors for more complex layouts. First, and most simply, it contains a one-inch plug that allows a second cable to be added for longer distances. Second, it contains a T-plug that allows one Macintosh to be connected to two cables, say to another Macintosh and to a printer. Using several of these T-plugs, it is possible to link several Macintoshes into a network.

Apple's sales figures on AppleTalk kits have always been impressive, but a large majority of AppleTalk "networks" only link a single Macintosh to a laser printer. Only a fraction of all kits are used for multimachine networking, and many of these networks are very simple, with two or three devices share a laser page printer and nothing else.

Apple was slow to deliver the network operating system needed for full networking. It was not until 1987 that it delivered the AppleShare software needed to do the job. Even then, AppleShare was a very limited offering. For instance, it required the server to be a dedicated server. As discussed in Chapter 12, this means that the server cannot be used as a user PC. Since many Macintosh networks consist of only two or three machines, dedicating a single machine to server functions is something of an extravagance. In addition, while Apple introduced an adapter board for IBM PCs, it did not extend AppleTalk software to run on IBM PCs. Over time, of course, AppleShare is likely to become much more powerful and flexible.

Because of Apple's slow entry into the network operating system market, other firms were able to get a firm foothold. Probably the most widely used of these network operating systems is **TOPS**. TOPS is a crude network that provides little more than simple printer sharing and disk sharing at the volume level (see Chapter 12), but is very easy to use and can link Macintoshes with IBM PCs and UNIX host computers. This multivendor operation is very important to most users, since most organizations have several IBM PCs and only one or two Macintoshes.

TOPS and other multivendor networks are becoming popular in many organizations, because networks designed for IBM PCs rarely include Macintosh support. Now that Macintoshes are proliferating, corporations need networks that support Macintoshes as well as IBM PCs and full compatibles.

Even AppleTalk cabling is beginning to get competition. AppleTalk cabling is sold in only a few sizes by Apple, and AppleTalk always uses coaxial cable, which is fairly expensive. In contrast, one competitor, PhoneNet, uses the same twisted-pair wire found in ordinary telephone wires. These wires are cheap, easy to lay, and easy to cut to length.

For the long run, AppleTalk is too slow to provide a solid base for networking. While its 0.23 Mbps speed is adequate for a small number of machines, it is totally inadequate for larger networks. Now that the Macintosh SE and the Macintosh II have included expansion slots that can be used for network expansion boards, we are likely to see Macintoshes using higher speed networks. Since Apple has a very large installed base of older machines, however, AppleTalk-based networks are likely to remain in use for some time.

PC Networking Services on LANs

When the first LANs were produced, they were designed for terminal-host communications. Once the importance of PCs became apparent, however, many LAN vendors began to connect PCs. Why have separate PC networks and risk incompatibility if the company's broad LAN can do the job?

The Need for Adapter Boards

At first, these LAN vendors let the PC come into the network via RS232C or the 3270 wiring approach. This allowed PCs to use the same external connectors as terminals did. RS232C was far too slow for file transfers, program downloading, graphics transfers, and many other popular PC applications. The 3270 "synchronous" links were typically also very slow, running at no more than 64 kbps in most cases.

To address these limitations, many LAN vendors, first developed adapter boards to let PCs communicate at bus speeds of several Mbps.

Second, they offered high-speed channels for PC traffic. If a LAN vendor says that it supports PCs, the first thing to look at is boards and channel speeds. If a network does not offer an Mbps adapter card and matching channel speed, it is a sham to say that it offers PC networking. Its speed will be far too low for any real office use.

Third, they offered server software to provide services crucial to PC networking.

Server Support

Transmission is not enough for PC networking on LANs. As mentioned earlier, PC networking only makes sense if servers are provided for print services, file services, communications services, and processing services for electronic mail, DBMS, and other processing chores.

To support PC networking, the LAN must either provide servers or offer software for using PCs as servers. In addition, unless this server software is extremely good, it will be a waste of money to do PC networking on a LAN. In the future, most LAN vendors may settle on the IBM Network Program or other standard server solutions, but for now, the server software picture is extremely mixed.

Bridges Between PC Networks and LANS

Although LANS offer PC networking and use it as a selling point by saying that now there is no need to build separate PC networks, many offer rather inferior service. The growing number of bridge products now on the market may make the use of dedicated PC networks linked to LANS for longer distance transmission the best alternative.

In the IBM world, of course, the Token-Ring Network for PCs should mesh smoothly with IBM's full token-ring LAN, which is moving rapidly to embrace all IBM products from PCs to mainframes.

Host-Based PC Networking

Many personal computers are already attached to host computers for analysis, data management, graphics, office automation, and data downloading to PCs. In some organizations, a majority of PCs are attached to host computers.

If an organization buys a PC network, it can reach a host through a network communications server. If many PCs are attached to the host already, however, a simpler solution to PC networking may be possible. This approach is to make the host itself act like a huge network server as well as like a network switch.

The host itself can do file serving, print serving, processing, and other PC networking server chores. In this way, the existing terminal/PC cabling can be used without modification and without waiting for a LAN to appear. In addition, the organization does not have to lay two sets of wires, one for PC-host connections and another for PC-PC work.

Furthermore, although PC networks are inherently small, host-based networking allows a company to set up one very large "PC net" for the company or, if a multiplicity of small systems is desired, a set of unrelated clusters of users and resources.

One of the biggest advantages of host-based servers is that certain network management chores can be handled by the existing operations staff. Disk backup is done automatically, every night, using file-by-file tape drives so that individual files accidentally destroyed by users as they work can be retrieved. Most host installations already have system software for diagnosing communications problems and for implementing various levels of security (see Chapter 13). The operations staff can even manage the operation of high-speed central laser printers.

The host software, of course, needs to be adequate. It must provide at least file locking and preferably record locking as well. Although host-based DBMSs are available (see Chapter 16), most of them are too complex for average users. Many host products do not do record locking or even file locking, and few run ordinary PC software. Hosts do provide sophisticated communications services—for instance, on System 36s, a PC emulating a 5250 terminal can be linked automatically to an IBM mainframe, including 3270 emulation—as well as links to host based analysis, data management, graphics, and office automation software. However, the lack of basic support for file locking and PC software usually causes too many troubles. At best, host-based networks must give up processing services such as popular PC multiuser DBMS service. They are most attractive if needs are limited to printer and program/data file storage.

FULL LOCAL AREA NETWORKS

To this point we have discussed only one kind of short distance network, the personal computer network. Now we will turn to full **local area networks** or **LANs.**

General Considerations

Scope

In contrast to PC networks, LANs have broad physical *scope.* Instead of serving a handful of PCs within a single office, LANs serve hundreds or even thousands of terminals, hosts, PCs, and other devices scattered throughout an entire building or campus of buildings.

This broader scope raises the implementation ante dramatically. Planning takes one to three years, and major engineering studies have to be done. Wire and cable have to be run through ceilings and walls instead of left on the floor, as is the case in most PC networks. Trenches have to be dug if the LAN runs between buildings.

Scope also changes the management of information, including security, data integrity, and the allocation of storage resources and priorities. Nearly every server can be accessed by anyone on the network if they find its security codes. Therefore, the informal security measures taken on most PC networks for individual offices will not be enough. In addition, as more and more vital information is stored on the network, its integrity must be maintained with formal planning.

Scope affects the management of the network hardware and software itself, including the difficulties of keeping a current list of users, the mechanics of adding and dropping users, problem diagnosis, adding enhancements, and analyzing statistics for facilities planning.

PC Networking on LANs

As noted earlier, some LANs support the high-speed communications needed for PC networking, as well as the server software for which PCs turn to networking. Because LANs were originally conceived as mere transmission systems, a major shift in conceptual thinking was required when LAN vendors began to see that PC networking must include server software as well as mere transmission.

Broadband LANs, Baseband LANs, and Data PBXs

There are two major types of LANs, each of which uses a different underlying technology and tends to have a different level of performance.

The superhighway of the LAN world is the **broadband LAN,** which provides a communications link of 100 to 400 Mbps and can span a campus of buildings spread over several miles and containing thousands of devices. Because the immense bandwidth of the broadband LAN is shared, no device can communicate at speeds that even approach its total bandwidth. More importantly, all broadband LANs divide their bandwidth into a number of channels, as noted earlier in this chapter, and some have small-channel bandwidths, reducing the peak burst speed available when devices transmit.

For smaller needs, **baseband LANs** span distances of about a thousand feet and support several hundred devices. Although their actual cable runs may be longer than a thousand feet, the need to snake wiring through walls and over obstructions limits nearly all to about a thousand feet between desks. Baseband networks are not for large installations, unless they use repeaters. So in selecting a baseband LAN, the availability of repeaters is critical. Even with repeaters, some baseband LANs have severe distance limitations.

Baseband networks are usually limited to speeds of only 4 Mbps to 40 Mbps, but this bandwidth is shared by fewer devices than broadband bandwidth, and there is only a single channel. Therefore, burst speeds in the Mbps range are routinely available to devices.

An alternative to both broadband and baseband LANs is the **data PBX**. PBXs are internal telephone switching systems that are owned by the user organization. Some PBXs, but by no means all, can carry data as easily as they can carry voice. In the past, most data PBXs could only transmit at 9600 bps to 64 kbps, but now higher speeds are becoming available.

Broadband LANs

CATV Cabling

As noted earlier, nearly all broadband LANs use standard cable television (CATV) cabling and amplifiers. This means that the underlying transmission technology is cheap and readily available.

It also simplifies installation. Many organizations let separate contracts for the underlying cable plant and for networking equipment (head end/transverters, controllers, etc.). The cabling contracts are usually awarded to local CATV companies, these companies may also handle the maintenance of the cable plant after the full system is installed.

Ordinary television uses channels that are 6 MHz wide. As a result, a recurrent theme in broadband system designs is the 6 MHz channel. One reason for extending the 6 MHz channel to the data world was the ready availability of transmitters and receivers with that bandwidth.

Because broadband signals attenuate with distance from an amplifier, careful engineering is needed, first, to ensure that there will be enough signal strength to drive the attached devices, and, second, to put controllers with appropriate "gains" (amplification levels) at each point along the cable run. Controllers farther away will obviously need stronger gains to boost the weaker signal at their location, and they will also have to transmit more strongly.

Sytek's Broadband Products

The IBM Personal Computer Network was jointly engineered by IBM and Sytek. Long before, however, Sytek had achieved a strong reputation for its broadband LANs.

Sytek uses traditional broadband transmission and a proprietary CSMA/CD access method that was developed before 802.3 and as a consequence is incompatible with the standard. (This is the CSMA/CD scheme used in the IBM Personal Computer Network.) Sytek supports both single-cable and dual-cable networks.

Sytek offers three installation approaches. For small systems with cable runs less than a thousand feet, there is a pre-engineered kit without amplifiers that can be assembled by unskilled labor. For cable runs of up to 2000 feet, there will be a few amplifiers, but pre-engineering can still be done, and unskilled labor can still be used. For longer distances, skilled labor, engineering, certification, and customer training will be needed.

Most devices are attached to the network through external controllers that handle the access method, physical interface with the network, and encryption if desired. These controllers come in models ranging from 2 to 32 ports. The external controller with 32 ports is a statistical multiplexer that attaches to a host. Up to 2000 of these external controllers can be attached to the network.

The controllers can accept both RS232C and 3270 devices. There is also an internal controller for PCs, the IBM PC network adapter card.

Sytek offers four basic services. For terminal-host transmission, there is Localnet 20 service, which provides channels with 128 kbps speeds. It does this by dividing standard 6 MHz television channels into 20 data channels of 300 Khz. Sending 128 kbps over a 300 Khz channel is relatively easy.

Localnet 40 services is for processor to processor communication at 2 Mbps. (This embraces the IBM Personal Computer Network.) Localnet 50 service, in turn, is a collection of network management services.

The main Localnet 50 product is the 50/100 Network Control Center, which automates network management services. This 16 bit processor, which sits on a desk or in a wall rack, is remotely accessible over the network. This server monitors network performance, provides encryption keys to controllers on a session-by-session basis, provides access and configuration control, and assigns names for devices.

Another major Localnet 50 product is the 50/201 interchannel bridge that links devices from up to eight 128 kbps channels so that they appear to be running on a single channel. The Localnet 50 family also includes the transverter/head end, a redundant head end for host backup, a cable test unit, a statistical monitor, and an intercable bridge that can link two entire cable plants so that they function as one.

We have emphasized Localnet 50 services because network management is often downplayed in analyses of local area networks. Without excellent automated support for network management, however, networks quickly get out of control or suffer from breakdowns and capacity problems that are totally unacceptable to users.

The last major service is PC networking. Sytek offers a stand-alone broadband PC networking services, the Sytek 6000 PC network, which is an expanded version of the IBM Personal Computer Network. It can support large numbers of PCs over large geographical areas. This service is mentioned in the context of local area networking because this service is also available on Sytek's LAN. Its frequencies do not overlap those of other services, so it can coexist easily with other Localnet services.

Ungerman-Bass Net One

Ungerman-Bass has long felt a need to support multiple standards, so that customers can have the system they wish and can upgrade over time. Ungerman-Bass has its own proprietary CSMA/CD method, has supported Ethernet, and has announced plans for supporting the full spectrum of IEEE 802 standards. Net One also supports both cable and optical fiber connections, as well as thin cable connections for PC networking.

This supermarket approach extends to Ungerman-Bass's controller family. In addition to supporting RS232C and IBM 3270 connections, the external controllers support IEEE 488 for instrumentation, Centronics (8-bit parallel for printers), and RS449 and V.35 interfaces. At the data link level, support is provided for asynchronous communications, bisynch, SDLC (SNA), HLDC (ISO), and DDCMP (military). External controllers also support several devices per controller. Net One supports board-level adapters for IBM personal computers and compatibles.

When two devices want to communicate, several types of sessions can be established. First, there are traditional virtual circuit and datagram connections (see Chapter 14). Second, these sessions can be established by users, by network administrators, and by data base tables that create permanent connections instead of transient connections.

Like Sytek's products, Net One provides extensive network management tools, bridges to link different cable networks, and PC networking. In contrast to Sytek, which focuses on adapter cards and software developed for the IBM Personal Computer Network, Net One provides its own PC adapter cards and server software. Although PCs can be networked via the full network, Ungerman-Bass also allows users to build PC-only networks using either full cabling or thin cabling for lower cost and ease of installation.

Wangnet

Wangnet is another major supplier of broadband LANs. Wangnet is interesting because it divides its cable capacity into a number of frequency bands that provide different services.

The Wangband is designed to link Wang host computers.

The Peripheral Attachment Band links Wang peripherals to Wang hosts via external controllers.

The Utility band can carry multiple television channels.

The Interconnect band provides a number of channels for linking non-Wang equipment. These channels have speeds of up to 64 kbps; the channels can be switched or dedicated (like leased lines).

As this list suggests, Wangnet was designed to connect Wang devices. This in itself is important because Wang hosts support speeds of 4.25 Mbps to each of their terminals. To connect Wang peripherals via RS232C produced dramatic performance degradation. Because Wang does not have an open architecture, few other networks link Wang peripherals.

Wang only recently began to support IBM host communications at speeds above 64 kbps. At the time of this writing, the only PCs it can support with internal controllers are Wang PCs, shutting off Wangnet users from IBM PC networking.

Baseband LANs

Because baseband networks are normally limited to short distances, their popularity has tended to wane. However, IBM's strategic office network architecture, 802.5, is a baseband network that takes advantage of the fact that each node regenerates the signal after receiving it to extend the distance of its network. Many organizations that have strong engineering groups are turning to 802.3 networks to support their engineering workstations and minicomputers.

IBMs Token-Ring Network

Since the early 1980s, IBM has signalled its clear intention to focus on 802.5 token-ring networks for office computing. Although only personal computer networking is supported, IBM has announced the directions in which it will move in the future.

As discussed in Chapter 14, a typical IBM Token-Ring Network of the future is likely to have a central backbone network running at 16 Mbps, as well as a number of subrings operating at 4 Mbps. Each device in a subring is attached to its subring by a concentrator that allows the rapid bypassing of the device in case its controller fails.

IBM initially announced two basic cable bundles to support the network in 1984. It also discussed the importance of building many wiring closets to make the ring connections. Therefore, only the details remain to be announced for the network hardware. Network software is another matter, of course. Although IBM's long-term strategy is SNA with APPC support, other networking software will be announced for SNA users who do not support APPC and for customers who do not have SNA. Network management programs will also be critical.

Ethernet (802.3)

Ethernet was pioneered in the 1970s by Xerox and fully developed by Xerox, Intel, and Digital Equipment Corporation. A number of organizations, including Xerox and 3Com, now sell and support Ethernet networks and the 802.3 standard that is a slight modification of Ethernet. Because IBM has indicated no intention of supporting 802.3, Ethernet exists mostly in engineering organizations or offices that moved into LAN technology before IBM developed its token-ring approach. The high speed of 802.3—10 Mbps—makes file transfers, program transfers, and other heavy operations virtually instantaneous.

The first Ethernet-based product was the Xerox 8000 Network System, which was introduced at about the same time as the IBM PC. This product introduced many of the terms and concepts now commonplace in PC networking. It had high-power workstations, with iconic interfaces, and it also introduced the concept of "servers," offering file, print, and communications servers with sophisticated software. This product was far too expensive for widespread use, although it did find homes in places where sophisticated technical documentation had to be developed.

Data PBXs

Companies have long purchased **private branch exchanges** or **PBXs** to handle their voice communications. As shown in Figure 15-3, a PBX allows a

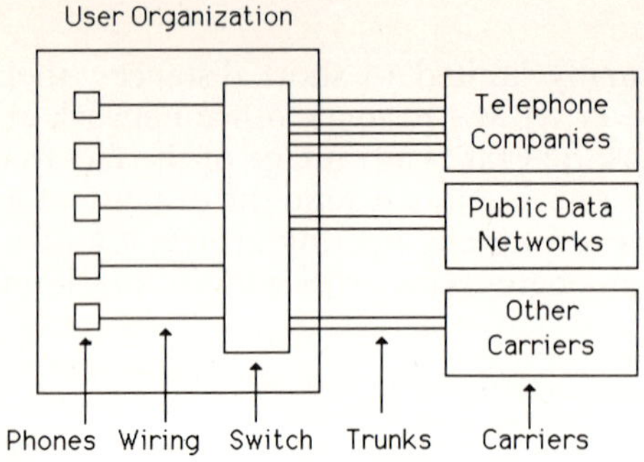

NETWORKING PRODUCTS

FIGURE 15-3 PRIVATE BRANCH EXCHANGE (PBX)

The user organization owns or leases the PBX system, including user devices such as telephones, modems, and other terminal equipment, wiring and the PBX switch or switches.

The user organization pays for trunk circuits to various common carriers for communications outside the company.

company to act like an independent country, handling its own internal telephone communications. The company controls its switch, its telephone instruments, and its transmission lines.

When communications are needed with the outside world, the user company contracts with a local telephone company, a public data network, a satellite transmission vendor, alternative long distance companies, and any other transmission source that may be appropriate.

PBXs for Voice Communications

PBXs were originally purchased strictly for voice communications. By purchasing its own system, the user organization avoided the cost of leasing its internal telephone system from the local telephone company. Even when implementation, maintenance, and operation costs were included, many users felt, PBXs offered lower costs than telephone leases.

PBXs would allow the company to get more control over its costs. Detailed use reports would allow the administrator to identify heavy users or even do chargeback to individual departments. Detailed circuit use reports would allow efficient capacity planning and information on the use of leased circuits. If low-cost WATS lines were available, the PBX would even do lowest cost routing automatically.

Data PBXs

If you had to build an entirely new wiring and switching system, many organizations eventually began to ask, why not handle data over the PBX system as well as voice? Vendors responded by providing **data PBXs** that could handle data as well as voice.

Of course, *all* voice PBXs can handle data simply by using a modem, but there are three problems with this approach. First, modems are expensive; second, modems only transmit at low speeds; and third, the user's telephone is tied up during every use session. Because many sessions last an hour or more, this seriously compromises the capability of the telephone system to reach people when they are needed.

The essence of a data PBX is not just the fact that it can carry data but that *it can bring simultaneous voice and data to any wall plug.* In other words, instead of the telephone jack providing a single transmission path, *two* transmission paths are multiplexed onto the single wire pair, one for voice and the other for data. This means that the voice handset is not tied up when the user works with a remote computer. It also means that transmission speeds are not limited by modem technology.

Even before data PBXs, most PBXs were using digital technology both in switching and in handsets. When the user spoke into the hand set, his or her voice was digitized for transmission through the system. At the other end, it was undigitized at the receiver's handset and converted into normal sounds. Although this sounds complicated, digital technology is more error-resistant and even cheaper than ordinary analog technology in many applications today.

Just because digital technology was used did not mean that a PBX was a data PBX. The important requirement, as noted earlier, is that there be simultaneous voice and data to any wall jack.

To digitize voice, 64 kbps must be used because 8000 samples must be taken each second to collect good information, and each sample is normally one byte long, giving 256 possible amplitude levels. To produce true data PBXs, most PBX designers added another 64 kbps channel to the one already going to handsets, giving each user 64 kbps for voice, 64 kbps for simultaneous data, and about 8 kbps for control signals.

As a result, most data PBXs have been limited to 64 kbps when working with synchronous data transmission. For RS232C devices, of course, the speed limit fell to the 19.2 kbps restriction of RS232C.

High-Speed Data PBXs

Although 64 kbps is more than most terminals can handle, IBM terminals and some others can send and receive much faster. PC networking would be positively stymied by a 64 kbps bottleneck. Many newer PBXs offer much higher transmission speeds for devices that can use them. The Northern Telecoms Meridian, in particular, can deliver a phenomenal 2.56 Mbps over its twisted pair wires. In addition, Meridian can connect PCs using an adapter card and the Microsoft Networks program, so that they can do PC networking.

Although higher speeds are now becoming popular, the number of devices that can use them is limited by the controllers needed to connect the devices to the network. Typically, only RS232C and IBM connections are supported, so Wang terminals and other non-IBM devices that work at high speed must use RS232C. In addition, adapter cards for PCs are usually offered only for IBM PCs.

Nonblocking PBXs

In the early days of PBXs, switching elements were expensive, so only enough were provided to support the average number of connections in use at any time. If only 10 percent of your units were expected to be in use at any given time, you only purchased enough switching elements to link 10 percent of your devices.

Although this produced occasional busy signals, the traditional statistics of telephone connect time were extremely stable, so it was possible to do cost/availability tradeoffs intelligently.

When data began to appear on PBXs, this traditional stability went out the window. Connect times became long and unpredictable, and data use was growing so rapidly that no one could predict future switching needs with any accuracy.

With switching costs falling rapidly, most new data PBXs are **nonblocking,** which means that they have enough switching elements to link everyone, even if every single device is active. Given the impossibilities inherent in demand forecasting, most organizations are buying nonblocking data PBXs.

In practice, few of these machines have a separate switching element for each pair of devices. Instead, most have a switch with very high bandwidth, say, 40 Mhz, and individual lines are multiplexed onto this high switching capacity with some proprietary scheme. As a result, although nonblocking is provided, slow-downs can occur if heavy demands are placed on the switch.

IBM'S DATA COMMUNICATIONS STRATEGIES

IBM sells roughly half of all mainframes and minicomputers. (1) In addition, many non-IBM mainframes are from **plug compatible manufacturers (PCMs).** These are the mainframe equivalents of PC cloners. No other host vendor has anything like IBM's market share. Because of the enormous market dominance of IBM, many corporate strategies revolve around IBM products. So a great deal of time and effort are spent trying to understand IBM's strategic directions in data communications.

Unfortunately, as noted earlier in this chapter, IBM has a tendency to switch its strategic direction rapidly if an approach fails to find market approval. Many highly touted "strategic products" lie on IBM's trash heap. In addition, IBM rarely puts all of its eggs into one strategic basket. It usually supports several competing approaches, letting the market decide which will survive. This makes sense from IBM's point of view, but it works a hardship on IBM's users.

IBM's Host-Based Strategies

Long before it got into networking, IBM was developing sophisticated strategies to link its host computers with the terminals attached to these hosts. In 1974, it brought order to its multiple strategies by introducing a comprehensive framework, SNA, which was discussed in Chapter 14. But users were slow to migrate to SNA, and even today, many non-SNA hosts are in use. In addition, many midsize IBM products, such as the System/36 and System/38, have yet to be brought into the SNA framework as completely as larger System/370 mainframes.

As discussed in Chapter 14, SNA itself is evolving. When it began, it was a pure master-slave system designed to link a single host with its many terminals. Since then, IBM has moved steadily toward a peer-to-peer architecture for SNA. As discussed in Chapter 14, this migration has been slow and includes several different strategies. It will be some time before anything like a simple peer-to-peer solution exists within SNA.

Short-Distance Networking

IBM has consistently disappointed its customers in short-distance networking. Its first PC network was a major market failure, and its Token-Ring Network for PCs was only a half-hearted performer at its first release, largely as a result of a limited network operating system.

In addition, IBM supports two network interfaces for program calls. The first is NetBIOS, which was introduced with the IBM Personal Computer Network and is now supported by the Token-Ring Network as well. The second is APPC/PC, which uses the more sophisticated LU 6.2 approach discussed in Chapter 14. Unfortunately, no software using APPC/PC was available when this interface was released.

To add to user confusion, the original IBM Network Program was poorly received, so many users turned to other network operating systems. IBM itself sold Novell's NetWare network operating system, and Microsoft introduced its own LAN Manager, as noted earlier in this chapter.

At the time of this writing, IBM has still not released a long-distance version for the Token-Ring Network network. One of the missing ingredients is a 16-Mbps backbone system to connect smaller 4-Mbps local rings, as discussed in Chapter 14. IBM's slow entry into the LAN market has effectively frozen users, who understandably wish to understand IBM's direction before committing to other approaches.

Data PBXs

Although IBM developed some PBXs in the 1970s, it moved into the data PBX market aggressively by purchasing a major PBX vendor, ROLM. IBM originally gave ROLM semi-independent status but has subsequently consolidated ROLM into the IBM system.

Although ROLM is doing reasonably well in the PBX market, voice PBXs still dominate its sales. In fact, few PBX vendors have been successful in getting customers to use data PBXs because of the cost problems discussed earlier in this chapter.

Openness

Originally, IBM tried to keep users from using any non-IBM equipment. Companies that followed this lead were called "true blue," because early IBM computers were almost always painted blue. But the number of true blue shops has declined steadily, and IBM has gradually adopted a more open position in data communications.

IBM has moved toward openness in three ways. The first has been to develop non-SNA products or at least bridges to the non-SNA world. IBM is moving fairly rapidly to develop gateways to international standards, such as X.25 and the IEEE LAN standards. IBM now seems fairly committed to the support of international standards, although the pace of IBM's development has been uneven.

Second, IBM has published the specifications for SNA, in order to encourage other vendors to link into SNA. While this has hurt IBM's computer sales somewhat, this form of openness in data communications design is mandatory in today's multivendor world.

Third, IBM hopes to keep control by providing network integration tools. At the heart of IBM's third strategy is a network management product called **NetView**. NetView can watch over a complex data communications system consisting of workstation–host systems, PC networks, LANs, and data PBXs. NetView calls have been published, so that equipment from other vendors can work with NetView. Early version of NetView, however, have been quite limited, and international network management standards are beginning to be firmed up.

Slow Evolution

Because IBM's user base is enormous, IBM does not have the luxury of throwing away its current data communications approaches and installing a completely different one. Its users would literally be thrown into chaos. While it is easy to criticize IBM's piecemeal approach to data communications products on grounds of elegance, hard reality will require a mixed approach to be supported for many years.

As a result, IBM moves very slowly, adding features to existing products, adding new products, and rarely discarding anything that already exists (although support for "losers" can become thin). The chaos and confusion that have marked IBM data communications in the past are likely to continue throughout the foreseeable future.

NETWORK PLANNING AND IMPLEMENTATION

Networks can create utter chaos unless carefully managed, and this includes personal computer networks. Greg Todd of Policy Management Systems once remarked that it is a fatal error to think of a network as a mere extension of the micro. (3) Giving some details to illustrate the importance of network management, Brad Gordon of Arthur Anderson and Company in Chicago said: (3)

> When you get into a networking environment, you get back all the same problems you had with a mainframe. You worry about backup, on-and-off-site storage, data integrity, someone corrupting the system, and handling throughput on a printer. When a company heads into networking, there is some front end planning and there should be someone who is a network administrator.

NETWORK PLANNING AND IMPLEMENTATION

We will look primarily at the management of personal computer networks because this is the area in which the information center will have to set standards. Setting standards for the use of corporate LANs may also be part of the information center's charter, but it is more likely that the information center will basically serve as an adviser or peer in the setting of these standards.

Initial Assessment

Benefits

Let us assume that a PC network is being planned for a department. The first step is to assess its likely benefits. Is peripheral sharing to reduce costs the main objective, or is this objective shared with cost containment due to the delegation of mundane operations and the elimination of floppy disk swaps?

Is there a clear need for multiuser software, for example, to support a multiuser data base? This can be a major reason for getting a PC network, but it may also mean that the department should be using a departmental minicomputer or DBMS software on a mainframe. Because few departmental minis support true relational multiuser DBMSs, departmental computers are likely to be good candidates only if a single file at a time is being processed, and some of these do not support multiuser record locking. Host computers with data management programs such as FOCUS are discussed in Chapter 16, but suffice it to say for the moment that they tend to be rather difficult to learn and are most useful for jobs that span a department's boundaries.

Network Hardware and Software Costs

The next step is to estimate costs, beginning with the prices the vendors charge for hardware and software. For the IBM Token-Ring Network, for example, the cost of the adapter board is $695, plus $35 for the NETBIOS, which is optional on this unit. But there also needs to be DOS 3.1, and this may require a low-cost upgrade. On top of DOS rests the Network Program, costing $75 per PC. Becuase the PCs may be more than 8 feet from the Multistation Access Unit, each PC will probably need a cable costing $35. When these numbers are totaled, the cost per PC comes to $840.

There are also costs for the network itself. The Multistation Access Unit costs $660, and the network management program about $1000. If two or three server programs are added, for instance, the IBM Asynchronous Communications Server Program, these will cost another $1000 or so. Overall, $3,000 is a good figure for the cost of a network serving up to eight personal computers.

Suppose, then, that five PCs are attached to the network. The network hardware and software will then cost $7200, or $1440 per PC. This is hardly the "average cost" of $800 to $900 touted for these networks.

Server Costs

If there are five personal computers in the network and if only one is a server, its performance is not likely to be very good if it is used as a stand-alone PC. As a result, the server PC is often dedicated to the server role and cannot be used as a user PC. Some people with experience in PC networking indicate that a PC AT server working as a dedicated server can serve about 10 user PCs. If this is so, then about $500 must be added per PC to make up the allocated cost of the server.

Planning Costs

Some time will have to be spent planning for the network. If five days is a good figure and the loaded cost of a manager (including fringe benefits and overhead) is $300 per day, about $1500 will have to be spent on planning. Many firms use consultants to reduce this cost or at least to spend the money on a source of expertise that is already at least halfway up the learning curve and is less likely to make serious elementary errors.

Implementation Costs

Putting the network in place will bring still more costs. Cables must be trimmed and covered to avoid accidents, and may have to be run through walls or drop ceilings. In addition, adapter cards will have to be placed in each PC.

After installation, the entire network will have to be tested. It may take a day or two to run all of the diagnostic tests that need to be done to ensure that the network is running well. If these diagnostics are not done, subtle faults may become very difficult to detect after the entire network begins operation.

In addition to the costs of the installers, implementation involves labor costs among the users. Files may have to converted, requiring large amounts of time, profiles will have to be developed on individuals and network resources, and labor productivity will decline for several weeks as people slowly get used to working with the new system.

Training Costs

Networks are not easy to use. The network administrator and individual users will have to receive extensive training. It is commonly said that an organization will have to spend about 25 percent of its network hardware and software budget on training. Administrators need detailed training, of course, but users also have to learn to do such tasks as redirecting output, changing the print queue, and using networked versions of their familiar application programs.

The Costs of Discarded Software

One cost that almost nobody anticipates is the cost of discarded software—software that has to be thrown away because it will not work with the network operating system. Nearly everyone who uses a network has to throw away several programs.

Network operating systems are RAM-resident programs (see Chapter 8), which intercept calls destined for the computer's basic operating system. As a result, they may conflict with other RAM-resident programs, including print spoolers, RAM disks, and pop-up desk accessories.

In addition, many programs are badly behaved (see Chapter 6), meaning that they bypass the operating systems at least some of the time. Since these programs do not give operating system calls when they bypass the operating system, there are no calls to intercept by the network operating system. So badly behaved programs also bypass the network operating system as well. Most badly behaved programs are careful not to use ROM service programs and sections of RAM in ways that conflict with the basic operating system, but no attempt is likely to be made to be compatible with network operating systems.

In some cases, the loss of a program is a mere inconvenience. In other cases, core programs will be lost, or the corporation must choose between the network operating system and a core program.

The Cost of Network Administrators

In a network—even a PC network—chaos is inevitable unless a single person has responsibility for the network. When a new user comes into the system, the network administrator must teach them how to use it, assign them passwords, and let the system software know that a new user exists with certain profile characteristics. Because the new user will presumably use the hard disk, he or she needs to be assigned a section of the disk to work on and be trained in how to organize files hierarchically, how to develop a good file retention and naming plan, and how to implement adequate data protection.

Later, the user will need continuing assistance when his or her disk space becomes full, when he or she wants to reorganize the file hierarchy, when the user will want to share files with certain other users, when the user wants to change a password or the security profile of some resource, when the user needs help changing the printing queue or using the communications service facility, or when the user accidentally deletes a file and wants the last version recovered from the backup tape. These actions are frequent and time consuming.

Then there is the everyday work of making backups, checking printer queues, and doing diagnostics to be sure the network is operating satisfactorily and is not running dangerously close to capacity.

At the more managerial level, the network administrator will need a map of the hard disk, including knowledge of where security is needed. As a watchdog, the network administrator should be sure that security is maintained, including the frequent changing of passwords.

It may well be that the network administrator role will be split between two people. The secretary or other support worker might handle day-to-day work, whereas a manager or professional works on higher level problems. Ideally, the support worker will be sufficiently trained to handle troubleshooting train users in advanced areas, and do difficult network operations without involving the manager.

The network administrator's time will be expensive. One chemist finds himself spending around 80 percent of his time handling 18 micros and 50 users. (1). In another company with only 50 employees, the network administrator devotes about 60 percent of her time working on the network. (1) For planning purposes, it might be wise to have one network administrator for every 50 users. So in a five-station network, about 10 percent of someone's time must be used up, and this has to be valued at about $5000 per year, including fringe benefits and overhead.

These human costs can be far larger than the obvious costs of hardware and software. Ease of installation, ease of use, and reliability are not merely nice conveniences. They have hard economic value and must be placed near the top of evaluation criteria.

The Bottom Line

All of these costs are a bit startling. PC networks are not nearly as cheap as their board costs might indicate. In fact, unless there are very strong benefits, networks do not make sense at today's high equipment costs and high maintenance loads.

Peripheral sharing alone rarely makes sense economically. Almost certainly, fast information sharing is the only way to justify a full PC network, and unless a department is already experiencing severe informationsharing difficulties, even information serving is not likely to be enough.

CONCLUSION

Networking requires a quantum leap in data communications expertise in the corporation. It also requires considerable expertise within the information center, so that the needs of end users can be championed, particularly in the area of PC networking.

Even small PC networks are surprisingly difficult to select, implement, and manage on an ongoing basis. The technology is new, options are many, and the simplicity of single-user environments gives way to the complexity and headaches of multiuser environments. Special care must be given to the quality of server software because server software is usually the most important factor in product selection.

LANs require vast commitments in time, money, talent, and ongoing management. From the viewpoint of end user computing, one of the most important considerations is the relationship between LANs and PC networks. Are they to be connected by gateways, or is the LAN itself to provide PC networking services?

Because networking is a new purchasing problem, it is very easy to make critical mistakes in product selection or to believe that a network will do more than it really can. For example, it is often believed that a network can link any device to any other device, but networking alone does not guarantee that two devices on the network will be able to make sense of what the other device sends. To give another example, networks often have capacities of tens of millions of bits per second, but there are often strong limits on the real transmission speed available to each device. These speed limits can be crippling to PC networking and even to terminal-host communications.

Networking must be viewed as part of a wider effort to develop true any-to-any communications among an organization's devices. To move to that ultimate step, a company must adopt a comprehensive standards architecture such as OSI or SNA, select individual standards within the broad framework, and implement these standards on all devices.

REVIEW QUESTIONS

1. What is the many-to-many myth? In what limited sense is it true? In what broader senses is it not true?
2. What are the LAN myths surrounding transmission speed? What are the several considerations that tend to reduce speeds far below popular expectations?
3. In networking, how are "synchronous" and "asynchronous" used in more restricted senses than the general concepts of synchronous and asynchronous transmission imply in the theoretical literature?
4. What are the limitations of many LANs for PC networking—one of the most important future uses of networks?
5. What problems face buyers if they forget to consider network management software in their purchasing decisions?
6. Why was IBM's first Personal Computer Network not very popular?
7. What were the technical characteristics of IBM's Token-Ring Network when it was first introduced in limited form for PC networking? Why was this second PC network more popular than the first?
8. In the IBM TRN, adapter boards can be purchased with NETBIOS ROM, APPC-PC ROM, or both. What is the advantage of each?
9. What must the user buy to implement an IBM Token-Ring Network for a dozen personal computers? Include one or two dedicated PC servers.
10. If you were a vendor developing a TRN-compatible network, what would you have to develop? What could you buy? What are the implications of the fact that the IBM TRN is not difficult to clone?
11. What would you do if you liked the TRN's hardware but not its network operating system?
12. Describe other approaches to networking if you have a group of IBM PCs and compatibles you wish to connect. What are the strengths and weaknesses of each approach?
13. How could you network an office with three IBM PCs, two IBM PC compatibles, and three Apple Macintoshes?
14. Why are LANs more complex to plan and implement than small PC networks?
15. What are the major management problems raised by LANs?
16. Compare the relative advantages and disadvantages of the three major alternatives for building short distance networking, namely, broadband LANs, baseband LANs, and data PBXs.
17. In an office, what are the main IEEE 802 standards you are likely to encounter when selecting a LAN?
18. Why is IBM's NetView important?
19. What are private branch exchanges (PBXs)? What are their main components? Why do organizations purchase them? What is the difference between data PBXs and other PBXs (any PBX can handle data by modems)? What advantage do data PBXs have for individuals? For the ability of corporations to communicate by voice over their telephone systems?

20. What are typical PBX speeds? What are speeds on the fastest PBXs? Under what conditions will high speeds not be possible for a particular device?
21. What are nonblocking PBXs? Why are they intelligent purchases?
22. Describe IBM's general approach toward short distance networking. Be sure to comment on Netview. What are the disadvantages of this fragmented approach for users? The advantages?
23. Discuss the total cost of a PC network serving seven (7) PCs, using IBM's Token-Ring network.

REFERENCES

1. CUMMINGS, STEVE, "Bying IBM: The Mainframe is the Message," *PC World,* August 1987, pp. 186–191.
2. PETROSKY, MARY, "The Thankless Job of LAN Administrator," *InfoWorld,* January 6, 1986, pp. 23–25.
3. WHITE, LEE, "Putting Network Management into Good Hands," *Computerworld Focus,* January 15, 1986, pp. 41–43.

DATA AND DECISION SUPPORT APPLICATIONS ON HOST COMPUTERS 16

When end user computing began, the only computers available were host computers. The applications served by these host computers generally fell into two categories: data applications and decision support applications.

Data applications are miniature data processing applications embracing all of the standard features of data processing systems, including data entry, file storage, computation, and report generation. Because most end user data applications are small, such tools as statement-based fourth-generation languages (4GLs) and menu-based applications generators (see Chapter 10) can be used to develop these applications. These tools are comparatively easy to master, and development time is short. The code they produce is somewhat inefficient compared to the tight code produced by good COBOL programmers, but running efficiency is a minor concern for small applications, compared to development costs.

Decision support applications support managers who are faced with decisions that are only partially structured. Decision support applications involve three major activities. (3)

Data retrieval The user must be able to extract data flexibly from corporate data processing files, from the files created in end user data applications, and from external data sources. Data retrieval tools include query languages, report generators, data extraction tools, and programs to download data to personal computers. Most of these tools were discussed in Chapter 10, but data downloading to personal computers was discussed in Chapter 13.

Analysis The user must be able to analyze data after they are retrieved. This requires the ability to model business situations, enter data into the model, and "interrogate" the model by testing various alternatives. Popular analysis tools include spreadsheet programs, financial analysis programs, and statistical analysis programs. Operations research programs are sometimes used by end users as well.

Presentation After results are generated, the user must be able to put the results in a form that will communicate these results clearly. Users often turn to analytical graphics tools to help them present their results. Report generators and word processing programs can be viewed as presentation tools, but they are normally classified separately.

Some decisions require only one of these three kinds of support, but many decisions require support from all three. These decisions often require integrated support, so that data retrieval functions can feed into analysis functions, which can in turn feed into presentation functions. Sprague (3) calls tools that embrace all three support activities **decision support systems** or **DSSs.**

In this chapter, we will examine the general characteristics of end user computing on time-shared hosts. We will begin with the general characteristics of tools on time-shared hosts and then look individually at financial analysis, statistical analysis, graphics, data management, and decision support systems.

A major theme of this chapter is good practice. Comparing host tools to PC tools for comparable applications is like comparing trucks to family cars. Host tools are normally used for larger and more complex applications, and size alone makes good practice critical. In addition, host applications tend to get users more deeply into such application-specific expertise as proper financial modeling, the selection of appropriate statistical tests, graphics discipline, data base design, and other matters that are difficult to master. It is not enough to know the hardware and software, to document applications, and to follow a disciplined development process. Users must also have application-specific expertise, and it may be up to the information center to train them in this application expertise, provide consulting and auditing services in these areas, or do both.

INTRODUCTION

Although data and decision support products vary enormously, several generalizations may be made about today's packages. Many of these contrast host-based data and decision support tools with comparable tools available on personal computers.

Difficulty of Learning

Many host-based tools tend to be difficult to master, for four reasons.

Host Operating System Environments

The first reason that host-based tools tend to be difficult to master is that host operating systems tend to be complex, in keeping with the many tasks that can be done on host computers. Older operating systems tend to be especially complex; a good example is IBM's MVS operating system, which began life as a batch processing system and then added successive layers of functionality. On many operating systems, even such simple functions as printing a file can lead the user into complex printer specification and queuing functions.

It is possible to hide much of this complexity from users. For most operating systems, you can build or buy a "shell" that presents a simple interface to users. These shells can use menus, fill-in forms, and other user interface techniques made popular in PCs—as long as the host uses at least a smart terminal (Chapter 13) and has a transmission facility with adequate speed (Chapter 13). These shells often limit the functionality inherent in the underlying operating system in order to support faster learning and easier use.

Aging User Interfaces in Application Programs
A second reason why data and decision support products tend to be difficult to learn is that many are 10 to 15 years old. When they were created, only conversational (TTY) terminals were available, and so they were designed for line-oriented editing. Most have gone on to support full-screen editing on smart terminals, but quite a few of them have adapted awkwardly. They also tend to show their age in other areas of user interface design.

Batch Operation
A third reason why data and decision support products are hard to learn is that many were designed to create batch programs. Batch operation separates the use of the program into two distinct phases. In the first phase, a program is created; and in the second, it is run. During the creation phase, the user cannot see results immediately.

In contrast, most PC application programs are interactive. When a user enters a formula into a spreadsheet, for instance, the results of the calculation appear immediately, giving instant feedback. For complex programs, failure to include interactive operation can lead to many frustrating creation/run cycles. Although the user *creates* these programs interactively, the separation of creation and run cycles is a major impediment to ease of use and user productivity.

Most batch procedures also tend to have complex syntax conventions. Because they are statement-based, rather than menu- or form-driven, some degree of syntax is always necessary, and the more complex the program becomes, the more syntax must be mastered. Furthermore, programs from different vendors use different conventions for such elementary things as the type of symbol used to indicate that a statement continues on the next line.

High Functionality
A fourth reason why these products are difficult to learn is that most users are "power users" who demand ever more power and functionality. Because difficulty of use has always tended to select against casual and occasional users, most organizations that have moved heavily into data and decision support have developed "SAS experts" and "IFPS gurus" to help other users or do advanced development work directly. Power users have put ex-

treme pressure on vendors to add ever greater functionality. In the statistical analysis world, for instance, functionality has been the main reason why users switch between SAS, SPSS, BMDP, and other products. Falling behind in the functionality race has been almost certain death, but adding functionality usually adds complexity and increases learning burdens.

Not all hosts computers programs have focused primarily on power at the sacrifice of simplicity. Among query languages, simplicity is the dominant driving force. Query languages are moving rapidly toward greater simplicity of use, as a result of natural language query programs, standardizing on a single interface (the ANSI SQL standard discussed later). Outside of retrieval, however, it is difficult to find another area in which simplicity is the *major* driving force.

Improving Ease of Use

Under pressure from PC products, many host vendors of application software have begun to improve the ease of use of their products. Several roads to this goal have been taken.

- The first is to build products designed specifically for end users who are not power users. These products have the limited functionality of many PC products but still provide the raw processing power and multiuser operation of host computers.
- The second is to build a shell on top of existing products, adding pop-down menus, fill-in forms, and other devices that aid ease of use. As noted above, shells tend to reduce power, but this does not have to be the case.
- The third approach is to build a PC version of the application program that can exchange files with the host. This allows a PC user interface while still permitting access to the host world.
- The fourth approach is to offer a sophisticated PC front end that effectively hides the details of working with a host computer from the end user. In contrast to the third approach, the PC front end does not have to be a PC clone of the host program. It is more comparable to an administrative assistant who helps the user deal with both PCs and hosts. Discussed at the end of the chapter, PC front ends also provide smooth integration among PC and host products.

Processing Speed and Multiuser Operation

The very fact that the user is working with a host rather than a PC tends to produce several advantages.

Processing Speed

A major advantage of host computers is the immense throughput of these machines. Their processing speed, which is typically measured in millions of instructions per second, is needed to handle large data bases, do statistical analysis on large data sets, or do optimization in large financial models. For large jobs with massive storage and speed requirements, there is no substitute for host computers, although advanced PCs of the 386 generation (see Chapters 6 and 7) now challenge hosts for many medium-size jobs.

If the host is heavily loaded, a specific user's share may be small, effectively shunting aside the advantage of immense processing speed. A heavily loaded machine is also sluggish for very simple operations and erratic in response time for many kinds of work. Sluggishness on simple tasks and inconsistency in response time are frustrating to users.

Multiuser Operation

Another benefit of data and decision support is multiuser access. Host-based applications can be designed by dozens of people in dozens of different locations. Although PC networks are beginning to bring some multiuser applications, PC networks are normally limited to single offices, and few sophisticated multiuser application packages are yet available. Where multiuser access is critical and distances between users are large, there is no real alternative to host processing.

Modular Pricing

Most advanced host data and decision support products are packaged as a series of modules. Figure 16-1 illustrates the major modules that go into Execucom's Interactive Financial Planning System (IFPS), a leading analysis tool for financially oriented decisions.

Module	First Year	Renewal
Main Module	$10,000	$5,000
Graphics	$8,000	$4,000
Application Development	$5,000	$3,000
Financial Analysis	$6,000	$3,000
Operations Research	$6,000	$3,000
Time Series	$6,000	$3,000
Quality Control	$6,000	$3,000
DBMS	$8,000	$4,000
Computer-Based Training	$4,000	$2,000
Total if All Purchased:	$59,000	$30,000

Notes:
These prices applied to a medium-size IBM mainframe.
Modules on PCs are not included.

FIGURE 16-1 MODULAR PACKAGING IN A HOST ANALYSIS PRODUCT

In most cases there are one to three core modules that nearly everyone must purchase. Beyond that are specialized modules that may or may not be attractive to individual firms. Because these additional modules are costly, firms only buy the ones they are likely to need.

The extra modules allow vendors to expand a product beyond its original core features. For example, additional modules allow IFPS to offer richer data file handling as well as graphics, spreadsheet, and optimization modules. Data management programs such as FOCUS, in turn, offer analysis and graphics modules. In general, most large host packages are moving gradually to embrace a wide variety of decision support functions. They are, in other words, moving toward becoming full decision support systems that embrace data management, analysis, and graphics.

Some modules provide links from the program to the outside world, including traditional mainframe file structures (such as ISAM and VSAM), and well as to host-based end user computing products from other vendors. An analysis tool, for instance, might have optional modules to let their users extract information from several popular DBMSs.

Managing Host Data and Decision Support Applications

Each host data and decision support product raises its own management needs, but three general statements may be made about the management of most of these products.

The first is that most require an adept system staff. In contrast to most PC packages such as Lotus 1-2-3, significant maintenance is needed to keep host data and decision support programs running. The information center staff is likely to have to do file extracts to move information from production data processing files to the files of end users programs.

The second is that training and ongoing consulting needs tend to be large. Manuals are often poor, and training is nearly always limited to vendor training at remote sites or (at considerable cost) at the user's sites. In addition, packages are so complex that occasional users and power users moving into new areas will need a good deal of one-on-one interaction. Nearly all information centers that deal with host data and decision support applications end up doing quite a number of complex tasks for users because training users to do complex one-time jobs would take far too long.

The third is that consultants need to be trained in the theoretical underpinnings of the tools. Most information center staff members have studied the theory of data bases and data modeling, but how many know the dangers lurking in factor analysis, understand how to set up financial models without making elementary financial errors, or are able create graphs that communicate well? Because quite a few information center analysts come from information systems departments, analysts will need extensive training in such topics as proper financial and statistical analysis. In fact, it may be far more efficient to hire consultants from functional departments and teach the computing instead of teaching statistics and finance to IS professionals. Nor can users be left to their own devices, for they will then make serious errors almost every time they do an analysis. Auditing financial and statistical models, may have to be a mandatory discipline enforced by the information center.

FINANCIAL ANALYSIS SOFTWARE

The most widely used class of analysis tools are **financial analysis** programs, also known as **financial planning** or **decision support** programs.

Financial analysis programs are used to build financial models. Their models often look like those produced in typical spreadsheet programs, but models built with financial analysis programs have three distinguishing characteristics:

1. Although a spreadsheet image can be used in financial analysis programs, the horizontal dimension is always time, in contrast to spreadsheet programs, which can have any horizontal dimension the modeler desires. Financial analysis programs are geared toward time-oriented decisions; as a result, they tend to be rich in functions to handle time lags and other time-related matters.
2. Financial analysis programs are built to model *financial* decisions, whose raw materials are revenues, expenses, taxes, incomes, and cash flows. As a result, they are rich in functions to handle depreciation, net present value, internal rate of return, and other calculations frequently encountered when dealing with financial variables.
3. Financial analysis systems are rich in "interrogation" functions that allow the model builder or user to study how the model behaves and see what it will predict under different circumstances. Interrogation features in financial analysis programs go far beyond the "what if" capabilities of most spreadsheet programs. Interrogation was discussed in detail in Chapter 9.

Financial analysis programs pay a price for these specific features. These features make them special-purpose packages adept only at financial problems, in comparison with spreadsheet programs, which can handle many types of modeling and analysis problems. For example, financial analysis programs are less adept at nonfinancial kinds of spreadsheet problems, and although they can be forced into other problem domains, they offer few specific functions to help model builders. Compared to Lotus 1-2-3, for instance, they are often poor in statistical calculation functions and other functions not used heavily in financial modeling. In addition, if the problem's horizontal dimension is not time, financial analysis programs tend to be very awkward to use.

Many financial analysis programs are now on the market. Later in this chapter, we will look at the most widely used financial analysis program, IFPS, later in this chapter.

Good Practice in Design

Although financial analysis is conducted widely in organizations, it is surprisingly difficult to do well, and without adequate training, end users are likely to make serious errors when they design statistical analysis. We will now look at just a few of the most important pitfalls in financial analysis.

Decision-Relevant Variables

A financial model of a business operation will have dozens of variables, including fixed startup costs and variable operating costs. Not all of these variables will be relevant to any particular decisions, and many decisions require new variables to be created. For example, suppose the decision is whether to build a new plant. Then, of course, startup costs will be relevant to the decision.

Suppose however, that the plant has already gotten started and it is now apparent that demand is far less than expectation, so the new plant will not be profitable. Now, a new and entirely different decision is present: *Should the plant continue in operation, or should it be shut down?* For this new decision, out-of-pocket cash outlays and revenues are still relevant. However, the amount originally paid for the factory has no bearing on the matter. As long as incremental revenues from the decision (to keep the plant in operation) outweigh the incremental costs, there is no reason to shut down the plant.

For this new decision, it is even necessary to add new variables to the model. Now the value of the decision to keep the plant going—the excess of incremental revenues over incremental expenses—needs to be compared to the scrap value of the plant or the value of other possible uses for the factory. Although the value of alternative uses should have been taken into account in the original decision, immediate scrap value was not part of the original model at all.

The moral of this story is that a user cannot begin to build a model until he or she has precisely stated the decision to be made. After a user has stated the decision, he or she may have to add new variables to an existing model while dropping existing variables from the model. The skill to think clearly about what variables are relevant to a particular decision takes considerable training.

NPV and IRR

So far, we have mentioned the "value" of a decision without saying how decisions are evaluated in financial decision making. In fact, the two most common methods of evaluating a decision are **net present value (NPV)** and **internal rate of return (IRR).**

Both methods are based on the idea that a dollar received today is better than a dollar received tomorrow. A dollar received today can be invested at about 20 percent and be worth $1.20 next year. If a firm cannot invest money in itself and receive good returns, then it should be out of business.

This line of reasoning, called **discounting,** allows a firm to evaluate alternative investments whose cash outlays and cash inflows span long periods of time. Most major business decisions involve such long-term cash flows. By comparing the net present values and internal rates of return of alternative investments, an analyst can quantify which decision would be better for the firm.

Most financial analysis programs calculate both NPV IRR, but this does not relieve the user from having to understand underlying concepts. For example, NPV and IRR give different pictures of the values of investments. An analyst must understand these differences if he or she is to interpret results intelligently. More subtly, the built-in NPV and IRR functions in most financial analysis programs have quirks that must be understood by the user. For example, some restrict the first year to being "year zero," and others to "year one." If these restrictions differ from what is appropriate in the analysis, the results can be off by 10 percent to 30 percent, and an unwary user will not even realize it.

In general, almost any of the built-in functions that give financial analysis systems their power must be used through blind trust or in the absence of good financial analysis knowledge. Like the magician's book, they can lead the sorcerer's apprentice to disaster.

Cash-Based Analysis

Both net present value and internal rate of return are computed on the basis of *cash flows*, not revenues and expenses. Cash flows are the basic realities in organizations. Incomes are merely artifacts created by accountants to give an overall scoreboard for the firm's *present period* performance.

Many revenues and expenses are not cash flows at all. For instance, accounts receivables cause real cash inflows to be out of synch with revenues, and incoming loans are not revenues at all, although they are cash flows that would impact on a decision. With regard to expenses, interest payments on loans are expenses, whereas capital repayments are not; yet both are cash flows. Another example of expenses versus cash flows is capital investment. The purchase cost of a factory is a cash outlay but not an expense, whereas annual depreciations are expenses but not cash outlays.

Most financial models include both income figures and cash flow figures because the two interact, particularly in regard to income taxes. Depreciation is not a cash flow in itself, but the way a company does depreciation will affect its income and so its income taxes. Taxes, of course, are normally real cash outflows.

Because most decision makers are more familiar with revenues, expenses, and income than they are with cash flows, they often find it difficult to accept the fact that "income is not important." Of course, income *is* important, but it is a concept invented by accountants to assess a company's operations in a specific year. Although investments must be profitable over the long run, the pattern of cash flows resulting from an investment is the more important variable.

Even business school graduates are more familiar with income accounting than cash flow accounting, and so they tend to misuse or not use cash flow accounting when evaluating alternative decisions.

Other Pitfalls

We have mentioned just a few of the most common pitfalls in financial analysis; in practice, there are many others. The basic lesson is that financial analysis is a difficult discipline that should not be handled by untrained users for large or important jobs, unless the information center is willing to play an active and knowledgeable role in major projects.

IFPS—A Financial Modeling System

Now that we have talked about decision modeling in general, we will take a closer look at one popular product, **IFPS**. IFPS—Interactive Financial Planning System—began life in the 1970s as a host-based product, although there is now IFPS Personal, which runs on PCs and can exchange information with its host-based cousin.

A Nonprocedural Language

Designed in the 1970s for host computers, many of which work only with dumb terminals, IFPS is a statement-based program. Its primary image of the model is the "equations image" discussed in Chapter 9 and uses the two-dimensional spreadsheet metaphor only when it prints results. Figure 16-2 illustrates an IFPS model that does a budget projection. The similarity to BASIC is clear. Statements have line numbers followed by keywords (sometimes optional) and then parameters.

Statement 110 is a comment statement, similar to the REM statement in BASIC. The asterisk is used in place of the keyword REM.

Statement 120 tells IFPS how many columns of data there will be and what their names will be. Four columns hold quarterly figures, and a Year column shows the total. There is nothing comparable in BASIC, since BASIC does not deal with multiple columns of information, except in arrays. The COLUMNS statement is vaguely like a DIM statement in BASIC.

Statements 130 through 180 are similar to LET statements in BASIC. In these "variable definition statements," there is a single variable on the left side of the equal sign. The variable name can be long—up to 31 characters—and it may have imbedded spaces.

On the right side of the equal signs are several values separated by commas. These refer to the time periods in the model, the four quarters. (The Year column is defined later in the model.)

In contrast to BASIC, which executes each statement in order, the variable definition statements (statements 120 through 180) are merely a set of simultaneous equations. The order in which simultaneous equations are given is not important, and such variables as Tax Rate in statement 180 can be used "before" they are defined, as shown in statement 160. Because IFPS models generally describe what is to be done, leaving to the program the chore of figuring out how to solve the simultaneous equations, IFPS is a nonprocedural language.

The last two statements are "COLUMN colname" statements and are not to be confused with the COLUMNS statement at the beginning of the model. COLUMN colname statements allow IFPS to do calculations across time periods. Statement 190 defines the Year figures for Revenues through income after tax as the sum of the four quarterly figures. Statement 200 defines Tax Rate as the average tax rate for the four quarters.

One nice aspect of IFPS, relative to Lotus 1-2-3, is the ability to specify simple equations such as "Income Before Tax = Revenues − Expenses,"

```
110   *Budget Projection Model
120   Columns Qtr1, Qtr2, Qtr3, Qtr4, Year
130   Revenues=200000, 220000, 240000, 380000
140   Expenses=180000, 190000, 190000, 220000
150   Income Before Tax=Revenues-Expenses
160   Tax=Income Before Tax*Tax Rate
170   Income After Tax=Income Before Tax-Tax
180   Tax Rate=42%, 41%, 38%, 36%
```

FIGURE 16-2 AN IFPS MODEL FOR BUDGET PROJECTION

instead of, say, placing **+B4-B5** in cell B6 and then copying this to columns C and D. Although 1-2-3 does allow ranges (including individual cells) to be named, formulas are still restricted to individual cells unless copied. Of course, this simplicity exists merely because financial analysis programs can exploit the fact that the horizontal dimension of the model is time. Lotus 1-2-3 is built for any type of problem and, as we will see below, IFPS is awkward when successive horizontal cells are not successive time periods. This is even true for total columns, and for many kinds of problems, IFPS would be prohibitively difficult to use.

Solving a Model

In BASIC, a program is **RUN.** In IFPS, a model is **SOLVED.** During the SOLVE process, the model is compiled, during which its simultaneous equations are solved.

The SOLVE command not only compiles the model, but it also allows the user to specify what will be printed. Figure 16-3 shows the output from a specialized listing that focuses only on selected columns (Qtr. 1, Qtr 4, Year) and the "bottom line" figure of income after tax. This kind of flexibility in output is impossible or at least very difficult to achieve in 1-2-3.

IFPS even has a more sophisticated printing option—report generation. With report generation, the user can exercise considerable control over what is printed and how it appears when it is printed. To use report generation, however, the user must enter a separate subsystem and build a statement-based format for the report. This is not simple, and there is no full-screen editing in the core package. Although report generation is reasonably powerful, it is not easy to use.

Interrogation

Lotus 1-2-3 allows users to do what if analysis. IFPS gives users far richer tools for asking questions about their model—in the terminology of IFPS, **interrogating** their model.

In all forms of IFPS interrogation, the original model remains unchanged. There is no need for users to remember their original assumptions, as is the case in 1-2-3. When the interrogation work is done, the model is still

```
?Solve

ENTER SOLVE OPTIONS
?Qtr1, Qtr4, Year
?Income After Tax

                  Qtr1    Qtr4    Year
Income After Tax  11600   102400  162700

ENTER SOLVE OPTIONS
?None
?
```

FIGURE 16-3 RESULTS FROM AN IFPS SOLVE

in its original state. This makes interrogation very easy in IFPS—much easier than in Lotus 1-2-3 and most other spreadsheet programs. It also makes it safer because there is no danger that the user will change the base model and either forget to undo one or two changes or not even remember what has to be changed to get it back to its base value.

Figure 16-4 shows a series of what if analyses conducted on our example mode. Note that IFPS even gives a sequence number to each case. The what if analyses are all independent, so changes made in one do not propagate to others. A WHAT IF CONTINUE command can be used in place of What if if a user wants to carry over assumptions from the previous case.

```
?What If
WHAT IF CASE 1
ENTER STATEMENTS
?Expenses = Expenses * 110%
?Solve
ENTER SOLVE OPTIONS
?Qtr1, Qtr4, Year
?Income After Tax

***** WHAT IF CASE 1 *****
1 WHAT IF STATEMENT PROCESSED

                    Qtr1      Qtr4      Year
Income After Tax    1160      88320     115190

ENTER SOLVE OPTIONS
?What If

WHAT IF CASE 2
ENTER STATEMENTS
?Expenses = Expenses * 80%
?Solve
ENTER SOLVE OPTIONS
?Qtr1, Qtr4, Year
?Income After Tax

***** WHAT IF CASE 2 *****
1 WHAT IF STATEMENT PROCESSED

                    Qtr1      Qtr4      Year
Income After Tax    32480     130560    257720

ENTER SOLVE OPTIONS
?None
```

FIGURE 16-4 WHAT IF ANALYSIS IN IFPS

Although IFPS's what if capabilities have some advantages over those of spreadsheet programs, IFPS comes into its own in more difficult forms of analysis, such as **goal seeking** analysis, which is also called **how can** analysis—how can I achieve a given result (say, breakeven incomes) by changing one of my assumptions. (How can analysis was discussed in Chapter 9.)

Suppose, for example, that a user is interested in breakeven conditions. As shown in Figure 16-5, he or she could specify that Expenses should be adjusted to make Income Before Tax equal zero in each time period. IFPS would then try various levels of Expenses and produce its results. This type of analysis would be extremely time consuming on a spreadsheet program.

IFPS allows users to combine what if and goal seeking analysis. For example, in a model that includes Price, Unit Sales, and Return on Investment, a user might specify that prices be raised by 20 percent and then ask what Unit Sales would be necessary to achieve a return on investment of 20 percent.

IFPS even has an optional subprogram called IFPS OPTIMUM, which is capable of *optimizing* a target variable subject to constraints on individual variables.

Overall, IFPS and other mainframe financial modeling systems offer far more powerful interrogation tools than their spreadsheet cousins. The penalty for this power is that the user must master a number of specific commands instead of just changing a number or two with a normal editing command and looking at the screen to see what happened. This tradeoff works against IFPS and its cousins in most departments, but in finance and other technical staff offices, financial modeling systems have a secure niche.

The Multiuser Dimension

Because most financial modeling systems run on host computers shared by many people, many financial modeling systems have made life easier for group work.

```
?GOAL SEEKING

GOAL SEEKING CASE 1
ENTER NAME OF VARIABLE TO BE ADJUSTED TO ACHIEVE PERFORMANCE
?Expenses
ENTER 1 COMPUTATIONAL STATEMENT FOR PERFORMANCE
?Income Before Tax = 0

***** GOAL SEEKING CASE 1 *****

              Qtr1    Qtr2    Qtr3    Qtr4    Year
Expenses    200000  220000  240000  380000  1040000

ENTER SOLVE OPTIONS
?None
```

FIGURE 16-5 GOAL-SEEKING ANALYSIS IN IFPS

For reasons discussed below, the crucial first step toward joint work is to separate models from their data. In the IFPS example in Figure 16-2, the model contained its own data, but it is also possible to divide the analysis into a model containing only logic and a data file containing only data.

One advantage of the separation is that now a group of analysts can create a central data file embodying all of the data they will work with jointly. Individual models built by the group members and perhaps stored in common areas can refer to whatever variables are needed in a particular analysis and ignore other data.

It is also possible to build a single model that works with many data files. If an organization wants to do budgeting in IFPS, it can create a single budgetary model and permit each department to have its own data file.

IFPS can also consolidate models and data files. Once individual departments have their individual budget proposals, for instance, these can be consolidated for the division, and division budget can be consolidated again into a corporate budget.

IFPS in Perspective

Almost anything IFPS does can be done with a spreadsheet program, but it is also fair to say that anything a spreadsheet program can do can be done in BASIC. The real issue is how much power users need and how much work users have to do to get their work done. For advanced users, IFPS takes longer to learn but saves time every time the user works. IFPS can be compared to a heavy rig for professional truckers.

In the past, financial modeling systems operated under another constraint—poor user interfaces stemming from their early emergence, when interface practices were crude, as well as from the need to work with dumb terminals lacking full-screen text editing.

Today, however, a growing percentage of mainframe products have been given better interfaces, and many financial modeling systems have been transported down to the PC level and given interfaces every bit as attractive as spreadsheet programs. (IFPS Personal is a good example.) These PC versions can also exchange files with their host-based versions, allowing the kinds of multiuser processing enjoyed by almost all host-based systems. Even host versions are getting facelifts for use on hosts that support full-screen interfaces (see Chapter 13), but these are basically grafted onto an underlying command-based structure.

Training, Support, and Control

Software Training

Financial analysis programs take about twice as long to learn as spreadsheet programs, primarily because they have many functions, some of whose purposes tend to be clear only after someone has struggled with the limitations of spreadsheet programs. In general, approximately three days of instruction are needed to learn these programs, not including the time needed to learn some advanced modules.

Given these kinds of learning burdens, it is questionable whether people without computer experience should be started on financial analysis programs. Even for experienced computer users, modularization is critical, although even a startup module for these programs should take at least one and a half to two days, and these startup modules do not even cover all core functions.

Many companies underestimate the training demands of financial analysis programs, because their thinking or training is guided by experiences with smaller packages with cleaner user interfaces. As a result, inadequate training is common.

Another training problem may appear when a multiuser application such as budgeting is implemented. In such cases, there is a strong tendency to give everyone but the designer a cursory overview of the software and injunctions to "just do these few steps." In practice, users do deviate from specified steps because of misunderstandings, typing mistakes, memory lapses, and the desire for exploration (which is a simple fact of life when intelligent users are on a system). If people are not to be given full training, it is at least critical to give them a "bullet-proof" menu system created in an internal programming language.

Content Training

As noted in the previous section on good practice, financial analysis quickly rises above the level of financial expertise possessed by the average manager or professional. Although computers have extended financial analysis outside of the finance and accounting department, this extension is likely to lead to trouble without adequate training in how to do financial analysis well.

It is often a good idea to have this training supervised by the finance department, an academic financial specialist, or an accounting firm. They have both the knowledge and the ability to organize the material.

At least a day of instruction is needed for even rudimentary knowledge; two full days are preferable. This instruction can stand alone, but it is better to tie it to the software training, so that the two forms of training can reinforce one another.

Support

For individual users who build applications for their own use, support needs are typical of those of other host packages. More support will be needed than for smaller packages, but this is a matter of degree, not kind. The biggest question mark for information center staff members is whether support will include consulting in how to do financial analysis well or whether consulting will be limited to the use of the software.

Support requirements are very different for large multiuser applications such as planning and budgeting systems. Large applications require menu front ends to be built, and the support needed to do this can be extensive, especially if the program code is to be testable and maintainable. It is also critical to ensure that clear instructions be produced and that adequate training classes be given.

Control

Host financial analysis products need careful control. One theme of this section on good practice has been that access to financial analysis software has spread much faster than financial knowledge. In most companies, dozens or even hundreds of critical financial projections are now being done by comparatively untrained managers and professionals.

One way to control this situation is to require **certified training,** in which analysts must pass an exam on financial analysis before being allowed to use a host financial analysis package. Another control tool is **auditing,** in which every major application must be audited to ensure compliance with financial analysis standards and good modeling practice. Of course, auditing and certified training are more powerful togehter than either alone.

A very different control problem is **access control** for reasons of security or privacy. Many financial analyses are highly proprietary, and care must be taken to avoid disclosure to competitors. Even confidential analyses that only affect employees can be dangerous—for example, financial analyses for wage negotiations or workforce reduction programs. Even privacy concerns may be present in some firms. Simple safeguards such as password controls may be sufficient, but callback modems and the security packages discussed in Chapter 13 may become mandatory in many cases.

However control is exercised, companies must treat large or important applications very differently than they do smaller applications. Although large applications are often done on PCs, large applications are the *rule* when host-based financial analysis tools are used.

STATISTICAL ANALYSIS TOOLS

A surprisingly large number of people in any organization need to do statistical analysis from time to time. As a result, statistical analysis has long been used by end users.

On mainframe computers, **statistical packages** have been commonplace since the 1970s. Exemplified by such programs as SAS and SPSS, these host "stat packages" are extremely powerful and versatile but are a bit intimidating to learn.

On micros, stat packages have been much slower to appear. For one thing, statistical analysis needs a great deal of computational power and megabytes of storage for the program and data sets. Early PCs were not up to the job. Even today's PCs with hard disks and AT-class microprocessors are only enough for small to medium-size data sets. In addition, host products were so mature by the time PCs began to be popular that it was hard for micro packages to make headway. Because of the time needed to master basic statistical concepts, many users have found the additional time needed to master host packages acceptable, and as their understanding of statistics broadens, more power is right there at their fingertips. PC software writers, in turn, were faced with costly development projects and a small market size. Today, PC packages are finally beginning to approach the functionality and throughput of mainframe systems, but for serious professional use, most analysts still turn to host systems.

One enduring advantage of host-based stat programs is that most can draw data from corporate data bases, end user data bases, and even external data bases. Although cooperative PC–Host software will eventually reduce this advantage, the ability of host-based statistical analysis programs to read host files directly, as well as data prepared statistically for the stat program, makes them the only game in town for doing statistical work on many corporate problems.

It is possible to describe statistical packages in terms of a simple dichotomy between **convenience programs** and **comprehensive programs.** Convenience programs provide only the most popular tools but are easy to learn and use. In contrast, comprehensive programs, provide virtually all possible statistical tools, as well as comprehensive data editing and recoding functions. They are very difficult to learn initially, but the user will almost never run out of power. PC programs span the two categories, but nearly every host product is a comprehensive program.

Statistical Problems

Although statistical packages offer a wide variety of tools, it is easy for an inexperienced user to use these tools inappropriately. We will survey just a few of the more common mistakes made by users.

Nonparametric Statistics

Nearly everyone is familiar with such statistical terms as means (averages), standard deviations, and correlation coefficients (Pearson's r). Even if they do not understand the calculations, they are used to seeing these terms used in presentations.

Unfortunately, these and many other statistics make certain assumptions about the kind of data being used in calculations. The first assumption is that the data are normally distributed. This is a poor assumption in many cases, although it only throws some statistical calculations into disarray.

More important is the second assumption, that the calculations are being done on something called **interval data.** This concept comes from an idea called "strength of measurement," which recognizes that some data are "stronger" than others, in the sense that more computations can be done on them. For example, it is possible to calculate a mean, median, and mode for salary data, whereas it is only possible to give a mode (the category with the most cases) for the cities in which suppliers reside. Statisticians recognize four strengths of measurement.

- For nominal data, modes can be computed, but not medians or means.
- For ordinal data, modes and medians can be computed, but not means.
- For interval data, modes, medians, and means can all be computed, as well as standard deviations.
- For ratio data, ratios can be computed.

The most common error involving strength of measurement is to treat ordinal data (for which means cannot be computed) as interval data. For example, a five-point scale from strongly agree to strongly disagree only produces ordinal data; therefore, computing a mean should not be done, although it often is. Moreover, if salary information is divided into categories (say, Under $20,000, $20,000 to $40,000, and Over $40,000, then it is reduced from interval data to ordinal data.

The user's first task is to recognize when data are interval data and normally distributed and when they are not. The user's second task is to find the appropriate statistical test to use with these data. Comprehensive stat programs are loaded with **nonparametric** statistical tests that work when data are not intervally scaled or normally distributed, but it takes some training to pick the most appropriate test.

In some cases, treating ordinal or even nominal data as interval produces only minor problems, but in other cases, violating the strength of measurement assumption underlying a statistical calculation may completely invalidate it. It is important to be sure that users understand strength of measurement and normal distributions, because programs cannot determine what variable has a given strength of measurement by simply looking at the data keyed into the system.

Other Statistical Assumptions

Most statistical tests have several assumptions, which must be carefully considered. For example, in order to compare means in two samples to determine whether one is larger, one would normally use a t-test. But the t-test assumes not only that the variable is both interval and normally distributed, but also that the standard deviations are the same in the two samples—an assumption that is often violated, since an effect often changes both the mean and the spread found in the data.

For such problems, statisticians normally have separate statistical tests that work even if an important assumption of a strong test is violated. Many users fail to realize that an assumption is violated because they often do not understand the assumptions underlying a test. As users move from simple cross-tabulations and frequency distributions to more advanced tests, knowledge of underlying assumptions becomes critical.

Inferences

Most people remember from their basic statistics courses that there are one-tail and two-tail statistical tests, but they tend to get confused about when each applies. It is important to resolve this issue because if the wrong choice is made, a bad inference can easily be drawn.

This issue can be resolved by making the decision *before looking at any data*. If one has reason to believe that the mean in Group 1 is greater than the mean in Group 2, then the user would use a one-tail t-test—and the user would reject the null hypothesis only if the mean of Group 1 was larger than the mean of Group 2. If the mean of Group 2 turns out to be larger, the user cannot switch to a two-tail t-test because the decision was made before looking at the data. Only if there was no reason to hypothesize that one is larger than another *before looking at the data* could a two-tail t-test be used. This practice is widely violated by inexperienced users, leading to many false positive results.

Another problem that leads to false positive results is the **multiple inference problem.** For example, suppose that a user wants to do 100 t-tests on data that are unrelated, so that none of the 100 t-tests should be positive. If one has a specific confidence level, say 0.05, then when one draws the 100 inferences, roughly 5 percent of all inferences will be falsely positive. If variables are correlated, there is no way to give a simple answer as to how many false positives will result from doing multiple inferences at a set confidence level. This is one of the most troublesome problems in all of statistics, and multiple inference errors appear in almost every questionnaire study or other data analysis dealing with multiple variables.

In general, users have many problems with inference work. First, they tend to use 0.05 or 0.01 confidence levels, even when they are totally inappropriate. There is nothing magical about either 0.05 or 0.01.

Second, they tend to ignore Type II errors (failing to reject the null hypothesis when one should). In business uses, Type II errors are often as bad as Type I errors, but because most statistics courses are oriented toward science, where only the Type I error is important, most businesspeople fail to take Type II errors into account. For example, in a statistical test to determine whether a warehouse should be expanded, a Type I error would be expanding the warehouse when it should not be done, whereas, a Type II error would be failing to expand the warehouse when it needs expansion. Both types of errors are about equally important, yet nearly all statistical inference tests focus only on Type I errors. Choosing a very stringent confidence interval for Type I errors (say 0.001) makes the chance of a Type II error rise astronomically.

Multivariate Analysis Tools

Many statistical calculations are performed on only one variable. The classic example is the mean. Others are performed on two related variables, for instance. Pearson's r to measure whether two variables are correlated. In many business problems, however, several variables must be taken into account. Statistical procedures that work with many variables are called **multivariate** procedures.

There are literally dozens of common multivariate tools, but all share one thing in common. All are very difficult to use well, because they depend on many subtle assumptions about the data. Multiple regression, ANOVA, factor analysis, and interaction analysis are all loaded with traps for the unwary user and even for experienced users. Without extreme knowledge and care, nearly every analysis will be misleading, perhaps seriously so.

Problems in Perspective

There are always two ways to deal with the application–specific knowledge required to avoid errors. The first is to teach the knowledge, and the second is to audit work for errors. The two, of course, are not mutually exclusive.

Although the potential number of problems is large, the danger of error depends on what a person is doing. Simple questionnaire analysis that involves only frequency distributions and cross-tabulations, for example, presents many difficult problems, but fewer than those presented by multivariate statistics. The degree of knowledge required by a user is therefore related less to statistics itself than to the specific kind of work the user will be doing. As a result, support and control strategies can be segmented in terms of the type of statistical analysis to be done.

A Comprehensive Package: SAS

Now that we have discussed the complex pitfalls facing the users of comprehensive statistical packages, we will turn to the mechanics of using these packages. One of the most popular host-based statistical packages is SAS. Although a personal computer version of SAS is now on the market, the PC version has only some of the host version's capabilities at the time of this writing.

Figure 16-6 shows a program written in SAS. The first part of the program defines the variables and their values. For example, in variable Q1F, the value "1" means "Strongly Disagree."

```
1    *--------------------------------------------------*
2    *    USER COMPUTING SURVEY:
3    *    MEASURE OF SUPPORT BY THE INFORMATION SYSTEMS GROUP
4    *--------------------------------------------------*
5    *   ;
6    PROC FORMAT;
7    /* DEFINE DESCRIPTIVE NAMES FOR INPUT VARIABLES    */
8      VALUE Q1F 1='STRONGLY DISAGREE'
9        2='DISAGREE'
10       3='NEITHER AGREE NOR DISAGREE'
11       4='AGREE'
12       5='STRONGLY AGREE'
13       OTHER='MISCODED';
14     VALUE Q2F 1='STRONGLY DISAGREE'
15       2='DISAGREE'
16       3='NEITHER AGREE NOR DISAGREE'
17       4='AGREE'
18       5='STRONGLY AGREE'
19       OTHER='MISCODED';
20     VALUE $Q3F 'M'='MALE'
21       'F'='FEMALE'
22       OTHER='MISCODED'
23     VALUE Q4F 1='UNDER 35'
24       2='35 TO 50'
25       3='OVER 50'
26       OTHER='MISCODED';
27     VALUE Q5F 1='WITHIN INFORMATION SYSTEMS'
28       2='OUTSIDE OF I.S.'
29       OTHER='MISCODED';
30     VALUE Q1GRPF 1='DISAGREE'
31       2='AGREE OR NEUTRAL'
32       3='NO ANSWER'
33       OTHER='MISCODED';
```

FIGURE 16-6 A SAS PROGRAM

```
34
35   DATA TEMP;    /* TEMPORARY SAS DATA SET */
36
37   /*  ASSOCIATE VARIABLES WITH FORMATS*/
38     FORMAT Q1 Q1F.;
39     FORMAT Q2 Q2F.;
40     FORMAT Q3 $Q3F.;
41     FORMAT Q4 Q4F.;
42     FORMAT Q5 Q5F.;
43     FORMAT Q1GRP Q1GRPF.;
44     INFILE TESTDATA;


45
46   /*  INPUT FORMAT: ONE POSITION PER QUESTION */
47    INPUT
48              Q1 1.
49              Q2 1.
50              Q3         $1.
51              Q4 1.
52              Q5 1.
53    ;
54
55    IF  Q1=1 OR Q1=2 OR Q1=3
56        THEN Q1GRP=1;
57        ELSE IF Q1=4 OR Q1=5
58                THEN Q1GRP=2;
59                ELSE Q1GRP=3;
60
61    LABEL Q1='USER COMPUTING'
62       Q2='ADEQUATE SUPPORT'
63       Q3='SEX'
64       Q4='AGE'
65       Q5='JOB AREA'
66    ;
67
68              PROC FREQ;
69                 TABLES Q1 Q3 Q1GRP;
70
71              PROC MEANS N NMISS MEAN STD RANGE SUM VAR;
72                 VAR Q1 Q2 Q1GRP;
73
74              PROC FREQ;
75                 TABLES Q1GRP*Q3 / CHISQ MISSING
76                    ;
```

The next section creates a temporary data set for the five variables in the model, as well as a sixth variable, Q1GRP. Q1GRP is a recoded variable that combines several data values in Q1. If Q1 is 1, 2, or 3, then Q1GRP1 is set to 1. If Q1 is 4 or 5, then Q1GRP is set to 2. Otherwise, Q1GRP is set to 3. This means that a variable with five choices, from strongly agree to strongly disagree, is reduced to two choices—one ranging from strongly disagree to neutral and the second from agree to agree strongly. Other values are labeled as miscodes and missing data. Recoding is often used when results are skewed or the number of categories must be reduced for chi square analysis or some other analysis.

The Label section labels the individual questions. For instance, Q2 is "Adequate Support." It asks if the person thinks support is adequate.

After the file has been described, the program moves on to procedures to be executed on the data. It begins with a frequency distribution on Q1, Q3, and Q1GRP, and it then computes a number of statistics for these variables, beginning with means. It uses PROC (procedure) FREQ to produce a crosstabulation of Q1GRP by Q3, resulting in a chi square statistic.

Although SAS takes some time to master, it is an extremely powerful tool with almost endless functionality. There is now a personal computer version of SAS that offers a somewhat better user interface but a great deal of power.

Good Practice

To conduct statistical analysis appropriately, a number of safeguards need to be implemented. If these are ignored, the results of statistical analysis can be extremely misleading because it is unlikely that the average reader of a report embodying statistics will have the knowledge to critique the analysis.

Faithfulness to Assumptions

The first concern is to avoid the errors mentioned at the beginning of this discussion on statistics, through training, auditing, or both. As discussed at the end of the section on problems, a different set of support and control tools can be supplied for such "simple" tasks as analyzing questionnaire data than for such complex tasks as multivariate studies or complex nonparametric analyses.

Data Quality

The second concern is data quality. If a user has a poor measurement instrument, for example, a survey that asks questions that people cannot be expected to respond to accurately or truthfully, the best statistical analysis tools will not be able to correct the problem. Many questionnaires have wording difficulties that could be avoided by asking a competent survey designer to review the questionnaire.

Even if the instrument is a good one, care must be taken to control the data collection if humans are involved. In the case of questionnaires, the interviewer must be carefully instructed to ask the question exactly, and a number of people interviewed should be contacted afterward to ensure that no interviewer cheating took place.

Other problems occur during data entry. In most cases, someone must key in the data. Keypunch errors are inevitable, and if a very large error is keyed in, a single data point may throw off the whole analysis. After the data are entered, they must be compared with the data input forms. This can be done by manual proofreading. Another approach is to **verify** the data; this involves keying in all data twice. The system will compare the two sets of entries and warn of differences. Verification was common when data were punched onto cards. It is somewhat less common now, and most statistical analysis packages do not support it directly.

Another check is to impose data entry rules for each variable, so that an unreasonable value will be flagged as soon as someone tries to enter it. Surprisingly, this capability is also missing from most stat packages. Instead, one usually plots each variable or asks the system to output the maximum and minimum values for individual variables. If **outliers**—points that fall outside expected values—are found, the analysts must decide whether the outlier can plausibly be eliminated.

After data have been keyed in, data backup is critical. The cost of keying data is usually substantial, and it may take a week or more to key in a good size data set. Loss of a data set can be extremely expensive, and the time it takes to reenter the data may be unacceptable given normal decision time horizons.

GRAPHICS

Graphics is the smallest member of the host data and decision support family, but it is also the most rapidly growing member of the family. Until recently, high-quality presentation graphics was restricted to host computers. First, the processing power needed to run the graphics software was far too much for personal computers. Second, expensive output devices were needed, and these output devices could only be justified by sharing them among many users.

Today, personal computers are the normal way to produce low-quality graphics such as Lotus 1-2-3 graphs, and they are also beginning to nip at the heels of host products for presentation graphics. For the time being, however, there is enough growth in both PC and host graphics systems to keep both growing rapidly.

As discussed in Chapter 11, graphics can be divided into analytical graphics, which deal with numbers, and into conceptual graphics, which portray concepts and their interrelationships. Graphics are also prominent in word processing, particularly in high-end publication systems. In the host world, analytical graphics is the primary application category. We will talk briefly about two programs from Integrated Software Systems Corporation, TELL-A-GRAF and CUECHART. The first is a powerful and flexible tool, and the second is designed to let users develop sophisticated tables and charts very easily.

Graphics Packages

Until recently, nearly all host graphics packages were quite sophisticated, requiring users to spend a good deal of time learning how to use them, even if simple designs were to be created.

At roughly the lower end of these sophisticated graphics packages is TELL-A-GRAF, one of the most popular host graphics package. As in the cases of IFPS and SAS, a TELL-A-GRAF user writes a statement-based description of the graph to be created and then executes the program to produce the graph. If problems are found, the statement-based description has to be modified. This approach requires a good deal of training, and statement-based systems tend to be intimidating to the new user.

In contrast to this batch processing approach, Lotus 1-2-3 and most PC graphics tools let the user describe the graph interactively. After giving the most essential information, namely, the kind of graph to be created and the data to be used, the user can preview the graph. The user can then add features one at a time, previewing the graph after each change, if desired. Only when the graph looks right does the user save it in preparation for printing.

Another limitation on sophisticated host systems is that not many terminals have full graphics capabilities. As a result, it is necessary to produce the graph, look at it, and then return to make changes. This is extremely time consuming. Although text-only PCs have the same problem, low-cost monochrome graphics adapter boards (see Chapter 7) can allow even the cheapest IBM PCs to preview a graph without color. Vendors offer similar capabilities.

Not all host packages use the obsolescent approach of creating batch files through text-only terminals. Most can use graphics terminals when they have them, and quite a few newer products use interactive design. Older systems, having had 10 to 20 years to mature, often provide many more features than newer competitors, and these features are often more fully developed.

As the use of host graphics increased, many one-time or occasional users began to produce charts. To respond to their more limited needs, companies began to produce simpler graphics programs. For instance, ISSCO, the maker of TELL-A-GRAF, produced the simpler product CUECHART.

In CUECHART, the user begins by logging in and then selecting a chart from a menu of over 400 options. Some are charts, such as line and pie charts, but the list also has a large number of table formats, since a presentation-quality table is the best way to present many data patterns.

The menu is rich is alternatives within each basic category. For example, there may be dozens of kinds of bar charts. Each alternative involves a variation on the basic theme, and the user merely chooses among possible presentation forms in a chart book instead of having to describe his or her format in exhaustive detail.

CUECHART is a variant of TELL-A-GRAF. Every CUECHART selection is a TELL-A-GRAF chart, and once a CUECHART option is selected, the user can turn to TELL-A-GRAF to add advanced features.

CUECHART has two advantages over TELL-A-GRAF. First, CUECHART allows novice users to specify complete chart descriptions through simple menus. Second, all CUECHART menu options were *developed by graphics professionals and so avoid the worst mistakes that novice chart builders tend to make in terms of clutter, the excessive use of color, and the other design errors discussed below.*

Good Practice

In graphics, as in almost everything else, users need training to help them avoid mistakes. Graphics design is new for most users, and it is easy to produce charts that are difficult to read. Several good articles (1,2,5) have been published on good practice in graphics, and far more will be produced as the use of graphics continues to explode. An excellent book on the field is Reference 4, Tufte's *The Visual Display of Quantitative Information.*

The biggest mistake to avoid is using a graph when words or tables would do the job. Tufte calls graphics produced just for graphics' sake "ducks" in honor of a store called Big Duck, a store that was built in the shape of a Duck. (5) The overuse of graphics can numb readers and listeners, diluting the impact of key graphs.

The second biggest mistake is to lose simplicity. A picture may be worth a thousand words, but unless it states a single simple message, it will communicate little. There should be few variables—no more than three to five—and a single pattern should be emphasized, perhaps by showing just that one feature in a contrasting color.

Simplicity requires that there be a clear flow to the figure. If several bars are shown, they should be shown in ascending or descending values of gray scale. If the graph is a pictorial graph showing relationships among concepts, there should be a clean and strong visual flow through the diagram.

Once emphasis and flow have been established, it is crucial to avoid any elaboration that detracts from the basic emphasis and flow. Grid lines should not be used, or, if they are absolutely necessary, they should be lighter than the data lines. (2) There should be a single type face and color, although a few size variations are possible. Parallel lines that are evenly spaced (Figure 16-7) produce jitter in the eye (2) and should be avoided. Unfortunately, Lotus 1-2-3 and many other programs use these lines routinely to represent shading on monochrome graphics screens.

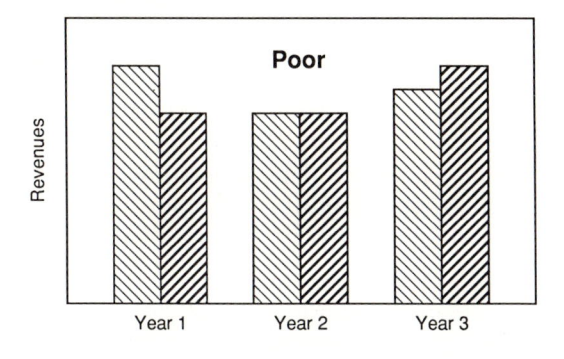

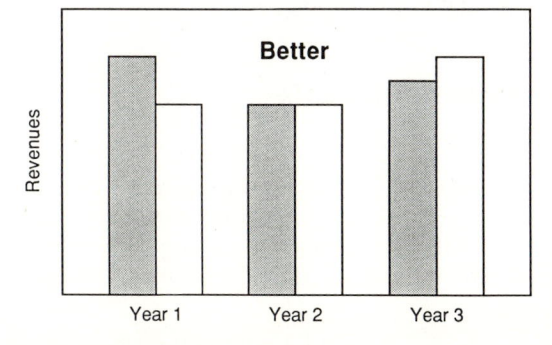

FIGURE 16-7 PARALLEL EVENLY SPACED LINES PRODUCE JITTER IN THE EYE

If analytical and pictorial graphs are used in live presentations, it is important to spend enough time on each illustration. A general rule of thumb is that a user should not show a figure unless he or she will talk about it for at least five minutes. After showing the audience the basic pattern, the user should spend some time discussing its implications. Users do not have to show this additional detail on the figure itself, since the audience should have a reduced size copy of the figure with plenty of room for side notes.

It is quite desirable to leave expansions off the basic image, so that the audience always has the full chart in front of them in a form simple enough to follow easily, without being distracted by clutter. Where details do need to be shown, a series of variations on the basic chart can be shown after the basic image has been developed. In each chart one area may be blown up to show the detail, or additional detail may be drawn in a way that shows the variation of this illustration from the basic theme.

The basic rules in graphics are (1) avoid it unless you need it, (2) tell a single message, and (3) elaborate in words at presentations, not by cluttering the chart with detail.

DATA MANAGEMENT SYSTEMS

Data management systems include both file management systems, which manage only a single file at a time, and data base management systems (DBMSs), which manage collections of files. Chapter 10 discussed the general features of data management systems; the reader may wish to review that chapter before reading this section.

Data management systems cut across the line drawn at the beginning of the chapter between data applications and decision support applications.

- When people use the retrieval tools found in these packages, including report generators and query languages, their work falls under the "decision support" category.
- When end users build their own miniature data processing systems, including data entry, manipulation, and fixed-format reporting, their work falls under the "data application" category.

Because of this dual use, we have postponed the discussion of data management systems until late in the chapter, following a disucssion of other decision support tools. In this way, the reader can consider data management systems from the viewpoints of both data applications and decision support applications.

The Evolution of Data Management Tools

The Early Years
During the 1970s, most data management programs were written in COBOL, a third-generation programming language oriented toward record manipulation in data files. Although COBOL is an excellent language, which can produce efficient and readable code, it is designed for large programs and

not for simple needs such as generating a report. COBOL programs are very time consuming to write.

During the 1970s, a number of fourth-generation tools began to appear on the market. These tools were easier to use than COBOL, and programmers could develop applications rapidly by using them. These fourth-generation tools soon became popular with programmers and information systems managers.

The code they produced was not very efficient, however, and so they could only be used for small jobs. Although they were popular and widely used, their use was limited to such simple tasks as generating one-time reports and other applications that would not be used heavily.

Types of Data Management Products

Most of these products were very limited in scope. For example, report generators (see Chapter 10) could create simple management reports, whereas sorting programs were limited to sorting the records in a file on the basis of one or more keys. A typical data processing shop might use a dozen or more of these limited tools.

Some of these products, on the other hand, were full file management systems or data base management systems. As discussed in Chapter 10, these products could build complete applications, including defining the database schema, managing data entry, supporting queries and report generation, and even developing applications using an embedded fourth-generation language or applications generator.

As shown in Figure 16-8, full data management systems generally fall into two categories. First, there are **production systems** which are designed to produce a company's main data processing systems. Characterized by IBM's IMS and DB2 products, these production systems produce efficient code but are difficult to use. They are designed for data processing professionals and tend to be difficult to learn and use.

Second, there are **stand-alone systems** which are designed for small applications. They are much easier to learn and use than production systems, but they cannot do as much. It would be tempting to call these "end user" data

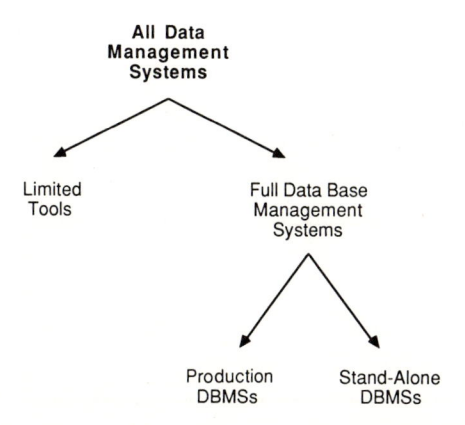

FIGURE 16-8 CATEGORIES OF DATA MANAGEMENT SYSTEMS

management systems, but they actually represent a compromise between the needs of end users and data processing professionals. In companies without production systems for data management, many small applications are built with stand-alone systems. Even when a production data management system is present, it is common for DP professionals to develop many small applications developed using stand-alone systems. Because of this dual market among DP professionals and end users, stand-alone data management systems tend to be feature-rich at the expense of ease of use. This situation is compounded by the fact that most end users who use these systems today are power users who also demand functionality, even at the expense of ease of use. The final result is that few of these stand-alone data management systems are suited to the needs of end users with modest needs.

End User Tools

Although few fourth-generation data management tools are designed specifically for the needs of end users, end users must turn to these tools if they want to get their work done. In this chapter, we will look at two of the many tools available to end users.

First, we will examine a tool with limited scope. This is SQL, a query language originally developed by IBM. SQL is important because it has become an ANSI national standard in the United States and, more importantly, is becoming the industry's de facto standard query language. It will soon be rare to see data management systems that fail to support SQL.

Second, we will consider a stand-alone DBMS, Information Builders' FOCUS. FOCUS is widely used, although its hierarchical structure appears to be an anachronism in these days of relational organization. As we will see, it is full featured but somewhat difficult to use.

We will not discuss production systems, which often involve end user tools, but we will include production systems at the end of the chapter, when we discuss integrated host systems. In the future, these integrated systems should be extremely important.

SQL

SQL (Structured Query Language) is a query language using the relational calculus (see Chapter 10). Originally developed by IBM, SQL is now an ANSI standard. Many products, including Oracle, implement SQL.

Simple Queries

The following query shows the simplest possible retrieval in SQL. The asterisk indicates that all columns are to be printed from the relation Payroll.

```
         SELECT *
         FROM Payroll
```

DATA MANAGEMENT SYSTEMS

The second example, shown below, illustrates a more precise query. This query prints columns: Firstname, Lastname, Salary/12, and (Salary−BaseSal). BaseSal is the person's base salary—the salary before bonuses, commissions, and other extras. The last two columns show that SQL can do calculations, demonstrating results that are inherent in the data but not stored in any single column.

```
SELECT   Firstname, Lastname, Salary/12, (Salary-BaseSal)
   FROM    Payroll
   WHERE   Salary > 30000
   ORDER   BY   Lastname, Firstname
```

The last clause, ORDER BY, tells SQL to sort the rows before printing them. The rows are sorted first on Lastname. If several rows have the same last name, they are printed in order of first name. In other words, the second field in the ORDER BY clause only comes into play if there is a tie on the first.

WHERE

The second to last clause in the previous example, WHERE, "filters" the rows before they are printed. Only rows passing the filter condition are printed.

As shown in Figure 16-9, SQL is rich in filtering conditions. Most obviously, it can compare a field value to a numerical quantity, using the six possible comparison conditions. In the last example, only rows in which Salary was more than $30,000 would pass the filter. SQL also has the WHERE operator BETWEEN, which allows the user to select field values between two limits.

Equal to	And	Between X and Y
Not Equal to	Or	IN(X,Y,Z)
Less Than	Not	LIKE "Text"
Not Less Than		
Greater Than		
Not Greater Than		

FIGURE 16-9 WHERE CONDITIONS IN SQL

In a step beyond this, it can do calculations on the two sides of the comparison conditions. It can, for instance, support this formulation:

```
WHERE (Salary/12)>(Bonus+1000)
```

Another WHERE clause capability is IN (A,B,C), which selects rows if the column contains one of the enumerated values A, B, or C. For example:

```
WHERE EmpID IN (125,438,12)
```

WHERE is also adept at handling text strings. In the simplest case, a field is compared to a quoted string, for example:

```
WHERE Lastname > 'Smith'
```

SQL can also work on partial string matches. For instance:

```
'%XYZ'      means any value ending in XYZ
'XYZ%'      means any value beginning with XYZ
'%XYZ%'     means any value with XYZ in its middle
'~XYZ'      means any value beginning with any
            single character, followed by XYZ
'X~Y~'      means any value beginning with X,
            followed by any character, then Y,
            then one other character
```

SQL has the AND, OR, and NOT operators to combine atomic comparisons into larger units. This capability is aided by the ability to use parenthesis, so that the user can express conditions like (A AND B) OR C.

Advanced Retrieval

SQL is able to do computations that summarize information in several records. For instance, the following query finds the average salary in the finance department:

```
SELECT   AVG (Salary)
  FROM   Payroll
 WHERE   DeptID='Fin'
```

The user may also want to summarize salaries in several departments instead of just seeing individual records. This brings into play two new clauses: GROUP BY and HAVING. Suppose, for instance, a user wants to know the average and minimum salaries in Accounting, Finance, and Marketing. The query to do so would be:

```
SELECT     DeptID, AVG(Salary), MIN (Salary)
  FROM     Payroll
GROUP BY   DeptID
HAVING     DeptID IN (Fin, Acctg, Mkt)
ORDER BY   DeptID
```

This query would produce output looking something like this:

```
Acctg    21650    11278
Fin      35675    20753
Mkt      27896    13529
```

As shown in this example, grouped output will not show information for individual records. Instead, it calculates statistics for several groups of records and then prints these summaries. In grouped output, HAVING is like the WHERE clause, but there HAVING *filters groups* defined in the GROUP BY clause, while WHERE *filters individual records.*

Multirelation Queries

All of the queries discussed so far have dealt with single relations, but single SQL queries can also pull data from two relations, using a syntax such as the following one:

```
SELECT Lastname, City, Salary
 FROM Payroll, Master
 WHERE (Emplnum=Idnum) AND State='NY'
```

Here, data are pulled from two relations, Payroll and Master. Payroll provides data for Lastname and Salary, whereas Master provides data for City and State. The equation of Emplnum with Idnum in the WHERE clause states that records in the two relations can be combined based on the values of Emplnum in Payroll and Idnum in Master.

Nonquery Operation

Although SQL is primarily a query operation, it can also be used to define a data base schema, insert new records, update records, and delete records. The following example gives the flavor of these operations.

```
CREATE TABLE Clients
  (Lastname    VARCHAR(15)    NOT NULL,
   Firstname   VARCHAR(15),
   Phone       CHAR (12),
   Sales Last  DECIMAL (8,2));
```

```
INSERT INTO Clients
  VALUES ("Smith," "Richard," 555-2672, 32765)
```

DATA MANAGEMENT SYSTEMS **687**

```
UPDATE Deptmgr
   SET  Manager='Hoover'
   WHERE DeptID='Fin'
```

```
DELETE
   FROM Product
   WHERE Prodid = 'Q39A'
```

These examples show that nonquery operations in SQL are cumbersome, but they are designed to be used within COBOL programs rather than in user queries. Within COBOL, it is possible to execute a set of SQL statements with a construction such as this one.

```
COBOL code
   EXEC SQL
      SQL statement(s)
   END-EXEC
```

Although it takes some time to learn how to use SQL effectively from within programs, it allows the programmer to create short, powerful programs that use the DBMS under SQL to do many complex tasks. For example, the following example shows how to do a data extraction in one statement. In COBOL, many statements would have been needed.

```
INSERT INTO NewTable
  SELECT Lastname, Firstname, Salary, JobCode
  FROM EMaster
  WHERE DeptID = "Shipping"
```

Overall

SQL has two major advantages. First, IBM is promoting it as the user query language for Database 2 (DB2) and future IBM relational products. Second, thanks to ANSI standardization, users may soon need to learn only a single query language to access relational DBMSs from different vendors running on mainframes, minis, and micros.

On the negative side, SQL is command-driven and lacks an integral fullscreen interface design. Although different vendors are likely to provide fullscreen interfaces, variations in their design will reintroduce learning difficulties. The other problem with SQL is that its query capability is more limited than other systems on the market. Therefore, heavier users may run out of functionality.

Finally, SQL is only a query language. It is not a report generator and cannot handle data entry and updating with the smooth full-screen interface users have come to expect. It is only one part of what end users will need to work with host data.

FOCUS—Describing FOCUS Data Bases

In contrast to SQL, which is primarily a query language, Information Builders' FOCUS is a full stand-alone DBMS. It allows users to define data bases, enter data, and generate reports, as well as to do the type of queries that are the forte of SQL. FOCUS is closer in spirit to dBASE III than to SQL.

Although FOCUS is much simpler than many host-based DBMSs, it still tries to appeal to professional programmers as well as to end users. As a result, it is not the kind of tool to give to most novice end users, nor is it the kind of tool to provide to anyone without extensive training.

Defining Data Files

FOCUS is a hierarchical data base management system, not a relational data base management system. Figure 16-10 illustrates a typical hierarchical data base structure within FOCUS. At the top level is the EmplMast segment, which holds basic information about each employee, namely, his or her ID number, last name, first name, and middle initial. At the next level down are the Salary and Deducts segments, which keep salary and deduction information about the employee. As shown in Figure 16-10, an employee may have several deduction segments, one for each type of deduction.

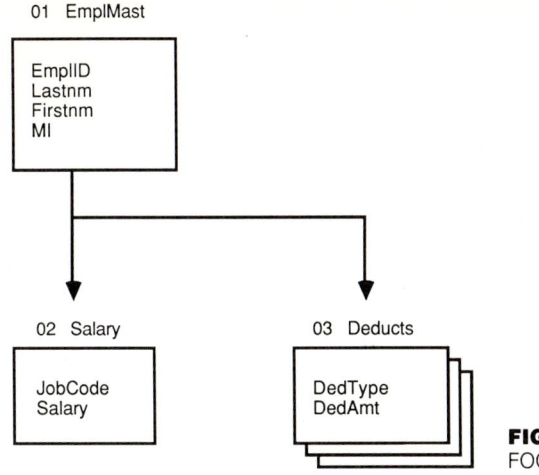

FIGURE 16-10 A HIERARCHICAL FOCUS DATA BASE

It is possible to "join," that is, associate two different data bases so that information in both can be used in various operations. The JOIN command produces a temporary association that is active only for the remainder of a session. FOCUS can also build permanent cross references between data bases.

In addition to its basic hierarchical structure, FOCUS users can also build simple sequential files, which are simple tables. Many end users remain with sequential files instead of mastering more complex hierarchical data bases. However, sequential files reduce FOCUS to being a file management system, since it is not possible to build data bases using several sequential files.

In addition to being able to work with hierarchical FOCUS files and simple sequential files, FOCUS can work with comma-delimited sequential files, ISAM files, VSAM files, IMS data bases, IDMS data bases, Total data bases, and ADABAS data bases.

Describing a FOCUS Data Base—Overview

Compared to products like dBASE III Plus which use full-screen interfaces, FOCUS is difficult to use. Figure 16-11 shows the procedure to define the FOCUS data base illustrated in Figure 16-10.

The first statement says that a file named Payroll is being defined. The SUFFIX, FOC, reveals that this is a FOCUS data base. The suffix SEQ would label it as a fixed format sequential file. There are other suffixes for the other kinds of files that FOCUS can use (ISAM, VSAM, etc.).

The next statement says that the following statements will describe the fields in the EmplMast segment. SEGTYPE S1 says that instances are to be logically sorted in lowest to highest order, based on values in the first field (EmplID). Different SEGTYPE parameters can cause records to be sorted in descending order, or based on values in a field other than the first.

```
FILENAME=Payroll,SUFFIX=FOCUS


SEGNAME=EmplMast,SEGTYPE=S1

    FIELDNAME=EmplID,ALIAS=ID,FORMAT=I5,$

    FIELDNAME=Lastnm,ALIAS=L,FORMAT=A20,$

    FIELDNAME=Firstnm,ALIAS=F,FORMAT=A20,$

    FIELDNAME=MI,ALIAS=M,FORMAT=A3,$


SEGNAME=Salary,PARENT=EmplMast,SEGTYPE=S1

    FIELDNAME=JobCode,ALIAS=J,FORMAT=I4,$

    FIELDNAME=Salary,ALIAS=S,FORMAT=D10.2,$


SEGNAME=Deducts,PARENT=EmplMast,SEGTYPE=S1

    FIELDNAME=DedType,ALIAS=DT,FORMAT=I3,$

    FIELDNAME=DedAmt,ALIAS=DA,FORMAT=D8.2,$
```

FIGURE 16-11 DEFINING A DATA BASE IN FOCUS

Skipping the next four lines, there is another SEGNAME statement, this time defining the Salary segment's records. This SEGNAME statement has a clause that is not found in the first, namely, PARENT=. This tells the segment to which the Salary segment is attached in the hierarchy; that segment is EmplMast. The Deducts segment has a similar definition.

Defining a FOCUS Data Base—Describing Fields

We previously skipped over FIELDNAME statements. We will now return to them. The first FIELDNAME statement defines the employee ID field in the Empinfo segment. The FIELDNAME= clause gives the name of the field, in this case EmplId. Next comes an ALIAS= field, which allows the user to create a shorthand for referring to the field in various commands. In this field, the alias is ID. The FORMAT=I5 clause describes the field as an integer field that is five characters wide. Finally, a dollar sign closes the definition. Note the precise use of commas.

In general, the FORMAT= keyword is followed by a Type, an optional length description, and zero or more edit options that determine how it will appear. The I type, already noted, is for integer information. There is also an alphanumeric type (A), a floating point type that allows decimals (F), a double precision floating point type (D), and several other miscellaneous types such as "packed."

Following the format type is the length of the field. Integer and alphanumeric fields require only a single number to specify them completely. Floating point fields need two numbers. The first shows the total number of characters, including sign and trailing decimal places, but not including the decimal point itself.

DATA MANAGEMENT SYSTEMS

The edit option, not shown in Figure 6-11, provides control over how values will be printed. C produces commas between thousands places, whereas M produces commas and a dollar sign before the first digit, B brackets negative values, and R puts credit (CR) after negative values. There are many options for date printing.

Aids

This whole process is complicated and tedious and places a heavy learning burden on users. To help users, Information Builders offers optional software to let users define data bases by choosing from menus and filling out forms. But even this software is no cure-all for FOCUS' complexity in defining data bases. Users still need to master underlying hierarchical network design principles, as well as FOCUS' particular approach to defining fields.

Even with this aid, it is still a heavy task to define a FOCUS data base. In many firms, an information center staff member does the creation work for the user. The user then only worries about working with the data base after its schema has been defined. Because setting up a FOCUS data base takes only an hour or so for an experienced FOCUS user, this practice does not place a heavy burden on the information center.

FOCUS—Queries and Reports

FOCUS does not have separate query and report generation tools.; a single method is used to produce both. In its simplest form, it can produce simple queries, but users may add optional clauses to produce a far richer form of output. There is literally a clear and simple line of development from the simplest queries to the most complex reports. As the user's needs and understanding grow, later learning builds incrementally and easily on earlier learning.

Basic Retrieval

The report definition shown below is the simplest form of query within FOCUS. It has three statements, the first saying that a table is being created, using the data base Wine; the second that two fields are to be printed from each record, Color (red, white, or rose) and UnitCost; and the third ending the report definition. If RUN is used instead of END, FOCUS will assume that more queries are to come on the data base, and the initial TABLE statement can be dropped.

```
TABLE FILE Wine
  Print Color, UnitCost
END
```

The next example shows the use of the BY clause. In this case, Country, Color, and Distributor are shown, with output sorted both by Country and Color. Figure 16-12 illustrates both the query and the results. Note that Country is shown only for the first record in the group, the same for Color. This produces a nicely formatted report.

In the BY clause, there is an optional phrase, IN-GROUPS-OF, which allows continuous data to be grouped into a few categories. For example, cars can be grouped by UnitCost, in IN-GROUPS-OF 5. The output will then show results for each UnitCost category.

Like SQL, FOCUS has a strong set of filtering conditions to specify what records will be printed, as well as the ability to do calculations. For simple tasks, the two are almost equally powerful, but for advanced retrievals, FOCUS rapidly pulls away from SQL.

Advanced Retrieval

The next example (Figure 16-13) shows a multiset request in which two requests are made. The first asks for a sum of Revenues by Country, and the second asks for Revenues by Country and Color. The figure shows that the two requests are shown side by side.

Most reports are vertically oriented, but FOCUS can also print information horizontally or even in the form of a matrix, as shown in Figure 16-14. Here, the ACROSS keyword with the Color field is used to create groups running horizontally, whereas Country is used to group vertically. There are even horizontal totals.

These abilities to do multiset requests and to produce a matrix form of output instead of a simple vertical listing are only two of FOCUS's advanced reporting features. These advanced features take FOCUS far beyond the capabilities of pure query languages such as SQL and even beyond the report generation capabilities of most PC DBMSs.

```
TABLE FILE Wine
PRINT Country Color Distributor
BY Country by Color
END


Country    Color    Distributor
-------------------------------
America    Red      Manheim
                    Franklin
                    ABRE
           White    Manheim
                    Prudholm
           Rose     ABRE
France     Red      Lefebre
                    Ami
...        ...      ...
```

FIGURE 16-12 A SIMPLE FOCUS REPORT

DATA MANAGEMENT SYSTEMS   **693**

```
TABLE FILE Wine
SUM Revenues BY Country
SUM Revenues BY Color
```

Country	Revenues	Color	Revenues
America	$4,040,155	Red	$2,347,290
		White	$1,125,428
		Rose	$567,437
France	$1,953,564	Red	$964,276
		White	$853,418
		Rose	$135,870
Italy	$3,282,760	Red	$1,437,503
		White	$1,296,531
		Rose	$548,726
...	...	...	...

FIGURE 16-13 A MULTISET REPORT IN FOCUS

Although we have surveyed a number of FOCUS capabilities, we have only scratched the surface of this remarkable product's ability to govern layout on the page. We have not talked at all, for instance, about page headings and footings, column titling, page breaks, subtotals, or other formatting refinements. Users with simple needs can do very simple things with ease, but users with more complex needs can do a wide spectrum of work with only incremental learning.

```
TABLE FILE Wine
SUM Revenues
ACROSS Color
BY Country
AND ROW-TOTAL
END
```

	Color			
Country	Red	White	Rose	Total
America	$2,347,290	$1,125,428	$567,437	$4,040,155
France	$964,276	$853,418	$135,870	$1,953,564
Italy	$1,437,503	$1,296,531	$548,726	$3,282,760
...	...	...	...	...

FIGURE 16-14 COMBINED HORIZONTAL AND VERTICAL PRINTING IN FOCUS

Training, Support, and Control

DBMSs need more extensive training and support than other host services.

- First, their higher functionality means that there is more to learn and more to correct if errors are made.
- Second, managers have to learn the terminology of data bases and queries and the concepts that underlie the terminology, including relational (or hierarchical/network) concepts and Boolean filtering. Even more needs to be learned if the user creates applications with an embedded 4GL.
- Third, building a schema involves modeling the data needs of a person or larger work group. Data modeling is a high art, even if the complications of normalization are ignored.
- Fourth, many DBMS users are intermittent users who may go several months between intense periods of use. Many details are lost during these "off periods," so relearning tends to be a serious problem. Moreover, most complex operations, such as defining the data base structure, are the least frequently used.
- Fifth, host DBMS applications tend to involve many people in different departments and different geographical areas. Users need to be taught how to develop consensus in application building.

Direct Support

End users on host data management systems tend to need a great deal of direct support. Many information centers do specific tasks, such as creating a schema or doing file extractions or conversions. Some information centers even do complete jobs for end users, from the creation of the schema to the creation of final reports. Whether or not to provide direct support, is always a complex issue.

Training Alternatives

For popular PC DBMS products, especially dBASE III, a number of training organizations are likely to provide instructions. However, few regions have any locally developed training available for host DBMS, even the most popular ones.

Vendors do provide training, but costs tend to be considerable. Training at the vendor's site usually involves expensive travel. Even if the vendor comes to the user's site, travel and lodging costs drive up training costs, and these customer premises training sessions normally appear only once or twice a year.

If the user organization does its own training, it must invest in the development of teaching materials. Unless a particular host product is widely used, the cost per teaching hour will be high. Computer-based training (CBT) promises to reduce these costs, but because most host products serve relatively small numbers of users, CBT has not developed as rapidly for host applications as it has for PC applications.

Modularization in Training

Modularization is needed in all application training, but it is especially critical in DBMS training. Most users are likely to start with a basic course that teaches them how to build a very simple data base, do a few simple queries, and use commands for exiting, printing, and other common chores.

An advanced retrieval class would take the retrieval-oriented user through advances queries, report generation, producing extract files, and perhaps importing data from external sources and exporting data into the format used in another host program or PC program. In addition to these technical matters, the course would teach policies for labeling data by data base, file/relation, field, filter condition, data, and time.

A data design module would take the user through data modeling, perhaps using some formal design techniques such as bubble charting.

Finally, one or more application development modules would take the user through the development of data entry screens, simple menu-driven programming, and advanced programming. These sessions would also teach error checking, crash recovery, backup, program verification, proper documentation, and user training.

System Maintenance

Most host DBMSs require the user support staff to do a good deal of hands-on maintenance work. This maintenance begins with initial installation in which the program is loaded onto the host and its parameters are configured for the particular system installation. If a package comes with many modules, each may have to be installed and checked separately. Then, about once or twice a year, updated versions must be installed or piecemeal updates must be added to the system.

Some DBMSs allow profiles to be established for individual users. These profiles govern what the user sees when he or she enters the system and also sets a number of defaults for actual system use. In addition, light or occasional users may need to be given menu-driven "front ends" from which to select commands. If a DBMS has many users, a good deal of the information center's time can be spent setting up profiles and menus, but the savings in user time are so large that these efforts are usually justified.

Much more time is spent developing data extract files. Few organizations like to have end users work directly with large production files. First, there is the danger that the production file will be accidentally or deliberately corrupted; second, most files have certain records and fields that should not be seen by everyone in the organization; and third, operations on small extract files will be faster for users and will consume fewer system resources. All of these considerations often lead the information center to produce extract files for users who want to do more than one or two simple and confidential queries.

There is yet another reason for doing data extracts; many stand-alone DBMSs either require it or work better with extract files that are converted into the DBMS's native data format.

File extraction and, to a lesser extent, conversion to a stand-alone DBMS's native file format tend to be difficult, requiring systems personnel in the information center to do the actual work.

Control Policies

Just as organizations must establish management policies for their large production data bases, end users must develop specific policies for managing every significant data base, and the information center needs to establish broad policies mandating the general content of these specific policies.

A major issue is "what is significant?" Only a red tape-crazed bureaucrat would require end users to establish written policies for his or her personal telephone book. As discussed in Chapter 1, however, many end user applications are large and could produce a substantial negative impact if mishandled.

Generally any application that gives beyond a purely personal use is potentially significant. In addition, because people leave companies or are transferred to other departments, even "personal" data may require significant protection.

One possibility for screening data bases is to require every data base with more than, say, 200 records to be brought to the attention of the information center, which could then assign it to one of three or so categories ranging from complete user control through formal review and certification.

Notification of the information center would come through a form detailing the number of fields and records, the source of the data, the number of people likely to use the information, and, most importantly, the possible consequences of data destruction or the unauthorized release of information.

Assigning Personal Responsibility

Once a data base is listed as significant, the first step is to assign **responsible users** for overall management and for backup management. The overall management is likely to be a manager or professional, and the backup a secretary. Each department should keep a list of project responsibilities for all staff members. If a person is transferred, part of the exit process should be the reassignment of responsibilities.

The Application Control Document

For each application, there should also be a written document describing the application and management. The application description should begin with a general description and then move into detail on files (or relations), field characteristics, data entry screens, automatic data validation rules, report formats, and programs. If programs exist, they should be well structured, validated, and documented.

The description of management should begin with a general assessment of risks if the data are destroyed or accessed improperly. It should then describe physical and software security, if any, a backup schedule, data entry validation procedures, a procedure to prevent data loss in case of accidental damage or erasure, and rules for who may sign off on changes.

To prevent users from being drowned in red tape, there should be a simple form for projects of low significance and one or more complex forms for projects of high significance.

Retention

A **retention policy**—deciding how long to keep data bases and particular data—is part of the general control plan, but we will discuss it separately because it is a major problem in most firms. Corporate hosts tend to get clogged with unused data bases, and active data bases tend to retain data too long, thus increasing the computer time needed to do most operations.

Each data base should have a retention date. As this date approaches, the data base should be deleted or its review data renewed. Many firms take an even more restrictive stance, automatically archiving data bases that have not been accessed in two to four months (one month is usually too short). Archived files are kept on tape for a certain period, generally one to four years.

Data in a data base should also have a maximum age. Periodically, data older than the maximum should either be deleted or archived. An archival function within the DBMS is a valuable aid to users and a good incentive to proper data management.

Sometimes, data summaries are kept online after details are archived. A sales manager is not likely to need to look at each transaction from two or three years ago, but he or she may wish to review weekly or monthly salesperson performance over a three-year period.

INTEGRATED DATA AND DECISION SUPPORT SYSTEMS

The Drive for Integration
Most large companies have a dozen or more host-based products for data and decision support applications. It would be nice to have a single integrated product capable of handling all data and decision support work. Having such a product would reduce costs and training time, and eliminate the file incompatibility problems that exist when applications cross product boundaries. For decision support applications, the need to combine data, analysis, and presentation capabilities makes integration especially crucial.

Although several products on the market today offer functionality in several major areas, they are strong in only one or two of these areas. Most began as DBMS, statistical analysis, or financial analysis programs, and then added capabilities in other areas. These extensions are useful for someone who works primarily with the program's main function and has a little work to do in other areas, but they are not strong enough for people with serious needs in these areas.

Tools
Figure 16-15 illustrates an idealized integrated system for data and decision support applications. We will examine each of the major modules in this figure.

Professional Data Tools
Professional data tools are designed for IS professionals who are developing large operations systems or doing smaller tasks. Professional development tools provide the rich working environment which professional pro-

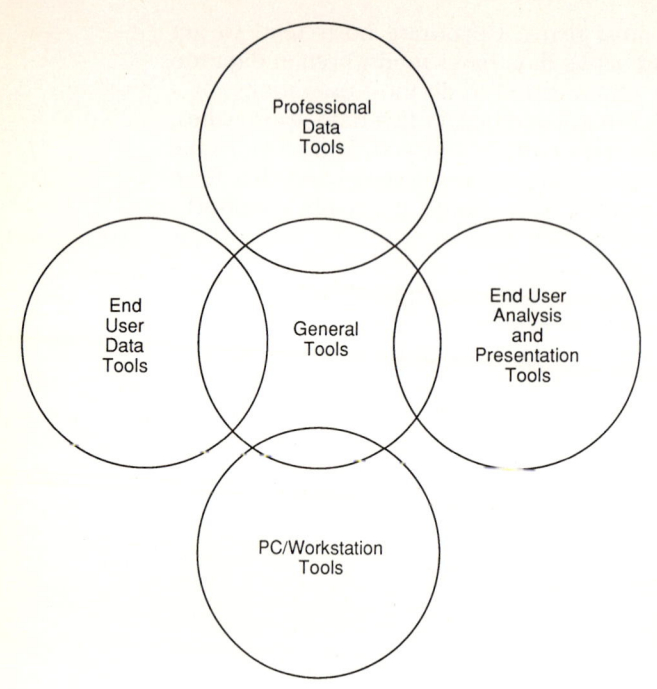

FIGURE 16-15 IDEALIZED INTEGRATED DATA/DECISION SUPPORT SYSTEM

grammers need if they are to work efficiently and effectively. Among the tools needed in this major function are the following.

- A production DBMS such as IBM's IMS or newer versions of DB2.
- An integrated data dictionary to provide a single reference point for the many people who need to understand data base schemas.
- Third-generation development tools such as COBOL that can issue calls to the DBMS.
- Fourth-generation application development tools for limited purposes, including query languages, report generators, sort programs, application generators, and fourth-generation languages.
- Perhaps stand-alone DBMSs for small jobs that would not benefit from being based on the full production DBMS.
- Links to other file structures, including ISAM, VSAM, and other common file structures on hosts and personal computers.

End User Data Tools

End user data tools are designed for end users who are working with data applications or doing retrieval aspects of decision support applications. The end user module should have similar tools to those in the professional data module, but these tools should be designed for the more limited needs of end users. There may even be separate tools for power users and for simple users among the EUC community.

When an end user does use the production DBMS, it should be possible to shield the full complexity of the product from the user, first by providing easy-to-use tools with limited functionality and vivid user interfaces, and second by limiting the user's "view" of a data base to certain files and certain information in the files. Ideally, the production DBMS should seem no more complex to an end user than an end user PC DBMS.

End User Analysis and Presentation Tools

End user analysis and presentation tools include analysis programs to work with data and analytical graphics programs to present results visually. End users need a broad spectrum of analysis tools, including general-purpose spreadsheet tools, financial analysis tools, statistical analysis tools, and operations research tools. These tools should be able to extract information from professional and end user DBMSs. They should also be able to work together on models. Ideally, there would be a single model structure with submodules to do different types of advanced analysis work.

Presentation tools should be able to create analytical graphics from any analysis tool and directly from data applications. These presentation tools should be extremely flexible.

PC/Workstation Tools

PC/workstation tools are programs that work on personal computers or more sophisticated workstations; these tools work symbiotically with host-based tools. The personal computer is rapidly becoming the normal environment for end user work. Most host data and decision support programs can already work with personal computers to some extent. As more powerful workstations become available, host tools will also have to work with these workstations.

At the simplest level, PC tools must be able to smooth the process of logging into and out of host computers, simplify general host operating system tasks, and, most importantly, allow information to be uploaded to the host and downloaded from the host simply, including file conversion between incompatible file formats.

Ideally, the PC will form a universal front end for all host data and decision support services. From a menu, the user will be able to select tools and use them equally well whether they are on the PC or on the host. The very existence of the host will be hidden from the user or at least muted in importance. All interactive work will be done on the PC, including selecting files, records, and fields in host data bases.

General Tools

General tools cut across individual modules. At the technical level, general tools should include a programming language or applications generator feature for building customized applications that span module boundaries, so that users of customized applications can do specific work without even being aware of distinctions between boundaries.

These general tools should also include links to the outside world, so that modules can issue calls to external programs outside the system and so that programs developed for third parties can access the tools within the system.

There is no way for every conceivable function to work within the system. External tools will include host tools from other vendors and PC tools such as Lotus 1-2-3 and dBASE III Plus.

Finally, there must be administrative tools to ensure security, privacy, billing, and other forms of management. Administrative tools should also allow profiles to be developed for individual users in order to reduce the apparent complexity of the overall system and to make the users' work efficient. Finally, administrative tools should be put into place to provide planning information for system expansion.

Roads to the Integrated System

No fully integrated systems such as the one shown in Figure 16-15 exist today, and it will take several years for such systems to be developed. This evolution toward a fully integrated system might take several different roads.

Multiple Integrated Systems

For the short run, the most likely scenario for integration calls for an expansion of a current trend: the support of several integrated products from different vendors. Although today's products have many of the functions discussed above, they are rarely strong in more than one area. Like the analysis package whose price structure was illustrated in Figure 16-1, there are usually one or two very strong modules as well as a number of weaker modules that are of value only for people with light needs in the other areas. As these secondary modules become more developed, however, companies may be able to replace their dozen or more host products with three or four.

Another major step forward would be cross-compatibility among these semi-integrated systems. For example, links to DB2 via SQL and other tools would be extremely valuable among analysis and graphics programs. Some of this is already beginning to happen. No vendor can afford to link its products with the dozens of competitors that are now on the market.

De facto standards could reduce this problem. For example, DBMS vendors other than IBM might offer interface software to make their products act like DB2 to other vendors. Neither DB2 nor any other data base product now dominates the market, and the same is true in other areas. Until one does, the spread of de facto standards is not likely. It would be even simpler if one integrated product family became dominant, so that others would be forced to be compatible with its basic file structures. Just as no products dominate individual areas, however, there is not even a good candidate for an integrated product standard.

At least for the foreseeable future, it will be necessary to continue supporting several different integrated products from different vendors, each with one or two strong points. In addition, it will probably continue to be necessary to build file format conversion bridges between different products in order to allow at least minimal interworking.

Full Standards

In several parts of data communications, users have been able to impose standards on vendors. In manufacturing, the MAP standards discussed in

Chapter 14 have provided a common framework for multivendor work. In office automation, CCITT/ISO and TOP standards (also discussed in Chapter 14) are beginning to bring order to chaos.

It is possible that customers or standards agencies will come together to agree on interconnection standards that will allow products from different vendors to work together. Among the standards needed will be the following.

- A relational data base description and manipulation language.
- An analytical modeling representation language.
- A graphics representation language.

Although there are obvious benefits to imposing such standards, the long time needed to develop today's multivendor standards for factory data communications and office automation suggests that it will be several years before data, modeling, and graphics standards appear and are widely implemented.

It would not even be necessary to standardize user interfaces—only calls to other programs. Individual vendors might offer integrated front ends that would present common faces to users no matter what tools were being used. As discussed in Chapter 14, standards deal with interactions among systems, not necessarily with the way users deal with individual systems.

At least for the foreseeable future, however, we will continue to be plagued by confusion and multiplicity among tools for data and decision support applications. Today, most application products are confined to individual tools, so that most users are inconvenienced only marginally. As rising user expectations create the demand for more integrated applications, the need to build a more integrated tool environment can be expected to grow rapidly.

CONCLUSION

In a few years, it may be possible to buy integrated host computing products containing financial analysis, statistical analysis, operations research analysis, graphics, data base management, and micro-mainframe links—all from a single vendor. And all of these modules will be excellent.

For the time being, however, the information center has to mix and match the products they support. Most choose a popular end user DBMS, a popular financial analysis program, a popular statistical analysis program, and a popular graphics program. They then try to build links among them through file transfer.

This technical work pales before the kind of teaching that must be done to train end users to support these powerful tools. High functionality and frequently obsolescent user interfaces make even basic tool training time consuming. Users need to know the professional statistical, financial, graphical, and data concepts that these tools draw on. Yet another problem is that these complex tools tend to be used for large and multiperson applications that must be developed rather formally. Host computing is industrial-strength end user computing.

REVIEW QUESTIONS

1. Define data applications and decision support applications. What distinguishes them?
2. What are the advantages and disadvantages of host data and decision support tools, compared to PC products in the same area? Specifically, why are host products difficult to use?
3. Summarize pricing and management differences between host and PC data and decision support tools.
4. What are the three distinguishing features of financial analysis programs, compared to general analysis programs such as spreadsheet programs? Why is each an advantage? A disadvantage?
5. What are the three most common pitfalls in financial analysis?
6. Is IFPS batch-oriented or interactive? How is IFPS's interrogation capability superior to that of Lotus 1-2-3?
7. Summarize the main statistical errors that are likely to be made by end users who are not familiar with statistical theory. Summarize the main points of good practice in statistical analysis.
8. Why may CUECHART be a model for good tool design in many areas of end user computing?
9. Summarize the most common mistakes likely to be made by end users who do not have a good understanding of graphics design.
10. What is the difference between production DBMSs and stand-alone DBMSs? Why is it not a good idea to refer to stand-alone DBMSs as "end user" DBMSs?
11. Why is SQL important? What are its limitations? When are its nonquery operations likely to be used?
12. Why do you think FOCUS was designed to work with so many different kinds of file structures? Do you think users would have more problems defining or querying FOCUS data bases? What are the advantages of combining query and report writing features into a single function (TABLE)? The disadvantages?
13. Describe the training, support, and control problems in each of these areas: financial analysis, statistical analysis, query languages, and stand-alone DBMSs.
14. What are the main functions of the idealized Integrated Data and Decision Support System discussed at the end of this chapter. Discuss how such a system might evolve.

REFERENCES

1. GROUT, BILL, "The Elements of Graphic Design," *Macworld,* February 1985, pp. 122–129.
2. MEILACH, DONA Z., "The Do's and Don'ts of Presentation Graphics," *PC Week,* August 6, 1985, pp. 47–50.
3. SPRAGUE, RALPH H., "A Framework for the Development of Decision Support Systems," *MIS Quarterly,* December 1980, pp. 1–26.
4. TUFTE, EDWARD R., "The Visual Display of Quantitative Information, Graphics Press, 1983.
5. VERITY, JOHN W., "Graphically Speaking with Dr. Edward R. Tufte," *DATAMATION,* April 1, 1985, pp. 88–92.

NONCLERICAL OFFICE AUTOMATION 17

Many corporations are merging their information centers and office automation departments; some have already completed the merger. Even where a full merger is not being considered, perceptive information systems managers are coordinating the activities of these two units very carefully because their products and services often serve the same individuals, especially managers and professionals.

In this chapter, we will focus on the major tools of nonclerical office automation (OA), including electronic mail, teleconferencing, and integrated office systems. We will, however, look briefly at office automation in Type I departments, such as word processing centers and records management centers. Information center staff members must understand at least the basic products and management issues of clerical office automation.

INTRODUCTION

The Two Worlds of Office Automation

Since its beginning in the 1960s, office automation has had two concerns.

- The support of Type I (clerical) departments, such as word processing centers, records management centers, central duplication groups, and mailrooms.
- The support of Type II (managerial and professional) departments, including electronic mail, integrated office systems, and many other products.

Of these two concerns, office automation in Type I departments was the first to bear fruit because needs in Type I departments could be supported with more primitive technology. Typing pools began to turn into word processing centers in the 1960s, and this process was virtually complete by the end of the 1970s. Records management centers, duplication departments, and mailrooms also saw revolutionary changes in technology, including microfilm, microfiche, computer-aided retrieval, high-volume copiers, and mailroom management systems.

Office automation in Type II departments had some impressive early demonstrations. For example, in 1967 Stanford Research Institute had a mouse-driven workstation with idea outlining, electronic messaging, and integrated text and graphics. In the mid-1970s, the Xerox Palo Alto Research Center introduced the iconic user interface made popular a decade later by the Macintosh.

The costs of these advanced systems for Type II departments were so high that they remained in the laboratory. Instead, OA first came into Type II departments in the form of individual products: copiers, electronic typewriters, answering machines, dictation machines, and low-speed facsimile devices. These and other modest changes became widespread during the early 1970s.

During the late 1970s, the success of these early devices and the falling costs of computers caused many vendors and analysts to envision an "office of the future," whose centerpiece would be the **integrated office system (IOS)**. The IOS would give each user a work station linked to other workstations and to host computers. In a single integrated package, the IOS would provide word processing, electronic mail, personal calendar management, group meeting scheduling, and other communication and activity management aids.

In 1979 and 1980, most computer and word processing vendors introduced IOS products, but early IOSs were too expensive and limited to attract widespread use. This did not bother IOS vendors, who envisioned their products spreading through corporations over a period of several years, as prices fell and as services expanded. This sense of security was destroyed by the personal computer explosion of the early 1980s. PCs did not offer all of the features of IOSs—especially the integration of functional modules and the integration of workstations with one another and with central computers. However, PCs did offer low entry costs, vivid user interfaces, and a rich software base. For several years, few corporations adopted integrated office systems on a large scale.

During this hiatus, several nonintegrated products from OA vendors did become successful. The first was electronic mail in all of its forms, including facsimile and electronic message systems. Although commercial electronic mail vendors, who switch mail among corporations, have had only limited success, internal corporate systems are beginning to thrive. In addition, teleconferencing is again receiving widespread attention, and there is hope that such factors as the falling costs of video teleconferencing will make teleconferencing more successful than it was in its earlier periods of high publicity during the 1960s and 1970s.

Today, even the integrated office system is beginning to make progress. Older IOSs have been extended to include personal computers as workstations, although they still tend to subordinate PCs and to work only with a few PC application programs. More importantly, vendors are beginning to design second-generation integrated office systems, that will work even more fully with PCs, comply with international standards, and therefore work with IOSs from other vendors. Such systems will go beyond communication and activity management products to provide a broad spectrum of end user computing services. We will end this book with a discussion of second-generation integrated office systems because these systems, if they fulfill their promise, will finally transform end user computing from the collection of separate products it is today into a single integrated service for users. Although this long-term vision will not be realized until the mid-1990s, it is an image that should mold our future thinking about the technostructure of end user computing.

Integrating the Management of OA and EUC

As noted at the start of this chapter, many organizations are merging their office automation departments and information centers. In quite a few firms, this merger has already taken place, and in many others, it is imminent.

In some cases, this merger is a marriage of convenience, based on the thin premise that neither OA nor EUC is classic data processing and so must have something in common. In these cases, the two departments remain basically separate but report to the same manager. Their internal operations are barely effected, and in many cases, they are not even located together.

In other cases, this merging is based on the strategic realization that Type II office needs cut freely across the product boundaries that vendors have long erected between office automation, decision support systems, perssonal computing, and other tools. Even if a firm wanted to separate OA from end user computing's classically defined service mix, this artificial separation would be doomed to failure.

Although combining OA with the information center probably is good strategically, it does raise three significant problems. First, and most importantly, information centers have traditionally focused on Type II office support, but OA is also concerned with word processing centers, mailrooms, and other Type I office departments. Unless the information center's management is astute and flexible, these Type I departments are likely to suffer from lack of concern or from a lack of the particular management skills that have been developed for each of these offices. It would probably be best if Type I OA operations were not put under the information center, leaving only Type II support—nonclerical office automation—under the information center.

The second problem is that OA needs to have a very large technical infrastructure in order to support electronic mail, integrated office systems, and other advanced applications. If this technical infrastructure can be built by adding software to existing host computers, then the problems of management will be similar to those found in host computing. If new hosts and networking systems must be built, however, a set of technical problems not found in all traditional information centers will have to be managed.

The third problem is that few information center specialists are familiar with communication products such as electronic mail or voice communication. OA began in the early 1970s, long before EUC, so its products tend to be much more mature than EUC products. This is particularly true in word processing, electronic mail, voice messaging, and teleconferencing. Because these products are mature and techniques to manage them have reached a high state of sophistication, a good deal of OA-specific knowledge is needed to make adequate purchase decisions and to establish management structures. Since relatively few EUC specialists have such knowledge, there is a danger that the information center staff will not be able to evaluate products as well as they should or will not be knowledgeable about their ongoing management. Many OA decisions are concerned with fundamental infrastructure matters that will have impact over many years. Consequently, this lack of experience with OA products could produce some long-term dangers.

Despite these problems, it seems likely that OA and EUC will be merged some time in the future. For convenience, we will assume that the "information center" title will be retained for this joint support team.

WORD PROCESSING CENTERS AND OTHER TYPE I DEPARTMENTS

As discussed earlier, putting the word processing center and other Type I OA departments under the information center may be an error because most information center staff members have little skill in the management of Type I operations. Because many information centers do manage Type I OA operations, however, we need to survey the management issues they raise.

Services in Word Processing Centers

Although the PC has brought word processing into most Type II departments, valuable services can still be provided through a word processing center. In most firms, the two most important services are central dictation and the handling of complex jobs. Some word processing centers also support desktop publishing (see Chapter 11) and other services.

Central Dictation

In centralized dictation, a manager or professional dials a number, dictates a letter, and then hangs up. In many systems, users control the dictation process by hitting keys on the telephone. By hitting keys, a user can review a letter just dictated, add an annotation for correction, re-record the letter, add special typing instructions, and do many other tasks.

After the dictation is completed, it is queued in a tape recorder, which often has several channels. The letter is then typed and returned to the user for signature or changes, typically within two or three hours.

Because it is faster to dictate than to write a draft long hand, a principal who has a number of letters to send can save as much as a half hour a day. Although the typist could work slightly faster from handwritten drafts, the time saved by managers and professionals is far more expensive.

Unfortunately, few managers and professionals are willing to dictate. Apart from a few professions such as medicine, where dictation is part of the basic educational process, it is difficult to get people to dictate. Unless the ordinary secretarial service is terrible, only 20 percent to 30 percent of all managers and professionals will dictate.

The relatively few firms that have successfully promoted dictation have provided strong incentives. First, they supply training programs to teach people how to dictate. Dictation is not a natural process for most people, and training helps users over their initial awkwardness and dislike of the process. Second, they provide user control of the dictation process through telephone keystroke commands, as noted earlier. Third, and most importantly, they provide excellent service, returning letters within two or three hours and training their word processing operators in the technical jargon of individual departments.

Complex Jobs

For complex production tasks, few Type II departments have either the equipment or the personnel to do the work efficiently and effectively, and the word processing center becomes a valuable way to do occasional complex jobs without disrupting the Type II department.

Form Letters For general form letters that are merged with personal information, the word processing center can maintain a list of personal information in a central file, do a mail merge operation to produce hundreds of letter images, and then print the output on a high-speed laser printer with a duty cycle that lets it run all day.

Contracts For legal contracts, the word processing center can assemble documents from standardized paragraphs.

Manuals The word processing center can handle the updating of large manuals. The center has the technical resources to do frequent large updates and to print rapidly. It also has the equipment to store versions of the document for later recovery in case questions appear.

Filing For projects with many documents, the word processing center can form a centralized locus for filing and later retrieval. In such cases, the word processing center alone may have the technical skills needed to master large document management systems such as IBM's Distributed Office Support System, DISOSS (discussed later). Project typing is especially attractive if the work originates from many departments. For multidepartment projects, the word processing center may be the only feasible way to support document management discipline.

Managing a Word Processing Center

Work Flow Management

Because word processing centers are production environments, they are usually run like paperwork assembly lines. Physically, they are laid out for good work flow. There is one central in-box near the entrance. From there, work flows smoothly to one or more operators. Each operator has a direct walking path to both the printer and to storage areas where paper documents and magnetic media are stored. Each workstation has ample room to lay out papers, and there is ample storage space to prevent crowding.

Great care is taken in the management of individual jobs. As each job comes in, it is given a buck slip with such essential information as who submitted it, what is to be done with it, what priority and time constraints it has, and whether it is to be stored as part of some project's or department's logical hierarchy in the center's online storage system. At the door, each buck slip is checked before it is accepted or, if the work arrives via interoffice mail, problems are clarified by phone before the work begins.

Each job is given a job number after acceptance and tracked throughout its stay. When it is assigned to a responsible operator, this is noted. Also noted are its finishing and delivery, as well as the physical location of its paper and magnetic media. Typing, proofing, and printing are kept as separate phases in this process. Users can check on the status of a job at any time, and when a job comes back for revisions, its history can be checked easily.

Training

Operators are given extensive training, because word processing center software and hardware fall under the heading of "heavy equipment" and can only be mastered with a week or two of training spread out over several months. Even more training is needed when the word processing center engages in additional work such as desktop publishing.

Automation

Another element in the management of word processing centers is the automation of as many processes as possible. Form letters should be set up for repeat use, and standard format shells for different kinds of documents should be set up and cataloged for fast access. In addition, most word processing systems have embedded programming languages (the best known is Wang's Glossary service), and as many operations as possible from setting up printing parameters to doing actual mail merge operations should be automated.

Integration with Corporate-Wide OA Systems

If an organization has an electronic mail system in place, the final delivery of much work may take place electronically, thus cutting delivery times. On the other hand, if a secretary has a merge document and a mailing list, he or she may ship it electronically to the word processing center for printing on high-speed printers.

If the word processing center is the main operator of the document management system, such as DISOSS, nonsensitive retrievals may still be made by people in other offices. Complex storage actions may be handled by sending the document to the word processing center, which then does the actual filing. As such links grow between the word processing center and activities in Type II offices, the role of the word processing center may become much larger than it is today.

Managing a Service

The last and most critical element in the management of the word processing center is managing the center as a *service business*. The center must process a high volume of complex transactions, do it rapidly and smoothly, and present a friendly, positive face to users. The word processing manager needs to be people-oriented and performance-oriented—in other words, a manager. The same is true of all other Type I operations.

Managing a service operation involves excellence in staffing, morale-building, handling personnel problems, establishing clear performance goals, measuring these goals, and contacting clients to obtain early warning of problems. It also involves working closely with personnel (human resources) on such issues as job design and the assignment of salary grades.

If the information center does get responsibility for Type I operations, it is important to put a service-oriented *and well-trained* person in charge of these units. Although the IS department has some experience in managing service operations, for example, data entry groups, word processing centers and other Type I OA operations increase the service business dramatically, bring new realms of complexity and diversity, and simply require a higher degree of competence. Giving the data entry supervisor control over these operations could be a major mistake.

One alternative is to leave the word processing center and other Type I operations under a functional manager but to have the information center specify technology. This will provide for consistency in Type I and Type II departments, but the drive for consistency can be devastating if it results in a feeling of powerlessness among clerical workers and their supervisors. Word processing center employees may feel that the information center's desire for consistency is extravagant to the point of giving clerical workers poor systems unsuited for their needs—either from lack of important functionality or from the selection of "state of the art technology" with operational flaws.

Other Type I Operations

Other Type I OA departments include records management centers, reproduction centers, and the mailroom. Even if they do not fall directly under the center's management, technical decisions must be at least reviewed by the information center's personnel because of growing links between Type I departmental services and Type II work.

Records Management Centers

Most large organizations have records management centers that store both documents and data processing output. Sometimes records are placed in storage for legal reasons and at other times because the output may need to be retrieved later in the course of projects.

The first key discipline in records management is **indexing**—developing a hierarchical or other kind of structure to describe an organization's stored documents. This is a difficult skill, and library scientists continue to work to develop better indexing approaches. Because the records management center has long been concerned with storage discipline, it may become the organization's manager of electronic document management systems as well as the manager of paper archives.

The second key discipline is **retention.** No document can be stored forever because space is expensive, and because when the number of items stored is doubled, the search time to retrieve a single item is tripled or quadrupled. A good retention policy is critical to maintaining control over stored information. Each class of documents will have some standard retention time, which may be overridden for individual documents. **Active** items are stored for fairly rapid retrieval, whereas **inactive** documents are stored in archives with longer access times, and **obsolete** items are completely discarded.

The third key discipline is the protection of **vital records,** which must be kept in place so that the business may be "re-created" after a major disaster. Companies have a legal obligation to protect vital records.

Although paper is the most common storage medium, many organizations have turned to microform storage to reduce space.

- **Microfilm** is produced on rolls.
- **Microfiche** is produced on cards with many individual frames. The cards are roughly the size of paper index cards.

Computer-assisted retrieval (CAR) combines microform storage with computerized indexing and retrieval. CAR is attractive when a great deal of labor is being devoted to retrieval.

Reproduction

Most firms have large central **reproduction departments** where high-speed copiers and duplicators are kept for large chores. **Copiers** reproduce directly from an original. The small to mid-size machines found near Type II departments are copiers. The copiers in reproduction centers use similar technology, but they can produce thousands of pages per day.

In contrast, **duplicators** require the creation of an intermediate master, and copies are made from this intermediate master instead of from the original. This method is less convenient than copying, but the cost is lower for large jobs. Duplicators have long been the preferred medium to handle large jobs, but high-volume copiers are beginning to rival duplicators in cost for all but the largest jobs.

Today, many vendors produce **communicating copiers,** which can take their input electronically instead of in the form of a paper sitting on the glass platen. These devices are essentially large page printers (see Chapter 7). Tied to a network, these high-speed communicating copiers can be used by remote departments to print large documents and do mass mailings.

The reproduction department is frequently the home of the organization's **graphics services department,** which has specialized skills for forms layout and the creation of illustrations. If this department's services can be linked to the rest of the organization electronically, the benefits can be considerable.

Mailrooms

Mailrooms have their own specialized needs such as electronic scales that may even be able to suggest a least cost routing scheme. Mailrooms in organizations with high volumes of form letters and billings tend to have specialized machines that at least stuff letters in envelopes and may even be able to print output on the spot before stuffing it.

ELECTRONIC MAIL

For many organizations, electronic mail is the first major office automation service beyond word processing and the first major OA service other than PC word processing to affect Type II departments.

The telecommunication department has long had clerical electronic mail service, in the form of facsimile rooms and Telex rooms, but new electronic mail services are used directly by managers and professionals and by secretaries in Type II departments. In addition, new standards are bringing electronic mail squarely into the world of data communications.

Internal and External Mail

Until recently, most electronic mail was handled by common carriers such as the Western Union Telegraph Company. Now, however, laws allow any company to offer electronic messaging and other advanced services without formally becoming a common carrier. As a result, organizations ranging from The Source to MCI have begun to offer electronic mail services.

Large companies can build their own internal electronic mail systems. Internal electronic mail is ideally suited for the 2 percent of all organizations that handle 78 percent of all intracompany mail in the United States. (6) Most of these companies are large and geographically dispersed. For basic worldwide services such as Telex, common carriers will always be dominant, but for advanced services such as document transfer and electronic messaging, large growth is expected to come first within companies. External vendors will primarily provide supplementary services, including switching messages between companies and focusing on niche markets, such as smaller firms or special interest groups with strong identities that cut across organizational boundaries.

Public Record Services

Services offered by regulated common carriers have traditionally been divided into two parts. Voice services, including the telephone, form the better known part of public telecommunications. The other part consists of **public record services,** which leave a permanent printed record of the transaction. Public record services are text services.

Telegraph

The first public record service was the telegraph, which Morse demonstrated in 1844. Almost immediately, the telegraph became used heavily. The Civil War and later the expansion of the nation's first large corporations further spurred the growth of the telegraph. The use of the telegraph peaked before World War II. Since then, it has been in steady decline.

TWX and Telex

Although the decline of telegraphy was due in large part to long distance telephone service, another factor was the emergence of competing text services, namely, teletypewriter networks, which put teletypewriter terminals right in the user corporation's offices instead of requiring users to walk down to a central telegraph office or call that office by phone.

Although teletypewriter terminals were introduced in the early 1900s, they were only used within telegraph companies for several years. AT&T introduced the first national public network in 1931. This was TWX, the Teletypewriter Exchange Service. After World War II, European telephone companies created the similar **Telex** service. Telex was selected as the international standard by the CCITT (see Chapter 14), and today TWX is a very small service limited primarily to the United States and Canada.

Because Telex emerged so many years ago, its technology is extremely crude:

- It uses the 5-bit Baudot code. This code has two shift codes, which move users to and from an extended set of characters. Even so, Telex cannot even handle lower case letters.
- It is extremely slow, plodding along at 50 bits per second. To send a typical page of 1500 characters requires almost three minutes.
- It is circuit-switched (see Chapter 14). Thus, if the receiving machine is busy sending, receiving, or even preparing an outgoing message, the sender gets a busy signal and has to call again later.

Despite these limitations, Telex flourished because it became the standard way to move information quickly over long distance and with minimum bother. It grew especially in international communications, where language barriers place a premium on written messages that can be studied at length. The "hot line" between the United States and Moscow is a text system.

In the United States, there is a basic distinction between **domestic record carriers** that operate within the United States and the **international record carriers** that operate internationally. This dividing line was once very strict, but today the Federal Communications Commission allows companies to operate in both arenas. For domestic Telex today, there are many vendors, and some offer such advanced features as store-and-forward communications. There are still few international record carriers, because foreign countries control the number of firms with whom they will work.

After World War II, Western Union absorbed the last of its major competitors and got a de facto monopoly over telegraphy. One condition imposed on the merger by the government was the separation of its domestic and international operations. The domestic operations became the Western Union Telegraph Company (WUTCO), and the international operations became Western Union International. The two now compete in the same markets, and when people say "Western Union," it is not clear which company they are discussing.

Most Telex users send only one or two messages a day. As a result, most users still employ cheap Telex terminals with no CRT and punch paper tape storage. However, both word processors and PCs can act as Telex terminals, linking directly to a Telex line or, in some services, dialing in. Heavier users normally use word processors attached to the Telex network.

Teletex

By the mid-1970s, the need for a faster and better text communication system was apparent to everyone. This led the CCITT to produce the advanced **Teletex** standard in 1980. The idea was to build Teletex and Telex as parallel services with interconnection—with Telex eventually disappearing as Teletex became more popular.

On the surface, the Teletex standard looks like just the right service: it communicates at 2400 bps (50 times faster than Telex); it uses an extended

ASCII character set that gives it international characters; it is built within the OSI standards architecture (see Chapter 14); it has advanced handshaking so that two terminals can set up and manage sessions efficiently; and its terminals can send and receive even while preparing an outgoing message. The standard Teletex terminal even has word processing functions. (In fact, Teletex has been offered primarily as a module on communicating word processors.)

Teletex also has two critical flaws. First, the basic Teletex standard is still circuit-switched, so that messages cannot be stored for later delivery if a terminal is offline or already engaging in transmission. Second, and more importantly, Teletex terminals are *required* to be online nearly 100 percent of the time, day and night. This eliminates PCs and most word processors. As a result, although Teletex has made some gains, it is not likely to be the wave of the future.

Other Record Services

Although telegraph, Telex, and Teletex are the main public record services, others do exist, most notably the Mailgram service created in 1971 by the U.S. Postal Service and the Western Union Telegraph Company. In Mailgram, messages are sent electronically to a post office near the receiver. At the post office, the letter is printed and then delivered as an ordinary letter. Money orders and other services also fall under the record category.

A number of large firms have **internal teletypewriter networks** that use Telex-like technology but usually add performance improvements. Typically, these private teletypewriter networks are installed to reduce costs when Telex use becomes high. To keep as many customers as possible, Western Union Telegraph Company offers a "shared public service," InfoCom, that gives each company internal service but shares system costs over many users.

Facsimile

Telex and Teletex send messages character by character, and as a result, they can only send text messages. Although this limits the kinds of documents they can send, it makes transmission efficient. An average typed page has about 1500 characters. At 10 bits per character, there are about 15,000 bits per page. Even at a leisurely 1200 bps, only 12 seconds are needed to send a page.

In contrast, **facsimile** scans an outgoing page like a television camera and converts this scanned image into an electrical transmission. It prints a copy of the original page at the other location. Because scanning can transmit any message, including forms, logos, figures, and signatures, facsimile is very efficient.

Scanning requires a great deal of information to be transmitted. Even a low-resolution fax machine will have 100 pixels (dots) per inch horizontally and 100 pixels per inch (ppi) vertically, for 10 Kpixels per square inch. An 8-1/2 by 11 or European A1 page has about 100 square inches; therefore, in facsimile, around 1 Mpixels must be sent per page. At one bit per pixel, this comes to a megabit—70 times the amount of data needed to transmit a page of text in character form. As a result, facsimile usually takes far longer to transmit a page than a modern character-based system such as Teletex, although data compression schemes in the newest facsimile standards have drastically reduced this disadvantage.

Group 1 Facsimile

General use facsimile began in 1966, when Magnavox and Xerox introduced the Telecopier and openly published their technical standards to encourage more vendors to build to their standard. Many vendors did follow suit, and this machine became the main basis for the Group 1 facsimile standard ratified later by the CCITT. The standard was laid down long after the fact, however, so that compliance with the standard was rather uneven.

Group 1 machines can transmit a page of information in six minutes, giving a resolution of 96 pixels per inch horizontally and vertically. This is extremely marginal resolution—only a third or a fourth of the resolution needed for true letter quality. Even cheap dot matrix printers can print around 150 pixels per inch horizontally and vertically.

Group 2 Facsimile

In 1976, the CCITT introduced its Group 2 standard. Although Group 2 machines have the same resolution as Group 1 machines, they transmit a page in only half the time, thus slashing transmission costs. Group 2 machines have pushed Group 1 machines off the market, but Group 2 machines also have the circuitry needed to talk to the large installed base of Group 1 machines.

Group 2 machines are often equipped with optional features outside the basic standard, including automatic operation for nighttime transmission and **vertical white space skipping.** Vertical blank spaces such as top and bottom margins and spaces between paragraphs are skipped automatically, thus slashing transmission time by 50 percent or more. Because of proprietary features, most firms standardize on a single Group 2 facsimile vendor.

Group 3 Facsimile

In 1980, the CCITT produced its Group 3 facsimile standard, bringing fax squarely into the world of data communications. Group 3 machines have resolutions of 200 pixels per inch (ppi) horizontally and 100 ppi vertically, with an option for 200 ppi vertically. Yet as a result of data compression techniques, they take less than a minute to transmit a typical page. Group 3 machines are completely digital, allowing for crisp, error-free transmission. It also allows the two devices to negotiate optional features to be used in a session without operator intervention. Just as Group 2 machines drove Group 1 machines off the market, Group 3 machines dominate the facsimile market today. Nearly all of these machines can talk with their slower Group 1 and Group 2 cousins.

Group 4 Facsimile

In 1984, the CCITT introduced its Group 4 standard. In contrast to earlier standards, Group 4 was not designed to be used over telephone lines. It was created specifically for high-speed digital data communications networks. A version for traditional analog telephone communications may be forthcoming in the future, but for now, Group 4 is not for most office environments.

Like many modern standards, Group 4 lets vendors and customers have many options. At the start of each transmission, the two machines trade information about what options each has and then jointly negotiate the options to be used in a particular session.

To reduce the need for negotiation, the CCITT defined classes of machines with different clusters of basic capabilities. Specifically, the CCITT defined three major classes.

- Class 1 machines are pure facsimile machines. They can send and receive Group 4 facsimile pages at resolutions of 200 ppi horizontally and vertically, with optional resolutions of 240, 300, and 400 ppi.
- Class 2 machines can send and receive Group 4 facsimile pages at resolutions of 200 and 300 ppi, with options of 240 and 400 ppi; these machines can also receive—but not send—both Teletex and T.73 mixed mode signals (discussed later). As sending machines, they are therefore limited to facsimile, but they can receive non-fax signals.
- At the high end, Class 3 machines have all of the abilities of Class 2 machines, as well as the ability to send (as well as receive) Teletex and T.73 mixed mode documents. They are true facsimile-Teletex hybrids.

Electronic Message Systems

Electronic message systems (EMSs) are store-and-forward systems that allow managers and professionals to do their own messaging via desktop terminals or personal computers. The sender composes a message, using either a word processor or the EMS's internal editor. The user then gives the name of the recipient or a series of names for multiparty distribution, and the system delivers the message in a few minutes or at most a few hours.

Incoming messages are delivered to the receiver's electronic in-box instead of to his or her terminal. Users can read messages whenever they choose, and messages can be delivered to the host computer in-box if the receiver is busy or even if the receiver's terminal or PC attached to the host is turned off.

The receiver has a broad spectrum of tools for reading, filing, forwarding, and replying to messages. This richness in noncreation services is important because message reading, filing, and disposal commands are used much more than message composing and sending commands. (11) EMSs are used far more for reading mail and for searching through old mail than they are for composition and transmission. Because this ability to dig through the in-box with Boolean searches is very important, it should be a major selection criterion when picking an EMS.

Costs

Apart from the cost of the terminal, which we will look at separately, electronic messages are cheap. (11) Commercial services such as MCI Mail cost only $0.50 to $2.00 per brief message. In 1986, the national average was $0.70 per message. (2) Internal corporate systems are even cheaper, costing only $0.20 to $0.40 per message. In other words, EMS is not much more expensive than postal delivery, and it will soon be cheaper.

These costs exclude the cost of a terminal, however. If the user purchases a terminal devoted exclusively to messaging, the cost per message is bound to be high on a permessage basis. Suppose a terminal costs $500 and is used for three years. A typical user sends 200 messages a year. (This is the long-standing average, and it has recently been reverified. (2)) The cost per message sent, for the terminal alone, will be $0.83, but if a terminal or communicating PC is already available, there is no additional cost. The cost is even reasonable if the user already has a noncommunicating PC and only needs to add a serial board, modem, and communications program. Because PCs can be used for many purposes, the cost of PC terminals is difficult to assess.

Because the average message is sent to three addresses in most systems, the cost per message received is one-third the cost per message sent. It is important to determine the cost per message received when comparisons are made with postal delivery.

User Reactions

Reactions to EMS tend to be extremely positive. The following comments are typical. (9)

> I used to get six inches of paper in my in-box every day. Now I get less than half an inch, and the things that come in by computer are easier to handle. I have a lot more time to spend with my managers, a lot more time to do my real job. (Bob Schiewe, VP, Continental Bank)
>
> It gives us *a real competitive advantage*. I have people in Europe and the Far East, and I can communicate with them as easily as I can with people here in Chicago. (Bob Champion, VP, Continental Bank).

In a survey of EMS users in a large geographically decentralized Army organization, nearly all users expressed positive comments about the system, and most ratings were strongly positive. Even managers who delegated the actual use of the system to their secretaries liked the system. (11)

EMS Failures

Despite favorable costs and strong positive user reactions to well-implemented systems, many electronic mail systems continue to fail. The sad thing is that the causes of these failures have been understood since the 1970s, and these problems have simple cures.

The biggest problem is **lax pickup,** that is, people not picking up their mail regularly or at all. An internal Wang study of voice messaging found that people only picked up their mail twice a week on the average. (7) Tucker documented lax pickup as the main source of one large failure. (13) Once lax pickup becomes an obvious problem, people stop using the system for fear that their message will not get through. In the case that Tucker documented, the system's use had stopped almost completely within a few weeks.

Another problem is secretarial overload. Many users have their secretaries handle the terminal work. In many organizations, the majority of all users delegate the use of the system, but most EMSs assume that people will handle their own mail and provide no easy way for secretaries to handle their delegators' mail efficiently. Secretaries often have to log into and out of a long series of EMS accounts—a process that is extremely time consuming and frustrating. In the survey of the Army organization mentioned earlier, almost all managers and professionals liked the system whether they worked directly with the EMS or delegated use. However, many secretaries complained about the system. (11)

A number of obvious measures can be taken to lessen these problems. First, make sure that the initial group has a high need to communicate, so that their traffic will be large enough for them to check their mail every day. (It is rarely best to start out with chief executives.) Second, make sure there are many terminals because people will not walk far to get to a terminal.

Third, establish a **universal service system;** build a comprehensive list of everyone in the organization; and then, give each person one of three levels of service—hands-on, departmental, or mailroom. Hands-on service provides messaging via the user's terminal. Departmental service requires that the department secretary handle the user's mail. Finally, mailroom service prints messages in the mailroom, which are then routed via interoffice mail. With this approach, everyone will be on the system from the very beginning, so that messages will be typed only once. In addition, mailroom receivers will get messages later, giving them the incentive to upgrade their service level.

Fourth provide a **bouncing** capability that automatically bounces messages that are not picked up promptly, say, within 24 hours, to the next lowest level. Therefore, even if a manager or professional with hands-on service is lax about pickup or is on vacation, the message will still get through, via his or her responsible secretary. If the secretary is lax, the messages still gets out, via the mailroom. This bouncing is the real key to success because it eliminates the lax pickup problem.

Fifth, when picking a system, give special attention to the needs of the responsible secretary. A secretary should be able to log-in just once to handle all accounts. This is not difficult to do technically, and this capability should be a major purchase consideration. The bottom line is that EMS systems need to be designed with organizational realities in mind instead of some simplistic stereotype of users as having terminals on their desks and logging into the system several times a day.

EMS Products

As noted in Chapter 12, a number of commercial online services offer EMS, including such firms as MCI, which specialize in EMS, and others, such as CompuServe, which offer it as one of many services. Firms that specialize usually offer better EMS service with less obvious but valuable add-ons. Firms that take the supermarket approach make it easy for users to use other online services after mastering comparatively simple EMS services.

Impacts of EMS

Although many claims have been made about the impact of EMS, most users send only one message per day and receive three. (2,11) As a result, it would be surprising if EMS had a massive impact on organizations. Indeed, surveys have shown that EMS is valuable but not revolutionary (see, for example, Reference 11).

Somewhat surprisingly, a number of studies have shown that EMS seems to substitute more for telephone communications than for letters. (1,2,11,12) The reason is probably **"telephone tag."** The odds of getting someone on the first call are about one in five. As a result, people call one another back and forth, driving up costs and lengthening the time needed to get through. With EMS, the norm is next day delivery, and this is fine for many informal messages.

Organizational Problems

In addition to lax pickup and the problems faced by the delegation of use to secretaries, firms that have adapted EMS tend to report two other significant organizational problems.

The first is the large amount of time that must be spent maintaining a list of people authorized to use the system. Personnel files can be used to keep track of people in the organization, but most EMSs are also used by people outside the organization, including suppliers, customers, and consultants. A significant amount of staff time is needed to keep track of both internal and external users.

The other problem is **flaming** which consists of three tendencies. The first is a tendency on the part of some people to send many long messages to other people on the system. These long and frequent messages tend to clog the in-boxes of other users and are strongly resented by the receivers. The second is a tendency to "shoot from the hip" when answering a question, often saying things that would not be said on a more leisurely medium such as a letter. The third is saying things in innocence that are misread by others. (Humor often fails to come through as such.)

Flaming is basically a problem in etiquette and communication experience. It tends to go away as people become experienced in using the system. However, many new systems, it is a serious problem, and etiquette and misinterpretation dangers should be discussed as part of the user training process.

Computer Conferencing

Computer conferencing is similar to electronic message systems, but it is also sufficiently different to merit a short discussion of its own. In **computer conferencing** systems, messages on a particular topic are sent to a central "bulletin board" instead of to individuals. Each topic has its own bulletin-board "conference." From time to time, each group member scans through the messages on the board and reads messages of personal interest.

Computer conferencing systems are very popular where there is a loose interest group of people who are concerned with a particular topic. Conferencing systems, often called **bulletin board** systems in the PC world, have proven very popular, especially in rapidly changing areas such as PC hardware and software. They allow many people in different organizations and in different parts of the world to exchange information in a wide-open manner.

Computer conferencing has not caught on widely in business, partly because conferences are almost impossible to control. It is nearly impossible to impose even the slightest discipline on users. Second, although these systems have proven highly beneficial for information exchange, they have not been effective in creating consensus. If a firm business decision needs to be made, a computer conference is not the tool to use.

Conferencing can also be done using the corporate EMS designed for person-to-person communication. Nearly all EMSs allow messages to be "broadcast" to mailing lists, so that groups can create conferences simply by creating mailing lists. Conferencing, however, is done via an EMS; some users do not want their mailboxes flooded by conference traffic. These users do not put their names on the mailing list for the conference. Instead, they periodically look through a dummy mailbox created in the name of the conference. This dummy mailbox will be on the mailing list and so will receive copies of all messages.

In both EMSs and conferencing systems, traffic appears to be very similar. Messages sent to only one or two people (conferencing systems offer "private" messaging as a subservice) will dominate the number of messages *sent*. Broadcast messages, while fewer in number, go to many more people, however, so they usually dominate in terms of the number of messages *received*.

Voice Messaging

Other than teleconferencing, which is discussed at the end of this chapter, voice messaging is the only nontext service to achieve significant support from OA specialists and user organizations. It has become a mainstay of OA service in many organizations and should grow even more popular in the future.

As the costs of digitizing and storing voice fell in the late 1970s, many organizations began to offer **voice messaging** in which the user sends a voice message instead of a text message. In contrast to traditional answering machines, voice message systems give the sender extensive control over message creation and sending.

- Messages can be reviewed and re-recorded if desired before being sent.
- There is no time pressure to begin a message, and the person can pause at any time without this pause being recorded.
- Messages can be sent to a distribution list ("Is Thursday a good time for the meeting?")
- Message delivery can be delayed to act as a reminder.

The receiver also has more control over reception, including the ability to skip over a message and return to it later. This degree of control in both reception and creation makes voice messaging attractive even to people who dislike answering systems.

Voice messaging is extremely cheap, its capital investment being only $200 to $400 per worker. This is far less than the cost of electronic mail systems, and as a result, many organizations see voice messaging as a good first step toward more sophisticated services.

Voice messaging suffers from the lax pickup problem. If there is no "message waiting" light on the telephone, lax pickup and nonpickup become epidemic. Even where waiting lights are present, pickup can still be a problem. The lack of a message waiting light is the greatest single cause of failure in voice messaging.

STANDARDS FOR TEXT COMMUNICATION

Both word processing and electronic message systems have long been plagued by a lack of good standards for interconnecting systems from different vendors. This situation is changing rapidly, however, and within a few years, we should have a solid body of standards for text communication.

Basic Categories of Standards

Document and Mail Delivery Standards

As shown in Figure 17-1, text communication standards cover two broad areas.

- **Document standards,** which allow word processing systems to exchange documents that are rich in formatting codes. Although ASCII can be used to exchange plain text (see Chapter 8), this is rarely sufficient for user needs because all formatting codes must be stripped out of the document sent as plain ASCII. Overall, document standards specify two things: content (text and graphics) and layout (formatting) information.
- **Mail delivery standards,** which allow two electronic mail programs to exchange messages. More specifically, these standards allow two electronic mail programs to exchange *envelopes* containing messages. It is not the business of the mail delivery standard to specify the contents of these envelopes; rather, document standards do so if the contents consist of a document. However, envelopes may also contain other kinds of files, including graphics files. Mail delivery standards are not limited to documents.

Document Standards

Figure 17-1 shows that document standards are subdivided into two major categories.

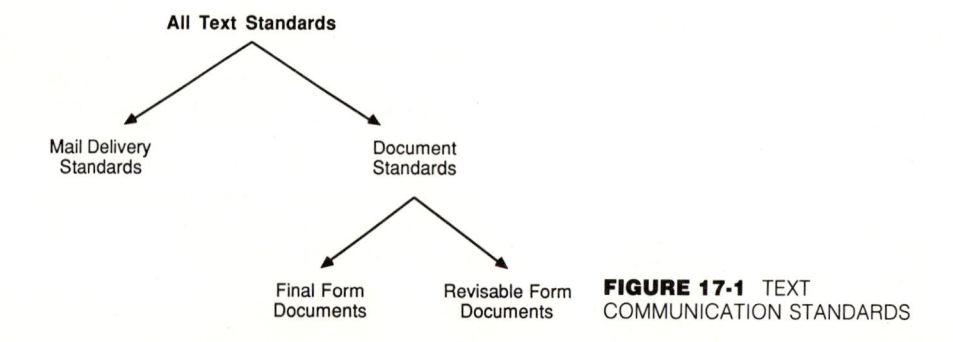

FIGURE 17-1 TEXT COMMUNICATION STANDARDS

- First, there are standards for **final form documents.** These documents are in their final form, ready for printing. Editing them further is difficult, if possible at all.
- Second, there are standards for **revisable documents.** These documents can be edited easily after delivery.

Revisable document standards are critically important because many corporations support multiple word processing programs on PCs, hosts, and dedicated word processors. With a revisable document standard, any program can exchange editable files with any other word processor that complies with the standard. Revisable document standards are basically word processing standards. Given the tremendous importance of word processing in every firm, most corporate IS managers place top priority on revisable document standards.

Final form standards are more restrictive because documents can only be printed once they are received. This restrictiveness does have one advantage: because they are page-oriented, it is easy for these standards to include sophisticated page layout functions. Final form document standards are good for printing documents created with desktop publishing programs, such as those discussed in Chapter 11, as well as for printing simple documents.

Standards-Setting Organizations

The CCITT has long been the source of electronic mail standards, including Telex, Teletex, and facsimile. In 1984, the CCITT introduced its X.400 standards for text communication. Given the CCITT's focus on communication, X.400 standards were aimed primarily at mail delivery.

Although a little attention was given to document standards, only simple final form standards were created in the initial round of standards in 1984. In electronic mail, documents are traditionally printed upon receipt and not edited further. The CCITT, being motivated primarily by a desire to improve electronic mail service, made sure that final form printing was possible.

Although the CCITT recognized the importance of revisable document standards, it left the task of creating these standards to ISO. Since 1984, ISO has been working to develop sophisticated document standards, first for final form documents and second for revisable documents. This effort has received little publicity, and there is a danger that, when ISO releases advanced standards, vendors may ignore these standards.

Another player in the standards game is IBM. In contrast to the CCITT, which was motivated primarily by a desire to improve electronic mail, IBM was motivated primarily by the desire to bring compatibility to its multiple lines of word processing programs by creating a common document standard for file exchange. Although the CCITT viewed revisable document standards as an extension to be added once good final form standards had been set, IBM viewed revisable document standards as the critical first step to take.

In the early 1980s, well before the CCITT released X.400, IBM introduced its text communication standards. Its document standard, called the **document content architecture (DCA),** was a fully revisable content standard. Its mail delivery standard was called the **document interchange architecture (DIA).** Together, they are referred to as **DIA/DCA.**

X.400 Standards

The CCITT called its X.400 standards **message-handling system (MHS)** standards. Released in 1984, X.400 was really a *series* of standards that were all in the CCITT's "X" series (for digital networks) and had numbers between X.400 and X.430.

Mail Delivery Standards

Figure 17-2 shows how X.400 views mail delivery. The model draws heavily on traditional postal delivery approaches.

- In postal delivery, the user prepares a document and then inserts it into an envelope. In the CCITT's vision, these tasks are handled by the sender's electronic mail program.

- In postal delivery, the user's envelope is sent to the corporate mailroom, which submits it to the postal service. In the CCITT's vision, the role of the corporate mailroom is handled by the sender's **user agent (UA)**. The user agent submits the message to the network, sheltering the user from all the details of the network's operations.

- In postal delivery, the postal service passes the message among its distribution systems, until it reaches the receiver's corporate mailroom. For international delivery, several national postal services may be involved. In X.400, **message transfer agents (MTAs)** are comparable to post offices and distribution centers. They pass on the message until the receiver's user agent accepts it for delivery. National electronic mail vendors, electronic mail authorities in other countries, and corporate systems can all be linked together.

- The receiver's user agent routes the message to the receiver's electronic mail system, which puts the message in the receiver's mailbox.

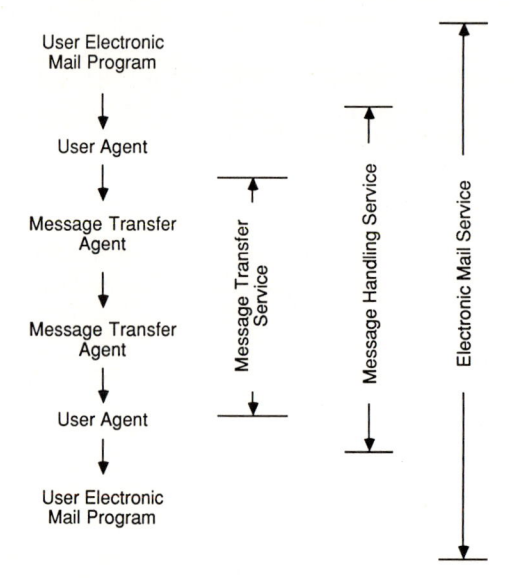

FIGURE 17-2 MAIL DELIVERY IN X.400

In CCITT terminology, a group of interconnected message transfer agents is called a **message transfer service,** as shown in Figure 17-2. When user agents are added to the picture, a group of interconnected MTAs and UAs form a **message handling service.** A group of interconnected MTAs, UAs, and electronic mail programs serving users directly is not defined in the standard, but we can plausibly call it an **electronic mail service.**

The X.400 standards specify two types of interaction.

- First, they specify MTA-MTA interactions, so that messages submitted to the systems are received properly, or at least so an inability to deliver the message will be noted to the sender.
- Second, they specify MTA-UA interactions, so that messages can be submitted to the MTA network and accepted for delivery.

The X.400 standards *do not* specify several other matters.

- First, they do not specify the workings of the sender's or receiver's electronic mail programs. Any electronic mail program that creates envelopes and document content (discussed later) in proper form is acceptable to the network. In other words, any vendor can be linked to any other that uses the same standard, even if their electronic mail systems are radically different.
- Second, they do not specify the interaction between a user's electronic mail program and the user's UA. This again is considered an "internal matter." As long as the user's electronic mail system has a proper UA or is linked to a proper UA, the standard has no interest in such items as how the message got to the proper user agent.

The Interpersonal Message System Standard

Although the mail delivery portion of the X.400 standards does not need to know anything about the content of the messages that lie within the envelopes it delivers, it makes no sense to specify envelope delivery unless the receiver can understand the sender's message. Thus, although the CCITT refused to prohibit any kinds of messages from going into X.400 envelopes, it did take the positive step of creating a simple document standard in 1984. This was the **interpersonal message system (IPMS)** standard. As the name suggests, the standard is designed for electronic message systems, which were discussed earlier in the chapter. As shown in Figure 17-3, an IPMS document has two parts: a header and a body.

The header contains a number of standard **fields,** such as the sender, the receiver (or list of receivers), and the date sent. The IPMS standards in X.400 specify a large number of mandatory and optional fields for the header. These fields are computer searchable, so that users can, for example, retrieve all messages from a certain person in the last two weeks.

The body contains the message itself. Although the IPMS is ideally suited to messaging, the CCITT left the body content format open-ended. The body can be Teletex, facsimile, or any other standardized message format. In other words, the body can consist of a long document or even a graphics file with no text at all.

NONCLERICAL OFFICE AUTOMATION

```
Header ──────▶  ┌──────────────┐
                │ Date:        │
                │ To:          │
                │ From:        │
                │ ...          │
                ├──────────────┤
                │              │
                │    Text,     │
Body   ──────▶  │  Graphics,   │
                │     or       │
                │    other     │
                │  Information │
                │              │
                └──────────────┘
```

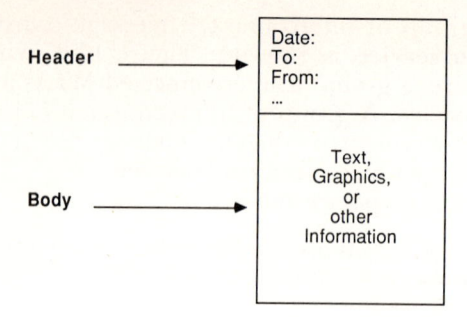

Note: An IPMS message has two parts. First, there is a header with multiple searchable fields. Second, there is a body consisting of text, graphics, or other information following an approved standard.

FIGURE 17-3 X.400 INTERPERSONAL MESSAGE SYSTEM STANDARD

When the body does not consist of text, the header fields identify its contents and label the message for later retrieval. Although envelopes may contain some of the information found in headers, the envelope is normally discarded upon receipt. Placing the information in header fields keeps it with its document.

By leaving the body format open, the CCITT made IPMS a standard useful in many contexts. By combining the ability to handle simple messaging and long documents, IPMS avoided the inconveniences that users experienced when they are handled separately, as in the case of IBM's PROFS. (Professional Office Support System). The open body format specification makes IPMS a broad-spectrum tool for specifying document content.

Although X.400 is currently too limited for file exchange among word processors, it is fine for electronic message systems. Several national telecommunications authorities have announced support for X.400, and commercial EMS vendors in the United States have already begun interconnecting via X.400 links. X.400 (including IPMS) has become the dominant standard for electronic message systems.

The Office Document Architecture Standards Effort

During the 1985–1988 study period, the CCITT has been extending both mail delivery and document portions of X.400. Although these efforts are important, the main spotlight has shifted to ISO, which has taken the lead in document standards.

The T.73 Standard

ISO's earliest efforts bore fruit in the 1984 **T.73** standards released by the CCITT. Although these were CCITT standards, ISO had a heavy role in creating them.

T.73 is not a revisable document standard, but it is a sophisticated final form document standard. As shown in Figure 17-4, T.73 specifies a complex

FIGURE 17-4 PAGE, PAGE SET, AND DOCUMENT IN T.73

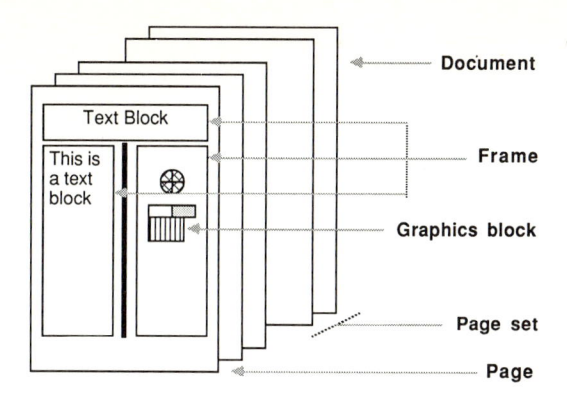

Note: A frame is a defined area on the page; a block is information within a frame--text, graphics, or other information. Frames are layout objects, while blocks are content objects.

page layout standard for final form printing. The heart of this standard is the layout of a single page.

- Each page is divided into **frames.**
- These frames can overlap, either transparently or opaquely.
- Each frame can be filled with **blocks** of text or graphics. (Frames, then, provide holding spaces for information, whereas blocks consist of the actual information on the page.
- Text was originally specified as Teletex text, whereas graphics was originally specified as Group 3 facsimile graphics. Extension will be added over time.

At higher levels, adjacent pages can be grouped into **page sets,** which have the same general format. This is also illustrated in Figure 17-4. A document consists of one or more pages, page sets, or combinations of the two. Overall, the standard specifies a sophisticated desktop publishing format.

Subsequent Office Document Architecture Standards Efforts

Since T.73 was created, ISO has been developing more sophisticated document structure standards under the general title of **office document architecture.** Little has appeared in the open literature about these efforts, but some statements can be made about them with some certainty.

First, future messages will have both specific and generic information. When the user fills out a traditional business form, both its layout and some parts of its content (titles, etc.) are generic information that is the same in all copies of the form. When the user fills out a form, however, he or she adds specific content information. The user may also add specific layout information to a document.

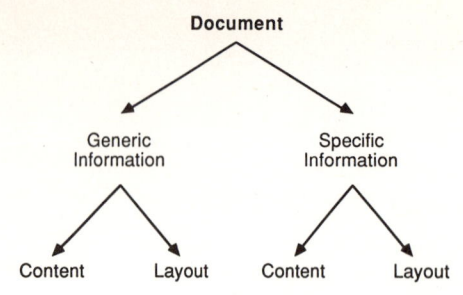

FIGURE 17-5 GENERIC AND SPECIFIC INFORMATION IN A DOCUMENT

As shown in Figure 17-5, future document standards will allow a message to contain both generic and specific information. For example, if a form is sent, the generic layout and content would probably be specified by giving the form's ID number. Then, specific layout and content information would be sent within the full document. This approach allows common forms to be sent with a minimum of bits transmitted. Only specific formatting and content need to be sent each time, as well as a small amount of information to identify the generic and specific content.

Another outcomes that can be predicted with some confidence is that ISO will produce a revisable document standard that will be analogous to IBM's DCA. There has recently been a trend toward adopting some IBM standards as international standards, particularly within the ISO. It would not be surprising if ISO standardized DCA as a standard for revisable documents, although it would probably not limit its standards to DCA.

Over the long run, ISO recognizes that it needs to combine the best features of final form and revisable document standards. It will eventually create documents with high levels of page layout complexity that are still revisable after receipt.

ISO also recognizes the need to produce true multimedia documents that will contain not only text and graphics, but also sound and even video images, in order to match the rich diversity of human communication. These multimedia standards may be in place by the time technology makes multimedia communication attractive to vendors and users.

IBM Efforts

We have already mentioned the key aspects of IBM's efforts, namely its creation of DIA/DCA in the early 1980s, even before the release of X.400. DIA (document interchange architecture) is a mail delivery standard, whereas DCA is a document standard. To use DIA, a company must also adopt IBM's **SNADS** (SNA Distribution Services), which provides for asynchronous communications among processes. Without SNADS, SNA only supports real-time interaction among processes.

Although the success of X.400 for standardizing mail delivery and the content of simple messages has limited the spread of IBM's document interchange architecture (even IBM offers X.400 links to the outside world), DCA the use of has been spreading rapdily. Because IBM began with a focus on revisable documents—it created DCA to connect the company's several incompatible lines of word processors—DCA was a revisable document standard the moment it was born. The need for such a standard, even a de facto one like DCA, was so strong that most of IBM's competitors soon adopted DCA as a way to handle document file exchange with other vendors. Today, nearly every word processing program can both import and export DCA files.

The obvious difference between DCA and IPMS is that DCA is a fully revisable document standard, whereas the IPMS body standards defined to date have been final form standards. Second, DCA lacks header fields. Therefore, unless envelopes are kept with documents, there is no way to annotate a transmitted document except to write on the document itself. As noted earlier, a good compromise would be to have the broad IPMS standard with DCA as a body standard within IPMS. The standards agencies seem to be moving in this direction, and DCA may become one of the approved body types for IPMS.

In general form, DIA is very similar to X.400's mail delivery standards. Both use the general concepts of MTAs and UAs, although IBM uses different terminology. This broad similarity is hardly surprising, inasmuch as the MTA/UA model has been around for many years, having been popularized and perhaps developed within the International Federation for Information Processing, (IFIP). Although the two are architecturally similar at a broad level, their details are radically different. Translating between DIA and X.400's mail transfer service is a complex task.

Conclusion

Today, we have two major standards for text exchange, and each is spreading rapidly within its own sphere of interest. First, IBM's DCA, which is used for exchanging revisable documents, has taken the word processing community by storm. Second, X.400 is becoming an international standard for mail delivery; it is being embraced by many commercial EMS vendors in the United States and by many national telecommunications authorities in other countries. A reconciliation of these two trends is very imporatant, so that X.400 carriers will be able to exchange DCA messages.

For the longer run, we can expect to see a growing stream of standards for more sophisticated document content, including desktop publishing standards and multimedia standards. Although the multimedia standards may be accepted by vendors quickly, the enormous pace of progress within desktop publishing makes it doubtful that an international standard for desktop publishing will soon be good enough to attract either vendors or users.

TELECONFERENCING

The telephone is fine if two people need to talk for a few minutes, but what if several people, perhaps in several locations, need to hold a two-hour conference? For these kinds of needs, users can turn to **teleconferencing**—the general term for systems that let more than two people communicate orally and perhaps with graphics and video as well.

The Audio Problem

In both audio and video teleconferencing systems, the biggest problem is engineering the audio parts of the system. The length of sound waves varies from a few inches to a few feet. This is the same general size range of objects found in rooms. As a result, when sound leaves the speaker, it tends to bounce around walls and objects in the room and then go back into the microphone.

When the reflected sound enters the microphone, it is amplified, sent out again through the speaker, and then reflected back into the microphone. Each cycle amplifies the sound, quickly producing the painful **screech** or **howl-around** that is all too familiar in public address systems.

There are several ways to reduce feedback, one of which is to give users directional microphones or lapel microphones. This reduces howl-around to some extent, but it restricts user mobility somewhat.

Another approach is **voice clipping,** in which a user's microphone is automatically shut off until it detects a sound above a certain loudness. This prevents howl-around but makes it difficult to interrupt someone talking at the other end, moreover, when a person does begin to talk, the first syllable is likely to be clipped off.

A more expensive approach is to treat the room with sound-absorbing materials. This method allows more natural sound at the two ends by reducing sound reflections and therefore howl-around. It also cuts out extraneous noise, such as paper shuffling and traffic noise, which can be a major distraction when amplified through the system. In practice, at least some acoustical treatment is necessary for decent sound quality.

The best (and most expensive) approach is to match the teleconferencing system's acoustical system to the individual room in which it is used. This process is called **voicing** the room. In voicing, sound of many frequencies is fed into the room in gradually increasing volume. When howl-around occurs, the frequencies at which it occurs are "notched out" of the system. This stops the howl-around. Volume is then increased until howl-around occurs again, and a new cycle of notching begins. After a while, natural sound is possible without suffering from howl-around.

Telephone Conferencing

Because nearly everyone has a telephone on his or her desk, an easy, low-tech, and low-cost way to move into teleconferencing is to use existing telephones. This can be done with loudspeaker telephones, conference calling, or a combination of the two.

Loudspeaker Telephones

With ordinary telephones, the user holds the handpiece to his or her mouth and ear. With **loudspeaker telephones,** the entire unit sits on the desk. A microphone picks up the user's voice and a speaker lets the user listen to the other person. Loudspeaker telephones give hands-free operation and also allow several people in the room to participate. Figure 17-6 shows a typical loudspeaking telephone.

Loudspeaker telephones in the 1960s and 1970s were subject to howl-around, excessive voice clipping, and a characteristic sound dubbed "voice at

FIGURE 17-6 AN AT&T SPEAKERPHONE

the bottom of the barrel." Some newer units are much better, although deregulation has brought many poor units into the market.

Conference Calling

Another desk-to-desk service is **telephone conference calling.** In conference calling, several telephones are linked via a **conference bridge,** as shown in Figure 17-7. This bridge serves two functions: (1), it serves as a switch, letting everyone hear what one person says; and (2) it compensates for loudness differences on different lines, so that one person will not be unpleasantly loud while another person can barely be heard.

Conference bridges are built into many corporate telephone systems. High-quality conference bridging services are offered by several common carriers and by companies that specialize in bridge services. When considering a service, important considerations are cost, the quality of sound equalization, automated meeting setup (in which people are automatically connected if they dial in), and the quality of service when operator-assisted setup is chosen.

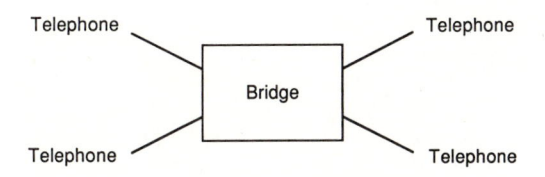

Note: The bridge connects all telephones so that everyone in the conference can hear everyone else. It also equalizes sound levels among the telephones.

FIGURE 17-7 TELEPHONE CONFERENCING BRIDGE

Room-to-Room Services

Loudspeaker telephones and conference calling serve people right at their desks. **Room-to-room** conferencing systems, however, require people to gather in conference rooms. In addition to requiring people to leave their desks, these systems require acoustical treatment for the room, as discussed earlier. In return, well-designed room-to-room systems provide a pleasant "shirtsleeve" environment with comfortable acoustics and sometimes graphics and video as well.

Portable Audio Conferencing Systems

The cheapest room-to-room systems are **portable audio conferencing systems.** These are basically grown-up loudspeaker telephones with several directional microphones and high-quality speakers, as shown in Figure 17-8. Costing anywhere from a few hundred dollars to about two thousand dollars, these units provide a low-cost way to get into teleconferencing, and they can be moved into whatever conference rooms are used by the participants. Their sound quality is still only moderate, however, and if they are taken into rooms without acoustical treatment and many hard surfaces, their sound quality may suffer considerably.

Portable Video Conferencing Systems

If you imagine a portable audio conferencing system with built-in cameras and a television monitor, you have the basic idea behind portable video conferencing systems.

This sounds like a simple extension of technology, but there is one catch. Although an audio system can work over ordinary long distance telephone lines, video of any sort requires video transmission lines. Without data compression, a full television channel costing thousands of dollars or more per hour would be needed. With suitable compression, a less expensive T.1 pri-

FIGURE 17-8 PORTABLE AUDIO CONFERENCING SYSTEM

vate line (discussed in Chapter 13) is sufficient, but these lines are still costly. moreover, the device needed to convert the television signal into T.1 digital signals and to reconvert incoming signals is quite expensive. This device is called a **codec**. Codec costs are falling rapidly, but the typical cost in 1987 was about $50,000. T.1 lines or wideband links to T.1 lines must be available in the rooms to which the portable system is taken.

The best codecs can squeeze reasonable full motion video over 56 kbps lines. AT&T's Accunet Switched 56 kbps lines provide switched service for twice the cost of a comparable long distance call over ordinary telephone lines. Codecs that can work over these lines are still extremely expensive, but as codec prices come down, 56 kbps lines may finally bring video conferencing transmission lines into a reasonable range.

To avoid these costs, some video systems use **slow scan television** in which continuous video is replaced by a series of video "snapshots." This allows ordinary telephone lines to be used for transmission, but it loses the impact of full motion video. In addition, snapshots often catch people in grimaces. Over 56 kbps lines, "fast slow scan" transmission can reduce the time between snapshots, giving much better service. So far vendors have not attacked this market, but they are likely to do so in the near future.

Dedicated Audio Conferencing Rooms

For high-quality audio conferencing, dedicated rooms provide the best solution. These rooms can be acoustically treated and voiced, and microphones, speakers, and a control booth can be built into walls and partitions. Leased lines can be purchased between the rooms in order to give slightly better sound than dial-up lines. Many dedicated rooms provide other features, including a second telephone for private discussions or administrative details and a facsimile machine for graphics. The cost of a typical dedicated audio conferencing room can be as much as $100,000, including electronics.

Dedicated Video Conferencing Rooms

Dedicated video conferencing rooms add video to basic audio service, and in most cases graphics support is also added. Figure 17-9 shows a dedicated video conferencing system. Although slow-scan video can be used, most dedicated video conferencing rooms use full motion video. The cost is high, with a typical pair of rooms costing around a half million dollars to modify and fill with equipment. Transmission can add another half million dollars per year, although this cost is falling rapidly. Another consideration is that an operator is normally needed to operate cameras, switch between the cameras, and take care of minor administrative details.

The Moderator's Role

The moderator is critical to productive teleconferencing of any type. His or her role is especially vital in audio conferencing, in which the participants cannot see one another.

- The moderator's first job is to maintain silence, except for the person talking. Acoustical systems are very good at picking up stray sounds, including side conversations and people tapping their pencils.

FIGURE 17-9 DEDICATED VIDEO CONFERENCING SYSTEM

- The second job is to ensure that each speaker gives his or her name before speaking. Even if participants know one another well, recognizing someone's voice is difficult.
- The third job is to bring taciturn participants into the conversation. This is a problem in any meeting, and it is amplified in conferencing.

When Does Teleconferencing Work?

Teleconferencing has been highly touted since the early 1960s. Since then, interest has flared and waned roughly every 10 years. In organization after organization, excellent systems have been built and promoted, but in every case, teleconferencing has been used in only a small fraction of all meetings.

There is a clear pattern to the kinds of meetings that tend to take place via teleconferencing. This pattern has been known since the 1970s. (5,8) In a nutshell, teleconferencing is used primarily when (1) a group of people needs to meet frequently (at least several times a year) and (2) finds travel burdensome. The Bank of America, for example, split its senior management staff between Los Angeles and San Francisco in the 1950s. These senior managers had to meet once a week or more. Travel became a major burden, and the bank's senior officers began using audio teleconferencing in the 1960s and have continued to use teleconferencing ever since. The National Aeronautics and Space Agency (NASA) has long used teleconferencing for its many project management meetings, because if engineers had to travel to these frequent meetings, there would be little time left for work.

Perhaps the reason for this pattern is that teleconferencing is not one of the standard ways of holding meetings, so psychological barriers have to be knocked down. In addition, a good deal of work goes into teleconferences, and it may take several conferences to work out social interactions. In any case, few exceptions exist to the general pattern just described. Even with heavy promotion, easy setup, and free service, teleconferencing still appeals to only a small fraction of all possible meetings.

Many firms find that a successful teleconferencing system merely points to a serious problem in the organization, in which two groups that need to work together closely are artificially split geographically. Many successful teleconferencing systems are discontinued after a year or two, as the result of a major reorganization that moves the conferencing groups together.

INTEGRATED OFFICE SYSTEMS

As noted earlier in the chapter, **integrated office systems (IOSs)** offer a broad spectrum of text communication and activity management tools in a single integrated package. With an IOS, a user does not have to create a document with a word processor, then convert the document to the file structure used by the electronic mail system, and finally use the electronic mail system to send a document. All of these and other functions are highly integrated.

Services

Word Processing

The most heavily used service is word processing. In some cases, the IOS is an extension of an existing word processing system. For instance, Wang Laboratories' Wang OFFICE is built on top of the company's standard word processing software.

Other integrated office systems offer only rudimentary word processors. These systems assume that the user will create anything except short messages in the corporation's normal PC or dedicated word processing system and then convert documents into the format used by the document distribution feature of the IOS. The most common distribution formats are ASCII, DCA, and X.400. Although this approach provides flexibility, it can be extremely wasteful of users' time unless the conversion is automatic and rapid. The specific implementation of conversion features—not just the mere presence of these features—is critical to product selection.

Electronic Messaging

The second widely used feature of the system is electronic messaging. Because research has shown that composition commands will be less used than scanning, reading, filing, and disposition commands, it is critical for the system to offer a broad set of tools for handling mail after it arrives. At the same time, the basic amenities in message creation should be demanded, including word wrap, easy handling of messages that are longer than a single screen, spell checking, and good editing aids.

As discussed in the earlier section on EMS, the proper handling of lax pickup and the easy handling of people who delegate terminal work to their secretaries should be critical to product selection. Many IOS vendors continue to ignore these two simple, yet extremely important, needs.

Ideally, document distribution should be integrated with the EMS feature. A user should be able to specify a document or part of a document as the body field for a message. To avoid overloading user mailboxes in the case of widely distributed documents, however, it may be desirable to keep only one copy of a document body on each computer. Whenever a user "reads" a message with this document as a body, the local copy of the full text is called automatically.

Group Meeting Scheduling

Most IOSs allow people to keep their appointment calendars online. Although this is less convenient for individuals than keeping their calendars on the paper appointment books they carry with them, it allows meetings to be scheduled easily.

Each individual is responsible for blanking out times when he or she has scheduled meetings or does not want to be disturbed for meetings. Although the content of these times is kept secret, the fact that certain meeting times are closed is not hidden.

If someone wants to schedule a meeting, he or she lists the people to be present, preferred meeting rooms, and preferred meeting times. The system automatically finds a good meeting time and meeting room. Some systems then write the meeting into the individual appointment calendars of the attendees. Others send an electronic message requesting individuals to add the meeting to their schedules.

Group meeting scheduling is accepted in some organizations, but widely rejected in others. It demands a discipline and commitment to enforcement that does not fit the organizational styles of many firms. Because it normally takes two to three dozen telephone calls to set up a meeting among a dozen or so people, however, many firms make the commitment to implement computerized group meeting scheduling as a normal part of corporate life.

Document Storage and Retrieval

One of the biggest problems facing electronic offices is how to keep track of documents. Some IOSs offer document storage and retrieval capabilities that attempt to automate document management. Most of these systems work by adding searchable fields to a document at the time it is stored. Boolean queries can then be done to retrieve documents.

Computerization does not relieve people, department managers, and task team leaders of the need to develop a comprehensive storage schema for documents. Index terms must be carefully selected and enforced, and hierarchies must be built in order to keep the schema comprehensible. Over time, as the schema changes in response to changing organizational work, existing documents may have to be assigned different search terms and moved to different branches of the hierarchy.

Central to all document management is a firm **retention discipline**—a policy for deciding how long each document is to be maintained online and a set of procedures for doing archiving or destruction. No system can survive a sloppy retention discipline.

Other Personal Services

The IOS may supply each user with other personal services. For example, there may be a filing system for telephone numbers or a general-purpose file management facility that the user can use for other purposes. There may also be a personal document filing system, so that the user can maintain a personal docubase of word processing files and electronic messages. In many cases, there will be customization features so that the user can customize his or her interaction with the service. Customization may go as far as an embedded programming language to automate common multistep tasks.

Administrative Services

An IOS is a complex undertaking that requires a full-time administrator and often support staff as well.

The administrator must be able to add and drop people from the system and maintain an up-to-date directory listing everyone authorized to use the system. This directory must be accessible to all authorized users, who will need the information to look up user addresses for electronic mail and group calendar management.

The administrator may also be able to build service profiles for individual users. These profiles will include such information as whether the user will retrieve messages online or whether messages should be printed for paper delivery. It may even be possible to customize the user interface, so that a menu will give a user access not only to all IOS services, but also to certain external services, such as spreadsheet programs.

Technology

Figure 17-10 illustrates a typical modern integrated office system. As shown in the figure, most IOSs allow several host computers to be linked together, including large mainframes, centralized minicomputers, and departmental minicomputers. IOS software is implemented on each host, and work that needs to flow from one host to another is routed automatically, often without

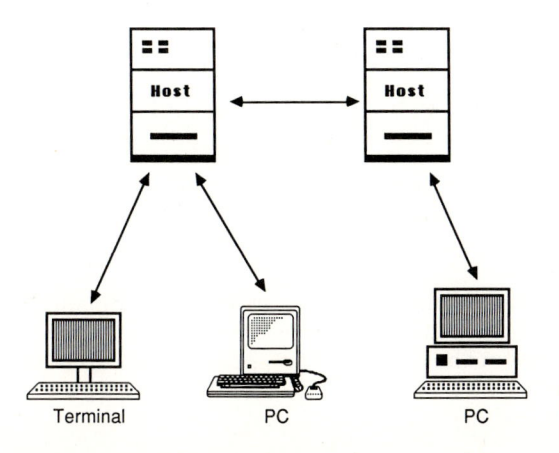

FIGURE 17-10 INTEGRATED OFFICE SYSTEM

the user's awareness. This flexibility allows as much processing as possible to be done close to the user, thus reducing communications costs.

For workstations, users can turn to either terminals or personal computers. Terminals are normally smart (see Chapter 13), so most editing tasks can be done locally instead of on the host. Personal computers, in turn, will have software implementing most or all of the IOS's functionality while adding snappy response and extensive graphics in the user interface. The PC software also reaches out to host computers automatically.

If personal computer networks are present, the server may implement some or all of the IOS functionality, providing this functionality to user PCs and reaching out to hosts as needed.

Wang Office

In contrast to the complex IBM approaches discussed later, Wang's approach to integrated office systems is limited to a single major product line today, Wang OFFICE. We will look at Wang OFFICE on the company's VS computers. The VS line is Wang's dominant minicomputer and mainframe line, and it is the environment on which Wang OFFICE is most completely developed today.

Wang offers two versions of Wang OFFICE. OFFICE I has nearly all the functionality an end user is likely to want, but OFFICE II offers two additional functions: Wang word processing and the Wang Office File Manager to keep track of documents. These additional functions integrate OFFICE into the full world of Wang document processing. We will look at the functions offered in OFFICE I and then turn to word processing and the Wang Office File Manager.

Directory Services

OFFICE has a general directory of everyone on the system. Users can look up basic information on any individual on the system, including the person's formal mailing address for electronic mail.

Electronic Mail

OFFICE has an advanced electronic messaging system, which includes the ability to send memos up to 32 screens long, online directory assistance, distribution lists for mailings to prespecified groups, phone message notices, invitations (which ask for replies), security levels, the ability to package several messages in a single outgoing package, and confirmation of receipt.

Time Management

OFFICE has calendars, reminder notices, invitations (handled through electronic messaging), an audible alarm, and security levels.

Other Features in OFFICE I

OFFICE I also provides an online phone book with space for detailed notes about each person, up to four interaction windows for different functions, and administration functions for the control of access and the establishment of customized user profiles.

Wang Word Processing

Wang word processing is widely used in industry and has many imitators. OFFICE II brings full Wang word processing to the individual user. It also brings extended features, including a list manager, a charts function, a spelling verifier, and even a readability index.

Wang Office File Manager

Any office or company that has been dealing with word processing for more than a few months understands the difficulty of keeping track of hundreds or thousands of documents. The Wang Office File Manager is an archive for documents, images, and other files. It provides the ability to locate and retrieve individual files and includes levels of security. As noted earlier, the Wang Office File Manager is available only in Wang OFFICE II.

Overall, Wang OFFICE follows the company's basic philosophy of offering simple and straightforward products that are easy to implement and can run without a large systems staff. The product is easy for end users to use and learn in greater detail when needs expand. Although it lacks some of the functionality found in IBM's DISOSS product discussed later in this chapter, its tractability makes it quite attractive to many businesses, especially those that already have extensive Wang equipment.

IBM Products

In addition to its individual office automation products, including the Displaywrite word processing software that runs on virtually all IBM computers from its personal computers to its largest mainframes, IBM has several integrated products: PROFS, DISOSS, and its Personal Services series.

PROFS, DISOSS, and Personal Services

PROFS, DISOSS, and Personal Services are not three components of a single system. As mentioned earlier, IBM often produces a number of competing products and lets the market decide which will succeed. If more than one succeeds, IBM builds bridges between them.

PROFS (Professional Office Support System) is the oldest of the three, dating back to 1972. It is oriented toward workstation functionality, offering 3270 terminal users and personal computer users a rich set of work functions, including messaging, word processing, and electronic messaging.

DISOSS aims at document services at the corporate level. It is a sophisticated document storage system, and it is also a large document post office with sophisticated delivery capabilities. It has the ability to run outside programs to work on the documents in its data base. The complexity of DISOSS and its high administrative overhead have restricted its spread. At the time of this writing, only a fraction of all IBM installations use DISOSS, and those that do use it for only a few document storage needs. (4)

PROFS runs on mainframes using the VM operating system, which is end-user oriented and runs most of IBM's end user analysis software. DISOSS, in turn, runs on mainframes using the MVS operating system, which is more heavily production-oriented and has comparatively little end user software. Unless an organization has two mainframes, one VM and one MVS, or unless it is willing to run MVS as a guest operating system in a partition on a VM machine (this is wasteful of resources), it must look either to PROFS or DISOSS today.

Personal Services is an attempt to provide some PROFS functionality to environments where MVS mainframes are dominant. DISOSS is primarily a document distribution and filing system. It does not even provide a messaging interface for individual users directly. Personal Services was created to provide electronic messaging service to individuals, then route messages and documents via DISOSS. IBM is now building bridges between the PROFS and DISOSS/Personal Services worlds, using its electronic mail standards, DIA and DCA.

PROFS

PROFS was developed in the early 1970s as a joint project between IBM and AMOCO for engineering and programmer users. Although PROFS has been improved constantly since that time, including being extended to personal computers, it has something of the feel of an early development.

Figure 17-11 shows the main screen image in PROFS. The screen is divided into two parts. The top is like a control panel, holding the meaning of various function keys on a 3270 terminal and calendar and time information. The lower portion of the screen is used to display information relative to a particular task. If the user has a 3279 or 3179 terminal, PROFS will use color to help the user identify information more rapidly. On the whole, this is a very attractive screen.

PROFS document creation is geared toward producing large documents with complex formatting. Because it was developed before WYSIWYG word

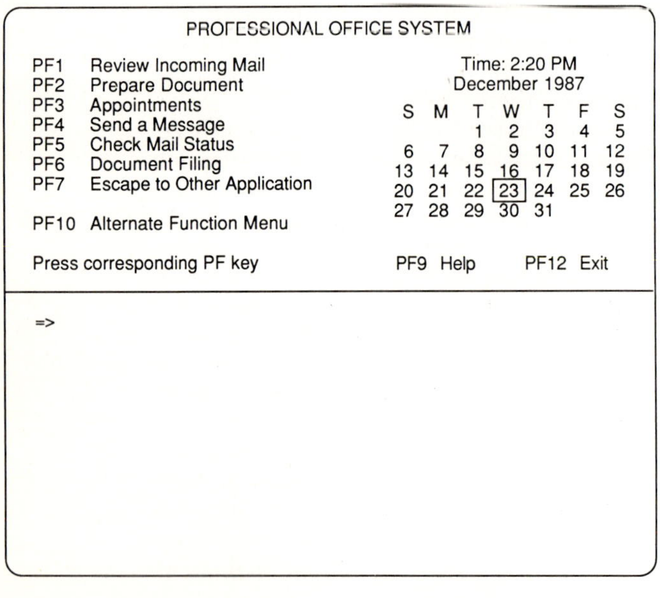

```
              PROFESSIONAL OFFICE SYSTEM
   PF1    Review Incoming Mail            Time: 2:20 PM
   PF2    Prepare Document                December 1987
   PF3    Appointments              S   M   T   W   T   F   S
   PF4    Send a Message                    1   2   3   4   5
   PF5    Check Mail Status         6   7   8   9  10  11  12
   PF6    Document Filing          13  14  15  16  17  18  19
   PF7    Escape to Other Application  20  21  22 [23] 24  25  26
                                    27  28  29  30  31
   PF10   Alternate Function Menu

   Press corresponding PF key        PF9 Help     PF12 Exit

   =>
```

FIGURE 17-11 THE MAIN PROFS SCREEN

processing (What You See Is What You Get), it handles all formatting through embedded formatting codes. The document is run through IBM's Document Composition Facility (DCF) for formatting at printing time. Although a very good spelling checker is available, document production within PROFS is very archaic on the whole, and most users create their documents in a word processor and then import them into PROFS.

PROFS has two separate electronic mail systems, instead of a single integrated electronic mail system: a simple electronic message system for brief messages; and a document transmission system.

The EMS function is simple to use, but it is also limited. Most disturbingly, the user cannot scan old mail with Boolean searches, for example, to see all messages from a certain person in the last two months. Because mail reading commands vastly outnumber composing and sending commands, this inability to search through old messages easily is disturbing.

The document distribution function is designed for the distribution of large documents, often to multiple users. This system does not actually send the full documents to each mailbox. Instead, it stores the original online and merely sends a message announcing the document's existence in the PROFS mail file. Users can then access the document as needed. PROFS does offer the ability to do Boolean searches on old documents, sent via this system.

For time management, PROFS offers personal calendar management (including reminders), the ability to create meetings based on the calendars of others (users can block out time slots they do not want scheduled), and a conference room scheduler.

Mindful of the limitations of PROFS on mainframe environments, IBM has put much of its development effort into moving PROFS down to the personal computer. Personal computer PROFS now has virtually all features of its mainframe cousins and is easier to use.

Another consideration with regard to PROFS is that it tends to need a maintenance staff to keep it running and a large systems staff effort to begin its use. This is true largely because PROFS must be tailored to the organization and to each individual.

DISOSS

During the 1970s, IBM's several divisions created a rash of incompatible word processing products, including the Displaywriter, the 5520 Administrative System, and 8100/DOSF. To bring some order to this chaos, IBM decided to develop a high-level mainframe product to allow these and future products to exchange messages. The resultant development effort produced the **Distributed Office Support System/370—DISOSS.**

DISOSS was the source of IBM's DIA and DCA standards. Although DISOSS has been described as merely the first implementation of these standards, the DISOSS project really produced these standards. As a result, DISOSS emerged with full-blown implementation of these standards.

DISOSS has two major functions. The first is **document delivery,** including data stream conversion between incompatible systems. With varying degrees of completeness and ease, DISOSS can convert and exchange messages among DisplayWriter, DisplayWrite software, the 5520 Administrative System, 8100/DOSF, PROFS, Personal Services, and Scanmaster I (a facsimile machine). This capability is very automatic, although deep differences among products, including naming conventions for electronic delivery, still require care and knowledge on the part of users.

The second major function of DISOSS is **Library Services.** DISOSS not only delivers documents, but it can also store them in a document base for later retrieval. DISOSS offers sophisticated keyword search capabilities as well as access control and deletion tools. DISOSS can contain information about external documents not produced on one of IBM's electronic systems, so that users can maintain information about paper files. DISOSS currently cannot store PROFS documents electronically.

Many users have complex document search needs. An **Application Program Interface,** using DIA, allows users to develop their own programs for retrieving, printing, and distributing documents. This extends the power of both DISOSS's distribution and library functions.

DISOSS also has two minor functions. **Host Services** allow users to use their word processor to prepare batch jobs for the mainframe computer. DISOSS then submits these batch jobs, thereby saving users from having to use a separate editor for creating batch jobs. **Service Aids** for the administrator and operator allow the monitoring of names and distribution, as well as the ability to delete entries from the distribution queue of documents, security checking, and user profile maintenance. Service Aids also include installation utilities for the whole system and the development of individual user profiles.

Although IBM has touted DISOSS widely, its use has been very limited. It is complex and difficult to use, and it is suited primarily to organizations with complex, tightly disciplined document filing and retrieval needs.

Personal Services

The Personal Services software series from IBM is designed for users who work in a DISOSS environment. Personal Services is implemented on IBM PCs, System 36s, and MVS mainframes, so that once a user learns how to work with Personal Services, it takes little relearning to switch to another technical environment.

Personal Services today focuses on electronic mail. It lets the user compose memos and documents and send them via DISOSS. Personal Services also gives the user access to DISOSS document storage and retrieval capabilities.

In the future, Personal Services seems destined to grow toward the fuller functionality now found in PROFS, giving MVS users a full set of IOS services without having to add a second machine running VM.

Perspective on Integrated Office Systems

Although we have only discussed products from a few vendors, most computer and OA vendors offer their own integrated OA products, as do a few vendors whose products run on more than one machine.

When evaluating products, a study team must consider the obvious, primarily what functions are offered and how well these functions are offered. Although most systems offer roughly the same functions, there are enormous differences in the scope of functionality within each function.

There are even more enormous differences in how smoothly each function is implemented and how long various jobs will take users to do. Extremely detailed product testing must be done.

At the same time, all products on the market are in an early stage of development, so picking the "best" product at this stage may be a serious mistake. The study team also needs to consider the long-term viability of each vendor as well as the directions the vendor is likely to take in the future.

Complicating of this picture is the technical environment in which the IOS will be embedded. Most IOSs run only on a single machine, and if the machine is an IBM mainframe, they may run only on one of the major IBM mainframe operating systems. Because user needs will include personal computing and the host computing applications discussed in Chapter 16, it is important to consider current and likely links between each candidate IOS and other software products which the organization is likely to use.

Unless the study team finds a product that is both excellent today and likely to become even more excellent in the future, it would probably be well advised to wait until the market situation clears somewhat. Instead, it can move forward to discrete services such as electronic mail and add more functionality later.

Second-Generation Integrated Office Systems

Although the original cohort of integrated office systems is beginning to be accepted in corporate life, vendors and users are now beginning to look forward to a second generation of integrated office systems.

Standards for Multivendor Environments

Second-generation IOSs will be based on international standards established by ISO and CCITT (see Chapter 14) or ad hoc standards—typically those of IBM. The word processing and electronic mail standards discussed earlier in this chapter are a major step in this direction because they allow both message and document exchange, but they are only a beginning.

First, they fail to provide many needed functions, such as group meeting scheduling and document storage and retrieval. If these functions are important, then lashing IOSs from different vendors together with electronic mail standards alone may not be satisfactory.

Second, multivendor integration needs to be very smooth. The existence of a multivendor EMS environment should be completely hidden from users if possible. In most multivendor environments today, it is *extremely* obvious when a user crosses vendor boundaries.

Multivendor IOS environments are certain to appear, but until much more development is done, multivendor service will remain a mere expedient that should be used where a single-vendor IOS environment cannot be implemented for practical reasons, such as the merger of two firms with different IOS vendors.

Multimedia Service

Today's first-generation IOSs are limited primarily to text. Although they may have some graphics features, these are usually minimal.

The graphics explosion in the PC environment will cause this situation to change. Second-generation IOSs will have to be rich in graphics capabilities. To avoid chaos, these graphics functions should obey the emerging international standards discussed in Chapter 7. Otherwise, we will be back to the single-vendor trap of first-generation IOSs.

Second-generation systems are even expected to leap beyond text and graphics to become true **multimedia** systems that will embrace not only text and graphics but also voice and even video. It will be possible, for example, to add voice annotation to documents. Some IOSs already provide limited multimedia functionality, but until international standards for multimedia documents appear, progress is expected to be "leisurely."

Extending Beyond Office Automation

OA has traditionally been limited to verbal communication and activity management tools, but Type II department needs cut freely across the synthetic boundary that the OA field has erected between these two functions and other EUC tools.

Second-generation IOSs will end this artificial separation by providing integrated access to most or all EUC tools, including the PC tools discussed in Chapters 9-12 and the host tools discussed in Chapter 16 and in this chapter. At first, this integration is likely to be limited to putting all of these functions under a menu and offering file conversion among selected tools, and even this limited integration will be valuable. In the longer term, second-generation IOSs should be able to provide seamless integration by offering a common set of user interface features, even if the underlying programs are diverse and, when used in stand-alone mode, offer different use interfaces.

PC Integration

First-generation IOSs already incorporate PC front ends, so that users can do most of their work on their personal PC. This takes advantage of PC response time and graphics for highly interactive work, turning to the mainframe only for heavy processing or shared data.

Although PC integration does not help define the transition from first-generation IOSs to second-generation systems, PC integration in second-generation systems is expected to be much tighter. Virtually all details of the larger system will be hidden from users, and system managers will be able to download profiles and other management information to PCs without additional work on the part of the users.

STUDYING CORPORATE NEEDS FOR OFFICE AUTOMATION

Before an advanced office automation system can be built, an empirical study nearly always needs to be done. In addition to pinpointing problem areas, this study will measure volumes of communications in different document categories. This empirical work is needed to select alternative systems, to estimate system costs, and to set various parameters in the system selected.

In contrast to the broad end user computing needs analysis study discussed in Chapter 2, the **office automation study** is aimed directly at the implementation of large OA systems. Here, we use the term "system" to include hardware, software, telecommunications, data structures, people, organization, and policies. To put it another way, the broad needs study in end user computing is designed to understand needs broadly and to test the match between current offerings and those needs. The office automation study is devoted to more concrete design matters—the specification of individual components in the system.

Mail Tagging

One of the first things that can be done is a mail tagging study. This study begins with the sampling of communication that goes through the corporate mailrooms at different sites. Without opening communications but only looking at addressing envelopes, the study team can complete a number of measurements.

- Current volume of traffic flowing within a site, via interoffice mail and direct distribution by secretaries.
- Current volume of traffic between corporate locations at different sites.
- Current volume of traffic going to or coming from external organizations.

The next step is to "tag" a sampling of all messages with a questionnaire. This questionnaire asks the receiver to answer certain questions about the content of the message. Among these questions would be the following.

- Its rough length (in pages)
- The number of people to whom it has been sent
- Its time urgency
- Its perceived relevancy to the receiver
- What will be done to it (disposal without reading, disposal after light reading, study and filing, etc.)
- Its general type: memo, progress report, etc.

As with any questionnaire, it is critical to create the instrument and then test it with a presample. In addition to answering the questions, subjects would be asked to comment on unclear questions and to suggest added questions as well. It is also critical to design the data collection instrument so that a data entry operator can key off the results easily. This is especially important since hundreds of questionnaires will be returned during a mail tagging exercise.

Personal Questionnaires

Although mail tagging gives a good sampling of corporate communication, it misses (1) the sender's point of view; and (2) the many notes left on desks and the many memos that stay within a department and so never get to the corporate mailroom.

A survey instrument can be created to ask people to keep one- or two-day records of their communication, including telephone calls, items sent through the mailroom, and items sent without going through the mailroom. For each communication, only a few pieces of information would be recorded. For telephone calls, for instance, failures to get through to the desired party would be logged, as well as whether the call was local or a toll call. For written communication, the questionnaire would ask length, number of recipients, form of delivery, and type of correspondence.

The data entry form might record only five to ten items on each page, leaving the rest of the page blank. In this blank space, the respondent would be asked a few questions about the last item on the page. These questions would ask about importance and any problems encountered. This would give a reasonably random sample of communication occasions.

The questionnaire would end with a set of questions to identify general problems encountered by the respondent, including the adequacy of various types of support currently being offered.

Focus Groups

To provide more detailed information, a series of focus groups should be held. Each group should be fairly homogeneous, each being limited to one occupational category (clerical workers, first line managers, middle managers etc.). Mixing people with different backgrounds and status levels almost always inhibits discussion.

The moderator should begin by having the group discuss general communication patterns. The questions should be noncontroversial and designed to be easy to answer. After posing a question, the moderator should go around clockwise or counterclockwise and get answers from everybody. This approach builds involvement and yields a good sampling of opinions.

Gradually, the discussion should focus on impediments to communication, including organizational constraints as well as service constraints. For instance, how often do people have to walk to the mailroom themselves, copy something themselves, or edit something themselves because help is not available when needed?

Finally, the groups should be presented with a few scenarios showing possible service offerings that are strategically possible. One might be a low-cost electronic message system with few organizational hurdles. Another might be a full IOS that will raise many implementation difficulties due to training, the reorganization of document storage procedures, and similar problems.

These systems should be presented one at a time, with different groups seeing them in different orders. At the end, each individual should select one preferred system, giving reasons for selecting it.

Research in Perspective

The purpose of this section has been not so much to lay out a step-by-step research program as to show the breadth of tools available when studying organizational communication needs. It is necessary to apply several of these tools if capacity planning is to be done intelligently. If the research is done properly, it can even help in product selection. Advanced OA systems cannot be implemented with the informality of many end user computing applications.

CONCLUSION

Office automation today embraces a broad spectrum of tools to aid human communication. Some OA systems are very small and can be implemented somewhat independently. Word processing and teleconferencing fall into this category. In contrast, other systems, including electronic mail systems and integrated office systems, are very large innovations that must be planned with extreme care, and their planning even requires empirical research studies.

Today, most users still deal with stand-alone tools, such as electronic message systems, facsimile, and teleconferencing systems. Integrated office systems already embrace a broad set of communication and activity management tools, however, and second-generation integrated office systems are expected to embrace not only OA tools but also other EUC tools, producing true integrated EUC systems.

As always, of course, the price of integration is great. The dollar costs of integrated office systems are high, and there are other costs as well, including limited functionality compared to stand-alone products. This last problem is extremely important today, and firms that opt for integration must be prepared to give up functionality. This integration-versus-functionality tradeoff often sets end users, who are unwilling to compromise their ability to do their daily work, against the information systems staff, which cannot continue to work out problems among the ever-growing stand-alone products in the corporation.

REVIEW QUESTIONS

1. Why is it a good idea to place the management of office automation in the information center? What problems are raised by this merger?
2. What are the main services offered by word processing centers? What are the main factors to take into account when managing a word processing center? What management issues do you think an information center is most likely to overlook? Why?
3. Why was Teletex a major leap forward over Telex? In what ways was it not enough of a leap forward?
4. Build a table summarizing the main features of Group 1, Group 2, Group 3, and Group 4 facsimile.
5. How do electronic message systems differ from traditional forms of electronic mail? What are the main components of EMS costs, and why is EMS cost assessment difficult?
6. What are the predictable management problems of EMS?
7. What are the differences, advantages, and disadvantages of EMS, computer conferencing, and voice messaging?
8. Argue that document standards are more important than mail delivery standards. Then argue the reverse. Which do you think is the stronger argument? What kinds of buyers would agree with your answer? What kinds would disagree?

9. What are the relative advantages of revisable and final form document standards?
10. What do X.400 and DIA/DCA specify? What do they not specify? Why do they not specify these things?
11. Contrast DCA with IPMS, T.73, and the Office Document Architecture.
12. What are the relative advantages of X.400 and DIA/DCA? How does your answer explain the markets in which each has been most successful?
13. What is the "audio problem" in teleconferencing?
14. What are the main components of videoconferencing costs? Which do you think will fall most rapidly? Discuss why slow scan video conferencing is likely to be successful and why it is not likely to be successful.
15. Create a tabular figure showing the relative advantages and disadvantages of various kinds of teleconferencing.
16. When does teleconferencing work?
17. What are the main services found in integrated office systems? What will be added in second-generation IOSs?
18. What are the strengths and weaknesses of IBM's IOS approach?
19. What information does mail tagging provide to OA planners? Personal questionnaires? Focus groups? How does each of these three methods supplement the weaknesses of the other two?

REFERENCES

1. BAIR, J. H., AND CONRATH, D. W., "The Computer as an Interpersonal Communication Device: A Study of Augmentation Technology and Its Apparent Impact on Organizational Communication," *Proceedings of the Second International Conference on Computer Communications,* Stockholm, Sweden, August 1974.
2. BAIRSTOW, JEFFREY, "The Electronic Mailbox: As Close as Your PC," *High Technology,* January 1987, pp. 16–22.
3. ELLIS, C. A., JOHANSEN, R., AND BAIR, J. H., "The ACM Workshop on Fundamental Issues in Office Automation: A Compilation of Notes," *ACM SIGOA Bulletin,* Association for Computing Machinery, 11 West 43nd Street, New York, Summer and Fall, 1985, pp. 3–9.
4. HOROWIT, ELISABETH, "Users Slow to Adopt DISOSS," *Computerworld,* August 4, 1986, pp. 1–6.
5. HOUGH, ROGER W., AND PANKO, RAYMOND R., *Teleconferencing Systems: A State of the Art Review,* Stanford Research Institute, Menlo Park, Calif., 1976.
6. Mackintosh International and Communications Studies and Planning, Ltd., special study on electronic mail, discussed in Connel, Steven and Galbraith, Ian, *Electronic Mail: A Revolution in Business Communications,* Knowledge Industry Publications, White Plains, N.Y., 1982.
7. MUNSON, VERNELL K., result of a survey conducted by Wang Laboratories, Inc., private communication with the author, 1984.
8. NOLL, A. MICHAEL, result of a survey conducted by AT&T, private communication with the author, 1985.

9. PANKO, RAYMOND R., "Electronic Mail," Chapter 9 in Quinn, Karen Tackle, *ed., Advances in Office Automation, Vol. 1,* John Wiley & Sons, Chichester, England, 1985.
10. PANKO, RAYMOND R., "The Costs of EMS," *Computer Networks,* March 1981, pp. 35–46.
11. PANKO, RAYMOND R., AND PANKO, ROSEMARIE U., "A Survey of EMS Users at DARCOM," *Computer Networks,* March 1981, pp. 19–23.
12. STEINFIELD, CHARLES W., "Explaining Task-Related and Socio-Emotional Uses of Computer-Mediated Communication in an Organizational Setting," speech at the annual meeting of the International Communication Association, Honolulu, 1985.
13. TUCKER, JEFFREY H. "Implementing Office Automation: Principles and an Electronic Mail Example," *Proceedings for the SIGOA Conference on Office Information Systems,* Association for Computing Machinery, June 21–23, 1982, pp. 93–100.

INDEX

3270:
   emulation, 557
     networking support, 625-626
     terminal emulation choices, 575
     terminal family, 550-556
     transmission, 572-575
802 LAN standards, 615-617
acceleration and control, 105-106
accelerator board, 243
activity management, 21
adapter, 202-203
adapter, 241-243
address space, 306-309
analysis, 20
analytical graphics, 394-395
analytical modeling:
   creation steps, 373-376
   good practice, 376-381
   images, 372-373
   interrogation, 382-388
   support, 406-407
analytical versus conceptual graphics, 466
APPC, 619
application development:
   DSS and EIS, 54
application generator, 456-458
applications:
   applications versus computers, 19
   generic versus hybrid, 19
   generic versus specific, 19
artificial intelligence, 355-362
   expert system, 363
   knowledge base, 356-359
   knowledge-based system, 355-356
   natural language input, 362
ASCII:
   code, 545-546
   files, 351-352
asynchronous network support, 625-626
asynchronous transmission, 547
@-functions, 395-399

BASIC, 528-529
backup, 253-255
bank switching, 318-319

baud, 543
breakthrough thinking, 56-57
bridge, 593
bus, 203
bus, 231-233
bus network layout, 600-601
business applications, 530
bypass, 577-578

C, 529
CATV, 602-605
cable, 594-595
CD-ROM, 255
CGA, 276
chargeback, 106-109
clip art, 491-492
clone, 216-219
cluster controller, 554
columns, multiple, 480-481
communication versus communications, 466
communications boards, 244
communications program, 513
communications program, 556-557
communications program, 558-564
compatible, 216-219
computer abuse policies, 153-157
computer conferencing, 718-719
computer families, 209-222
control, 39-40
control, 143-144
coprocessor, 237-238
core program, 316-317
costs and benefits, 57
CRT radiation, 159-160
critical success factors, 55-56
CSMA/CD, 606-607

dBASE III Plus, 441-459
data applications, 20-21
data file:
   form image, 417-418
   table image, 417
   terminology, 417-420
data management system, 412-413

I-2 Index

data modeling, 430-441
data processing, 1
DBMS, 20-21
DBMS, 415
    application generator, 456-458
    data modeling, 430-441
    fourth-generation language, 455-456
    host, 680-697
    index file, 446-447
    information center support, 459-463
    query language, 447-451
    report generator, 452-454
    support, 694-697
DCA, 726-727
decision support applications, 655-656
decision support system, 22, 75-80
    development, 77-79
delegated development, 28-32
demographics of office work, 10-12
department management, 72-75
department management matrix, 72
department manager's roles, 73
desk accessory program, 527-528
desk accessory program, 347-348
desktop publishing, 496-505
DIF, 353
DISOSS, 739-740
disk:
    backup, 253-255
    Bernoulli, 255
    floppy, 251-252
    hard, 252-253
    management program, 344-345
    optical, 255-256
    technology, 248-251
display, 272-281
    flat panel, 278-279
    full-page, 279-280
    monochrome versus color, 274-275
    projection system, 280-281
    RGB versus analog color, 274-275
    text versus graphics, 274
document content architecture, 354
DSS (see decision support)
dumb terminal, 544-545

EBCDIC, 551
echo, 549-550
EGA, 276-277
electronic mail, 710-719
electronic message systems, 715-718
entity, 432-435
entity-Relationship Modeling, 433-435
ergonomics, 157-160
Excel, 403
executive information system, 22
executive information system, 75-80
executive information system development, 77-79

expansion board, 204-205
expansion board, 240-245
expert system, 363
expert system, 531-538
expert system shell, 362-363
external contribution analysis, 56
external memory, 247-256
external program, 316-317

facsimile, 713-715
feasibility, 58
fifth environment, 32-34
file format conversion, 350-354
file management systems, 415
file transfer protocol, 562
financial analysis software, 651-670
first environment, 26-27
FOCUS, 688-693
fourth environment, 28-32
fourth environment, 54
fourth-generation language, 411
fourth-generation language, 455-456
frames knowledge base, 358
full duplex, 549-550
functional specialist, 137-138

gateway, 593
graphics, 22
    analytical versus conceptual, 466
    analytical versus conceptual, 483-484
    embedded in text, 481-482
    good practice, 678-689
    host, 677-680
    monochrome and color, 260-261
    object, 262-267
    overview of technology, 256-272
    pixel versus object, 484-485
    presentation, 484
    standards, 267-272
graphics coprocessor, 238
graphics kernel standard, 271
gray scale, 260-261

HDLC, 553
Hercules Graphics Card, 276
hierarchical design, 63-64
host security software, 579-580
host-specific terminals, 550-556
hybrid applications, 22

IBM personal computers, 211-216
IFPS, 663-670
IFPS/Personal, 404
images:
    analytical model, 372-373
inference engine, 359-361
information center, 1, 15-16
    and Type II departments, 132

Index I-3

bridging functions, 130-132
critical success factors, 92-94
development for users, 109-112
history, 34-39
mobilizing end users, 136-138
placement in the organization, 126-132
planning, 112-122
proactive, 40
problems, 89-92
promption, 139-140
services, 86-90
staffing, 133-136
technological infrastructure, 141-153
training, 178
work space, 132
installation, 149-150
integrated Office Systems, 733-742
integrated data and decision support systems, 697-701
integrated personal productivity applications, 22
integrated software, 346-347, 521-526
integration, 346-355
    ASCII, 351-352
    DCA, 354
    DIF, 353
    file format conversion, 350-354
    incompatible file format, 346
    integrated software, 346-347
    screen capture, 349-350
interactive program, 316-317
internal memory, 202
internal program, 316-317
international Data Corporation, 5
interrupt, 311-312
ISND standards, 614-615
interactive development, 52-53

jump with return, 310-311

keyboard enhancer, 342-344
keyboard explosion, 5
knowledge base, 356-359
knowledge-based system, 355-356

LAP, 553
LATA, 576-577
layered software, 309-310
learning research, 172-177
leased lines, 576-579
LISP, 361-362
life cycles, 84-86
    Gibson and Nolan, 85
    Guimaraes, 85-86
    Henderson and Treacy, 86
line driver, 570
line sharing, 554-555
lotus 1-2-3, 388-405
LU 6.2, 619

MAP/TOP, 621
MacDraw, 492-496
MacPaint, 271
Macintosh, 486-492
    operating system, 219-222
    Lotus 1-2-3, 330-334
macro, 400-402
maintenance, 151-152
management mix, 26
math coprocessor, 238
memory map, 307
micro-mainframe links, 563-564
microprocessor, 201-202
microprocessor, 233-237
microwave, 577-578
modem, 512, 564-568
    callback, 568
    intelligent, 567
    internal and external, 567-568
    short haul, 570
    standards, 566
modular design, 63-64
mother board, 203-204
mouse, 298
MS-DOS, 321-326
multidrop line, 554-555
multifunction board, 244
multiplexer, 570-572
multitasking, 326-327

NAPLPS, 270, 512
natural language input, 362
needs assessment, corporate, 58-60
network:
    administrator, 651-652
    baseband, 599-602
    baseband products, 643
    broadband, 599-600
    broadband, 602-605
    broadband products, 640-642
    controller, 626-627
    internal and external controllers, 589-590
    management, 628-629
    often-overlooked considerations, 586-587
    planning, 648-652
    purchasing, 624-652
    purchasing pitfalls, 624-629
    standards, 590-593
    standards, 608-621
    switched versus nonswitched, 589
network data base, 421-422
newsletters, 140-141
no programming dogma, 35
noise, 543-544
noise, 594
normalization, 423-425

I-4 Index

object graphics, 262-267
objective-critical applications, 57
Office Document Architecture, 724-726
office automation, 22
    Type I department, 706-710
    Type I versus Type II, 703-706
office document architecture, 270
online services, 509-515
open design, 208
operating system:
    environment, 341-342
    MS-DOS, 321-326
    Macintosh, 330-3334
    multitasking, 326-327
    multiuser, 327-328
    OS/2, 335-338
    simple, 321-326
optical fiber, 578, 595
OS/2, 335-338
OSI, 610-612
outlining, 482
overlay program, 316-317

PBX, 643-646
PC networking:
    services, 512
packet, 551
packet switching, 596-598
page description language, 481
page layout, 498-502
parallel adapter, 242
parity, 546-547
PC network, 629-639
    3 Com, 634-635
    IBM products, 629-633
    Macintosh, 636
    Microsoft, 635
    Novell Netware, 634
    service on LANs, 637-638
    service on hosts, 638-639
personal computer:
    desktop, 199
    engineering work station, 200
    hardware, 231-304
    home computers, 200-201
    laptop, 199-200
    portable, 199-200
    prices, 223-229
    standards, 196-230
personal computers versus hosts, 18-19, 95-98
personal computers versus hosts, 656-659
piracy, 155-157
pixel, 257-258
    storage requirements, 260-262
planning, 39
    annual, 121-122
planning study, 117-121

post-DP revolution, 1
PostScript, 268-270
PostScript, 481
power (electrical), 245-247
power user's roles, 74
PROFS, 738-739
PROLOG, 362
primary keys, 435-436
printer, 281-296
    color, 294-295
    daisywheel, 283-285
    dot matrix, 284-289
    page (laser), 289-293
    plotter, 293-294
printer driver, 267
privacy, 153-157
product research and selection, 144-146
programming languages, 528-529
project assessment, 54-57
project construction, 66-68
project cutover, 70-72
project design, 60-66
    second environment, 64-65
    third environment, 65-66
project implementation, 68-72
project justification, 98-105
project management, 21, 530
project selection, 57-58
protocol, 608
protocol converter, 557-558
purchasing, 146-149

query language, 447-451

RAM, 238-240
RAM disk, 319
records management center, 709-710
relational DBMs, 422-430
relational algebra, 426-429
relational calculus, 429-430
repeating field, 419-420
report generator, 447-449, 452-454
reserved system memory, 307-308
resolution, 259-260
ring layout, 601-602
ROM, 240
RS232C, 547-548
    cabling and null modems, 568-570

SAS, 674-676
satellite transmission, 578-579
scanner, 299-300
screen capture, 561
SDLC, 553
second environment, 26-27, 53
secondary key field, 446-447
secretary's roles, 73-74
security, 153-157

semantic network, 357-358
sequential development, 51-52
serial adapter, 242-243
service program lookup table, 312
site licenses, 148
skills hierarchy, 167-172
smart terminals, 550-551
software upgrades, 150-151
spelling checker, 482
spreadsheet software, 402-405
SQL, 682-688
standards:
   data communications, 608-621
      layering, 609
      protocol, 608
      text and electronic mail, 720-727
statistical analysis software, 670-677
stress, 160
structural analysis, 58-59
style sheets, 481
support mix, 165
   in different environments, 191
switching, 595-599
   circuit switching, 596
   datagram, 597-598
   hierarchical, 598-599
   message and packet switching, 596
   peer, 598-599
   virtual-circuit, 597-598
synchronous network support, 625-626
synchronous transmission, 551-553
systems Application Architecture, 338-341
systems Network Architecture, 618-621
systems development life cycle, 49-51

tactical management initiatives, 56
TCP/IP, 618
technological infrastructure, 141-153
teleconferencing, 727-733
telephone deregulation, 576-577
Teletex, 712
Telex, 711-712
terminal emulation, 555-557
terminate and stay resident, 206, 311
text characteristics, 472-474
theft, 153-157

third environment, 53, 27-28
token passing, 607-608
training:
   audio and video, 185-186
   classroom training, 180-182
   comprehensive programs, 186-191
   computer-based, 183-185
   modular training, 179
transmission media, 594-595
transmission speed, 542-544
TTY, 512-513, 544-550
   emulation, 556
twisted pair wire, 594
Type I, 6-7
Type I and Type II, 6-10
Type I versus Type II, 703-706
Type II, 8-10, 15-16
Type II and the information center, 132

UNIX, 327-328
unauthorized software copying, 155-157
use of time studies, 12-15
user groups, 136-137

vandalism, 153-157
VDI, 270
verbal communication, 20
vertical software, 531-532
VGA, 277
Videotex, 512-513
virtual memory, 317-318
voice input and output, 300-302
voice messaging, 719-720

Wang OFFICE, 736-737
what if analysis, 383-384, 393-394
windows, 328-330
word processing center, 706-709
word processing software, 467-483
work systems, 68-70
workstation, 540
WYSIWYG, 480

X.25 and X.75, 612-614
X.400 electronic mail standards, 722-724
XON/XOFF, 561-562